Fourth Edition

PROGRAMMING LANGUAGES
Design and Implementation

Terrence W. Pratt
Center of Excellence in Space Data and Information Sciences
NASA Goddard Space Flight Center, Greenbelt, MD
(retired)

Marvin V. Zelkowitz
Department of Computer Science and
Institute for Advanced Computer Studies
University of Maryland, College Park, MD

PRENTICE HALL, Upper Saddle River, New Jersey 07458

Library of Congress Cataloging-in-Publication Data

Pratt, Terrence W.
Programming languages : design and implementation / Terrence W. Pratt, Marvin V. Zelkowitz. -- 4th ed.
p. cm.
Includes bibliographical references and index.
ISBN 0-13-027678-2 (alk. paper)
1. Programming languages (Electronic computers) I. Zelkowitz, Marvin V., 1945- II. Title.
QA76.7 P7 2000
005.13--dc20 95-19011
CIP

Vice president and editorial director, ECS: Marcia Horton
Acquisition editor: Petra Recter
Associate editor: Sarah Burrows
Editorial assistant: Karen Schultz
Production editor: Leslie Galen
Managing editor: David A. George
Executive managing editor: Vince O'Brien
Art director: Heather Scott
Assistant art director: John Christiana
Cover design: Marjory Dressler
Marketing manager: Jennie Burger
Manufacturing buyer: Dawn Murrin
Manufacturing manager: Trudy Pisciotti
Assistant vice president of production and manufacturing: David W. Riccardi

Prentice Hall

Printed in the United States of America

10 9 8 7 6 5 4 3 2

ISBN 0-13-027678-2

Prentice-Hall International (UK) Limited, London
Prentice-Hall of Australia Pty. Limited, Sydney
Prentice-Hall Canada Inc., Toronto
Prentice-Hall Hispanoamericana, S. A., Mexico
Prentice-Hall of India Private Limited, New Delhi
Prentice-Hall of Japan, Inc., Tokyo
Pearson Education Asia, Pte. Ltd.
Editora Prentice-Hall do Brasil, Ltda., Rio de Janeiro

For Kirsten, Randy, Laurie, Aaron, and Elena

Preface

This fourth edition of *Programming Languages: Design and Implementation* continues the tradition developed in the earlier editions to describe programming language design by means of the underlying software and hardware architecture that is required for execution of programs written in those languages. This provides the programmer with the ability to develop software that is both correct and efficient in execution. In this new edition, we continue this approach, as well as improve on the presentation of the underlying theory and formal models that form the basis for the decisions made in creating those languages.

Programming language design is still a very active pursuit in the computer science community as languages are born, age, and eventually die. This fourth edition represents the vital languages of the early 21st century. Postscript, Java, HTML, and Perl have been added to the languages discussed in the third edition to reflect the growth of the World Wide Web as a programming domain. The discussion of Pascal, FORTRAN, and Ada has been deemphasized in recognition of these languages' aging in anticipation of possibly dropping them in future editions of this book.

At the University of Maryland, a course has been taught for the past 25 years that conforms to the structure of this book. For our junior-level course, we assume the student already knows C, Java, or C++ from earlier courses. We then emphasize Smalltalk, ML, Prolog, and LISP, as well as include further discussions of the implementation aspects of C++. The study of C++ furthers the students' knowledge of procedural languages with the addition of object-oriented classes, and the inclusion of LISP, Prolog, and ML provides for discussions of different programming paradigms. Replacement of one or two of these by FORTRAN, Ada, or Pascal would also be appropriate.

It is assumed that the reader is familiar with at least one procedural language, generally C, C++, Java, or FORTRAN. For those institutions using this book at a lower level, or for others wishing to review prerequisite material to provide a framework for discussing programming language design issues, Chapters 1 and 2 provide a review of material needed to understand later chapters. Chapter 1 is a general introduction to programming languages, while Chapter 2 is a brief overview of the underlying hardware that will execute the given program.

The theme of this book is language design and implementation issues. Chapter 3, and 5 through 12 provide the basis for this course by describing the underlying grammatical model for programming languages and their compilers (Chapter 3), elementary data types (Chapter 5), data structures and encapsulation (Chapter 6), inheritance (Chapter 7), statements (Chapter 8), procedure invocation (Chapter 9), storage management (Chapter 10), distributed processing (Chapter 11) and network programming (Chapter 12), which form the central concerns in language design.

Chapter 4 is a more advanced chapter on language semantics that includes an introduction to program verification, denotational semantics, and the lambda calculus. It may be skipped in the typical sophomore- or junior-level course. As with the previous editions of this book, we include a comprehensive appendix that is a brief summary of the features in the 12 languages covered in some detail in this book.

The topics in this book cover the 12 knowledge units recommended by the 1991 ACM/IEEE Computer Society Joint Curriculum Task Force for the programming languages subject area [TUCKER et al. 1991].

Although compiler writing was at one time a central course in the computer science curriculum, there is increasing belief that not every computer science student needs to be able to develop a compiler; such technology should be left to the compiler specialist, and the hole in the schedule produced by deleting such a course might be better utilized with courses such as software engineering, database engineering, or other practical use of computer science technology. However, we believe that aspects of compiler design should be part of the background for all good programmers. Therefore, a focus of this book is how various language structures are compiled, and Chapter 3 provides a fairly complete summary of parsing issues.

The 12 chapters emphasize programming language examples in FORTRAN, Ada, C, Java, Pascal, ML, LISP, Perl, Postscript, Prolog, C++, and Smalltalk. Additional examples are given in HTML, PL/I, SNOBOL4, APL, BASIC, and COBOL as the need arises. The goal is to give examples from a wide variety of languages and let the instructor decide which languages to use as programming examples during the course.

Although discussing all of the languages briefly during the semester is appropriate, we do not suggest that the programming parts of this course consist of problems in each of these languages. We think that would be too superficial in one course. Ten programs, each written in a different language, would be quite a chore and would provide the student with little in-depth knowledge of any of these languages. We assume that each instructor will choose three or four languages and emphasize those.

All examples in this book, except for the most trivial, were tested on an appropriate translator; however, as we clearly point out in Section 1.3.3, correct execution on our local system is no guarantee that the translator is processing programs according to the language standard. We are sure that Mr. Murphy is at work here, and some of the trivial examples may have errors. If so, we apologize for any problems that may cause.

To summarize, our goals in producing this fourth edition were as follows:

- Provide an overview of the key paradigms used in developing modern programming languages;
- Highlight several languages, which provide those features, in sufficient detail to permit programs to be written in each language demonstrating those features;
- Explore the implementation of each language in sufficient detail to provide the programmer with an understanding of the relationship between a source program and its execution behavior;
- Provide sufficient formal theory to show where programming language design fits within the general computer science research agenda;
- Provide a sufficient set of problems and alternative references to allow students the opportunity to extend their knowledge of this important topic.

We gratefully acknowledge the valuable comments received from the users of the third edition of this text and from the hundreds of students of CMSC 330 at the University of Maryland who provided valuable feedback on improving the presentation contained in this book.

Changes to the Fourth Edition. For users familiar with the third edition, the fourth edition has the following changes:

1. A chapter was added (Chapter 12) on the World Wide Web. Java was added as a major programming language, and an overview of HTML and Postscript were added to move the book away from the classical "FORTRAN number–crunching" view of compilers.

2. The material on object-oriented design was moved earlier in the text to indicate its major importance in software design today. In addition, numerous other changes were made by moving minor sections around to better organize the material into a more consistent presentation.

3. We have found that the detailed discussions of languages in Part II of the third edition were not as useful as we expected. A short history of each of the 12 languages was added to the chapter that best represents the major features of that language, and the language summaries in Part II of the third edition were shortened as the appendix. Despite these additions, the size of the book has not increased because we deleted some obsolete material.

Terry Pratt, Howardsville, Virginia

Marv Zelkowitz, College Park, Maryland

Contents

Chapter 1

Language Design Issues

Any notation for the description of algorithms and data structures may be termed a programming language; however, in this book we are mostly interested in those that are implemented on a computer. The sense in which a language may be implemented is considered in the next two chapters. In the remainder of this book, the design and implementation of the various components of a language are considered in detail. The goal is to look at language features, independent of any particular language, and give examples from a wide class of commonly used languages.

Throughout the book, we illustrate the application of these concepts in the design of 12 major programming languages and their dialects: Ada, C, C++, FORTRAN, Java, LISP, ML, Pascal, Perl, Postscript, Prolog, and Smalltalk. In addition, we also give brief summaries about other languages that have made an impact on the field. This list includes APL, BASIC, COBOL, Forth, PL/I, and SNOBOL4. Before approaching the general study of programming languages, however, it is worth understanding why there is value in such a study to a computer programmer.

1.1 WHY STUDY PROGRAMMING LANGUAGES?

Hundreds of different programming languages have been designed and implemented. Even in 1969, Sammet [SAMMET 1969] listed 120 that were fairly widely used, and many others have been developed since then. Most programmers, however, never venture to use more than a few languages, and many confine their programming entirely to one or two. In fact, practicing programmers often work at computer installations where use of a particular language such as Java, C, or Ada is required. What is to be gained, then, by study of a variety of different languages that one is unlikely ever to use?

There are excellent reasons for such a study, provided that you go beneath the superficial consideration of the "features" of languages and delve into the underlying design concepts and their effect on language implementation. Six primary reasons come immediately to mind:

1. *To improve your ability to develop effective algorithms.* Many languages provide features, that when used properly, are of benefit to the programmer but, when used improperly, may waste large amounts of computer time or lead the programmer into time-consuming logical errors. Even a programmer who has used a language for years may not understand all of its features. A typical example is *recursion*—a handy programming feature that, when properly used, allows the direct implementation of elegant and efficient algorithms. When used improperly, it may cause an astronomical increase in execution time. The programmer who knows nothing of the design questions and implementation difficulties that recursion implies is likely to shy away from this somewhat mysterious construct. However, a basic knowledge of its principles and implementation techniques allows the programmer to understand the relative cost of recursion in a particular language and from this understanding to determine whether its use is warranted in a particular programming situation. New programming methods are constantly being introduced in the literature. The best use of concepts like object-oriented programming, logic programming, or concurrent programming, for example, requires an understanding of languages that implement these concepts. New technology, such as the Internet and World Wide Web, change the nature of programming. How best to develop techniques applicable in these new environments depends on an understanding of languages.

2. *To improve your use of your existing programming language.* By understanding how features in your language are implemented, you greatly increase your ability to write efficient programs. For example, understanding how data such as arrays, strings, lists, or records are created and manipulated by your language, knowing the implementation details of recursion, or understanding how object classes are built allows you to build more efficient programs consisting of such components.

3. *To increase your vocabulary of useful programming constructs.* Language serves both as an aid and a constraint to thinking. People use language to express thoughts, but language also serves to structure how one thinks, to the extent that it is difficult to think in ways that allow no direct expression in words. Familiarity with a single programming language tends to have a similar constraining effect. In searching for data and program structures suitable to the solution of a problem, one tends to think only of structures that are immediately expressible in the languages with which one is familiar. By studying the constructs provided by a wide range of languages, a programmer increases his programming vocabulary. The understanding of implementation techniques is particularly important because, to use a construct while programming in a language that does not provide it directly, the programmer must provide an implementation of the construct in terms of the primitive elements actually provided by the language. For example, the subprogram control structure known as a *coroutine* is useful in many programs, but few

languages provide a coroutine feature directly. A C or FORTRAN programmer, however, may readily design a program to use a coroutine structure and then implement it as a C or a FORTRAN program if familiar with the coroutine concept and its implementation.

4. *To allow a better choice of programming language.* A knowledge of a variety of languages may allow the choice of just the right language for a particular project, thereby reducing the required coding effort. Applications requiring numerical calculations can be easily designed in languages like C, FORTRAN, or Ada. Developing applications useful in decision making, such as in artificial-intelligence applications, would be more easily written in LISP, ML, or Prolog. Internet applications are more readily designed using Perl and Java. Knowledge of the basic features of each language's strengths and weaknesses gives the programmer a broader choice of alternatives.

5. *To make it easier to learn a new language.* A linguist, through a deep understanding of the underlying structure of natural languages, often can learn a new foreign language more quickly and easily than struggling novices who understand little of the structure even of their native tongue. Similarly, a thorough knowledge of a variety of programming language constructs and implementation techniques allows the programmer to learn a new programming language more easily when the need arises.

6. *To make it easier to design a new language.* Few programmers ever think of themselves as language designers, yet many applications are really a form of programming language. A designer of a user interface for a large program such as a text editor, an operating system, or a graphics package must be concerned with many of the same issues that are present in the design of a general-purpose programming language. Many new languages are based on C or Pascal as implementation models. This aspect of program design is often simplified if the programmer is familiar with a variety of constructs and implementation methods from ordinary programming languages.

There is much more to the study of programming languages than simply a cursory look at their features. In fact, many similarities in features are deceiving. The same feature in two different languages may be implemented in two very different ways, and thus the two versions may differ greatly in the cost of use. For example, almost every language provides an addition operation as a primitive, but the cost of performing an addition in C, COBOL, or Smalltalk may vary by an order of magnitude.

In this book, numerous language constructs are discussed, accompanied in almost every case by one or more designs for the implementation of the construct on a conventional computer. However, no attempt has been made to be comprehensive in covering all possible implementation methods. The same language or construct, if implemented on the reader's local computer, may differ radically in cost or detail of structure when different implementation techniques have been used or when the underlying computer hardware differs from the simple conventional structure assumed here.

1.2 A SHORT HISTORY OF PROGRAMMING LANGUAGES

Programming language designs and implementation methods have evolved continuously since the earliest high-level languages appeared in the 1950s. Of the 12 languages described in some detail, the first versions of FORTRAN and LISP were designed during the 1950s; Ada, C, Pascal, Prolog, and Smalltalk date from the 1970s; C++, ML, Perl, and Postscript date from the 1980s; and Java dates from the 1990s. In the 1960s and 1970s, new languages were often developed as part of major software development projects. When the U.S. Department of Defense did a survey as part of its background efforts in developing Ada in the 1970s, it found that over 500 languages were being used on various defense projects.

1.2.1 Development of Early Languages

We briefly summarize language development during the early days of computing, generally from the mid-1950s to the early 1970s. Later developments are covered in more detail as each new language is introduced later in this book.

Numerically based languages. Computer technology dates from the era just before World War II through the early 1940s. Determining ballistics trajectories by solving the differential equations of motion was the major role for computers during World War II, which led to them being called *electronic calculators.*

In the early 1950s, symbolic notations started to appear. Grace Hopper led a group at Univac to develop the A-0 language, and John Backus developed Speedcoding for the IBM 701. Both were designed to compile simple arithmetic expressions into executable machine language.

The real breakthrough occurred in 1957 when Backus managed a team to develop FORTRAN, or FORmula TRANslator. As with the earlier efforts, FORTRAN data were oriented around numerical calculations, but the goal was a full-fledged programming language including control structures, conditionals, and input and output statements. Because few believed that the resulting language could compete with hand-coded assembly language, every effort was put into efficient execution, and various statements were designed specifically for the IBM 704. Concepts like the three-way arithmetic branch of FORTRAN came directly from the hardware of the 704, and statements like *READ INPUT TAPE* seem quaint today. It wasn't very elegant, but in those days, little was known about *elegant* programming, and the language was fast for the given hardware.

FORTRAN was extremely successful and was the dominant language through the 1970s. FORTRAN was revised as FORTRAN II in 1958 and FORTRAN IV a few years later. Almost every manufacturer implemented a version of the language, and chaos reigned. Finally in 1966, FORTRAN IV became a standard under the name FORTRAN 66 and has been upgraded twice since, to FORTRAN 77 and FORTRAN 90. However, the extremely large number of programs written in these early dialects has caused succeeding generations of translators to be mostly backward compatible with these old programs and inhibits the use of modern programming features.

Because of the success of FORTRAN, there was fear, especially in Europe, of the domination by IBM of the industry. The German society of applied mathematics (GAMM) organized a committee to design a universal language. In the United States, the Association for Computing Machinery (ACM) also organized a similar committee. Although there was concern by the Europeans of being dominated by the Americans, the committees merged. Under the leadership of Peter Naur, the committee developed the International Algorithmic Language (IAL). Although ALGOrithmic Language (ALGOL) was proposed, the name was not approved. However, common usage forced the official name change, and the language became known as ALGOL 58. A revision occurred in 1960, and ALGOL 60 (with a minor revision in 1962) became the standard academic computing language from the 1960s to the early 1970s.

Although FORTRAN was designed for efficient execution on an IBM 704, ALGOL had very different goals:

1. ALGOL notation should be close to standard mathematics.
2. ALGOL should be useful for the description of algorithms.
3. Programs in ALGOL should be compilable into machine language.
4. ALGOL should not be bound to a single computer architecture.

These turned out to be very ambitious goals for 1958. To allow for machine independence, no input or output was included in the language; special procedures could be written for these operations. Although that certainly made programs independent of a particular hardware, it also meant that each implementation would necessarily be incompatible with another. To keep close to pure mathematics, a subprogram was viewed as a macro substitution, which led to the concept of *call by name* parameter passing; as we see in Section 9.3, call by name is extremely hard to implement efficiently.

ALGOL never achieved commercial success in the United States, although it did achieve some success in Europe. But it had a major impact on languages that followed. As one example, Jules Schwartz of System Development Corporation (SDC) developed a version of IAL (Jules' Own Version of IAL, or JOVIAL), which became a standard for U.S. Air Force applications.

Backus was editor of the ALGOL report defining the language [BACKUS 1960]. He used a syntactic notation comparable to the context free language concept developed by Chomsky [CHOMSKY 1959]. This was the introduction of formal grammar theory to the programming language world (Section 3.3). Because of his and Naur's role in developing ALGOL, the notation is now called Backus Naur Form (BNF)..

As another example of ALGOL's influence, Burroughs, a computer vendor that has since merged with Sperry Univac to form Unisys, discovered the works of the Polish mathematician, Lukasiewicz. Lukasiewicz had developed a technique that enabled arithmetic expressions to be written without parentheses using an efficient stack-based evaluation process. This technique has had a profound effect on compiler theory. Using methods based on Lukasiewicz's technique, Burroughs developed the B5500 computer using a stack architecture and soon had an ALGOL compiler that was much faster than any existing FORTRAN compiler.

At this point, the story starts to diverge. The concept of user-defined types developed in the 1960s, and neither FORTRAN nor ALGOL had such features. Simula-67, developed by Nygaard and Dahl of Norway, introduced the concept of classes to ALGOL. This gave Stroustrup the idea for his C++ classes (Appendix A.3) as an extension to C in the 1980s. Wirth developed ALGOL-W in the mid-1960s as an extension to ALGOL. This met with only minor success; however, around 1970, he developed Pascal, which became *the* computer science language of the 1970s. Another committee tried to duplicate ALGOL 60's success with ALGOL 68, but the language was much too complex for most to understand or implement effectively.

With the introduction of its new 360 line of computers in 1963, IBM developed NPL (New Programming Language) at its Hursley Laboratory in England. After some complaints by the English National Physical Laboratory, the name was changed to MPPL (Multi-Purpose Programming Language), which was then shortened to just PL/I. PL/I merged the numerical attributes of FORTRAN with the business programming features of COBOL. PL/I achieved modest success in the 1970s (e.g., it was one of the featured languages in the second edition of this book), but its use today is dwindling as it is replaced by C, C++ and Ada. The educational subset PL/C achieved modest success in the 1970s as a student PL/I compiler (page 87). BASIC (page 79) was developed to satisfy the numerical calculation needs of the nonscientist but has been extended far beyond its original goal.

Business languages. Business data processing was an early application domain to develop after numerical calculations. Grace Hopper led a group at Univac to develop FLOWMATIC in 1955. The goal was to develop business applications using a form of Englishlike text. In 1959, the U.S. Department of Defense sponsored a meeting to develop Common Business Language (CBL), which would be a business-oriented language that used English as much as possible for its notation. Because of divergent activities from many companies, a Short Range Committee was formed to quickly develop this language. Although they thought they were designing an interim language, the specifications, published in 1960, were the designs for COBOL (COmmon Business Oriented Language). COBOL was revised in 1961 and 1962, standardized in 1968, and revised again in 1974 and 1984. (Additional comments are found on page 315.)

Artificial-intelligence languages. Interest in artificial-intelligence languages began in the 1950s with Information Processing Language (IPL) by the Rand Corporation. IPL–V was fairly widely known, but its use was limited by its low-level design. The major breakthrough occurred when John McCarthy of MIT designed LIst PRocessing (LISP) for the IBM 704. LISP 1.5 became the standard LISP implementation for many years. More recently, Scheme and Common LISP have continued that evolution (Appendix A.6).

LISP was designed as a list-processing functional language. Game playing was a natural test bed for LISP because the usual LISP program would develop a tree of possible moves (as a linked list) and then walk over the tree searching for the optimum strategy. Automatic machine translation, where strings of symbols could be replaced by other strings, was another natural application domain. COMIT, by Yngve of MIT, was an early language in this domain. Each program statement was very similar to a context-free production (Section 3.3.1) and represented the set of replacements that could be made if that string were found in the data. Because Yngve kept his code proprietary, a group at AT&T Bell Labs decided to develop their own language, which resulted in SNOBOL (page 331).

Although LISP was designed for general-purpose list-processing applications, Prolog (Appendix A.11) was a special-purpose language whose basic control structure and implementation strategy were based on concepts from mathematical logic.

Systems languages. Because of the need for efficiency, the use of assembly language held on for years in the systems area long after other application domains started to use higher level languages. Many systems programming languages, such as CPL and BCPL, were designed, but were never widely used. C (Appendix A.2) changed all that. With the development of a competitive environment in UNIX written mostly in C during the early 1970s, high-level languages have been shown to be effective in this environment as well as others.

1.2.2 Evolution of Software Architectures

Development of a programming language does not proceed in a vacuum. The hardware that supports a language has a great impact on language design. Language, as a means to solve a problem, is part of the overall technology that is employed. The external environment supporting the execution of a program is termed its *operating* or *target environment*. The environment in which a program is designed, coded, tested, and debugged, or *host environment*, may be different from the operating environment in which the program ultimately is used. The computing industry has now entered its third major era in the development of computer programs. Each era has had a profound effect on the set of languages that were used for applications in each time period.

Mainframe Era

From the earliest computers in the 1940s through the 1970s, the large mainframe dominated computing. A single expensive computer filled a room and was attended to by hordes of technicians.

Batch environments. The earliest and simplest operating environment consists only of external files of data. A program takes a set of data files as input, processes the data, and produces a set of output data files (e.g., a payroll program processes two input files containing master payroll records and weekly pay-period times and produces two output files containing updated master records and paychecks). This operating environment is termed *batch-processing* because the input data are collected in *batches* on files and are processed in batches by the program. The 80-column punched card or Hollerith card, named after Herman Hollerith who developed the card for use in the 1890 U.S. census, was the ubiquitous sign of computing in the 1960s.

Languages such as FORTRAN, COBOL, and Pascal were initially designed for batch-processing environments, although they may be used now in an interactive or in an embedded-system environment.

Interactive environments. Toward the end of the mainframe era, in the early 1970s, interactive programming made its appearance. Rather than developing a program on a deck of cards, cathode ray tube terminals were directly connected to the computer. Based on research in the 1960s at MIT's Project MAC and Multics, the computer was able to *time share* by enabling each user to have a small slice of the computer's processor time. Thus, if 20 users were connected to a computer, and each user had a time slice of 25 milliseconds, then each user would have two such slices or 50 milliseconds of computer time each second. Because many users spent much of their time at a terminal thinking, the few who were actually executing programs would often get more than their quota of two slices per second.

In an interactive environment, a program interacts directly with a user at a display console during its execution, by alternately sending output to the display and receiving input from the keyboard or mouse. Examples include word-processing systems, spreadsheets, video games, database management systems, and computer-assisted instruction systems. These examples are all tools with which you may be familiar.

Effects on language design. In a language designed for batch processing, files are usually the basis for most of the input-output (I/O) structure. Although a file may be used for interactive I/O to a terminal, the special needs of interactive I/O are not addressed in these languages. For example, files are usually stored as fixed-length records, yet at a terminal, the program would need to read each character as it is entered on the keyboard. The I/O structure also typically does not address the requirement for access to special I/O devices found in embedded systems.

In a batch-processing environment, an error that terminates execution of the program is acceptable but costly because often the entire run must be repeated after the error is corrected. In this environment, too, no external help from the user in immediately handling or correcting the error is possible. Thus, the error- and exception-handling facilities of the language emphasize error/exception handling within the program so that the program may recover from most errors and continue processing without terminating.

A third distinguishing characteristic of a batch-processing environment is the lack of timing constraints on a program. The language usually provides no facilities for monitoring or directly affecting the speed at which the program executes.

The characteristics of interactive I/O are sufficiently different from ordinary file operations that most languages designed for a batch-processing environment experience some difficulty in adapting to an interactive environment. These differences are discussed in Section 5.3.3. As an example, C includes functions for accessing lines of text from a file and other functions that directly input each character as typed by the user at a terminal. The direct input of text from a terminal in Pascal, however, is often very cumbersome. For this reason, C (and its derivative C++) has grown greatly in popularity as a language for writing interactive programs.

Error handling in an interactive environment is given different treatment. If bad input data are entered from a keyboard, the program may display an error message and ask for a correction from the user. Language features for handling the error within the program (e.g., by ignoring it and attempting to continue) are of lesser importance. However, termination of the program in response to an error is usually not acceptable (unlike batch processing).

Interactive programs must often utilize some notion of timing constraints. For example, in a video game, the failure to respond within a fixed time interval to a displayed scene would cause the program to invoke some response. An interactive program that operates so slowly that it cannot respond to an input command in a reasonable period is often considered unusable.

Personal Computer Era

In hindsight, the mainframe time-sharing era of computing was very short-lived, lasting perhaps from the early 1970s to the mid-1980s. The Personal Computer (PC) changed all that.

Personal computers. The 1970s could be called the *era of the minicomputer.* These were progressively smaller and cheaper machines than the standard mainframe of that era. Hardware technology was making great strides forward, and the microcomputer, which contained the entire machine processor on a single 1- to 2-inch square piece of plastic and silicon, was becoming faster and cheaper each year. The standard mainframe of the 1970s shrunk from a room full of cabinets and tape drives to a decorative office machine perhaps 3 to 5 feet long and 3 to 4 feet high.

In 1978, Apple released the Apple II computer, the first true commercial PC. It was a small desktop machine that ran BASIC. This machine had a major impact on the educational market; however, business was skeptical of minisized Apple and its minisized computer.

In 1981, all of this changed. The PC was released by IBM, and Lotus developed 1-2-3 based on the Visi-Calc spreadsheet program. This program became the first of the *killer applications* (killer aps) that industry had to run. The PC became an overnight success.

The modern PC era can be traced to January 1984 during the U.S. football Superbowl game. During a commercial on television, Apple announced the Macintosh computer. The Macintosh contained a windows-based graphical user interface with a mouse for point-and-click data entry. Although previously developed at the Xerox Palo Alto Research Center (PARC), the Macintosh was the first commercial application of this technology. Quickly mimicked by Microsoft for its Windows operating system, this interface design has become the mainstay of the PC.

Since that time, the machines have gotten cheaper and faster. The PC used to write this book is about 200 to 400 times faster, has 200 times the main memory, 3,000 times the disk space, and costs only one third of the $5,000 cost of the original PC 20 years earlier. It is more powerful than the mainframe computers that it replaced.

Embedded-system environments. An offshoot of the PC is the embedded computer. A computer system that is used to control part of a larger system such as an industrial plant, an aircraft, a machine tool, an automobile, or even your toaster is termed an *embedded computer system.* The computer system has become an integral part of the larger system, and the failure of the computer system usually means failure of the larger system as well. Unlike in the PC environment, where failure of the program often is simply an inconvenience requiring the program to be rerun, failure of an embedded application can often be life-threatening, from failure of an automobile computer causing a car to stall at high speeds on a highway, to failure of a computer causing a nuclear plant to overheat, to failure of a hospital computer causing patient monitoring to cease, down to failure of your digital watch causing you to be late for a meeting. Reliability and correctness are primary attributes for programs used in these domains. Ada, C, and C++ are used extensively to meet some of the special requirements of embedded-system environments.

Effects on language design. The PC has again changed the role of languages. Performance is now less of a concern in many application domains. With the advent of user interfaces such as windows, each machine executes under control of a single user. With prices so low, the need to time-share is not present. Developing languages with good interactive graphics becomes of primary importance.

Today windows-based systems are the primary user interface. PC users are quite familiar with the tools of the windows interface. They are familiar with windows, icons, scroll bars, menus, and the assorted other aspects of interacting with the computer. However, programming such packages can be complex. Vendors of such windowing systems have created libraries of these packages. Accessing these libraries to enable easy development of windows-based programs is a primary concern of application developers.

Object-oriented programming is a natural model for this environment. The use of languages like Java and C++ with its class hierarchy allows for easy incorporation of packages written by others.

Programs written for embedded systems often operate without an underlying operating system and without the usual environment of files and I/O devices. Instead, the program must interact directly with nonstandard I/O devices through special procedures that take account of the peculiarities of each device. For this reason, languages for embedded systems often place much less emphasis on files and file-oriented I/O operations. Access to special devices is often provided through language features that give access to particular hardware registers, memory locations, interrupt handlers, or subprograms written in assembly or other low-level languages.

Error handling in embedded systems is of particular importance. Ordinarily, each program must be prepared to handle all errors internally, taking appropriate actions to recover and continue. Termination, except in the case of a catastrophic system failure, is often not an acceptable alternative, and usually there is no user in the environment to provide interactive error correction.

Embedded systems almost always operate in *real time*; that is, the operation of the larger system within which the computer system is embedded requires that the computer system be able to respond to inputs and produce outputs within tightly constrained time intervals. For example, a computer controlling the flight of an aircraft must respond rapidly to changes in its altitude or speed. Real-time operation of these programs requires language features for monitoring time intervals, responding to delays of more than a certain length of time (which may indicate failure of a component of the system), and starting up and terminating actions at certain designated points in time.

Finally, an embedded computer system is often a *distributed system* composed of more than one computer. The program running on such a distributed system is usually composed of a set of tasks that operate concurrently, each controlling or monitoring one part of the system. The main program, if there is one, exists only to initiate execution of the tasks. Once initiated, these tasks usually run concurrently and indefinitely, because they need to terminate only when the entire system fails or is shut down for some reason.

Networking Era

Distributed computing. As machines became faster, smaller, and cheaper during the 1980s, they started to populate the business environment. Companies would have central machines for handling corporate data, such as payroll, and each department would have local machines for providing support to that department, order processing, report writing, and so on. For an organization to run smoothly, information on one machine had to be transferred and processed on another. For example, the sales office had to send purchase order information to the production department's computer and the financial department needed the information for billing and accounting. Local area networks (LANs) using telecommunication lines between the machines were developed within large organizations using a *client-server* model of computing. The *server* would be a program that provided information and multiple *client* programs would communicate with the server to obtain that information.

An airline reservation system is one well-known example of a client-server application. The database of airline flight schedules would be on a large mainframe. Each agent would run a client program that conveyed information to the agent (or traveler) about flights. If a new flight was desired, the client program would send information to the server program to receive or download information from the server to the client application about the new flights. In this way, a single-server application could serve many client programs.

Internet. The mid-1990s saw the emergence of the distributed LAN into an international global network, the Internet. In 1970, the Defense Advanced Research Projects Agency (DARPA) started a research project to link together mainframe computers into a large reliable and secure network. The goal was to provide redundancy in case of war so that military planners could access computers across the nation. Fortunately, the ARPANET was never put to that use, and in the mid-1980s, the military ARPANET evolved into the research-oriented Internet. Over time, additional computers were added to the network, and today any user worldwide can have a machine added to the network. Millions of machines are connected in a complex and dynamically changing complex of network server machines.

Accessing the Internet in its early days required two classes of computers. A user would be sitting at a client personal computer. To access information, the user would connect to an appropriate server machine to get that information. The protocols for performing those were telnet and file transfer protocol (FTP). The *telnet* protocol made it appear as if the user were actually executing as part of the distant server, whereas FTP simply allowed the client machine to send or receive files from the server machine. In both cases, the user had to know what machine contained the information that was desired.

At the same time a third protocol was being developed – Simple Mail Transfer Protocol (SMTP). *SMTP* is the basis for today's e-mail. Each user has a local login name on the client machine, and each machine has a unique machine name (e.g., mvz as the login name of an author of this book and aaron.cs.umd.edu as the unique name for the machine connected to the Internet). Sending a message to an individual was then a simple manner of using a program that adhered to the SMTP protocol and sending mail to a user at a specific machine (e.g., mvz@aaron.cs.umd.edu). What is important here is that the specific location of the machine containing the user is often unnecessary (e.g., mvz@cs.umd.edu is sufficient). There was no need to actually know the address of the machine on the Internet.

A goal in the late 1980s was to make the retrieval of information as easy to accomplish as sending e-mail. The breakthrough came in 1989 at CERN, the European nuclear research facility in Geneva, Switzerland. Berners-Lee developed the concept of the *HyperText markup Language* (HTML) *hyperlink* as a way to navigate around the Internet. With the development of the Mosaic web browser in 1993 and the *HyperText Transfer Protocol* (HTTP) addition to Internet technology, the general population discovered the Internet. By the end of the 20th century, everyone was *web surfing*, and the entire structure of knowledge acquisition and search worldwide had changed.

Effects on language design. The use of the World Wide Web (WWW) has again changed the role of the programming language. Computing is again becoming centralized, but in a way much different from the earlier mainframe era. Large information repository servers are being created worldwide. Users will access servers via the Web to obtain information and use their local client machines for local processing, such as word processing the information into a report. Rather than distributing millions of copies of a new software product, a vendor can simply put the software on the Web and have users download the copies for local use. This requires the use of languages that allow interaction between the client and server computers, such as the user being able to download the software and the vendor being able to charge the user for the privilege of downloading the software. The rise of Electronic commerce (E-commerce) depends on these features.

The initial Web pages were static. That is, text, pictures, or graphics could be displayed. Users could click on a Uniform Resource Locator (*URL*) to access a new Web page. In order for E-commerce to flourish, however, information had to flow both ways between client and server, and Web pages needed to be more active. Use of languages like Perl and Java provide such features.

The Web poses programming language issues that were not apparent in the previous two eras. Security is one. A user visiting a web site wants to be certain the owner of that site is not malicious and will not destroy the client machine by erasing the disk files of the user. Although a problem with time-sharing systems, this problem did not exist on single user PCs. Access to local user files from the server web site has to be restricted.

Performance is another critical problem. Although PCs have gotten extremely fast, the communication lines connecting a user to the Internet are often limited in speed. In addition, although the machines are fast, if many users are accessing the same server, then server processing power may be taxed. A way out of that is to process the information at the client site rather than on the server. This requires the server to send small executable programs to the client to offload work from the server to the client. The problem is that the server does not know what kind of computer the client is, so it is not clear what the executable program needs to look like. Java was developed specifically to handle this problem, and we discuss it later.

Era	Application	Major languages	Other languages
1960s	Business	COBOL	Assembler
	Scientific	FORTRAN	ALGOL, BASIC, APL
	System	Assembler	JOVIAL, Forth
	Artificial intelligence	LISP	SNOBOL
Today	Business	COBOL, C++, Java, spreadsheet	C, PL/I, 4GLs
	Scientific	FORTRAN, C, C++, Java	BASIC
	System	C, C++, Java	Ada, BASIC, Modula
	Artificial intelligence	LISP, Prolog	
	Publishing	TeX, Postscript, word processing	
	Process	UNIX shell, TCL, Perl, Javascript	AWK, Marvel, SED
	New paradigms	ML, Smalltalk	Eiffel

Table 1.1. Languages for various application domains.

1.2.3 Application Domains

The appropriate language to use often depends on the application domain for the problem to be solved. The appropriate language to use for various application domains has evolved over the past 30 years. The languages discussed in this book, plus a few others, are summarized in Table 1.1.

Applications of the 1960s

During the 1960s, most programming could be divided into four basic programming models: business processing, scientific calculations, systems programming, and artificial-intelligence applications.

Business processing. Most of these applications were large data processing applications designed to run on *big iron* mainframes. These included order-entry programs, inventory control, personnel management, and payroll. They were characterized by reading in large amounts of historical data on multiple tape drives, reading in a smaller set of recent transactions, and writing out a new set of historical data. For a view of what this looked like, watch any 1960s science fiction movie. They liked to show lots of spinning tapes to indicate *modern computing.*

COBOL was developed for these applications. The COBOL designers took great pains to ensure that such data processing records would be processed correctly.

Business applications also include business planning, risk analysis, and what-if scenarios. In the 1960s, it often required several months for a COBOL programmer to put together a typical what-if application.

Scientific. These applications are characterized by the solution of various mathematical equations. They include numerical analysis problems, solving differential or integral functions, and generating statistics. It is in this realm that the computer was first developed—for use during World War II to generate ballistics tables. FORTRAN has always been the dominant language in this domain. Its syntax has always been close to mathematics, and scientists find it easy to use.

System. For building operating systems and implementing compilers, no effective language existed. Such applications must be able to access the full functionality and resources of the underlying hardware. Assembly language was often the choice to gain efficiency. JOVIAL, a variation on ALGOL, was used on some U.S. Department of Defense projects, and toward the end of the 1960s, languages like PL/I were used for this application.

A related application domain is process control, the controlling of machinery. Because of the expense and size of computers during this era, most process control applications were large, such as controlling a power station or automatic assembly line. Languages like Forth were developed to address this application domain, although assembly language was often used.

Artificial Intelligence. Artificial intelligence (AI) was a relatively new research area, and LISP was the dominant language for AI applications. These programs are characterized by algorithms that search through large data spaces. For example, to play chess, the computer generates many potential moves and then searches for the best move within the time it has to decide what to do next.

Applications of the 21st Century

Although Ada was developed to eliminate much of the duplication among competing languages, the situation today is probably more complex than it was during the 1960s. We have more application domains where programming languages are especially well adapted with multiple choices for each application domain.

Business processing. COBOL is still the dominant language in this domain for data processing applications, although C and C++ are sometimes used. However, the what-if scenario has totally changed. Today the spreadsheet on the PC has totally reformed this application domain. Whereas it once took a programmer several months for a typical business planning program, today an analyst can *cook up* many spreadsheets in just a few hours.

Fourth-generation languages (4GLs) have also taken over some of this market. 4GLs are languages adapted for specific business application domains and typically provide a window-based programmer interface, easy access to database records, and special features for generating fill-in-the-blank input forms and elegant output reports. Sometimes these 4GL compilers generate COBOL programs as output.

E-commerce, a term referring to business activity conducted over the WWW, did not even exist when the previous edition of this book was published in 1996, yet it has greatly changed the nature of business programming. Tools that allow for interaction between the user (i.e., purchaser) and company (i.e., vendor) using the Web as the intermediary has given rise to new roles for languages. Java was developed as a language to ensure privacy rights of the user, and process languages such as Perl and Javascript allow for vendors to obtain critical data from the user to conduct a transaction.

Scientific. FORTRAN is still hanging on here, too, although FORTRAN 90 is being challenged by languages like C++ and Java.

System. C, developed toward the end of the 1960s, and its newer variant C++, dominate this application domain. C provides very efficient execution and allows the programmer full access to the operating system and underlying hardware. Other languages like Modula and modern variations of BASIC are also used. Although intended for this application, Ada has never achieved its goal of becoming a major language in this domain. Assembly language programming has become an anachronism.

With the advent of inexpensive microprocessors running cars, microwave ovens, video games, and digital watches, the need for real-time languages has increased. C, Ada, and C++ are often used for such real-time processing.

Artificial Intelligence. LISP is still used, although modern versions like Scheme and Common LISP have replaced the MIT LISP 1.5 of the early 1960s. Prolog has developed a following. Both languages are adept at searching applications.

Publishing. Publishing represents a relatively new application domain for languages. Word processing systems have their own syntax for input commands and output files. This book was composed using the TeX text processing system. For lack of a better term, chapters were *compiled* as they were written to put in figure and table references, to place figures, and to compose paragraphs.

The TeX translator produces a program in the Postscript page description language. Although Postscript is usually the output of a processor, it does have a syntax and semantics and can be compiled by an appropriate processor. Often this is the laser printer that is used to print the document. We know of individuals who insist on programming directly in Postscript, but this seems to be about as foolish today as programming in assembly language was in the 1960s. (See Section 12.1.)

Process. During the 1960s, the programmer was the active agent in using a computer. To accomplish a task, the programmer would write an appropriate command that the computer would then execute. However, today we often use one program to control another (e.g., to back up files every midnight, to synchronize time once an hour, to send an automatic reply to incoming e-mail when on vacation, to automatically test a program whenever it compiles successfully, etc.). We call such activities *processes*, and there is considerable interest in developing languages where such processes can be specified and then translated to execute automatically.

Within UNIX, the user command language is called the *shell*, and programs are called *shell scripts*. These scripts can be invoked whenever certain enabling conditions occur. Various other scripting languages have appeared; both TCL and Perl are used for similar purposes.

New paradigms. New application models are always under study. ML has been used in programming language research to investigate type theory. Although not a major language in industry, its popularity is growing. Smalltalk is another important language. Although commercial Smalltalk use is not very great, it has had a profound effect on language design. Many of the object-oriented features in C++ and Ada had their origins in Smalltalk.

Languages for various application domains are a continuing source of new research and development. As our knowledge of compiling techniques improves, and as our knowledge of how to build complex systems evolves, we are constantly finding new application domains and require languages that meet the needs of those domains.

1.3 ROLE OF PROGRAMMING LANGUAGES

Initially, languages were designed to execute programs efficiently. Computers, costing in the millions of dollars, were the critical resource, whereas programmers, earning perhaps $10,000 annually, were a minor cost. Any high-level language had to be competitive with the execution behavior of hand-coded assembly language. John Backus, chief designer of FORTRAN for IBM in the late 1950s, stated a decade later [IBM 1966]:

> Frankly, we didn't have the vaguest idea how the thing [FORTRAN language and compiler] would work out in detail. ... We struck out simply to optimize the object program, the running time, because most people at that time believed you really couldn't do that kind of thing. They believed that machine-coded programs would be so terribly inefficient that it would be impractical for very many applications.
>
> One result we didn't have in mind was this business of having a system that was designed to be utterly independent of the machine that the program was ultimately to run on. It turned out to be a very valuable capability, but we sure didn't have it in mind.
>
> There was nothing organized about our activities. Each part of the program was written by one or two people who were complete masters of what they did with very minor exceptions—and the thing just grew like Topsy. ... [When FORTRAN was distributed] we had the problem

of facing the fact that these 25,000 instructions weren't all going to be correct, and that there were going to be difficulties that would show up only after a lot of use.

By the middle of the 1960s, when the previous quote was made, after the advent of FORTRAN, COBOL, LISP, and ALGOL, Backus already realized that programming was changing. Machines were becoming less expensive, programming costs were rising, there was a growing need for moving programs from one system to another, and maintenance of the resulting product was taking a larger share of computing resources. Rather than compiling programs to work efficiently on a large, expensive computer, the task of a high-level language was to make it easier to develop correct programs to solve problems for some given application area.

Compiler technology matured in the 1960s and 1970s (Chapter 3), and language technology centered on solving domain-specific problems. Scientific computing generally used FORTRAN, business applications were typically written in COBOL, military applications were written in JOVIAL, artificial-intelligence applications were written in LISP, and embedded military applications were to be written in Ada.

Just like natural languages, programming languages evolve and eventually pass out of use. ALGOL from 1960 is no longer used, replaced by Pascal, which in turn is being replaced by C++ and Java. COBOL use is dropping for business applications, also being replaced by C++. APL, PL/I, and SNOBOL4, all from the 1960s, and Pascal from the 1970s have all but disappeared.

The older languages still in use have undergone periodic revisions to reflect changing influences from other areas of computing. Newer languages like C++, Java, and ML reflect a composite of experience gained in the design and use of these and the hundreds of other older languages. Some of these influences include the following:

1. *Computer capabilities.* Computers have evolved from the small, slow, and costly vacuum-tube machines of the 1950s to the supercomputers and microcomputers of today. At the same time, layers of operating system software have been inserted between the programming language and the underlying computer hardware. These factors have influenced both the structure and cost of using the features of high-level languages.

2. *Applications.* Computer use has spread rapidly from the original concentration on military, scientific, business, and industrial applications in the 1950s, where the cost could be justified, to the computer games, PCs, Internet, and applications in every area of human activity seen today. The requirements of these new application areas affect the designs of new languages and the revisions and extensions of older ones.

3. *Programming methods.* Language designs have evolved to reflect our changing understanding of good methods for writing large and complex programs and

to reflect the changing environment in which programming is done.

4. *Implementation methods.* The development of better implementation methods has affected the choice of features to include in new language designs.

5. *Theoretical studies.* Research into the conceptual foundations for language design and implementation, using formal mathematical methods, has deepened our understanding of the strengths and weaknesses of language features, which has influenced the inclusion of these features in new language designs.

6. *Standardization.* The need for standard languages that can be implemented easily on a variety of computer systems, which allow programs to be transported from one computer to another, has provided a strong conservative influence on the evolution of language designs.

To illustrate, Table 1.2 briefly lists some of the languages and technology influences that were important during the latter half of the 20th century. Many of these topics are taken up in later chapters. Of course, missing from this table are the hundreds of languages and influences that have played a lesser but still important part in this history.

1.3.1 What Makes a Good Language?

Mechanisms to design high-level languages must still be perfected. Each language in this book has shortcomings, but each is also successful in comparison with the many hundreds of other languages that have been designed, implemented, used for a period of time, and then allowed to fall into disuse.

Some reasons for the success or failure of a language may be external to the language itself. For example, use of COBOL or Ada in the United States was enforced in certain areas of programming by government mandate. Likewise, part of the reason for the success of FORTRAN may be attributed to the strong support of various computer manufacturers that have expended large efforts in providing sophisticated implementations and extensive documentation for these languages. Part of the success of SNOBOL4 during the 1970s can be attributed to an excellent text describing the language [GRISWOLD 1975]. Pascal and LISP have benefited from their use as objects of theoretical study by students of language design as well as from actual practical use.

Attributes of a Good Language

Despite the major importance of some of these external influences, it is the programmer who ultimately, if sometimes indirectly, determines which languages live and die. Many reasons explain why programmers prefer one language over another. Let us consider some of these.

Years	Influences and New Technology
1951–55	**Hardware:** Vacuum-tube computers; mercury delay line memories **Methods:** Assembly languages; foundation concepts: subprograms, data structures **Languages:** Experimental use of expression compilers
1956–60	**Hardware:** Magnetic tape storage; core memories; transistor circuits **Methods:** Early compiler technology; BNF grammars; code optimization; interpreters; dynamic storage methods and list processing **Languages:** FORTRAN, ALGOL 58, ALGOL 60, LISP
1961–65	**Hardware:** Families of compatible architectures; magnetic disk storage **Methods:** Multiprogramming operating systems; syntax-directed compilers **Languages:** COBOL, ALGOL 60 (revised), SNOBOL, JOVIAL
1966–70	**Hardware:** Increasing size and speed and decreasing cost; microprogramming; integrated circuits **Methods:** Time-sharing systems; optimizing compilers; translator writing systems **Languages:** APL, FORTRAN 66, COBOL 65, ALGOL 68, SNOBOL4, BASIC, PL/I, SIMULA 67, ALGOL-W
1971–75	**Hardware:** Minicomputers; small mass storage systems; semiconductor memories **Methods:** Program verification; structured programming; software engineering **Languages:** Pascal, COBOL 74, PL/I (standard), C, Scheme, Prolog
1976–80	**Hardware:** Microcomputers; mass storage systems; distributed computing **Methods:** Data abstraction; formal semantics; concurrent, embedded, and real-time programming techniques **Languages:** Smalltalk, Ada, FORTRAN 77, ML
1981–85	**Hardware:** Personal computers; workstations; video games; local-area networks; ARPANET **Methods:** Object-oriented programming; interactive environments; syntax-directed editors **Languages:** Turbo Pascal, Smalltalk-80, use of Prolog, Ada 83, Postscript
1986–90	**Hardware:** Age of microcomputer; engineering workstation; RISC architectures; Internet **Methods:** Client/server computing **Languages:** FORTRAN 90, C++, SML (Standard ML)
1991–95	**Hardware:** Very fast inexpensive workstations and microcomputers; massively parallel architectures; voice, video, fax, multimedia **Methods:** Open systems; environment frameworks **Languages:** Ada 95, Process languages (TCL, PERL), HTML
1996-2000	**Hardware:** Computers as inexpensive appliances; Personal digital assistants; World wide web; Cable-based home networking; Gigabyte disk storage **Methods:** E-commerce **Languages:** Java, Javascript, XML

Table 1.2. Some influences on programming language development.

1. *Clarity, simplicity, and unity.* A programming language provides both a conceptual framework for thinking about algorithms and a means of expressing those algorithms. The language should be an aid to the programmer long before the actual coding stage. It should provide a clear, simple, and unified set of concepts that can be used as primitives in developing algorithms. To this end, it is desirable to have a minimum number of different concepts, with the rules for their combination being as simple and regular as possible. We call this attribute *conceptual integrity.*

   The syntax of a language affects the ease with which a program may be written, tested, and later understood and modified. The readability of programs in a language is a central issue here. A syntax that is particularly terse or cryptic often makes a program easy to write (for the experienced programmer) but difficult to read when the program must be modified later. APL programs are often so cryptic that their own designers cannot easily decipher them a few months after they are completed. Many languages contain syntactic constructs that encourage misreading by making two almost identical statements actually mean radically different things. For example, the presence of a blank character, which is an operator, in a SNOBOL4 statement may entirely alter its meaning. A language should have the property in which constructs that *mean* different things look different; that is, semantic differences should be mirrored in the language syntax.

2. *Orthogonality.* The term *orthogonality* refers to the attribute of being able to combine various features of a language in all possible combinations, with every combination being meaningful. For example, suppose a language provides for an expression that can produce a value, and it also provides for a conditional statement that evaluates an expression to get a true or false value. These two features of the language, expression and conditional statement, are orthogonal if any expression can be used (and evaluated) within the conditional statement.

   When the features of a language are orthogonal, the language is easier to learn and programs are easier to write because there are fewer exceptions and special cases to remember. The negative aspect of orthogonality is that a program will often compile without errors even though it contains a combination of features that are logically incoherent or extremely inefficient to execute.

3. *Naturalness for the application.* A language needs a syntax that, when properly used, allows the program structure to reflect the underlying logical structure of the algorithm. Ideally, it should be possible to translate such a program design directly into appropriate program statements that reflect the structure of the algorithm. Sequential algorithms, concurrent algorithms, logic algorithms, and others all have differing natural structures that are represented by programs in those languages.

The language should provide appropriate data structures, operations, control structures, and a natural syntax for the problem to be solved. One of the major reasons for the proliferation of languages is this need for naturalness. A language particularly suited to a certain class of applications may greatly simplify the creation of individual programs in that area. Prolog, with its bias toward deduction properties, and C++, for object-oriented design, are two languages with an obvious slant toward particular classes of applications.

4. *Support for abstraction.* Even with the most natural programming language for an application, there is always a substantial gap remaining between the abstract data structures and operations that characterize the solution to a problem and the particular primitive data structures and operations built into a language. For example, C may be an appropriate language for constructing a program to do class scheduling for a university, but the abstract data structures of *student*, *class section*, *instructor*, *lecture room* and the abstract operations of *assign a student to a class section* and *schedule a class section in a lecture room*, which are natural to the application, are not provided directly by C.

   A substantial part of the programmer's task is to design the appropriate abstractions for the problem solution and then implement these abstractions using the more primitive features provided by the actual programming language. Ideally, the language should allow data structures, data types, and operations to be defined and maintained as self-contained abstractions. The programmer may use them in other parts of the program knowing only their abstract properties without concern for the details of their implementation. Both Ada and C++ were developed because of just these shortcomings in the earlier languages of Pascal and C, respectively.

5. *Ease of program verification.* The reliability of programs written in a language is always a central concern. There are many techniques for verifying that a program correctly performs its required function. A program may be proved correct by a formal verification method (see Section 4.2), it may be informally proved correct by *desk checking* (reading and visually checking the program text), it may be *tested* by executing it with test input data and checking the output results against the specifications, and so on. For large programs, some combination of all these methods is often used. A language that makes program verification difficult may be far more troublesome to use than one that supports and simplifies verification, even though the former may provide many more features that superficially appear to make programming easier. Simplicity of semantic and syntactic structure is a primary aspect that tends to simplify program verification.

6. *Programming environment.* The technical structure of a programming language is only one aspect affecting its utility. The presence of an appropriate programming environment may make a technically weak language easier to

work with than a stronger language that has little external support. A long list of factors might be included as part of the programming environment. The availability of a reliable, efficient, and well-documented implementation of the language must head the list. Special editors and testing packages tailored to the language may greatly speed the creation and testing of programs. Facilities for maintaining and modifying multiple versions of a program may make working with large programs much simpler. Of the languages discussed in this book, only Smalltalk was specifically designed around a programming environment consisting of windows, menus, mouse input, and a set of tools to operate on programs written in Smalltalk.

7. *Portability of programs.* One important criterion for many programming projects is the *transportability* of the resulting programs from the computer on which they are developed to other computer systems. A language that is widely available and whose definition is independent of the features of a particular machine forms a useful base for the production of transportable programs. Ada, FORTRAN, C, and Pascal all have standardized definitions allowing for portable applications to be implemented. Others, like ML, come from a single-source implementation allowing the language designer some control over portable features of the language.

8. *Cost of use.* The tricky criterion of cost has been left for last. Cost is certainly a major element in the evaluation of any programming language, but cost means many different things:

   (a) Cost of program execution. In the early years of computing, questions of cost were concerned almost exclusively with program execution. Research on the design of optimizing compilers, efficient register allocation, and the design of efficient run-time support mechanisms was important. Cost of program execution, although always of some importance in language design, is of primary importance for large production programs that will be executed repeatedly. Today, however, for many applications, speed of execution is not of highest concern. With desktop machines running at many million instructions per second and sitting idle much of the time, a 10% or 20% increase in execution time can be tolerated if it means better diagnostics or easier user control over development and maintenance of the program.

   (b) Cost of program translation. When a language like FORTRAN or C is used in teaching, the question of efficient translation (compilation) rather than efficient execution may be paramount. Typically, student programs are compiled many times while being debugged but are executed only a few times. In such a case, it is important to have a fast and efficient compiler rather than a compiler that produces optimized executable code.

   (c) Cost of program creation, testing, and use. Yet a third aspect of cost in a programming language is exemplified by the language Smalltalk and process languages like Perl. For a certain class of problems, a solution may be designed, coded, tested, modified, and used with a minimum investment of programmer time and energy. Smalltalk and Perl are cost-effective in that the overall time and effort expended in solving a problem on the computer is minimized even though execution time of the program may be higher than with other languages.

(d) Cost of program maintenance. Many studies have shown that the largest cost involved in any program that is used over a period of years is not the cost of initial design, coding, and testing of the program, but total *life cycle costs* including development costs and the cost of maintenance of the program while it is in production use. Maintenance includes the repair of errors discovered after the program is put into use, changes in the program required as the underlying hardware or operating system is updated, and extensions and enhancements to the program that are needed to meet new needs. A language that makes it easy for a program to be repeatedly modified, repaired, and extended by different programmers over a period of many years may be, in the long run, much less expensive to use than any other.

Syntax and Semantics

The *syntax* of a programming language is what the program looks like. To give the rules of syntax for a programming language means to tell how statements, declarations, and other language constructs are written. The *semantics* of a programming language is the meaning given to the various syntactic constructs. For example, in C, to declare a 10-element vector, *V*, of integers, you would give a declaration, such as

int V[10];

In contrast, in Pascal, it would be specified as

V: **array**[0..9] **of** integer;

Although both create similar data objects at run time, their syntax is very different. To understand the meaning of the declaration, you need to know the semantics of both Pascal and C for such array declarations. That is, you need to know that such a declaration placed at the beginning of a subprogram means to create the vector on each entry to that subprogram and destroy the vector on exit. The vector can be referenced by the name *V* during execution of the subprogram. In both examples, the elements of *V* are V_0, ..., V_9.

However, if *V* is created as a list in LISP, then you need to know that the size of the object is arbitrary and determined when the object is created, it can be created at arbitrary times during the execution of the program, and the first member is referenced as (*car V*) or (*head V*).

In programming language manuals and other language descriptions, it is customary to organize the language description around the various syntactic constructs in the language. Typically the syntax is given for a language construct such as a particular type of statement or declaration, then the semantics for that construct is also given, describing the intended meaning. In Chapter 3, we describe BNF as the major notation used to describe programming language syntax.

In this text, a different organization is used; it is organized around the structure associated with the execution of the program. Sometimes these data structures and operations are tied directly to particular constructs in the syntax of the language, but often the tie is much less direct. For example, an executing C program may use a vector V, where V has a structure that is given by the prior declaration. However, the compiled program may have other data structures, such as a central stack of subprogram activation records, that are not seen directly in the syntax of programs at all.

These hidden structures are as important to an understanding of the language as are the visible structures that correspond directly to something that the programmer has written in the program. For this reason, the discussion of language elements here is organized around the executable structures, rather than in terms of syntactic elements. A particular element may have no syntactic representation in a program, may be directly represented by a single syntactic element, or may be represented by several separate syntactic elements that are brought together by the language translator to produce one virtual computer element.

1.3.2 Language Paradigms

When proponents of various languages meet, the discussions often take the form of political rallies. Great debates ensue about the efficiency of the array declaration in C++ versus the array declaration in Java or the value of interpreting versus compiling a program. In truth, however, the array declarations and translation issues have very little to do with distinguishing between these languages. There are often minor syntactic variations that simply reflect the wishes of the language designers, which have little concrete effect upon the programs written in those languages. We need to look deeper to understand how languages are constructed.

There are four basic computational models that describe most programming today: imperative, applicative, rule based, and object oriented. We briefly describe each of these models.

Imperative languages. *Imperative* or *procedural languages* are command-driven or statement-oriented languages. The basic concept is the machine state, the set of all values for all memory locations in the computer. A program consists of a sequence of statements, and the execution of each statement causes the computer to change the value of one or more locations in its memory, that is, to enter a new state. The syntax of such languages generally has the form

$$statement_1;$$
$$statement_2;$$
$$\ldots$$

Figure 1.1(a) describes this process. Memory consists of a collection of *marbles in boxes*, and the execution of a statement (e.g., adding together two variables to get a third) can be represented as accessing the memory locations (the boxes), combining these values (the marbles) in some way, and storing the result (a new marble) in the new location. Program development consists of building the successive machine states needed to arrive at the solution. This is often the first view one has of programming, and many widely used languages (e.g., C, C++, FORTRAN, ALGOL, PL/I, Pascal, Ada, Smalltalk, and COBOL) support this model. This model follows from the hardware of the conventional computer that executes instructions sequentially. It is not surprising that most conventional languages follow this model.

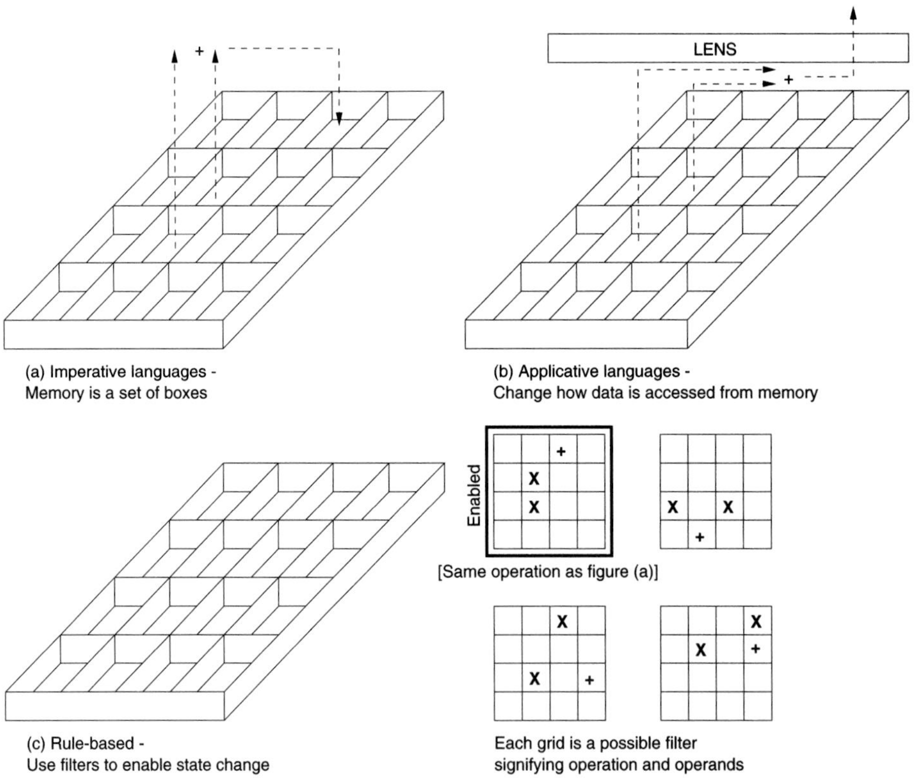

Figure 1.1. Computational models of programming languages.

Applicative languages. An alternative view of the computation performed by a programming language is to look at the function that the program represents rather than just the state changes as the program executes, statement by statement. We can achieve this by looking at the desired result rather than at the available data. In other words, rather than looking at the sequence of states that the machine must pass through in achieving an answer, the question to be asked is: What is the function that must be applied to the initial machine state by accessing the initial set of variables and combining them in specific ways to get an answer? Languages that emphasize this view are called *applicative* or *functional languages.*

We can view this model [Figure 1.1(b)] as a lens that takes the initial data and, by manipulating the view of memory (e.g., as through a lens), produces the desired answer. Program development proceeds by developing functions from previously developed functions to build more complex functions that manipulate the initial set of data until the final function can be used to compute an answer from the initial data. Rather than looking at the successive machine states of a computation, we consider the successive functional transformations that we must make on data to arrive at our answer. Once we have our final answer, we apply this to the initial data to arrive at a result. The syntax of such languages generally is similar to

$$function_n(\ldots function_2(function_1(data))\ldots)$$

LISP and ML are two functional languages in this book that support this model.

Rule-based languages. *Rule-based languages* execute by checking for the presence of a certain enabling condition and, when present, executing an appropriate action. The most common rule-based language is Prolog, also called a *logic programming language*, because the basic enabling conditions are certain classes of predicate logic expressions (to be discussed more fully in Section 8.4.2). We can describe rule-based languages in Figure 1.1(c) as a set of filters to apply to the data storage. Execution of a rule-based language is similar to an imperative language except that statements are not sequential. Enabling conditions determine the order of execution. The syntax of such languages generally is similar to the following:

$$\begin{array}{l} enabling\ condition_1 \rightarrow action_1 \\ enabling\ condition_2 \rightarrow action_2 \\ \ldots \\ enabling\ condition_n \rightarrow action_n \end{array}$$

(Sometimes the rules are written as *action if enabling condition* with the action on the left.)

Although Prolog is the most well-known language in this class, many other languages exist that use this paradigm. The common business application of decision tables is a form of rule-based programming. In this case, enabling conditions on data are governed by the presence or absence of enabling data values in a data record. Programming often consists of building a matrix (or table) of possible conditions and then giving appropriate actions if such a condition occurs (hence its name). BNF parsing techniques (described in chapter 3) and tools like YACC (Yet Another Compiler Compiler) to parse programs are rule-based techniques that use the formal syntax of the program as the enabling condition.

Object-oriented programming. As we discuss more fully in chapter 7, object-oriented programming is becoming an increasingly important computational model. In this case, complex data objects are built, then a limited set of functions are designed to operate on those data. Complex objects are designed as extensions of simpler objects, inheriting properties of the simpler object. As we show, what is actually happening is that we are trying to use the best of two of the other computational models. By building concrete data objects, an object-oriented program gains the efficiency of imperative languages. By building classes of functions that use a restricted set of data objects, we build the flexibility and reliability of the applicative model.

Generality of Computational Model

The preceding discussion was careful to use the word *supports* in describing a given computational model rather than the word *implements.* How one uses a programming language depends upon the programmer. Imperative languages simplify statement-oriented programming that manipulates the internal machine states of a computer, but it is possible to write both LISP or Prolog programs that execute sequentially to perform the same function. It is also relatively easy to write a C program that consists solely of function calls, and hence seems applicative. It is important to keep that in mind as we discuss language features later.

Historically, the imperative languages were the first widely used class of languages and are the dominant form in use today. One of the more interesting research results of the 1970s and 1980s was that applicative techniques provide for effective ways to verify programs and show that they are correct. To see this, observe the two flowgraphs of Figure 1.2. Figure 1.2(a) represents a flowchart of a typical program design of the 1960s. There is no obvious structure to the program, and control seems to jump almost randomly. Such programs today are often called *spaghetti code*, because the control paths resemble a bowl of spaghetti. In such programs, it is often difficult to understand the program state at any point during the execution of the program.

However, Figure 1.2(b) represents a more structured design. We can surround each segment of the flowgraph by a dotted box. Each of the four dotted boxes in this figure has a single arrow entering the box and a single arrow leaving. We can view this program as the composition of four functions, and we can define the behavior of the program as a function that takes a given state on entering a dotted box and transforms it into the result state on leaving the dotted box. This, however, is simply a form of the applicative model we just described. We will discuss this further

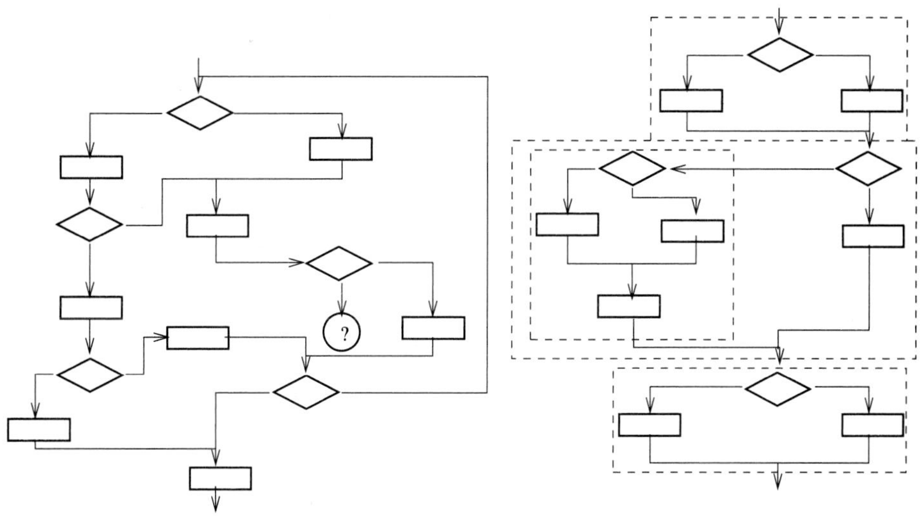

(a) Spaghetti code (b) Structured code

Figure 1.2. Applicative techniques in imperative languages.

when we describe prime programs in Section 8.3.3. Applying applicative techniques to imperative programs is behind much of the research in program verification, the use of formal proofs to show that a program is correct. Some of the predicate and algebraic techniques discussed in chapter 4 are based on this applicative model. We also see that object-oriented programming is another approach which, is based on applying the applicative model to imperative programs.

1.3.3 Language Standardization

What describes a programming language? Consider the following C code:

int i; i = (1 && 2) + 3;

Is this valid C? What is the value of *i*? How would you answer these questions?[1] The following three approaches are most often used:

1. Read the definition in the language reference manual to decide what the statement means.
2. Write a program on your local computer system to see what happens.
3. Read the definition in the language standard.

Option 2 is probably the most common. Simply sit down and write a two- or three-line program that tests this condition. Therefore, the concept of a programming

[1]Note that the answers are "yes" and "4," respectively, for the curious.

language is closely tied into the particular implementation on your local computer system. For the more scholarly, a language reference manual, typically published by the vendor of your local C compiler, can also be checked. Because few have access to the language standard, Option 3 is rarely employed.

Options 1 and 2 mean that a concept of a programming language is tied to a particular implementation. But is that implementation correct? What if you want to move your 50,000-line C program to another computer that has a compiler by a different vendor? Will the program still compile correctly and produce the same results when executed? If not, why not? Often language design involves some intricate details, and one vendor may have a different interpretation from another, yielding a slightly different execution behavior.

However, one vendor may decide that a new feature added to the language may enhance its usefulness. Is this legal? For example, if you extend C to add a new dynamic array declaration, can you still call the language C? If so, programs that use this new feature on the local compiler will fail to compile if moved to another system.

To address these concerns, most languages have standard definitions. All implementations should adhere to this standard. Standards generally come in two flavors:

1. *Proprietary standards.* These are definitions by the company that developed and owns the language. For the most part, proprietary standards do not work for languages that have become popular and widely used. Variations in implementations soon appear with many enhancements and incompatibilities.

2. *Consensus standards.* These are documents produced by organizations based on an agreement by the relevant participants. Consensus standards, or simply *standards*, are the major method to ensure uniformity among several implementations of a language.

Each country typically has one or more organizations assigned with the role of developing standards. In the United States, that is the American National Standards Institute (ANSI). Programming language standards are assigned to committee X3 of the Computer Business Equipment Manufacturers Association (CBEMA). The Institute of Electrical and Electronic Engineers (IEEE) also may develop such standards. In the United Kingdom, the standards role is assumed by the British Standards Institute (BSI). International standards are produced by the International Standards Organization (ISO) with headquarters in Geneva, Switzerland.

In the United States, standards are voluntary. The National Institute of Standards and Technology (NIST), an agency of the United States government, develops federal standards. These standards are only requirements on vendors that wish to sell products to federal agencies. Private companies are free to ignore such standards. However, because of the size of the federal government, these standards often become adopted, and NIST, ANSI, IEEE, and ISO often work together to develop many of these standards.

Standards development follows a similar process in all of these organizations. At some point, a group decides that a language needs a standard definition. The standards body charters a working group of volunteers to develop that standard. When the working group agrees on their standard, it is voted on by a larger voting block of interested individuals. Disagreements are worked out, and the language standard is produced.

Although it sounds good in theory, the application of standards making is partially technical and partially political. For example, vendors of compilers have a strong financial stake in the standards process. After all, they want the standard to be like their current compiler to avoid having to make changes in their own implementation. Not only are such changes costly, but users of the compiler, which employ the features that have changed, now have programs that do not meet the standard. This makes for unhappy customers.

Therefore, as stated earlier, standards making is a consensus process. Not everyone gets their way, but one hopes that the resulting language is acceptable to everyone. Consider the following simple example. During the deliberations for the 1977 FORTRAN standard, it was generally agreed that strings and substrings were desirable features, since most FORTRAN implementations already had such features. However, there were several feasible implementations of substrings: If M = "abcdefg," then the substring "bcde" could be the string from the second to fifth character of M (M[2:5]) or could be the string starting at Position 2 and extending for four characters (M[2:4]). It could also be written M[3:6] by counting characters from the right. Because no consensus could be reached, the decision was simply to leave this out of the standard. Although not fulfilling most of the goals for a language as expressed by this chapter, it was the expedient solution that was adopted. For this reason, standards are useful documents, but the language definition can get colored by the politics of the day.

To use standards effectively, we need to address three issues:

1. *Timeliness.* When do we standardize a language?

2. *Conformance.* What does it mean for a program to adhere to a standard and for a compiler to compile a standard?

3. *Obsolescence.* When does a standard age, and how does it get modified?

We consider each question in turn.

Timeliness. One important issue is *when* to standardize a language. FORTRAN was initially standardized in 1966 after there were many incompatible versions. This led to problems because each implementation was different from the others. At the other extreme, Ada was initially standardized in 1983, before there were any implementations; therefore, it was not clear when the standard was produced whether the language would even work. The first effective Ada compilers did not even appear until 1987, and several idiosyncrasies were identified by these early implementations. One would like to standardize a language early enough so that there is enough experience in using the language, yet not so late as to encourage many incompatible implementations.

Of the languages in this book, FORTRAN was standardized fairly late, when there were many incompatible variations; Ada was standardized very early, before any implementations existed; and C and Pascal were standardized while use was growing and before there were too many incompatible versions.

Conformance. If there exists a standard for a language, we often talk about *conformance* to that standard. A program is *conformant* if it only uses features defined in the standard. A *conforming compiler* is one that, when given a conformant program, produces an executable program that produces the correct output.

Note that this does not say anything about extensions to the standard. If a compiler adds additional features, then any program that uses those features is not conformant, and the standard says nothing about what the results of the computation should be. Standards generally address conformant programs. Because of this, most compilers have features that are not addressed by the standard. This means that one must be careful in using the local implementation as a final authority as to the meaning of a given feature in a language. (For example, see the Pascal program *anomaly* in Figure 9.5 on page 356.)

Obsolescence. As our knowledge and experience of programming evolve, new computer architectures require new language features. Once we standardize a language, it seems quaint a few years later. The original FORTRAN 66 standard is quite out of date without types, nested control structures, encapsulation, block structure, and the numerous other features in more modern languages.

The standardization process already takes some of this into account. Standards have to be reviewed every 5 years and either be renewed or dropped. The 5-year cycle often gets stretched out somewhat, but the process is mostly effective. FORTRAN was first standardized in 1966, revised in 1978 (called FORTRAN 77, although the proposed finalization date of 1977 was missed by a few months), and again in 1990. Ada was standardized in 1983 and revised in 1995.

One problem with updating a standard is what to do with the existing collection of programs written for the older standard. Companies have significant resources invested in their software, and to rewrite all of this code for a new version of a language is quite costly. Because of this, most standards require backward compatibility; the new standard must include older versions of the language.

There are problems with this. For one, the language can get unwieldy with numerous obsolete constructs. More damaging, some of these constructs may be detrimental to good program design. The FORTRAN EQUIVALENCE statement is one such feature. If A is a real number, and I is an integer, then

```
EQUIVALENCE (A,I)
A=A+1
I=I+1
```

assigns A and I to the same storage location. The assignment to A accesses this location as a real number and adds 1 to it. The assignment to I accesses this location assuming it is an integer and adds 1 to it. Because the representation of integers and reals on most computers is different, the results here are very unpredictable. Leaving this feature in the language is not a good idea.

Recently, the concepts of obsolescent and deprecated features have developed. A feature is *obsolescent* if it is a candidate feature that may be dropped in the next version of the standard. This warns users that the feature is still available, but in the next 5 to 10 years, it will be dropped. That gives a fair warning to rewrite any code using that feature. A *deprecated* feature may become obsolescent with the next standard, and hence may be dropped after two revisions. This gives a longer 10- to 20-year warning. New programs should not use these features.

Because standard-conforming compilers are allowed to have extensions to the language, as long as they compile standard-conforming programs correctly, most compilers have additions that the vendor thinks are useful and will increase market share for that product. This allows innovation to continue and the language to evolve. Of course, within the academic community, most faculty do not care about such standards and will develop their own products that extend and modify languages as they see fit. This provides a fertile atmosphere where new language ideas get tried, and some of the better ones make it into commercial languages and compilers.

1.3.4 Internationalization

With the globalization of commerce and the emergence of the WWW, programming is increasingly a global activity, and it is important for languages to be readily usable in multiple countries. There is increasing need for computers to "speak" many different languages. For example, use of an 8-bit byte, which can store up to 256 different character representations, to represent a character is often insufficient. This issue has generally gone under the name of *internationalization.*[2]

Often local conventions affect the way data are stored and processed. Such issues as character codes, collating sequences, formats for date and time, and other local standards affect input and output data. Some of the relevant issues are as follows[MARTIN 1992]:

Collating sequences. In what collating sequence should the characters be ordered?

- *Sorting.* The position of non-Roman characters, such as Å, Ø, ß, ö, and others is not uniformly defined and may have different interpretations in different countries.

[2]Also called the I18N issue, internationalization has 20 characters, and calling it I18N avoids the arguments as to whether it should be spelled with the British "s" or American "z."

- *Case.* Some languages like Japanese, Arabic, Hebrew, and Thai have no uppercase–lowercase distinction.

- *Scanning direction.* Most languages read from left to right, but others exist (e.g., right to left, top to bottom).

Country-specific date formats. 11/26/02 in the United States is 26/11/02 in England; 26.11.02 in France; 26-XI-02 in Italy, etc.

Country-specific time formats. 5:40 p.m. in the United States is 17:40 in Japan, 17.40 in Germany, 17h40 in France,and so on.

Time zones. Although the general rule is 1 hour of change for each 15 degrees of longitude, it is more a guideline than a reality. Time zones are generally an integral number of hours apart, but some vary by 15 or 30 minutes. Time changes (e.g., daylight savings time in the United States and summer time in Europe) do not occur uniformly around the world. Translating local time into a worldwide standard time is nontrivial. In the southern hemisphere, the transformation for summer time is opposite that of the northern hemisphere.

Ideographic systems. Some written languages are not based on a small number of characters forming an alphabet, but instead use large numbers of ideographs (e.g., Japanese, Chinese, and Korean). Often 16 bits might be needed to represent text in those languages.

Currency. Representation of currency (e.g., $, £, ¥) varies by country.

1.4 PROGRAMMING ENVIRONMENTS

A *programming environment* is the environment familiar to most readers of this book. It is the environment in which programs are created and tested, and it tends to have less influence on language design than the operating environment in which programs are expected to be executed. A programming environment consists primarily of a set of support tools and a command language for invoking them. Each support tool is another program that may be used by the programmer as an aid during one or more of the stages of creation of a program. Typical tools in a programming environment include editors, debuggers, verifiers, test data generators, and pretty printers.

1.4.1 Effects on Language Design

Programming environments have affected language design primarily in two major areas: features aiding separate compilation and assembly of a program from components and features aiding program testing and debugging.

Separate compilation. In the construction of any large program, it is ordinarily desirable to have different programmers or programming groups design, code, and test parts of the program before a final assembly of all the components into a complete program. This requires the language to be structured so that individual subprograms or other parts can be separately compiled and executed, without the other parts, and then later merged without change into the final program.

Separate compilation is made difficult by the fact that in compiling one subprogram, the compiler may need information about other subprograms or shared data objects, as in the following situation:

1. The specification of the number, order, and type of parameters expected by any subprogram called allows the compiler to check whether a call of the external subprogram is valid. The language in which the other subprogram is coded may also need to be known so that the compiler may set up the appropriate calling sequence of instructions to transfer data and control information to the external subprogram during execution in the form expected by that subprogram.

2. The declaration of data type for any variable referenced is needed to allow the compiler to determine the storage representation of the external variable so that the reference may be compiled using the appropriate accessing formula for the variable (e.g., the correct offset within the common environment block).

3. The definition of a data type that is defined externally but is used to declare any local variable within the subprogram is needed to allow the compiler to allocate storage and compute accessing formulas for local data.

To provide this information about separately compiled subprograms, shared data objects, and type definitions either (1) the language may require that the information be *redeclared* within the subprogram (in FORTRAN); (2) it may prescribe a particular *order of compilation* to require compilation of each subprogram to be preceded by compilation of the specification of all called subprograms and shared data (in Ada and to some extent in Pascal); or (3) it may require the presence of a library containing the relevant specifications during compilation so that the compiler may retrieve them as needed (in Java and C++).

The term *independent compilation* is usually used for Option 1. Each subprogram may be independently compiled without any external information; the subprogram is entirely self-contained. Independent compilation has the disadvantage that ordinarily there is no way to check the consistency of the information about external subprograms and data that are redeclared in the subprogram. If the declarations within the subprogram do not match the actual structure of the external data or subprogram, then a subtle error appears in the final assembly stage that will not have been detected during testing of the independently compiled program parts.

Options 2 and 3 require a means for specifications of subprograms, type definitions, and common environments to be given or placed in a library prior to the compilation of a subprogram. Usually it is desirable to allow the *body* (local variables and statements) of a subprogram to be omitted, with only the *specification* given. The body may be complied separately later. In Ada, for example, every subprogram, task, or package is split into two parts, a specification and a body, which may be separately compiled or placed in a library as required to allow compilation of other subprograms. A subprogram call made to a subprogram that has not yet been compiled is termed a *stub*. A subprogram containing stubs may be executed; when a stub is reached, the call causes a system diagnostic message to be printed (or other action taken) rather than an actual call on the subprogram. Thus, a separately compiled subprogram may be executed for testing purposes, even though code for some of the routines it calls is not yet available.

Another aspect of separate compilation that affects language design is in the use of shared names. If several groups are writing portions of a large program, it is often difficult to ensure that the names used by each group for subprograms, common environments, and shared type definitions are distinct. A common problem is to find, during assembly of the final complete program, that several subprograms or other program units have the same names. This often means a tedious and time-consuming revision of already-tested code. Languages employ three methods to avoid this problem:

1. Each shared name, such as in an *extern* statement in C, must be unique, and it is the obligation of the programmer to ensure that this is so. *Naming conventions* must be adopted at the outset so that each group has a distinct set of names they may use for subprograms (e.g., "all names used by your group must begin with QQ"). For example, names used within the standard C #include files are usually prefixed with _, so programmers should avoid variable names beginning with the underscore.

2. Languages often use *scoping* rules to hide names. If one subprogram is contained within another subprogram, only the names in the outermost subprogram are known to other separately compiled subprograms. Languages like Pascal, C, and Ada use this mechanism. We discuss block structure and scope of names more fully in Section 9.2.2.

3. Names may be known by explicitly adding their definitions from an external library. This is the basic mechanism of *inheritance* in object-oriented languages. By including an externally defined class definition into a subprogram, other objects defined by that class become known, as in Ada and C++. In Ada, names may also be *overloaded* so that several objects may have the same name. As long as the compiler can resolve which object is actually referenced, no change is needed in the calling program. Overloading is discussed more fully in Chapter 7.

Testing and debugging. Most languages contain some features to aid program testing and debugging. A few typical examples are the following:

1. *Execution trace features.* Prolog, LISP, and many other interactive languages provide features that allow particular statements and variables to be tagged for tracing during execution. Whenever a tagged statement is executed or a tagged variable is assigned a new value, execution of the program is interrupted, and a designated trace subprogram is called (which typically prints appropriate debugging information).

2. *Breakpoints.* In an interactive programming environment, languages often provide a feature where the programmer can specify points in the program as *breakpoints*. When a breakpoint is reached during execution, execution of the program is interrupted, and control is given to the programmer at a terminal. The programmer may inspect and modify values of variables and then restart the program from the point of interruption.

3. *Assertions.* An assertion is a conditional expression inserted as a separate statement in a program, for example,

   assert(X>0 **and** A=1) **or** (X=0 **and** A>B+10).

   The assertion states the relationships that must hold among the values of the variables at that point in the program. When the assertion is enabled, the compiler inserts code into the compiled program to test the conditions stated. During execution, if the conditions fail to hold, then execution is interrupted, and an exception handler is invoked to print a message or take other action. After the program is debugged, the assertions may be disabled so that the compiler generates no code for their checking. They then become useful comments that aid in documenting the program. This is a simple concept that exists in several languages, including C++.

1.4.2 Environment Frameworks

A support environment consists of infrastructure services called the *environment framework* to manage the development of a program. This framework supplies services such as a data repository, graphical user interface, security, and communication services. Programs are written to use these services. Programmers need to use the infrastructure services as part of their program design. Accordingly, languages are sometimes designed to allow for easy access to these infrastructure services.

For example, programs written in the 1960s all included specific I/O routines to handle communication with the user. With the growth of interactive systems, the concept of windows displayed on a screen has become the standard output format. Today, an environment framework would contain an underlying window manager, such as Motif, which uses the X Window System, and the program would only need to call on specific Motif functions to display windows, menus, and scroll bars and to perform most of the common windowing actions. The X Windows interfaces are part of the environment framework, which gives all programs that use it a common behavior pattern for the user at a terminal. Systems like Visual Basic and Microsoft's Visual Studio provide for libraries of services for C++ , Java, and BASIC programs to build window-based applications.

1.4.3 Job Control and Process Languages

Related to environment frameworks is the concept of *job control.* Today, if you want to execute a program such as the C compiler or a word processor, you move the mouse to the appropriate picture or icon on the screen and click the mouse. The appropriate program starts to execute. Before the age of windows-based systems, you would type in the name of the program to run (e.g., as you would do with the MS-DOS window on a PC today). Earlier still, during the punched-card era of computing, you would place a punched card naming the program to run ahead of the cards containing your data.

All of these allow the user to be in direct control of determining what steps to perform. If the compilation fails, the user could invoke an editor to correct the program; if the compilation succeeds, the user could invoke a loader and execute the program.

As we briefly described in Section 1.2.3, the 1960s saw the rise of processes as a computer took over the management of executing other programs. Rather than have an operator wait for each step to successfully finish, each program would produce a *return code,* and the command for the next step could test that return code and decide whether to execute. Thus, a sequence of steps—compile, load, execute program 1, execute program 2,—could be preloaded into the computer, and the operating system would sequence through these steps in a predefined manner. IBM used this approach in its Job Control Language for its System 360 beginning in 1963.

The developers of UNIX extended this concept. Rather than simply checking a return code on a previous job step, the control language could be a more complex structure with data, operations, and statements. In this case, the data objects would be the programs and files of the existing computer system. Thus, users could write programs that linked together various operations from other programs. One could then program the operation of a sequence of steps based on the contents of data files and the results of previous operations. This led to the UNIX *shell* including variations such as the Bourne shell, C shell, Korn shell, and so on. The $*$.*bat* file on the PC is a simple form of shell program.

From the concept of a shell, many related languages developed. These all go under the general category of a *process* or *scripting language.* They are generally interpreted and have the property that they view programs and files as the primitive data to manipulate. Languages such as AWK, Perl, and TCL have been used for years to develop such scripts and, for most of the past 20 years, have been viewed as part of the arcane province of the systems programmer. However, their popularity has increased with the advent of the Web. Such scripting languages are important for conveying information back and forth between a user at a web browser and a web server. Later (Section 12.2.2) we look at how one such language, Perl, is used in the development of Web programs.

Today we are in an environment where every organization is trying to provide products "faster, better, and cheaper." The term *Internet time* has been coined to describe the process that software development needs to proceed at the speed of the Internet—at megabits per second. The use of interpreted languages, such as these job control and scripting process languages, permits developers to *rapidly prototype* applications. A language like Perl allows developers to build simple algorithms that invoke other previously written software using shell scripts in a very rapid manner.

1.5 C OVERVIEW

C is one language that is closely allied with its programming environment.

History. C is a language developed in 1972 by Dennis Ritchie and Ken Thompson of AT&T Bell Telephone Laboratories. It is related to ALGOL and Pascal in style, with attributes of PL/I thrown in. Although a general-purpose programming language, its compact syntax and efficient execution characteristics have made it popular as a systems programming language.

In the late 1960s, AT&T Bell Telephone Laboratories dropped out of the MIT and GE project to develop the Multics operating system; however, developing a useful system was still the goal of Ken Thompson. Thus, began UNIX, whose name is a pun on the Multics name. Multics was programmed in PL/I, and there was a strong desire to also build this new system using a higher level language, although PL/I was deemed too cumbersome. Having some previous experience with the systems language BCPL (which was too low level and lacking in any run-time support), Thompson designed a language named B as a minimal subset of BCPL for systems programming ("BCPL squeezed into 8K bytes of [PDP-7] memory" [RITCHIE 1993]). Today, it is hard to realize how strong a constraint limited memory size was only 30 years ago.

In 1970, the UNIX project acquired a PDP-11 with its huge 24K memory. At this time, the small, but growing, embryonic UNIX community felt limited by the restrictions of B. Types, structure definitions, and additional operators were added, and the new language became known as C.

Although it is a general-purpose programming language, it has been closely associated with systems programming activities. It was first used to write the kernel of the UNIX operating system and has been closely tied to UNIX implementations every since, although versions of C exist on most computing systems today.

During the 1970s, C was mostly a university curiosity due to the university fascination with UNIX. However, as commercial versions of this operating system began to appear in the 1980s, the exposure of C caused its popularity to grow. In 1982, an ANSI working group began to develop a standard for the language, which was finally produced in 1989 [ANSI 1989] and was accepted as an international Standard (ISO/IEC 9899) in 1990.

Today, C programmers are probably the fastest growing segment of the programming world. With its C++ and Java derivatives, they are major influences in programming today. Most new languages today (e.g., Java, Perl) have a syntax and semantics partially based on their C roots.

Brief overview of the language. When discussing C, you almost always consider the C environment and not just the language defined by a specific grammar. C programming almost always consists of the following:

- *The C language.* This is a relatively small language with a limited number of control structures and features. (Remember its roots as a minimal compiler executing on a PDP 7 and then later on a small PDP 11.)

- *The C preprocessor.* Because almost every C compiler includes # preprocessor statements, most users do not realize that these are not really part of the C language.

- *The C interface assumptions.* A set of conventions has grown up over the use of C features. For example, interface definitions between modules are assumed to be defined in an appropriate ".h" (header) file. The statement

  #include "myfcn.h"

  uses both the C preprocessor and this third convention in specifying the interface to module *myfcn*.

- *The C library.* Many functions, such as *printf*, *getchar*, *malloc*, *fork*, and *exec*, have been written with C language interfaces, although they are not officially part of the C language definition. However, ANSI C includes these functions as required library functions for conforming compilers. The inclusion of a large library allows for a relatively small kernel language, which can be enhanced with such library functions.

A C module consists of global declarations and a sequence of functions. Multiple modules are loaded together to form one executable program. Each function may invoke other functions and access data local to that function or global.

With this structure, data storage is very simple. Each function has local storage or a local activation record, which is dynamic and allows for recursion, and each function has access to global data. There is no real block structure. Each data item has an efficient implementation. For example, multidimensional arrays are built out of one-dimensional arrays, and one-dimensional arrays have indices beginning with 0. This avoids the need for descriptors, which avoids all complex array calculations.

C has pointers, and there is an equivalence between arrays and pointers, permitting programs to use whichever method of access is most appropriate. Strings are implemented as arrays of characters. This implementation is completely transparent so that strings may be accessed as strings, as arrays, or, as just indicated, as pointers to individual characters.

C has a large set of arithmetic operators that give rise to very efficient and sometimes very terse programs. C has a full set of control structures with very flexible semantics, allowing for strange uses at times.

C has a flexible type definition facility; however, you can claim (correctly) that C is both strongly typed and not strongly typed. That is because most data items are subtypes of integers. Although the translator will find typing errors, because most data items are ultimately integers, many errors are missed.

C has always been closely tied to operating system functionality. In UNIX, operating system functions (e.g., the *malloc* function for allocating dynamic storage) are specified as C language function calls. By convention, these are specified in ".h" system files. So, for example, to call *malloc* from a C program, the program would include

#include <malloc.h>

at the beginning of the program, and simply use $malloc(StorageSize)$ when needed in the program. When such a program is compiled and loaded, the appropriate function definitions (e.g., *malloc*) are included from the C library.

The C compiler executes by invoking the preprocessor first. Commands like $\#define$ and *#include* are evaluated first, and then the complete program is compiled by the C translator.

I/O statements are patterned after the FORMAT concept of FORTRAN but address interactive program execution better than FORTRAN READ and WRITE statements. Most of the useful functions are defined in the system file stdio.h, which should be included in every C program. This provides an easy way to extend a language; a set of functions are written to add new functionality.

Comments (any text bounded by /* ... */) may appear wherever a blank may be used in a program. Because text is free format in the source files, continuation lines are generally not needed; however, macro preprocessor statements are defined as one line of input. Therefore, a macro preprocessor statement uses the symbol \ to indicate that the preprocessor statement continues on the next line.

1.6 SUGGESTIONS FOR FURTHER READING

Numerous texts discuss particular programming languages at an introductory level. The books by [DERSHEM and JIPPING 1995], [LOUDEN 1993], [SEBESTA 1998], and [SETHI 1996] provide alternative views of many of the issues treated here. The early history of programming languages is treated extensively in [SAMMET 1969, SAMMET 1972] and [ROSEN 1967]. Wexelblat [WEXELBLAT 1981] edited a collection of papers from the original designers of many major languages that are also of interest, including ALGOL, APL, COBOL, FORTRAN, and PL/I. A second History of Programming Languages conference was held in 1993 [ACM 1993]. This volume gives further information on the history of Prolog, C, LISP, C++, Ada, and Pascal, as well as several other languages not discussed in this book. The role of language standardization is discussed in [RADA and BERG 1995].

Each language in the book shows influences from its programming and operating environments. Ada, C, Java, LISP, ML, and Prolog are strongly influenced by these considerations. [BROWN et al. 1992] and [PERRY and KAISER 1991] summarized many modern environment designs. Program correctness and the limitations of verification techniques are summarized in [ABRAMS and ZELKOWITZ 1994]. The *IEEE Transactions on Software Engineering*, *ACM Transactions on Software Engineering and Methodology*, and *Software Practice and Experience* are three journals that often carry relevant articles in this area.

1.7 PROBLEMS

1. For a language that is heavily used on your local computer system, evaluate the reasons for its success according to the list of criteria given in Section 1.3.1. Should the list be extended?

2. Choose a standardized language for which you have access to the compiler. Write a program that is nonconformant yet compiles and executes. List several nonstandard features that the compiler accepts.

3. When the standard definition of a language is revised (usually every 5 to 10 years), a major influence on the revision is the requirement to make programs written in the earlier version portable to implementations of the revised version. Thus, there is pressure during the revision to make the new version include features of the earlier version. For the several standard definitions of Ada, COBOL, or FORTRAN, compare the features and list several poor ones whose appearance in a later standard is attributable primarily to the desire to maintain compatibility with the first.

4. Consider the following simple language. a and b represent names of integer variables. Each statement may have a label as a prefix. Statements in the language are as follows:

a = b	Assign a the value of b
a = a+1	Add 1 to a
a = a−1	Subtract 1 from a
if a=0 then goto L	If a=0, transfer control to statement L
if a>0 then goto L	If a>0, transfer control to statement L
goto L	Transfer control to statement L
halt	Stop execution

For example, the program that computes $a = a + b$ can be given by:

```
L:  a=a+1
    b=b-1
    if b>0 then goto L
    halt
```

(a) Write the following programs in this language:

(1) Given a and b, compute $x = a + b$
(2) Given a and b, compute $x = a \times b$
(3) Given a, b, c, and d, compute $x = a \times b$ and $y = c \times d$

(b) Discuss a minimal set of extensions needed to make this language easy to use. Consider concepts like subprograms, new statements, declarations, and so on.

5. Take one short program you have written in an imperative language (e.g., FORTRAN, C, and Pascal) and rewrite it to be applicative.

6. Features in C allow the same meaning to be expressed many ways. How many different statements can you write in C that add 1 to a variable X (i.e., equivalent to $X = X + 1$)? Discuss the advantages and disadvantages of this aspect in the design of C.

7. The **assert** statement on page 37 can be implemented as a run-time test that is executed each time the statement is reached, or it can be a property proved to be true at that point in the program.

(a) Discuss how each approach could be implemented. What is the difficulty in implementing each approach?

(b) What is the ultimate truth of each assertion for all executions of that program (i.e., when will that assertion always be true) for each implementation method?

8. Early computers were designed as electronic calculators to solve numerical problems. Speculate on what programming languages would be like if these early machines were developed for a different purpose (e.g., word processing, robot control, game playing).

9. Suppose a new language design provides three basic data types: *integer*, *real*, and *character*. It also provides the ability to declare *arrays* and *records* of data. Arrays have elements of the same type and records have elements of mixed types. Use the concept of *orthogonality* to critique the following two variants of this new design:

(a) Elements of arrays and records may be of any of these basic data types and may themselves also be arrays or records (e. g., an element of a record may be an array).

(b) Elements of arrays and records may be of type *integer* or *real*. Arrays of characters are called *strings* and get special treatment. Record elements may be of type *character*. Records may have arrays as elements, but arrays may not have records as elements. Arrays may not have arrays as elements, but multidimensional arrays are provided to get the same effect.

Chapter 2

Impact of Machine Architectures

As described in Section 1.2, early languages were designed to permit programs to run efficiently on expensive hardware. Therefore, the early languages (e.g., FORTRAN for arithmetic computation, LISP for list processing) had a design that translated into efficient machine code, even if the programs were hard to write. However, machines today are inexpensive, machine cycles are usually plentiful, but programmers are expensive. There is a greater emphasis in designing programs that are easy to write correctly even if they execute somewhat more slowly. The data typing features of ML, the **class** object of C++, and the **package** specification of Ada all take their toll on execution speed, but all have the advantage of easing the correctness problem of writing good programs. However, how do we design such languages?

In developing a programming language, the architecture of the software influences the design of a language in two ways: (1) the underlying computer on which programs written in the language will execute; and (2) the execution model, or virtual computer, that supports that language on the actual hardware. In this chapter, we briefly discuss these topics.

2.1 THE OPERATION OF A COMPUTER

A *computer* is an integrated set of algorithms and data structures capable of storing and executing programs. A computer may be constructed as an actual physical device using wires, integrated circuits, circuit boards, and the like, in which case it is termed an *actual computer* or *hardware computer*. However, it may also be constructed via software by programs running on another computer, in which case it is a *software-simulated* computer. A programming language is implemented by construction of a *translator*, which translates programs in the language into machine language programs that can be directly executed by some computer. The computer that executes the translated programs may either be a hardware computer or a

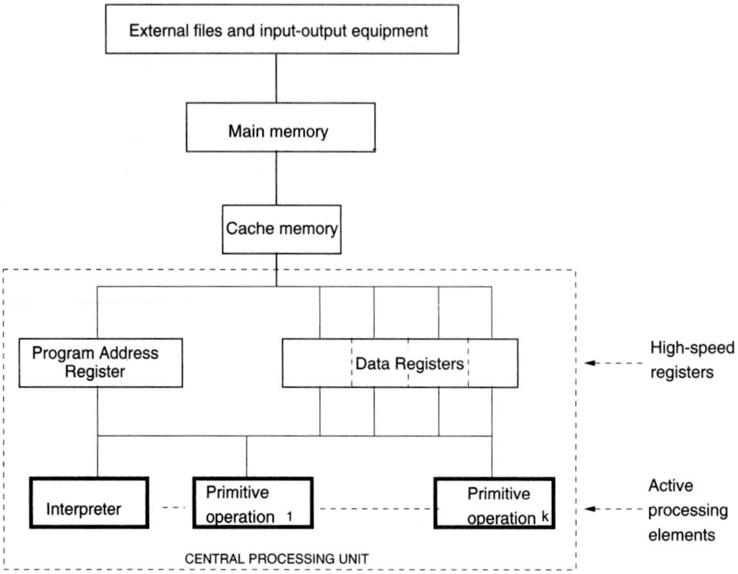

Figure 2.1. Organization of a conventional computer.

virtual computer composed partially of hardware and partially of software.

A computer consists of six major components that correspond closely to the major aspects of a programming language:

1. *Data.* A computer must provide various kinds of elementary data items and data structures to be manipulated.

2. *Primitive operations.* A computer must provide a set of primitive operations useful for manipulating the data.

3. *Sequence control.* A computer must provide mechanisms for controlling the sequence in which the primitive operations are to be executed.

4. *Data access.* A computer must provide mechanisms for controlling the data supplied to each execution of an operation.

5. *Storage management.* A computer must provide mechanisms to control the allocation of storage for programs and data.

6. *Operating environment.* A computer must provide mechanisms for communication with an external environment containing programs and data to be processed.

These six topics form the features from which languages are designed. However, before looking at these topics in the rather complex context of high-level programming languages, it is instructive to view them within the simple context of an actual hardware computer.

2.1.1 Computer Hardware

Hardware computer organizations vary widely, but Figure 2.1 illustrates a fairly typical conventional organization. A *main memory* contains programs and data to be processed. Processing is performed by an *interpreter*, which takes each machine language instruction in turn, decodes it, and calls the designated primitive operation with the designated operands as input. The primitives manipulate the data in main memory and in high-speed *registers* and also may transmit programs or data between memory and the external operating environment. Let us consider the six major parts of the computer in more detail.

Data. The schematic of Figure 2.1 shows three major data storage components: main memory, high-speed registers, and external files. *Main memory* is usually organized as a linear sequence of bits subdivided into fixed-length words (typically 32 or 64 bits) or 8-bit bytes (typically 4 or 8 bytes per word). The high-speed *registers* consist of word-length bit sequences and may have special subfields that are directly accessible. The contents of a register may represent data or the address in main memory containing the data or next instruction. A high-speed *cache memory* is often situated between main memory and the registers as a mechanism to speed up access to data from this main memory. *External files*, stored on magnetic disk, magnetic tape, or CD-ROM, are usually subdivided into records, each of which is a sequence of bits or bytes.

A computer has certain built-in data types that can be manipulated directly by hardware primitive operations. A common set might include integers, single-precision (e.g., one-word) reals, also called *floating-point numbers*, fixed-length character strings, and fixed-length bit strings (where the length is equal to the number of bits that fit into a single word of storage).

Besides these obvious hardware data elements, programs are also a form of data. As with the other built-in data types, there must be a built-in representation for programs, termed the *machine language representation* of the computer. Typically, a machine language program would be structured as a sequence of memory locations, each containing one or more instructions. Each instruction in turn is composed of an operation code and a set of operand designators.

Operations. A computer must contain a set of built-in primitive operations, usually paired one to one with the operation codes that may appear in machine language instructions. A typical set would include primitives for arithmetic on each built-in numeric data type (e.g., real and integer addition, subtraction, multiplication, and division), primitives for testing various properties of data items (e.g., test for zero,

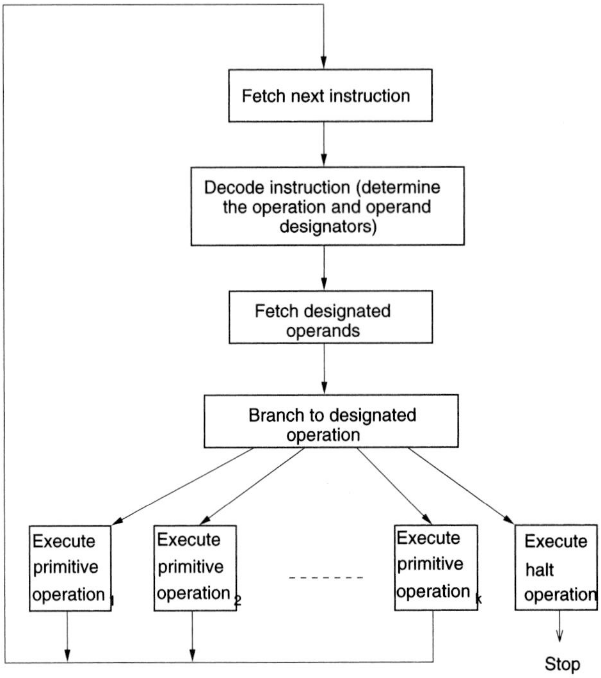

Figure 2.2. Program interpretation and execution.

positive, and negative numbers), primitives for accessing and modifying various parts of a data item (e.g., retrieve or store a character in a word and retrieve or store an operand address in an instruction), primitives for controlling input–output (I/O) devices, and primitives for sequence control (e.g., unconditional and return jumps).

As conventional machines (*complex instruction set computers* or CISC) have evolved, the set of available instructions have become more numerous and more powerful as a mechanism to increase the effective speed of the machine. However, alternatively, it has been found that faster computers can be built by designing them with fewer primitive instructions, which simplify the internal logic of the central processing unit (CPU). These *reduced instruction set computers* (RISC) are discussed in Section 11.3.

Sequence control. The next instruction to be executed at any point during execution of a machine language program is usually determined by the contents of a special *program address register* (also called the *location counter*), which always contains the memory address of the next instruction. Certain primitive operations are allowed to modify the program address register to transfer control to another part of the program, but it is the *interpreter* that actually uses the program address register and guides the sequence of operations.

The interpreter is central to the operation of a computer. Typically, the interpreter executes the simple cyclic algorithm shown in Figure 2.2. During each cycle, the interpreter gets the address of the next instruction from the program address register (and increments the register value to be the next instruction address), fetches the designated instruction from memory, decodes the instruction into an operation code and a set of operand designators, fetches the designated operands (if necessary), and calls the designated operation with the designated operands as arguments. The primitive operation may modify data in memory or registers, access I/O devices, or change the execution sequence by modifying the contents of the program address register. After execution of the primitive, the interpreter simply repeats the previously described cycle.

Data access. Besides an operation code, each machine instruction must specify the operands that the designated operation is to use. Typically an operand might be in main memory or in a register. A computer must incorporate a means of designating operands and a mechanism for retrieving operands from a given operand designator. Likewise, the result of a primitive operation must be stored in some designated location. We term these facilities the *data access control* of the computer. The conventional scheme is to simply associate integer *addresses* with memory locations and provide operations for retrieving the contents of a location given its address (or, alternatively, for storing a new value in a location whose address is given). Similarly, registers are also often designated by simple integer addresses.

Storage management. One driving principle in machine design is to keep all resources of the computer (e.g., memory, central processor, external data devices) operating as much as possible. The central conflict in achieving this principle is that operations within the CPU typically happen at the nanosecond level (e.g., 5–10 nanoseconds for a typical operation on a modern processor), accessing memory occurs at the microsecond level (50–70 nanoseconds), and external data operations occur at the millisecond level (10–15 milliseconds). This corresponds to a factor of 1,000,000 between the internal speed of a microprocessor and the speed of a disk. To balance these speeds appropriately, various storage management facilities are employed.

In the simplest design (e.g., a low-cost personal computer (PC) for home use), only simple storage management facilities are built into the hardware; programs and data reside in memory throughout program execution, and often only one program may be ready for execution at one time. Although the CPU must wait for appropriate data to be made available, it is cost-effective not to add additional hardware to speed up the process.

For speeding up the imbalance between external data access and the central processor, *multiprogramming* is often used by the operating system. While waiting the many milliseconds for data to be read (e.g., from disk), the computer will execute another program. To allow for many programs to be coresident in memory at the same time, it is now common to include facilities for *paging* or *dynamic program relocation* directly in the hardware. *Paging* algorithms exist that try to anticipate which program and data addresses will be most likely used in the near future so that the hardware can make them available to the central processor. Programs execute as long as the correct page of instruction or data is in main memory. If there is a *page fault* (i.e., the correct location is not in main memory), then the operating system will retrieve that page from the external data storage and in the meantime execute another program whose pages are in main memory.

For speeding up the imbalance between main memory and the central processor, a *cache memory* is used. A cache memory is a small high-speed data storage that is between main memory and the central processor. (See Figure 2.1.) This memory, typically $1K$ (where K is standard computer jargon for 1,024, or 2^{10}) to $512K$ bytes, contains the data and instructions most recently used by the central processor, and hence contains the data and instructions most likely to be needed again in the near future. The data in the cache are made available immediately to the central processor if there is a *hit* of the correct data in the cache, and changed data in the cache are stored in main memory at the slower main memory rate. If the specified address is not in the cache, the hardware will retrieve a block of data containing that address, as well as the next few addresses, to prefetch other data that probably will be needed shortly.

A cache allows the computer to operate as if the main memory had essentially the same speed as the central processor. With even small cache memories of 32K, hit rates of over 95% are generally achieved, yielding performance of the system as if the main memory operated essentially at the faster processor rate.

Operating environment. The operating environment of a computer ordinarily consists of a set of peripheral storage and I/O devices. These devices represent the outside world to the computer, and any communication with the computer must be by way of the operating environment. Often there are hardware distinctions between various classes of devices in the environment based on differences in use or speed of access (e.g., high-speed storage [extended memories], medium-speed storage [magnetic disks, CD-ROM], low-speed storage [tapes], and I/O devices [readers, printers, displays, data communication lines]).

Alternative computer architectures. The organization of the computer hardware often takes alternative forms. The previous discussion is often referred to as a *von Neumann architecture.* Other alternative architectures are possible,

von Neumann architecture. The von Neumann computer is named after the mathematician John von Neumann, who developed this initial design in the early 1940s as part of the design of ENIAC, which was one of the first electronic computers. A computer, in his design, consisted of a small controlling *central processing unit* (CPU) consisting of the primitive operations, sequence control and registers for storing the results of the primitive operations, a larger main memory, and a process for retrieving and storing words of data between the CPU and larger memory. Most computers sold today still adhere to this basic design, although additions like cache memory, many CPU registers, and virtual memory have increased performance.

Multiprocessors. As we just discussed, one problem with the von Neumann design is the great imbalance in the slow speed of external data devices and the high speed of the CPU registers. An alternative approach toward this imbalance is the use of multiple CPUs in a given system. Such *multiprocessing* systems have been in use for over 30 years. By coupling several relatively inexpensive CPUs with single sets of memory, disks, tapes, and so on, an effective system can be designed. The operating system runs different programs on different CPUs in the system and overall performance is improved.

For the most part, these developments are outside of the realm of programming language design because each CPU executes an independent program. However, language and system design is evolving so that programs are now being written to execute on multiple computers and communicate among one another. In Section 11.3.2 we discuss alternative machine architectures that provide for variations on this basic von Neumann design and look at their effects on programming language design and translation.

Computer states. An understanding of the *static organization* of a computer in terms of data, operations, control structures, and the like provides only part of the picture. Full understanding requires that we also see clearly the *dynamic operation* of the computer during program execution. What are the contents of the various storage components at the start of execution? What operations are executed in what sequence? How are the various data components modified as execution proceeds? What is the final result of program execution?

A convenient means of viewing the dynamic behavior of a computer is through the concept of *computer state.* Consider the process of program execution by the computer to proceed through a series of states, each defined by the contents of memory, registers, and external storage at some point during execution. The initial contents of these storage areas define the *initial state* of the computer. Each step in program execution transforms the existing state into a new state through modification of the contents of one or more of these storage areas. This transformation of state is termed a *state transition.* When program execution is complete, the *final state* is defined by the final contents of these storage areas. Program execution may be seen as the sequence of state transitions made by the computer.

2.1.2 Firmware Computers

Earlier we defined a computer as an integrated set of algorithms and data structures capable of storing and executing programs. The programs executed by a computer are, of course, written in the machine language of the computer. Ordinarily we think of computers as operating on a rather low-level machine language, with simple instruction formats and operations such as "add two numbers" and "load a register with the contents of a memory location." However, machine languages are not restricted to be low level. Choose any programming language (e.g., C, FORTRAN, ML) and specify precisely a set of data structures and algorithms that define the rules for execution of any program written in the language. In so doing, you are necessarily defining a computer—a computer whose machine language is the programming language you chose. Each program defines an initial state for the computer, and the rules for program execution define the sequence of state transitions that the computer will make during program execution. The result of program execution is determined by the final state of the computer when program execution is complete (if ever).

Given a precise definition of a computer, it is always possible to *realize the computer in hardware* (i.e., to construct a hardware device whose machine language is precisely that of the defined computer). This is true even if the machine language is C, Ada, or some other high-level language (e.g., the Burroughs B5500 mentioned in Section 1.2.1). In suggesting this possibility, we are appealing to an important basic principle behind computer design: *Any precisely defined algorithm or data structure may be realized in hardware.* Because a computer is simply a collection of algorithms and data structures, we may assume that its hardware realization is a possibility, regardless of the complexity of the computer or its associated machine language.

Actual hardware computers usually have a rather low-level machine language because of practical considerations. A computer with C or Ada as its machine language is likely to be considerably more complex (and hence more costly) and considerably less flexible in a variety of computing tasks than a computer with a low-level machine language. A hardware computer with a low-level general-purpose instruction set and a simple, unstructured main memory and register set may be programmed to look like any of a broad range of computers relatively efficiently, as we see in the following sections. Computers with high-level machine languages have occasionally been constructed, but other techniques for implementation of high-level languages are usually preferable over hardware realization.

A common alternative to the strict hardware realization of a computer is the *firmware computer* simulated by a *microprogram* running on a special *microprogrammable hardware computer.* The machine language of this computer consists of an extremely low-level set of *microinstructions,* which usually specify simple transfers of data between main memory and high-speed registers, between the registers themselves, and from registers through processors such as adders and multipliers to other registers. A special microprogram is coded, using this simple instruction set, that defines the interpretation cycle and the various primitive operations of the desired computer. The microprogram *simulates* the operation of the desired computer on the microprogrammable *host* computer. Ordinarily the microprogram resides in a special read-only memory in the host computer and is executed at high speed by the host computer hardware. This microprogram simulation of a computer is essentially the same, in concept, as the software simulation technique discussed in the next section, except that the host computer in this case is especially designed for microprogramming and provides execution speeds for the simulated computer comparable to those obtained by direct hardware realization.

Microprogram simulation of a computer is sometimes termed *emulation.* We also refer to the resulting computer as a *virtual computer* because it is simulated by the microprogram; without this microprogrammed simulation, the machine would not exist.

2.1.3 Translators and Virtual Architectures

In theory it may be possible to construct a hardware or firmware computer to execute directly programs written in any particular programming language, and thus to construct a LISP, Prolog, or C computer, but it is not ordinarily economical to do so. Practical considerations tend to favor actual computers with rather low-level machine languages on the basis of speed, flexibility, and cost. Programming, of course, is most often done in a high-level language far removed from the hardware machine language. The question, then, is how to get programs in the high-level language executed on the actual computer at hand, regardless of its machine language.

There are two basic solutions to this implementation question:

1. *Translation* (or *compilation*). A translator could be designed to translate programs in the high-level language into equivalent programs in the machine language of the actual computer. The interpreter and primitive operations built into the hardware then directly execute this machine language program. The general term *translator* denotes any language processor that accepts programs in some *source language* (which may be high or low level) as input and produces functionally equivalent programs in another *object language* (which may also be high or low level) as output. Several specialized types of translator have particular names:

a. An *assembler* is a translator whose object language is also some variety of machine language for an actual computer but whose source language, an *assembly language,* represents for the most part a symbolic representation of the object machine code. Most instructions in the source language are translated one for one into object language instructions.

b. A *compiler* is a translator whose source language is a high-level language and whose object language is close to the machine language of an actual computer, either being an assembly language or some variety of machine language. C, for example, is usually compiled into an assembly language, which is then converted into machine language by an assembler.

c. A *loader* or *link editor* is a translator whose object language is actual machine code and whose source language is almost identical; it usually consists of machine language programs in *relocatable* form together with tables of data specifying points, where the relocatable code must be modified to become truly executable. For example, subprogram P might be compiled for Addresses 0 to 999, and subprogram Q might be compiled to use Addresses 0 to 1,999. In addition, these subprograms may use library functions that are defined for addresses 0 to 4,999. The loader's function is to create a single *executable program* whose addresses are compatible, as in the following table:

Subprogram	Compiled Addresses	Executable Addresses
P	0-999	0-999
Q	0-1,999	1,000-2,999
library	0-4,999	3,000-7,999

The executable program will look as if it were a single program using addresses from 0 to 7,999.

d. A *preprocessor* or a *macroprocessor* is a translator whose source language is an extended form of some high-level language such as C++ or Java and whose object language is the standard form of the same language. The object program produced by a preprocessor is then ready to be translated and executed by the usual processors for the standard language. Most C compilers include such a preprocessor for first translating C macro references into standard C source statements.

Translation of a high-level source language into executable machine language programs often involves more than one translation step. For example, it is not uncommon to have C++ programs first translated into C programs, compiled into assembly language, assembled to produce relocatable machine code, and finally link-edited and loaded to produce executable machine code. Moreover, the compilation step may involve a number of passes that progressively translate the program into various intermediate forms before producing the final object program.

2. *Software simulation* (*software interpretation*). Rather than translating the high-level language programs into equivalent machine-language programs, we might instead *simulate,* through programs running on another host computer, *a computer whose machine language is the high-level language.* To do this, we construct a set of programs in the machine language of the host computer that represent the algorithms (and data structures) necessary for the execution of programs in the high-level language. In other words, we construct with software running on the host computer the high-level language computer that we might otherwise have constructed in hardware. This is termed a *software simulation* (or *software interpretation*) of the high-level language computer on the host computer. The simulated computer accepts as input data a program in the high-level language. The main simulator program performs an interpretation algorithm similar to that of Figure 2.2 decoding and executing each statement of the input program in the appropriate sequence and producing the specified output from the program.

In such a case, we say that the host computer creates a *virtual machine* simulating the high-level language. When the host computer is executing the high-level program, it is not possible to tell whether the program is being executed directly by the hardware or is first converted to the low-level machine language of the hardware computer.

Note the difference between software simulation and translation. Both translator and simulator accept programs in the high-level language as input. However, the

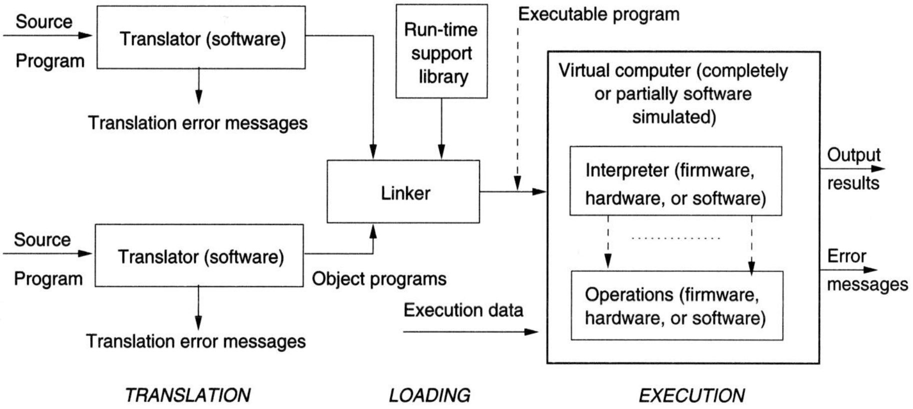

Figure 2.3. Structure of a typical language implementation.

translator simply produces an equivalent program in its object language, which must then be executed by an interpreter for the object language. The simulator executes the input program directly. If we were to follow the processing of the input program by both translator and simulator, we would observe the translator processing the program statements in their physical input sequence and the simulator following the logical flow of control through the program. The translator would ordinarily process each program statement exactly once, whereas the simulator might process some statements repeatedly (if they were part of a loop) and might ignore others completely (if control never reached them).

Pure translation and pure simulation form two extremes. In practice, pure translation is seldom used except in cases where the input language is in fact quite similar to the machine language, as in the case of assembly languages. Pure simulation is also relatively rare except in the case of operating system control languages or interactive languages. More commonly, a language is implemented on a computer by a combination of translation and simulation, as shown in Figure 2.3. A program is first translated from its original form into a form that is more easily executable. This is usually done via several independent pieces, called *procedures*, *subprograms*, or *subroutines*. These separate pieces are combined during the loading phase with a set of run-time support routines that represent software-simulated operations into an executable form of the program, which is decoded and executed by simulation.

Translation and simulation provide different advantages in a programming language implementation. Some aspects of program structure are best translated into simpler forms before execution; other aspects are best left in their original form and processed only as needed during execution. Statements in the original source language program that are executed repeatedly (e.g., statements within program loops or statements in subprograms that are called more than once) are more efficient if translated. These statements often require a complicated decoding process to determine the operations to be executed and their operands. Most or all of this process is identical each time the statement is executed. Thus, if the statement is executed 1,000 times, the identical decoding must be performed 1,000 times. If instead the statement is translated into a form that is simple to decode (e. g., as a sequence of machine-language instructions), then the complex decoding process need be executed only once by the translator, and only a simple decoding of the translated statement is needed during each of the 1,000 repetitions during execution.

The major disadvantage of translation is loss of information about the program. If data from the source program are translated to a sequence of machine-language addresses, and there is an error in the program (e.g., one of these data objects is divided by 0), it is often difficult to determine which source language statement was executing and which data objects were being manipulated. With simulation, all of this information is still available for displaying to the user. In addition, because a high-level language statement conveys more information than a single machine-language instruction, an object program is usually much larger than the source program that produced it.

Simulation provides almost an inverted set of advantages. By leaving statements in their original form until they need to be executed, no space is needed to store multiple copies of long code sequences; the basic code need be stored only once in the simulation routine. However, the total cost of decoding must be paid each time the statement is to be executed.

The key question in a language implementation tends to be whether the base representation of the program during execution is that of the machine language of the actual computer being used. This provides the basis for the common division of languages (more precisely, language implementations) into those that are *compiled* and those that are *interpreted:*

1. *Compiled languages.* C, C++, FORTRAN, Pascal, and Ada are commonly thought of as languages that are compiled. This means that programs in these languages are usually translated into the machine language of the actual computer being used before execution begins, with simulation being confined to a set of *run-time support routines* that simulate primitive operations in the source language that have no close analogue in the machine language. Typically, the translator for a compiled language is relatively large and complex, and the emphasis in translation is on the production of a translated program that executes as efficiently as possible.

2. *Interpreted languages.* LISP, ML, Perl, Postscript, Prolog, and Smalltalk are often implemented by use of a software interpreter. In such a language implementation, the translator does not produce machine code for the computer being used. Instead, the translator produces some intermediate form of the program that is more easily executable than the original program form yet that is different from machine code. The interpretation procedure for execution of this translated program form must be represented by software because the hardware interpreter cannot be used directly. Use of a software interpreter ordinarily results in relatively slow program

execution. Translators for interpreted languages tend to be rather simple, with most of the complexity of the implementation coming in the simulation software.

Java and the WWW have changed some of these rules. Java, a language more like C++ and Pascal than LISP, is nevertheless often processed as an interpreted language with the Java compiler producing an intermediate set of *bytecodes* for a Java virtual machine. For Web applications, major inefficiency is due to the transmission time of web pages over the network and not in host machine time. By transmitting the bytecodes to the local machine, execution is often faster, even on a slow computer, than transmitting the results from the Web server. However, the Web server does not know the underlying machine architecture of the host computer. In this case, the Web browser creates a Java virtual machine that executes the standard set of Java bytecodes.

2.2 VIRTUAL COMPUTERS AND BINDING TIMES

In the previous section, a computer was defined as an integrated set of algorithms and data structures capable of storing and executing programs. We considered ways in which a given computer might actually be constructed:

1. Through a *hardware realization,* representing the data structures and algorithms directly with physical devices.

2. Through a *firmware realization,* representing the data structures and algorithms by microprogramming a suitable hardware computer.

3. Through a *virtual machine,* representing the data structures and algorithms by programs and data structures in some other programming language.

4. Through some *combination* of these techniques, representing various parts of the computer directly in hardware, in microprograms, or by software simulation as appropriate.

When a programming language is implemented, the run-time data structures and algorithms used in program execution define a computer. Similar to the firmware implementation of a computer, we speak of this as the *virtual computer defined by the language implementation.* The machine language of this virtual computer is the executable program produced by the translator for the language, which may take the form of actual machine code if the language is compiled, or, alternatively, may have some arbitrary structure if the language is interpreted. The data structures of this virtual computer are the run-time data structures that are used during program execution. The primitive operations are those operations that are actually executable at run time. Sequence control, data control, and storage management structures are those used at run time regardless of representation by software, hardware, or microprogram.

2.2.1 Virtual Computers and Language Implementations

If programming languages are defined in terms of their virtual computers so that each language is associated with a single commonly understood virtual computer, then description of the semantics of each language in terms of its virtual computer is straightforward. Unfortunately, because languages are usually defined by giving a semantics for each syntactic construct individually, language definitions specify only implicitly an underlying virtual computer. Each time the language is implemented on a different computer, the implementor tends to see a slightly (or very) different virtual computer in the language definition. Thus, two different implementations of the same language may utilize a different set of data structures and operations in the implementation, particularly for data structures and operations that are hidden in the program syntax. Each implementor has wide latitude in determining the virtual computer structures that are the basis for a particular implementation.

When a programming language is being implemented on a particular computer, the implementor first determines the virtual computer that represents an interpretation of the semantics of the language and then constructs that virtual computer out of the hardware and software elements provided by the underlying computer. For example, if the virtual computer contains both an integer-addition operation and a square-root operation, the implementor may choose to represent the integer-addition operation using an integer-addition operation provided directly by the underlying hardware, whereas the square-root operation may be represented by a software simulation as a subprogram for computing square roots. If the virtual computer contains a simple integer variable X, then the implementor may choose to represent X directly by a storage location in memory containing the value of X or may choose to represent X by a storage location that contains a type tag designating integer together with a pointer to another storage location that contains the value of X. The organization and structure of an implementation of a language are determined by these many detailed decisions made by the implementor, taking into account the various hardware and software facilities available in the underlying computer and the costs of their use.

The implementor must also determine precisely what is to be done during translation of a program and what during execution. Often a particular way of representing a virtual computer data structure or operation during program execution can be used only if certain kinds of actions are taken during program translation to set up the run-time structure. If the implementor chooses to simplify the translator by omitting these actions, then different run-time representations may be necessary.

Thus, three factors lead to differences among implementations of the same language:

1. Differences in each implementor's conception of the virtual computer that is implicit in the language definition.

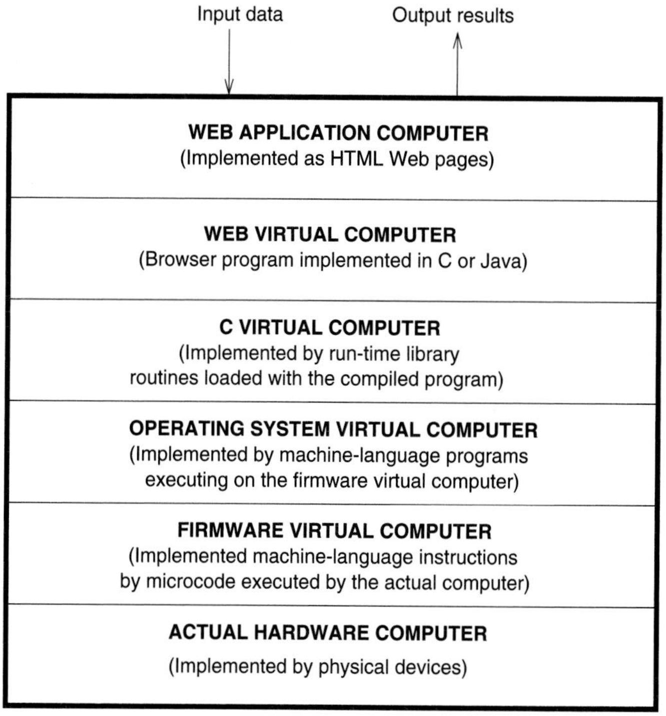

Figure 2.4. Layers of virtual computers for a Web application.

2. Differences in the facilities provided by the host computer on which the language is to be implemented.

3. Differences in the choices made by each implementor as to how to simulate the virtual computer elements using the facilities provided by the underlying computer and how to construct the translator so as to support these choices of virtual computer representation.

2.2.2 Hierarchies of Virtual Machines

The virtual machine that a programmer uses to create an application is in fact formed from a *hierarchy of virtual computers.* At the bottom, there must, of course, lie an actual hardware computer. However, the ordinary programmer seldom has any direct dealing with this computer. Instead, this hardware computer is successively transformed by layers of software (or microprograms) into a virtual machine that may be radically different. The second level of virtual computer (or the third if a microprogram forms the second level) is usually defined by the complex collection of routines known as the *operating system.*

Typically the operating system provides simulations for a number of new operations and data structures that are not directly provided by the hardware (e.g., external file structures or time-of-day functions). The operating system also deletes certain hardware primitives from the operating-system-defined virtual computer so that they are not accessible to the operating system user (e.g., hardware primitives for I/O, turning the machine off, multiprogramming, and multiprocessing). The operating-system-defined virtual computer is usually that which is available to the implementor of a high-level language. The language implementor provides a new layer of software that runs on the operating-system-defined computer and simulates the operation of the virtual computer for the high-level language. The implementor also provides a translator for translating user programs into the machine language of the language-defined virtual computer.

The hierarchy in fact does not end with the high-level language implementation. The programs that a programmer builds add yet more levels to the hierarchy. Figure 2.4 illustrates such a hierarchy of virtual machines as they might appear to a user on the WWW.

On top of the C-language virtual machine created by the C-language compiler, a programmer builds a program called a Web browser using the C (or equivalent) language. This browser creates the Web virtual machine, which can process the basic data structures of the WWW, the hyperlinks (URLs) to visit new web sites, the basic HTML language for displaying Web pages, and the ability to run interactive programs (i.e., applets) for users of that browser. At the highest level in this particular hierarchy is the Web application computer. The Web developer uses the features of the Web virtual machine (HTML, applets, etc.) to provide services to users of that Web page.

Implicit in this discussion is a central concept: *the equivalence of programs and data.* We are accustomed to considering certain kinds of objects in programming as program and others as data. This is often a useful intuitive distinction, but, as the prior discussion makes clear, it is a distinction that is more apparent than real. That which is program in one context is likely to become data in another. For example, the HTML describing a Web page is data to the Web virtual machine, which processes the commands to determine how to display the information, but it is a program to the Web developer who uses HTML to process information for users of that particular web site.

This equivalence between programs and data can be taken a step further. In languages like C and FORTRAN, the storage representing the executable program is generally separated from the storage containing the data used by that program. In other languages, such as Prolog and LISP, there is no real distinction. Programs and data are all intermixed, and it is only the execution process that keeps them separate.

2.2.3 Binding and Binding Time

Without attempting to be too precise, we may speak of the *binding* of a program element to a particular characteristic or property as simply the choice of the property from a set of possible properties. The time during program formulation or processing when this choice is made is termed the *binding time* of that property for that element. There are many different varieties of bindings in programming languages, as well as a variety of binding times. We also include within the concepts of binding and binding time the properties of program elements that are fixed either by the definition of the language or its implementation.

Classes of Binding Times

Although there is no simple categorization of the various types of bindings, a few main binding times may be distinguished if we recall our basic assumption that the processing of a program, regardless of the language, always involves a translation step followed by execution of the translated program:

1. *Execution time* (*run time*). Many bindings are performed during program execution. These include bindings of variables to their values, as well as (in many languages) the binding of variables to particular storage locations. Two important subcategories may be distinguished:

a. On entry to a subprogram or block. In most languages, bindings are restricted to occur only at the time of entry to a subprogram or block during execution. For example, in C and C++, the binding of formal to actual parameters and the binding of formal parameters to particular storage locations may occur only on entry to a subprogram.

b. At arbitrary points during execution. Some bindings may occur at any point during execution of a program. The most important example here is the basic binding of variables to values through assignment, whereas some languages like LISP, Smalltalk, and ML permit the binding of names to storage locations to also occur at arbitrary points in the program.

2. *Translation time* (*compile time*). Three different classes of translation time bindings may be distinguished:

a. Bindings chosen by the programmer. In writing a program, the programmer consciously makes many decisions regarding choices of variable names, types for variables, program statement structures, and so on, that represent bindings during translation. The language translator makes use of these bindings to determine the final form of the object program.

b. Bindings chosen by the translator. Some bindings are chosen by the language translator without direct programmer specification. For example, the relative location of a data object in the storage allocated for a procedure is generally handled without knowledge or intervention by the programmer. How arrays are stored and how descriptors for the arrays, if any, are created are decisions made by the language translator. Different implementations of a given language may choose to provide these features in different ways.

c. Bindings chosen by the loader. A program usually consists of several subprograms that must be merged into a single executable program. The translator typically binds variables to addresses within the storage designated for each subprogram. However, this storage must be allocated actual addresses within the physical computer that will execute the program. This occurs during *load time* (also called *link time*).

3. *Language implementation time.* Some aspects of a language definition may be the same for all programs that are run using a particular implementation of a language, but they may vary between implementations. For example, often the details associated with the representations of numbers and arithmetic operations are determined by the way that arithmetic is done in the underlying hardware computer. A program written in the language that uses a feature whose definition has been fixed at implementation time will not necessarily run on another implementation of the same language; even more troublesome, it may run and give different results.

4. *Language definition time.* Most of the structure of a programming language is fixed at the time the language is defined, in the sense of specification of the alternatives available to a programmer when writing a program. For example, the possible alternative statement forms, data structure types, program structures, and so on are all often fixed at language definition time.

To illustrate the variety of bindings and binding times, consider the simple assignment statement

$$X = X + 10$$

written in a language L. We might inquire into the bindings and binding times of the following elements of this statement:

1. *Set of types for Variable X.* Variable X in the statement usually has a data type associated with it, such as *real, integer,* or *Boolean.* The set of allowable types for X is often fixed at language definition time (e.g., only types *real, integer, Boolean, set,* and *character* might be allowed). Alternatively, the language may allow each program to define new types, as in C, Java, and Ada, so that the set of possible types for X is fixed at translation time.

2. *Type of variable X.* The particular data type associated with variable X is often fixed at translation time through an explicit declaration in the program such as *float X*, which is the C designation for a real data type. In other languages, such as Smalltalk and Perl, the data type of X may be bound at execution time through assignment of a value of a particular type to X. In these languages, X may refer to an integer at one point and to a string at a later point in the same program.

3. *Set of possible values for variable X.* If X has data type *real,* then its value at any point during execution is one of a set of bit sequences representing real

numbers. The precise set of possible values for X is determined by the real numbers that can be represented and manipulated in the virtual computer defining the language, which ordinarily is the set of real numbers that can be represented conveniently in the underlying hardware computer.

4. *Value of Variable X.* At any point during program execution, a particular value is bound to Variable X. This value is determined at execution time through assignment of a value to X. The assignment $X = X + 10$ changes the binding of X, replacing its old value by a new one that is 10 more than the old one.

5. *Representation of the constant 10.* The integer 10 has both a representation as a constant in the text of the program, using the string 10, and a representation at execution time, commonly as a sequence of bits. The choice of decimal representation in the program (i.e., using 10 for ten) is usually made at *language definition time,* whereas the choice of a particular sequence of bits to represent 10 at execution time is usually made at *language implementation time.*

6. *Properties of the operator +.* The choice of symbol + to represent the addition operation is made at *language definition time.* However, it is common to allow the same symbol + to be overloaded by representing *real addition, integer addition, complex addition,* and so on, depending on the context. In a compiled language, it is common to make the determination of which operation is represented by + at *compile time.* The mechanism for specifying the binding desired is usually the typing mechanism for variables: If X is type integer, then the + in $X + 10$ represents integer addition; if X is type real, then the + represents real addition, and so on.

   The detailed definition of the operation represented by + may also depend on the underlying hardware computer. In our example, if X has the value 2^{49}, then $X + 10$ may not even be defined on some computers.

   In summary, for a language like C, the symbol + is bound to a set of *addition operations* at language definition time, each addition operation in the set is defined at language implementation time, each particular use of the symbol + in a program is bound to a particular addition operation at translation time, and the particular value of each particular addition operation for its operands is determined only at execution time.

Importance of Binding Times

In the analysis and comparison of programming languages in the following chapters, many distinctions are based on differences in binding times. We are continuously in the process of asking this question: Is this done at translation time or at execution time? Many of the most important and subtle differences among languages involve differences in binding times. For example, almost every language allows numbers as data and allows arithmetic operations on these numbers. Yet not all languages are equally suited for programming problems involving a great deal of arithmetic. For example, although both ML and FORTRAN allow one to set up and manipulate arrays of numbers, solving a problem requiring large arrays and large amounts of arithmetic in ML would probably be most inappropriate if it could also be done in FORTRAN. If we were to trace the reason for this by comparing the features of ML and FORTRAN, we ultimately would ascribe the superiority of FORTRAN in this case to the fact that in ML most of the bindings required in the program will be set up at execution time, whereas in FORTRAN most will be set up at translation time. Thus, an ML version of the program would spend most of its execution time creating and destroying bindings, whereas in the FORTRAN version most of the same bindings would be set up once during translation, leaving only a few to be handled during execution. As a result, the FORTRAN version would execute much more efficiently.

Nevertheless, we might turn around and ask a related question: Why is FORTRAN so inflexible in its handling of strings as compared with ML? Again the answer turns on binding times. Because most bindings in FORTRAN are performed at translation time, before the input data are known, it is difficult in FORTRAN to write programs that can adapt to a variety of different data-dependent situations at execution time. For example, the size of strings and the type of variables must be fixed at translation time in FORTRAN. In ML, bindings may be delayed during execution until the input data have been examined and the appropriate bindings for the particular input data determined.

A language like FORTRAN, in which most bindings are made during translation, early in the processing of a program, is said to have *early binding;* languages with *late binding,* such as ML or HTML, delay most bindings until execution time.

The advantages and disadvantages of early binding versus late binding revolve around a conflict between efficiency and flexibility. In languages where execution efficiency is a prime consideration, such as FORTRAN, Pascal, and C, it is common to design the language so that as many bindings as possible may be performed during translation. Where flexibility is the prime determiner, as in ML and LISP, most bindings are delayed until execution time so that they may be made data dependent. In a language designed for both efficient execution and flexibility, such as Ada, multiple options are often available that allow choices of binding times.

Binding Times and Language Implementations

Language definitions are usually permissive in specifying binding times. A language is designed so that a particular binding may be performed at translation time, but the actual time at which the binding is performed is in fact defined only by the implementation of the language. For example, Pascal is designed to permit the type of variables to be determined at compile time, but a particular Pascal implementation might instead do type checking at execution time. Thus, although the definition of Pascal permits compile-time type checking, it does not require it. In general, a language design specifies the earliest time during program processing at which a particular binding is possible, but any implementation of the language may in fact delay the binding. However, usually most implementations of the same language will perform most bindings at the same time. If the language is designed to permit compile-time bindings, then to delay these bindings until execution time will probably lead to less efficient execution at no gain in flexibility, such as the prior example of execution-time type checking in Pascal.

One additional caution is needed, however. Often seemingly minor changes in a language may lead to major changes in binding times. For example, in FORTRAN 90, the change to allow recursion modifies many of the binding times of important FORTRAN features. Because binding times are implementation dependent, we place emphasis on knowing the language implementation. When approaching your own local implementation of a language, it is important to ask about the binding times in that implementation. Are they the usual ones, or have local modifications to the language caused the usual binding times to be modified?

2.2.4 Java Overview

History. Java development began in 1991 at Sun Microsystems, where James Gosling led the Green Team in a project to develop a language for use on consumer digital devices. In the summer of 1992, they had a working version, but they were *ahead of the curve*, as the saying goes, and industry was not ready for this language.

In 1993, the Mosaic Web Browser was released. This had the effect of moving the Internet from the domain of the academic researcher to the world at-large. The Green Team immediately saw the role of their language as a way to enhance Web browsers.

With Mosaic, and its underlying HTML Web pages and URLs to navigate around the Web, users could download information from distant sites. (See a discussion of this in chapter 12.) However, there were three limitations to using the Web:

1. Transmission speeds to consumer homes were limited to about 33,000 bits per second in 1993. (Now it is generally around 50,000 bits per second.)

2. If a site were popular, its own processing speed would be severely impacted if many users were accessing its Web pages at the same time.

3. Each Web object (e.g., document, picture, video, audio) required a separate protocol in each Web browser. New formats could not be added to the set until all browsers included this new protocol.

Because most users of the Web were waiting for information to appear on their screen, their own computers were often idle. A way around the first two limitations would be to have some of the information processed on the user's machine and not on the Web server. This could be accomplished by having the Web server download a small application program (i.e., an applet) that would run on the user's computer, thus freeing up the Web server to process more users at the same time. Similarly, the Web server could download an applet that could handle any new protocols that were needed. using this same feature.

The Sun group saw the value of their development as an adjunct to Web technology. However, to be effective, their language had to fulfill several requirements:

1. *Architectural independence.* The Web server would not know what machine the user's browser was executing on. To solve this problem, a Java virtual machine was designed and the applet would be compiled into a series of bytecodes for that virtual machine. Thus, any browser that handled the Java virtual machine would be able to execute a Java applet.

2. *Security.* A critical need for consumer acceptance of Java would be that the Web server must not be able to access information from the user's computer and pass that information back to the Web server. If web sites had that ability, users would be reluctant to use the Web to access unknown sites, and the growth of the Web would be stunted.

In 1994, Sun developed the HotJava browser that contained the Java virtual machine to demonstrate its applicability. Finally on May 23, 1995, Marc Andreessen, cofounder of Netscape Communications, which at the time had a 70% market share of the Web browser market, announced that Netscape had incorporated the Java virtual machine as part of its Netscape browser. Since that time, Java use has mushroomed. Although designed to execute applets as part of a Web browser, it has also gained acceptance as a general programming language, often replacing C++ or C as a first programming language for student use.

Brief overview of the language. Java is similar to C and C++. Looking at these languages historically shows the relationship among them. C was developed in the 1970s as a language for building operating systems (principally UNIX). As such, the language designers wanted a language that would allow access to the underlying architecture of the hardware computer. When Stroustrup developed C++, he included the class concept from Simula and inheritance from Smalltalk. However, the basic C language was not modified, so features of C that were useful for systems programming were carried along into C++. When Sun developed Java, they kept the basic syntax, class, and inheritance concepts from C++, but deleted unnecessary features. This resulted in Java as a smaller language than C++, but with a more rational syntax and semantics as a useful programming language.

For the most part, Java is C++ with the excess baggage of C, which yields poor programs, removed. Data are strongly typed, with integers, Booleans, and characters all being separate types. Arrays are also separate types, and a string is not simply an array of characters. All of these permit the compiler to perform more complete error checking on Java programs.

There are fewer ways to perform some actions, such as method invocation being the only subroutine linkage. Because all objects are part of classes, there is no need for separate function or procedure calls. *Struct* objects are also not needed because the same effect can be achieved via instance variables in class definitions.

Pointers are implicit in the language, but there is no pointer data type. That means that all of the problems with memory fragmentation, dangling references, and other pointer mishaps are hidden from the users. Pointer allocation is implicit by the instantiation of class objects and the *new* operator.

To create a Java program, a file *name.java* is created. The name of the file should be the same as the class created by the Java program. A Java compiler is called and a file of bytecodes is produced in the file *name.class*. This file may be executed by the Java interpreter (Java virtual machine).

Java is basically a simple language: It has the clean C++ design without some of C's clumsiness. However, this is at a cost in execution efficiency because many of these structures need run-time validation. In addition, because Java is often interpreted as an applet in a Java virtual machine, there is certainly an execution cost over compiled machine language. For the application domain it was designed for, Web browsers, workstation speed is higher than either the terminal display processor or Internet communication. Therefore, the inefficiency of the Java execution model is mostly hidden from the user, who will still spend most of the time waiting for network response to transmit the desired information.

2.3 SUGGESTIONS FOR FURTHER READING

Alternative computer organizations based on radically different principles from the von Neumann architecture have not been discussed here, although there is a brief summary of such topics in chapter 11. The Turing Award Lecture of Backus [BACKUS 1978] critiques the von Neumann computer organization and offers an alternative. Today, there is increasing emphasis in parallel architectures and massively parallel machines (e.g., thousands of computers working in parallel) to increase performance (e.g., January 1991 issue of *IEEE Computer* on experimental research in computer architecture or [MANO and KIME 1999]).

2.4 PROBLEMS

1. Analyze the implementation of a programming language with which you are familiar. What is the executable form of a program (i.e., what is the output of the translator)? What sorts of translations are made in translating the various statements and expressions into executable form? What software simulation is necessary during program execution? Is the interpreter software simulated? Which of the primitive operations require software simulation?

2. On your computer, determine the structure of the virtual computer defined by the operating system. How does this virtual computer differ from the actual hardware computer? Are there features of the hardware that are restricted by the operating system (e.g., hardware instructions that are not allowed in user programs in the operating-system-defined virtual computer)? What new features are provided directly in the operating system virtual computer that could be simulated only by complex software on the basic hardware computer (e.g., I/O)?

3. The use of an operating system to provide the programmer with a virtual computer different from the basic hardware computer has three advantages. It allows the user to work with a simpler computer than is provided directly by the hardware (e.g., by providing simpler and more powerful I/O facilities). It also protects the computer system from the user, in that each user may be effectively sealed off in a separate virtual computer so that any errors will only hurt that virtual computer and not bring down the whole system and its other users as well. It also allows the operating system to allocate the resources of the system more appropriately to different users. Analyze your local operating system and the virtual computer it provides the programmer. How well does it achieve these goals?

4. The BASIC programming language is often implemented using a complete software simulation of the BASIC virtual computer. If the programs that simulate the BASIC virtual computer were written in FORTRAN (as they might well be), then another layer would be added to the layers of virtual computer in Figure 2.4 on page 59. Draw the new layer. If you know both BASIC and FORTRAN, explain the parts of the BASIC virtual computer that the FORTRAN programs might simulate. Where does the *translator* that translates BASIC programs into their executable form fit into this diagram?

5. Write a statement in a language with which you are familiar. For each syntactic component of the statement (variable names, operation symbols, etc.), list the various bindings that are necessary to completely determine the semantics of the statement when it is executed. For each binding, identify the binding time used in the language.

6. Do Problem 5, but use a *declaration* instead of a statement. Declarations are usually said to be *elaborated* instead of executed, so list the bindings (and their binding times) necessary for a complete elaboration of the declaration.

7. Consider all the languages in the appendix. Which ones do you think should be dropped from a later edition? Which ones will dominate programming in the next decade? Consider binding time for features, virtual computer needed to execute programs, attributes for effective use, and any other relevant attributes.

Chapter 3

Language Translation Issues

During the early days of language design (e.g., during the formative era of developing FORTRAN, ALGOL, COBOL, and LISP around 1960), it was believed that a formal syntax was all that was required for specifying programs. The concept of a context-free grammar or Backus-Naur form (BNF) grammar was developed (and is discussed later in this chapter) and used successfully for specifying the syntax of a language. It is still the major technique today for describing the components of a program. However, over time it was realized that syntax was insufficient. In Chapter 4 we give a brief introduction to the issue of programming semantics or the understanding of what a program means.

3.1 PROGRAMMING LANGUAGE SYNTAX

Syntax, which is defined as "the arrangement of words as elements in a sentence to show their relationship,"[1] describes the sequence of symbols that make up valid programs. The C statement $X = Y + Z$ represents a valid sequence of symbols, whereas $XY + -$ does not represent a valid sequence of symbols for a C program.

Syntax provides significant information needed for understanding a program and provides much-needed information toward the translation of the source program into an object program. For example, almost everyone reading this text will interpret the expression $2+3\times 4$ as having the value of 14 and not 20. That is, the expression is interpreted as if written $2+(3\times 4)$ and is not interpreted as if written $(2+3)\times 4$. We can specify either interpretation, if we wish, by syntax and hence guide the translator into generating the correct operations for evaluating this expression.

As with the ambiguous English sentence "They are flying planes," developing a language syntax alone is insufficient to unambiguously specify the structure of a statement. In a statement like $X = 2.45 + 3.67$, syntax cannot tell us whether Variable X was declared or declared as type real. Results of $X = 5$, $X = 6$, and $X = 6.12$ are all possible if X and $+$ denote integers, X denotes an integer and $+$ is real addition, and X and $+$ denote real values, respectively. We need more

[1] *Webster's New World Dictionary,* Fawcett, 1979.

than just syntactic structures for the full description of a programming language. Other attributes, under the general term *semantics*, such as the use of declarations, operations, sequence control, and referencing environments, affect a variable and are not always determined by syntax rules.

Although syntactic descriptions of a programming language are insufficient for the complete understanding of the language, they are important attributes in this description. For the most part, description of syntax is a "solved problem." When we discuss translator design later in this chapter, the first phase of syntactic understanding of the source program is fairly mechanical. Tools such as YACC (Yet Another Compiler Compiler) automatically produce this syntactic description of a given program. Applying semantic understanding to generate an efficient object program from a given source program still requires a great deal of skill, as well as the application of some formal methods to the process.

3.1.1 General Syntactic Criteria

The primary purpose of syntax is to provide a notation for communication between the programmer and the programming language processor. The choice of particular syntactic structures, however, is constrained only slightly by the necessity to communicate particular items of information. For example, the fact that a particular variable has a value of type *real number* may be represented in any of a dozen different ways in a program—through an explicit declaration as in C, through an implicit *naming convention* as in FORTRAN, and so on. The details of syntax are chosen largely on the basis of secondary criteria, such as readability, which are unrelated to the primary goal of communicating information to the language processor.

There are many secondary criteria, but they may be roughly categorized under the general goals of making programs easy to read, easy to write, easy to translate, and unambiguous. We consider some of the ways that language syntactic structures may be designed to satisfy these often conflicting goals.

Readability. A program is readable if the underlying structure of the algorithm and data represented by the program is apparent from an inspection of the program text. A readable program is often said to be *self-documenting*—that is, it is understandable without any separate documentation (although this goal is seldom achieved in practice). Readability is enhanced by such language features as natural statement formats, structured statements, liberal use of keywords and noise words, provision for embedded comments, unrestricted length identifiers, mnemonic operator symbols, free-field formats, and complete data declarations. Readability, of course, cannot be guaranteed by the design of a language, because even the best design may be circumvented by poor programming. However, syntactic design can force even the best-intentioned programmer to write unreadable programs (as is often the case in APL). The COBOL design emphasizes readability most heavily, often at the expense of ease of writing and translation.

Readability is enhanced by a program syntax in which syntactic differences reflect underlying semantic differences so that program constructs that do similar things look similar and program constructs that do radically different things look different. In general, the greater the variety of syntactic constructs used, the more easily the program structure may be made to reflect different underlying semantic structures.

Languages that provide only a few different syntactic constructs in general lead to less readable programs. In APL or SNOBOL4, for example, only one statement format is provided. The differences among an assignment statement, a subprogram call, a simple goto statement, a subprogram return, a multiway conditional branch, and various other common program structures are reflected syntactically only by differences in one or a few operator symbols within a complex expression. It often requires a detailed analysis of a program to determine even its gross control structure. Moreover, a simple syntax error, such as a single incorrect character in a statement, may radically alter the meaning of a statement without rendering it syntactically incorrect. In LISP, errors in matching parentheses cause similar problems; one of Scheme's extensions to LISP is to circumvent this problem.

Writeability. The syntactic features that make a program easy to write are often in conflict with those features that make it easy to read. Writeability is enhanced by use of concise and regular syntactic structures, whereas for readability a variety of more verbose constructs are helpful. C unfortunately has this attribute of providing for very concise programs that are hard to read, although it does have a full complement of useful features.

Implicit syntactic conventions that allow declarations and operations to be left unspecified make programs shorter and easier to write but harder to read. Other features advance both goals (e.g., the use of structured statements, simple natural statement formats, mnemonic operation symbols, and unrestricted identifiers usually make program writing easier by allowing the natural structure of the problem algorithms and data to be directly represented in the program).

A syntax is *redundant* if it communicates the same item of information in more than one way. Some redundancy is useful in programming language syntax because it makes a program easier to read and also allows for error checking during translation. The disadvantage is that redundancy makes programs more verbose and thus harder to write. Most of the default rules for the meaning of language constructs are intended to reduce redundancy by eliminating explicit statement of meanings that can be inferred from the context. For example, rather than require explicit declaration of the type of every function parameter, ML uses data type induction to derive the type of a function's argument. However, if there is an error in writing such a function, the translator will be unable to detect this error. Because of this effect of masking errors in programs, languages that lack all redundancy are often difficult to use.

Ease of verifiability. Related to readability and writeability is the concept of program correctness or *program verification.* After many years of experience, we now understand that understanding each programming language statement is relatively easy, but the overall process of creating correct programs is extremely difficult. Therefore, we need techniques that enable the program to be mathematically proved correct. We discuss this further in chapter 4.

Ease of translation. A third conflicting goal is that of making programs easy to translate into executable form. Readability and writeability are criteria directed to the needs of the human programmer. Ease of translation relates to the needs of the translator that processes the written program. The key to easy translation is regularity of structure. The LISP syntax provides an example of a program structure that is neither particularly readable nor particularly writable but that is extremely simple to translate. The entire syntactic structure of any LISP program may be described in a few simple rules because of the regularity of the syntax. Programs become harder to translate as the number of special syntactic constructs increases. For example, COBOL translation is made extremely difficult by the large number of statement and declaration forms allowed, although the semantics of the language is not particularly complicated.

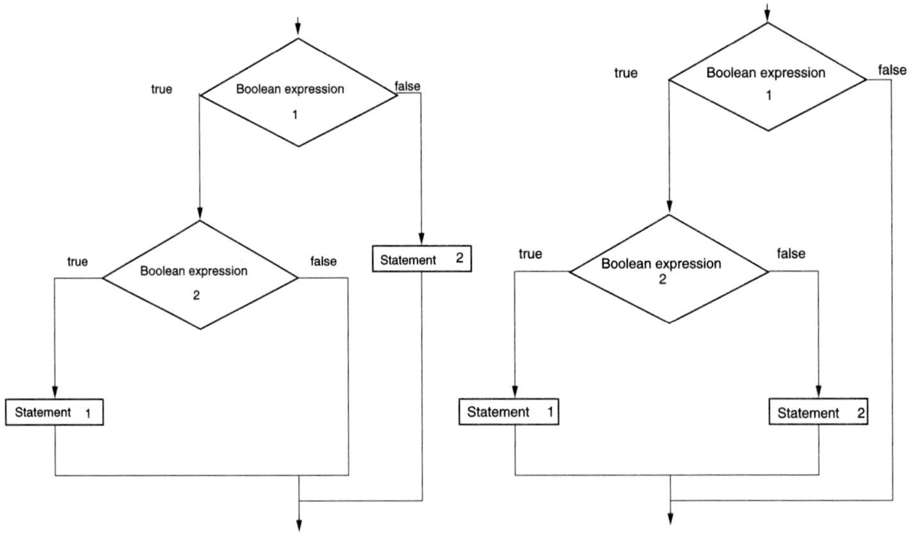

Figure 3.1. Two interpretations of a conditional statement.

Lack of ambiguity. Ambiguity is a central problem in every language design. A language definition ideally provides a unique meaning for every syntactic construct that a programmer may write. An ambiguous construction allows two or more different interpretations. The problems of ambiguity usually arise not in the structure of individual program elements but in the interplay between different structures.

For example, both Pascal and ALGOL allow two different forms of conditional statement:

1. **if** *Boolean expression* **then** $statement_1$ **else** $statement_2$
2. **if** *Boolean expression* **then** $statement_1$

The interpretation to be given to each statement form is clearly defined. However, when the two forms are combined by allowing $statement_1$ to be another conditional statement, then the structure

> **if** *Boolean* $expression_1$ **then if** *Boolean* $expression_2$ **then**
> $statement_1$ **else** $statement_2$

termed a *dangling else*, is formed. This statement form is ambiguous, because it is not clear which of the two execution sequences of Figure 3.1 is intended. FORTRAN syntax provides another example. A reference to A(I,J) might be either a reference to an element of the two-dimensional array A or a call of the function subprogram A because the syntax in FORTRAN for function calls and array references is the same. Similar ambiguities arise in almost every programming language.

The ambiguities in FORTRAN and ALGOL mentioned earlier have in fact been resolved in both languages. In the ALGOL conditional statement, the ambiguity has been resolved by changing the syntax of the language to introduce a required **begin** ... **end** delimiter pair around the embedded conditional statement. Thus, the natural but ambiguous combination of two conditional statements has been replaced by the two less natural but unambiguous constructions, depending on the desired interpretation:

1. **if** *Boolean* $expression_1$ **then begin if** *Boolean* $expression_2$ **then** $statement_1$ **end else** $statement_2$
2. **if** *Boolean* $expression_1$ **then begin if** *Boolean* $expression_2$ **then** $statement_1$ **else** $statement_2$ **end**

A simpler solution is used in Ada: Each **if** statement must end with the delimiter **end if**. In C and Pascal, another technique is used to resolve the ambiguity. An arbitrary interpretation is chosen for the ambiguous construction—in this case, the final **else** is paired with the nearest **then** so that the combined statement has the same meaning as the second of the previous ALGOL constructions. The ambiguity of FORTRAN function and array references is resolved by the rule: The construct $A(I, J)$ is assumed to be a function call if no declaration for an array A is given. Because each array must be declared prior to its use in a program, the translator may readily check whether there is in fact an array A to which the reference applies. If none is found, then the translator assumes that the construct is a call to an external Function A. This assumption cannot be checked until load time when all the external functions (including library functions) are linked into the final executable program. If the loader finds no Function A, then a loader error message is produced. In Pascal, a different technique is used to distinguish function calls from array references: A syntactic distinction is made. Square brackets are used to enclose subscript lists in array references (e.g., $A[I, J]$), and parentheses are used to enclose parameter lists of function calls (e.g., $A(I, J)$).

3.1.2 Syntactic Elements of a Language

The general syntactic style of a language is set by the choice of the various basic syntactic elements. We consider briefly the most prominent of these.

Character set. The choice of character set is one of the first to be made in designing a language syntax. There are several widely used character sets, such as the ASCII set, each containing a different set of special characters in addition to the basic letters and digits. Usually one of these standard sets is chosen, although occasionally a special nonstandard character set may be used, as, for example, in APL. The choice of character set is important in determining the type of input–output (I/O) equipment that can be used in implementing the language. For example, the basic C character set is available on most I/O equipment. However, the APL character set cannot be used directly on most I/O devices.

The general use of 8-bit bytes to represent characters seemed like a reasonable choice when the computer industry went from 6- to 8-bit characters in the early 1960s. Two hundred fifty-six characters seemed like more than enough to represent the 52 upper and lower case letters, 10 digits, and a few punctuation symbols. However, today the computer industry is much more international. Not many (in fact, few) countries use the same 26 letters. Spanish adds the tilde ($\sim$), French uses accents($'$), and other characters are present in some languages (e.g., å, ß, ö). In addition, there are languages like Greek, Hebrew, and Arabic with totally different character sets. Representing languages like Chinese or Japanese, where each ideograph represents a word or phrase, requires a character set on the order of 10,000 symbols. Single-byte characters clearly do not work in all such cases, and language implementors increasingly have to consider 16-bit (i.e., 65,536) representations for the character set.

Identifiers. The basic syntax for identifiers—a string of letters and digits beginning with a letter—is widely accepted. Variations among languages are mainly in the optional inclusion of special characters such as `.` or `-` to improve readability and in length restrictions. Length restrictions, such as the early BASIC restriction to a single letter and digit, force the use of identifiers with little mnemonic value in many cases and thus restrict program readability significantly.

Operator symbols. Most languages use the special characters $+$ and $-$ to represent the two basic arithmetic operations, but beyond that there is almost no uniformity. Primitive operations may be represented entirely by special characters, as is done in APL. Alternatively identifiers may be used for all primitives, as in the LISP PLUS, TIMES, and so on. Most languages adopt some combination, utilizing special characters for some operators, identifiers for others, and often also some character strings that fit in neither of these categories (e.g., the FORTRAN .EQ. and **, for equality and exponentiation, respectively).

Keywords and reserved words. A *keyword* is an identifier used as a fixed part of the syntax of a statement (e.g., *if* beginning a C conditional statement or *for* beginning a C iteration statement). A keyword is a *reserved word* if it may not also be used as a programmer-chosen identifier. Most languages today use reserved words, thus improving the error-detecting capabilities of the translators. Most statements begin with a keyword designating the statement type: READ, IF, WHILE, and so on.

Syntactic analysis during translation is made easier by using reserved words. FORTRAN syntactic analysis, for example, is made difficult by the fact that a statement beginning with DO or IF may not actually be an iteration or conditional statement. Because DO and IF are not reserved words, a programmer may legitimately choose these as variable names. COBOL uses reserved words heavily, but there are so many identifiers reserved that it is difficult to remember them all; as a result, one often inadvertently chooses a reserved identifier as a variable name. The primary difficulty with reserved words, however, comes when the language needs to be extended to include new statements using new reserved words (e.g., as when COBOL is periodically revised to prepare an updated standard). Addition of a new reserved word to the language means that every old program that uses that identifier as a variable name (or other name) is no longer syntactically correct, although it has not been modified.

Noise words. Noise words are optional words that are inserted in statements to improve readability. COBOL provides many such options. For example, in the **goto** statement, written GO TO *label*, the keyword GO is required, but TO is optional; it carries no information and is used only to improve readability.

Comments. Inclusion of comments in a program is an important part of its documentation. A language may allow comments in several ways: (1) Separate comment lines in the program, as in the BASIC REM statement; (2) delimited by special markers, such as the C /* and */ with no concern for line boundaries; or (3) beginning anywhere on a line but terminated by the end of the line, as the - - in Ada, // in C++ or ! in FORTRAN 90. The second alternative suffers from the disadvantage that a missing terminating delimiter on a comment will turn the following statements (up to the end of the next comment) into comments, so that, although they appear to be correct when reading the program, they are not in fact translated and executed.

Blanks (spaces). Rules on the use of blanks vary widely between languages. In C, for example, blanks are not significant anywhere except in literal character-string data. Other languages use blanks as separators so that they play an important syntactic role. In SNOBOL4, the primitive operation of concatenation is represented by a blank, and the blank is also used as a separator between elements of a statement (leading to much confusion). In C, blanks are generally ignored, but not always. In early versions of C, the symbol =+ was a single operator, whereas = + represented two operations. To prevent such errors, the current C definition uses the symbol += as the combined operator because + = would be a syntax error.

Delimiters and brackets. A *delimiter* is a syntactic element used simply to mark the beginning or end of some syntactic unit such as a statement or expression. *Brackets* are paired delimiters (e.g., parentheses or **begin** ... **end** pairs). Delimiters may be used merely to enhance readability or simplify syntactic analysis, but more often they serve the important purpose of removing ambiguities by explicitly defining the boundaries of a particular syntactic construct.

Free- and fixed-field formats. A holdover from the early punched card era of computing is the *fixed field.* A syntax is *free field* if program statements may be written anywhere on an input line without regard for positioning on the line or for breaks between lines. A *fixed-field* syntax utilizes the positioning on an input line to convey information. Strict fixed-field syntax, where each element of a statement must appear within a given part of an input line, is most often seen in assembly languages. Fixed-field syntax is increasingly rare today, and free field is the norm.

Expressions. Expressions are functions that access data objects in a program and return some value. Expressions are the basic syntactic building block from which statements (and sometimes programs) are built. In imperative languages like C, expressions form the basic operations that allow for the machine state to be changed by each statement. In applicative languages like ML or LISP, expressions form the basic sequence control that drives program execution. We discuss expression building more fully in chapter 8.

Statements. Statements are the most prominent syntactic component in imperative languages, the dominant class of languages in use today. Their syntax has a critical effect on the overall regularity, readability, and writeability of the language. Some languages adopt a single basic statement format, whereas others use a different syntax for each different statement type. The former approach emphasizes regularity, whereas the latter emphasizes readability. SNOBOL4 has only one basic statement syntax, the pattern-matching-replacement statement, from which other statement types may be derived by omitting elements of the basic statement. Most languages lean toward the other extreme of providing different syntactic structures for each statement type. COBOL is most notable in this regard. Each COBOL statement has a unique structure involving special keywords, noise words, alternative constructions, optional elements, and so on. The advantage of using a variety of syntactic structures, of course, is that each may be made to express in a natural way the operations involved.

A more important difference in statement structures is that between *structured* or *nested* statements and *simple* statements. A simple statement contains no other embedded statements. APL and SNOBOL4 allow only simple statements. A structured statement may contain embedded statements. The advantages of structured statements are discussed at length in chapter 8.

3.1.3 Overall Program-Subprogram Structure

The overall syntactic organization of main program and subprogram definitions is as varied as the other aspects of language syntax.

Separate subprogram definitions. C illustrates an overall organization in which each subprogram definition is treated as a separate syntactic unit. Each subprogram is compiled separately and the compiled programs linked at load time. Object orientation requires information to be passed among the separately compiled units. The inheritance of class definitions requires that the compiler process some of these separate subprogram issues before the program is loaded prior to execution.

Separate data definitions. An alternative model is to group together all operations that manipulate a given data object. For example, a subprogram might consist of all operations that address a specific data format within the program, operations to create the data record, operations to print the data record, and operations to compute with the data record. This is the general approach of the **class** mechanism in languages like Java, C++, and Smalltalk.

Nested subprogram definitions. Nested subprogram definition was an important concept for building modular programs during the early days of ALGOL, FORTRAN, and Pascal, but the concept is disappearing with the rise of object-oriented languages such as C++ and Java. Pascal illustrates a nested program structure in which subprogram definitions appear as declarations within the main program and may contain other subprogram definitions nested within their definitions to any depth. These nested subprogram definitions serve to provide a nonlocal referencing environment for subprograms that is defined at compile time and that allows static type checking and compilation of efficient executable code for subprograms containing nonlocal references.

Separate interface definitions. The structure of FORTRAN permits the easy compilation of separate subprograms, but it has the disadvantage that data used across different subprograms may have different definitions that the compiler will not be able to detect at compile time. However, Pascal allows the compiler to have access to all such definitions to aid in finding errors. The disadvantage is that the entire program, even if it is many thousands of statements long, must be recompiled each time a single statement needs to be changed. C, ML, and Ada use aspects of both of these techniques to improve compilation behavior.

In these languages, a program *implementation* consists of several subprograms that are intended to interact together. All such components, called *modules*, are linked together, as in FORTRAN, to create an executable program, but only any changed components need be recompiled each time. However, data passed among the procedures in a component must have common declarations as in Pascal, permitting efficient checking by the compiler. However, to pass information between two separately compiled components, additional data are needed. This is handled by a *program-specification* component. In C, the approach is to include certain operating system file operations into the language by allowing the program to include files that contain these interface definitions. The C ".h" files form the specification components and the source program ".c" files form the implementation components[2]. In Ada, the approach was to build such features directly into the language. Programs are defined in components called *packages*, which contain either the specification of the interface definitions or the source program implementation (in the package *body*) that will use these definitions.

Data descriptions separated from executable statements. COBOL contains an early form of component structure. In a COBOL program, the data declarations and the executable statements for all subprograms are divided into separate program *data divisions* and *procedure divisions.* A third *environment division* consists of declarations concerning the external operating environment. The procedure division of a program is organized into subunits corresponding to subprogram bodies, but all data are global to all subprograms, and there is nothing corresponding to the usual local data of a subprogram. The advantage of the centralized data division containing all data declarations is that it enforces the logical independence of the data formats and the algorithms in the procedure division. Minor changes in data structure can be made by modification of the data division without modifying the procedure division. It is also convenient to have the data descriptions collected in one place rather than scattered throughout the subprograms.

Unseparated subprogram definitions. SNOBOL4 represents the extreme in overall program organization (or lack of organization). No syntactic distinction is made in SNOBOL4 between main program statements and subprogram statements. Regardless of the number of subprograms it contains, a program is syntactically just a list of statements. The points where subprograms begin and end are not differentiated syntactically. Programs simply execute, and execution of a function call starts a new subprogram, and execution of a RETURN function ends a subprogram. Behavior of the program is totally dynamic. In fact, any statement may be part of the main program as well as of any number of subprograms at the same time, in the sense that it may be executed at one point during execution of the main program and later executed again as part of execution of a subprogram. This rather chaotic program organization is valuable only in allowing run-time translation and execution of new statements and subprograms with relatively simple mechanisms.

BASIC [KURTZ 1978] is another example that runs contrary to some of these programming language design goals. Developed at Dartmouth College in the 1960s,

[2]The popular UNIX program *make* is used to determine which ".c" and ".h" files have been altered to recompile only changed components of a system.

Language Summary 3.1: BASIC

Features: A language with an extremely simple syntax and semantics: statements numbered, variable names are single letter plus digit, simple IF, FOR loop and GOSUB (subroutine) linkage.

History: BASIC (Beginner's All-purpose Symbolic Instruction Code) was developed at Dartmouth College by Thomas Kurtz and John Kemeny in the early 1960s. The goals were to provide a simple computing environment, especially to those students not in the sciences. Also, to increase the effectiveness of computing, BASIC was designed as an interactive language years before time-sharing became standard in system architecture.
BASIC is also a good example of the self-contradiction in programming. Critics say "BASIC" is the answer to the question: What is a one word oxymoron (contradictory phrase)? While the syntax is extremely easy to learn, the complexity of putting a program together makes BASIC code unreadable if greater than about a page of source statements are used. Because of this, more recent versions of BASIC have included longer variable names, subroutine names, and greater flexibility in control structures, thus making BASIC look more like languages like Pascal or FORTRAN than the simple language developed in the 1960s.

Example: Compute sum of $1^2 + 2^2 + \ldots + 10^2$

```
100 REMARK S IS SUM; I IS INDEX
200 LET S=0
300 FOR I=1 TO 10
400 LET S = S + I * I
500 NEXT I
600 REMARK NEXT IS END OF LOOP
700 PRINT "SUM IS ", S
800 STOP
900 REMARK OTHER STATEMENTS: IF S>400 THEN 200 – (branch to 200)
1000 REMARK OTHER STATEMENTS: DIM A(20) – A array of 20
1100 REMARK OTHER STATEMENTS: GOSUB 100; RETURN – Subroutines
1200 REMARK OTHER STATEMENTS: READ A – Input
```

Reference: T. E. Kurtz, "BASIC," *ACM History of Programming Languages Conference*, Los Angeles (June 1978) *(SIGPLAN Notices (13)8 [August 1978])*, 103–118.

its major goal was to bring computing in an easy manner to the nonscientist. As such, it had an extremely simple syntax. Although long BASIC programs are extremely hard to understand, it is a very effective language for building small throwaway programs that need to be executed a few times and then discarded. Language Summary 3.1 summarizes the BASIC language. Since the 1960s, however, successive versions of BASIC have become more complex, often reaching the structure of languages like Pascal in power, syntax, and complexity.

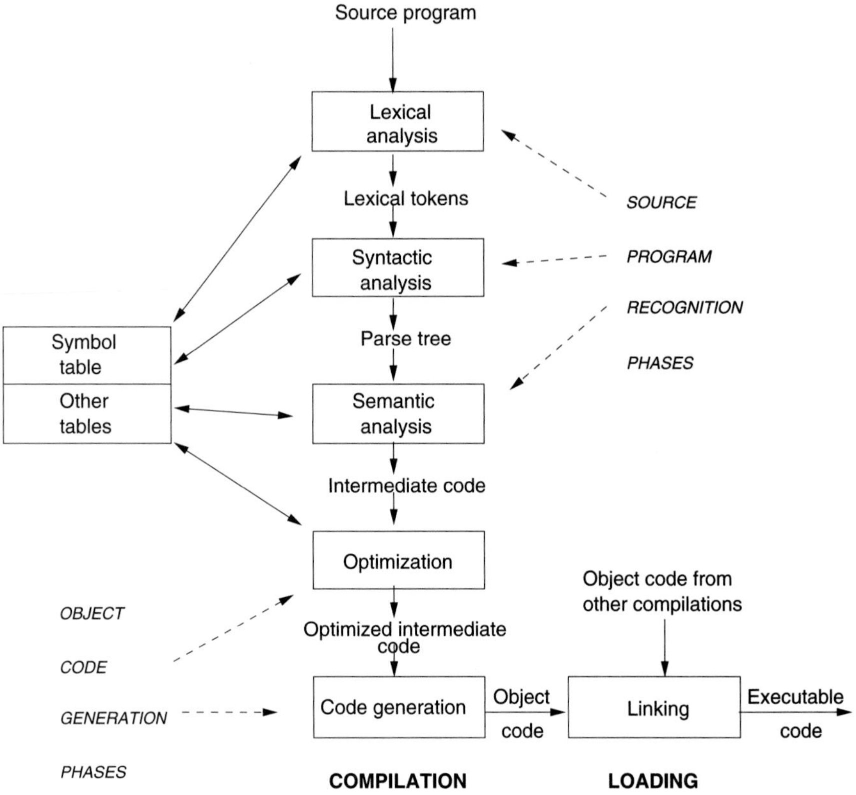

Figure 3.2. Structure of a compiler.

3.2 STAGES IN TRANSLATION

The process of translation of a program from its original syntax into executable form is central in every programming language implementation. The translation may be quite simple, as in the case of Perl, Prolog, or LISP programs, but more often the process can be quite complex. Most languages could be implemented with only trivial translation if one were willing to write a software interpreter and if one were willing to accept slow execution speeds. However, efficient execution is such a desirable goal that major efforts are made to translate programs into efficiently executable structures. The translation process becomes progressively more complex as the executable program form becomes further removed in structure from the original program. At the extreme, an optimizing compiler for a complex language like Ada may radically alter program structures to obtain more efficient execution.

Logically, we may divide translation into two major parts: the *analysis* of the input source program and the *synthesis* of the executable object program. In most translators, these logical stages are not clearly separate but instead are mixed so that analysis and synthesis alternate—often on a statement-by-statement basis. Figure 3.2 illustrates the structure of a typical compiler.

Translators are crudely grouped according to the number of *passes* they make over the source program. A simple compiler typically uses two passes. The first analysis pass decomposes the program into its constituent components and derives information, such as variable name usage, from the program. The second pass typically generates an object program from this collected information.

If compilation speed is important (such as in an educational compiler), a one-pass strategy may be employed. In this case, as the program is analyzed, it is immediately converted into object code. Pascal was designed so that a one-pass compiler could be developed for the language. However, if execution speed is paramount, a three- (or more) pass compiler may be developed. The first pass analyzes the source program, the second pass rewrites the source program into a more efficient form using various well-defined optimization algorithms, and the third pass generates the object code.

As our knowledge of compiler technology has improved, the relationship between number of passes and compiler speed is no longer clear. What is more important is the complexity of the language rather than the number of passes needed to analyze the source program.

3.2.1 Analysis of the Source Program

To a translator, the source program appears initially as one long undifferentiated sequence of symbols composed of thousands or tens of thousands of characters. Of course, a programmer seeing such a program almost instinctively structures it into subprograms, statements, declarations, and so forth. To the translator, none of this is apparent. An analysis of the program's structure must be laboriously built up character by character during translation.

Lexical analysis (scanning). The initial phase of any translation is to group this sequence of characters into its elementary constituents: identifiers, delimiters, operator symbols, numbers, keywords, noise words, blanks, comments, and so on. This phase is termed *lexical analysis,* and the basic program units that result from lexical analysis are termed *lexical items* (or *tokens*). Typically the lexical analyzer (or scanner) is the input routine for the translator, reading successive lines of input program, breaking them down into individual lexical items, called *lexemes*, and feeding these lexemes to the later stages of the translator to be used in the higher levels of analysis. The lexical analyzer must identify the type of each lexeme (number, identifier, delimiter, operator, etc.) and attach a type tag. In addition, conversion to an internal representation is often made for items such as numbers (converted to internal binary fixed- or floating-point form) and identifiers (stored in a symbol table and the address of the symbol table entry used in place of the character string). The formal model used to design lexical analyzers is the *finite-state automata,* which is briefly described in Section 3.3.2.

Although lexical analysis is simple in concept, this phase of translation often requires a larger share of translation time than any other. This fact is in part due simply to the necessity to scan and analyze the source program character by character. It is also true that in practice it is sometimes difficult to determine where the boundaries between lexical items lie without rather complex context-dependent algorithms. For example, the two FORTRAN statements

DO 10 I = 1,5 and DO 10 I = 1.5

have entirely different lexical structures. The first is a DO statement and the second is an assignment, but this fact cannot be discovered until either the "," or "." character is read, because blanks are ignored in FORTRAN.

Syntactic analysis (parsing). The second stage in translation is *syntactic analysis* or *parsing*. Here the larger program structures are identified (statements, declarations, expressions, etc.) using the lexical items produced by the lexical analyzer. Syntactic analysis usually alternates with semantic analysis. First, the syntactic analyzer identifies a sequence of lexical items forming a syntactic unit such as an expression, statement, subprogram call, or declaration. A semantic analyzer is then called to process this unit. Commonly, the syntactic and semantic analyzers communicate using a stack. The syntactic analyzer enters in the stack the various elements of the syntactic unit found, and these are retrieved and processed by the semantic analyzer. Much research has centered on discovery of efficient syntactic-analysis techniques, particularly techniques based on the use of formal grammars (as described in Section 3.3.1).

Semantic analysis. Semantic analysis is perhaps the central phase of translation. Here the syntactic structures recognized by the syntactic analyzer are processed, and the structure of the executable object code begins to take shape. Semantic analysis is thus the bridge between the analysis and synthesis parts of translation. A number of other important subsidiary functions also occur in this stage, including symbol-table maintenance, most error detection, expansion of macros, and execution of compile-time statements. The semantic analyzer may actually produce the executable object code in simple translations, but more commonly the output from this stage is some internal form of the final executable program, which is then manipulated by the optimization stage of the translator before executable code is actually generated.

The semantic analyzer is ordinarily split into a set of smaller semantic analyzers, each of which handles one particular type of program construct. The semantic analyzers interact among themselves through information stored in various data structures, particularly in the central symbol table. For example, a semantic analyzer that processes type declarations for simple variables may often do little more than enter the declared types into the symbol table. A later semantic analyzer that processes arithmetic expressions may then use the declared types to generate the appropriate type-specific arithmetic operations for the object code. The exact functions of the semantic analyzers vary greatly depending on the language and logical organization of the translator. Some of the most common functions may be described as follows:

1. *Symbol-table maintenance.* A *symbol table* is one of the central data structures in every translator. The symbol table contains an entry for each different identifier encountered in the source program. The lexical analyzer makes the initial entries as it scans the input program. The symbol-table entry contains more than just the identifier. It contains additional data concerning the attributes of that identifier: its type (simple variable, array name, subprogram name, formal parameter, etc.), type of values (integer, real, etc.), referencing environment, and whatever other information is available from the input program through declarations and usage. The semantic analyzers enter this information into the symbol table as they process declarations, subprogram headers, and program statements. Other parts of the translator use this information to construct efficient executable code.

   The symbol table in translators for compiled languages is usually discarded at the end of translation. However, it may be retained during execution (e.g., in languages that allow new identifiers to be created at run time or as an aid in debugging). ML, Prolog, and LISP implementations all utilize a symbol table initially created during translation as a central run-time system-defined data structure. *dbx* is a popular UNIX program that uses a run-time symbol table to debug C programs.

2. *Insertion of implicit information.* Often in the source program, information is implicit and must be made explicit in the lower level object program. Most of this implicit information goes under the general heading of *default conventions*, which are interpretations to be provided when the programmer gives no explicit specification. For example, a FORTRAN variable that is used but not declared is automatically provided with a type declaration depending on the initial letter of its name.

3. *Error detection.* The syntactic and semantic analyzers must be prepared to handle incorrect as well as correct programs. At any point, the lexical analyzer may send to the syntactic analyzer a lexical item that does not fit in the surrounding context (e.g., a statement delimiter in the middle of an expression, a declaration in the middle of a sequence of statements, an operator symbol where an identifier is expected). The error may be more subtle, such as a real variable where an integer variable is required or a subscripted variable reference with three subscripts when the array was declared to have only two dimensions. At each step in translation, a multitude of such errors might occur. The semantic analyzer must not only recognize such errors when they occur and produce an appropriate error message, but must also, in all but the most drastic cases, determine the appropriate way to continue with syntactic analysis of the remainder of the program.

4. *Macro processing and compile-time operations.* Not all languages include macro features or provision for compile-time operations. Where these are present, however, processing is usually handled during semantic analysis.

   A *macro,* in its simplest form, is a piece of program text that has been separately defined and that is to be inserted into the program during translation whenever an appropriate macro call is encountered in the source program. Thus, a macro is much like a subprogram except that, rather than being separately translated and called at run time (i.e., the binding of the subprogram name with its semantics occurs at run time), its body is simply substituted for each call during program translation (i.e., the binding occurs at translation time). Macros may be just simple strings to be substituted (e.g., substitution of 3.1416 for PI whenever the latter is referenced). More commonly, they look much like subprograms with parameters that must be processed before the substitution for the macro call is made.

   Where macros are allowed, the semantic analyzers must identify the macro call within the source program and set up the appropriate substitution of the macro body for the call. Often this task involves interrupting the lexical and syntactic analyzers and setting them to work analyzing the string representing the macro body before proceeding with the remainder of the source string. Alternatively, the macro body may have already been partially translated so that the semantic analyzer can process it directly, inserting the appropriate object code and making the appropriate table entries before continuing with analysis of the source program.

   A *compile-time operation* is an operation to be performed during translation to control the translation of the source program. C provides a number of such operations. The C "#define" allows for constants or expressions to be evaluated before the program is compiled. The "#ifdef" (if-defined) construct allows for alternative sequences of code to be compiled depending on the presence or absence of certain variables. These switches allow the programmer to alter the sequence of statements that are compiled. For example, a common source file can be used to compile alternative versions of a program:

```
#define pc          /* Set to PC or UNIX version of program */
   ...
ProgramWrite(...)
   #ifdef pc        /* If defined then PC code needed */
   ...              /* Do PC version code */
                    /* e.g., write Microsoft Windows output */
   #else
   ...              /* Do UNIX version code */
                    /* e.g., write Motif X Windows output */
   #endif
```

3.2.2 Synthesis of the Object Program

The final stages of translation are concerned with the construction of the executable program from the outputs produced by the semantic analyzer. This phase involves code generation necessarily and may also include optimization of the generated program. If subprograms are translated separately, or if library subprograms are used, a final linking and loading stage is needed to produce the complete program ready for execution.

Optimization. The semantic analyzer ordinarily produces as output the executable translated program represented in some *intermediate code,* an internal representation such as a string of operators and operands, or a table of operator-operand sequences. From this internal representation, the code generators may generate the properly formatted output object code. Before code generation, however, there is usually some optimization of the program in the internal representation. Typically the semantic analyzer generates the internal program form piecemeal as each segment of input program is analyzed. The semantic analyzer generally does not have to worry about the surrounding code that has already been generated. In doing this piecemeal output, however, extremely poor code may be produced (e.g., a register may be stored at the end of one generated segment and immediately reloaded from the same location at the beginning of the next segment). For example, the statement

$$\mathrm{A} = \mathrm{B} + \mathrm{C} + \mathrm{D}$$

may generate the intermediate code
(a) Temp1 = B + C
(b) Temp2 = Temp1 + D
(c) A = Temp2
which may generate the straightforward, but inefficient, code
1. Load register with B (from (a))
2. Add C to register
3. Store register in Temp1
4. Load register with Temp1 (from (b))
5. Add D to register
6. Store register in Temp2
7. Load register with Temp2 (from (c))
8. Store register in A.

Instructions 3, 4, 6, and 7 are redundant because all the data can be kept in the register before storing the result in A. Often it is desirable to allow the generation of poor code sequences by the semantic analyzers and then during optimization replace these sequences by better ones that avoid obvious inefficiencies.

Many compilers go far beyond this sort of simple optimization and analyze the program for other improvements that can be made (e.g., computing common subexpressions only once, removing constant operations from loops, optimizing the use of registers, and optimizing the calculation of array-accessing formulas). Much research has been done on program optimization, and many sophisticated techniques are known (see the references at the end of this chapter).

Code generation. After the translated program in the internal representation has been optimized, it must be formed into the assembly language statements, machine code, or other object program form that is to be the output of the translation. This process involves formatting the output properly from the information contained in the internal program representation. The output code may be directly executable, or there may be other translation steps to follow (e.g., assembly or linking and loading).

Linking and loading. In the optional final stage of translation, the pieces of code resulting from separate translations of subprograms are coalesced into the final executable program. The output of the preceding translation phases typically consists of executable programs in almost final form, except where the programs reference external data or other subprograms. These incomplete locations in the code are specified in attached *loader tables* produced by the translator. The *linking loader* (or *link editor*) loads the various segments of translated code into memory and then uses the attached loader tables to link them together properly by filling in data and subprogram addresses in the code as needed. The result is the final executable program ready to be run.

Bootstrapping

Often the translator for a new language is written in that language. For example, the initial Pascal compiler was written in Pascal and designed to execute on a P-code virtual machine. One problem with this is how to get started. If the original Pascal compiler were written in Pascal, how did this first compiler get compiled? This is called *bootstrapping.* One way is to compile the compiler by hand into its P-code. Although tedious, it is not very difficult. Once that is done, the P-code interpreter can execute this hand-translated compiler. One then has a Pascal compiler running, and optimizations in the generated code can be made to improve the process. Moving to a new machine is not difficult because one now has the old Pascal compiler on the prior machine to use to develop P-code. One still has to redo the P-code interpreter, but that is not very difficult.

Diagnostic Compilers

A variation on this approach was popular during the 1960s, when batch-processing computers caused long delays in receiving the results of a compilation. Language Summary 3.2 summarizes the experience of Cornell University in developing diagnostic compilers for CORC [CONWAY and MAXWELL 1963], CUPL, and PL/C [CONWAY and WILCOX 1973]. In this case, rapid turnaround and compilation

Language Summary 3.2: CORC, CUPL, and PL/C

Features: Compilers provided for automatic correction of invalid progams.

History: During the batch-processing era of the 1960s until the mid-1970s, it often took over a day for return of a compiled program. Compilation errors were therefore very costly. Cornell University, led by Richard Conway, developed a series of compilers (CORC, Cornell Compiler; CUPL, Cornell University Programming Language; PL/C, Cornell dialect for PL/I) that performed error corrections automatically in order to fix simple syntax and semantic errors as an aid to get programs to execute sooner. On simple mistakes, the systems were fairly effective. With the growth of time-sharing systems in the 1970s and the personal computer and workstation of the 1980s, the need for automatic error correction has declined.

Example:

```
/* PL/C EXAMPLE OF ERROR CORRECTION IN PL/I */
SAMPLE: PROCEDURE OPTIONS(MAIN);      /* MAIN PROCEDURE */
    DECLARE VAR1 FIXED BINARY /* VAR1 integer; Fix missing ; at end */
    DECLARE VAR2 FIXED BINARY;
    VAR1 = 1;
    VAR2 = 2;
    IF (VAR1 < VAR2 /* Add missing ) at end of line */
        THEN PUT SKIP LIST(VAR1, 'less than ', VAR2) /* Add ; at end */
                /* Print: 1 less than 2 */
                /* SKIP goes to new line */
        ELSE PUT SKIP LIST(VAR2, 'less than ', VAR1);
    DO WHILE(VAR2>0);
        PUT SKIP ('Counting down ', VAR2);      /* Add missing LIST term */
        VAR2 VAR2 - 1;          /* = inserted after first VAR2 */
        END;                    /* END DO WHILE */
    END;                        /* END PROCEDURE SAMPLE */
```

Reference: R. W. Conway and T. Wilcox, "Design and Implementation of a Diagnostic Compiler for PL/I," *Comm. ACM* (16)3 (1973), 169–179.

time were the major goals because student programs typically executed for only a fraction of a second and, once executed correctly, were discarded.

3.3 FORMAL TRANSLATION MODELS

As stated in the previous section, the syntactic recognition parts of compiler theory are fairly standard and generally based on the context-free theory of languages. We briefly summarize that theory in the next few pages. The formal definition of the syntax of a programming language is usually called a *grammar*, as an analogy with the common terminology for natural languages. A grammar consists of a set of rules (called *productions*) that specify the sequences of characters (or lexical items) that form allowable programs in the language being defined. A *formal grammar* is just a grammar specified using a strictly defined notation. The two classes of grammars useful in compiler technology include the *BNF grammar* (or *context-free grammar*) and the *regular grammar*, described in the following subsections. A brief summary of other grammar classes, not particularly useful for compiler development but extremely important in understanding the general computational powers that computers provide, is given in Section 4.1.

3.3.1 BNF Grammars

When we consider the structure of an English sentence, we usually describe it as a sequence of categories. That is, a simple sentence is often given as

subject / verb / object,

with examples being

The girl / ran / home.
The boy / cooks / dinner.

Each category can be further subdivided. In the previous examples, *subject* is represented by *article noun*, making the structure of these sentences

article / noun / verb / object.

There are other possible sentence structures besides the simple declarative ones just given. Simple interrogative sentences (questions) often have a syntax of

auxiliary verb / subject / predicate,

as in

Did / the girl / run home?
Is / the boy / cooking dinner?

We can represent these sentences by a set of rules. We can say a sentence may be a simple declarative sentence or a simple interrogative sentence, or notationally as

$$\langle sentence \rangle ::= \langle declarative \rangle \mid \langle interrogative \rangle,$$

with ::= signifying "is defined as" and | signifying "or." Each sentence type can be further defined as follows:

$$\begin{array}{ll} \langle declarative \rangle ::= & \langle subject \rangle \langle verb \rangle \langle object \rangle. \\ \langle subject \rangle ::= & \langle article \rangle \langle noun \rangle. \\ \langle interrogative \rangle ::= & \langle auxiliary\ verb \rangle \langle subject \rangle \langle predicate \rangle? \end{array}$$

This specific notation is called *BNF* (Backus-Naur form). It was developed by John Backus [BACKUS 1960] in the late 1950s as a way to express the syntactic definition of ALGOL. Peter Naur was chair of the committee that developed ALGOL. At about the same time, a similar grammatical form, the *context-free grammar*, was developed by linguist Noam Chomsky [CHOMSKY 1959] for the definition of natural language syntax. The BNF and context-free grammar forms are equivalent in power; the differences are only in notation. For this reason, the terms *BNF grammar* and *context-free grammar* are usually interchangeable in discussion of syntax.

Syntax

A BNF grammar is composed of a finite set of BNF grammar rules, which define a *language*—in our case, a programming language. Before we look at these grammar rules in detail, the term *language* deserves some further explanation. Because syntax is only concerned with form rather than meaning, a (programming) language, considered syntactically, consists of a set of *syntactically correct programs*, each of which is simply a sequence of characters. A syntactically correct program need not make any sense semantically (e.g., if it were executed, it would not need to compute anything useful, or anything at all for that matter).

For example, looking at our simple declarative and imperative sentences highlighted earlier, the syntax *subject verb object* is also fulfilled by the sequence

The home / ran / girl,

which does not make sense under normal interpretations of these words.

With programming language syntax, we carry this lack of concern with meaning one step further: A *language* is *any set of* (finite-length) *character strings* with characters chosen from some fixed finite alphabet of symbols. Under this definition, the following are all languages:

1. The set of all C assignment statements
2. The set of all C programs
3. The set of all LISP atoms
4. The set composed of sequences of *a*s and *b*s where all the *a*s precede all the *b*s (e.g., *ab*, *aab*, *abb*, ...)

A language may consist of only a finite set of strings (e.g., the language composed of all Pascal delimiters: **begin**, **end**, **if**, **then**, etc.), or an infinite number of strings (e.g., the string of *a*s and *b*s given as number 4 in the prior list). The only restriction on a language is that each string in it must be of finite length and must contain characters chosen from some fixed finite alphabet of symbols.

Studying the prior list of sample languages indicates some of the problems in using natural language (English in this case) in describing programming languages. Consider number 4 again. Is *b* by itself a member of this language? It is true that all *a*s (none in this case) precede all the *b*s in the string, but must a string contain at least one a? Similarly, is a by itself in the language? As stated, the description is incomplete.

We solve this problem by giving a formal mathematical set of rules for determining exactly which strings are in the language. In the simplest case, a grammar rule may simply list the elements of a finite language—for example:

$$\langle digit \rangle ::= 0 \mid 1 \mid 2 \mid 3 \mid 4 \mid 5 \mid 6 \mid 7 \mid 8 \mid 9$$

This rule defines a language composed of the 10 single-character strings 0, 1, 2, 3, 4, 5, 6, 7, 8, and 9 by listing a set of alternatives. This grammar rule is read, "A *digit* is either a '0' or a '1' or a '2' or a ... ." The term *digit* is called a *syntactic category* or a *nonterminal*: It serves as a name for the language defined by the grammar rule. The symbols making up strings in our language—in this case the digits from 0 to 9 are called *terminal* symbols. Often the ::= symbol is given as →, especially if the syntactic categories are written as single upper case letters (e.g., the rule $\langle X \rangle ::= \langle B \rangle | \langle C \rangle$ is often written as $X \rightarrow B|C$). Both notations are used in this book.

Once we have defined a basic set of syntactic categories, we can use these in constructing more complex strings. For example, the rule

$$\begin{aligned} &\langle conditional\ statement \rangle ::= \\ &\quad \textbf{if}\ \langle Boolean\ expression \rangle\ \textbf{then}\ \langle statement \rangle \textbf{else}\ \langle statement \rangle \\ &\qquad \mid \textbf{if}\ \langle Boolean\ expression \rangle\ \textbf{then}\ \langle statement \rangle \end{aligned}$$

defines the language composed of $\langle conditional\ statement \rangle$ constructs, using the syntactic categories $\langle Boolean\ expression \rangle$ and $\langle statement \rangle$, which must be defined in turn using other grammar rules. Note that the earlier rule shows two alternative forms of conditional statement (separated by the | symbol). Each alternative is constructed from the concatenation of several elements, which may be literal strings (e.g., **if** or **else**) or syntactic categories. When a syntactic category is designated, it means that any string in the sublanguage defined by that category may be used at that point. For example, assuming that *Boolean expression* consists of a set of strings representing valid Boolean expressions, the prior rule allows any one of these strings to be inserted between the **if** and **then** of a conditional statement.

The syntactic category defined by the rule may be used in that rule to specify repetition. Such a rule is called a *recursive* rule. For example, the recursive rule

$$\langle unsigned\ integer \rangle ::= \langle digit \rangle \mid \langle unsigned\ integer \rangle \langle digit \rangle$$

defines an unsigned integer as a sequence of $\langle digit \rangle$s. The first alternative $\langle digit \rangle$ defines an unsigned integer as a single digit, whereas the second alternative adds a second digit to this initial digit, a third digit onto the second, and so forth.

A complete BNF grammar is just a set of such grammar rules, which together define a hierarchy of sublanguages leading to the top-level syntactic category, which

$$
\begin{array}{ll}
\langle assignment\ statement\rangle ::= & \langle variable\rangle = \langle arithmetic\ expression\rangle \\
\langle arithmetic\ expression\rangle ::= & \langle term\rangle \mid \langle arithmetic\ expression\rangle + \langle term\rangle \mid \\
 & \quad \langle arithmetic\ expression\rangle - \langle term\rangle \\
\langle term\rangle ::= & \langle primary\rangle \mid \langle term\rangle \times \langle primary\rangle \mid \\
 & \quad \langle term\rangle / \langle primary\rangle \\
\langle primary\rangle ::= & \langle variable\rangle \mid \langle number\rangle \mid (\langle arithmetic\ expression\rangle) \\
\langle variable\rangle ::= & \langle identifier\rangle \mid \langle identifier\rangle[\langle subscript\ list\rangle] \\
\langle subscript\ list\rangle ::= & \langle arithmetic\ expression\rangle \mid \\
 & \quad \langle subscript\ list\rangle, \langle arithmetic\ expression\rangle
\end{array}
$$

Figure 3.3. Grammar for simple assignment statements.

for a programming language is usually the syntactic category $\langle program\rangle$. Figure 3.3 illustrates a more complex grammar defining the syntax of a class of simple assignment statements that assumes the basic syntactic categories $\langle identifier\rangle$ and $\langle number\rangle$ already have been defined.

Parse Trees

Given a grammar, we can use a single-replacement rule to generate strings in our language. For example, the following grammar generates all sequences of balanced parentheses:

$$S \rightarrow SS \mid (S) \mid ()$$

Given any string, we may replace any nonterminal with the right-hand side of any production containing that nonterminal on the left. For example, we can generate the string $(()())$ from S by

1. Replacing S using rule $S \rightarrow (S)$ giving (S)
2. Replacing S in (S) using rule $S \rightarrow SS$ giving (SS)
3. Replacing first S in (SS) using rule $S \rightarrow ()$ giving $(()S)$
4. Replacing S in $(()S)$ using rule $S \rightarrow ()$ giving $(()())$

We use the symbol $\Rightarrow$ to indicate that one string is derived from another string. The entire derivation can be written as

$$S \Rightarrow (S) \Rightarrow (SS) \Rightarrow (()S) \Rightarrow (()())$$

Each term in the derivation is called a *sentential form*, and we formally define a *language* as the set of sentential forms, each consisting of only terminal symbols that can be derived from the initial symbol of a grammar.

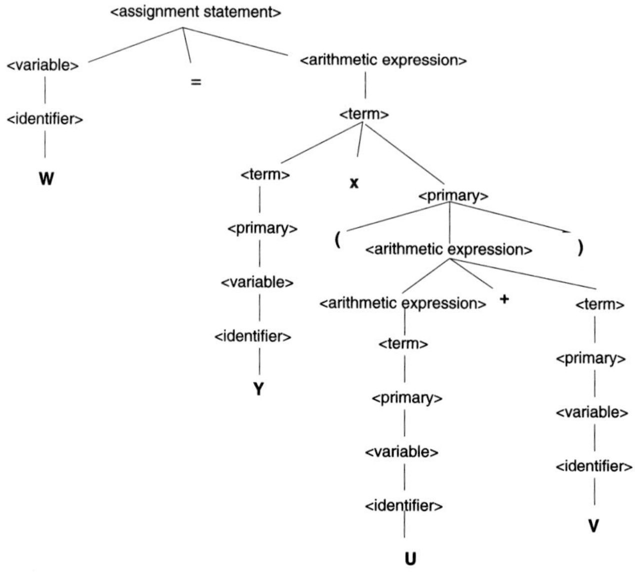

Figure 3.4. Parse tree for an assignment statement.

The use of a formal grammar to define the syntax of a programming language is important to both the language user and language implementor. The user may consult it to answer subtle questions about program form, punctuation, and structure. The implementor may use it to determine all the possible cases of input program structures that are allowed and thus with which the translator may have to deal. Both programmer and implementor have a common agreed-on definition that may be used to resolve disputes about allowed syntactic constructs. A formal syntactic definition also helps eliminate minor syntactic differences between implementations of a language.

To determine if a given string in fact represents a syntactically valid program in the language defined by a BNF grammar, we must use the grammar rules to construct a syntactic analysis or parse of the string. If the string can be successfully parsed, then it is in the language. If no way can be found of parsing the string with the given grammar rules, then the string is not in the language. Figure 3.4 illustrates the *parse tree* that results from a syntactic analysis of the statement $W = Y \times (U + V)$ using the BNF grammar of Figure 3.3.

A BNF grammar assigns a structure to each string in the language defined by the grammar, as seen in Figure 3.4. Note that the structure assigned is necessarily a tree because of the restrictions on BNF grammar rules. Each leaf of this parse tree is a single character or lexical item in the input string. Each intermediate branch point in the tree is tagged with a syntactic category that designates the class to

$$
\begin{aligned}
\langle assignment\ statement\rangle ::= \quad & \langle variable\rangle = \langle arithmetic\ expression\rangle \\
\langle arithmetic\ expression\rangle ::= \quad & \langle term\rangle \mid \langle arithmetic\ expression\rangle \times \langle term\rangle \mid \\
& \quad \langle arithmetic\ expression\rangle + \langle term\rangle \\
\langle term\rangle ::= \quad & \langle primary\rangle \mid \langle term\rangle - \langle primary\rangle \mid \\
& \quad \langle term\rangle / \langle primary\rangle \\
\langle primary\rangle ::= \quad & \langle variable\rangle \mid \langle number\rangle \mid (\langle arithmetic\ expression\rangle) \\
\langle variable\rangle ::= \quad & \langle identifier\rangle \mid \langle identifier\rangle[\langle subscript\ list\rangle] \\
\langle subscript\ list\rangle ::= \quad & \langle arithmetic\ expression\rangle \mid \\
& \quad \langle subscript\ list\rangle, \langle arithmetic\ expression\rangle
\end{aligned}
$$

Figure 3.5. Alternative BNF grammar.

which the subtree below it belongs. The root node of the tree is tagged with the syntactic category designating the whole language—in this case, the category $\langle assignment\ statement\rangle$.

The parse tree provides an intuitive semantic structure for much of a program. Thus, for example, the BNF grammar for Pascal specifies a structure for a program as a sequence of declarations and statements with nested blocks. The statements, in turn, are structured using expressions of various kinds, and the expressions are composed of simple and subscripted variables, primitive operators, functions calls, and so on. At the lowest level, even identifiers and numbers are broken down into their constituent parts. By studying the grammar, a programmer may gain a direct insight into various structures that combine to form correct programs. It is important to note that no grammar must necessarily assign the structure one would expect to a given program element. The same language may be defined by many different grammars, as may easily be seen by playing with the grammar of Figure 3.3. Figure 3.5, for example, gives a grammar defining the same language as the grammar of Figure 3.3, but note that the structures assigned by this new grammar are quite at odds with the structures one would intuitively assign.

In spite of its exceedingly simple structure, the BNF grammar can be used to do a surprisingly good job of defining the syntax of most programming languages. The areas of syntax that cannot be defined by a BNF grammar are those that involve contextual dependence. For example, the restrictions "the same identifier may not be declared twice in the same block," "every identifier must be declared in some block enclosing the point of its use," and "an array declared to have two dimensions cannot be referenced with three subscripts" are each unspecifiable using only a BNF grammar. Restrictions of this sort must be defined by an addendum to the formal BNF grammar. In chapter 4, we discuss some formal theories that try to address these shortcomings of the BNF model.

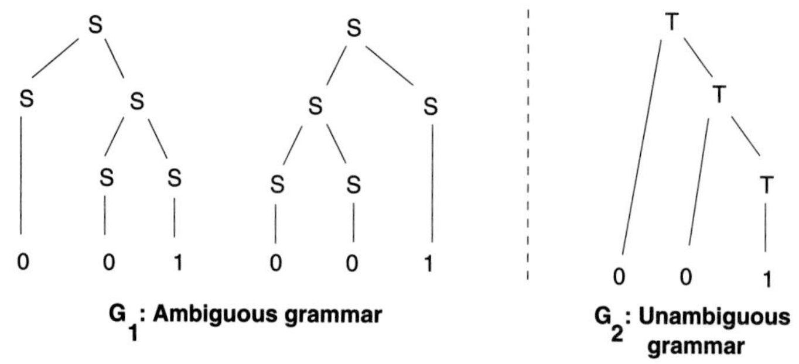

Figure 3.6. Ambiguity in grammars.

The process by which a BNF grammar is used to develop parse trees for a given program is a well-understood process. In Section 3.4 we briefly describe one simple parsing strategy—recursive descent—to give an appreciation of the problems involved.

Ambiguity

As stated earlier, ambiguity is a problem with syntax. Consider the sentence "They are flying planes." We can represent it two ways:

They / are / flying planes.
They / are flying / planes.

Both have an appropriate, but very different, meaning. In the first case, *They* refers to the planes, with *flying* being an adjective modifying planes. In the second case, *They* refers to others engaged in the act of flying airplanes.

Ambiguity is often a property of a given grammar and not of a given language. For example, grammar G_1, which generates all binary strings, is ambiguous:

$$G_1: \quad S \rightarrow SS \mid 0 \mid 1$$

We know that it is ambiguous because there is some string in the language that has two distinct parse trees (Figure 3.6).

If every grammar for a given language is ambiguous, we say the language is *inherently ambiguous*. However, the language of all binary strings is not inherently ambiguous, because there is an unambiguous grammar that generates the same strings, grammar G_2:

$$G_2: \quad T \rightarrow 0T \mid 1T \mid 0 \mid 1$$

$$
\begin{array}{ll}
\langle assignment\ statement\rangle ::= & \langle variable\rangle = \langle arithmetic\ expression\rangle \\
\langle arithmetic\ expression\rangle ::= & \langle term\rangle \ \{[+ \mid -]\ \langle term\rangle\}^\star \\
\langle term\rangle ::= & \langle primary\rangle \ \{[\times \mid /]\langle primary\rangle\}\star \\
\langle primary\rangle ::= & \langle variable\rangle \mid \langle number\rangle \mid (\langle arithmetic\ expression\rangle) \\
\langle variable\rangle ::= & \langle identifier\rangle \mid \langle identifier\rangle[\langle subscript\ list\rangle] \\
\langle subscript\ list\rangle ::= & \langle arithmetic\ expression\rangle \\
 & \quad \{, \langle arithmetic\ expression\rangle\}^\star
\end{array}
$$

Figure 3.7. Extended BNF for simple assignment statements.

Extensions to BNF Notation

Despite the power, elegance, and simplicity of BNF grammars, they are not an ideal notation for communicating the rules of programming language syntax to the practicing programmer. The primary reason is the simplicity of the BNF rule, which forces a rather unnatural representation for the common syntactic constructs of optional elements, alternative elements, and repeated elements within a grammar rule. For example, to express the simple syntactic idea "a *signed integer* is a sequence of digits preceded by an optional plus or minus," we must write in BNF a fairly complex set of recursive rules such as

$$
\begin{array}{ll}
\langle signed\ integer\rangle ::= & +\langle integer\rangle \mid -\langle integer\rangle \\
\langle integer\rangle ::= & \langle digit\rangle \mid \langle integer\rangle\langle digit\rangle
\end{array}
$$

We can describe extensions to BNF that avoid some of these unnatural ways to specify simple syntactic properties of some grammars.

Extended BNF notation. To extend BNF, the following notational extensions do not change the power of the BNF grammar but allow for easier descriptions of languages:

- An optional element may be indicated by enclosing the element in square brackets, [...].
- A choice of alternatives may use the | symbol within a single rule, optionally enclosed by parentheses ([,]) if needed.
- An arbitrary sequence of instances of an element may be indicated by enclosing the element in braces followed by an asterisk, $\{\ldots\}^\star$.

Examples of this notation include the following:

$$
\begin{array}{lll}
\textit{signed integers:} & \langle signed\ integer\rangle ::= & [+ \mid -]\ \langle digit\rangle\{\langle digit\rangle\}^\star \\
\textit{identifier:} & \langle identifier\rangle ::= & \langle letter\rangle\ \{\langle letter\rangle \mid \langle digit\rangle\}^\star
\end{array}
$$

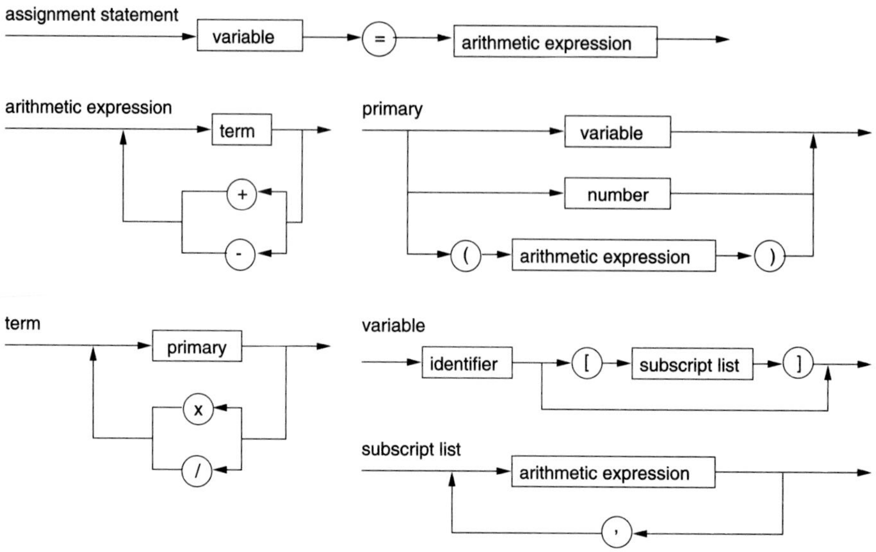

Figure 3.8. Syntax charts for simple assignment statements.

As another example, arithmetic expressions, such as described by Figure 3.3, can be described more intuitively using extended BNF. Rules such as

$$\langle arithmetic\ expression\rangle ::= \ \langle term\rangle \mid \langle arithmetic\ expression\rangle + \langle term\rangle$$

reflect the relationship that an arithmetic expression is really an arbitrary number of terms and can be expressed using extended BNF as:

$$\langle arithmetic\ expression\rangle ::= \ \langle term\rangle \ \{\ +\ \langle term\rangle\}^{\star}$$

The entire expression grammar can be restated in extended BNF as given in Figure 3.7.

Syntax charts. A syntax chart (also called a *railroad diagram* because it looks like the switching yard of a railroad) is a graphical way to express extended BNF rules. Each rule is represented by a path from the input on the left to the output on the right. Any valid path from input to output represents a string generated by that rule. If we represent other rules by boxes and terminal symbols by circles, we can represent the grammar of Figure 3.7 by the syntax charts of Figure 3.8.

For example, the production $\langle term\rangle$ is satisfied by any path that either goes through $\langle primary\rangle$ and exits on the right, or goes through $\langle primary\rangle$ and then loops one or more times through one of the operators and then goes through $\langle primary\rangle$ again— that is, the extended BNF rule:

$$\langle term\rangle ::= \langle primary\rangle \ \{[\times \ \mid /]\langle primary\rangle\}^{\star}$$

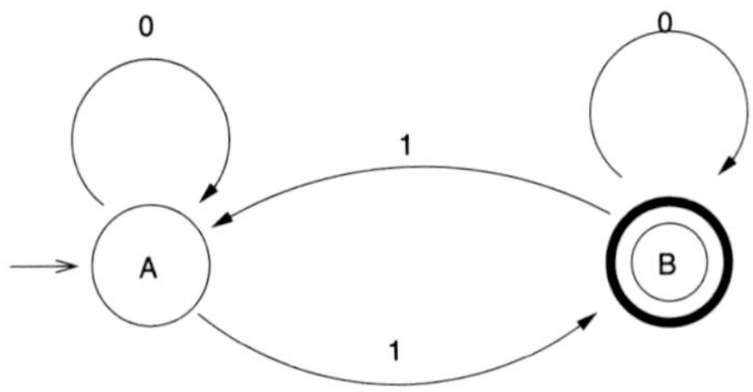

Figure 3.9. FSA to recognize an odd number of 1s.

3.3.2 Finite-State Automata

Tokens for a programming language all have a simple structure. As mentioned previously, the lexical analysis phase of the compiler breaks down the source program into a stream of such tokens. Taking a different perspective here, compared with the previous section on BNF grammars, we describe a machine model for recognizing tokens.

An identifier begins with a letter; as long as successive characters are letters or digits, they are part of the identifier's name. An integer is just a sequence of digits. The **if** reserved word is just the letter i followed by the letter f. In all of these cases, there is a simple model called a *finite-state automaton* (FSA) or a *state machine* that recognizes such tokens. As long as we know which state we are in, we can determine whether the input we have seen is part of the token for which we are looking.

Figure 3.9 describes a simple FSA that recognizes an odd number of 1s. Starting in State A (containing an input arc that does not come from another state), each successive input moves the machine to either State A or State B by moving along the arc labeled with the next input symbol. Whenever we are in State B (a *final state* indicated by a double circle), the string up to the current symbol is valid and accepted by the machine. Whenever we are in State A, the string is not accepted.

Operation of the machine for Input 100101 would proceed as follows:

Input	Current state	Accept string?
null	A	no
1	B	yes
10	B	yes
100	B	yes
1001	A	no
10010	A	no
100101	B	yes

We see that after inputs 1, 10, 100, and 100101, we are in State B, have an odd number of 1s, and accept the input.

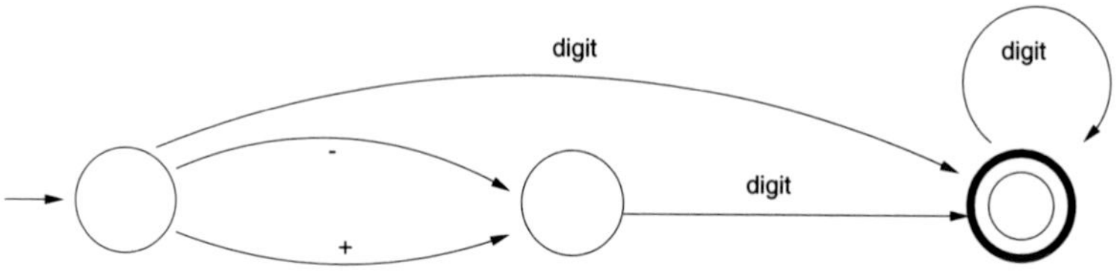

Figure 3.10. FSA to recognize optionally signed integers.

In general, an FSA has a starting state, one or more final states, and a set of transitions (labeled arcs) from one state to another. Any string that takes the machine from the initial state to a final state through a series of transitions is accepted by the machine.

Figure 3.10 is another example that defines an FSA to recognize signed integers. In extended BNF from the last section, this would be $[+ \mid -]$ *digit* { *digit* }*. This example also demonstrates another important characteristic. There is a duality between abstract machines and grammars. An FSA can be modeled by a grammar, as is described later in this chapter.

Nondeterministic finite automata. In the discussion on finite automata so far, we have implicitly assumed that all transitions are uniquely specified by the current state and the next input symbol. That is, for each state of the FSA and each input symbol, we have a unique transition to the same or different state. Such an FSA is called *deterministic.* If there are n states and the input alphabet has k symbols, then the FSA will have $n \times k$ transitions (labeled arcs). Figure 3.10 is such a deterministic FSA. Missing arcs are not the issue—we can always add arcs to an absorbing nonfinal error state. The issue of nondeterminism is the presence of multiple arcs from a state with the same label so that you have a choice as to which way to go.

We define a *nondeterministic* finite automaton as an FSA with

1. A set of states (nodes in a graph)
2. A start state (one of the nodes)
3. A set of final states (a subset of the nodes)
4. An input alphabet (labels on the arcs between nodes), and
5. A set of arcs from nodes to nodes, each labeled by an element of the input alphabet.

From any particular node, there may be any number of (or no) arcs going to other nodes, including multiple arcs with the same label. Such transitions are nondeterministic, because there are several possible moves for that particular input symbol (e.g., Figure 3.12). In this case, we say that a string is *accepted* by the nondeterministic FSA if there is *some* path from the start node to one of the final nodes, although there may be other paths that do *not* reach a final state. In the deterministic case, you would always wind up in a specific state that can be determined from the input symbols. See Problem 12 for additional comments on FSAs.

Regular Grammars

Regular grammars are special cases of BNF grammars that turn out to be equivalent to the FSA languages just described. These grammars have rules of the form

$$\langle nonterminal \rangle ::= \langle terminal \rangle \; \langle nonterminal \rangle \; \mid \; \langle terminal \rangle$$

Each rule consists of a terminal that may optionally be followed by a nonterminal. A grammar to generate binary strings ending in 0 is given by

$$A \;\rightarrow\; 0A \mid 1A \mid 0$$

The first two alternatives are used to generate any binary string, and the third alternative is used to end the generation with a final 0.

There is a close association between FSA and regular grammars; we can show that the two generate the same set of languages. (See problems at end of chapter.)

Regular Expressions

Regular expressions represent a third form of language definition that is equivalent to the FSA and regular grammar. We define a regular expression recursively as follows:

1. Individual terminal symbols are regular expressions.
2. If a and b are regular expressions, then so are: $a \vee b$, ab, (a), and $a^\star$.
3. Nothing else is a regular expression.

ab represents the concatenation or sequencing of regular expressions a and b, and $a \vee b$ represents the alternation of a or b. $a^\star$ is called the Kleene closure of regular expression a and represents zero or more repetitions of a (i.e., the null string [often written as ϵ], a, aa, aaa, $\ldots$).

We can use regular expressions to represent any language defined by a regular grammar or FSA, although converting any FSA to a regular expression is not always obvious. The following table is illustrative:

Language	**Regular expression**
Identifiers	$letter(letter \vee digit)^\star$
Binary strings divisible by 2	$(0 \vee 1)^\star 0$
Binary strings containing 01	$(0 \vee 1)^\star 01(0 \vee 1)^\star$

Converting any regular expression to an FSA is fairly easy. The $\vee$ operator simply represents alternative paths from State A to State B, concatenation represents a sequence of states, and Kleene closure represents loops (Figure 3.11). The

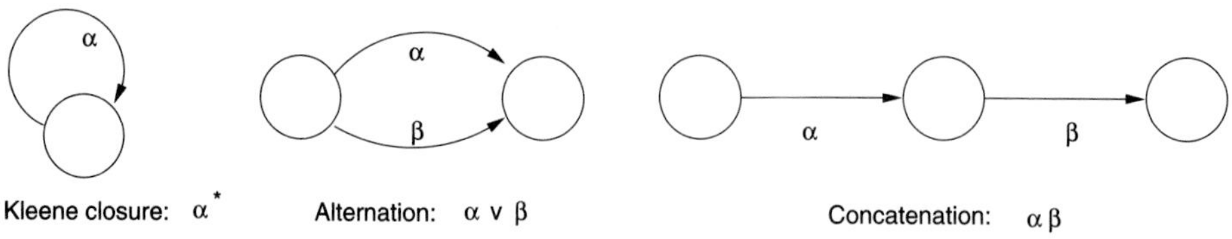

Figure 3.11. Converting regular expressions into an FSA.

FSA for the third regular expression is given by Figure 3.12. Note that this process results in a nondeterministic FSA, which we know can also be converted into an equivalent deterministic FSA (Problem 12). As we demonstrate in Section 3.3.3, the complexity of regular expressions and FSA are well understood, and tools such as Perl have been implemented to easily process such expressions.

Computational Power of an FSA

Finite-state automata have a finite amount of information—the set of states. Therefore, the set of strings they can recognize is limited. For example, the set a^nb^n cannot be recognized by any FSA. To see this, assume a^nb^n is recognized by an FSA with k states. For any input a^nb^n with $n > k$, the machine must enter the same state at least twice while reading the symbol a. So some subset of this string causes a loop within the FSA. This means that $a^n = wxy$ where substring x causes a loop back to the same state in the FSA. It is easy to see that $wx^{\star}yb^n$ is accepted by the FSA. These will be strings of the form $a^{m+i \times p}b^n$ for integers m and p and for all i, which is not the same as a^nb^n.

3.3.3 Perl Overview

Perl is a language well suited for the handling of regular expressions as described earlier in this chapter. As discussed in Section 1.4.2, with UNIX came the introduction

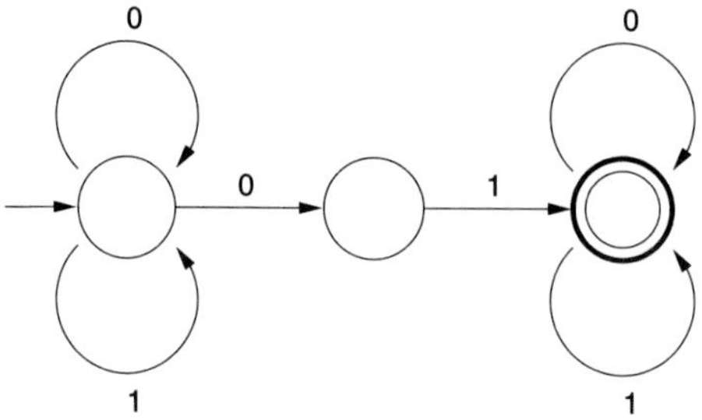

Figure 3.12. Converting $(0 \vee 1)^{\star}01(0 \vee 1)^{\star}$ to an FSA.

of the shell script as a programmable process language for controlling the execution of programs on a computer. The various data items used by the script were the files and programs within that computer system. As an aid to programming the shell, various string processing languages were developed. Two of the earliest were AWK in 1977 (named after its designers Alfred V. Aho, Peter J. Weinberger, and Brian W. Kernighan) and SED, a stream editor, patterned after the early UNIX *ed* editor.

For example, because AWK was designed to handle files that had regular patterns, if you have a file consisting of a list of names and e-mail addresses, AWK can be used to send an e-mail message to each name in the file. By writing a loop command in the shell and then invoking AWK to extract the e-mail address of the next name for each pass through the loop, an e-mail message can be sent to each name. The process of sending a message to each name in a file is now a process: a shell program that loops, and for each loop iteration AWK extracts the e-mail address and an e-mail program sends the message. Knowing the UNIX shell and the pattern-matching capabilities of AWK allows the programmer to build such a mailing list process fairly easily.

History. Many such shell-scripting languages, like AWK, developed as new uses for process control languages were found to aid in UNIX shell programming. Perl (Practical Extraction and Report Language) was developed by Larry Wall in 1986 in response to a management need for a configuration management system to control several computers on a network. Initially he used a tool called *B-news*, but it was inadequate to handle the necessary reports. AWK was insufficient for opening and closing multiple files. The result was a new language, Perl, that had some features similar to the earlier scripting languages like AWK and SED, but was better tuned for this new application.

The language was originally called PEARL, but a conflict with an existing graphics language resulted in the shortening of the name. The language included pattern matching, file handling, and scalar data. Newer versions of the language have evolved with the times and now include object-oriented classes. The growth of the WWW has led to Perl being a language well suited for Web interaction to process information that is entered on a Web page.

Brief overview of the language. Perl is an interpreted language designed for efficient text-processing applications. It has syntax patterned after C and was originally designed to operate as a shell script on a UNIX operating system where C is the predominant programming tool. Because of its similarity with C, it is either as readable or unreadable as a C program depending on whether you consider C readable.

Variables in Perl are either integers or strings and begin with the symbol $. It also has arrays and associative arrays. Associative arrays are also called *content addressable* arrays because information can be accessed by content and not necessarily with a subscript. For example, associated with a program in most modern systems is an environment. In Perl, this is accessible by the associative array $\$ENV$. One of the items in this environment (in UNIX systems) is the user's login ID. In Perl, one can just write:

```
print "The user of this program is: $ENV{'USER'}\n";
```

and the name of the user (environment variable $USER$) will be printed without the need to determine where in the environment the ID is stored. This shows the easy integration of Perl with the operating system to develop process scripts.

A simple Perl program consists of a series of **print** statements. It includes the usual sequence of control structures such as a **for**, **while**, and **until** loops and the **if** conditional. The **foreach** loop is particularly useful because it enables a program to loop through all members of an array, performing some action on each member without knowing a priori how large the array is.

Perl shares an ability to process regular expressions like several other process languages. =~ is the logical operator for matching a string. $\$ENV\{'USER'\}$ =~ mvz will be true if login name mvz is in the string $\$ENV\{'USER'\}$ (i.e., is the user running this program). ! ~ is the operator for not matching.

Regular Expressions in Perl

Perl provides a direct translation of regular expressions. For example, recognizing the regular expression a^+b^+ is the following Perl script:

```
#!/usr/bin/perl            # Inform operating system that this is a Perl script
$_ = <STDIN>;              # Read in input to default argument $_
if (/^a+b+$/) then { print "yes\n";}
        else { print "no\n";}
```

The pattern $/X/$ is matched against the string argument. This pattern succeeds if the regular expression a^+b^+ extends from the initial character of the input line (∧) to the end of the input line ($). To succeed if a^+b^+ is contained *within* a string, we only need the pattern /a+b+/. (See Appendix A.9 for additional regular expression operators.)

Perl allows for easy matching and substitution of strings, as in the following script:

```
$_ = 'aaabbbb';            # Give the default string the value 'aaabbbb'
if (s/(a+)/c/) { print "$_ and $1\n";}
        else {print "fail\n";};
```

In this example, $s/X/Y/$ means to find Pattern X and replace it with String Y. The pattern $a+$ matches the string aaa and c is substituted for the matched part. Because of the parentheses around the pattern, the Perl variable $1 is assigned the value of the matched string so the print statement will print *cbbbb and aaa*, showing the substitution of the pattern and assignment of the matched part.

3.3.4 Pushdown Automata

In the previous section, we described the finite-state automaton and stated that the set of languages accepted by such an FSA were equivalent to the languages generated by regular grammars. There is a certain duality here. Similarly, we use BNF grammars to generate strings in a language, and we can use an abstract machine to recognize that a given string is in the language. In this case, we can create a machine called a *pushdown automaton* that is equivalent to the BNF grammars we discussed previously.

A *pushdown automaton* (PDA) is an abstract model machine similar to the FSA. It also has a finite set of states. However, in addition, it has a pushdown stack. Moves of the PDA are as follows:

1. An input symbol is read and the top symbol on the stack is read.

2. Based on both inputs, the machine enters a new state and writes zero or more symbols onto the pushdown stack.

3. Acceptance of a string occurs if the stack is ever empty. (Alternatively, acceptance can be if the PDA is in a final state. Both models can be shown to be equivalent.)

It is easy to see that such PDAs are more powerful than the FSAs of the previous section. Strings like $a^n b^n$, which cannot be recognized by an FSA, can easily be recognized by the PDA. Simply stack the initial a symbols and, for each b, pop an a off the stack. If the end of input is reached at the same time that the stack becomes empty, the string is accepted.

It is less clear that the languages accepted by PDAs are equivalent to the context-free languages. However, consider the process of producing the leftmost derivation of a string. In such cases, the sentential form can be saved on the stack. Operation of the PDA is as follows:

1. If the top of the stack is a terminal symbol, compare it to the next input and pop if off the stack if the same. It is an error if the symbols do not match.

2. If the top of the stack is a nonterminal symbol X, replace X on the stack with some string α, where α is the right hand side of some production $X \rightarrow \alpha$.

This PDA now simulates the leftmost derivation for some context-free grammar. This construction actually develops a nondeterministic PDA that is equivalent to the corresponding BNF grammar. In Step 2 of the construction, there may be more than one rule of the form $X \rightarrow \alpha$, and it is not clear which one to use. We define a *nondeterministic pushdown automaton* in a manner similar to the nondeterministic FSA. A string is accepted if there is a possible sequence of moves that accepts the string.

Comparing with the FSA case, what is the relationship between deterministic PDAs and nondeterministic PDAs? In this case, they are different. Consider the set of palindromes, strings reading the same forward and backward, generated by the grammar

S ::= 0S0 | 1S1 | 2

We can recognize such strings by a deterministic PDA simply:

1. Stack all 0s and 1s as read.
2. Enter a new state upon reading a 2.
3. Compare each new input to the top of stack, and pop stack.

However, consider the following set of palindromes:

S ::= 0S0 | 1S1 | 0 | 1

In this case, we never know where the middle of the string is. To recognize these palindromes, the automaton must guess where the middle of the string is. As an example, given the palindrome 011010110, the pushdown automaton could:

Stack:	**Middle**	**Match Stack With:**
	0	11010110
0	1	1010110
01	1	010110
011	0	10110
0110	1	0110
01101	0	110
011010	1	10
0110101	1	0
01101011	0	

Only the fifth option—where the machine guesses that 0110 is the first half—terminates successfully. If some sequence of guesses leads to a complete parse of the input string, then the string is valid according to the grammar.

3.3.5 General Parsing Algorithms

It has been understood from the time of Chomsky's work that each type of formal grammar is closely related to a type of automaton—a simple abstract machine that is usually defined to be capable of reading an input tape containing a sequence of characters and producing an output tape containing another sequence of characters. Unfortunately, a problem arises. Because a BNF grammar may be ambiguous, the automaton must be *nondeterministic* (i. e., it may have several choices of moves to make and must guess which one is most appropriate at any given time).

Nondeterministic pushdown automata can recognize any context-free grammar by utilizing this guessing strategy. For programming language translation, however, a more restricted automaton that never has to guess (called a *deterministic* automaton) is needed.

Although for regular grammars there is always a corresponding deterministic automaton, for BNF grammars there is none unless the grammar is unambiguous and meets some other restrictions as well. For unambiguous BNF grammars, straightforward parsing techniques have been discovered. One of the earliest practical techniques was recursive descent. A major advance came with Knuth's discovery of a class of grammars called *LR grammars* (or left to right parsing algorithms), which describe all BNF grammars recognized by deterministic pushdown automata. The LR(1) grammars describe all grammars where one only needs to look one symbol ahead to make a parsing decision. The SLR (Simple LR) and LALR (Lookahead LR) are subclasses of LR grammars that lead to efficient parsing algorithms. In addition, an alternative top–down technique called LL, as a generalization of recursive descent, also provides a practical parsing alternative. Most languages today are designed to be either SLR, LR, or LL, and parser generating tools such as YACC may be used to automatically generate the parser given the grammar.

Deterministic PDAs are equivalent to the LR(k) grammars and are important in the design of practical compilers for programming languages. Most languages based on grammars use an LR(k) grammar for their syntax. The full study of LR(k) grammars is beyond the scope of this book. However, in Section 3.4 we briefly describe recursive descent parsing as a simple example of parsing context-free languages.

3.4 RECURSIVE DESCENT PARSING

It is beyond the scope of this book to cover the complete spectrum of parsing algorithms. However, recursive descent is relatively simple to describe and implement, and an example recursive descent parser serves to show the relationship between the formal description of a programming language and the ability to generate executable code for programs in the language.

Recall that we may often rewrite a grammar using extended BNF. For example, for the assignment statement syntax of Figure 3.7, we stated that an arithmetic expression was described as

$$\langle \mathit{arithmetic\ expression} \rangle ::= \langle \mathit{term} \rangle \ \{[+ \mid -] \ \langle \mathit{term} \rangle\}^{\star}$$

This states that we first recognize a $\langle \mathit{term} \rangle$. As long as the next symbol is either a $+$ or $-$, we recognize another $\langle \mathit{term} \rangle$. If we make the assumption that the variable *nextchar* always contains the first character of the respective nonterminal and that the function *getchar* reads in a character, then we may directly rewrite the prior extended BNF rule as the following recursive procedure:

Identifier and *Number* are functions to read in those syntactic categories using a finite state scanner.

```
procedure AssignStmt;
    begin
    Variable;
    if nextchar <> '=' then Error
        else begin
        nextchar := getchar;
        Expression
        end
    end;
procedure Expression;
    begin
    Term;
    while ((nextchar='+') or (nextchar='-')) do
        begin
        nextchar := getchar;
        Term
        end
    end;
procedure Term;
    begin
    Primary;
    while ((nextchar='×') or (nextchar='/')) do
        begin
        nextchar := getchar;
        Primary
        end
    end;
procedure Primary;
    begin if nextchar = letter then Variable
    else if nextchar = digit then Number
    else if nextchar= '(' then
        begin
        nextchar := getchar;
        Expression;
        if nextchar=')' then
            nextchar := getchar
            else Error /* Missing ')' */
        end
    else Error /* Missing '(' */
    end;
procedure Variable;
    begin Identifier;
    if nextchar= '[' then
        begin
        nextchar := getchar;
        SubList;
        if nextchar = ']' then
            nextchar := getchar
        else Error /* Missing ']' */
        end
    end;
procedure SubList;
    begin Expression;
    while nextchar=',' do
        begin
        nextchar := getchar;
        Expression
        end
    end;
```

Figure 3.13. Recursive descent parser for arithmetic statements.

```
procedure Expression;
begin
    Term; /* Call procedure Term to find first term */
    while ((nextchar='+') or (nextchar='-')) do
    begin
        nextchar := getchar; /* Skip over operator */
        Term
    end
end
```

Figure 3.13 gives a complete recursive descent parser for the assignment statement grammar of Figure 3.7. To finish the parsing problem, as we discuss later in Section 8.2.1, one only has to realize that, given the expression $term_1 + term_2$, the postfix for this expression is simply $term_1$ $term_2$ +. As we later show, converting the input source statement into postfix permits an easy-to-implement execution strategy for the expression. Given the procedures to recognize arithmetic expressions, the postfix can be produced almost as easily. Assume that each procedure produces the postfix for its own subexpression using the procedure *output*. The postfix for the expression procedure may be produced as follows:

```
procedure Expression;
begin var PlusType: char;
    Term; /* Call procedure Term to find first term */
    while ((nextchar='+') or (nextchar='-')) do
    begin
        PlusType := nextchar; nextchar := getchar;
        Term; output(PlusType)
    end
end
```

Each of the other procedures may be modified in a similar manner. The postfix for *variable* = *expression* is just *variable expression* =, the postfix for $factor_1 \times factor_2$ is just $factor_1$ $factor_2$ $\times$, and so on.

3.5 PASCAL OVERVIEW

History. Pascal was designed in the 1968 to 1970 time period by Niklaus Wirth to overcome many of the deficiencies of the earlier ALGOL language. It was named after the French mathematician, Blaise Pascal, who developed a digital calculator in 1642. From the late 1970s through the late 1980s, it was the dominant language in beginning computer science courses, but has since been replaced by C, C++, and Java.

ALGOL 60 was the first attempt at a formal definition of a programming language; however, implementation of the language was difficult. Call-by-name parameters, although elegant, were hard to implement. There was no I/O statement because those were considered implementation dependent at the time, and own static storage was difficult to implement. In addition, more modern practices like data types and structured programming were developing during the 1960s. Languages like FORTRAN, although inelegant, were popular due to run-time efficiency.

In 1965, Wirth developed an extension to ALGOL 60 that included data structures and pointers for the IBM 360 computer while at Stanford University. This language, ALGOL W, was used by several universities, but its implementation remained solely on IBM 360 computers. The language required a rather large run-time support package to handle the string processing, double precision (real), and complex data types. As such, it turned out not to be effective as a systems programming language.

In 1968, Wirth returned to Switzerland and began work on a successor to ALGOL W. The goal was to design a language that could be compiled in one pass, and a recursive descent parsing algorithm was used to develop the initial compiler. This compiler executed on a Control Data computer and developed the now-famous P-code interpreter. Pascal compiler first translated the Pascal source program into a hypothetical machine language for a machine that was based on a stack architecture. Because of this structure, Pascal was relatively easy to transport to other computer systems. The Pascal compiler was written in Pascal. All that was necessary was to rewrite the P-code interpreter to execute on the new system.

Once developed in 1970, use spread. An American standard was developed in 1983 (IEEE 770/ ANSI X3.97 [LEDGARD 1984]) and an ISO standard soon followed (ISO 7185).

Brief overview of the language. Pascal is a language with a run-time structure much like C. However, it also has the ability to declare internal local procedures and create a full-nested name hierarchy of data objects. A Pascal program is always formed from a single main program block, which contains within it definitions of the subprograms used.

Pascal has a fairly large set of primitive and structured data types: integers, reals, characters, enumerations, Booleans, arrays, records, sequential files, and a limited form of sets. A **type** statement allows the programmer to develop new types, although it does not provide grouping and encapsulation of the type definition with a set of subprograms for operating on data objects of the new type. In addition, a pointer type and an operation to create new data objects of any type allow the programmer to construct new linked data objects during program execution.

Subprograms take the form of functions (if they return a single value) or procedures (if they act by modifying their parameters or global variables). Statement-level sequence control is based on structured control statements: compound statements, conditional and **case** statements, and three forms of iteration statement, although the language does have a **goto** statement, which is seldom used and never needed. Subprograms are invoked with the usual call-return structure with recursion.

Because Pascal is a block-structured language, most of its data-control structure for variable references uses the standard static scope rules and nested-program format characteristic of block structure. Parameters may be transmitted either by value or reference.

Pascal may be implemented efficiently on conventional computer hardware. The design includes only language features for which there exist well-understood and efficient implementations. During translation, static type checking for almost all operations is possible so that little dynamic checking is required, but full security of execution is still provided. Translation is ordinarily into executable machine code, although some Pascal implementations instead translate into a virtual machine code, which is interpreted and executed by a software interpreter.

During execution of a Pascal program, a central stack is used for subprogram activation records, with a heap storage area for data objects created directly for use with pointer variables and a static area for subprogram code segments and run-time support routines. Few run-time support routines are required beyond the standard procedures for I/O to sequential files and procedures for storage management.

Although a very useful language, Pascal does have its flaws. Among these are:

1. The language definition confuses language design with the underlying implementation. For example, the **forward** construct is solely to allow for one-pass compilers under the assumption that one-pass compilers would necessarily be the most efficient. This is not necessarily true. For example, the PL/C compiler for PL/I used three passes, but was one of the most efficient compilers for any common language in its time [CONWAY and WILCOX 1973]. In addition, today, with fast inexpensive computers, compilation speed is of little consequence.

2. Perhaps the biggest weakness is that arrays are considered a type, rather than an aggregation of objects of a type, thus,

   array [1..10] **of** integer

   is a different type from

   array [1..20] **of** integer

   This makes general array processing algorithms difficult, because arrays of differing sizes cannot be passed into a common subprogram (e.g., a common dot-product or matrix multiplication subprogram). Strings are implemented as arrays of characters, making string processing difficult because variable length results are hard to develop.

3. The procedure definition has the syntax

   procedure heading
   local variables
   local procedures
   begin *procedure_body* **end**

   Because there may be many large-nested local procedures, the definition of the local variables for a procedure may be very far, syntactically, from their use in the body of the procedure. This makes documentation and understanding of large Pascal programs difficult.

4. Features in the language should occur not by *omission* of information, but by *commission* of that information. Pascal parameters violate this rule. Parameters are all call by value unless an explicit **var** attribute is added to the parameter list, making the parameter call by reference. More than one novice (and also an author of this book) has spent many hours staring at listings trying to discover the error of the missing **var**.

5. Pascal implementation was defined as one monolithic compilation. There is no concept of independently compiled modules. Extensions in most implementations make this a relatively minor problem, because most Pascal systems have adopted a convention similar to the C ".h" header files to create external procedures. However, such nonstandard extensions limit portability of Pascal programs across various machines.

6. Although Pascal has user-defined types to support abstractions, it has no real encapsulation and information-hiding attributes. This is not so much a criticism of the language, but a comment about the state of knowledge around 1970 when the language was developed.

3.6 SUGGESTIONS FOR FURTHER READING

The literature on the syntax and translation of programming languages is extensive. Books by Aho, Sethi, and Ullman [AHO et al. 1988] and Fischer and LeBlanc [FISCHER and LEBLANC 1988] provide details of the translation process. Chapter 10 in [BIERMANN 1990] provides a simple overview of the translation process. Diagnostic compiler design is described in the description of the Cornell University languages CORC [CONWAY and MAXWELL 1963] and the PL/I variant PL/C [CONWAY and WILCOX 1973]. Spelling correction is discussed by Morgan [MORGAN 1970].

Practical considerations in the design of the syntax of languages have also received attention. Sammet [SAMMET 1969] surveyed much of the relevant material. Rationale documents, such as for Ada [ISO 1994], provide insights into decisions made in developing such languages.

3.7 PROBLEMS

1. Consider the following BNF grammar rules:

$$\begin{aligned} \langle pop \rangle ::= &\quad [\langle bop \rangle, \langle pop \rangle] | \langle bop \rangle \\ \langle bop \rangle ::= &\quad \langle boop \rangle | (\langle pop \rangle) \\ \langle boop \rangle ::= &\quad x|y|z \end{aligned}$$

For each of the following strings, indicate all the syntactic categories of which it is a member, if any:

(*a*) z
(*b*) (x)
(*c*) [y]
(*d*) ([x,y])
(*e*) [(x),y]
(*f*) [(x),[y,x]]

Chapter 4

Modeling Language Properties

During the early days of compiler technology, experts originally believed that a formal syntax such as BNF would be sufficient for describing the attributes of a programming language so that the behavior of a program could be explicitly described. However, in Section 3.3.1, we gave some examples of where BNF is insufficient to accurately describe the behavior of a program.

BNF is an excellent notation for answering the question, What does a program in a specific language look like? In this chapter[1], we introduce several formal theories that extend BNF to try and answer the question, What does a program do? We will do this by introducing the following formal models:

1. **Formal grammars.** BNF and regular grammars are just two examples of a more complex structure developed by Professor Noam Chomsky of MIT in the 1950s. We introduce the Chomsky hierarchy and briefly give the properties of these grammars. As we demonstrate, unfortunately, only the BNF and regular grammars already studied have a role in our discussion of programming languages. However, the other classes of grammars have important properties into the nature of computing, and we give an introduction to the concepts of undecidability and algorithmic complexity.

2. **Language semantics.** Other approaches besides formal grammars have been used to develop models of programming languages. One of the earliest is the attribute grammar by Professor Donald Knuth of Stanford University. This model appends semantic information to the usual BNF description of a language. A more formal model is denotational semantics, which embeds a program into a mathematical functional notation.

3. **Program verification.** A third approach is program verification. Rather than giving a formal description of a program, the goal here is to show the equivalence between a program and another notation—for example, predicate logic. If one wants to develop a program to output the cube of the input variable, the con-

[1]This chapter is more advanced than the others in this book and should be studied only by students wanting additional information. Except for the ML introduction in Section 4.2.3, this chapter may be skipped.

dition to prove is that the program and the equation *output* $=$ *input*^{3} have the same behavior. In this case, we are not as interested in what the program means, only that it has the required behavior. Originally developed by Robert Floyd and Tony Hoare in the 1960s, it is a technique that, although difficult to apply, is quite important in certain applications where program correctness is a critical property, such as nuclear power plant control.

4.1 FORMAL PROPERTIES OF LANGUAGES

Modern civilization is based on science and engineering working together to help explain nature and enable new techniques to be developed as an aid for future advances. The general model is

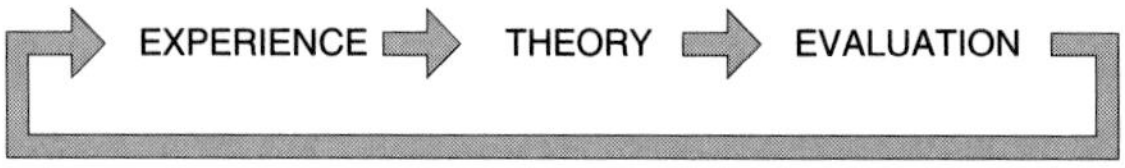

We experience nature (e.g., programs have bugs, programming is hard), develop theories of language design (e.g., structured programming, BNF grammars, data abstractions), and evaluate those theories (e.g., build languages using these concepts), which lead to further improvements (e.g., development of object-oriented classes as an improvement over data abstractions, development of SLR[1] and LALR[1] parsing techniques over LR[1] parsing), further improving the overall process. In this book, we have discussed some of the techniques that have generally found their way into language design. In this section, we briefly outline some of the other theoretical models that affect programming language design.

Much of early language design and implementation was based on practical concerns: What can we do to make this primitive piece of computer hardware usable for constructing the large programs needed for practical problems such as designing aircraft, analyzing radar data, or monitoring nuclear reactions? Many early language designs grew out of such needs, with little input from theory. The flaws, failures, and successes of this practice led to some early formal models of programming language syntax and semantics, which led in turn to better languages. Although better, these languages still had numerous flaws in both design and implementation. Better theoretical models led to yet further refinements in design.

A theoretical model may be *conceptual* (i.e., qualitative), describing practice in terms of an underlying set of basic concepts, without an attempt to provide a formal mathematical description of the concepts. In this sense, the preceding chapters have constructed a theoretical model of the basic concepts underlying programming language design and implementation. Alternatively, a theoretical model may be *formal* (i.e., quantitative), describing practice in terms of a precise mathematical model that can be studied, analyzed, and manipulated using the tools of mathematics. The theoretical models of this section are formal models. The treatment here is not meant to be complete, but it should provide sufficient details for the

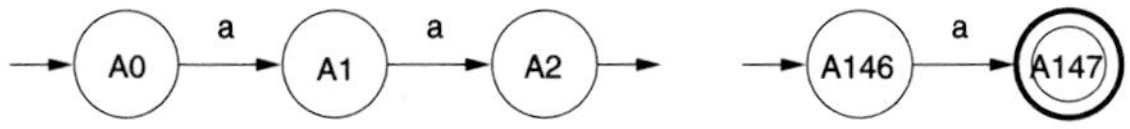

Figure 4.1. Using an FSA to count.

reader to understand the problem and the proposed solution.

4.1.1 Chomsky Hierarchy

As described in Section 3.3.1, BNF grammars have proved to be very useful in describing the syntax of programming languages. However, these BNF, or context-free, grammars are only one component of a class of grammars described by Noam Chomsky in 1959 [CHOMSKY 1959]. We briefly outline the model of grammars that Chomsky initially defined.

Grammar Types

In Section 3.3.1, we gave the basic syntax for BNF rules or *productions.* A *grammar* is defined by a set of nonterminal symbols, a set of terminal symbols, a start symbol (one of the nonterminals), and a set of productions. Each class of grammar is differentiated by the set of production rules that are permitted.

As given in the BNF case, a *language* is just a set of finite sequences of symbols from some arbitrary alphabet derived from the start symbol. The alphabet is just the set of characters that can be used in programs, and each finite sequence of these characters represents one complete valid program. We can talk about the set of strings *generated* by a grammar (i.e., the terminal strings produced from the start symbol) or, alternatively, we can say that the grammar *recognizes* the strings (i.e., beginning with a string, we can produce its syntax tree back to the start symbol).

A type n language is one that is generated by a type n grammar, where there is no grammar of type $n+1$ that also generates it. (As you see here, every grammar of type n is, by definition, also a grammar of type $n-1$.)

The Type 3 grammars are just the regular grammars defining the finite-state languages that model the lexical tokens of a language. Type 2 grammars are our familiar BNF grammars. Type 1 and Type 0 grammars have few practical purposes for programming language issues, but are important in theoretical computer science areas. We summarize each type in the following subsections.

Regular Grammars — Type 3

As stated earlier, finite-state automata and regular grammars provide a model for building lexical analyzers in a translator for a programming language (Section 3.3.2). Regular grammars have the following properties:

- Most properties of such grammars are decidable (e.g., Does the grammar generate any strings? Is a given string in the language generated by the grammar? Are there a finite number of strings in the language?).

- Regular grammars can generate strings of the form α^n for any finite sequence α and any integer n. That is, the grammar can recognize any number of patterns of finite length.

- Regular grammars can count up to any finite number. For example, you can recognize $\{a^n \mid n = 147\}$ by building an FSA with at least 148 states, as given in Figure 4.1. It will fail for the first 146 inputs, but will accept input number 147. With only 148 states, no FSA can reliably accept an input of any specific number greater than 147.

- These grammars are often used in scanners of compilers to recognize keywords or tokens of a language (if, while, begin, identifiers, numbers, strings).

As an example, a regular grammar to generate identifiers in Pascal (a letter followed by any number of letters or digits—i.e., $letter\{letter \vee digit\}^\star$) is given by

Ident→ **aX**| ... | **zX**| **a**| ... | **z**
X→ **aX**| ... | **zX**| 0 **X**| ... | 9 **X**| **a**| ... | **z**| 0 | ... | 9

Context-Free Grammars — Type 2

These are the BNF production rules with which you are already familiar. Productions are of the form $\mathbf{X} \rightarrow \alpha$, where α is any sequence of terminal and nonterminal symbols.

These grammars have the following properties:

- Many properties of such grammars are decidable (e.g., Does the grammar generate any strings? Is a given string in the language generated by the grammar? Is the language empty?)

- These grammars can be used to count two items and compare them. That is, they are characterized by strings such as $a^n cb^n$ for any n.

- Context-free grammars can be "implemented" via stacks. For the previous example of recognizing $a^n cb^n$, you can stack a^n, ignore the c, and then compare the stack with b^n to compare the two strings.

- These grammars can be used to automatically develop parse trees of programs, as described in chapter 3.

- For the most part, Type 2 and Type 3 grammars are no longer interesting research topics. All relevant properties seem to be solved.

As an example, the usual expression grammar is given by

$$\begin{array}{l} \mathbf{E} \rightarrow \mathbf{E} + \mathbf{T} \mid \mathbf{T} \\ \mathbf{T} \rightarrow \mathbf{T} * \mathbf{P} \mid \mathbf{P} \\ \mathbf{P} \rightarrow \mathrm{i} \mid (\mathbf{E}) \end{array}$$

Context-Sensitive Grammars — Type 1

These grammars are characterized by productions of the form

$$\alpha \rightarrow \beta$$

where α is any string of nonterminals, β is any string of terminals or nonterminals, and the number of symbols in α is less than or equal to the number of symbols in β.

Some properties of context-sensitive grammars are the following:

- All strings derived from the start symbol have length *nondecreasing* because every production must keep the length of the string the same or increase it.
- Context-sensitive grammars generate strings that need a fixed amount of memory. For example, they can recognize $a^n b^n c^n$, which cannot be recognized by a context-free grammar.
- Context-sensitive grammars are generally too complex to be useful for programming language applications.
- Some properties of context-sensitive grammars are unknown. In Section 4.1.3, we briefly outline the theoretical problem of showing NP-completeness or whether nondeterminism with context sensitivity is the same as determinism.

As an example, the following grammar generates $xa^n b^n c^n$:

$$\begin{array}{l} \mathbf{X} \rightarrow \mathbf{ABCX} | \mathbf{Y} \\ \mathbf{CB} \rightarrow \mathbf{BC} \\ \mathbf{CA} \rightarrow \mathbf{AC} \\ \mathbf{BA} \rightarrow \mathbf{AB} \\ \mathbf{CCY} \rightarrow \mathbf{CYc} \\ \mathbf{BCY} \rightarrow \mathbf{BYc} \\ \mathbf{BBY} \rightarrow \mathbf{BYb} \\ \mathbf{ABY} \rightarrow \mathbf{AYb} \\ \mathbf{AAY} \rightarrow \mathbf{AYa} \\ \mathbf{AY} \rightarrow \mathbf{xa} \end{array}$$

Unrestricted Grammars — Type 0

These grammars are characterized by unrestricted productions of the form $\alpha \rightarrow \beta$, where α is any string of nonterminals and β is any string of terminals and nonterminals. These grammars have the following properties:

- They can be used to recognize any computable function. For example, a grammar can be given (although not easily) for the string $a^n b^{f(n)}$ representing the function f. Given n as, the grammar generates $f(n)$ bs.
- Most properties are *undecidable* (Section 4.1.3). That is, there is no process by which you can determine whether a given property is true for all Type 0 grammars (e.g., is the language empty?). This differs from the context-sensitive case where many properties are simply unknown and may be true, false, or undecidable.

4.1.2 Undecidability

In discussing the Chomsky hierarchy, it was apparent that as we moved from Type 3 to Type 2 to Type 1 to Type 0 grammars, the resulting languages became more and more complex. We know that today's computers are extremely fast and often seem to have magical solution properties. So we may want to consider the question: Is there a limit to what we can compute with a computer?

Consider the following practical problem. Rather than testing a C program, can you write another program that reads a description of the C program (e.g., its source file) and determines whether the C program will halt when it is executed? If we had such a program, it would be extremely useful; we could avoid much testing of programs that eventually go into infinite loops by first checking them out with this new test program.

If you try to write this program, you will find it extremely difficult, impossible even. The problem is not that you are not clever enough; no one could write this program. It is one of the limitations of our mathematical system that a study of the Type 0 languages reveals. We discuss some of the aspects of this problem in this section.

Turing Machines

When programming in a language, say Language A, it is usually apparent that an equivalent program might be written in Language B. For example, if you write a payroll computation program in COBOL, the same program might equivalently be written in C or FORTRAN and perhaps with more difficulty in ML or LISP. Is there a program that can be written in one language for which there is really no equivalent program possible in one of the other languages? For example, is there a program that can be written in LISP or Prolog that has no equivalent in FORTRAN? A *universal programming language* is a language that is general enough to allow any computation to be expressed. Our problem might be expressed by asking: *Are all the standard programming languages universal?* If not, then what sorts of programs can one express that another cannot. If so, then why do we need all these different languages? If all are universal, then perhaps we should find the simplest universal programming language and dispense with the others altogether.

Note first that the question may be phrased in terms of the function computed by a program. To say that Program P written in Language A is equivalent to Program Q written in Language B must mean that the two programs compute the same function. That is, each program takes the same sets of possible input data and produces the same results in each case. A universal programming language is one in which any *computable function* can be expressed as a program. A function is computable if it can be expressed as a program in some programming language. This statement of the problem sounds a bit circular because we are up against a fundamental difficulty: how to define the concept of a computable function. To say that a function is computable means, intuitively, that there is some procedure that can be followed to compute it, step by step, in such a way that the procedure always terminates. However, to define the class of all computable functions, we must give a programming language or virtual computer that is universal in which any computable function can be expressed. The problem is that we do not know how to tell whether a language is universal.

This problem was already considered before the invention of computers. Mathematicians in the 1930s studied the problem of defining the class of computable functions. Several invented simple abstract machines or automata that might serve to define the class of computable functions. The most widely known of these is the *Turing machine,* named for its inventor, Alan Turing [TURING 1936].

A Turing machine has only a single data structure, a variable-length linear array called the *tape.* Each component of the tape contains just a single character. There is also a single pointer variable, called the *read head,* that points to some component of the tape at all times. The Turing machine is controlled by a program that involves only a few simple operations:

1. The character at the tape position designated by the read head can be read or written (replaced by another character). The program can branch depending on the value read. It can also use unconditional **goto**s to construct loops. (That is, the internal logic of the Turing machine is similar to the finite state automaton given earlier.)

2. The read-head pointer can be modified to point to the tape component one to the left or one to the right of its current position. If this shift of the read head moves its pointer off the end of the tape, then a new component is inserted at that end, with an initial value of the null character.

The operation of a Turing machine begins with its tape containing the input data and its read head positioned at the leftmost character in the input data. The

Turing machine performs a sequence of the prior simple operations while modifying the contents of its tape (and possibly extending it as well). If it finally halts, the tape contains the results computed.

A Turing machine is an extremely simple abstract machine. Note that it cannot even do arithmetic. If you wish it to add two numbers, it must be programmed using only the operations described earlier. No other variables or data structures are allowed; only the single tape for storage (but note that the storage capacity of the tape is unlimited).

Can a Turing machine do *anything* useful? Several example programs might be given to convince you that it can at least be programmed to do some simple things like addition and subtraction. However, the argument that we really wish to make is a lot stronger: A Turing machine can do *everything* useful (in the realm of computations)! That is, we would like to show that every computation can be expressed as a program for a Turing machine, and thus the language used for programming a Turing machine is a universal language despite that it allows only one vector and no arithmetic, no subroutines, and none of the other structures that we associate with ordinary programming languages.

The formal statement of this idea is known as *Church's thesis* (the same Church mentioned in Section 4.2). *Any computable function can be computed by a Turing machine.* Church's thesis is not a theorem that can be proved. It is a hypothesis that might be disproved if a computation could be defined in some other programming language and be shown to have no equivalent as a computation for a Turing machine. However, Church's thesis has been considered for many years by many mathematicians. Many different real and abstract computers and languages have been invented, and it has been proved repeatedly that each alternative method proposed for producing a universal machine or language is in fact no more powerful than a Turing machine. That is, each function that can be computed using the new language or machine can be represented as a program for a Turing machine.

One result relevant to our discussion of programming languages is that Turing machines are equivalent to the Type 0 grammars discussed earlier in this chapter. It is fairly easy to show that any state of a Turing machine can be simulated by a derivation with a Type 0 grammar. Similarly, any Type 0 grammar can be recognized by a (nondeterministic) Turing machine. Unlike the context-free case, surprisingly enough, nondeterministic and deterministic Turing machines are equivalent. That is, any computation computed by a nondeterministic Turing machine can be computed by an equivalent deterministic Turing machine.

The central fact that the Turing machine illustrates is this: *It takes almost no machinery to achieve universality, other than some sort of unlimited storage capacity.* Even an extremely simple set of data structures and operations is sufficient to allow any computable function to be expressed.

The Halting Problem

The study of Turing machines and languages has led to some other important results. Among these are a number of results showing that certain problems are *undecidable*. That is, there is no general algorithm for their solution even in the context of these simple machines.

Consider the problem of the program to check if a given C program will ever halt, as described at the beginning of this section. We certainly know about subcases of C programs that halt. For example, the program

```
main()
    {int i;
    i=0;
    }
```

certainly halts. In fact, the set of all C programs consisting of only declarations and assignment statements all halt. We can even easily build a program that determines this for us as follows:

1. Take some C compiler.
2. From the BNF grammar defining C, delete all productions that include any branching, procedure call, or loop statements.
3. Execute the compiler using this reduced set of productions for C.

Any program correctly compiled by this modified C compiler only consists of assignment statements and will halt. The interesting cases are those programs that do not compile on this modified C compiler. Some obviously are correct and will halt (e.g., all those programs you have written that contain loops that work correctly), but others may not halt and will loop forever. The problem is that you cannot tell in general which case you have.

Assume that you have such a universal checking program and you give it an extremely long program to analyze. Assume that you let it run for up to 3 years; if it doesn't conclude within that time period that the program halts, assume that it never will.

If you let it run for 3 years and then stop and say the program it is analyzing will never halt, perhaps the answer could have been found if you ran the program for 3 years and 10 minutes. The problem is that for items not in the computable set, we just don't know when to stop trying to compute the answer.

This is an intuitive discussion of what has become known as the *halting problem:* Is there a general algorithm for determining whether any given Turing machine will ever halt when given any particular character string as its input data? Turing's original theoretical studies in 1936 showed that the halting problem was undecidable: There could exist no general algorithm to solve the problem for all Turing machines and all input data sets.

To show that any particular problem is undecidable, we show that it is equivalent to the halting problem. If we could then solve this problem of interest, we could also solve the halting problem, which we know is undecidable. Therefore, the original problem must also be undecidable.

The study of these simple universal languages and machines leads to the conclusion that any programming language that might reasonably be used in practice is undoubtedly a universal language if bounds on execution time and storage are ignored. Thus, the programmer who steadfastly refuses to use any language other than, for example, LISP, because "anything can be done in LISP," is, in fact, correct. It may be difficult, but it certainly can be done. The differences among programming languages are not *quantitative* differences in what can be done, but only *qualitative* differences in how elegantly, easily, and effectively things can be done.

Ambiguity

The Chomsky hierarchy of grammar forms is an example of a common phenomenon in theoretical work: Many different theoretical models of a practical situation may be constructed, each abstracting the practical problem in different ways. Some of these theoretical models turn out to be less useful than others and are studied for a while and then forgotten. Others turn out to capture some important element of the practical problem and enter into general use. The context-sensitive and unrestricted grammars in Chomsky's hierarchy turned out to be the wrong models for programming languages. Although more powerful than BNF, they were also more complex to understand, analyze, and use in practice. Many of the later grammar forms were developed in an attempt to overcome the limitations of these models.

BNF grammars have a number of nice properties. They are rather easy to use in practical situations and are powerful enough to express most (but not all) of the syntactic constraints that are required for programming languages (linguists found them less useful for natural languages). They are also easy to mathematically analyze to discover obscure facts about the languages they define.

For example, one important practical question is whether a given BNF grammar for a programming language is *ambiguous* (i.e., does the grammar define a unique parse for each valid program, or are multiple parses possible?) Ordinarily each parse corresponds to a different meaning given to the program, so multiple parses lead to multiple meanings. This question arises: Can you find a general procedure for determining whether a BNF grammar is ambiguous? The result from theoretical studies is surprising: Don't bother to find such a procedure. There is none. In formal terms, the question of determining the ambiguity of a BNF grammar is said to be *undecidable;* there can be no general procedure for answering the question for any BNF grammar. The result is disappointing because, faced with a complex BNF grammar containing hundreds of productions, it would be nice to have a program that could check whether it is ambiguous. We might write a program that could give a yes or no answer most of the time, but the undecidability of the question

Chomsky Level	Grammar Class	Machine Class
0	Unrestricted	Turing machine
1	Context sensitive	Linear-bounded automaton
2	Context free	Pushdown automaton
3	Regular	Finite-state automaton

Table 4.1. Classes of grammars and abstract machines.

tells us that no program could *always* give an answer. For some grammars, it would have to fail to produce an answer no matter how long we let it run.

4.1.3 Algorithm Complexity

The Chomsky hierarchy is still a fascinating topic of study in formal computer science. Although the lexical analysis and parsing issues are largely resolved, there are many interesting questions needing a solution. We summarize some of these remaining problems.

Grammars and machines. For each class of grammar we said that there was a duality between that grammar class and an abstract machine class. Table 4.1 and Figure 4.2 summarize this discussion:

1. A finite-state automaton [Figure 4.2(a)] consists of a finite state graph and a one-way tape. For each operation, the automaton reads the next symbol from the tape and enters a new state.

2. A pushdown automaton [Figure 4.2(b)] adds a stack to the finite automaton. For each operation, the automaton reads the next tape symbol and the stack symbol, writes a new stack symbol, and enters a new state.

3. A linear-bounded automaton [Figure 4.2(c)] is similar to the finite-state automaton with the additions that it can read and write to the tape for each input symbol and it can move the tape in either direction.

4. A Turing machine [Figure 4.2(d)] is similar to a linear-bounded automaton except that the tape is infinite in either direction.

We have discussed all of these previously except for the linear-bounded automaton. We define a *linear-bounded automaton* (LBA) as a Turing machine that can use only the amount of tape containing its input data. Thus, its storage grows with the size of the input, and it can recognize more complex strings. However, its data storage capabilities are limited compared with the Turing machine, because it cannot extend its tape indefinitely.

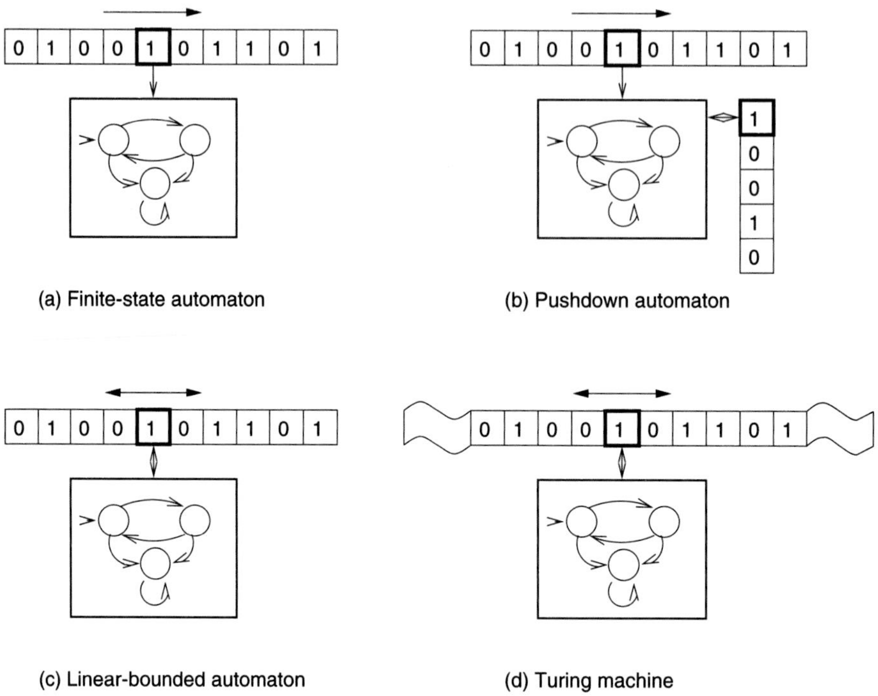

Figure 4.2. Abstract machine models.

When we discuss the computational power of both the deterministic and nondeterministic form of each abstract machine, we have the following interesting results:

Machine Type	Determinism versus Nondeterminism
Finite-state automaton	Same
Pushdown automaton	Not Same
Linear-bounded automaton	?
Turing machine	Same

For both Type 3 and Type 0 languages, nondeterminism does not add any additional power to the abstract machine. The functionality of the nondeterministic machine can be duplicated by an equivalent deterministic machine. However, for Type 2 languages, we know that nondeterminism does increase power. We can recognize the set of palindromes by a nondeterministic pushdown automaton (as described in Section 3.3.5) by having the nondeterministic machine guess where the midpoint of the string is, but we cannot recognize this string with a deterministic pushdown automaton. The deterministic pushdown automaton recognizes the *deterministic context-free languages,* which turn out to be the LR(k) languages that form the basis for compiler syntactic analysis theory.

Unfortunately, we have no answer for the linear-bounded case. We simply do not know whether nondeterministic LBAs are equivalent to deterministic LBAs. This problem has plagued theoretical computer scientists for over 30 years.

Polynomial time computations. Because of the difficulty of solving the nondeterminism question for LBAs, an entire specialty in theoretical computer science has evolved, determining the complexity of an algorithm. Determinism can be related to computation in *polynomial time*. That is, given an input of length n, the abstract machine will execute for at most $p(n)$ time units for some polynomial p [where $p(x) = a_1x^n + a_2x^{n-1} + \ldots + a_{n-1}x + a_n$]. In contrast, nondeterminism can be reduced to showing that a computation cannot be completed in polynomial time. The equivalence of the nondeterministic LBA and the deterministic LBA has been shown to be equivalent to this problem: Given a computation that can be completed in nonpolynomial time (NP), is there another machine that can compute this same result in polynomial time (P)? In other words, does P = NP? We call this problem for LBAs *NP-completeness* and state that any problem equivalent to this question is *NP-complete*. The nondeterminism question for LBAs is therefore NP-complete.

There are many related problems that have been shown to be NP-complete, but so far we have no answer to the basic question. Many theoreticians now believe that there is no answer to this question. It is simply outside of the axiom system of our mathematical formalism.

Value of Formal Models

Practicing programmers often fail to appreciate the value of theoretical models and studies in the advancement of programming languages and programming techniques. The abstraction necessary as the first step in constructing a theoretical model of a practical problem sometimes appears to simplify to the point that the core of the practical problem is lost. In fact, this can and often does happen. By choosing the wrong abstraction, the theoretician may study a theoretical model and produce results that cannot be translated back into a solution to the original practical problem. However, as this section has tried to indicate, when the right abstraction is found, theoretical studies may produce results of the deepest practical impact.

4.2 LANGUAGE SEMANTICS

Although much is known about programming language syntax, we have less knowledge of how to correctly define the semantics of a language. A manual for a programming language must define the meaning of each construct in the language, both alone and in conjunction with other language constructs. The problem is quite similar to the problem of definition of syntax. A language provides a variety of different constructs, and both the language user and implementor require a precise definition of each construct. The programmer needs the definition to be able to write correct programs and predict the effect of execution of any program statement. The implementor needs the definition to construct a correct implementation of the language.

In most language manuals, the definition of semantics is given in ordinary prose. Typically a rule (or set of rules) from a BNF or other formal grammar is given to define the syntax of a construct, and then a few paragraphs and some examples are given to define the semantics. Unfortunately, the prose is often ambiguous in its meaning so that different readers come away with different interpretations of the semantics of a language construct. A programmer may misunderstand what a program will do when executed, and an implementor may implement a construct differently from other implementors of the same language. As with syntax, some method is needed for giving a readable, precise, and concise definition of the semantics of an entire language.

The problem of semantic definition has been the object of theoretical study for as long as the problem of syntactic definition, but a satisfactory solution has been much more difficult to find. Many different methods for the formal definition of semantics have been developed. The following are some of these.

Grammatical models. Some of the earliest attempts to add semantics to a programming language involved adding extensions to the BNF grammar that defined the language. Given a parse tree for a program, additional information could be extracted from that tree. We shortly discuss attribute grammars as a way to extract this additional information.

Imperative or operational models. An *operational* definition of a programming language is a definition that defines how programs in the language are executed on a virtual computer. Typically the definition of the virtual computer is described as an automaton, but an automaton that is far more complex than the simple automata models used in the study of syntax and parsing. The automaton has an internal state that corresponds to the internal state of a program when it is executing; that is, the state contains all the values of the variables, the executable program, and various system-defined housekeeping data structures. A set of formally defined operations are used to specify how the internal state of the automaton may change, corresponding to the execution of one instruction in the program. A second part of the definition specifies how a program text is translated into an initial state for the automaton. From this initial state, the rules defining the automaton specify how the automaton moves from state to state until a final state is reached. Such an operational definition of a programming language may represent a fairly direct abstraction of how the language might actually be implemented. In contrast, it may represent a more abstract model that might be the basis for a software interpreter for the language, but not for an actual production implementation.

The *Vienna Definition Language* (VDL) is an operational approach from the 1970s. It extends the syntactic parse tree to include the machine interpreter as well. A *state* of a computation is the program tree as well as a tree describing all data in the machine. Each statement moves the tree state to another tree state.

Applicative models. An applicative definition of a language attempts to directly construct a definition of the function that each program in the language computes. This definition is built up hierarchically through definition of the function computed by each individual program construct. Corresponding to the applicative languages described in chapter 1, this method is an applicative approach toward semantic modeling.

Each primitive and programmer-defined operation in a program represents a mathematical function. The sequence-control structures of the language may be used to compose these functions into larger sequences represented in the program text by expressions and statements. Statement sequences and conditional branching are readily represented as functions constructed out of the functions represented by their individual components. The function represented by a loop is usually defined recursively, as a recursive function constructed from the components of the loop body. Ultimately, a complete functional model of the entire program is derived. The method of *denotational semantics* of Scott and Strachey and the method of *functional semantics* of Mills are examples of this approach to semantic definition. In Section 4.2.2, we present a short introduction to denotational semantics.

Axiomatic models. This method extends the predicate calculus to include programs. We can define the semantics of each syntactic construct in the language as axioms or rules of inference that may be used to deduce the effect of execution of that construct. To understand the meaning of an entire program, one uses the axioms and rules of inference somewhat as in ordinary proofs in mathematics. Beginning with the initial assumption that the values of the input variables meet certain constraints, the axioms and rules of inference may be used to deduce the constraints met by the values of other variables after execution of each program statement. Ultimately the results of the program are proved to meet the desired constraints on their values in relation to the input values. That is, it is proved that the output values represent the appropriate function computed from the input values. The method of *axiomatic semantics* developed by Hoare is an example of this method (Section 4.2.4).

Specification models. In the *specification model*, we describe the relationship among the various functions implementing a program. As long as we can show that an implementation obeys this relationship between any two functions, we claim that the implementation is correct with respect to the specification.

The *algebraic data type* is a form of formal specification. For example, in building a program that implements stacks, *push* and *pop* are inverses in the sense that, given any stack S, if you push something onto S and then pop S, you get the original stack back. We might state this as the axiom

$$pop(push(S, x)) = S$$

Any implementation that preserved this property (along with several others) can be said to be a correct implementation of a stack. In Section 4.2.5, we present a short introduction to algebraic data types.

Formal semantic definitions are becoming an accepted part of definition of a new language. The standard definition of PL/I includes a VDL-like notation for describing the semantic behavior of PL/I statements, and a denotational semantic definition was developed for Ada. However, the effect of formal semantic definition studies on the practice of language definition has not been as strong as the effect of study of formal grammars on definition of syntax. No single semantic definition method has been found useful for both user and implementor of a language. The operational methods may provide a good formal model of implementation that an implementor can use, but these definitions are usually too detailed to be of much value to the user. Functional and denotational methods do not provide much guidance to the implementor and have usually proved too complex to be of direct value to users. Axiomatic methods are more directly understandable by a language user, but they cannot generally be used to define a language completely without becoming extremely complex, and they provide no guidance to the implementor.

We briefly describe the attribute grammar as a form of semantic model of a programming language. In Section 4.2, we describe other language semantic models.

4.2.1 Attribute Grammars

One of the earliest attempts to develop a semantic model of a programming language was the concept of *attribute grammars*, developed by Knuth [KNUTH 1968]. The idea was to associate a function with each node in the parse tree of a program giving the semantic content of that node. Attribute grammars were created by adding functions (*attributes*) to each rule in a grammar.

An *inherited* attribute is a function that relates nonterminal values in a tree with nonterminal values higher up in the tree. In other words, the functional value for the nonterminals on the right of any rule are a function of the left-hand side nonterminal.

A *synthesized* attribute is a function that relates the left-hand side nonterminal to values of the right-hand side nonterminals. These attributes pass information up the tree (i.e., were synthesized from the information below in the tree).

Consider this simple grammar for arithmetic expressions:

$$\begin{aligned} &\mathrm{E} \to \mathrm{T} \mid \mathrm{E+T} \\ &\mathrm{T} \to \mathrm{P} \mid \mathrm{T} \times \mathrm{P} \\ &\mathrm{P} \to \mathrm{I} \mid (\mathrm{E}) \end{aligned}$$

We can define the semantics of this language by a set of relationships among the nonterminals of the grammar. For example, the following functions produce the value of any expression generated by this grammar:

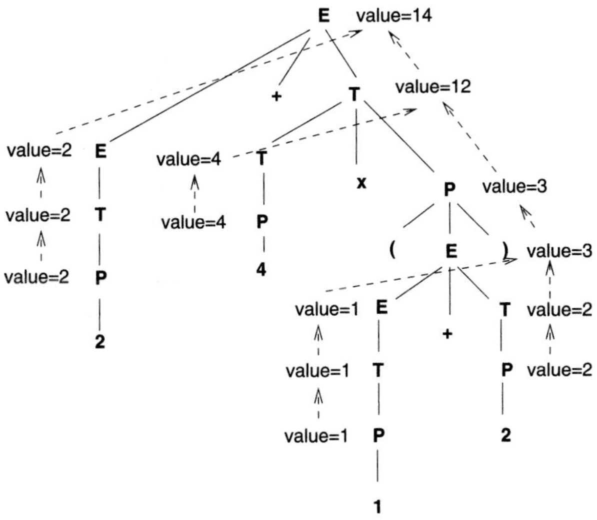

Figure 4.3. Attribute value example.

Production	**Attribute**
$E \to E + T$	$value(E_1) = value(E_2) + value(T)$
$E \to T$	$value(E) = value(T)$
$T \to T \times P$	$value(T_1) = value(T_2) \times value(P)$
$T \to P$	$value(T) = value(P)$
$P \to I$	$value(P) = value\ of\ number\ I$
$P \to (E)$	$value(P) = value(E)$

Here, we labeled X_1 and X_2 to be the first or second reference of nonterminal X in the production. Figure 4.3 shows an attributed tree giving the value of the expression $2 + 4 \times (1 + 2)$.

Attribute grammars can be used to pass semantic information around the syntax tree. For example, declaration information can be collected by the declaration productions of a language and that symbol table information passed down the tree to be used to generate code for expressions.

For example, the following attributes can be added to the nonterminals ⟨*decl*⟩ and ⟨*declaration*⟩ to create a set of names declared in a program:

Production	Attribute
$\langle declaration\rangle ::= \langle decl\rangle\langle declaration\rangle$	$decl\_set(declaration_1) = decl\_name(decl)$ $\cup decl\_set(declaration_2)$
$\langle declaration\rangle ::= \langle decl\rangle$	$decl\_set(declaration) = decl\_name(decl)$
$\langle decl\rangle ::=$ **declare** x	$decl\_name(decl) = x$
$\langle decl\rangle ::=$ **declare** y	$decl\_name(decl) = y$
$\langle decl\rangle ::=$ **declare** z	$decl\_name(decl) = z$

The synthesized attribute *decl_set* associated with the nonterminal $\langle declaration\rangle$ will always contain the set of names that are declared in any particular program. This attribute can then be passed down the tree via an inherited attribute and used to help generate the correct code for that data.

If a grammar has only synthesized attributes (as in this example), they can be evaluated by the compiler at the same time that the syntax tree is generated during the syntactic analysis phase of translation. This is how systems like YACC work. Each time YACC determines a BNF production rule to apply, a subroutine (e.g., its attribute function) executes to apply semantics to the syntax tree.

4.2.2 Denotational Semantics

Denotational semantics is a formal applicative model for describing programming language semantics. Before briefly discussing denotational semantics, we first introduce the lambda calculus as a simpler functional model developed during the 1930s as a way to explain mathematical computations. From the lambda calculus, more complex structures can be developed, including the concepts of data types and programming language semantics. Later (Section 4.2.3) we introduce ML as an applicative language based on some of the functional style of denotational semantics.

Lambda Calculus

Perhaps the earliest model of programming language semantics was the *Lambda calculus* (λ calculus) developed in the 1930s by A. Church as a theoretical model of computation comparable to the Turing machine (Section 4.1.3). Although predating the earliest computers by several years and programming languages by about 15, the λ calculus served as a good model for programming language function invocation. In fact, both ALGOL and LISP can trace their function call semantics to the λ calculus model; λ calculus substitution is a direct mapping of the call-by-name parameter passing mechanism defined in ALGOL (Section 9.3). The λ calculus was extended by Scott [SCOTT 1972] into a general theory of data types, which is known today as *denotational semantics.* This notation has had an impact on the design of the ML theory of data types. Full discussion of both the λ calculus and denotational semantics is beyond the scope of this book; however, we present a brief overview of these ideas and show their relationship to programming language design.

λ expressions are defined recursively as follows:

1. If x is a variable name, then x is a λ expression.
2. If M is a λ expression, then $\lambda x.M$ is a λ expression.
3. If F and A are λ expressions, then (FA) is a λ expression. F is the *operator* and A is the *operand.*

We can also define λ expressions by a context-free grammar:

$$\lambda\_expr \;\rightarrow\; identifier \mid \lambda identifier.\lambda\_expr \mid (\lambda\_expr\ \lambda\_expr).$$

The following are all examples of λ expressions generated by this grammar:

$$\begin{array}{lll} x & \lambda x.x & \lambda x.y \\ \lambda x.(xy) & (\lambda x.(xx)\lambda x.(xx)) & \lambda x.\lambda y.x \end{array}$$

Variables may be bound or free. Intuitively, a *bound variable* is a locally declared variable, whereas a free variable has no declaration. In λ expression x, x is *free.* If x is free in M, then x is bound in $\lambda x.M$. x is free in $(F\ A)$ if x is free in F or x is free in A.

Any bound variable may have its name changed, just like the renaming of function parameters. Thus, the λ expression $\lambda x.x$ is equivalent to $\lambda y.y$. $\lambda x.\lambda x.x$ is equivalent to $\lambda x.\lambda y.y$ because the variable x is bound to the rightmost λx. Informally, bound variables are parameters to the function described by the λ expression; free variables are global. This analogy shows that the λ expression is a simple approximation to the procedure or subroutine concept in most algorithmic programming languages like Pascal, C, Ada, or Fortran.

Operations on Lambda Expressions

λ expressions have only one *reduction* operation. If (FA) is a λ expression and $F = \lambda x.M$, then A may be substituted for all free occurrences of x in M. This is written as: $(\lambda x.M\ A) \Rightarrow M'$. This operation is analogous to substituting an argument for a formal parameter in a function call.

Some examples of λ expression reductions are as follows:

$$\begin{array}{llll} (\lambda x.x\ y) & \Rightarrow y & & \\ (\lambda x.(xy)\ y) & \Rightarrow (yy) & & \\ (\lambda x.(xy)\ \lambda x.x) & \Rightarrow (\lambda x.x\ y) & \Rightarrow y & \\ (\lambda x.(xx)\ \lambda x.(xx)) & \Rightarrow (\lambda x.(xx)\ \lambda .x(xx)) & \Rightarrow & \ldots \end{array}$$

Note that the reduction operation does not always result in a λ expression that is simpler than the original expression; the fourth example does not terminate. This leads us to the *Church–Rosser property*; if two different reductions of a λ expression terminate, then they are members of the same value class. Stated another way, if

λ expression M has the reductions $M \Rightarrow P$ and $M \Rightarrow Q$, then there is a unique λ expression R such that $P \Rightarrow R$ and $Q \Rightarrow R$. We call R the *normal form* for the value class represented by M.

Parameter passing with λ expressions. In any λ expression, consider two standard approaches toward reduction: (1) Reduce innermost left term first, and (2) reduce outermost left term first. For example, in the λ expression: $(\lambda y.(yy)\ (\lambda x.(xx)\ a))$, the outmost term is the entire expression, whereas the innermost term is $(\lambda x.(xx)\ a)$. Two reduction sequences are possible:

Outermost first	**Innermost first**
$(\lambda y.(yy)\ (\lambda x.(xx)\ a))$	$(\lambda y.(yy)\ (\lambda x.(xx)\ a))$
$\Rightarrow ((\lambda x.(xx)\ a)\ (\lambda x.(xx)\ a))$	$\Rightarrow (\lambda y.(yy)\ (aa))$
$\Rightarrow ((aa)(aa))$	$\Rightarrow ((aa)(aa))$

Both get the same answer; however, the outermost reduction substituted the function $(\lambda x.(xx)\ a)$ for parameter y and evaluated this function for each occurrence of y. This is just the call-by-name mechanism described in Section 9.3. However, the innermost first reduction evaluated the constant (aa) before substituting for y. This is just the call-by-value mechanism.

If there is a normal form, call-by-name evaluation will find it, although as shown earlier, neither reduction method need terminate. Call by name is a form of lazy evaluation (Section 8.2.2), so only expressions used in the final solution need be evaluated. Call by value, however, always evaluates arguments, so nonterminating arguments will be evaluated even if not needed.

We can use this to create simple examples of terms that terminate via call by name and do not terminate via call by value. All we need is to compose a nonterminating λ expression as an argument that is never referenced. We already know that $(\lambda x.(xx)\ \lambda x.(xx))$ doesn't terminate, and trivially in $\lambda y.z$, the parameter y is never referenced. Hence,

$$(\lambda y.z\ (\lambda x.(xx)\ \lambda x.(xx)))$$

has the normal form z, which is easily determined if call by name is used, but represents a nonterminating λ expression if call by value is employed.

Modeling Mathematics with Lambda Expressions

The λ calculus was originally developed as a logical model of computation. We can use such expressions to model our understanding of arithmetic. First λ expressions are used to model the predicate calculus; using predicate calculus, we can model integers.

Boolean values. We model Boolean values as λ expressions:

True (T) is defined as: $\lambda x.\lambda y.x$. (The interpretation of this expression may be clearer by stating that *true* means: of a pair of values, choose the first. The following example demonstrates this.)
False (F) is defined as: $\lambda x.\lambda y.y$. (Of a pair, choose the second.)

We have defined these objects, so the following properties are true:

$$\begin{array}{ll} ((T\ P)Q) \Rightarrow P & i.e., ((T\ P)Q) \Rightarrow ((\lambda x.\lambda y.x\ P)Q) \Rightarrow (\lambda y.P\ Q) \Rightarrow P \\ ((F\ P)Q) \Rightarrow Q & i.e., ((F\ P)Q) \Rightarrow ((\lambda x.\lambda y.y\ P)Q) \Rightarrow (\lambda y.y\ Q) \Rightarrow Q \end{array}$$

Given the definitions for these constants T and F, we can define the following Boolean functions:

$$\begin{aligned} not = &\ \lambda x.((xF)T) \\ and = &\ \lambda x.\lambda y.((xy)F) \\ or = &\ \lambda x.\lambda y.((xT)y) \end{aligned}$$

With these definitions, we need to show that our interpretation of them is consistent with our rules of predicate logic. For example, *not*, when applied to T, returns F, and *not*, when applied to F, returns T:

$$\begin{aligned} (not\ \ T) = (\lambda x.((x\ F)T)T) \Rightarrow ((T\ F)T) \Rightarrow F \\ (not\ \ F) = (\lambda x.((x\ F)T)F) \Rightarrow ((F\ F)T) \Rightarrow T \end{aligned}$$

We can show that *and* and *or* have the usual logical properties in an analogous manner.

Integers. Given the Boolean functions, we can now develop the integers:

$$\begin{aligned} 0 = &\ \lambda f.\lambda c.c \\ 1 = &\ \lambda f.\lambda c.(fc) \\ 2 = &\ \lambda f.\lambda c.(f(fc)) \\ 3 = &\ \lambda f.\lambda c.(f(f(fc))) \\ \ldots &\ \ \ldots \end{aligned}$$

c is the zero element, and f is the successor (i.e., add 1) function applied sufficiently often to the c element. From these definitions, we can define our usual arithmetic operations:

Integer N is written as the λ expression $(N\ a)$, which is $\lambda c.(a \ldots (a\ c) \ldots)$. Applying reduction to $((N\ a)b)$, we get $(a \ldots (a\ b) \ldots)$.

Consider $((M\ a)((N\ a)b))$ by applying constant $((N\ a)b)$ to λ expression $(M\ a)$. The substitution of $((N\ a)b)$ for c in $(M\ a)$ yields $(a \ldots (a\ b) \ldots)$ where there are now $(M + N)$ a's in the list. We have just shown that we can *add* λ expressions

$$[M + N] \quad = \lambda a.\lambda b.((M\ a)((N\ a)b))$$

or the + operator is defined as

$$+ \quad = \lambda M.\lambda N.\lambda a.\lambda b.((M\ a)((N\ a)b))$$

Similarly, we can also show the following:

$$\begin{array}{lll} \textbf{Multiplication}: & [M \times N] = & \lambda a.(M(N\ a)) \\ \textbf{Exponentiation}: & [M^N] = & (N\ M) \end{array}$$

Continuing in this manner, we can develop all of the computable mathematical functions. However, let's apply these ideas toward programming language semantics.

Modeling Programming Languages

Given the previous discussion of lambda expressions, we can extend the concept to use lambda expressions to model data types; from that we can extend the model to include programming language semantics.

When the reduction operation is applied to an expression, λ expressions either reduce to constants or other λ expressions. Thus, all λ expressions are solutions to the functional equation:

$$\lambda expression = constant + (\lambda expression \Rightarrow \lambda expression)$$

Without getting too lost in the details of denotational semantics, we simply state that a *data type* is a solution to this equation. Note, however, that there is a direct analog between this formal model of a data type and type definitions in ML—that is,

$$\begin{array}{ll} \textbf{datatype}\ \text{Mylist} = & \text{var}\ \textbf{of}\ \text{int}\ | \\ & \text{listitem}\ \textbf{of}\ \text{int} * \text{Mylist}; \end{array}$$

which defines a list of integers (constructor $Mylist$) using constructors (like λ expressions) var and $listitem$.

Using this concept, we can define a *denotational semantics* model of a simple programming language. The model is a form of operational semantics because we are tracing through the execution of each statement type to determine its effect on a higher level interpreter. However, unlike traditional interpreters, such as described in chapter 2, we consider a program to be a function, similar to the earier λ calculus treatment. Each statement of the language is a function, and we model the execution of successive statements by determining what the composition function of the two must be.

We can write down a data-type equation for each statement type:

$$\begin{array}{rll} Stmt = & (Id \times Exp) & \text{Domain of assignments} \\ & +(Stmt \times Stmt) & \text{Domain of sequences} \\ & +(Exp \times Stmt \times Stmt) & \text{Domain of conditionals} \\ & +(Exp \times Stmt) & \text{Domain of iterations} \end{array}$$

As with any interpreter, we need to understand the underlying virtual computer. We assume that each identifier refers to a specific location in memory. Aliasing, parameter passing, and pointers are not allowed in this simple example. Therefore, for each identifier, there is a unique location in memory containing its value. Stated another way, we can model our concept of memory as a function that returns for each identifier—its unique value. We call such a function a *store.*

The store for a program is a function that maps each location (or id) into its appropriate value. The effect of executing a statement is to create a slightly modified store. We have a new function (similar to the previous one) that now maps each *id* into a value, possibly the same or a different one. Thus, we are viewing execution as the composition of the value store function followed by the function that describes the execution of a particular statement.

We view a store as a mapping from identifiers to storable values with a signature of type $id \rightarrow value$, where *id* are the set of identifiers in the language. We call this the *program state.*

In defining the semantics for a programming language, there are three basic functions we need to represent:

1. We need to describe the semantics of a *program.* In this case, the syntax of a program defines a function that has the effect of mapping a number to another number. In other words, we are looking for a function $\mathcal{M}$ with signature
$$\mathcal{M} : prog \rightarrow [num \rightarrow num]$$

2. We need to describe a statement in the language. Each statement maps a given state to another state, or
$$\mathcal{C} : stmt \rightarrow [state \rightarrow state]$$
This simply says that each syntactic statement (domain of $\mathcal{C}$) is a function from *state* to *state*. Therefore, each unique statement takes a program state (or mapping from identifier to value) and produces a new mapping from identifier to value that is the result of all previous statements, including this new statement.

3. The statement function $\mathcal{C}$ depends on the value of various expressions, so we need to understand the effects of expression evaluation in our language. Each expression is a syntactic entity involving identifiers, and each one accesses the storage to produce a value. Thus, from the set of syntactic expressions, a set of storable values produces an expression value. This gives the signature for expression evaluation as
$$\mathcal{E} : exp \rightarrow [state \rightarrow eval]$$

As a simple example, if exp is the expression $a+b$, then the evaluation function is: $\mathcal{E}(a+b) : state \rightarrow eval$, and applying this function to the state s gives us the function

$$\mathcal{E}(a+b)(s) = a(s) + b(s)$$

We usually write $\mathcal{E}(a+b)$ as $\mathcal{E}\{\!\{a+b\}\!\}$ by putting syntactic arguments in set braces rather than parentheses.

We can now model the domains for our programming language:

$state = id \rightarrow value$	$program\ states$
id	$identifiers$
$value = eval$	$values$
$eval = num + bool$	$expression\ values$
num	$integers$
$bool$	$booleans$
exp	$expressions$
$stmt$	$statements$

To define our language, we need to define a function of type $state \rightarrow state$ for each of the syntactic statement types. For ease in readability, we use a λ-like *let* construct (similar to the let in ML). The term

$$\text{let x} \leftarrow \text{a in } body$$

is used to mean $((x) : body)(a)$ and has a meaning similar to the λ expression $(\lambda x.\ body\ a)$

If x is of domain type $D \rightarrow D'$, then the expression $x[v/e]$ is defined as

$$\text{x[v/e]} = \text{(D d) D': } \textbf{if } \text{d=v } \textbf{then } \text{e } \textbf{else } \text{x(d)}$$

This has the intuitive meaning of changing the v component of x to e and represents the basic model of an assignment.

Statement Semantics

We now give the semantic definition for each statement of our language in terms of transformations on the state of a computation.

begin statement end: The **begin . . . end** sequence has no effect on the internal state of a computation, so it is effectively an identity function on the state space. We represent this as

$$\mathcal{C}\{\!\{begin\ stmt\ end\}\!\} = \mathcal{C}\{\!\{stmt\}\!\}$$

composition: In this case, we would like to apply the resulting state after executing $stmt_1$ on $stmt_2$. We represent this as function composition:

$$\mathcal{C}\{\!\{stmt_1\ ;\ stmt_2\}\!\} = (state\ s)state : \mathcal{C}\{\!\{stmt_2\}\!\}(\mathcal{C}\{\!\{stmt_1\}\!\}(s))$$

The argument to $\mathcal{C}\{\!\{stmt_2\}\!\}$ is just the resulting state after evaluating $stmt_1$.

assignment: Create a new storage map resulting from evaluating exp in the current state:

$$\mathcal{C}\{\!\{id \leftarrow exp\}\!\} = (state\ s)state : ((value\ v)state : s[id/v])(\mathcal{E}\{\!\{exp\}\!\}(s))$$

if: This simply determines which of two functions to evaluate by first evaluating $\mathcal{E}$ on the expression and applying this to the Boolean function, which then evaluates $stmt_1$ or $stmt_2$ as appropriate:

$$\begin{array}{l}\mathcal{C}\{\!\{if\ exp\ then\ stmt_1\ else\ stmt_2\}\!\} = \\ \quad (state\ s)state : ((bool\ b)state \rightarrow state : \\ \quad (\textbf{if}\ b\ \textbf{then}\ \mathcal{C}\{\!\{stmt_1\}\!\})\textbf{else}\ \mathcal{C}\{\!\{stmt_2\}\!\})(\mathcal{E}\{\!\{exp\}\!\}(s))(s)\end{array}$$

while: This requires a recursive (i.e., rec) definition because the **while** function is part of the definition:

$$\begin{array}{l}\mathcal{C}\{\!\{while\ exp\ do\ stmt\}\!\} = \\ \quad rec(state\ s)state : ((bool\ b)state \rightarrow state : \\ \quad (\textbf{if}\ b\ \textbf{then}\ \mathcal{C}\{\!\{stmt\}\!\} \circ \mathcal{C}\{\!\{while\ exp\ do\ stmt\}\!\}) \\ \qquad \textbf{else}\ ((state\ s')state : s')) \\ \quad (\mathcal{E}\{\!\{exp\}\!\}(s))(s)\end{array}$$

Note that in the prior definition for $\mathcal{C}\{\!\{while\}\!\}$, we actually use $\mathcal{C}\{\!\{while\}\!\}$ in its definition (as part of the **then** expression). This accounts for the term rec standing for $recursive$ in the prior definition. So the **while** is actually of the form

$$\mathcal{C}\{\!\{while\}\!\} = f(\mathcal{C}\{\!\{while\}\!\})$$

More simply, we say that the **while** statement is a solution to an equation of the form

$$x = f(x)$$

Such solutions are called *fixed points*, and what we want is the least fixed point that solves this equation. A complete analysis of fixed-point theory is beyond the scope of this book. However, the earlier description gives an indication of how systems like the lambda calculus can be extended to model programming languages.

4.2.3 ML Overview

History. ML (MetaLanguage) is an applicative language with programs written in the style of C or Pascal. However, it is an applicative language with an advanced concept of data type. ML supports polymorphism and, through its type system, supports data abstractions. The basic language is relatively compact, especially when compared with the definition of a language like Ada. However, its type extensibility gives it great power to develop complex programs. It includes exceptions, imperative and functional programming, rule-based specifications, and most of the concepts presented in other languages in this book. If one were limited to one language in which to study many language concepts, then ML would make a reasonable choice as long as one were not concerned about the commercial viability of the language.

ML has made significant inroads into the computer science educational and research communities. The exposure of the type mechanism at the source language level is a feature not available in other widely used languages. However, commercial applications of ML programs are few, and so far it remains mostly a vehicle for computer science research and educational use.

ML was developed by Robin Milner, along with others, as a mechanism for machine-assisted formal proofs in the Edinburgh Logic for Computable Functions system developed in the mid-1970s. However, it was also found useful as a general symbol-manipulation language. In 1983, the language was redesigned and extended with concepts like modules to become Standard ML. Although usually implemented as an interpreter, ML can be compiled relatively easily. The first compilers appeared in 1984 [CARDELLI 1984].

Use of Standard ML spread through the programming languages research community during the late 1980s. One popular version was developed by David Appel of Princeton University and David MacQueen of AT&T Bell Telephone Laboratories [APPEL and MACQUEEN 1991]. It is this version that was used to check the examples of ML presented in this book.

Brief overview of the language. ML is a language with static types, strong typing, and applicative execution of programs. However, it differs from other languages we have studied in that types need not be specified by the programmer. There is a type inference mechanism that determines the types of resulting expressions. This type inference allows for overloading and pattern matching using unification, much like Prolog.

As in LISP, an ML program consists of several function definitions. Each function is statically typed and may return values of any type. Because it is applicative, variable storage is handled differently from languages like C or FORTRAN. There is only a limited form of assignment. Because of the functional nature of execution, all parameters to functions are call by value with ML creating a new copy of any complex object using a heap store.

Comments in ML use the notation (* ... *). Unlike most other languages, in

ML, comments may be nested within other comments. ML includes most of the features we have studied in this book. It provides for records, abstract data types, and exceptions. Its I/O capabilities are fairly limited due to the research nature of its major users who don't need the ability to process multiple databases using complex formats. The syntax is fairly concise compared with languages such as Ada or C++.

4.2.4 Program Verification

In building programs, we are becoming more concerned about correctness and reliability in our finished products. Languages are being designed with features that enhance these attributes. We can use some of the previous discussion on language semantics to aid in correctness issues in three ways:

1. Given Program P, what does it mean? That is, what is its Specification S?
2. Given Specification S, develop Program P that implements that specification.
3. Do Specification S and Program P perform the same function?

The first of these conditions is just the semantic modeling issue of the last section. The second condition is just the problem of how to build a good program from its specification (i.e., the central problem in software engineering today). The third condition is the central problem in program verification (i.e., do the program and its specification mean the same?). Although we can phrase this question in three different ways, they are all similar.

Question 3 was popular to study in the 1970s, Question 1 was popular from about 1975 to the late 1980s, and Question 2 is currently of major interest. However, similar techniques are needed to work on all three issues. Testing a program cannot ensure that the program is without errors except in very simple cases. A program is tested with some test data sets, and the results are compared with the input data. If the results are consistently correct for a substantial number of test cases, then the program is usually pronounced debugged. However, in truth, only those test data sets actually tried are known to work correctly. The program may still be in error for other input data sets. To test all the possible input data sets for a program is ordinarily impossible. Thus, the tester must be satisfied with a less-than-complete guarantee of a correct program. If some method could be found that would guarantee correctness of a program without relying on testing, then programs could consistently be made more reliable.

A program computes a function. The programmer must know what function the program should compute. Suppose a separate specification of the function were made as part of the initial design of the program. Suppose that from the program, it were possible to determine the function that the program actually computed. If the program could in fact be shown to compute exactly the specified function, then it would have been proved to be correct without testing.

The *predicate calculus* is a notation from formal logic that is particularly useful for specifying complex functions precisely. Several approaches to proving the correctness of programs rely on the basic idea that the function desired is specified using the predicate calculus, and the program is then analyzed to determine whether the function it computes is in fact that specified by the predicate-calculus formula.

The notation generally used is $\{P\}S\{Q\}$, which means that if predicate P is true before execution of statement S, and if S executes and terminates, then Q will be true after termination of S. By adding some inference rules, we can embed this structure in predicate-calculus proofs as demonstrated by the following table:

Rule	**Antecedent**	**Consequent**
1. *consequence*$_1$	$\{P\}S\{Q\}, (Q \Rightarrow R)$	$\{P\}S\{R\}$
2. *consequence*$_2$	$(R \Rightarrow P), \{P\}S\{Q\}$	$\{R\}S\{Q\}$
3. *composition*	$\{P\}S_1\{Q\}, \{Q\}S_2\{R\}$	$\{P\}S_1; S_2\{R\}$
4. *assignment*	$x := expr$	$\{P(expr)\}x := expr\{P(x)\}$
5. *if*	$\{P \wedge B\}S_1\{Q\}$, $\{P \wedge \neg B\}S_2\ \{Q\}$	$\{P\}$**if** B **then** S_1 **else** $S_2\{Q\}$
6. *while*	$\{P \wedge B\}S\{P\}$	$\{P\}$**while** B **do** $S\{P \wedge \neg B\}$

If the antecedent in each inference rule can be shown to be true, then we can replace the antecedent with the consequent. This allows us to embed proofs of program constructs within our knowledge of predicate calculus.

Axiomatic verification typically works by going backward through a program. Knowing what the postcondition to a statement is, derive what precondition must be true before the statement executes. For example, if the postcondition to the assignment statement $X := Y + Z$ is $X > 0$, then, by the assignment axiom

$$\{P(expr)\}x := expr\{P(x)\}$$

where $P(x) = X > 0$, we get

$$\{Y + Z > 0\}X := Y + Z\{X > 0\}$$

So the precondition to the assignment statement must be $Y + Z > 0$. Continuing in this manner, we can prove (with some difficulty) sequences of statements containing assignment **if** and **while** statements.

The proof rule for the **while** statement is perhaps most interesting:

$$\text{if } \{P \wedge B\}S\{P\} \text{ then } \{P\}\textbf{while } B \textbf{ do } S\{P \wedge \neg B\}.$$

Predicate P is known as an *invariant* and must be true before and after the body of the **while** loop. Although there are heuristics for finding invariants, the general problem is impossible to solve (see Section 4.1.3). However, for many reasonable programs, invariants can be determined.

```
{B ≥ 0 }
MULT(A,B) ≡{
    a := A;
    b := B;
    y := 0;
    while b>0 do
        begin
        y := y+a;
        b := b-1;
        end}
{y = A × B}
```

Figure 4.4. Program to compute $y = A \times B$.

Example 4.1 presents the proof of the program $MULT$ of Figure 4.4 that computes $y = A \times B$. In this case, if we study the program, we see that each pass through the **while** loop adds a to y, whereas the product $a \times b$ decreases by a because b is decremented by 1. Therefore, we get an invariant $y + a \times b = A \times B \wedge b \geq 0$.

The condition $\{P\}S\{Q\}$ states that *if* S terminates and if P is true before execution of S, then Q will be true after S terminates. For the assignment and **if** statement, there is no problem. Both are assumed to terminate. But this is not necessarily so for **while** statements. To prove that loops do terminate, we need an external proof of this fact. The method generally used is as follows:

1. Show that there is some integer function f such that $f > 0$ whenever the loop executes.

2. If f_i represents function f during the ith execution of the loop, then $f_{i+1} < f_i$.

If both conditions can be shown to be true, then the loop must terminate. (See Problem 8 at end of chapter.)

This notation can only be practical if we can automate this process of proving the correctness of a program; the proof methods developed in these studies tend to be tedious to apply to real programs. An error in the proof may make it appear that a program is correct when in fact it is not. For these reasons, it is desirable to automate the proof procedure so that, from the functional specification of the program and the program, an automatic program-proving system can derive the complete proof with little or no human intervention.

Methods for program proving are now widely understood to be useful primarily during the design of a program so that, in a sense, the program is proved as it is written. The use of program proofs for programs that have been written in ordinary ways, without being structured so as to be easy to prove correct, has been found to be difficult or impossible. The methods for program proof, although useful, are not powerful enough to deal with extremely complex program structures such as those found in older programs that have been modified repeatedly in production use. Program proof methods are commonly taught to practicing programmers, as

EXAMPLE 4.1. Axiomatic Proof of program MULT.

Generally work backwards deriving antecedent from consequent.

Need to develop "invariants" for **while** loop on lines 5–7:

y is increased by a as b is decremented by 1. This gives an invariant of:

$(y + ab = AB) \ \wedge \ (b \geq 0)$

	Statement	Reason
a	$\{y + a(b-1) = AB \wedge (b-1) \geq 0\}$ $b := b - 1\{y + ab = AB \wedge b \geq 0\}$	*assignment* (line 7)
b	$\{y + ab = AB \wedge b - 1 \geq 0\} y := y + a$ $\{y + a(b-1) = AB \wedge b - 1 \geq 0\}$	*assignment* (line 6)
c	$\{y + ab = AB \wedge b - 1 \geq 0\}$ $y := y + a; b := b - 1$ $\{y + ab = AB \wedge b \geq 0\}$	*composition* (a, b)
d	$(y + ab = AB) \wedge (b \geq 0) \wedge (b > 0) \Rightarrow$ $(y + ab = AB) \wedge b - 1 \geq 0$	*theorem*
e	$\{y + ab = AB \wedge (b \geq 0) \wedge (b > 0)\}$ $y := y + a; b := b - 1$ $\{y + ab = AB \wedge b \geq 0\}$	*consequence*$_2$ (c, d)
f	$\{y + ab = AB \wedge b \geq 0\}$**while**$\cdots$ $\{y + ab = AB \wedge b \geq 0 \wedge \neg b > 0\}$	*while* (line 5, e)
g	$\{0 + ab = AB \wedge b \geq 0\}$ $y := 0\{y + ab = AB \wedge b \geq 0\}$	*assignment* (line 4, f)
h	$\{0 + aB = AB \wedge B \geq 0\} b := B$ $\{0 + ab = AB \wedge b \geq 0\}$	*assignment* (line 3, g)
i	$\{0 + AB = AB \wedge (B \geq 0)\} a := A$ $\{0 + aB = AB \wedge B \geq 0\}$	*assignment* (Line 2, h)
j	$B \geq 0 \Rightarrow 0 + AB = AB \wedge B \geq 0$	*theorem*
k	$\{B \geq 0\} a := A\{0 + AB = AB \wedge B \geq 0\}$	*consequence*$_2$
l	$\{B \geq 0\} a := A; b := B; y := 0$ $\{y + ab = AB \wedge b \geq 0\}$	*composition* (k, h, g)
m	$\{B \geq 0\} MULT(A, B)$ $\{y + ab = AB \wedge b \geq 0 \wedge \neg b > 0\}$	*composition* (l,f)
n	$(y + ab = AB) \wedge (b \geq 0) \wedge \neg(b > 0) \Rightarrow$ $(b = 0) \wedge (y = AB)$	*theorem*
o	$\{B \geq 0\} MULT(A, B)\{y = AB\}$	*consequence*$_1$ (m, n)

Must also show that the program terminates. This reduces to showing that all **while** statements terminate. The usual way is:

1. Show there is some property that is always positive in loop (e.g., $b \geq 0$).
2. Show that this property decreases in loop (e.g., In loop $b := b - 1$).

If both properties are to remain true, loop must terminate.

well as being part of many introductory programming courses.

The impact of this work has been in its effect on the design of languages. Language features that inhibit proof of the correctness of programs are now generally considered undesirable if an adequate substitute is available that is more amenable to correctness proof. For example, work on correctness proofs has been instrumental in showing the undesirability of *aliasing* in language design, as discussed in Section 9.2.1. Some languages such as C++ include an **assert** capability based somewhat on this axiomatic method. (See Section 11.1.1.) The assertion is placed in the source program and the program *tests* the assertion as it executes. It is not an *a priori* proof of correctness, but the placing of the assertion does catch many errors later in the life of the program.

4.2.5 Algebraic Data Types

The operations of term rewriting and unification, described earlier, play an important role in developing the algebraic data type model. If we describe the relationship among a series of functions, we state that any implementation that adheres to that relationship is a correct implementation.

For example, a *stack* of integers can be defined by the following operations:

$$\begin{array}{ll}
push: & stack \times integer \rightarrow stack \\
pop: & stack \rightarrow stack \\
top: & stack \rightarrow integer \cup \{undefined\} \\
empty: & stack \rightarrow Boolean \\
size: & stack \rightarrow integer \\
newstack: & \rightarrow stack
\end{array}$$

push and *pop* have their usual interpretation, *top* returns the top of the stack without removing the entry, *empty* checks for an empty stack, *size* is the number of elements in the stack, and *newstack* creates a new instance of a stack.

Generation of Algebraic Axioms

Given the set of operations that specify a data type, we can give several heuristics for developing the relationships among these operations. We divide these operations into three classes: generators, constructors, and functions:

Generators. For abstract data type x, a generator g constructs a new instance of the type. Thus, it has the signature

$$g : not\_x \rightarrow x$$

(not_x is any type except x.) In our *stack* example, *newstack* is a generator.

Constructors. Constructors c modify instances of our abstract type x and have signatures

$$c : x \times not\_x \rightarrow x$$

push is a constructor in this example.

Functions. All other operations on abstract type x are functions. In our *stack* example, *top*, *pop*, *size*, and *empty* are functions.

Intuitively, we state that any object y of abstract type x can be created by an application of a generator and repeated application of constructors. For stacks, this states that any stack is the result of using *newstack* to create an empty stack followed by repeated applications of *push* to place things on the stack. For example, the stack containing $1, 5, 3$ can be created as

$$push(push(push(newstack, 1), 5), 3)$$

Although there is no formal model for developing algebraic axioms, the following heuristic works well. Generate an axiom for each function with each constructor and generator. Because our stack example has three functions, one constructor, and one generator, that yields six axioms. Once you write down the left side of the axiom, its value is usually easy to determine. For example, with function *top* and constructor *push*, the axiom looks like

$$top(push(S, I)) = \ldots$$

Intuitively, we want the top of the stack to be what we just added to the stack, so we get the axiom

$$top(push(S, I)) = I$$

Continuing in this way, we get the following axioms:

$$\begin{array}{ll}
1: \; pop(newstack) = & newstack \\
2: \; pop(push(S, I)) = & S \\
3: \; top(newstack) = & undefined \\
4: \; top(push(S, I)) = & I \\
5: \; empty(newstack) = & true \\
6: \; empty(push(S, I)) = & false \\
7: \; size(newstack) = & 0 \\
8: \; size(push(S, I)) = & size(S) + 1
\end{array}$$

These axioms are often thought of as rewrite rules. We can take one instance of an object and use the rules to rewrite the instance in a simpler way. According to the specification, the *push* operation returns an instance of *stack* constructed from another instance of *stack* and some *integer*. For example, one query might be formed by calling *newstack*, then applying a *push*, then another *push*, then a *pop*, and then applying the function *empty* as in

$$empty(pop(push(push(newstack, 42), 17)))$$

Unification of this expression with axiom 2 gives us a simplification of the outermost composition of *pop* with *push*, and we can rewrite the sentence as

$$empty(push(newstack, 42))$$

At this point, we can use Axiom 6 and simplify the string to $false$. We were able to modify the expression to only generators and constructors before applying the definition of *empty* to get our answer $false$. This illustrates our point in the earlier discussion about constructors. An algebraic expression using only constructors and generators will be in *canonical* or *normal* form.

Data Type Induction

Given the set of axioms (i.e., relationships) among the set of operations in an algebraic data type, we often need to verify that certain properties are true. These then become requirements on any program (e.g., in C or Pascal) that implements this specification. *Data type induction* is one technique to verify these properties. It is closely related to natural induction of the positive integers.

Let $P(y)$ be some predicate concerning $y \in x$. Under what conditions will P be true for every member of type x? Similar to natural induction, we can show that P is true for primitive objects of the type. Then we can show that, when these primitive objects are used to construct new objects of the type, the property P remains true.

We define *data type induction* as follows:

1. Given type x with generator functions f_i, constructors g_i and and other functions h_i and predicate $P(y)$ for $y \in x$:

2. Show that $P(f_i)$ is valid. This is the base case showing the generator value is correct.

3. Assume $P(y)$ is valid. Show that this implies $P(g_i(y))$ is valid. This allows us to extend predicate P to all objects created by application of a generator followed by constructor applications.

4. We then conclude $P(y)$ for any y of type x.

For our stack example, we need to show $P(newstack)$ and $P(push(x, i))$. Using data type induction, we can show that pushing a value on a stack increases the size of the stack—that is,

$$size(push(S, X)) > size(S)$$

Example 4.2 gives the proof of this.

EXAMPLE 4.2. Data Type Induction.

1. We prove P(S) $\equiv$ size(push(S,X))>size(S) by using the axioms as rewrite rules until no more simplifications are possible:

size(push(S,X))>size(S) - Theorem hypothesis
size(S)+1>size(S) - By axiom 8

2. At this point, we need data type induction to show size(S)+1>size(S) for generators newstack and push, i.e., we need to show P(newstack) and P(push(S,i)):

(a) Base case: First replace S by newstack and show that the base case holds:

0+1 > 0+0 - Simple mathematical fact
size(newstack)+1>size(newstack) - By axiom 7

which shows that the base case is true for S=newstack.

(b) Induction case: Assume that the theorem holds for S, i.e., size(S)+1>size(S). Show the theorem holds for S'=push(S,X):

size(S)+1>size(S) - Inductive hypothesis
size(S)+1+1>size(S)+1 - Add 1 to both sides
size(push(S,X))+1¿size(push(S,X)) - By axiom 8

which shows that the inductive step also holds.

Conclusion: We have now shown that:

size(push(S,X))>size(S)

is a true result holding for all stacks S.

4.3 SUGGESTIONS FOR FURTHER READING

Formal models of syntax, parsing, and translation are widely used in the analysis and implementation of compilers and translators. (See the references at the end of chapter 3). The application of the λ calculus and denotational semantics toward the design of programming languages is presented in greater detail by Stansifer [STANSIFER 1995].

Marcotty et al. [MARCOTTY et al. 1976] surveyed the issues in formal semantic definition and described several methods. The 1974 Hoare and Lauer paper [HOARE 1974] is a good comparison of several methods to define the semantics of a simple language. Lucas and Walk [LUCAS and WALK 1969] described the operational method called the *Vienna Definition Language*, which was used for a formal semantic definition of PL/I. A denotational semantic definition of most of Ada has been written [ADA 1980]; an axiomatic definition of most of Pascal is given by Hoare and Wirth [HOARE 1973].

Program verification methods are surveyed in [ZELKOWITZ 1993] and in the book by Gannon, Purtilo, and Zelkowitz [GANNON et al. 1994]. Algebraic data types were developed by Guttag [GUTTAG 1980]. The formal specification method *Vienna Development Method* (VDM) is described in the book [JONES 1990], and the method Z is described in the paper [SPIVEY 1989]. This chapter has been able to touch on only a few of the many fascinating theoretical models and results in the study of program semantics, universal languages, and abstract automata such as the Turing machine.

4.4 PROBLEMS

1. Append the grammar of Figure 3.3 on page 91 with the following BNF rules:

$$\begin{array}{ll} \langle program \rangle ::= & \langle declaration \rangle\ \langle stmt\ list \rangle \\ \langle declaration \rangle ::= & \langle decl \rangle\ \langle declaration \rangle \mid \langle decl \rangle \\ \langle decl \rangle ::= & \textbf{declare}\ \langle variable \rangle\ ; \\ \langle stmt\ list \rangle ::= & \langle assignment\ statement \rangle\ \langle stmt\ list \rangle \mid \\ & \quad \langle assignment\ statement \rangle \end{array}$$

Develop an attribute grammar such that

(a) $valid(assignment\ statement) = true$ if and only if every variable in the statement has been declared.

(b) $valid(program) = true$ if and only if every assignment statement in the program is valid.

2. Show that the language generated by the following grammar is a regular language:

$$S \to aSa|a$$

3. A palindrome is a string that reads the same forward and backward.

(a) Show that the set of odd-length palindromes over the alphabet {a, b} is a context-free language.

(b) Show that the set of odd-length strings over the alphabet {a, b} that are **not** palindromes is context free.

(c) Why does the set of odd-length palindromes require a nondeterministic pushdown automaton for recognition rather than a deterministic pushdown automaton?

4. Given the context-free grammar

S ::= 0S0 | 1S1 | 0 | 1

give the derivation tree for 0110110.

5. We know that strings of the form $a^n b^n$ require a context-free grammar for their generation. Consider the following regular grammar:

S ::= aS | bS | a | b

A claim is made that it can generate $a^n b^n$. For example, $a^3 b^3$ is generated by the following derivation:

$$S \Rightarrow aS \Rightarrow aaS \Rightarrow aaaS \Rightarrow aaabS \Rightarrow aaabbS \Rightarrow aaabbb$$

Explain this apparent contradiction in using a Type 3 grammar to generate a Type 2 language.

6. Modify each of the procedures of Figure 3.13 on page 106 to produce postfix for arithmetic statements.

7. Can this language for a subset of expressions be recognized by a regular grammar? Explain. Also, explain the major difference between this grammar and the full expression grammar

$$\begin{array}{l} \mathrm{E} \rightarrow \mathrm{E} + \mathrm{T} \mid \mathrm{T} \\ \mathrm{T} \rightarrow \mathrm{T} * \mathrm{P} \mid \mathrm{P} \\ \mathrm{P} \rightarrow \mathrm{i} \end{array}$$

8. With axiomatic correctness,

(a) Show that the two termination conditions for **while** loops do indeed force the loop to terminate. (Hint: What happens if both conditions are true, and the loop doesn't terminate?)

(b) Why do we put the constraint that f must be an integer function?

9. Prove the following program for integer division:

```
{x ≥ 0 ∧ y > 0}
q := 0;
r := x;
while y ≤ r do
    begin
    r := r − y;
    q := q + 1
    end
{y > r ∧ x = r + y × q}
```

10. In Figure 4.4, discuss what happens when B is less than 0. What is the complete domain for Variables A and B for which the program halts and gives the correct answer?

11. Using the definitions given for *not*, *and*, and *or* as λ expressions, show that *(a)* ((*and* A) B) is true if and only if both A and B are true, and *(b)* ((*or* A) B) is true if and only if either A or B is true. That is, the definitions for *and* and *or* agree with our usual interpretation of them.

12. Using the definitions for the integers as λ expressions, show that $2 + 3 = 5$.

13. In the example algebraic data type for stacks, an assumption is made that stacks are unbounded. *push* could be applied to any stack. However, most stacks have a finite limit. Rewrite the axioms for *stack* to limit stacks to some maximum value $MaxStack$.

14. Create axioms for other data types. For example: queues and sets. What are the operations needed to specify such data types?

15. Implement stacks, queues, or sets in C++, and show that your implementation fulfills each relevant axiom.

16. Consider the following axioms for addition (*succ* stands for the *successor* function, the addition of 1):

add(0,X) = X
add(succ(X),Y) = succ(add(X,Y))

Using only these two axioms with data type induction, prove that

(a) add(X,Y) = add(Y,X)
(b) add(add(X,Y),Z) = add(X,add(Y,Z))

17. Consider the axioms for a stack in Section 4.2.5. If we consider these rewrite rules to be rules in Prolog, we can implement many of the algebraic properties as Prolog programs. Develop a set of Prolog rules that convert a sequence of *push* and *pop* operations to simply being *push* operations (i.e., converting to a normal form). For example: $pop(push(S, I))$ would result in S, and $push(pop(push(pop(push(S, I)), J)), K)$ would reduce to $push(S, K)$.

18. Show the equivalence between

(a) Finite automata and regular languages.
(b) Pushdown automata and context-free languages.
(c) Linear-bounded automata and context-sensitive languages. An LBA is a Turing machine that is limited to a tape containing only the input data. (Hence, it grows with the size of the input, but is not unlimited.)
(d) Turing machines and unrestricted languages.

19. Show either the equivalence or nonequivalence between the nondeterministic and deterministic models for

(a) Finite-state automata.
(b) Pushdown automata.
(c) Linear-bounded automata.
(d) Turing machines.

(a) and (d) are fairly easy, (b) is difficult, and (c) is worth an instant Ph.D. degree and fame and fortune in the computer science community. It is an unsolved problem related to the NP-completeness of Section 4.1.3.

Chapter 5

Elementary Data Types

All programs specify a set of operations that are to be applied to certain data in a certain sequence. Basic differences among languages exist in the types of data allowed, in the types of operations available, and in the mechanisms provided for controlling the sequence in which the operations are applied to the data. These three areas—data, operations, and control—form the basis for much of the discussion and comparison of the languages in this book. This chapter considers the data, types, and operations that are usually built into languages; Chapter 6 extends this concept to programmer-defined extensions to these basic data types—a concept called *abstraction.*

5.1 PROPERTIES OF TYPES AND OBJECTS

We first investigate the properties that define data objects in a programming language. We then discuss typical types in most programming languages in terms of features available from the hardware of the actual computer (i.e., elementary data types). In chapter 6 we consider data that are usually software simulated (i.e., structured data types).

5.1.1 Data Objects, Variables, and Constants

The data storage areas of an actual computer, such as the memory, registers, and external media, usually have a relatively simple structure as sequences of bits grouped into bytes or words. However, data storage of the virtual computer for a programming language tends to have a more complex organization, with arrays, stacks, numbers, character strings, and other forms of data existing at different points during execution of a program. It is convenient to use the term *data object* to refer to a run-time grouping of one or more pieces of data in a virtual computer. During execution of a program, many different data objects of different types exist. Moreover, in contrast to the relatively static organization of the underlying storage areas of an actual computer, these data objects and their interrelationships change dynamically during program execution.

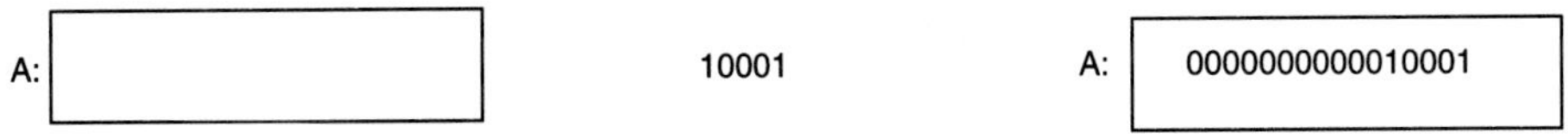

(a) **Data object:** A location in computer memory with the name A.

(b) **Data value:** A bit pattern used by the translator whenever the number 17 is used in a program

(c) **Bound variable:** Data object bound to data value 17

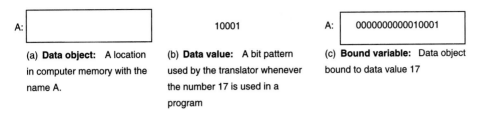

Figure 5.1. A simple variable data object with value 17.

Some of the data objects that exist during program execution are *programmer defined* (i.e., they are variables, constants, arrays, files, etc.); the programmer explicitly creates and manipulates through declarations and statements in the program. Other data objects are *system defined* (i.e., they will be data objects that the virtual computer sets up for housekeeping during program execution and are not directly accessible to the programmer, such as run-time storage stacks, subprogram activation records, file buffers, and free-space lists). System-defined data objects are ordinarily generated automatically as needed during program execution without explicit specification by the programmer.

A data object represents a *container for data values*—a place where data values may be stored and later retrieved. A data object is characterized by a set of *attributes*, the most important of which is its *data type*. The attributes determine the number and type of values that the data object may contain and also determine the logical organization of those values.

A *data value* might be a single number, character, or possibly a pointer to another data object. A data value is ordinarily represented by a particular pattern of bits in the storage of a computer. For now we consider two values to be the same if the patterns of bits representing them in storage are identical. However, this simple definition is insufficient for more complex data items. It is easy to confuse data objects and data values and, in many languages, the distinction is not clearly made. The distinction is perhaps most easily seen by noting the difference in implementation: A data object is usually represented as storage in the computer memory. A data value is represented by a pattern of bits. To say that a data object A contains the value B means that the block of storage representing A is set to contain the particular bit pattern representing B, as shown in Figure 5.1.

If we observe the execution of a program, some data objects exist at the beginning of execution and others are created dynamically during execution. Some data objects are destroyed during execution; others persist until the program terminates. Thus, each object has a lifetime during which it may be used to store data values. A data object is *elementary* if it contains a data value that is always manipulated as a unit. It is a *data structure* if it is an aggregate of other data objects.

A data object participates in various bindings during its lifetime. Although the attributes of a data object are invariant during its lifetime, the bindings may change dynamically. The most important attributes and bindings are as follows:

1. *Type.* This associates the data object with the set of data values that the object may take.

2. *Location.* The binding to a storage location in memory where the data object is represented ordinarily is not directly modifiable by the programmer but is set up and may be changed by the storage management routines of the virtual computer, as discussed in Section 10.

3. *Value.* This binding is usually the result of an assignment operation.

4. *Name.* The binding to one or more names by which the object may be referenced during program execution is usually set up by declarations and modified by subprogram calls and returns, as discussed in chapter 9.

5. *Component.* The binding of a data object to one or more data objects of which it is a component is often represented by a pointer value, and it may be modified by a change in the pointer, as discussed in Section 5.3.2.

Variables and Constants

A data object that is defined and named by the programmer explicitly in a program is termed a *variable.* A *simple variable* is an elementary data object with a name. We usually think of the value (or values) of a variable as being modifiable by assignment operations (i.e., the binding of data object to value may change during its lifetime). If there is no difference between upper and lower case letters in a name (e.g., $MYVARIABLE$ and *myvariable* refer to the same object), the names are said to be *case insensitive.* If they are different objects, the names are *case sensitive.*

A *constant* is a data object with a name that is bound to a value (or values) permanently during its lifetime. A *literal* (or *literal constant*) is a constant whose name is just the written representation of its value (e.g., "21" is the written decimal representation of the literal constant that is a data object with value 21). A *programmer-defined constant* or a *manifest constant* is a constant whose name is chosen by the programmer in a definition of the data object.

Because the value of a constant is bound to its name permanently during its lifetime, that binding is also known to the translator. Therefore, if a programmer writes in C: $\#define\ MAX$ 30, that information is known at translation time. The C compiler may make use of that information, knowing that the value may not be altered. (For example, the assignment statement $MAX = 4$ would be invalid because MAX is always the constant 30; it makes as much sense as writing the assignment statement $30 = 4$.) Sometimes the compiler can use information about

EXAMPLE 5.1. C Simple Variables.

A C subprogram may include the declaration:

$int\ N;$

which declares a simple data object N of type *integer*. Subsequently in the subprogram, the assignment:

$N = 27;$

may be used to assign the data value 27 to N. We would describe the situation somewhat more completely as follows:

1. The declaration specifies an elementary data object of type *integer*.
2. This data object is to be created on entry to the subprogram and destroyed on exit; thus its lifetime is the duration of execution of the subprogram.
3. During its lifetime, the data object is to be bound to the name "N," through which it may be referenced, as happens in the assignment statement above. Other names may be bound to the data object if it is passed as an argument to another subprogram.
4. No value is bound to the data object initially, but the assignment statement binds the value 27 to it temporarily until some later assignment to N changes the binding.
5. Hidden from the programmer are other bindings made by the virtual computer: the data object N is made a component of an *activation record*, a data object that contains all the local data for the subprogram, and this activation record is allocated storage in a *run-time stack* (another hidden data object) at the time that execution of the subprogram begins. When the subprogram terminates, this storage is freed for reuse, and the binding of data object to storage location is destroyed (discussed in greater detail in chapter 6).

---

constant values to avoid generating code for a statement or expression. For example, in the **if** statement

$$\textbf{if}\ (\text{MAX} < 2)\{\ \ldots\}$$

the translator already has the data values for the constants MAX and 2, can compute that it is false that 30 is less than 2, and hence can ignore completely any code for the **if** statement.

Persistence. Most programs today are still developed using the batch processing model (Section 1.2.2). That is, the programmer assumes the following sequence of events:

EXAMPLE 5.2. C Variables, Constants, and Literals.

A C subprogram may include the declarations:

```
const int MAX=30;
int N;
```

We may then write the assignments:

```
N = 27;
N = N + MAX;
```

N is a simple variable; MAX, 27, and 30 are constants. N, MAX, "27," and "30" are names for data objects of type *integer*. The constant declaration specifies that the data object named MAX is to be bound permanently (for the duration of execution of the subprogram) to the value 30. The constant MAX is a *programmer-defined constant* because the programmer explicitly defines the name for the value 30. The name "27," on the other hand, is a *literal* that names a data object containing the value 27. Such literals are defined as part of the language definition itself. The important but confusing distinction here is between the *value* 27, which is an integer represented as a sequence of bits in storage during program execution, and the *name* "27," which is a sequence of two characters "2" and "7" that represents the same number in decimal form as it is written in a program. C both has constant declarations, as in this example, and macro definitions such as #define MAX 30, which is a compile-time operation that causes all references to MAX in the program to be changed to the constant 30.

Note that in this example, the constant 30 has two names, the programmer-defined name "MAX" and the literal name "30," both of which may be used to refer to a data object containing the value 30 in the program.

One should also realize that

```
#define MAX 30
```

is a command, which the translator uses to equate MAX with the value 30, whereas the *const* attribute in C is a translator directive stating that variable MAX will always contain the value 30.

---

1. The program is loaded into memory.
2. Appropriate external data (e.g., tapes, disks) are made available to the program.
3. The relevant input data are read into variables in the program, the variables are manipulated, and the result data are written back to its external format.
4. The program terminates.

The lifetime of the variables in the program are determined by the execution time of the program; however, the lifetime of the data often extends beyond that single execution. We say that the data are *persistent* and continue to exist between executions of the program.

Many applications today do not easily fit within this model. Consider an airline reservation system. To reserve a seat, you call a travel agent who interrogates the reservation system and invokes programs that check on schedules, prices, and destinations. The data and the programs coexist essentially indefinitely. In this case, having a language that represented persistent data would allow designing such transaction-based systems more efficiently. With such a language, variables would be declared whose lifetime extended beyond the execution of the program. Programming would be simpler because there would be no need to specify the form of data in an external file before manipulating it. The language translator would already know where the data were stored and their form. In Section 11.4.1, we discuss current research on the development of persistent languages. However, until such languages become widely used, in Section 5.3.3 we discuss the use of files for transferring persistent data into local program variables.

5.1.2 Data Types

A *data type* is a class of data objects together with a set of operations for creating and manipulating them. Although a program deals with particular *data objects* such as an array A, the integer variable X, or the file F, a programming language necessarily deals more commonly with *data types* such as the class of arrays, integers, or files and the operations provided for manipulating arrays, integers, or files.

Every language has a set of *primitive* data types that are built into the language. In addition, a language may provide facilities to allow the programmer to define new data types. One of the major differences between older languages such as FORTRAN and COBOL and newer languages such as Java and Ada lies in the area of programmer-defined data types—a subject taken up in Section 6.4. The newest trend is to allow for types to be manipulated by the programming language. This is a major feature added to ML and is one of the features present in the object-oriented programming models discussed in chapter 7.

The basic elements of a *specification* of a data type are as follows:

1. The *attributes* that distinguish data objects of that type,
2. The *values* that data objects of that type may have, and
3. The *operations* that define the possible manipulations of data objects of that type.

For example, in considering the specification of an array data type, the attributes might include the number of dimensions, the subscript range for each dimension, and the data type of the components; the values would be the sets of numbers that form valid values for array components; and the operations would include subscripting to select individual array components and possibly other operations to create arrays, change their shape, access attributes such as upper and lower bounds of subscripts, and perform arithmetic on pairs of arrays.

The following are basic elements of the *implementation* of a data type:

1. The *storage representation* that is used to represent the data objects of the data type in the storage of the computer during program execution, and

2. The manner in which the operations defined for the data type are represented in terms of particular *algorithms* or *procedures* that manipulate the chosen storage representation of the data objects. The implementation of a data type defines the *simulation* of those parts of the virtual computer in terms of the more primitive constructs provided by the underlying layer of virtual computer, which may be directly the hardware computer or a hardware/software combination defined by an operating system or microcode.

The last concern connected with a data type lies in its *syntactic representation.* Both specification and implementation are largely independent of the particular syntactic forms used in the language. Attributes of data objects are often represented syntactically by *declarations* or *type definitions.* Values may be represented as literals or defined constants. Operations may be invoked by using special symbols, built-in procedures, or functions such as *sin* or *read*, or implicitly through combinations of other language elements. The particular syntactic representation makes little difference, but the information present in the program syntax provides information to the language translator that may be vital in determining the binding time of various attributes, and thus in allowing the translator to set up efficient storage representations or perform checking for type errors.

Specification of Elementary Data Types

An *elementary* data object contains a single data value. A class of such data objects over which various operations are defined is termed an *elementary data type.* Although each programming language tends to have a somewhat different set of elementary data types, the types *integer*, *real*, *character*, *Boolean*, *enumeration*, and *pointer* are often included, although the exact specification may differ significantly between two languages. For example, although most languages include Boolean data, it is treated quite differently in Java and C++.

Attributes. Basic attributes of any data object, such as data type and name, are usually invariant during its lifetime. Some of the attributes may be stored in a *descriptor* (also called a *dope vector*) as part of the data object during program execution; others may be used only to determine the storage representation of the data object and may not appear explicitly during execution. Note that the *value of an attribute* of a data object is different from the *value that the data object contains.* The value contained may change during the data object's lifetime and is always represented explicitly during program execution.

Values. The type of a data object determines the set of possible values that it may contain. For example, the *integer* data type determines a set of integer values that may serve as the values for data objects of this type. C defines the following four classes of integer types: *int*, *short*, *long*, and *char*. Because most hardware implements multiple precision integer arithmetic (e.g., 16-bit and 32-bit integers or 32-bit and 64-bit integers), C permits the programmer to choose among these hardware-defined implementations. *Short* uses the shortest value of the integer word length, *long* uses the longest value implemented by the hardware, and *int* uses the most efficient value that the hardware implements. This may be the same as *short*, the same as *long*, or some value intermediate to those. It is interesting to note that in C, characters are stored as 8-bit integers in the type *char*, which is a subtype of integer.

The set of values defined by an elementary data type is usually an *ordered set* with a least value and a greatest value; for any pair of distinct values, one is greater than the other. For example, for an integer data type, there is usually a greatest integer corresponding to the greatest integer that can be conveniently represented in memory, a least integer, and the integers between arranged in their usual numerical ordering.

Operations. The set of operations defined for a data type determine how data objects of that type may be manipulated. The operations may be *primitive operations*, which means they are specified as part of the language definition, or they may be *programmer-defined operations*, in the form of subprograms or method declarations as part of class definitions. This chapter emphasizes primitive operations; programmer-defined operations are considered in greater detail in subsequent chapters.

EXAMPLE 5.3. Signatures of simple operations.

(a) Integer addition is an operation that takes two integer data objects as arguments and produces an integer data object as its result (a data object usually containing the sum of the values of its two arguments). Thus its specification is:

$$+ : integer \times integer \rightarrow integer$$

(b) The operator "=" that tests for equality of the values of two integer data objects and produces a data object containing a Boolean (true or false) result is specified:

$$=: integer \times integer \rightarrow Boolean$$

(c) A square-root operation, SQRT, on real number data objects is specified:

$$SQRT : real \rightarrow real$$

An operation is a *mathematical function*; for a given input *argument* (or arguments); it has a well-defined and uniquely determined *result*. Each operation has a *domain* (the set of possible input arguments on which it is defined) and a *range* (the set of possible results that it may produce). The *action* of the operation defines the results produced for any given set of arguments.

An *algorithm* that specifies how to compute the results for any given set of arguments is a common method for specifying the action of an operation, but other specifications are possible. For example, to specify the action of a multiplication operation, you might give a multiplication table that simply lists the result of multiplying any two pairs of numbers, rather than an algorithm for multiplying any two numbers.

To specify the *signature* of an operation, the number, order, and data types of the arguments in the domain of an operation are given as well as the order and data type of the resulting range. It is convenient to use the usual mathematical notation for this specification:

$$op\ name : arg\ type \times arg\ type \times \ldots arg\ type \rightarrow result\ type$$

In C, we call this the function *prototype.*

An operation that has two arguments and produces a single result is termed a *binary* (or *dyadic*) operation. If it has one argument and one result, it is a *unary* (or *monadic*) operation. The number of arguments for an operation is often called the *arity* of the operation. Most of the primitive operations in programming languages are binary or unary operations.

A precise specification of the action of an operation ordinarily requires more information than just its signature. In particular, the storage representation of argument types usually determines how arguments of those types may be manipulated. For example, an algorithm for multiplication of two numbers, where the numbers are represented in binary notation, is different from a multiplication algorithm for decimal numbers. Thus in the specification of an operation, an informal description of the action is usually given. A precise specification of the action then is part of the implementation of the operation after the storage representations for the arguments have been determined.

It is sometimes difficult to determine a precise specification of an operation as a mathematical function. There are four main factors that combine to obscure the definition of many programming language operations:

1. *Operations that are undefined for certain inputs.* An operation that is defined over some domain may in fact be undefined for certain inputs in the domain (e.g., the square-root function on the negative integer domain). The exact domain on which an operation is undefined may be extremely difficult to specify, as, for example, the sets of numbers that cause underflow or overflow in arithmetic operations.

2. *Implicit arguments.* An operation in a program ordinarily is invoked with a set of explicit arguments. However, the operation may access other implicit arguments through the use of global variables or other nonlocal identifier references. Complete determination of all the data that may affect the result of an operation is often obscured by such implicit arguments.

3. *Side effects (implicit results).* An operation may return an explicit result, as in the sum returned as the result of an addition, but it may also modify the values stored in other data objects, both programmer- and system-defined. Such implicit results are termed *side effects.* A function may modify its input arguments as well as return a value. Side effects are a basic part of many operations, particularly those that modify data structures. Their presence makes exact specification of the range of an operation difficult.

4. *Self-modification (history sensitivity).* An operation may modify its own internal structure, either local data that are retained between executions or its own code. The results produced by the operation for a particular set of arguments then depend not only on those arguments, but on the entire history of preceding calls during the computation and the arguments given at each call. The operation is said to be *history sensitive* in its actions. A common example is the *random number generator* found as an operation in many languages. Typically this operation takes a constant argument and yet returns a different result each time it is executed. The operation not only returns its result but also modifies an internal *seed number* that affects its result on the next execution. Self-modification through changes in local data retained between calls is common; self-modification through change in the code of an operation is less common but possible in languages such as LISP.

Subtypes. When describing a new data type, we often want to say that it is similar to another data type. For example, C defines the types of *int*, *long*, *short*, and *char* as variations on integers. All behave similarly, and we would like some operations, such as + and ×, to be defined in an analogous manner. If a data type is part of a larger class, we say it is a *subtype* of the larger class, and the larger class is a *supertype* of this data type. For example, in Pascal, we may create subranges of integers as in

type SmallInteger= 1..20;

being a subtype of *integer* with values limited to 1, 2, 3, ..., 20.

With a subtype, we assume that the operations available to the larger class of objects are also available to the smaller class. How can we determine this? In Pascal and Ada, subranges of types are explicitly part of the language. How do we extend this to other data types that are not primitive to the language? The important concept of *inheritance*, discussed in chapter 7, is a generalization of this subtype property. We would say that the C *char* type *inherits* the operations of integer type *int*.

Implementation of Elementary Data Types

The implementation of an elementary data type consists of a *storage representation* for data objects and values of that type, and a set of *algorithms* or *procedures* that define the operations of the type in terms of manipulations of the storage representation.

Storage representation. Storage for elementary data types is strongly influenced by the underlying computer that will execute the program. For example, the storage representation for integer or real values is almost always the integer or floating-point binary representation for numbers used in the underlying hardware. The reason for this choice is simple: If the hardware storage representations are used, then the basic operations on data of that type may be implemented using the hardware provided operations. If the hardware storage representations are not used, then the operations must be software simulated, and the same operations will execute much less efficiently.

The *attributes* of elementary data objects are treated similarly:

1. For efficiency, many languages are designed for data attributes to be determined by the compiler. The attributes are not stored in the run-time storage representation. This is the usual method in C, where efficiency of storage use and execution speed are primary goals.

2. The attributes of a data object may be stored in a *descriptor* as part of the data object at run time. This is the usual method in languages such as LISP and Prolog, where flexibility rather than efficiency is the primary goal. Because most hardware does not provide storage representations for descriptors directly, descriptors and operations on data objects with descriptors must be software simulated.

The representation of a data object is ordinarily independent of its location in memory. The storage representation is usually described in terms of the size of the block of memory required (the number of memory words, bytes, or bits needed) and the layout of the attributes and data values within this block. Usually the address of the first word or byte of such a block of memory is taken to represent the location of the data object.

Implementation of operations. Each operation defined for data objects of a given type may be implemented in one of three main ways:

1. *Directly as a hardware operation.* For example, if integers are stored using the hardware representation for integers, then addition and subtraction are implemented using the arithmetic operations built into the hardware.

2. *As a procedure or function subprogram.* For example, a square-root operation is usually not provided directly as a hardware operation. It might be implemented as a square-root subprogram that calculates the square root of its argument.

3. *As an inline code sequence.* An *inline code sequence* is also a software implementation of the operation. However, instead of using a subprogram, the operations in the subprogram are copied into the program at the point where the subprogram would otherwise have been invoked. For example, the absolute-value function on numbers, defined by

$$\text{abs(x)} = \textbf{if } \text{x} < 0 \textbf{ then } -\text{x} \textbf{ else } \text{x}$$

is usually implemented as an inline code sequence:

(a) Fetch value of x from memory.
(b) If $x > 0$, skip the next instruction.
(c) Set $x = -x$.
(d) Store new value of x in memory.

Here, each line is implemented by a single-hardware operation.

5.1.3 Declarations

In writing a program, the programmer determines the name and type of each data object that is needed. Also the lifetime of each data object, during what part of program execution it is needed, as well as the operations to be applied to it, must be specified.

A *declaration* is a program statement that serves to communicate to the language translator information about the name and type of data objects needed during program execution. By its placement in the program (e.g., within a particular subprogram or class definition), a declaration may also serve to indicate the desired lifetimes of the data objects. For example, the C declaration

float A, B;

at the start of a subprogram indicates that two data objects of type *float* are needed during execution of the subprogram. The declaration also specifies the binding of the data objects to the names A and B during their lifetimes.

The previous C declaration is an *explicit* declaration. Many languages also provide *implicit* or *default* declarations, which are declarations that hold when no explicit declaration is given. For example, in a FORTRAN subprogram, a simple variable $INDEX$ may be used without explicit declaration; by default, it is assumed by the FORTRAN compiler to be an integer variable because its name begins with one of the letters I–N. In Perl, simply assigning a value to a variable declares it:

```
$abc = 'a string';      # $abc is now a string variable
$abc = 7;               # $abc is now an integer variable
```

A declaration may also specify the value of the data object if it is a constant or the initial value of the data object, if not. Other bindings for the data object may also be specified in the declaration: a name for the data object or the placement of the data object as a component of a larger data object. Sometimes implementation details such as binding to a particular storage location or to a particular specialized storage representation are also specified. For example, the COBOL designation of an integer variable as COMPUTATIONAL usually indicates that a binary rather than a character-string storage representation for the value of that data object is needed (to allow more efficient arithmetic operations to be used).

Declarations of Operations

The information required during translation is primarily the signature of each operation. No explicit declaration of argument types and result types for primitive operations that are built into a language is ordinarily required. Such operations may be invoked as needed in writing a program, and the argument and result types are determined implicitly by the language translator. However, argument and result types for programmer-defined operations must usually be made known to the language translator before the subprogram may be called. For example, in C, the head of a subprogram definition, its *prototype*, provides this information. Thus,

```
float Sub(int X, float Y)
```

declares *Sub* to have the signature

$$Sub : int \ \times float \rightarrow float$$

Purposes for Declarations

Declarations serve several important purposes:

1. *Choice of storage representations.* If a declaration provides information to the language translator about the data type and attributes of a data object, then the translator can often determine the best storage representation for that data object.

2. *Storage management.* Information provided by declarations about the lifetimes of data objects often makes it possible to use more efficient storage management procedures during program execution. In C, for example, data objects declared at the beginning of a subprogram all have the same lifetime (equal to the duration of execution of the subprogram) and thus may be allocated storage as a single block on entry to the subprogram, with the entire block being freed on exit. Other C data objects are created dynamically by use of a special function *malloc*. Because the lifetimes of these data objects are not declared, they must be allocated storage individually.

3. *Polymorphic operations.* Most languages use special symbols such as + to designate any one of several different operations depending on the data types of the arguments provided. $A + B$ in C, for example, means "perform integer addition" if A and B are of integer type or "perform real addition" if A and B are of *float* type. Such an operation symbol is said to be *overloaded* because it does not designate one specific operation, but rather denotes a *generic* "add" operation that may have several different *type-specific* forms for arguments of different types. In most languages, the basic operation symbols such as +, *, and / are overloaded (i.e., they denote generic operations); and other operation names uniquely identify a particular operation. However, Ada allows the programmer to define overloaded subprogram names and add additional meanings to existing operation symbols. ML expands this concept with full *polymorphism*, where a function name may take on a variety

of implementations depending on the types of arguments. When we discuss object-oriented designs, polymorphism is a major feature that allows the programmer to extend the language with new data types and operations.

Declarations usually allow the language translator to determine at compile time the particular operation designated by an overloaded operation symbol. For example, in C, the compiler determines from the declarations of Variables A and B which of the two possible operations (integer addition or float addition) is designated by $A + B$. No run-time checking is required. In Smalltalk, in contrast, because there are no declarations of types for variables, the determination of which + operation to perform must be made each time a + operation is encountered during program execution.

4. *Type checking.* The most important purpose for declarations, from the programmer's viewpoint, is that they allow for *static* rather than *dynamic* type checking.

5.1.4 Type Checking and Type Conversion

Data storage representations that are built into the computer hardware usually include no type information, and the primitive operations on the data do no type checking. For example, a particular word in the computer memory during execution of a program may contain the bit sequence 11100101100...0011. This bit sequence might represent an integer, a real number, a sequence of characters, or an instruction; there is no way to tell. The hardware primitive operation for integer addition cannot check whether its two arguments represent integers; they are simply bit sequences. Thus, at the hardware level, conventional computers are particularly unreliable in detecting data type errors.

Type checking means checking that each operation executed by a program receives the proper number of arguments of the proper data type. For example, before executing the assignment statement

$$X = A + B * C$$

the compiler must determine for each operation—addition, multiplication, and assignment—that each receives two arguments of the proper data type. If + is defined only for integer or real arguments and A names a character data object, then there is an argument *type error.* Type checking may be done at run time (*dynamic type checking*) or at compile time (*static type checking*). A major advantage of using a high-level language in programming is that the language implementation can provide type checking for all (or almost all) operations, and thus the programmer is protected against this particularly insidious form of programming error.

Dynamic type checking is run-time type checking usually performed immediately before the execution of a particular operation. Dynamic type checking is usually implemented by storing a type tag in each data object that indicates the data type of the object. For example, an integer data object would contain both the integer value and an integer type tag. Each operation is then implemented to begin with a type-checking sequence in which the type tag of each argument is checked. The operation is performed only if the argument types are correct; otherwise an error is signaled. Each operation must also attach the appropriate type tags to its results so that subsequent operations can check them.

Some programming languages such as Perl and Prolog are designed to require dynamic type checking. In these languages, no declarations for variables are given and no default declaration of type is assumed (in contrast to the default typing structures of FORTRAN). The data types of variables such as A and B in the expression $A + B$ may change during the course of program execution. In such circumstances, the types of A and B must be checked dynamically each time the addition is performed at run time. In languages without declarations, the variables are sometimes said to be *typeless* because they have no fixed type.

The major advantage of dynamic types is the flexibility in program design: No declarations are required, and the type of data object associated with a variable name may change as needed during program execution. The programmer is freed from most concerns about data types. However, dynamic type checking has several major disadvantages:

1. Programs are difficult to debug (i.e., tO completely remove all argument type errors). Because dynamic type checking checks data types at the time of execution of an operation, operations on program execution paths that are not executed are never checked. During program testing, not all possible execution paths can be tested, in general. Any untested execution paths may still contain argument type errors.

2. Dynamic type checking requires that type information be kept during program execution. The extra storage required can be substantial.

3. Dynamic type checking must ordinarily be implemented in software because the underlying hardware seldom provides support. This reduces the speed for executing the operation.

Most languages attempt to eliminate or minimize dynamic type checking by performing type checking at compile time. *Static type checking* is performed during translation of a program. The needed information is usually provided in part by declarations that the programmer provides and in part by other language structures. The information required includes the following:

1. *For each operation, the number, order, and data types of its arguments and results* (i.e., its signature).

2. *For each variable, the type of data object named.* The type of the data object associated with a variable name must be invariant during program execution as well. However, in checking an expression such as $A + B$, it can be assumed that the type of data object named by A is the same on each execution of the expression even if the expression is executed repeatedly with different bindings of A to particular data objects.

3. *The type of each constant data object.* The syntactic form of a literal usually indicates its type (e.g., 2 is an integer, 2.3 is a real number). Each defined constant must be matched with its definition to determine its type.

During the initial phases of program translation, the compiler (or other translator) collects information from declarations in the program into various tables, primarily a symbol table (see chapter 3) that contains type information about variables and operations. After all the type information is collected, each operation invoked by the program is checked to determine whether the type of each argument is valid. Note that if the operation is a polymorphic one, as discussed earlier, then any of several argument types may be valid. If the argument types are valid, then the result types are determined and the compiler saves this information for checking later operations. Note that the polymorphic operation name may also be replaced by the name of the particular *type-specific operation* that uses arguments of the designated types.

Because static type checking includes all operations that appear in any program statement, all possible execution paths are checked, and further testing for type errors is not needed. Thus, type tags on data objects at run time are not required, and no dynamic type checking is needed. The result is a substantial gain in efficiency of storage use and execution speed.

Concern for static type checking tends to affect many aspects of the language: declarations, data-control structures, and provisions for separate compilation of subprograms, to name a few. In most languages, static type checking is not possible for some language constructs in certain cases. These flaws in the type-checking structure may be treated in two ways:

1. *By dynamic type checking.* Often the storage cost of this option is high because type tags for data objects must be stored at run time, although the type tags are rarely checked.

2. *By leaving the operations unchecked.* Unchecked operations can cause serious and subtle program errors, as noted earlier, but sometimes they are accepted where the cost of dynamic checking is considered too great.

Strong typing. If we can detect all type errors statically in a program, we say that the language is *strongly typed*. In general, strong typing provides a level of security to our programs. We call a function f, with signature $f : S \to R$, *type safe* if execution of f cannot generate a value outside of R. For any operations that are type safe, we know statically that the results will be of the correct type and that no dynamic checking need be done. Obviously, if every operation is type safe, the language is strongly typed.

Few languages are truly strongly typed. For example, in C, if X and Y are of type *short* (i.e., short integers), then $X + Y$ and $X * Y$ may have a result outside of the range allowable for short integers and cause a type error. Although true strong typing is difficult, if we restrict conversion between one type and another, we come close to strong typing. We discuss such conversion in the subsection that follows.

Type inference. ML has an interesting approach toward data types. Type declarations are not necessary if the interpretation is unambiguous. The language implementation will infer any missing type information from other declared types. The language has a relatively standard syntax for declaring arguments to functions, as in

fun area(length:int, width:int):int = length * width;

which declares the function *area* to return the area (as an integer) if given the integer sides of a rectangle. In this case, once the type of one of *length*, *width*, or *area* is determined, then the other two are also determined. Leaving out any two of these declarations still leaves the function with only one interpretation. Knowing that $*$ can multiply together either two reals or two integers, ML interprets the following as equivalent to the prior example:

fun area(length, width):int = length * width;
fun area(length:int, width) = length * width;
fun area(length, width:int) = length * width;

However,

fun area(length, width) = length * width;

is invalid because it is now ambiguous as to the type of arguments. They could all be *int* or they could all be *real*.

Type Conversion and Coercion

If, during type checking, a mismatch occurs between the actual type of an argument and the expected type for that operation, then either

1. The type mismatch may be flagged as an error and an appropriate error action taken, or

2. *A coercion* (or *implicit type conversion*) may be applied to change the type of the actual argument to the correct type.

A *type conversion* is an operation with the signature

$$conversion\_op : type_1 \rightarrow type_2$$

That is, the conversion takes a data object of one type and produces the corresponding data object of a different type. Most languages provide type conversions in two ways:

1. As a set of *built-in functions* that the programmer may explicitly invoke to effect the conversion. For example, Pascal provides the function *round* that converts a real-number data object to an integer data object with a value equal to the rounded value of the real. In C, we *cast* an expression to coerce it to the correct type. (int) X, for *float* X converts the value of X to type integer.

2. As *coercions* invoked automatically in certain cases of type mismatch. For example, in Pascal, if the arguments for an arithmetic operation such as "+" are of mixed real and integer types, the integer data object is implicitly converted to type real before the addition is performed. Unlike in C++, Java permits implicit coercions if the operation is a widening. Thus, an *int* value can be assigned to a *float* variable in Java, but in C++ an explicit cast to *float* must be given.

The basic principle driving coercions is not to lose information. Because every short integer (in C) can be represented as a long integer, no information is lost by automatically invoking a *short int* → *long int* conversion. Such coercions are called *widenings* or *promotions*. Similarly, because integers (in most languages) can be exactly represented as a real data object, small-valued integers are usually widened to reals with no loss of information.

However, the coercion of a real to an integer may lose information. Although 1.0 is exactly equal to the integer 1, 1.5 is not so representable as an integer. It will be converted to either 1 or 2. In this case, we call the coercion a *narrowing*, and information gets lost.

With dynamic type checking, coercions are made at the point that the type mismatch is detected during execution. For such languages, narrowing conversions could be allowed if the data object had an appropriate value (e.g., 1.0 could be converted to type integer, but 1.5 could not). For static type checking, extra code is inserted in the compiled program to invoke the conversion operation at the appropriate point during execution. because efficient execution is usually a desired attribute, narrowing coercions are usually prohibited so that run-time code would not have to be executed to determine whether the coercion would be legal.

A type-conversion operation may require extensive change in the run-time storage representation of the data object. For example, in COBOL and PL/I, numbers often are stored in character-string form. To perform addition of such numbers on most machines, the character-string storage representation must be converted to a hardware-supported binary-number representation, with the result being converted back to character-string form before it is stored. The type-conversion operations here may take hundreds of times longer than the actual addition.

Implementors of language translators, however, sometimes confuse the semantics of a data object and its storage representation. Decimal data in COBOL and PL/I are a case in point. PL/I translators normally store FIXED DECIMAL data in packed decimal format. This is a hardware representation, but one that executes rather slowly. In the PL/C compiler [CONWAY and WILCOX 1973], FIXED DECIMAL data are stored as 16-digit double-precision floating-point data. By storing it as 16 digits, there is no loss of precision (important for storing decimal data). For example, computing $123.45 + 543.21$ requires a rather slow packed decimal add (or even slower software simulation if packed decimal data are not hardware implemented), whereas PL/C performs this as a single, faster, floating-point add of $12345 + 54321$. The compiler keeps track of the decimal point (e.g., divide by 10^2 to get true value) as a compile-time attribute of the resulting value.

Two opposed philosophies exist regarding the extent to which the language should provide coercions between data types. In Pascal and Ada, almost no coercions are provided; any type mismatch, with few exceptions, is considered an error. In C, coercions are the rule; a type mismatch causes the compiler to search for an appropriate conversion operation to insert into the compiled code to provide the appropriate change of type. Only if no conversion is possible is the mismatch flagged as an error.

Type mismatch is a common minor programming error and type conversion is a common need, particularly in languages that have a large number of data types. There are also subtle questions as to the meaning of the notion type mismatch. (See Section 6.4.) Coercions often free the programmer from concern with what otherwise would be tedious detail — the invocation of numerous-type conversion operations explicitly in a program. However, coercions may also mask serious programming errors that might otherwise be brought to the programmer's attention during compilation.

PL/I, in particular, is infamous for the propensity of its compilers to take a minor programming error, such as a misspelled variable name, and, through a sometimes subtle coercion, hide the error so that it becomes a program bug that is difficult to detect. Because PL/I's conversion operations permit narrowing coercions, results are surprising. For example, $9 + 10/3$ is invalid! To see this, observe that $10/3$ is coerced into 3.33333333... up to the implementation-defined maximum number of digits. But $9 + 3.333...$ has one additional digit in the result, giving rise to an OVERFLOW exception. If this exception is disabled (i.e., ignored), then the result is converted automatically to 2.333..., not quite what was expected.

5.1.5 Assignment and Initialization

Most of the operations for the common elementary data types—in particular, numbers, enumerations, Booleans, and characters—take one or two argument data objects of the type; perform a relatively simple arithmetic, relational, or other operation; and produce a result data object, which may be of the same or different type. The operation of assignment, however, is somewhat more subtle and deserves special mention.

Assignment is the basic operation for changing the binding of a value to a data object. This change, however, is a *side effect* of the operation. In some languages, such as C and LISP, assignment also returns a value, which is a data object containing a copy of the value assigned. These factors become clear when we try to write a specification for assignment. In Pascal, the specification for assignment of integers would be

$$assignment(:=) : integer_1 \times integer_2 \rightarrow void$$

with this action: Set the value contained in data object $integer_1$ to be a copy of the value contained in data object $integer_2$ and return no explicit result. (The change to $integer_1$ is an implicit result or side effect.) In C, the specification is

$$assignment(=) : integer_1 \times integer_2 \rightarrow integer_3$$

with this action: Set the value contained in data object $integer_1$ to be a copy of the value contained in data object $integer_2$ and also create and return a new data object $integer_3$, containing a copy of the new value of $integer_2$.

Consider the assignment: $X := X$. What is interesting about this statement is the different interpretation given to both references of the variable X. The rightmost X refers to the value contained in the named data object. Such references are often called the *right-hand side (of the assignment operator) value* or *r-value* of a data object. Similarly, the leftmost X refers to the location of the data object that will contain the new value. Such references are called the *left-hand side (of the assignment operator) value* or *l-value.* We can then define an assignment operation as

1. Compute the l-value of the first operand expression.
2. Compute the r-value of the second operand expression.
3. Assign the computed r-value to the computed l-value data object.
4. Return the computed r-value as the result of the operation.

If we have an assignment operator (as in C), we then say that the operator returns the r-value of the newly assigned data object. In addition, C contains a set of unary operators for manipulating l-values and r-values of expressions that gives C programs the ability to perform many useful, and strange, manipulations of such assignments. This dual use of the assignment operator, as a mechanism to change a data object's value (via its l-value) and as a function that also returns a value (its r-value), is heavily exploited by C and is discussed further in chapter 8.

Using l-values and r-values gives a more concise way to describe expression semantics. Consider the C assignment $A = B$ for integers A and B. In C, as in many other languages, this means "Assign a copy of the value of variable B to variable A" (i.e., assign to the l-value of A the r-value of B). Now consider the assignment $A = B$, where A and B are pointer variables. If B is a pointer, then B's r-value is the l-value of some other data object. This assignment then means, "Make the r-value of A refer to the same data object as the r-value of B" (i.e., assign to the l-value of A the r-value of B, which is the l-value f some other data

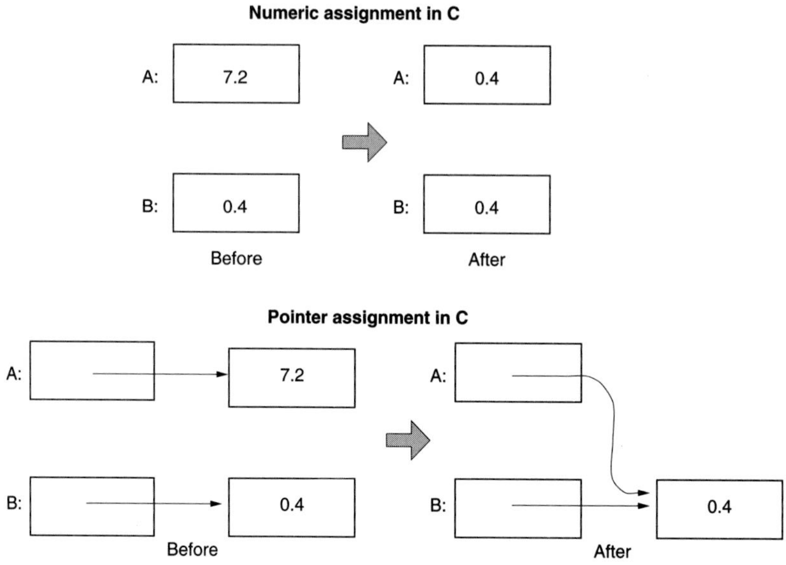

Figure 5.2. Two views of assignment.

object). Thus, the assignment $A = B$ means "Assign a copy of the pointer stored in variable B to variable A," as shown in Figure 5.2.

Equality and equivalence. The assignment statement is so pervasive in languages that few question its semantics. However, there is a major issue that needs to be resolved. Consider the assignment to A in some new language *Zork*:

$$A \leftarrow 2 + 3.$$

Does this mean

1. Evaluate the expression $2 + 3$ and assign its equivalent value of 5 to A? or
2. Assign the operation "2+3" to A?

For languages with static types for data, the type for A decides which semantics to follow: If A is of type integer, then only the assignment of 5 to A makes sense; if A is of type *operation*, then only the second is appropriate. However, for a dynamically typed language, where A is given a type by virtue of the assignment of a value to it, both semantics may be applicable and the prior assignment may be ambiguous.

Exactly this situation arises within Prolog. The operator *is* means assign the equivalent value, whereas the operator = means assign the pattern. Equality is then determined by the current value of the assigned variable. Thus, in Prolog, the first clause in the following succeeds because X is first assigned the value 5 and its type is set to integer, whereas the second clause fails because X is assigned the operation "2+3," which is not the same as the integer 5:

1 X is 2 + 3, X = 5.
2 X = 2 + 3, X = 5.

Note that, in this case, the symbol = appears to stand for both an assignment operator and a Boolean comparison operator depending on context. Actually, this is an example of Prolog's unification principle (i.e., in the second clause, the assignment of both 2 + 3 and 5 to X are not mutually compatible). This is further explained in Section 8.4.3.

Initialization. An *uninitialized variable*, or more generally, an *uninitialized data object,* is a data object that has been created but not yet assigned a value (i.e., an l-value with no corresponding r-value). Creation of a data object ordinarily involves only allocation of a block of storage. Without any further action, the block of storage retains whatever bit pattern it happened to contain when the allocation was made. An explicit assignment is ordinarily required to bind a data object to a valid value. In some languages (e.g., Pascal), initialization must be done explicitly with assignment statements. In other languages (e.g., APL), initial values for each data object must be specified when the object is created; the assignment of initial values is handled implicitly without use of the assignment operation by the programmer.

Uninitialized variables are a serious source of programming error for professional programmers as well as beginners. The random bit pattern contained in the value storage area of an uninitialized data object ordinarily cannot be distinguished from a valid value because the valid value also appears as a bit pattern. Thus, a program often may compute with the value of an uninitialized variable and appear to operate correctly, when in fact it contains a serious error. Because of the effect of uninitialized variables on program reliability, immediate initialization of variable values on creation is often considered good programming practice, and newer languages such as Ada provide facilities to do this more easily. For example, in Ada, each variable declaration may also include an initial value for the variable using the same syntax used for ordinary assignment. For instance,

A: **array**(1..3) **of** float := (17.2, 20.4, 23.6);

creates an array A and assigns each element an initial value explicitly in the declaration. Because ordinarily the array A is created dynamically during program execution, the implementation of initial-value assignment requires the generation of code by the compiler that, when executed, explicitly assigns the specified initial values of the data object.

5.2 SCALAR DATA TYPES

We first consider a class of elementary data objects known as *scalar data objects.* These are objects that have a single attribute for its data object. For example, an integer object has an integral value (e.g., 1, 3, 42), and no other information can be obtained from that object. Next (Section 5.3) we consider composite data where an object may have multiple attribute values. For example, a character string contains a sequence of characters as its data value, but also may have other attributes, such as a string size, as an additional attribute value.

In general the scalar objects follow the hardware architecture of a computer (e.g., integers, floating point numbers, characters). Composite data are usually complex structures created by the compiler that are not primitive hardware-implemented objects (e.g., strings).

5.2.1 Numeric Data Types

Some form of numeric data is found in almost every programming language. Integer and real number types are the most common because they are often directly supported in the computer hardware. The properties of numeric data representations and arithmetic on computers differ substantially from the numbers and arithmetic operations discussed in ordinary mathematics. The fascinating subject of computer arithmetic has been treated in other books, however, and is not central to an understanding of the larger structure of programming languages, so only a brief treatment is given here.

Integers

Specification. The set of integer values defined for the type forms an ordered subset, within some finite bounds, of the infinite set of integers studied in mathematics. The maximum integer value is sometimes represented as a defined constant (e.g., in Pascal, it is the constant *maxint*). The range of values is then ordinarily defined to be from $-maxint$ to $maxint$. As given earlier, C has four different integer specifications: *int*, *short*, *long*, and *char*.

Operations on integer data objects typically include the main groups:

Arithmetic operations. Binary arithmetic operations have the signature

$BinOp : integer \times integer \rightarrow integer$

where *BinOp* may be *addition* (+), *subtraction* (−), *multiplication* (×), *division* (/ or div), *remainder* (mod), or a similar operation. Unary arithmetic operations have the signature

$UnaryOp : integer \rightarrow integer$

where, for example, *UnaryOp* may be *negation* (−) or *identity* (+). Commonly other arithmetic operations are included as well, often as library function subprograms (e.g., *absolute value*).

Relational operations. The relational operations each have the signature

$RelOp : integer \times integer \rightarrow Boolean$

where *RelOp* may be *equal*, *not equal*, *less-than*, *greater-than*, *less-than-or-equal*, and *greater-than-or-equal*. The relational operation compares the values of its two argument data values and returns a Boolean (true or false value) data object as its result.

Assignment. Assignment between integer data objects may be specified as one of

$assignment : integer \times integer \rightarrow void$

and

$assignment : integer \times integer \rightarrow integer$

as discussed in the preceding section.

Bit operations. In a language with few primitive data types, integers fulfill many roles. In C, integers also play the role of Boolean values. Therefore, additional bit operations are also defined using the signature

$BinOp : integer \times integer \rightarrow integer$

C includes operations to *and* the bits together (&), *or* the bits together (|), and shift the bits (<<), among others.

Implementation. The language-defined integer data type is most often implemented using a hardware-defined integer storage representation and set of hardware arithmetic and relational primitive operations on integers. Figure 5.3 shows three possible storage representations for integers. The first has no run-time descriptor; only the value is stored. This representation is possible where the language provides declarations and static type checking for integer data objects. The second form stores the descriptor in a separate memory location, with a pointer to the full-word integer value. This representation is often used in LISP. Its disadvantage is that it potentially may double the storage required for a single integer data object; its advantage is that the value is stored using the built-in hardware representation so that hardware arithmetic operations may be used. The third form stores the descriptor and value in a single memory location by shortening the size of the integer sufficiently to provide space for the descriptor. Here storage is conserved, but the hardware arithmetic operations cannot be used without first clearing the descriptor from the integer data object, performing the arithmetic, and then reinserting the descriptor. Because a sequence of hardware instructions must be executed to perform a single arithmetic operation, arithmetic is inefficient. This form is only practical for hardware-implemented type descriptors, which are not common on the processors in use today.

Subranges

Specification. A subrange of an integer data type is a subtype of the integer data type and consists of a sequence of integer values within some restricted range (e.g., the integers in the range 1 to 10 or in the range −5 to 50). A declaration of the form: $A : 1..10$ (Pascal) or A : *integer* **range** 1..10 (Ada) is often used. A subrange type allows the same set of operations to be used as for the ordinary integer type; thus, a subrange may be termed a *subtype* of the *base type* integer.

Implementation. Subrange types have two important effects on implementations:

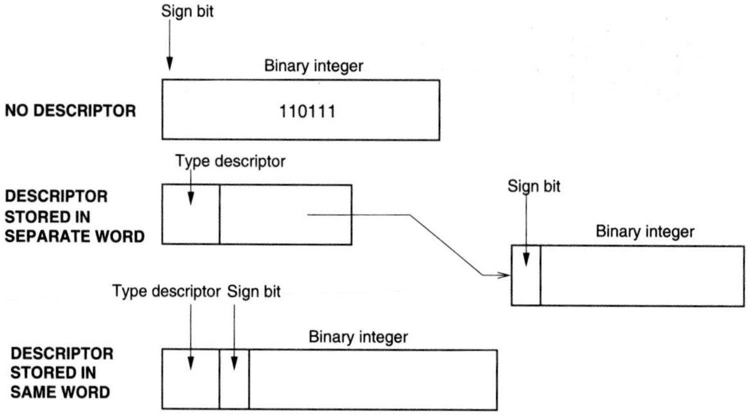

Figure 5.3. Three storage representations for integers.

1. *Smaller storage requirements.* Because a smaller range of values is possible, a subrange value can usually be stored in fewer bits than a general integer value. For example, an integer in the subrange 1 .. 10 requires only four bits of storage for its representation, whereas a full integer value might require 16, 32, or more on typical machines. However, because arithmetic operations on shortened integers may need software simulation for their execution (and thus be much slower), subrange values are often represented as the smallest number of bits for which the hardware implements arithmetic operations. This can generally be 8 or 16 bits. In C, for example, characters are stored as 8-bit integers that may be directly manipulated by most microprocessor hardware.

2. *Better type checking.* Declaration of a variable as being of a subrange type allows more precise type checking to be performed on the values assigned to that variable. For example, if variable $Month$ is: $Month$: 1..12, then the assignment

   Month := 0

   is invalid and can be detected at compile time. In contrast, if $Month$ is declared to be of integer type, then the assignment is valid and the error must be found by the programmer during testing. Many subrange type checks cannot be performed at compile time, however, if the check involves a computed value. For example, in

   Month := Month + 1

   run-time checking is needed to determine whether the new value assigned to $Month$ is still within the bounds declared. In this case, the bounds must be available at run time to allow the checking (e.g., $Month = 12$ would be legal; $Month = 13$ would be invalid).

Floating-Point Real Numbers

Specification. A floating-point real-number data type is often specified with only the single data type attribute *real*, as in FORTRAN, or *float*, as in C. As with type *integer*, the values form an ordered sequence from some hardware-determined minimum negative value to a maximum value, but the values are not distributed evenly across this range. Alternatively, the precision required for floating-point numbers, in terms of the number of digits used in the decimal representation, may be specified by the programmer, as in Ada.

The same arithmetic, relational, and assignment operations described for integers are usually also provided for reals, although the Boolean operations are sometimes restricted. Due to roundoff issues, equality between two real numbers is rarely achieved. Programs that check for equality to exit a loop may never terminate. For this reason, equality between two real numbers may be prohibited by the language designer to prevent this form of error. In addition, most languages provide other operations as built-in functions, such as the *sine* and *maximum value* functions

$$sin : real \rightarrow real$$

and

$$max : real \times real \rightarrow real$$

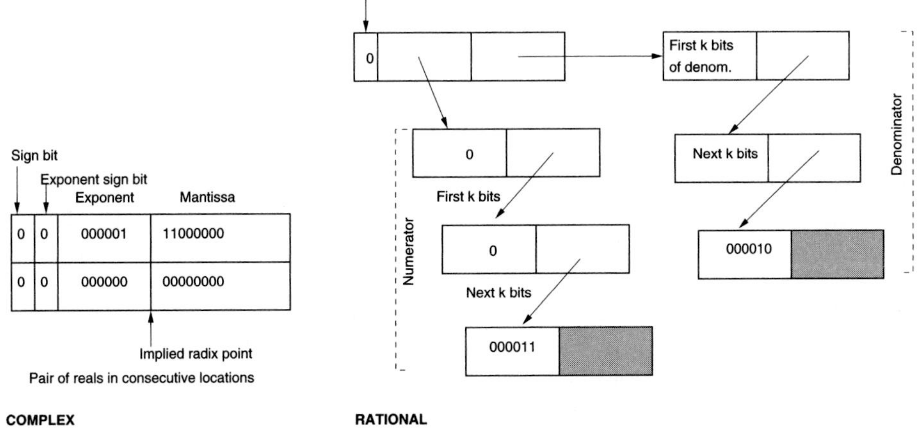

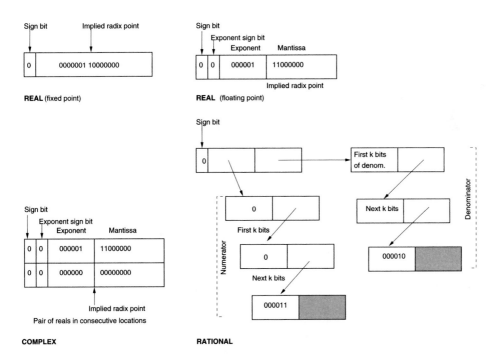

Figure 5.4. Representations of 1.5 without descriptors.

Implementation. Storage representations for floating-point real types are ordinarily based on an underlying hardware representation in which a storage location is divided into a mantissa (i.e., the significant digits of the number) and an exponent, as shown in Figure 5.4. This model emulates scientific notation, where any number N can be expressed as $N = m \times 2^k$ for m between 0 and 1 and for some integer k. IEEE Standard 754 [IEEE 1985] has become the accepted definition for floating-point format in many implementations (see Example 4.4). A double-precision form of floating-point number is also often available, in which an additional memory word is used to store an extended mantissa. Both single and double precision (if available) are generally supported by hardware arithmetic operations for addition, subtraction, multiplication, and division. Exponentiation is usually software simulated. Where both single- and double-precision real numbers are supported, the precision declaration for the number of digits in the value of a particular real data object is used to determine whether single- or double-precision storage representation must be used. Alternatively the programmer may simply declare a real variable to be *double* or *long real* to specify use of double precision as the storage representation.

Fixed-Point Real Numbers

Specification. Although most hardware includes both integer and floating-point data objects, there are many applications where specific rational numbers are needed. For example, data objects representing money contain dollars and cents, which are rational numbers written to two decimal places. These cannot be written as integers and, if written as floating-point values, may have roundoff errors. A form of fixed-point data can be used to represent such values.

A fixed-point number is represented as a digit sequence of fixed length, with the decimal point positioned at a given point between two digits. In COBOL, the declaration is given as a PICTURE clause—for example,

```
X PICTURE 999V99.
```

which declares X as a fixed-point variable with three digits before the decimal and two digits after.

Implementation. A fixed-point type may be directly supported by the hardware or, as stated earlier, may be simulated by software. For example, in PL/I, fixed data are of type FIXED DECIMAL. We can write

```
DECLARE X FIXED DECIMAL (10,3),
        Y FIXED DECIMAL (10,2),
        Z FIXED DECIMAL (10,2);
```

signifying X is 10 digits with three decimal places: Y and Z are also 10 digits, but have two decimal places. We store such data as *integers*, with the decimal point being an *attribute* of the data object. If X has the value 103.421, the r-value of X

EXAMPLE 5.4. IEEE Floating-Point Format.

IEEE standard 754 specifies both a 32- and 64-bit standard for floating-point numbers. The 32-bit standard is as follows:

S	exponent	mantissa
1	8	23

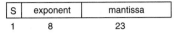

Numbers consist of three fields:

S – a one-bit sign field. 0 is positive.

E – an exponent in excess-127 notation. Values (8 bits) range from 0 to 255, corresponding to exponents of 2 that range from -127 to 128.

M – a mantissa of 23 bits. Since the first bit of the mantissa in a normalized number is always 1, it can be omitted and inserted automatically by the hardware, yielding an extra 24th bit of precision.

S determines the sign of the number. Given E, and M, the value of the representation is:

Parameters	Value
E=255 and M $\neq$ 0	An invalid number
E=255 and M=0	∞
$0 < E < 255$	$2^{E-127}(1.M)$
E=0 and M $\neq$ 0	$2^{-126}.M$
E=0 and M=0	0

Some examples:

+1 = $2^0 \times 1$ = $2^{127-127} \times (1).0(binary)$ =	0 01111111 000000...
+1.5 = $2^0 \times 1.5$ = $2^{127-127} \times (1).1(binary)$ =	0 01111111 100000...
-5 = $-2^2 \times 1.25$ = $2^{129-127} \times (1).01(binary)$ =	1 10000001 010000...

This gives a range from 10^{-38} to 10^{38}. In 64-bit format, the exponent is extended to 11 bits giving a range from -1022 to $+1023$, yielding numbers in the range 10^{-308} to 10^{308}.

---

will be 103,421, and the object X will have an attribute *scale factor* (*SF*) of three, implying that the decimal point is three places to the left. That is, in

$$value(X) = rvalue(X) \times 10^{-SF}$$

SF will always be 3 regardless of the r-value of X. Similarly, if Y has the value 102.34, then it will be stored as the integer 10,234 with $SF = 2$.

Consider the execution of the statement

$$\text{Z} = \text{X+Y}$$

If you perform this task with paper and pencil, your first task is to line up the decimal points. Because X has three positions and Y has two, you need to shift Y left one position, and you know that the sum will have three decimal digits— that is, $SF = 3$:

X =	103.421	
Y =	102.34x	← Shift left 1 position
Sum =	205.761	Sum has SF = 3

The shift is equivalent to multiplying the integral r-value of Y by 10. The actual code to compute $X + Y$ is therefore $X + 10 \times Y$ with $SF = 3$. Because Z has only two decimal places ($SF = 2$) and the sum has three, we need to remove one place (divide by 10). Therefore, the code produced is

$$\mathrm{Z} = (\mathrm{X} + 10 \times \mathrm{Y}) \; / \; 10$$

As long as the scaling factor is known at compile time (and it always is), the translator knows how to scale the results. Similarly, for multiplication $X \times Y$, we get the product by multiplying the two arguments together and adding the scale factors:

$$\begin{aligned} \text{Product} &= \text{rvalue(X)} \times \text{rvalue(Y)} \\ \text{SF} &= \text{SF(X)} + \text{SF(Y)} \end{aligned}$$

Subtraction and division are handled in an analogous manner.

Other Numeric Data Types

Complex numbers. A complex number consists of a pair of numbers representing the number's real and imaginary parts. A complex-number data type may be easily provided by representing each data object as a block of two storage locations containing a pair of real values. Operations on complex numbers may be software simulated because they are unlikely to be hardware implemented. (For example, addition would simply be the two additions on the corresponding real and imaginary parts of each argument, whereas multiplication is a more complex interaction involving all four real and imaginary components of the arguments.)

Rational numbers. A rational number is the quotient of two integers. The usual reason for including a rational number data type in a language is to avoid the problems of roundoff and truncation encountered in floating- and fixed-point representations of reals. As a result, it is desirable to represent rationals as pairs of integers of unbounded length. Such long integers are often represented using a linked representation. Figure 5.4 illustrates some of these number representations.

5.2.2 Enumerations

We often want a variable to take on only one of a small number of symbolic values. For example, a variable *StudentClass* might have only four possible values representing freshman, sophomore, junior, and senior. Similarly, a variable *EmployeeSex* might have only two values representing male and female. In older languages such as FORTRAN or COBOL, such a variable is ordinarily given the data type *integer*, and the values are represented as distinct, arbitrarily chosen integers (e.g., $Freshman = 1$, $Sophomore = 2$, and so on, or $Male = 0$, $Female = 1$). The program then manipulates these values as integers. The use of subranges for these special types often saves in storage requirements. However, in such cases, the programmer is responsible for ensuring that no operations are applied to the integer variables that make no sense in terms of the intended meaning. Assigning 2 to variable *EmployeeSex* or multiplying *StudentClass* by *Female* (e.g., the integer 1) would make no sense here, but would be allowed by the translator.

Languages such as C, Pascal, and Ada include an *enumeration* data type that allows the programmer to define and manipulate such variables more directly.

Specification. An enumeration is an ordered list of distinct values. The programmer defines both the literal names to be used for the values and their ordering using a declaration such as the following in C:

```
enum   StudentClass {Fresh, Soph, Junior, Senior};
enum   EmployeeSex {Male, Female};
```

Because ordinarily many variables of the same enumeration type are used in a program, it is common to define the enumeration in a separate type definition and give it a type name that can then be used to specify the type of several variables. In Pascal, the prior C definition can be specified as

```
type Class = (Fresh, Soph, Junior, Senior);
```

followed by declarations for variables such as

```
StudentClass: Class;
TransferStudentClass: Class;
```

Note that the type definition introduces the type name *Class*, which may be used wherever a primitive type name such as *integer* might be used. It also introduces the *literals* of *Fresh*, *Soph*, *Junior*, and *Senior*, which may be used wherever a language-defined literal such as "27" might be used. Thus, we can write

```
if StudentClass = Junior then ...
```

instead of the less understandable

```
if StudentClass = 3 then ...
```

which would be required if integer variables were used. In addition, static type checking by the compiler could find programming errors such as

if StudentClass=Male **then** ...

The basic operations on enumeration types are the relational operations (equal, less-than, greater-than, etc.), assignment, and the operations *successor* and *predecessor,* which give the next and previous value, respectively, in the sequence of literals defining the enumeration (and are undefined for the last and first values, respectively). Note that the full set of relational operations is defined for enumeration types because the set of values is given an ordering in the type definition.

Implementation. The storage representation for a data object of an enumeration type is straightforward: Each value in the enumeration sequence is represented at run time by one of the integers $0, 1, 2, \ldots$ Because only a small set of values is involved and the values are never negative, the usual integer representation is often shortened to omit the sign bit and use only enough bits for the range of values required, as with a subrange value. For example, the type $Class$ defined earlier has only four possible values, represented at run time as $0 = Fresh$, $1 = Soph$, $2 = Junior$, and $3 = Senior$. Because only two bits are required to represent these four possible values in memory, a variable of type $Class$ needs to be allocated only two bits of storage. The successor and predecessor operations involve simply adding or subtracting one from the integer representing the value and checking to see that the result is within the proper range.

In C, the programmer may override this default and set any values desired for enumeration values—for example,

enum class {Fresh=14, Soph=36, Junior=4, Senior=42}

Given this storage representation for enumeration types, implementation of the basic operations on enumerations is also straightforward because the hardware-provided operations on integers may be used. For example, relational operations such as $=, >$, and $<$ may be implemented using the corresponding hardware primitives that compare integers.

5.2.3 Booleans

Most languages provide a data type for representing $true$ and $false$, usually called a *Boolean* or *logical* data type.

Specification. The Boolean data type consists of data objects having one of two values—*true* or *false.* In Pascal and Ada, the Boolean data type is considered simply a language-defined enumeration, viz.,

type Boolean = (false, true);

which both defines the names *true* and *false* for the values of the type and defines the ordering $false < true$.

The most common operations on Boolean types include assignment as well as the following logical operations:

and:	$Boolean \times Boolean \rightarrow Boolean$	(conjunction)
or:	$Boolean \times Boolean \rightarrow Boolean$	(inclusive disjunction)
not:	$Boolean \rightarrow Boolean$	(negation or complement)

Other Boolean operations such as equivalence, exclusive or, implication, nand (not-and), and nor (not-or) are sometimes included. *Short-circuit* forms of the operations *and* and *or* are discussed in Section 8.2.

Implementation. The storage representation for a Boolean data object is a single bit of storage provided no descriptor designating the data type is needed. Because single bits may not be separately addressable in memory, often this storage representation is extended to be a single addressable unit such as a byte or word. Then the values *true* and *false* might be represented in two ways within this storage unit:

- A particular bit is used for the value (often the sign bit of the number representation), with $0 = false$, $1 = true$, and the rest of the byte or word ignored; or
- A zero value in the entire storage unit represents *false*, and any other nonzero value represents *true*.

Because a large amount of storage may be used by either of these representations, provision is often made in a language for collections of bits. The *bit-string* data type of PL/I and the *packed array of Boolean* and *set* data types of Pascal are examples.

Java has an explicit Boolean type, but C does not. In C, integer is used. *true* is any nonzero value, and *false* is 0. This can potentially cause some problems. For example,

```
int flag;
flag = 7
```

sets *flag* to 7 or 111 in binary, which would represent a true value. However, if you negate *flag* by changing all the bits in its representation, then the value of *flag* in binary would be ...1111000, or still true. Similarly, combining flags using the bitwise *or* operation | instead of the logical *or* operation || or using the bitwise *and* operation & instead of the logical *and* && leads to similar problems. In C, it is always safer to represent *true* by the integer value 1 and not try to pack multiple Boolean values in the same multibit integer.

5.2.4 Characters

Most data are input and output in character form. Conversion during input and output to other data types is usually provided, but processing of some data directly in character form is also important. Sequences of characters (character strings) are often processed as a unit. Provision for character-string data may be provided either directly through a *character-string* data type (as in ML and Prolog) or through a *character* data type, with a character string considered as a linear array of characters (as in C, Pascal, and Ada). Character strings are considered in Section 5.3.1.

Specification. A character data type provides data objects that have a single character as their value. The set of possible character values is usually taken to be a language-defined enumeration corresponding to the standard character sets supported by the underlying hardware and operating system, such as the ASCII character set. The ordering of the characters in this character set is called the *collating sequence* for the character set. The collating sequence is important because it determines the alphabetical ordering given to character strings by the relational operations. Because the ordering includes all characters in the set, character strings that include spaces, digits, and special characters may be alphabetized as well. Operations on character data include only the relational operations, assignment, and sometimes operations to test whether a character value is one of the special classes letter, digit, or special character.

Implementation. Character data values are almost always directly supported by the underlying hardware and operating system because of their use in input–output. Occasionally, however, the language definition prescribes use of a particular character set (such as the ASCII set) that is not supported by the underlying hardware. Although the same characters may be represented in both character sets, their storage representation, and thus their collating sequences, may differ; in other cases, some special characters in one set may not exist in the other. Because characters arrive from the input–output system in the hardware-supported representation, the language implementation may have to provide appropriate conversions to the alternative character-set representation or provide special implementation of the relational operations that take account of differences in the collating sequences. If the language-defined character representation is the same as that supported by the hardware, then the relational operations also are usually represented directly in the hardware or may be simulated by short inline code sequences.

5.3 COMPOSITE DATA TYPES

The data types in this section are usually considered elementary data objects. However, their implementation usually involves a complex data structure organization by the compiler. Multiple attributes are often given for each such data type.

5.3.1 Character Strings

A *character string* is a data object composed of a sequence of characters. A character-string data type is important in most languages, owing in part to the use of character representations of data for input and output.

Specification and syntax. At least three different treatments of character-string data types may be identified:

1. *Fixed declared length.* A character-string data object may have a fixed length that is declared in the program. The value assigned to the data object is always a character string of this length. Assignment of a new string value to the data object results in a length adjustment of the new string through truncation of excess characters or addition of blank characters to produce a string of the correct length.

2. *Variable length to a declared bound.* A character-string data object may have a *maximum* length that is declared in the prior program, but the actual value stored in the data object may be a string of shorter length—possibly even the empty string of no characters. During execution, the length of the string value of the data object may vary, but it is truncated if it exceeds the bound.

3. *Unbounded length.* A character-string data object may have a string value of any length, and the length may vary dynamically during execution with no bound (beyond available memory).

The C case is actually a bit more complicated. In C, strings are arrays of characters, but C has no string declaration. However, there is a convention that a null character ("\0") follows the last character of a string. A string constant written as "This string has null terminator" will have the null character appended to the string constant by the C translator; that is, the string, when stored in an array, will have a null character appended. However, for strings made from programmer-defined arrays, it is the programmer's responsibility to make sure that strings include the final null character.

The first two methods of handling character-string data allow storage allocation for each string data object to be determined at translation time; if strings have unbounded length, then dynamic storage allocation at run time is required. The different methods also make different sorts of operations on strings appropriate.

A wide variety of operations on character-string data are provided. Some of the more important are briefly described here:

1. *Concatenation.* Concatenation is the operation of joining two character strings to make one long string. For example, if || is the symbol for the concatenation operation, then "BLOCK" || "HEAD" gives "BLOCKHEAD".

2. *Relational operations on strings.* The usual relational operations (equal, less-than, greater-than, etc.) may be extended to strings. The basic character set always has an ordering as described in Section 5.2.4. Extending this ordering to character strings gives the usual *lexicographic* (alphabetic) ordering, in which String A is considered to be less than String B (i.e., comes before it in the ordering) if either the first character of A is less than the first character of B, if the first characters are equal and the second character of A is less than the second character of B, and so on, with the shorter of Strings A and B sometimes extended with blank characters (spaces) to the length of the longer.

3. *Substring selection using positioning subscripts.* Manipulation of character-string data often involves working with a contiguous substring of the overall string. For example, a string may often contain a leading sequence of blank characters or be composed of words separated by blanks and punctuation marks. To facilitate manipulation of substrings of a string, many languages provide an operation for selecting a substring by giving the positions of its first and last characters (or first character position and length of the substring), as in the FORTRAN $NEXT = STR(6:10)$, which assigns the five characters in Positions 6 through 10 of string STR to string variable $NEXT$. The meaning of the substring selection operation is particularly troublesome to define if it is allowed to appear on both sides of an assignment (i.e., it is both an r-value and l-value function so that a new value may be assigned to the selected substring). Consider the FORTRAN expression

$$\text{STR(1:5)} = \text{STR(I:I+4)}$$

which might be used to move a five-character substring beginning in Position I to the first five-character positions of the string. If the substrings referenced on the left and right of the assignment happen to overlap, the meaning of this statement must be carefully defined.

4. *Input–output formatting.* Operations for manipulating character strings are often provided primarily to aid in formatting data for output or for breaking up formatted input data into smaller data items. The formatted input-output features of FORTRAN and C are examples of extensive sets of operations provided for this purpose.

5. *Substring selection using pattern matching.* Often the position of a desired substring within a larger string is not known, but its relation to other substrings is known. For example, we might want to select the first nonblank character of a string, a sequence of digits followed by a decimal point, or the word following the word *THE*. A *pattern-matching operation* takes as one argument a pattern data structure, where the pattern specifies the form of the substring desired (e.g., its length, or that it is composed of a sequence

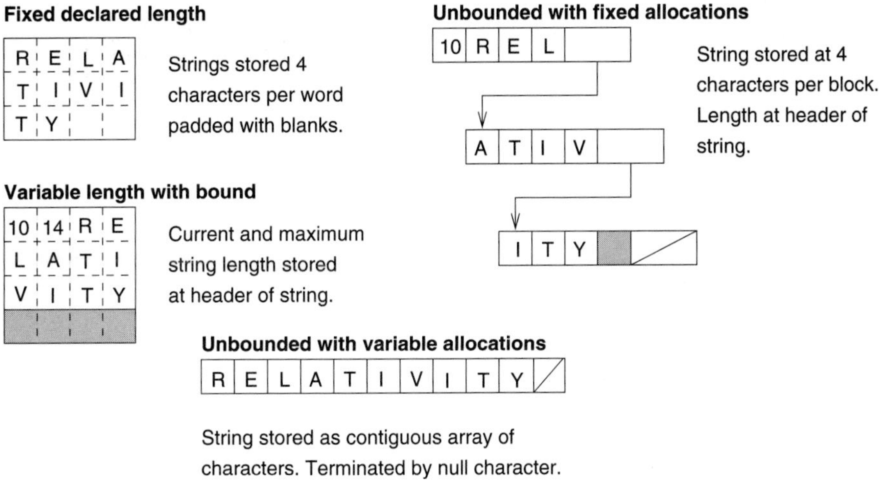
Fixed declared length
R E L A
T I V I
T Y
Strings stored 4 characters per word padded with blanks.
Variable length with bound
10 14 R E
L A T I
V I T Y
Current and maximum string length stored at header of string.
Unbounded with fixed allocations
10 R E L
A T I V
I T Y
String stored at 4 characters per block. Length at header of string.
Unbounded with variable allocations
R E L A T I V I T Y
String stored as contiguous array of characters. Terminated by null character.

Figure 5.5. Storage representation for strings.

of decimal digits) and possibly other substrings that should adjoin it (e.g., a following decimal point or a preceding sequence of blank characters). The second argument to the pattern-matching operation is a character string that is to be scanned to find a substring that matches that specified by the pattern. We have already encountered this in Perl in its handling of regular expressions (Section 3.3.3).

6. *Dynamic strings.* String values may be either static or dynamic. Perl is an example where both are possible. The string '$ABC' is static, and the statement

   print '$ABC';

   will print the value $\$ABC$. However, the string "$ABC" is dynamic and the statement

   print "$ABC";

   will cause the string to be evaluated, and the value of the Perl variable $\$ABC$ is printed instead.

Implementation. Each of the three methods for handling character strings utilizes a different storage representation, as shown in Figure 5.5. Storage representations for characters are discussed in Section 5.2.4. For a string of fixed, declared length, the representation is essentially that used for a packed vector of characters, as described in Section 6.1.5. For the variable-length string to be a declared bound, the storage representation utilizes a descriptor containing both the declared maximum length and the current length of the string stored in the data object. For strings of unbounded length, either a linked storage representation of fixed-length data objects may be used or a contiguous array of characters may be used to contain the string. This latter method is the technique used in C, which often requires dynamic run-time storage management to allocate such storage.

Hardware support for the simple fixed-length representation is usually available, but other representations for strings must usually be software simulated. Operations on strings such as concatenation, substring selection, and pattern matching are ordinarily entirely software simulated.

5.3.2 Pointers and Programmer-Constructed Data Objects

Commonly, rather than including a variety of types of variable-size, linked data objects into a programming language, facilities are provided to allow the construction of any structure using pointers to link together the component data objects as desired. Several language features are needed to make this possible:

1. An elementary data type *pointer* (also called a *reference* or *access* type). A pointer data object contains the location of another data object (i.e., its l-value) or may contain the null pointer, *nil* or *null.* Pointers are ordinary data objects that may be simple variables or components of arrays and records.

2. A *creation operation* for data objects of fixed size, such as arrays, records, and elementary types. The creation operation both allocates a block of storage for the new data object and returns its l-value, which may then be stored as the r-value of a pointer data object. The creation operation differs in two ways from the ordinary creation of data objects caused by declarations: (a) The data objects created need have no names because they are accessed through pointers, and (b) data objects may be created in this way at any point during execution of a program, not just on entry to a subprogram.

3. A *dereferencing operation* for pointer values that allows a pointer to be followed to the data object to which it points.

Specification. A pointer data type defines a class of data objects whose values are the locations of other data objects. A single data object of pointer type might be treated in two ways:

1. *Pointers may reference data objects only of a single type.* The pointers (locations) that are allowed as a value of the pointer data object may be restricted to point only to data objects of the same type. This is the approach used in C, Pascal, and Ada, where type declarations and static type checking are used. To declare a pointer variable in C (e.g., that may point to any data object of type *List*), use

List *P;

The * designates the type of P as type pointer. The type *List* designates that the value of P may be the l-value of an object of type *List*. A separate type definition must be given to define the structure of data objects of type *List*:

struct List { int ListValue; List *NextItem; };

2. *Pointers may reference data objects of any type.* An alternative is to allow a pointer data object to point to data objects of varying types at different times during program execution. This is the approach used in languages like Smalltalk, where data objects carry type descriptors during execution and dynamic type checking is performed.

In some languages (e.g., C and C++), pointers are data objects that may be manipulated by the program. In others (e.g., Java), pointers are part of the hidden data structures managed by the language implementation.

The creation operation allocates storage for (and thus creates) a fixed-size data object and also creates a pointer to the new data object that may be stored in a pointer data object. In Ada, this operation is named *new*. In C, the system function *malloc* (memory-allocator) provides this function. (C++ and Java simplify C by restoring the function *new* as an allocator.) Consider a subprogram containing a declaration of pointer variable P (as defined earlier). On entry to the subprogram, only space for the data object P is allocated (storage for a single pointer value). Later during execution of the subprogram, data of type *List* may be created by executing the statement

P = malloc(sizeof(List))

Because P has been declared to point to objects only of the type *List*, this statement has the meaning "Create a two-word block of storage to be used as an object of type *List*, and store its l-value in P."

The selection operation allows a pointer value to be followed to reach the data object designated. Because pointers are ordinary data objects, the pointer data object may also be selected using only the ordinary mechanisms for selection. For example, in C, the selection operation that follows a pointer to its designated object is written *. To select a component of the vector pointed to by P, you write $*P.first$. The * operator simply takes the r-value of the pointer and makes it an l-value. Thus, $*P.first$ accesses the value in P, assumes it is now an l-value, and uses this to access the $first$ component of the record pointed to by P.

Implementation. A pointer data object is represented as a storage location containing the address of another storage location. The address is the base address of the block of storage representing the data object pointed to by the pointer. Two major storage representations are used for pointer values:

1. *Absolute addresses.* A pointer value may be represented as the actual memory address of the storage block for the data object.

2. *Relative addresses.* A pointer value may be represented as an *offset* from the *base address* of some larger *heap* storage block within which the data object is allocated.

If absolute addresses are used for pointer values, then data objects created by the creation operation, *new*, may be allocated storage anywhere in memory. Usually this allocation takes place within a general *heap* storage area. Selection using absolute addresses is efficient because the pointer value provides direct access to the data object using the hardware memory-accessing operation. The disadvantage of absolute addresses is that storage management is more difficult because no data object may be moved within memory if there exists a pointer to it stored elsewhere, unless the pointer value is changed to reflect the new position of the data object. Recovery of storage for data objects that have become garbage is also difficult because each such data object is recovered individually and its storage block must be integrated back into the overall pool of available storage. These issues are treated in chapter 10.

The use of relative addresses as pointers requires the initial allocation of a block of storage within which subsequent allocation of data objects by *new* takes place. There may be one area for each type of data object to be allocated, or a single area for all data objects. Each area is managed as a *heap* storage area. Assuming one area for each type of data object, then *new* may allocate storage in fixed-size blocks within the area, which makes storage management particularly simple. Selection using this form of pointer value is more costly than for an absolute address because the offset must be added to the base address of the area to obtain an absolute address before the data object may be accessed. However, the advantage of relative pointers lies in the opportunity to move the area block as a whole at any time without invalidating any of the pointers. For example, the area might be written out to a file and later read back into a different place in primary memory. Because the offset of each pointer value is unchanged, access to a data object in the new area may use the same offset with the new base address of the area. An additional advantage is that the entire area may be treated as a data object that is created on entry to a subprogram, used by *new* within that subprogram (and any subprograms it calls), and then deleted on exit. No storage recovery of individual data objects within the area is necessary; they may be allowed to become garbage because the entire area is recovered as a whole when the subprogram is exited.

Static type checking is possible for references using pointer values if each pointer data object is restricted to point to other data objects of a single type, as described earlier. Without this restriction, it cannot be determined during translation what type of data object a pointer will designate at run time, so dynamic type checking is necessary. In some languages, selections using pointer values are simply left unchecked. Run-time checking for a *nil* pointer value is also required before selection.

The major implementation problem associated with pointers and programmer-constructed data objects that use pointer linkages is the storage allocation associated with the creation operation. Because this operation may be used to create data objects of different sizes at arbitrary times during program execution, it requires an underlying storage management system capable of managing a general *heap* storage area. For C, the other parts of the language requires only a stack-based storage management system, so the addition of pointers and the *malloc* operation to the language requires a substantial extension of the overall run-time storage management structure. Pointer data objects introduce the potential for generating garbage if all pointers to a created data object are lost. Dangling references are also possible if data objects can be destroyed and the storage recovered for reuse. These issues are treated again in chapter 6.

5.3.3 Files and Input–Output

A *file* is a data structure with two special properties:

1. It ordinarily is represented on a secondary storage device such as a disk or tape and thus may be much larger than most data structures of other types.

2. Its lifetime may encompass a greater span of time than that of the program creating it.

Sequential files are the most common type of file, but many languages also provide *direct-access files* and *indexed sequential files*. Two general uses for files are seen: for input and output of data to an external operating environment (see chapter 1) and as temporary *scratch storage* for data when not enough high-speed memory is available. The components of a file are often termed *records*, but this use of the term is avoided here because of the conflict with the record data structure discussed in Section 6.1.6.

Sequential Files

A *sequential file* is a data structure composed of a linear sequence of components of the same type. It is of varying length with no fixed maximum bound (beyond available storage). In Pascal, a file is declared by giving its name and the type of component it contains. For example,

Master: **file of** EmployeeRec;

defines a file named $Master$ whose components are of type *EmployeeRec*. Variable-size data structures ordinarily cannot be components of files (thus, no files of files or files of stacks). In addition, data structures that are in linked representation or that include pointer values are often not allowed as components of files because the pointer values usually become meaningless after the lifetime of the program creating the file. When the data are later read from the file, the storage locations referenced by the pointer values may be in use for another purpose.

For input–output, data are usually represented in character form. Each component of such a file is then a single character, and the file is known, in Pascal, as a *textfile.* Most languages provide a special set of input–output operations for textfiles, in addition to the ordinary file operations. A textfile also commonly divides character sequences into groups called *lines.* We consider ordinary sequential files first and then note some special characteristics of textfiles.

Typically the file may be accessed in either *read* mode or *write* mode. In either mode, there is a *file-position pointer* that designates a position before the first file component, between two components, or after the last component. In write mode, the file-position pointer is always positioned after the last component, and the only operation possible is to assign (*write*) a new component to that position, thus extending the file by one component. In read mode, the file-position pointer may be positioned anywhere in the file, and the only access provided is access (*read*) to the component at (immediately following) the position designated. No assignment of new components or component values is provided.

Specification. The major operations on sequential files are as follows:

1. *Open.* Ordinarily, before a file may be used, it must be opened. The *open* operation is given the name of a file and the access mode (read or write). If the mode is *read,* then the file is presumed to already exist. The *open* operation ordinarily requests information from the operating system about the location and properties of the file, allocates the required internal storage for buffers and other information (see the following implementation discussion), and sets the file-position pointer to the first component of the file. If the mode is *write,* then a request is made to the operating system to create a new empty file or, if a file already exists with the given name, delete all the existing components of the file so that it is empty. The file position pointer is set to the start of the empty file.

   Ordinarily, an explicit *open* statement is provided. In Pascal, the procedure *reset* opens a file in read mode, and procedure *rewrite* opens a file in write mode. Sometimes a language provides for an implicit *open* operation on a file at the time of the first attempt to read or write the file.

2. *Read.* A *read* operation transfers the contents of the current file component (designated by the file-position pointer) to a designated variable in the program. The transfer is usually defined as having the same semantics as an assignment from the file component to the program variable.

3. *Write.* A *write* operation creates a new component at the current position in the file (always at the end) and transfers the contents of a designated program

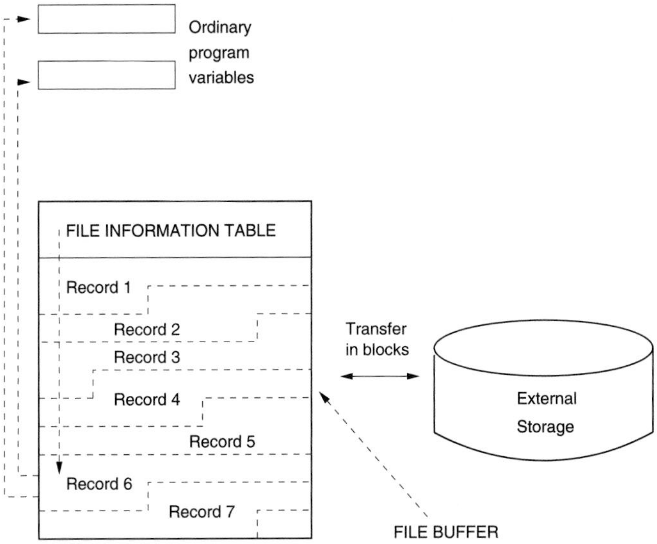

Figure 5.6. File representation using a buffer.

variable to the new component. Again this transfer is usually defined as a form of assignment.

4. *End-of-file test.* A *read* operation fails if the file position pointer designates the end of the file. Because the file is of variable length, an explicit test for the end-of-file position is needed so that the program may take special action.

5. *Close.* When processing of a file is complete, it must be closed. Ordinarily, this operation involves notification to the operating system that the file can be detached from the program (and potentially made available to other programs) and possibly also deallocation of internal storage used for the file (such as buffers and buffer variables). Often files are closed implicitly when the program terminates without explicit action by the programmer. However, to change the mode of access to a file from write to read, or vice versa, the file must often be explicitly closed and then reopened in the new mode.

Implementation. In most computer systems, the underlying operating system has the primary responsibility for the implementation of files because files are created and manipulated by various programming language processors and utilities. File operations are primarily implemented by calls on primitives provided by the operating system.

From the language viewpoint, the primary implementation problem comes from the need to provide storage for system data and buffers required by the operating system primitives. Typically when a program opens a file during its execution, storage for a *file information table* and a *buffer* must be provided. The operating system *open* primitive stores information about the location and characteristics of the file in the file information table. Assume the file is opened in *write* mode. When a *write* operation transfers a component to be appended to the end of the file, the data are sent to an operating system *write* primitive. The *write* primitive stores the data in the next available position in the buffer, in memory, and updates pointers to this buffer in the file information table. No actual transfer of data to the file takes place until enough *write* operations have been performed to allow a complete block of components to have accumulated in the buffer. At this time, the block of components is transferred from the buffer to the external storage device (e.g., disk or tape). The next sequence of *write* operations executed by the program again fills the buffer until a complete block may be transferred to external storage. When a file is read, the inverse process occurs: Data are transferred from the file into the buffer in blocks of components. Each *read* operation executed by the program transfers a single component from the buffer to the program variable. The buffer is refilled as needed. This organization is shown in Figure 5.6.

Textfiles

A *textfile* (the term comes from Pascal) is a file of characters. Textfiles are the primary form of file for input–output to the user in most languages because textfiles may be printed and may be created directly from keyboard input. Files with components of other types ordinarily are only written and read by programs. Textfiles are a form of ordinary sequential file and may be manipulated in the same ways. However, special operations are often provided for textfiles that allow numeric data (and sometimes other types of data) to be automatically converted to internal storage representations during input without storage in character form. Similar operations on output allow conversion of numbers and other data from internal representations to character form. Along with these conversions, provision is ordinarily made for formatting the data on output into lines of the appropriate length that include headings, spaces, and converted data items as desired for printed output. This *output formatting* is an important part of the implementation of output operations for textfiles. Similar formatting operations may be used for input, or the input operations may be *free format,* allowing numbers to appear anywhere on a line separated by spaces. The free-format *read* operation scans the line (or lines) as necessary to find the numbers needed to satisfy the read request.

Interactive Input–Output

Consider a textfile that represents an interactive terminal at which a programmer is sitting. During execution of the program, a *write* operation on this file is interpreted as a command to display the characters on the terminal screen. A *read* operation is a command that requests input of data from the keyboard, usually beginning with display of a prompt character on the screen. In this setting, several aspects of the ordinary view of sequential files described earlier are modified:

1. The file must be in *both* read and write mode at the same time because ordinarily *read* and *write* operations alternate. First some data are displayed, then some input data are requested, and so on.

2. Buffering of data on input and output is restricted. Seldom can more than one line of data be collected in an input buffer before it is processed. Data collected in an output buffer must be displayed before a read request is made to the terminal.

3. The file-position pointer and end-of-file test have relatively little significance. An interactive file has no position, in the sense described earlier, and it has no end because the programmer may continue to enter data indefinitely. A special control character may be used by the programmer to signal the end of a portion of the input from the terminal, but the usual notions of end-of-file test and end-of-file processing are often inappropriate.

Because of these substantial differences between interactive files and ordinary sequential files, many language designs have experienced difficulty accommodating interactive files within an input–output structure designed for ordinary sequential files.

Direct-Access Files

In a sequential file, the components must be accessed in sequence in the order in which they appear on the file. Although limited operations to advance or backspace the file-position pointer are usually available, access to any component at random is usually not possible. A *direct-access file* is organized so that any single component may be accessed at random, just as in an array or a record. The subscript used to select a component is called its *key* and may be an integer or other identifier. If an integer, the key looks much like an ordinary subscript used to designate a component of the file. However, because a direct-access file is stored on a secondary storage device rather than in central memory, the implementation of the file and the selection operation is quite different from that for an array.

A direct-access file is organized as an unordered set of components, with a key value associated with each component. Initially the file is empty. A *write* operation is given a component to copy to the file and the key value to be associated with that component. The *write* operation creates a new component on the external storage device and copies the designated value into it. The key value is ordinarily associated with the location of the component (on the external storage device) by storing the pair (key, location) in an index. An *index* is a vector of such pairs. Each *write* operation that writes a component with a new key value adds another pair to the index. However, if a *write* operation is given the key of an existing component, that component is *overwritten* with the new value. Thus, writing on a direct-access file is similar to assignment to a component of a vector, where the key value is the subscript. A *read* operation is given the key of the desired component in the file. The index is searched to find the pair with that key, and then the component is read from the designated location in secondary storage.

Indexed Sequential Files

An indexed sequential file is similar to a direct-access file, with the additional facility to access components in sequence, beginning from a component selected at random. For example, if component with key value 27 is selected (read), then the subsequent *read* operation may choose the next component in sequence, rather than giving a key value. This file organization provides a compromise between the pure sequential and pure direct-access organizations.

An indexed sequential file requires an index of key values, just as for a direct-access file, but the entries in the index must be *ordered* by key values. When a *read* or *write* operation selects a component with a particular key value, that pair in the index becomes the *current component* of the file (e.g., the file-position pointer is positioned at that component). To advance to the next file component in sequence, the next entry in the index is accessed, and that entry becomes the current component. Thus, sequential access to components is possible without a major change from the direct-access organization.

5.4 FORTRAN OVERVIEW

History. FORTRAN is one of the first and still widely used language for scientific and engineering computation. It has undergone much evolution in its 40-year life, has been deemed obsolete and irrelevant numerous times, and yet is still with us and still evolving.

FORTRAN was the first high-level programming language to become widely used. It was first developed in 1957 by IBM for execution on the IBM 704 computer. At that time, the utility of any high-level language was open to question by programmers schooled in assembly language programming. Their most serious complaint concerned the efficiency of execution of code compiled from high-level language programs. As a result, the design of the earliest versions of FORTRAN was oriented heavily toward providing execution efficiency. The success of this early FORTRAN and its dependence on features oriented toward efficient execution on the IBM 704 computer have been a problem with the language, as we later indicate. The first standard definition of the language was adopted in 1966, and a major revision was made in this standard in the 1970s, leading to FORTRAN 77 and FORTRAN 90 in the 1990s.

FORTRAN is generally implemented using traditional compiler technology. A text editor is used to create the program, a FORTRAN compiler translates the program into executable form; a linker is used to merge subprograms, the main program, and run-time library routines into one executable program; and an execution step executes the translated program.

Brief overview of the language. The design of FORTRAN centers on the goal of execution efficiency. The language structures are generally simple and much of the design rather inelegant, but the goal of execution efficiency is achieved. In discussing FORTRAN, we can almost consider FORTRAN 77 and FORTRAN 90 to be distinct languages. FORTRAN 90 adds most of the modern data and control features, classically missing from FORTRAN, to give it the power of languages like C and Pascal.

A FORTRAN program consists of a main program and a set of subprograms, each of which is compiled separately from all the others, with the translated programs linked into final executable form during loading. Each subprogram is compiled into a statically allocated code segment and activation record. No run-time storage management is provided. All storage is allocated statically before program execution begins, although FORTRAN 90 changes the execution model to allow for dynamic storage.

Only a restricted set of data types is provided in FORTRAN: four types of numeric data (integer, real, complex, and double-precision real), Boolean data (called *logical*), arrays, character strings, and files. An extensive set of arithmetic operations and mathematical functions is provided, reflecting the orientation of the language toward engineering and scientific computation. Relational and Boolean operations and simple selection from arrays using subscripting are provided. Both sequential and direct-access files are supported, and a flexible set of input–output facilities and format specification features are available.

Sequence-control structures include expressions with the usual infix and prefix operations and function calls. Statement sequence control relies heavily on statement labels and GOTO statements, although each revision of the language has been adding more nested control structures. FORTRAN 66 was heavily influenced by the underlying computer architecture on which it was executed. FORTRAN 77 added some modern control structures (e.g., the IF ... THEN ... ELSE conditional), and FORTRAN 90 extended this concept to the extent that it is now possible to write FORTRAN programs with no GOTO statements. FORTRAN 90 includes the concept of the *deprecated* feature, such as the arithmetic IF statement that is considered obsolete and will be deleted in a later version of the language standard. Because most of the machine-based features of FORTRAN 66 are now deprecated, by the time of the next revision of the standard, FORTRAN should be a modern language.

Only two levels of referencing environment are provided: global and local. However, FORTRAN 90 does add the concept of *nested subroutines*. The global environment may be partitioned into separate common environments (called *COMMON blocks*, now on the deprecated list) that are shared among sets of subprograms, but only data objects may be shared in this way. Parameters are uniformly transmitted by reference (or value result).

5.5 SUGGESTIONS FOR FURTHER READING

Most general texts on programming languages discuss the issues of types and type checking (see the references at the end of chapter 1). The *Ada Rationale* ([ISO 1994]) is particularly relevant; it also includes a discussion of the design problems associated with fixed-point and floating-point real-number types. The three volumes by Knuth [KNUTH 1973] contain a wealth of material on data structures and their manipulation.

5.6 PROBLEMS

1. For an elementary data type in a language with which you are familiar, do the following:

(a) Describe the set of values that data objects of that type may contain.

(b) Determine the storage representation for values of that type (used in your local implementation of the language).

(c) Define the syntactic representation used for constants of that type.

(d) Determine the set of operations defined for data objects of that type; for each operation, give its signature and syntactic representation in the language.

(e) For each operation, determine whether it is implemented through software simulation or directly as a single-hardware instruction.

(f) Describe any attributes that a data object of that type may have other than its data type.

(g) Determine if any of the operation symbols or names used to represent operations of the type are overloaded. For each overloaded operation name, determine when (compile time or run time) the specific meaning of each use of the overloaded name in a statement is determined.

(h) Determine whether static or dynamic type checking is used to determine the validity of each use of each operation of the type.

2. For an elementary data type in a language with which you are familiar, do the following:

(a) Explain the difference among the type, variables of that type, and constants of that type.

(b) Show a situation during execution where a data object of that type exists that is neither a variable nor a constant.

(c) Explain the difference between data objects of that type and the values that those data objects may contain.

3. For a language with which you are familiar, find an example of a primitive operation that

(a) Has an implicit argument.
(b) Has a side effect.
(c) Is undefined for some data objects in its specified domain.
(d) That is self-modifying.

4. Give a formula for determining the maximum number of bits required for storage of any value in the integer subrange $M..N$, where M and N are any two integers such that $M < N$.

5. For a language with which you are familiar and uses static type checking, give two examples of constructs that cannot be checked statically. For each construct, determine by running a test program whether the language implementation provides dynamic type checking or leaves the construct unchecked during execution.

6. Give an example of an operation in a programming language that

(a) Is implemented directly in hardware.
(b) Is implemented as a subprogram.
(c) Is implemented as an inline code sequence.

7. The potential for overloading of enumeration literal names is a problem in languages that provide enumeration types. In defining an enumeration type in a large program, the programmer may inadvertently use one of the same literal names that is used in another enumeration (e.g., the literal $Junior$ might be used in the definition of enumeration $Class$ and in the definition of another enumeration $OfficerGrade$). A later reference to the literal $Junior$ is then ambiguous. Propose a means by which a language might allow the programmer to resolve the ambiguity without prohibiting overloaded enumeration literals altogether. (Note: Ada permits this form of overloading, which is discussed in Section A.1.)

8. Figure 5.3 illustrates two number representations for integers with a run-time type descriptor. One uses extra space to gain speed in arithmetic; the other sacrifices speed for a more compact storage structure. Design two similar representations for your local computer assuming the run-time descriptor requires at most 6 bits. Write the programs necessary for addition, subtraction, multiplication, and division of numbers in these forms. Compare the relative advantages and disadvantages of the two representations.

9. *(a)* Describe the elementary data types that are built into the hardware of your local computer. Determine whether any hardware data types carry descriptors.

(b) Design a complete set of descriptors for the hardware data types. Each descriptor should include enough information so that from the descriptor alone the location, length, and format of the data item it describes can be determined.

(c) Design a *storage structure* for the descriptors whose logical organization was set up in Part b. Because you do not wish to get into the problem of descriptors for descriptors, design the storage structure so that descriptors are *self-describing* (i.e., given the location of the first bit [on a binary computer] of any descriptor, it should be possible to determine the length and format of the descriptor without additional information).

10. Consider a substring selection operation, ⟨*string variable*⟩(⟨*first char. pos.*⟩ : ⟨*last char. pos.*⟩), such as described in Section 5.3.1. Give two different possible definitions for the meaning of this selection operation when used as both the source and object in an assignment, such as

$$\text{STR(I:J)} := \text{STR(K:L)}$$

where the selected substrings may overlap.

11. *Concatenation* is a central operation on character strings.

(a) Assuming the representation of Figure 5.5 for character strings of variable length with a declared bound, design a concatenation operation $CAT1$. $CAT1$ is called with three parameters: A, B, and C. A and B are pointers to the two storage blocks containing the strings to be concatenated, and C is the receiving block that initially contains some other character string. The string composed of the characters of String B concatenated to the characters of String A is to be stored in Block C (with the appropriate descriptor, of course). Blocks A and B are to be unchanged by the operation.

(b) Strings without a declared bound may also be stored sequentially using the same storage representation with the maximum length deleted from the descriptor. Design an appropriate storage structure assuming that characters may be packed four per word. Then design the concatenation operation $CAT2$. $CAT2$ has two parameters, A and B, representing the strings to be concatenated and returns a pointer to a new block of storage containing the concatenated strings. Assume $CAT2$ calls a function $ALLOCATE(N)$ that returns a pointer to a newly allocated block of N words of storage.

(c) Design $CAT3$—a routine that concatenates strings represented as linked lists in the manner of Figure 5.5.

12. For a language that provides a *pointer* type for programmer-constructed data objects and operations such as *new* and *dispose*, which allocate and free storage for data objects, write a program segment that generates *garbage* (in the storage management sense). Write a program segment that generates a *dangling reference.* If one or the other program segment cannot be written, explain why.

13. In many SNOBOL4 implementations, the set of character strings that exist at any point during program execution is kept in a *central strings table.* This table is organized as a hash table in which each entry is a pointer to a linked bucket list. A *double-hashing* scheme is used to test for membership of a given string X in the set. X is hashed twice to produce both a hash address, which is used to index the central table to obtain a pointer to the appropriate bucket, and a *bucket order number.* Each entry on a bucket list is composed of a bucket order number and a pointer to a string. Entries on a given bucket list are ordered by bucket order number. To determine whether X is stored in the bucket designated by its hash address, the bucket is searched matching X's bucket order number against those in the bucket list until either a match is found or a bucket order number greater than that of X is found. In the latter case, X is immediately inserted in the list and otherwise a character-by-character match of X with any other strings in the list with the same bucket order number is required. Program this double-hashing scheme assuming that strings are stored in sequential blocks with a length descriptor. The function coded would accept a pointer to a string as input, look up the string in the table, enter it if it were not found, and return the address of the old entry if found and the address of the new entry if not.

14. File input and end-of-file tests are usually done in advance of the need for the data or for the result of the test because input is done through a buffer in blocks, as shown in Figure 5.6. An alternative, *lazy input*, is more appropriate with interactive input–output. Neither input of data nor an end-of-file test is ever performed until required by the program being executed. Design a *read* operation and an *end of file* test for lazy input from an interactive file. The user should be able to input several values at once when input is requested, so a buffer may still be needed.

Chapter 6

Encapsulation

In the construction of large programs, the programmer is almost inevitably concerned with the design and implementation of new data types. For example, in constructing a program to generate registration assignments and class rolls for a university, one of the early steps in the design might be to define a type of data object that represents a single *section* of a course. Certain information would be stored in such a data object: the instructor's name, room assignment, maximum enrollment, and so on. These might be considered the attributes of the data type *section* because they would not be expected to change over the lifetime of such a data object. A section would also contain a list of the students enrolled, which might be considered the components of the data object. A particular data object of this type would represent a particular class section, with values assigned for each attribute and for the current student list. A set of operations would then be defined to provide the basic manipulations of such *section* data objects: create a new section, assign a student to a section, destroy a section, and so on. All of this design activity might properly be considered as designing the *specification* of the *abstract data type section* (i.e., designing the attributes and operations required).

Implementation of the *section* data type comes at a later step in constructing the program. A particular representation for section data objects must be chosen using the data types provided by the language or perhaps using other abstract data types such as a type student, a type instructor, and so on. Thus, the instructor's name might be implemented as a character string of 10 characters or fewer or as an integer (the identification number of the instructor), while the student roll list might be represented as a linear array of integers (student identification numbers). Once this representation for *section* data objects is defined, the operations on sections may be implemented as subprograms whose arguments represent such data objects.

Programmers who are designing and coding other parts of the larger program now may use the *section* data type. They may use the defined representation and subprograms to create and manipulate *sections* using the specification given for the subprograms without much concern with exactly how sections are implemented. For these programmers, the effect is similar to the addition of a new data type to the language. The base language provides a primitive type *integer* and operations on integers that effectively make it unnecessary for the programmer to be concerned with the details of the underlying representation of integers as bit sequences. Now there exists a higher level type *section* and a set of operations on sections that make it unnecessary for the programmer to be concerned with the details of the implementation of sections as arrays, records, character strings, and the like.

The current goal in programming language design is to make the distinctions in the various forms of data transparent to the programmer who uses the data types. A programmer who needs an *integer* variable and one who needs a *section* variable should see the same syntax. Similarly, the operation signatures of $add : integer \times integer \rightarrow integer$ and $add\_to\_course : student \times section \rightarrow section$ should have the same syntax and comparable semantics.

Four basic mechanisms exist to provide the programmer with the ability to create new data types and operations on that type:

1. *Structured data.* Virtually all languages have included features for creating complex data objects out of the elementary data objects defined by the language designers. Arrays, lists, and sets are ways to create homogeneous collections of objects. Records are a mechanism for creating nonhomogeneous collections of data objects.

2. *Subprograms.* The programmer could create subprograms that perform the functionality of a new type; however, correct use of the new type is the responsibility of the programmer with little automated support provided by the programming language.

3. *Type declarations.* The language includes the ability to define new types and operations on that type. The concept of *abstract data types* (Section 6.2) is available in languages like C and Ada for creating new programmer-defined types.

4. *Inheritance.* The concepts of object-oriented programming and inheritance greatly expand the ability of the programmer to create new types, build operations to use those types, and have the programming language detect improper uses of the type. We cover inheritance separately in chapter 7.

6.1 STRUCTURED DATA TYPES

A data structure is a data object that contains other data objects as its elements or components. In the preceding chapter, the concepts of data object and data type are considered in the simple setting of elementary data types. In this section, the same issues are taken up again in the more complex setting of data structures. The important data types of arrays, records, stacks, lists, and sets are considered.

6.1.1 Structured Data Objects and Data Types

A data object that is constructed as an aggregate of other data objects, called *components,* is termed a structured data object or *data structure.* A component may be elementary or it may be another data structure (e.g., a component of an array may be a number or it may be a record, character string, or another array).

Many of the issues and concepts surrounding data structures in programming languages are the same as for elementary data objects and have been treated. As with elementary data objects, some are programmer defined and others are system defined during program execution. The bindings of data structures to values, names, and locations are important and somewhat more complex in this setting.

With structured data, the specification and implementation of structural information become a central problem: how to indicate the component data objects of a data structure and their relationships in such a way that selection of a component from the structure is straightforward. Second, many operations on data structures bring up storage management issues that are not present for elementary data objects.

6.1.2 Specification of Data Structure Types

The major attributes for specifying data structures include the following:

1. *Number of components.* A data structure may be of *fixed size* if the number of components is invariant during its lifetime or of *variable size* if the number of components changes dynamically. Variable-size data structure types usually define operations that insert and delete components from structures. *Arrays* and *records* are common examples of fixed-size data structure types; *stacks, lists, sets, tables,* and *files* are examples of variable-size types. Variable-size data objects often use a *pointer* data type that allows fixed-size data objects to be linked together explicitly by the programmer.

2. *Type of each component.* A data structure is *homogeneous* if all its components are of the same type. It is *heterogeneous* if its components are of different types. Arrays, sets, and files are usually homogeneous, whereas records and lists are usually heterogeneous.

3. *Names to be used for selecting components.* A data structure type needs a *selection* mechanism for identifying individual components of the data structure. For an array, the name of an individual component may be an integer subscript or sequence of subscripts; for a table, the name may be a programmer-defined identifier; for a record, the name is usually a programmer-defined identifier. Some data structure types such as stacks and files allow access to only a particular component (e.g., the top or current component) at any time, but operations are provided to change the component that is currently accessible.

4. *Maximum number of components.* For a variable-size data structure such as a stack, a maximum size for the structure in terms of number of components may be specified.

5. *Organization of the components.* The most common organization is a simple linear sequence of components. Vectors (one-dimensional arrays), records, stacks, lists, and files are data structures with this organization. Array, record, and list types, however, are usually extended to multidimensional forms: multidimensional arrays, records whose components are records, and lists whose components are lists. These extended forms may be treated as separate types or simply as the basic sequential type in which the components are data structures of similar type. For example, a two-dimensional array (matrix) may be considered as a separate type (as in FORTRAN's $A(i, j)$) or as a vector of vectors (as in C's $A[i][j]$)—a vector in which the components (the rows or columns) are vectors. Records also may include variants: alternative sets of components of which only one is included in each data object of that type.

Operations on Data Structures

Specification of the domain and range of operations on data structure types may be given in much the same manner as for elementary types. Some new classes of operations are of particular importance:

1. *Component selection operations.* Processing of data structures often proceeds by retrieving each component of the structure. Two types of *selection operations* access components of a data structure and make them available for processing by other operations: *random selection,* in which an arbitrary component of the data structure is accessed, and *sequential selection,* in which components are selected in a predetermined order. For example, in processing a vector, the subscripting operation selects a component at random (e.g., $V[4]$), and subscripting combined with a **for** or **while** loop is used to select a sequence of components— as in

   for I := 1 **to** 10 **do** ... V[I] ...;

2. *Whole-data structure operations.* Operations may take entire data structures as arguments and produce new data structures as results. Most languages provide a limited set of such whole-data structure operations (e.g., addition of two arrays, assignment of one record to another, or a union operation on sets). Languages such as APL and SNOBOL4 provide rich sets of whole-data structure operations, however, so that the programmer need seldom select individual components of data structures for processing.

3. *Insertion/deletion of components.* Operations that change the number of components in a data structure have a major impact on storage representations and storage management for data structures, as discussed in the next section.

4. *Creation/destruction of data structures.* Operations that create and destroy data structures also have a major impact on storage management for data structures.

Selection (or *accessing*) of a component or data value in a data object should be distinguished from the related operation of *referencing,* as discussed in chapter 9. Ordinarily a data object is given a name (e.g., the vector previously named V). When we write $V[4]$ in a program to select the fourth component of V, we actually invoke a two-step sequence composed of a *referencing operation* followed by a *selection operation.* The referencing operation determines the current location of the name V (i.e., its l-value), returning as its result a pointer to the location of the entire vector data object designated by the name V. The selection operation takes the pointer to the vector, together with the subscript 4 of the designated component of the vector, and returns a pointer to the location of that particular component within the vector. Only the selection operation is of concern in this section. Discussion of the referencing operation (which may be far more complex and costly than the selection operation) must await a detailed consideration of the problems of names, scope rules, and referencing environments in chapter 9.

6.1.3 Implementation of Data Structure Types

Implementation considerations for data structure types include the same issues as for elementary types. In addition, two new issues develop that strongly affect the choice of storage representations: efficient selection of components from a data structure, and efficient overall storage management for the language implementation.

Storage Representations

The storage representation for a data structure includes (1) storage for the components of the structure, and (2) an optional *descriptor* that stores some or all of the attributes of the structure. The two basic representations are shown in Figure 6.1:

1. *Sequential representation,* in which the data structure is stored in a single contiguous block of storage that includes both descriptor and components.

2. *Linked representation,* in which the data structure is stored in several noncontiguous blocks of storage, with the blocks linked together through pointers. A *pointer* from Block A to Block B, called a *link,* is represented by storing the address of the first location of Block B in a location reserved for the purpose in Block A.

Sequential representations are used for fixed-size structures and sometimes for homogeneous variable-size structures such as character strings or stacks. Linked representations are commonly used for variable-size structures such as lists. Several

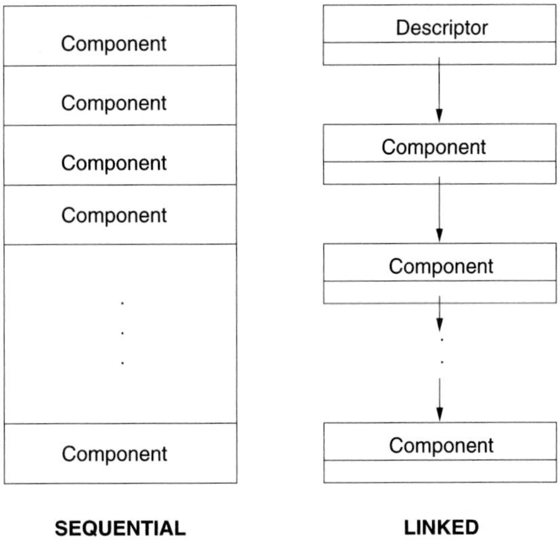

Figure 6.1. Storage representations for linear data structures.

different varieties of sequential and linked representations are seen in subsequent sections.

Memories in general are structured simply as a sequence of bytes. Hardware operations for accessing components of data structures are usually lacking beyond the provision of simple index registers, base registers, and indexing operations that allow efficient access to vectors stored sequentially in memory. Most hardware lacks provisions for data structure descriptors, manipulation of linked representations, storage management for data structures, and easy manipulation of external files. Thus, data structures and operations that work with data structures must usually be software simulated in the programming language's virtual computer implementation, in contrast to elementary data types, where direct hardware-supported storage representations and operations are common.

Implementation of Operations on Data Structures

Component selection is of primary importance in the implementation of most data structures. Efficiency of both random-selection and sequential-selection operations is needed. For example, for Vector A, selection of component $A[I]$ must be efficient. It is also desirable to step through the array sequentially, selecting $A[1]$, $A[2], \ldots$ more efficiently than simply as a sequence of random selections. These two basic types of component selection are implemented differently for sequential and linked storage representations.

Sequential representation. Random selection of a component often involves a *base-address-plus-offset* calculation using an *accessing formula.* The relative location of the selected component within the sequential block is called its *offset.* The starting location of the entire block is the *base address.* The accessing formula, given the name or subscript of the desired component (e.g., the integer subscripts of an array component), specifies how to compute the offset of the component. The offset is then added to the base address to get the actual location in memory of the selected component, as shown in Figure 6.2. For example, in the C array *char* $A[10]$, storage for A is arranged sequentially as $A[0]$, $A[1], \ldots, A[9]$. The address of $A[1]$ will be the base address of the array A (i.e., the l-value of array element $A[0]$) with an offset of 1, or, in general, for C *char* arrays, the address of $A[I]$ will be $lvalue(A)+I$. Note that this calculation may be very efficient; if constant subscripts are used, then the translator can calculate the accessing formula during compile time and generate code to directly access the component.

For a homogeneous structure such as an array that is stored sequentially, selection of a sequence of components from the structure is possible by these steps:

1. To select the first component of the sequence, use the base-address-plus-offset calculation described earlier.

2. To advance to the next component in the sequence, add the size of the current component to the location of the current component. For a homogeneous structure, the size of each component is the same, and thus each component in the sequence is found by adding a constant value to the location of the preceding component.

Linked representation. Random selection of a component from a linked structure involves following a chain of pointers from the first block of storage in the structure to the desired component. For this selection algorithm, the position of the link pointer within each component block must be known. Selection of a sequence of components proceeds by selecting the first component and then following the link pointer from the current component to the next component for each subsequent selection.

Data structure representations are sometimes extended to include system-defined structures that allow efficient component selection. For example, random selection of components of an ordinary sequential file is difficult unless an index is added to the storage representation, as described in Section 5.3.3. Hash-coded tables for set storage are another example.

Storage Management and Data Structures

The lifetime of any data object begins when the binding of the object to a particular storage location is made (i.e., when a block [or blocks] of storage is allocated and the storage representation for the data object is initialized). The lifetime ends when

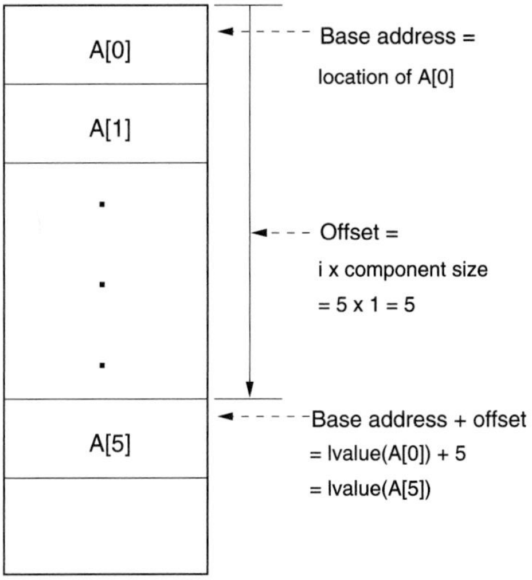

Figure 6.2. Accessing components in a C char array.

this binding of object to storage block is dissolved. For a data structure of variable size, individual components of the structure have their own lifetimes, which are determined by the time at which they are created and inserted into the structure and by the time at which they are deleted from the structure.

At the time that a data object is created (i.e., at the start of its lifetime), an *access path* to the data object must also be created so that the data object can be accessed by operations in the program. Creation of an access path is accomplished either through association of the data object with an identifier, its *name,* in some referencing environment (see chapter 9) or through storage of a pointer to the structure in some other existing, already accessible structure. In the latter case, the data object becomes a component of the older structure.

During the lifetime of a data object, additional access paths to it may be created (e.g., by passing it as an argument to a subprogram or creating new pointers to it). Access paths may also be destroyed in various ways (e.g., by assigning a new value to a pointer variable or by return from a subprogram), with the consequent loss of its referencing environment. Thus, at any point during the lifetime of a data object, several access paths to it may exist.

Two central problems in storage management arise because of the interplay between the lifetime of a data object and the access paths to it that exist:

1. *Garbage.* When all access paths to a data object are destroyed but the data object continues to exist, the data object is said to be *garbage.* The data object can no longer be accessed from other parts of the program, so it is of no further use. However, the binding of data object to storage location has

not been broken, so the storage is not available for reuse.

2. *Dangling references.* A *dangling reference* is an access path that continues to exist after the lifetime of the associated data object. An access path ordinarily leads to the location of a data object (i.e., to the beginning of the block of storage for the object). At the end of the lifetime of the object, this block of storage is recovered for reallocation at some later point to another data object. However, the recovery of the storage block does not necessarily destroy the existing access paths to the block, and thus they may continue to exist as dangling references.

Dangling references are a particularly serious problem for storage management because they may compromise the integrity of the entire run-time structure during program execution. For example, an assignment to a nonexistent data object via a dangling reference can modify storage already allocated to another data object of an entirely different type (thus violating the security of the type-checking structure). Or it can modify housekeeping data (such as a link to a free space list) that has been stored there temporarily by the storage management system (thus destroying the integrity of the storage management system).

Garbage is a less serious, but still troublesome, problem. A data object that has become garbage ties up storage that might otherwise be reallocated for another purpose. Because storage is finite, even in large megabyte machines, a buildup of garbage can force the program to terminate prematurely because of insufficient memory in which to execute. Storage management structures for dealing with garbage and dangling references are treated in chapter 10.

6.1.4 Declarations and Type Checking for Data Structures

The basic concepts and concerns surrounding declarations and type checking for data structures are similar to those discussed for elementary data objects. However, structures are ordinarily more complex because there are more attributes to specify. For example, the C declaration

float A[20];

at the beginning of a subprogram P specifies the following attributes of Array A:

1. Data type is an array.
2. Number of dimensions is one.
3. Number of components is 20.
4. Subscripts naming the rows are the integers from 0 to 19.
6. Data type of each component is float.

Declaration of these attributes allows a sequential storage representation for A and the appropriate accessing formula for selecting any component $A[I]$ of A to be determined at compile time, as described in the next section, despite that A is not created until entry to subprogram P at run time. Without the declaration, the attributes of A would have to be determined dynamically at run time, with the result that the storage representation and component accessing would be much less efficient.

Type checking is somewhat more complex for data structures because component selection operations must be taken into account. There are two main problems:

1. *Existence of a selected component.* The arguments to a selection operation may be of the right types, but the component designated may not exist in the data structure. For example, a subscripting operation that selects a component from an array may receive a subscript that is out of bounds for the particular array (i.e., that produces an invalid l-value for the array component). This is not a type-checking problem provided that the selection operation fails gracefully by noting the error and raising an exception (e.g., a subscript range error). However, if run-time type checking is disabled for efficiency and the exception is not raised, the result of a selection operation is almost always used immediately as an argument by some other operation. If the selection operation produces an incorrect l-value, the effect is similar to a type-checking error. The operation receiving the result is given an invalid argument (the location of a block of storage that may contain data of the wrong type, executable code, etc.). Component-selection operations that use an accessing formula to compute the offset of the selected component within a sequential block are particularly prone to this sort of error; run-time checking is often required to determine whether the selected component exists before the formula is used to determine its precise l-value.

2. *Type of a selected component.* A selection sequence may define a complex path through a data structure to the desired component. For example, the C:

   A[2][3].link -> item

   selects the contents of the component named item in the record reached via the pointer contained in the component named link of the record that is the component in Row 2 and Column 3 of Array A. To perform static type checking, it must be possible to determine at compile time the type of the component selected by any valid composite selector of this sort. As noted earlier, it cannot be assumed in general that the selected component exists when needed at run time. Instead, static type checking only guarantees that if the component does exist, then it is of the right type.

6.1.5 Vectors and Arrays

Vectors and arrays are the most common types of data structures in programming languages. A *vector* is a data structure composed of a fixed number of components of the same type organized as a simple linear sequence. A component of a vector is selected by giving its *subscript,* an integer (or enumeration value) indicating the position of the component in the sequence. A vector is also termed a *one-dimensional array* or *linear array.* A *two-dimensional array,* or *matrix,* has its components organized into a rectangular grid of rows and columns. Both a row subscript and a column subscript are needed to select a component of a matrix. Multidimensional arrays of three or more dimensions are defined in a similar manner.

Vectors

The attributes of a vector are as follows:

1. *Number of components,* usually indicated implicitly by giving a sequence of subscript ranges, one for each dimension.
2. *Data type of each component,* which is a single data type, because the components are all of the same type.
3. *Subscript to be used to select each component,* usually given as a range of integers, with the first integer designating the first component, the second designating the second component, and so on. This may be either a range of values as $-5..5$ or an upper bound with an implied lower bound, as $A(10)$.

A typical declaration for a vector is the Pascal declaration

V: **array** [-5 .. 5] **of** real;

which defines a vector of 11 components, each a real number, where the components are selected by the subscripts, -5, -4, ... 5. C declarations are simpler:

float a[10];

declares a C array of 10 components with subscripts ranging from 0 to 9.

In languages that allow for a range of subscript values, the subscript range need not begin at 1 as demonstrated with the previous Pascal array V. The subscript range need not even be a subrange of integers; it may be any enumeration (or a subsequence of an enumeration)—for example,

type class = (Fresh,Soph,Junior,Senior);
var ClassAverage: **array** [class] **of** real;

Operations on vectors. The operation that selects a component from a vector is called *subscripting*; it is usually written as the vector name followed by the subscript of the component to be selected (e.g., $V[2]$ or $ClassAverage[Soph]$). However, the subscript may generally be a computed value, in which case an expression may be given that computes the subscript (e.g., $V[I+2]$). As we discussed previously, the subscripting operation returns the l-value or location of the relevant data object.

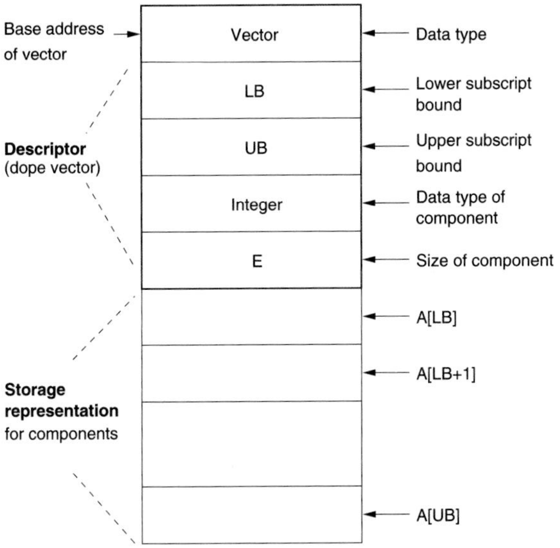

Figure 6.3. Full descriptor representation of Vector A.

Accessing its value (its r-value), given the location, is then a simple operation that may follow if the r-value rather than the location is required.

Other operations on vectors include operations to create and destroy vectors, assignment to components of a vector, and operations that perform arithmetic operations on pairs of vectors of the same size, such as addition of two vectors (add corresponding components). Because vectors are of fixed size, insertion and deletion of components are not allowed; only the value of a component may be modified. Most languages provide only a limited set of such operations, but APL contains a large set that allows vectors to be decomposed and new vectors to be constructed in quite general ways.

Implementation. The homogeneity of components and fixed size of a vector make storage and accessing of individual components straightforward. Homogeneity implies that the size and structure of each component is the same, and fixed size implies that the number and position of each component of a vector are invariant throughout its lifetime. A sequential storage representation is appropriate, as shown in Figure 6.3, where components are stored sequentially. A descriptor may also be included to store some or all of the attributes of the vector, especially if all such information is not known until execution time. The upper and lower bounds of the subscript range, not needed for accessing components, are commonly stored in the descriptor if range checking for computed subscript values is required. The other attributes often are not stored in the descriptor at run time; they are needed only during translation for type checking and for setting up the storage representation.

Beginning at the initial component, the Ith component can be addressed by skipping $I - 1$ components. If E is the size of each component, then we must skip $(I - 1) \times E$ memory locations. If LB is the lower bound on the subscript range, then the number of such components to skip is $I - LB$, or $(I - LB) \times E$ memory locations. If the first element of the vector begins at location α, we get the *accessing formula* for the l-value of a vector component:

$$lvalue(A[I]) = \alpha + (I - LB) \times E$$

This can be rewritten as

$$lvalue(A[I]) = (\alpha - LB \times E) + (I \times E)$$

Note that once storage for the vector is allocated, $(\alpha - LB \times E)$ is a constant (call it K) and the accessing formula reduces to

$$lvalue(A[I]) = K + I \times E$$

For languages like FORTRAN, K is a constant and can be computed at translation time. This makes vector accessing quite fast. Even in languages like Pascal, where each argument of K can be variable, it need be computed only once when the storage for the vector is allocated. Hence, even in Pascal, array accessing is efficient. Because the size of each component (E) is known at translation time, if the value of subscript I is also known to the translator (e.g., $A[2]$), then the entire accessing formula reduces to a compile-time value. Note that, in C *char* arrays, E is 1; because LB is always 0, the equivalent C accessing formula reduces to the extremely efficient

$$lvalue(A[I]) = \alpha + I$$

Virtual origin. Let us now address the element with subscript 0 of our vector. Our accessing formula gives us

$$\begin{aligned} lvalue(A[0]) &= (\alpha - LB \times E) + (0 \times E) \\ &= (\alpha - LB \times E) \\ &= K \end{aligned}$$

K represents the address that the element 0 of the vector would occupy *if it existed.* Because the zeroth element may not be part of the array (because the array may have a lower bound greater than 0), this address is called the *virtual origin* (VO). This then gives an algorithm for building vectors and generating the accessing formula:

1. *On creation of vector storage:* Allocate storage for N components of the vector of size E and descriptor of size D. (Allocate $D + N \times E$ memory locations.) Call α the address where the first vector element is stored.

2. Compute the virtual origin $VO = \alpha - LB \times E$.

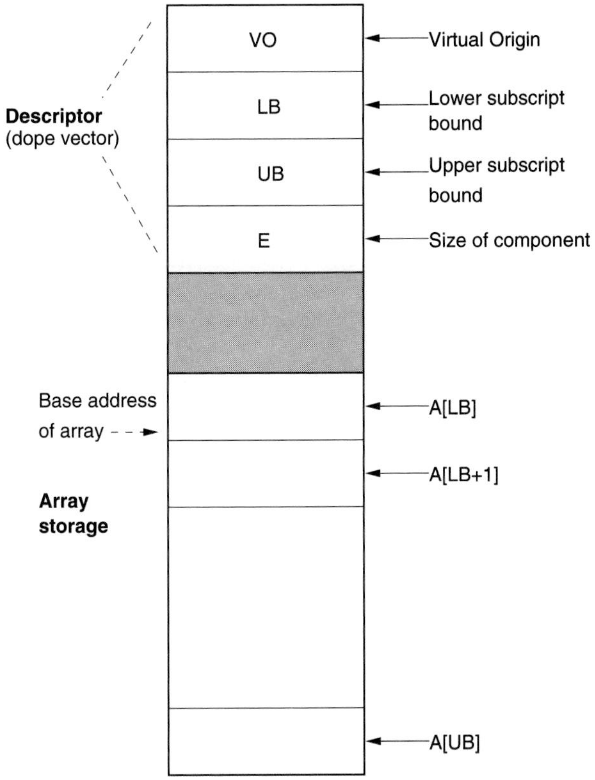

Figure 6.4. Separate storage areas for descriptor and components.

3. *On accessing a vector component:* The l-value of any component $A[I]$ is computed as

$$lvalue(A[I]) = VO + I \times E$$

The prior formula assumes that the value of I is known to be a valid subscript for A. To check for a subscript range error, the test $LB \leq I \leq UB$ must precede use of the accessing formula, and the values of both LB and UB must be present in the run-time descriptor. In general, the exact variation of the accessing calculation (and range checking) that is most efficient depends on the particular hardware configuration and hardware operations available. It is this range test, which ensures that, even if the subscript I is not within the range $LB \leq I \leq UB$, storage can never be accessed as an l-value, which does not represent a valid subscript.

Note that the prior accessing formula uses the virtual origin to determine where a given array element is located. If the virtual origin is stored in the array descriptor, then the actual array need not be contiguous with its descriptor (Figure 6.4). This is the usual case where descriptors for array parameters may be passed to subprograms and the actual array storage stored elsewhere. (Note that the type of the descriptor and data type of component are omitted from Figure 6.4. For languages like C and Pascal, this information is bound at translation time, and there is no need to carry this information in the run-time descriptor.)

Packed- and unpacked-storage representations. The accessing formula given earlier presumes that the size, E, of each component is an integral number of addressable storage units (words or bytes). For example, if the basic unit of addressable storage in the computer is a word, then each component is presumed to fill one word, two words, and so on, as appropriate for the declared component type. If the component type is *Boolean* or *character,* only a small part of a word may be required to store one component, and thus several components might be packed into a single word. A *packed-storage representation* is one in which components of a vector (or other structure) are packed into storage sequentially without regard for placing each component at the beginning of an addressable word (or byte) of storage. A packed-storage representation may allow substantial savings in the amount of storage required for a vector. Unfortunately, access to a component of a packed structure is usually much more expensive because the simple accessing formula above cannot be used. Instead, a more complex series of calculations is required to access the memory word that contains the component.

Because of the cost of a packed vector's access, vectors are often stored in *unpacked* form; each component is stored beginning at the boundary of an addressable unit of storage. Accessing is then possible, but at a cost in lost storage. However, with the growth of byte-addressable machines and the subsequent decline of word-addressable machines, this is rarely an issue in most systems today.

Whole-vector operations. Operations that work an entire vector as a unit are readily implemented using the sequential storage representation for vectors. Assignment of one vector to another with the same attributes is implemented by simply copying the contents of the storage block representing the first into the storage block representing the second. (The descriptors for each vector do not have to be copied because they do not change.) Arithmetic operations on vectors, or specialized operations such as inner product, are implemented as loops that process the elements of the vectors in sequence.

A major implementation problem with such whole-vector operations concerns the storage required for the result. The result of adding two vectors of 100 components each is a vector of 100 components. Storage must be allocated temporarily to store the r-value of this result unless it is immediately assigned to an existing l-value location. If a program involves many whole-vector operations, a substantial amount of storage for temporary results may be required, and the management of this temporary storage may increase the complexity and cost of program execution.

Multidimensional Arrays

A vector is a one-dimensional array; a matrix composed of rows and columns of components is a two-dimensional array; a three-dimensional array is composed of planes of rows and columns; similarly, arrays of any number of dimensions may be constructed from arrays of fewer dimensions. The storage representation and accessing formula for vectors generalize readily to multidimensional arrays.

Specification and syntax. A multidimensional array differs from a vector in its attributes only in that a subscript range for each dimension is required, as in the Pascal declaration

B: **array** [1 .. 10,-5 .. 5] **of** real;

Selection of a component requires that one subscript be given for each dimension (e.g., $B[2,4]$).

Implementation. A matrix is conveniently implemented by considering it as a vector of vectors; a three-dimensional array is a vector whose elements are vectors of vectors, and so on. Note that all the subvectors must have the same number of elements of the same type.

Whether a matrix is viewed as a column of rows or a row of columns is important in some contexts (most often, where a matrix is to be passed as an argument to a subprogram written in another language). Most common is the column-of-rows structure in which the matrix is considered as a vector in which each element is a subvector representing one row of the original matrix. This representation is known as *row-major order.* In general, an array of any number of dimensions is organized in row-major order when the array is first divided into a vector of subvectors for each element in the range of the first subscript, then each of these subvectors is subdivided into subsubvectors for each element in the range of the second subscript, and so on. *Column-major order* is the representation in which the matrix is treated as a single row of columns.

The storage representation for a multidimensional array follows directly from that for a vector. For a matrix, we store the data objects in the first row (assuming row-major order), followed by the data objects in the second row, and so on. The result is a single sequential block of memory containing all the components of the array in sequence. The descriptor for the array is the same as that for a vector, except that an upper and a lower bound for the subscript range of each dimension are needed. Figure 6.5 illustrates this storage representation for a matrix.

The subscripting operation, using an accessing formula to compute the offset of a component from the base address of the array, is similar to that for vectors: To find the l-value of $A[I,J]$, first determine the number of rows to skip over, $(I-LB_1)$, multiply by the length of a row to get the location of the start of the Ith row, and then find the location of the Jth component in that row, as for a vector. Thus, if A is a matrix with M rows and N columns and A is stored in row-major order, the

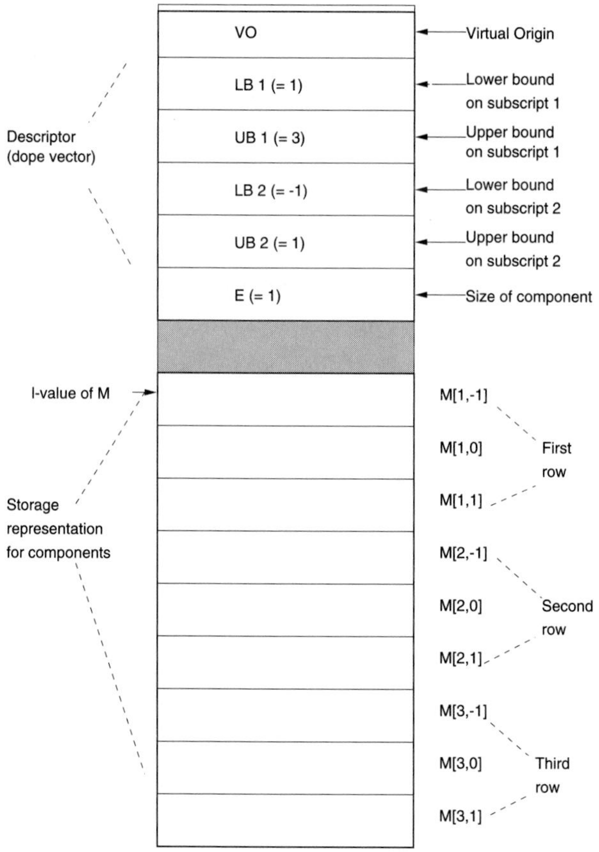

Figure 6.5. Storage representation for two-dimensional array.

location of element $A[I, J]$ is given by

$$lvalue(A[I,J]) = \alpha + (I - LB_1) \times S + (J - LB_2) \times E$$

where

$$\begin{aligned} \alpha &= \text{base address} \\ S &= \text{length of a row} = (UB_2 - LB_2 + 1) \times E \\ LB_1 &= \text{lower bound on first subscript} \\ LB_2, UB_2 &= \text{lower and upper bounds on the second subscript} \end{aligned}$$

Collecting constant terms, this simplifies to

$$\begin{aligned} &S = (UB_2 - LB_2 + 1) \times E \\ &VO = \alpha - LB_1 \times S - LB_2 \times E \\ &lvalue(A[I,J]) = VO + I \times S + J \times E \end{aligned}$$

Similar to the vector case, E is the size of each component and S is the size of each row of the matrix. This allows VO to be easily computed.

Note that VO, S, α, and E are fixed when the array is created and thus need be computed only once and stored. VO, as in the vector case, is the virtual origin and represents the location for $A[0,0]$, if it would exist in the array. The worst-case computation necessary on each access then becomes

$$lvalue(A[I,J]) = VO + I \times S + J \times E$$

Higher dimensionality arrays. The generalization of these formulas to higher dimensions is straightforward. The following general algorithm can be used to allocate descriptors on array creation and for accessing array elements.

Assume we have an array $A[L_1 : U_1, \ldots, L_n : U_n]$ of n dimensions where L_i are the lower bounds, U_i are the upper bounds, and e is the size of each array element. The array will be stored beginning at address α.

- *Computation of multipliers:* Each multiplier m_i is computed as follows:
  $m_n = e$
  For each $i = n-1$ down to 1, compute: $m_i = (U_{i+1} - L_{i+1} + 1) \times m_{i+1}$.
- *Computation of virtual origin:*
  $VO = \alpha - \Sigma_{i=1}^{n}(L_i \times m_i)$
  The multipliers m_i and virtual origin VO can be stored in the run-time descriptor for the array.
- *Address of array element:* The address of element $A[s_1, \ldots, s_n]$ is given by $VO + \Sigma_{i=1}^{n}(s_i \times m_i)$.

Slices

Specification. A *slice* is a substructure of an array that is an array. Figure 6.6 gives some examples, Figure 6.6(a) represents Column 2 of a three-column matrix, Figure 6.6(b) represents Row 3 of a 4-row matrix, and Figure 6.6(c) represents the third plane of a three-dimensional array.

PL/I was one of the earliest languages to implement slices. If array A is declared $A(4,3)$, then the slice in Figure 6.6(a) is referenced as $A(*,2)$, meaning that subscript 1 (the row) ranges from 1 to 4. Similarly, the other two slices are specified as $B(3,*)$ and $C(3,*,*)$. Slices may be passed as arguments to subprograms.

FORTRAN permits programmers to pass parts of one array as parameters to subprograms. Because FORTRAN uses column-major ordering, passing the element $A(1,3)$ to vector parameter B sets up the correspondence $A(1,3)$ with $B(1)$, $A(2,3)$ with $B(2)$, $A(3,3)$ with $B(3)$, and so on. This provides an efficient way for programmers to develop matrix algorithms to manipulate subparts of a given larger matrix. However, this requires the programmer to know about the internal storage mechanisms used by FORTRAN.

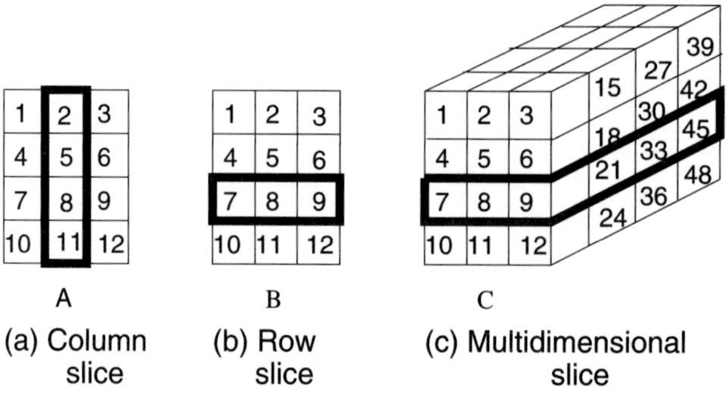

Figure 6.6. Array slices.

Because this design goes against the current philosophy in language design, FORTRAN 90 introduced the concept of slices. The arrays in Figure 6.6 can be specified in FORTRAN 90 as $A(1:4, 2)$, $B(3, 1:3)$, and $C(3, 1:3, 1:4)$.

Implementation. The use of descriptors permits an efficient implementation of a slice. For example, the 3-by-4 array A can be described by the descriptor

VO	α
LB 1	1
UB 1	4
Multiplier 1	3
LB 2	1
UB 2	3
Multiplier 2	1

The address of $A(I, J)$, given by the formula at the end of the last section, is simply:

$$lvalue(A[I, J]) = VO + I \times 3 + J \times 1.$$

Note that, in this case, $Multiplier$ 2, which represents the size of the data object, is also the distance between successive elements of the array. In this case, the elements are contiguous. However, this need not be true. A slice has the property that all elements of one dimension may not be contiguous, but are equally spaced. Therefore, we can represent the slice $A(*, 2)$ as a descriptor based on the descriptor for A as follows:

VO	$\alpha - 3$
LB 1	1
UB 1	4
Multiplier 1	3

which represents a one-dimensional vector of length 4, starting one location after A, with each element three locations apart. We can represent slices for B and C (which returns a two-dimensional descriptor) in an analogous manner.

Associative Arrays

The essential feature of arrays, so far, is the method for accessing a particular element by using an enumerated data type called the *subscript.* Array elements are ordered by this subscript, and moving through the values of the subscript allows one to access each array element.

In some applications, there is a desire to access information by name without having a predefined ordering or enumeration of the appropriate subscripts. For example, a class roster can be given by two arrays, where $name[i]$ is the student's name and $grade[i]$ is the grade for student i. In this case, there is an implied ordering using the integer subscript i.

An alternative method is to use the name as the index. Because the sequence of names (i.e., strings of letters) is essentially infinite, there is no implied enumeration that is feasible. Instead, the set of names are used as the enumeration set; if a new name is added, this enumeration is increased. Such an array is called an *associative array.* They were available in SNOBOL4 as a **table** and are an important feature in process languages like Perl.

In Perl, an associative array is created with the % operator. Thus,

```
%ClassList = ( "Michelle", 'A', "Doris", 'B', "Michael", 'D' );
```

creates a three-element associative array. The first members of each pair are the *keys*, and the second members are the *values.* The array is accessed as in the following examples:

```
$ClassList{'Michelle'}      # has the value "A".
@y=%ClassList;             # Make array y a 6-element enumeration array
for ($i=0; $i<6; $i++){print "I=, $i, $y[$i]\n;"};
            I=, 0, Doris
            I=, 1, B
            I=, 2, Michael
            I=, 3, D
            I=, 4, Michelle
            I=, 5, A
```

This last example gives a clue to the implementation of associative arrays. Although the initial order was given as Michelle, Doris, and Michael, the array is stored in alphabetical order by key. This allows for an efficient binary search of the keys to find a match when the array is accessed.

6.1.6 Records

A data structure composed of a fixed number of components of different types is usually termed a *record.*

Specification and syntax. Both records and vectors are forms of fixed-length linear data structures, but records differ in two ways:

1. The components of records may be *heterogeneous*, of mixed data types, rather than homogeneous.
2. The components of records are named with *symbolic names* (identifiers), rather than indexed with subscripts.

The C syntax for a record declaration (**struct** in C) is fairly typical:

```
struct EmployeeType
        {int ID;
        int Age;
        float SALARY;
        char Dept;
        } Employee;
```

The declaration defines a record of type *EmployeeType* consisting of four components of types: *integer*, *integer*, *real*, and *character*, with component names *ID*, *Age*, *SALARY*, and *Dept*, respectively. *Employee* is declared to be a variable of type *EmployeeType.* (Subsequent declarations of other variables of type *EmployeeType* do not need to give the record structure for *EmployeeType.*) To select a component of the record, one writes in C,

```
Employee.ID
Employee.SALARY
```

The attributes of a record are seen in the prior declaration:

1. The number of components
2. The data type of each component
3. The selector used to name each component

The components of a record are often called *fields,* and the component names then are the *field names.* Records are sometimes called *structures* (as in C).

Component selection is the basic operation on a record, as in the selection *Employee.SALARY*. This operation corresponds to the subscripting operation for arrays, but with one crucial difference: The subscript here is always a *literal component name;* it is never a computed value. For example, the prior selection of the third component of the record Employee corresponds to the selection VECT[3] of the third component of a vector, but there is no selection for records that corresponds to *VECT*[*I*], where the value of *I* is computed.

Operations on entire records are usually few. Most commonly assignment of records of identical structure is provided, as in

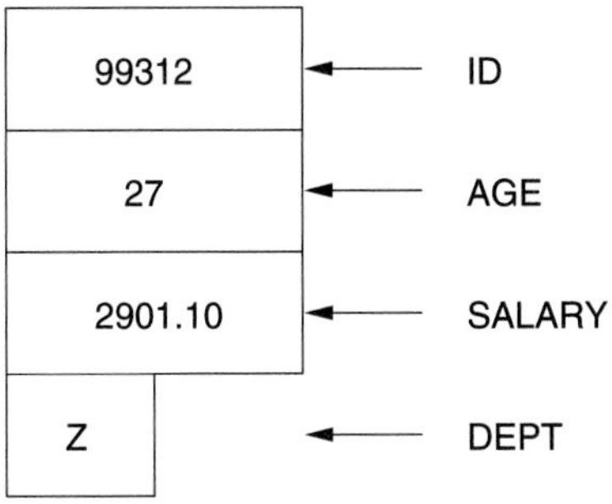

Figure 6.7. Storage representation for struct Employee.

struct EmployeeType INPUTREC;
...
Employee = INPUTREC

where $INPUTREC$ has the same attributes as *Employee*. The correspondence of component names between records is also made the basis for assignment in COBOL and PL/I—for example, in the COBOL

MOVE CORRESPONDING INPUTREC TO EMPLOYEE

which assigns each component of $INPUTREC$ to the corresponding component of $EMPLOYEE$, where corresponding components must have the same name and data type but need not appear in the same order in each record.

Implementation. The storage representation for a record consists of a single sequential block of memory in which the components are stored in sequence (Figure 6.7). Individual components may need descriptors to indicate their data type or other attributes, but ordinarily no run-time descriptor for the record is required.

Component selection is easily implemented because subscripts (field names) are known during translation rather than being computed during execution. The declaration for the record also allows the size of each component and its position within the storage block to be determined during translation. As a result, the *offset* of any component may be computed during translation. The basic accessing formula used to compute the location of the Ith component is

$$lvalue(R.I) = \alpha + \sum_{j=1}^{I-1}(size\ of\ R.j)$$

where α is the base address of the storage block representing R and R.j is the jth component. The summation is necessary because of the possibly differing sizes of each component. However, the summation may always be computed during translation to give the offset, K_I, for the Ith component, so that during execution only the base address for the storage block need be added:

$$lvalue(R.I) = \alpha + K_I$$

With some data types, storage must begin on specific address boundaries. For example, integers may have to begin on a word boundary, which on a byte-addressable machine is an address divisible by 4 (i.e., binary address ends in 00). Therefore, the various pieces may not fit together. For example, in the C statement

```
struct EmployeeDivision
    { char Division;
    int IdNumber; } Employee
```

IdNumber must begin on a word boundary, and three bytes between *Division* and *IdNumber* are unused and are considered *padding.* The storage representation would be as if the following were declared:

```
struct EmployeeDivision
    {char Division;
    char UnusedPadding[3];
    int IdNumber; } Employee
```

The operation of assignment of an entire record to another of identical structure may be implemented as a simple copy of the contents of the storage block representing the first record into the storage block representing the second record. The more complex MOVE CORRESPONDING operation may be implemented as a sequence of assignments of individual components of one record to another.

Records and Arrays with Structured Components

In languages that provide both arrays and records as basic data types, provision is usually made for components of the two types to be intermixed with components of elementary types (and usually of other structured types such as character strings). For example, a vector in which each component is a record is often useful, as in the C declaration

```
struct EmployeeType
        {int ID;
        int Age;
        float SALARY;
        char Dept;
        } Employee[500];
```

which declares a vector of 500 components, each of which is an *EmployeeType* record. A component of such a composite data structure is selected by using a

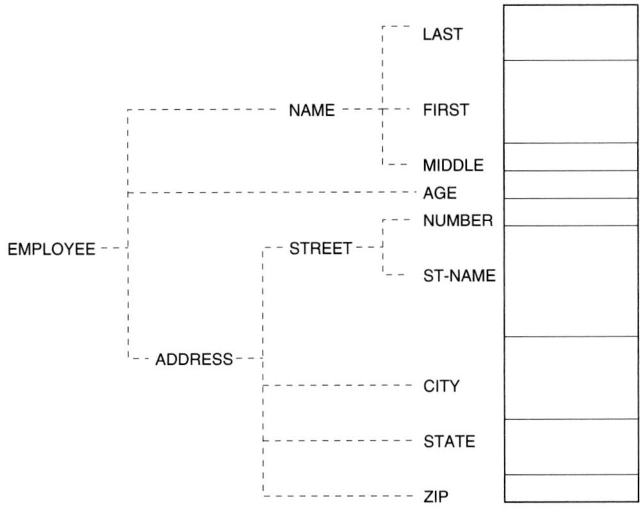

Figure 6.8. Storage representation for multilevel PL/I record.

sequence of selection operations to select first a component of the vector and then a component of the record, as in *Employee*[3].*SALARY*.

A record may also have components that are arrays or other records, leading to records that have a hierarchical structure consisting of a top level of components, some of which may be arrays or records. The components of these second-level components may also be arrays or records. In COBOL and PL/I, this hierarchical organization is indicated syntactically by assigning *level numbers* to specify each new level of components. The PL/I declaration is typical:

```
1 Employee,
    2 Name,
        3 Last CHARACTER(10),
        3 First CHARACTER(15),
        3 Middle CHARACTER(1),
    2 Age FIXED(2),
    2 Address,
        3 Street,
            4 Number FIXED(5),
            4 St-Name CHARACTER(20),
        3 City CHARACTER(15),
        3 State CHARACTER(10),
        3 Zip FIXED(5);
```

This declaration syntax resembles that of an outline, with major headings, subheads, and so on. The data structure resulting from this declaration is composed of a single record *Employee*, whose components are those at Level 2 with names *Name*, *Age*, and *Address*. *Age* is an elementary component (an integer), but *Name* and *Address* are each records, and their components are at Level 3. The component *Street* of record *Address* is a record, and its components are at Level 4.

Implementation. The storage representations for simple vectors and records extend without change to vectors and records whose components are vectors or records. We considered vectors of vectors in Section 6.1.5. A vector of records has the same storage representation as a vector of integers or any other elementary type, except that the storage block representing a component in the larger block representing the vector is the storage block for a record. Thus, a vector of records is stored much as the vector of vectors in Figure 6.5, but with each row replaced by the storage representation of a record. Similarly a record whose components are records (or vectors) retains the same sequential storage representation, but with each component represented by a subblock that may be the representation of an entire record. Figure 6.8 shows the storage representation for the PL/I data structure declared earlier. Selection of components requires only a sequence of selections—starting from the base address of the complete structure and computing an offset to find the location of the first-level component, followed by computation of an offset from this base address to find the second-level component, and so on.

Variant Records

A record may often be used to represent similar, but distinct data, objects—for example, an employee who may be paid either hourly or monthly. It may be useful to have a single record type that has several variants. Such a record ordinarily has one or more components that are common to all variants, and then each variant has, in addition, several other components with names and data types that are unique to that variant. For example, a record containing employee payroll information may have two variants: one for salaried employees paid by the month and one for employees paid by the hour. The Pascal declaration

```
type PayType = (Salaried, Hourly);
var Employee: record
              ID: integer;
              Dept: array [1..3] of char;
              Age: integer;
              case PayClass: PayType of
                 Salaried: (MonthlyRate: real;
                            StartDate: integer);
                 Hourly: (HourRate: real;
                          Reg: integer;
                          Overtime: integer)
              end
```

defines such a variant record. The record always has components *ID*, *Dept*, *Age*, and *PayClass*. When the value of *PayClass* = *Salaried*, then the record also has the components *MonthlyRate* and *StartDate*, whereas if the value of *PayClass* = *Hourly*, then it has components *HourRate*, *Reg*, and *Overtime*. The component *PayClass* is called the *tag* (Pascal) or *discriminant* (Ada) because it serves to indicate which variant of the record exists at a given point during program execution.

The selection operation for components of a variant record is the same as that for an ordinary record. For example, *Employee.MonthlyRate* and *Employee.Reg* select components from the variants defined previously. For ordinary records, each component exists throughout the lifetime of the record, but for a component in a variant, the component may exist at one point during execution (when the tag component has a particular value), may later cease to exist (when the value of the tag changes to indicate a different variant), and later may reappear (if the tag changes back to its original value). Thus, the selection *Employee.Reg* may attempt to select a component during execution that does not exist at that time. This problem of selection of a nonexistent component of a variant record is similar to the subscript range error discussed in the preceding section, and the possible solutions are similar:

1. *Dynamic checking.* The tag component may be checked at run time before the component is accessed to ensure that the tag value indicates that the component exists. If the tag has the proper value, then the component is accessed; if not, then it is a run-time error, and some special exception processing is invoked, much as is done when checking for subscript range errors.

2. *No checking.* The language design may allow variant record definitions without an explicit tag component that may be checked at run time, so that selection of a component of a variant record is presumed to be valid whenever executed. Because of the implementation of variant records, described next, such a selection is always possible. However, if the component does not exist, values in the current variant that does exist may be inadvertently retrieved or overwritten. COBOL, PL/I, and Pascal provide forms of variant records without designated tag fields, and the C *union* declaration does not permit a tag. The implementations of these forms cannot provide checking.

Record types with variants are also commonly known as *union types* because each variant may be considered as a separate class of record data object, and then the overall record type appears as the union of these sets of data objects. If there is no designated tag field (as in the C *union* type), then it is a *free-union* type; if there is, then it is a *discriminated-union* type. The term *discriminated* refers to the fact that it is possible (by checking the tag field) to discriminate the variant class to which each data object of the overall type belongs.

Implementation. Implementation of a variant record is easier than using it correctly. During translation, the amount of storage required for the components of

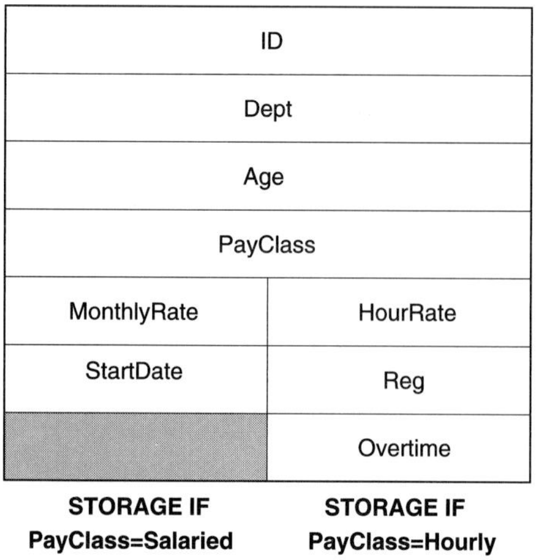

Figure 6.9. Storage representation for variant records.

each variant is determined, and storage is allocated in the record for the *largest* possible variant, as shown in Figure 6.9. Within this storage block, each variant describes a different layout for the block in terms of number and types of components. Because the block is large enough for the largest variant, there is space in the block for any one of the variants at a given time during program execution, but smaller variants may not use some of the allocated storage. The layouts are determined during translation and are used to compute offsets for component selection. During execution, no special descriptor is needed for a variant record because the tag component is considered just another component of the record.

Selection of a component of a variant is identical to selection of a component of an ordinary record, when no checking is to be done. During translation, the offset of the selected component within the storage block is computed; during execution, the offset is added to the base address of the block to determine the location of the component. If the component does not exist, this accessing calculation gives the location where the component *would be stored* if it did exist, but the location instead will contain a value (or part of a value or several values) representing a component of the current variant. An assignment to a component that does not exist, if unchecked, changes the contents of the location accessed. If that location is currently being used as part of a component in the current variant, then unpredictable changes are made in the value of that component (with possibly disastrous results).

If dynamic checking is provided for selection of components of variants, then at run time the base-address-plus-offset calculation to locate the component is the same, but first the value of the tag field must be checked to ensure that the tag indicates that the proper variant currently exists.

6.1.7 Lists

A data structure composed of an ordered sequence of data structures is usually termed a *list.*

Specification and syntax. Lists are similar to vectors in that they consist of an ordered sequence of objects. That is, one may refer to the first member of a list (usually called the *head* of the list), the second member, and so on. However, lists differ from vectors in several important respects:

1. Lists are rarely of fixed length. Lists are often used to represent arbitrary data structures, and typically lists grow and shrink during program execution.
2. Lists are rarely homogeneous. The data type of each member of a list may differ from its neighbor.
3. Languages that use lists typically declare such data implicitly without explicit attributes for list members.

The LISP syntax represents a typical list structure:

$$(FunctionName\ Data_1\ Data_2\ \ldots\ Data_n)$$

LISP executes by applying $FunctionName$ to arguments $Data_1$ through $Data_n$.

Most operations in LISP take list arguments and return list values. For example, *cons* takes two list arguments and returns a list whose first argument is appended to the beginning of the second argument:

$$\text{(cons '(a b c) '(d e f)) = ((a b c) d e f)}$$

This example shows that the result is a list of four members, the first member being the list $(a\ b\ c)$. The four members of the resulting list are not of the same type, the first being a list, whereas the remaining three are primitive elements or atoms.

This example also shows an important characteristic of LISP. All arguments to functions are first evaluated. If the expression were written as

$$\text{(cons (a b c) (d e f))}$$

then LISP would have first tried to evaluate the function a with arguments b and c and then tried to evaluate the function d with arguments e and f. This would probably be an error. The function $(quote\ x)$, or more simply $'x$, just returns the literal value (the l-value) of its argument, thus avoiding the improper evaluation in this case.

ML also provides for lists with the syntax $[a, b, c]$. However, lists in ML are homogeneous, so you can have lists of integers (as in $[1, 2, 3]$) or lists of strings (as in ["abc","def","ghi"]).

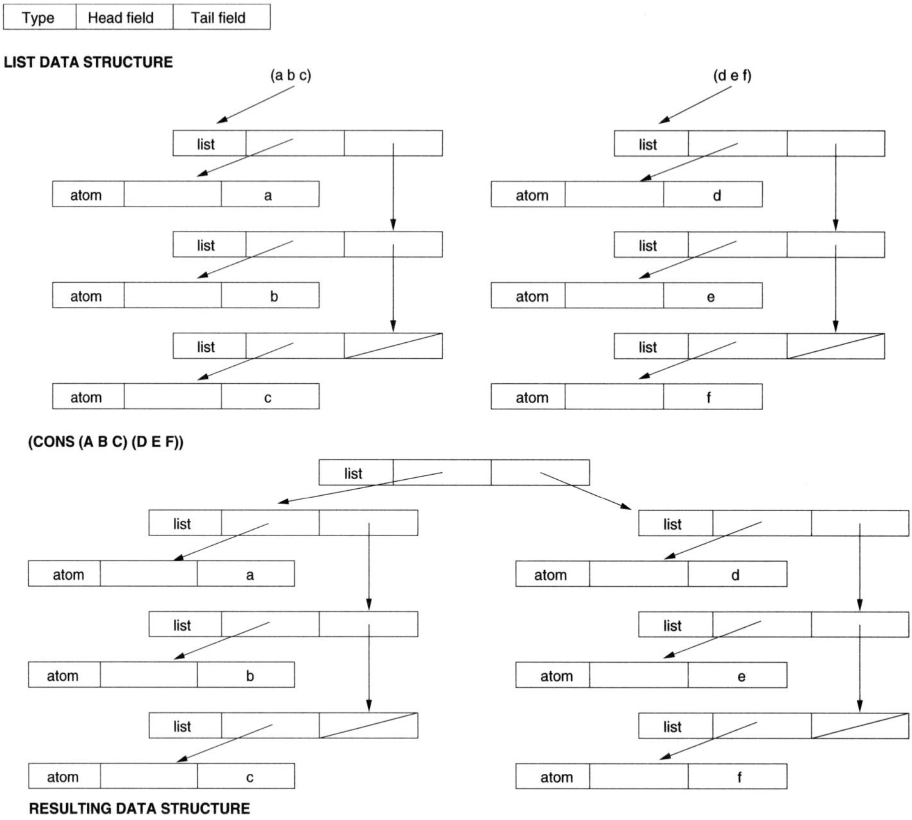

Figure 6.10. Representation of storage for lists.

Implementation. The dynamic nature of most list implementations and the fact that items in a list are rarely homogeneous means that the regular storage management useful for vectors and arrays will not work. In such cases, a *linked-list* storage management organization is typically used. A *list item* is the primitive element and usually consists of a fixed-size data object. For LISP, we usually need three fields of information: a type field and two list pointers. If the type field says atom, then the remaining fields are descriptors describing the atom. If the type field is a list, then the first pointer is the *head* of the list (its first member), whereas the second is the *tail* of the list (its remaining members). Figure 6.10 describes the storage structure for the prior example: $(cons\ '(a\ b\ c)\ '(d\ e\ f)) = ((a\ b\ c)\ d\ e\ f)$. The similarity between the middle and bottom structures in Figure 6.10 shows the efficiency of this implementation for list structures:

1. *cons.* A *cons* or a *join* operation is implemented by creating a new list node and making the head field the first argument of the *cons* and making the tail field the second argument of the *cons*.

2. *head.* The *head* of a list is the contents (r-value) of the head field of the list item.

3. *tail.* The *tail* of a list is the contents of the tail field of the list item.

LISP was initially implemented in the early 1960s on an IBM 704 computer. This was a 36-bit word machine where two addresses of 18 bits could be stored in the one 36-bit register. The upper 18 bits were called the *address register* and the lower 18 bits were called the *decrement register*. Hence, a *head* operation was simply the "contents of the address register" (CAR) and a *tail* operation was simply the "contents of the decrement register" (CDR). CAR and CDR are now ingrained in the folklore of LISP, and LISP purists would never refer to such operations as *head* and *tail*.

Lists are primitive data objects in languages like ML, LISP, and Prolog, but do not appear in the usual compiled languages like C, Pascal, or Ada. The dynamic storage management needed to maintain lists is at odds with the regular efficient storage management often used in the compiled languages. However, we shortly show that programmers using these languages still have access to lists, but must make them programmer-defined data types instead.

Variations on Lists

Variations on the typical list structure appear in some languages:

Stacks and queues. A *stack* is a list in which component selection, insertion, and deletion are restricted to one end. A *queue* is a list in which component selection and deletion are restricted to one end and insertion is restricted to the other end. Both sequential and linked storage representations for stacks and queues are common.

Trees. A list in which the components may be lists as well as elementary data objects is termed a *tree,* provided that each list is only a component of at most one other list. Most of the LISP examples in this book, such as Figure 6.10, are really trees.

Directed graphs. A data structure in which the components may be linked together using arbitrary linkage patterns (rather than just linear sequences of components) is termed a *directed graph.*

Property lists. A *record* with a varying number of components is usually termed a *property list* if the number of components may vary without restriction. (The variant record structure of Pascal allows variation only within a predefined set of alternatives). In a property list, both the component names (field names) and their

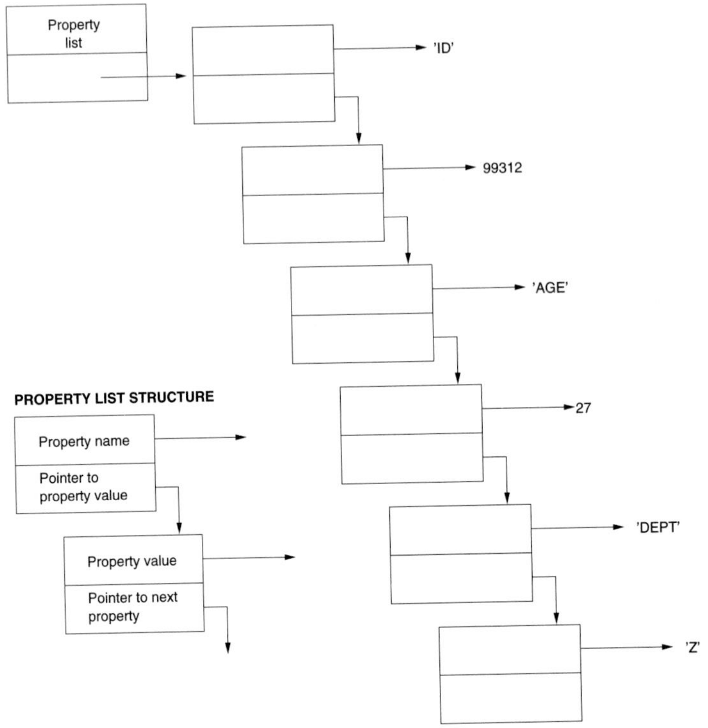

Figure 6.11. Storage representation of property lists.

values must be stored. Each field name is termed a *property name;* the corresponding value of the field is the *property value.* A common representation for a property list is as an ordinary linked list, with the property names and their values alternating in a single long sequence, as illustrated in Figure 6.11. To select a particular property value (e.g., the value for the *Age* property), the list is searched, looking only at the property names, until the desired property is found. The next list component is then the value for that property. When a new property is inserted in the property list, two components are inserted: the property name and its value. Property lists are found under a variety of names in programming languages; in LISP, they are called property lists as well as *tables* (and a mixed sequential and linked representation is sometimes used for their storage). The terms *attribute-value list* and *description list* are also used.

Variable-size data objects are natural to use when the amount of data in a problem is not known in advance. Variable-size data structures instead allow storage to be allocated gradually as needed during program execution.

There are two fundamentally different approaches to these data types in programming languages. In some languages, such as ML and LISP, a list structure, property list, stack, or queue data type is provided directly. It is built into the language, and the language implementation provides a hidden storage management system that automatically manages the allocation and recovery of storage for these structures. In other languages, such as C, Pascal, and Ada, a *pointer* data type is provided, along with facilities for the dynamic allocation of storage explicitly by the programmer, and the programmer builds linked structures, as described in Section 5.3.2.

Stacks, queues, trees, and other types of variable-size data objects are important in many phases of the implementation of a language. For example, a run-time stack is a central system-defined data object in most language implementations (chapter 9), trees are often used to represent the symbol table in a compiler (chapter 3), and queues are often used in the scheduling and synchronization of concurrent subprograms (chapter 9).

6.1.8 Sets

A *set* is a data object containing an *unordered* collection of *distinct* values. In contrast, a list is an ordered collection of values, some of which may be repeated. The following are the basic operations on sets:

1. *Membership.* Is data value X a member of set S (i.e., is $X \in S$)?

2. *Insertion and deletion of single values.* Insert data value X in set S provided it is not already a member of S. Delete data value X from S if a member.

3. *Union, intersection, and difference of sets.* Given two sets, S_1 and S_2, create set S_3 that contains all members of both S_1 and S_2 with duplicates deleted (*union* operation), create S_3 to contain only values that are members of both S_1 and S_2 (*intersection* operation), or create S_3 to contain only values that are in S_1 but not in S_2 (*difference* operation).

Note that accessing of components of a set by subscript or relative position plays no part in set processing.

Implementation. In programming languages, the term *set* is sometimes applied to a data structure representing an *ordered* set. An ordered set is actually a list with duplicate values removed; it requires no special consideration. The unordered set, however, admits two specialized storage representations that merit attention.

Bit-string representation of sets. The bit-string storage representation is appropriate where the size of the underlying universe of values (the values that may appear in set data objects) is known to be small. Suppose that there are N elements in the universe. Order these elements arbitrarily as e_1, e_2, $/ldots$, e_N. A set of elements chosen from this universe may then be represented by a bit string of length N, where the ith bit in the string is a 1 if e_1 is in the set and 0 if not. The bit string represents the *characteristic function* of the set. With this representation, insertion of an element into a set consists of setting the appropriate bit to 1, deletion consists of setting the appropriate bit to 0, and membership is determined simply by interrogating the appropriate bit. The union, intersection, and difference operations on whole sets may be represented by the Boolean operations on bit strings that are usually provided by the hardware: The Boolean *or* of two bit-strings represents union, *and* represents intersection, and the *and* of the first string and the complement of the second represents the difference operation.

The hardware support for bit-string operations, if provided, makes manipulation of the bit-string representation of sets efficient. However, the hardware operations usually apply only to bit strings up to a certain fixed length (e.g., the word length of the central memory). For strings longer than this maximum, software simulation must be used to break up the string into smaller units that can be processed by the hardware.

Hash-coded representation of sets. A common alternative representation for a set is based on the technique of *hash coding* or *scatter storage.* This method may be used when the underlying universe of possible values is large (e.g., when the set contains numbers or character strings). It allows the membership test, insertion, and (with some methods) deletion of values to be performed efficiently. However, union, intersection, and difference operations must be implemented as a sequence of membership tests, insertions, and deletions of individual elements so they are inefficient. To be effective, hash-coding methods also require a substantial allocation of storage. Most commonly, a language does not provide this representation for a set *data type* available to the user, but the language implementation uses this representation for some of the system-defined data required during translation or execution. For example, most LISP implementations use this storage representation for the set called the *object list*, which consists of the names of all the atomic data objects in use by a LISP program during its execution. Almost every compiler uses hash coding to look up names in its symbol table (chapter 3).

In a vector, every subscript designates a unique component that is easily addressable with a simple accessing function. The goal with hash coding is to duplicate this property so that efficient accessing of a component is maintained. However, the problem is that the potential set of valid names is huge compared with the available memory. If we allocate memory, called the *hash table*, at least twice as large as what we expect to use, then hash coding can be very efficient (e.g., if our set will have 1,000 members, then allocate space for 2,000 members). Rather than storing elements of the set in sequential locations within this block, however, the elements are scattered randomly through the block. The trick is to store each new element in such a way that its presence or absence can later be immediately determined without a search of the block.

Consider how this may be done. Suppose that we wish to add a new element x, represented by bit string B_x, to the set S, represented by the block of storage M_S. First, we must determine whether x is already a member of S and, if not, add it to the set. We determine a position for B_x within the block M_S by the application of a *hashing function* to the bit string B_x. The hashing function hashes (chops up into little pieces and mixes together) the bit string B_x and then extracts a hash address

I_x from the result. This hash address is used as an index pointing to a position in the block M_S. We look at that position in the block; if X is already in the set, then it must be stored at that position. If not, then we store the bit string B_x at the location designated by I_x. Any later attempt to find whether x is a member of S will be answered by hashing the new bit string B_x representing x, obtaining I_x, accessing the block M_S at that position, and finding the previously stored string B_x. No search of the table is ever needed.

Exactly how the hashing function works is not critical as long as it is relatively fast and generates hash addresses that are fairly randomly distributed. An example illustrates the idea more directly. Suppose that we allocate a block of 1,024 words (a block length equal to a power of 2 for a binary computer is most convenient) for the block M_S. Suppose also that the data items to be stored are character strings represented by double-word bit strings. We may represent a set of up to 511 distinct elements within this block. Suppose that the starting address of the block in memory is α. An appropriate hash address for such a table would be a string I_x of 9 bits because the formula $\alpha + 2 \times I_x$ would always generate an address within the block. We might compute I_x from a given two-word-long bit string B_x by the following algorithm (assuming that B_x is stored in words a and b):

1. Multiply a and b, giving c (two-word product).
2. Add together the two words of c, giving one word value d.
3. Square d, giving e.
4. Extract the center nine bits of e, giving I_x.

Even the best hashing function cannot guarantee that different data items will generate different hash addresses when hashed. Although it is desirable that the hashing function spread the generated hash addresses throughout the block as much as possible, almost inevitably two data items may be hashed to the same hash address, leading to a *collision*. A collision occurs when we have a data item to be added to the set, go to the block at the designated hash address, and find the block entry at that point filled with a data item different from the one to be stored (but that just happened to hash to the same hash address). (That is, two different data items x and y produce the same hash value I_x.) Many techniques for handling collisions are known:

1. *Rehashing.* We might modify the original bit string B_x (e.g., by multiplication by a constant) and then rehash the result, generating a new hash address. If another collision occurs, we rehash again until either B_x is found or an empty block location is encountered.

2. *Sequential scan.* From the original point of the collision in the block, we might begin a sequential (end-around) search until either B_x is found or an empty block location is encountered.

3. *Bucketing.* In place of direct storage in the block we might substitute pointers to linked *bucket lists* of the elements having the same hash addresses. After

hashing B_x and retrieving the pointer to the appropriate bucket list, we search the list for B_x and, if not found, add it to the end of the list.

Different hashing functions are appropriate depending on the properties of the bit-string representations of the data to be stored. With a good hashing function and the table at most half full, collisions rarely occur. Collision resolution is why the 512-entry table in the prior example can only be used to store 511 entries. Eventually collision resolution must find an empty entry or else the resolution process may never terminate.

6.1.9 Executable Data Objects

In most languages, especially compiled languages like C and Ada, executable source programs and the data objects they manipulate are separate structures. However, this is not necessarily always true. In languages like LISP and Prolog, executable statements may be data that are accessible by the program, and that may be manipulated by it. For example, LISP stores all of its data in lists. The Scheme expression

(define myfunction (cons (a b c) (d e f)))

simply defines the function name *myfunction* to be the *cons* operation defined earlier. This is stored as a linked list much like any other list structure.

The same may be said of Prolog and its *consult* operation for its lists of rules. Although handling such data is easy using the list structures described here, the ability to enter, modify, and execute a program during its execution lifetime has a profound effect on its execution structure. We discuss this further in Section 6.3.

6.2 ABSTRACT DATA TYPES

Early languages, such as FORTRAN and COBOL, limit the creation of new data types to subprogram definitions. As the concept of data type has evolved, new language designs have provided better facilities for specifying and implementing entire abstract data types, such as the Ada **package** and C++ or Java **class**. In this chapter, we study the more classical approach toward programmer-defined data via the construction of subprograms: how procedures, subroutines, and functions are defined and implemented. In Chapter 7, we look at how Ada extended this concept with its data encapsulation facilities called *packages*. We also extend these ideas with the concept of a **class** and the ability to link executable procedures (e.g., *methods*) with these data objects to build what are called today *object-oriented programs*.

6.2.1 Evolution of the Data Type Concept

Because actual computers ordinarily include no provision for defining and enforcing data type restrictions (e.g., the hardware cannot tell the difference between a bit string representing a real number, character, or integer), higher level languages provide a set of basic data types, such as *real, integer,* and *character string.* Type checking is provided to ensure that operations such as + or × are not applied to data of the wrong type. The early notion of data type defines a *type* as a *set of values* that a variable might take on. Data types are directly associated with individual variables so that each declaration names a variable and defines its type. If a program uses several arrays, each containing 20 real numbers, each array is declared separately and the entire array description is repeated for each.

Around 1970, Pascal extended the concept to a general type definition applicable to a set of variables. A *type definition* defines the structure of a data object with its possible value bindings. To get a particular data object of the defined type, a declaration requires only the variable name and the name of the type to be given.

During the 1970s, the concept of data type was extended beyond just a *set of data objects* to also include the *set of operations* that manipulate those data objects. For primitive types such as *real* and *integer,* a language provides a facility to declare variables of that type and a set of operations on reals and integers that represent the *only way* that reals and integers can be manipulated by the programmer. Thus, the storage representation of reals and integers is effectively *encapsulated* (e.g., it is hidden from the programmer). The programmer may use real and integer data objects without knowing or caring exactly how they are represented in storage. All the programmer sees is the name of the type and the list of operations available for manipulating data objects of that type.

Data abstraction. In order to extend this encapsulation concept to programmer-defined data, we define an *abstract data type* as

1. A set of *data objects,* ordinarily using one or more type definitions,
2. A set of *abstract operations* on those data objects, and
3. *Encapsulation* of the whole in such a way that the user of the new type cannot manipulate data objects of the type except by use of the operations defined.

The entire definition should be encapsulated in such a way that the user of the type needs to know only the type name and semantics of the available operations. In this chapter we discuss how abstractions can be designed using the subprogram feature available in most languages. In chapter 7 we extend this concept to include language features, as embodied, for example, in the Ada **package** or C++ and Smalltalk **class**, which aid in this encapsulation process.

6.2.2 Information Hiding

To understand the design of language facilities for programmer-defined operations and data types, it is important to understand *abstraction.* A large program, or even one of moderate size, when all its details are considered at once, easily exceeds the intellectual grasp of a single person. To construct a large program, a form of divide-and-conquer strategy must be used. The program is divided into a set of components often called *modules.* Each module performs a limited set of operations on a limited amount of data. This keeps intellectual control over the program design process.

Module design has generally followed two approaches: (1) Modules represent a *functional* decomposition of the program, or (2) modules represent a *data* decomposition of the program. The former approach was the common model of program design during the 1960s, and the typical subprogram structure, procedures, and functions derived from it.

A functional design has been the method of choice for many years. However, to see what is wrong with that method, consider the *section* data type mentioned earlier. To decompose the program into functional units, one programmer might develop the *registration* functions that would create *sections*, add *students* to *sections*, and assign an *instructor* to a *section*. Another programmer might perform *class maintenance* functions, such as drop/add of a *student* from or to a *section*, entering grades for each *student*, and sending home bills to pay for each such course. In each case, the programmer must know the details of what both a *section* and a *student* are. There is little simplification of the knowledge required to build each component. However, by creating modules based on data modularization, called *simple abstractions*, most of the drawbacks in the prior discussion are avoided.

Building a *section* abstraction and then using it in other modules are just such a simple abstraction. The specification of the data type is all that must be understood to make use of it; the implementation details are hidden and can be ignored. Thus, the programmer designing the overall strategy for assigning students to sections in the program can forget about exactly how sections are implemented and remember only that students can be assigned to sections, sections have instructors and room numbers, and so on.

Abstraction is so pervasive in programming activities that it often goes without notice. The layering of software and hardware described in chapter 2 is another example of abstraction. A flowchart is an abstraction of the statement-level control structure of a program. Methods for designing programs—given various names such as *stepwise refinement, structured programming, modular programming,* and *top-down programming*—are concerned with the design of abstractions.

A programming language provides support for abstraction in two ways. First, by providing a virtual computer that is simpler to use and more powerful than the actual underlying hardware computer, the language directly supplies a useful set of abstractions that we think of as the features of the language. Second, the language provides facilities that aid the programmer to construct abstractions—the abstractions that together form the virtual computer defined by a particular program. Subprograms, subprogram libraries, type definitions, classes, and packages are some of the facilities provided by different languages to support programmer-defined abstractions.

Information hiding is the term used for the central principle in the design of programmer-defined abstractions: Each such program component should hide as much information as possible from the component users. Thus, the language-provided square-root function is a successful abstract operation because it hides the details of the number representation and the square-root computation algorithm from the user. Similarly a programmer-defined data type is a successful abstraction if it may be used without knowledge of the representation of objects of that type or of the algorithms used by its operations.

When information is *encapsulated* in an abstraction, it means that the user of the abstraction

1. *Does not need to know* the hidden information in order to use the abstraction, and

2. *Is not permitted* to directly use or manipulate the hidden information even if desiring to do so.

For example, the integer data type in a programming language such as FORTRAN or C not only hides the details of the integer number representation, but also effectively encapsulates the representation so that the programmer cannot manipulate individual bits of the representation of an integer (except by use of flaws in the encapsulation mechanism of the language to get invalid access to the bits). It is much more difficult for the user of FORTRAN or C to encapsulate the representation of a new data type. Although a set of subprograms can be constructed that allows *sections* to be created and manipulated as abstractions in those languages (thus giving information hiding), it is impossible to encapsulate the data representation used for sections so that the user of the abstraction cannot write another subprogram that will manipulate sections in improper ways. For example, if the student roll list is represented as a linear array of integers, a subprogram could be written that would add 3 to each integer in the array. Such an operation is meaningless in terms of the abstraction, where the integers represent student identification numbers, but it is perfectly valid in terms of the particular data representations used.

Encapsulation is particularly important in permitting easy modification of a program. If the *section* data type were encapsulated, then we could modify the representation of sections at any time by simply modifying the subprograms that manipulate sections so that they work with the new representation instead of the old. However, if not encapsulated, then other parts of the program may presume a particular representation for sections. Any change in the representation will invalidate those other parts. Often it is difficult to determine which subprograms are dependent on a particular representation for data objects if there is no encapsulation, and thus changes in a data representation give rise to subtle errors in other parts of the program that seemingly should not be affected by the change.

Subprograms form a basic encapsulation mechanism that is present in almost every language. Mechanisms that allow encapsulation of entire data type definitions are more recent and, of the languages presented here, appear only in Ada and

C++. Note that information hiding is primarily a question of *program design;* information hiding is possible in any program that is properly designed regardless of the programming language used. Encapsulation, however, is primarily a question of *language design;* an abstraction is effectively encapsulated only when the language prohibits access to the information hidden within the abstraction.

6.3 ENCAPSULATION BY SUBPROGRAMS

A subprogram is an abstract operation defined by the programmer. Subprograms form the basic building block out of which most programs are constructed, and facilities for their definition and invocation are found in almost every language. Two views of subprograms are important here. At the *program design* level, we may ask about the sense in which a subprogram represents an abstract operation that the programmer defines, as opposed to the primitive operations that are built into the language. At the *language design* level, the concern is with the design and implementation of the general facilities for subprogram definition and invocation. Although the views overlap, it is helpful to take them up separately.

6.3.1 Subprograms as Abstract Operations

As with primitive operations, a subprogram definition has two parts: a *specification* and an *implementation.* However, for a subprogram, both parts are provided by the programmer when the subprogram is defined.

Specification of a subprogram. Because a subprogram represents an abstract operation, we should be able to understand its specification without understanding how it is implemented. The specification for a subprogram is the same as that for a primitive operation. It includes

1. The *name* of the subprogram;
2. The *signature* (also called prototype) of the subprogram giving the number of *arguments,* their order, and the data type of each, as well as the number of *results,* their order, and the data type of each; and
3. The *action* performed by the subprogram (i.e., a description of the function it computes).

A subprogram represents a mathematical function that maps each particular set of arguments into a particular set of results. If a subprogram returns a single-result data object explicitly, it is usually termed a *function subprogram* (or simply, *function*). A typical syntax for its specification is the C expression

float FN(float X, int Y)

which specifies the signature

$$FN : real \times integer \rightarrow real$$

Note that the specification also includes the names X and Y by which the arguments may be referenced within the subprogram; these *formal parameters* and the general topic of transmission of parameters to a subprogram are taken up in Section 9.3. In addition, some languages also include a keyword in the declaration, such as **procedure** or **function**, as in the Pascal statement

function FN(X: real; Y: integer): real;

If a subprogram returns more than one result or if it modifies its arguments rather than returning results explicitly, it is usually termed a *procedure* or *subroutine,* and a typical syntax for its specification is the C expression

void Sub(float X, int Y, float *Z, int *W);

In this specification, *void* indicates a null function, a subprogram that does not return a value. A formal parameter name preceded by $*$ may indicate a result value or an argument that may be modified. (These are actually pointer arguments, as is discussed more fully in Section 9.3.) The syntax in Ada for this specification clarifies these distinctions:

procedure Sub(X: **in** REAL; Y: **in** integer;
Z: **in out** REAL; W: **out** BOOLEAN)

This heading specifies a subprogram with the signature

$$Sub : real_1 \times integer \times real_2 \rightarrow real_3 \times Boolean$$

The tags **in**, **out**, and **in out** distinguish the three ways to invoke arguments to a subprogram, **in** designates an argument that is not modified by the subprogram, **in out** designates an argument that may be modified, and **out** designates a result. These ideas are treated more extensively in Section 9.3.

Although a subprogram represents a mathematical function, problems arise in attempting to describe precisely the function computed:

1. A subprogram may have *implicit arguments* in the form of nonlocal variables that it references.

2. A subprogram may have *implicit results* (*side effects*) returned as changes to nonlocal variables or as changes in its in–out arguments.

3. A subprogram may not be defined for some possible arguments so that it does not complete execution in the ordinary way if given those arguments, but instead transfers control to some external exception handler (chapter 11) or terminates execution of the entire program abruptly.

4. A subprogram may be *history sensitive* so that its results depend on the arguments given over the entire past history of its calls and not just on the arguments given in a single call. History sensitivity may be due to the subprogram's retaining local data between invocations.

Implementation of a subprogram. A *subprogram* represents an operation of the virtual computer layer constructed by the programmer, and thus a subprogram is implemented using the data structures and operations provided by the programming language. The implementation is defined by the subprogram *body,* which consists of *local data declarations* defining the data structures used by the subprogram and *statements* defining the actions to be taken when the subprogram is executed. The declarations and statements are usually encapsulated so that neither the local data nor the statements are accessible separately to the user of the subprogram; the user may only invoke the subprogram with a particular set of arguments and receive the computed results. The C syntax for the body of a subprogram is typical:

```
float FN(float X, int Y)    - Signature of subprogram
    {float M(10); int N;    - Declarations of local data objects
    .                       - Sequence of statements defining
    . }                         the actions of the subprogram
```

In some languages (e.g., Pascal, Ada, but not in C), the body may also include definitions of other subprograms that represent programmer-defined operations used only within the larger subprogram. These local subprograms are also encapsulated so they cannot be invoked from outside the larger subprogram.

Each invocation of a subprogram requires arguments of the proper types, as given in the subprogram specification. The types of the results returned by a subprogram must also be known. The type-checking issues are similar to those for primitive operations. Type checking may be performed statically, during translation, if declarations are given for the argument and result types of each subprogram. Alternatively, type checking may be dynamic during program execution. *Coercion* of arguments to convert them to the proper types may also be provided automatically by the language implementation. These problems and implementation methods are straightforward generalizations of the concepts presented in chapter 5 for primitive operations. The major difference comes from the need for the programmer to explicitly declare information about argument and result types that is implicit for primitive operations. Once this information is provided, however, the type-checking problems are treated similarly.

6.3.2 Subprogram Definition and Invocation

The design of facilities for subprogram definition and invocation is a central problem—perhaps *the* central problem—in the design of most languages. Much of the overall implementation structure is determined by this subprogram structure. Some general concepts are taken up here. In chapter 7, we consider methods for providing full encapsulation and information hiding of data.

Subprogram Definitions and Subprogram Activations

A subprogram definition is a static property of a program. During execution of the program, if the subprogram is called (or *invoked*), an *activation* of the subprogram is created. When execution of the subprogram is complete, the activation is destroyed. If another call is made, a new activation is created. From a single subprogram definition, many activations may be created during program execution. The definition serves as a *template* for creating activations during execution.

The distinction between definitions and activations of subprograms is important. A definition is what is present in the program as written and is the only information available during translation (e.g., the type of subprogram variables is known, but not their value or location [r-value or l-value]). Subprogram activations exist only during program execution. During execution, code to access a variable's l-value or r-value can be executed, but the type of a variable may not be available unless the translator saved such information in a variable's descriptor.

This distinction is quite similar to the distinction between a type definition and a data object of that type, as taken up in the next section. The type definition is used as a template to determine the size and structure of the data objects of that type. However, the data objects are usually created during execution, either when a subprogram is entered or on execution of a creation operation such as *malloc*. The use of *malloc* to create new data objects as needed during program execution corresponds to the use of *call* to create new subprogram activations as needed. In fact, a subprogram activation is a type of data object. It is represented as a block of storage that contains certain component data items relevant to the subprogram activation. Storage must be allocated when it is created, and storage is freed when it is destroyed. An activation has a *lifetime*—the time during execution between the *call* that creates it and the *return* that destroys it. However, there are concepts surrounding subprogram activations that have no direct analog for other data objects (e.g., the concept of *executing* an activation and the concept of referencing and modifying other data objects during this execution). Because of these differences, and because intuitively a strong distinction is made in most languages between subprograms and other data objects, the term *data object* is not used here to refer to a subprogram activation.

Implementation of Subprogram Definition and Invocation

Consider a C subprogram definition (Figure 6.12). This definition defines the components needed for an activation of the subprogram at run time:

1. FN's signature line provides information for storage for *parameters* (the data objects X and Y) and storage for the *function result,* a data object of type *float.*

2. Declarations provide for storage for *local variables* (Array M and Variable N).

3. Storage for *literals* and *defined constants.* $Initval$ is the defined Constant 2,

```
float FN( float X, int Y)
     {const initval=2;
     #define finalval 10
     float M(10); int N;
     N = initval;
     if(N<finalval){ ... }
     return (20 * X + M(N)); }
```

Figure 6.12. C subprogram definition.

finalval is the defined Constant 10, and 10 and 20 are literals.

4. Storage for the *executable code* generated from the statements in the subprogram body.

Note one important feature of C. The **const** attribute informs the C compiler that data object *Initval* has the literal value of integer 2. However, the **#define** statement is a preprocessor (macro) command that converts each appearance of *finalval* to the characters "10". The C translator never processes the name *finalval*. The practical effects of each statement on the executable subprogram are the same, but their meanings are quite different. *Initval* will have an l-value whose r-value is 2, whereas *finalval* will only have an r-value of 10.

The definition of the subprogram allows these storage areas to be organized and the executable code determined during translation. The result from translation is the template used to construct each particular activation at the time the subprogram is called during execution. Figure 6.13 shows the subprogram definition as translated into a run-time template.

To construct a particular activation of the subprogram from its template, the entire template might be copied into a new area of memory. However, rather than making a complete copy, it is far better to split the template into two parts:

- A static part, called the *code segment,* consisting of the constants and executable code. This part should be invariant during execution of the subprogram, and thus a single copy may be shared by all activations.

- A dynamic part, called an *activation record*, consisting of parameters, function results, and local data, plus other implementation-defined housekeeping data such as temporary storage areas, return points, and linkages for referencing nonlocal variables (discussed in Section 9.2). This part has the same structure for each activation, but it contains different data values. Thus, each activation necessarily has its own copy of the activation record part.

The resulting structure during execution is shown in Figure 6.14. For each subprogram, a single code segment exists in storage throughout program execution. Activation records are dynamically created and destroyed during execution each time the subprogram is called and each time it terminates with a return.

The size and structure of the activation record required for a subprogram can ordinarily be determined during translation (e.g., the compiler [or translator] can determine how many components are needed to store the necessary data within the activation record and the position of each component within the activation record). Access to the components may then be made using the base-address-plus-offset calculation, as described in Section 6.1.3 for ordinary record data objects. For this reason, an activation record is in fact ordinarily represented in storage just as any other record data object. To create a new activation record requires only that the size of the record storage block be known, rather than its detailed internal structure (because the offsets into the block are already computed during translation, and only the base address is needed to complete the accessing calculation during execution). Rather than storing a complete activation record template at run time, only the size of the activation record must be stored for use by the *call* operation in creating the activation record. Storage management on subprogram call and return involves only allocation of a block of the appropriate size when a subprogram is called and freeing of the block on return. As we discuss in chapter 9, a simple stack is normally used to manage the allocation and deallocation of activation records.

When a subprogram is called, a number of hidden actions take place that are concerned with the setting up of the activation record, the transmission of param-

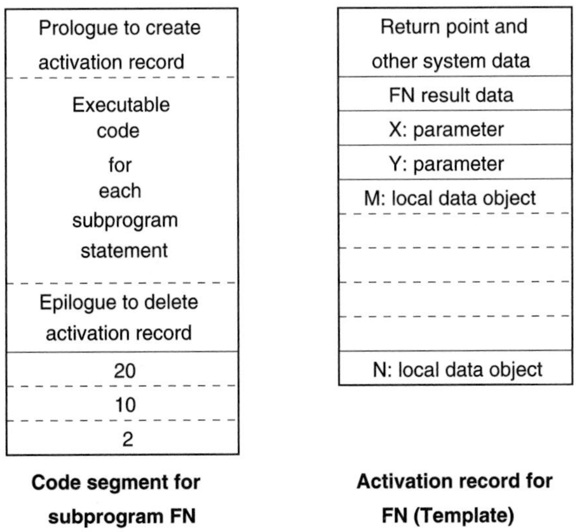

Figure 6.13. Structure of a subprogram activation.

eters, the creation of linkages for nonlocal referencing, and similar housekeeping activities. These actions must take place before the actual code for the statements in the body of the subprogram is executed. The execution of this *prologue* before the execution of the code block for the subprogram is usually handled by the translator inserting a block of code to perform these actions at the start of the subprogram. On termination of a subprogram, a similar set of housekeeping actions is required to return results and free the storage for the activation record. An *epilogue* is a set of instructions inserted by the translator at the end of the executable code block to perform these actions. Further details are found later in this chapter.

Generic Subprograms

The specification of a subprogram ordinarily lists the number, order, and data types of the arguments. A *generic subprogram* is one with a single name but several different definitions, distinguished by a different signature. A generic subprogram name is said to be *overloaded.* The general concepts of a generic operation and an overloaded operation name are treated in Chapter 5 in relation to primitive operations. Subprograms may also be generic in the same manner. For example, in writing a set of subprograms for a university class registration program, two routines might be needed: one to enter a section in a table of class sections and another to enter a student in a class roll for a section. Both subprograms might be defined using the name *Enter*:

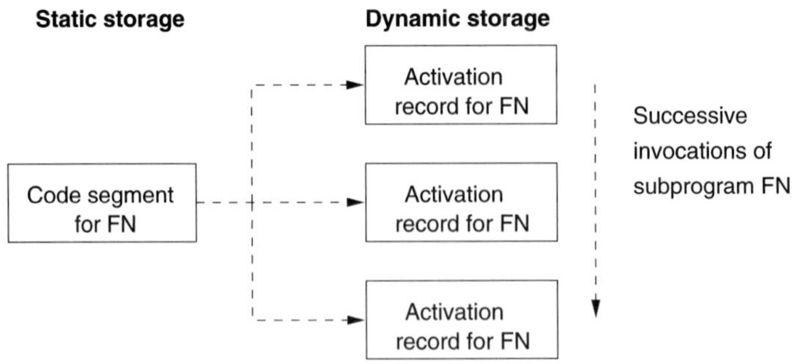

Figure 6.14. Shared code and separate activation records.

```
INTERFACE ENTER
    SUBROUTINE ENTER_STUDENT(STUDENT, SECT)
        INTEGER :: STUDENT
        SECTION :: SECT
        END SUBROUTINE ENTER_STUDENT
    SUBROUTINE ENTER_SECTION(S, TAB)
        SECTION :: S
        CLASSLIST :: TAB
        END SUBROUTINE ENTER_SECTION
END INTERFACE ENTER
```

Figure 6.15. FORTRAN 90 interface block.

```
procedure Enter(Student: in integer;
                Sect: in out Section) is
    begin – statements here to enter student in a section roll list
    end;
procedure Enter(S: in Section;
                Tab: in out Classlist) is
    begin – statements here to enter section in a classlist
    end;
```

The name *Enter* is overloaded and has become the name of a generic *Enter* subprogram. When a call to *Enter* is made ($Enter(A, B)$), the translator must resolve the types of the arguments A and B with the appropriate types for the two *Enter* procedures. In this case, if A is of type *integer,* then the call is a call on the first definition of the *Enter* subprogram; if A is of type *section,* then it is a call on the second. Because this resolution is made during translation, in a language such as Ada there is no effect on the run-time organization of the language. Once the overloading is resolved, translation of the subprogram call proceeds as for any other subprogram call.

In FORTRAN 90, overloaded procedures are specified via an INTERFACE block. The previous example would be specified as given in Figure 6.15. In this example, subroutine $ENTER$ was defined to take either a parameter of type *integer* or a parameter of type *section.* We can extend this to include the type as a parameter, as in ML's *polymorphic* type mechanism.

Generic subprograms introduce no major change in the language or its possible implementation, but can have great impact on how the language gets used. Therefore, rather than making overloading an extra feature in languages like Ada, it becomes a central property of programming in ML. This is discussed in greater detail in chapter 7.

6.3.3 Subprogram Definitions as Data Objects

In most compiled languages, such as C, C++, and Java, subprogram definition is independent from subprogram execution. The source program is first processed into run-time form by a compiler. During execution, the static part of the subprogram definition is both inaccessible and invisible. However, in languages such as LISP, Perl, and Prolog (which are usually implemented by software interpreters), there is typically no distinction between these two phases. Facilities allow subprogram *definitions* to be treated as run-time data objects.

Translation is an operation that takes a subprogram definition in the form of a character string and produces the run-time data object representing the definition. *Execution* is an operation that takes a definition in run-time form, creates an activation from it, and executes the activation. The execution operation is invoked by the usual *call* primitive, but the translation operation is often considered a separate *metaoperation* that takes place for all subprograms before the execution of the overall program begins. In LISP and Prolog, however, translation is also an operation that may be invoked at *run time* on a character-string data object to produce the executable form of a subprogram body. These languages provide an operation *define* that takes a subprogram body and specification and produces a complete callable subprogram definition (e.g., *define* in LISP, *consult* in Prolog).

Thus, in both languages it is possible to begin program execution without having a particular subprogram in existence. During execution, the subprogram body may be read in or created as a character-string data object and then translated into executable form. The *define* operation may then be used to provide a name and define parameters for the body so that a complete definition results. Subsequently, the subprogram may be called as needed. Later the definition of the subprogram may be modified. Subprogram definitions thus become true data objects in these languages.

6.4 TYPE DEFINITIONS

In defining a complete new abstract data type, some mechanism is required for definition of a class of data objects. In languages such as C, Pascal, and Ada, this mechanism is termed a *type definition* (but note that a type definition does not define a complete abstract data type because it does not include definition of the *operations* on data of that type).

In a type definition, a *type name* is given, together with a declaration that describes the structure of a class of data objects. The type name then becomes the name for that class of data objects. When a particular data object of that structure is needed, we need give only the type name, rather than repeating the complete description of the data structure. In Pascal, for example, if several records, A, B, and C are needed, each of which has the same structure (e.g., a record describing a rational number), then the program may contain the type definition

```
type Rational = record
        numerator: integer;
        denominator: integer
        end
```

followed by the declaration

```
var A, B, C: Rational;
```

so that the definition of the structure of a data object of type *Rational* is given only once rather than being repeated three times for each of A, B, and C.

In C, the situation is similar, but not quite as clean as in the Pascal example. New types can only be defined by the **struct** feature. Therefore, type *Rational* may be given as

```
struct RationalType
        {int numerator;
        int denominator; }
```

Use of a new type in C, however, requires the indication of the **struct** in the declaration, with the resulting program looking like

```
struct RationalType A, B, C;
```

This violates one of our data abstraction principles. We would like the new data type to appear as an extension of the language and be syntactically and semantically similar to the primitive data types. The inclusion of the keyword **struct** seems out of place. This effect is due to the age of the C language, developed initially during the early 1970s when concepts of encapsulation and information hiding were not as well formed. Fortunately, C does have a way out of this—the **typedef** construct:

```
typedef definition name
```

This is really a substitution of *name* for the *definition* contained in the typedef statement, much like a macro substitution. Therefore, we would write our *Rational* example in C as

```
typedef struct RationalType
        {int numerator;
        int denominator; } Rational;
```

followed by the declaration

```
Rational A, B, C;
```

which now has a syntax similar to the prior Pascal example. *Rational* means the new type **struct** *RationalType*. It is important to remember that new types in C are generated by the **struct** feature, whereas the **typedef** does not create a new type and is only a macro substitution of its definition—the name typedef notwithstanding. However, most of the time, typedef is used to create new types, and for most applications it behaves much like a new type declaration.

Besides simplifying program structure, type definitions have other advantages for the programmer. Should the structure of a *Rational* need to be modified, the use of a type definition allows the modification to be made only to the single type definition, rather than to many separate instances of declarations of individual variables. Also, if a data object is transmitted as an argument to a subprogram, the subprogram definition must usually include a description of the argument. Here again, rather than repeating the entire structure description, we need use only the type name.

A type definition is used as a *template* to construct data objects during program execution. A data object of the type may be created on entry to a subprogram (if a declaration for a variable of that type is included among the local data declarations for the subprogram) or it may be created dynamically through use of a creation operation, such as the *malloc* operation discussed in Section 5.3.2 with subsequent access through pointer variables. In its role as a template, a type definition is quite similar to a subprogram definition, as described in the preceding section.

Type definitions allow the separation of the definition of the *structure* of a data object from the definition of the points during execution at which data objects of that structure are to be *created.* However, also note that we potentially have a new form of *encapsulation* and *information hiding.* A subprogram may declare a variable to be of a particular type by simply using the type name. The type definition effectively hides the internal structure of data objects of that type. If a subprogram only creates objects of the type, using the type name, but never accesses the internal components of the data objects, then the subprogram becomes independent of the particular structure declared in the type definition. The definition may be modified without changing the subprogram. If the language design enforces the restriction so that only a few designated subprograms can access the internal components of the data objects, then the type definition has effectively encapsulated the structure of data objects of the type. In the next section, we consider how this encapsulation allows construction of a complete programmer-defined abstract data type.

Implementation. The information contained in the declaration of a variable is used primarily during translation to determine the storage representation for the data object and for storage management and type-checking purposes. Declarations are not present at run time; they are used only to set up the appropriate run-time data objects. Similarly, a type definition is only used during translation. The language translator enters the information from a type definition into a table during translation and, whenever the type name is referenced in a subsequent declaration, uses the tabled information to produce the appropriate executable code for setting

```
program main(input, output);
type Vect1: array [1 .. 10] of real;
        Vect2: array [1 .. 10] of real;
var X,Z: Vect1; Y: Vect2;
procedure Sub(A: Vect1);
        ...
        end;
begin                   – main program
    X: = Y;
    Sub(Y)
end.
```

Figure 6.16. Type equality.

up and manipulating the desired data objects during execution. The type definition allows some aspects of translation, such as determining storage representations, to be done only once for a single type definition rather than many times for different declarations. However, inclusion of type definitions in a language does not ordinarily change the run-time organization of the language implementation.

6.4.1 Type Equivalence

Type checking, whether static or dynamic, involves a comparison between the data type of the actual argument given to an operation and the data type of the argument that is expected by the operation. If the types are the same, then the argument is accepted and the operation proceeds. If they are different, then it is either considered an error or a coercion is used to convert the type of the argument to match what was expected.

Type equivalence brings up two related concepts:

1. What does it mean to say that two types are "the same"?
2. What does it mean to say that two data objects of the same type are "equal"?

The first is a data type issue. If we can determine this statically, as we said in the last chapter, the language will be strongly typed. The second is a semantic issue in determining the r-value of a data object.

Type equality. When is type X the same as type Y? This is a subtle question that we have mostly ignored when dealing with primitive data types such as integers or arrays (although the question was addressed when we discussed subtypes of primitive types). Type definitions require that the question be answered if a language is to have a clear definition.

Consider the type definitions and declarations of the program in Figure 6.16. The question is whether Variables X, Y, Z, and A have the same type to permit the assignment $X := Y$ and the procedure invocation $Sub(Y)$ to be valid, or whether they have different types, making the use of Y as an argument in either case invalid.

The two general solutions to this problem are name equivalence and structural equivalence.

Name equivalence. Two data types are considered equivalent only if they have the same name. Thus, types $Vect1$ and $Vect2$ are different types, although the defined data objects have the same structure. An assignment $X := Z$ is valid, but $X := Y$ is not. Name equivalence of types is the method used in Ada, C++, and for subprogram parameters in Pascal (although not for other cases in Pascal).

Name equivalence has these disadvantages:

1. Every object used in an assignment must have a type name; there can be no *anonymous types.* In Pascal,

var W: **array** [1..10] **of** real;

variable W has a distinct type, but W cannot be used as an argument to a subprogram because its type has no name.

2. A single type definition must serve all or large parts of a program because the type of a data object transmitted as an argument through a chain of subprograms cannot be defined again in each subprogram; the single global type definition must be used. Class definitions in C++, package specification names in Ada, and ".h" include files in C ensure that this is so.

Structural equivalence. Two data types are considered equivalent if they define data objects that have the same *internal components.* Usually "the same internal components" means that the same storage representation may be used for both classes of data objects. For example, $Vect1$ and $Vect2$ are equivalent types under this definition because each data object of type $Vect1$ and each data object of type $Vect2$ have exactly the same number of components of equivalent types in the same order. The storage representation for data objects of either type is the same so that the same accessing formulas can be used to select components; in general, the run-time implementation of the data types is identical.

Structural equivalence does not have the disadvantages of name equivalence, but it has its own set of problems:

1. Several subtle questions arise as to when two types are structurally equivalent. For example, for records, must the component names be identical or does it suffice to have the same number and type of components in the same order? If record component names must be identical, then must the components be in the same order? Must array subscript ranges be identical or is it sufficient to have the same number of components? Must the literals in two enumeration types be the same and in the same order?

2. Two variables may inadvertently be structurally equivalent, although the programmer declares them as separate types, as in the simple example

```
type Meters = integer;
     Liters = integer;
var Len: Meters;
     Vol: Liters;
```

Variables *Len* and *Vol* have structurally equivalent types, and thus an error such as computing $Len + Vol$ would not be detected by static type checking. Where several programmers are working on a program, inadvertent type equivalence may destroy much of what is gained from static type checking because many type errors may go undetected.

3. Determining whether two complex type definitions are structurally equivalent, if done frequently, may be a costly part of translation.

The issues involved in the choice of a definition of type equivalence are important in the design of languages such as Ada and Pascal, where type definitions play a central role. In older languages, such as FORTRAN, COBOL, and PL/I, there are no type definitions, and thus some form of structural equivalence of types is used. The Pascal design raises the issues but does not consistently use either method. C uses structural equivalence. However, as stated earlier, C++ uses name equivalence—a subtle distinction between the languages. The Ada design consistently uses name equivalence, but the issue is still considered a research question (see the references and problems at the end of this chapter).

Data object equality. Once the compiler determines that two objects are the same type, are the two objects equal? Assume variables A and B are both of some type X. Under what conditions can you say $A = B$? Unfortunately, the language cannot help the programmer much in this respect. Much of the design of a data type is in how it will be used. Consider the following two type definitions in C for a *stack* and a *set*:

```
struct stack                    struct set
    {int TopStack;                  {int NumberInSet;
    int Data[100]; } X, Y;          int Data[100]; } A, B;
```

X, Y, A, and B have structurally equivalent types, an integer, and an array of 100 integers. However, the conditions on which we may want to have $X = Y$ and $A = B$ are very different:

- *Stack equality.* If we assume that *TopStack* refers to the data object in *Data* that is at the top of the stack, then we would want equality between X and Y to be as follows:

  1. $X.TopStack = Y.TopStack$
  2. For all I between 0 and $TopStack - 1$: $X.Data[I] = Y.Data[I]$

  This would indicate that both X and Y represented equivalent stacks.

- *Set equality.* If we assume that $NumberInSet$ refers to the number of data objects in sets A and B, then we would want equality between A and B to be defined as:

    1. $A.NumberInSet = B.NumberInSet$
    2. $A.Data[0] \ldots A.Data[NumberInSet-1]$ is a permutation of $B.Data[0] \ldots B.Data[NumberInSet-1]$ because the order of insertion of items in a set is not relevant.

    Of course, how we implement *stack* operations like *push* and *pop* and *set* operations like *insert* and *delete* affects these definitions. For example, if we implement *set* insertion so that all members of the set are in increasing value in *Data* by sorting the array each time a new *insert* is called, then the definition of *stack* equality would be correct for these sets.

As can be seen, we currently do not have the mechanisms to easily formalize equality for complex data objects. The usual approach, then, for building programmer-defined data is to also include a separate operation for equals. Therefore, if you are building a *stack* data type, besides the usual operations of *push*, *pop*, *empty*, and *top*, you would also need to include a *StackEquals* operation if that function is to be used in your program.

6.4.2 Type Definitions with Parameters

Where many similar type definitions are needed, a language may provide for parameterizing the type definition to be used repeatedly with different substitutions for the parameters. Array sizes have been the classical example of type parameters. For example, suppose we wish to define a type *Section* as a record, as in the Ada definition

```
type Section is
        record
            Room: integer;
            Instructor: integer;
            ClassSize: integer range 0 .. 100;
            ClassRoll:array (1 .. 100) of Student_ID;
        end record;
```

Note the problem. This definition of *Section* defines a section of at most 100 students; to get larger sections requires a new type definition.

A parameterized type definition for *Section* allows the type definition to have a $MaxSize$ parameter that determines the maximum class size:

```
type Section(MaxSize: integer) is
    record
        Room: integer;
        Instructor: integer;
        ClassSize: integer range 0 .. MaxSize;
        ClassRoll:array (1 .. MaxSize) of Student_ID;
    end record;
```

With this type definition, the maximum class size may be declared as part of the declaration of each individual variable:

```
X: Section(100)   – gives maximum size 100
Y: Section(25)    – gives maximum size 25
```

ML extends this concept by allowing the type to be a parameter:

```
signature OrderedItem =
    sig
        type elem
        val lessthan: elem * elem -> bool
    end;
```

OrderedItem is defined to be a type (*signature* in ML) that takes: (1) a parameter of type *elem*, and (2) a function *lessthan* that takes two elements of type *elem* and returns a Boolean value.

We declare data types using this signature (i.e., type) as follows:

```
(* Define intitem as a variant of type integer *)
structure intitem: OrderedItem =
    struct type elem = int
    fun less(i:elem, j:elem) = (i<j)
    end;

(* Define realitem as a variant of type real *)
structure realitem: OrderedItem =
    struct type elem = real
    fun less(i:elem, j:elem) = (i<j)
    end;
```

We then use the following invocation:

```
- intitem.less(5,6);
val it = true : bool
```

Intitem.less is a function *less* that takes arguments of type *int*, as defined by the signature for *intitem*.

Implementation. Type definitions with parameters are used as templates during compilation, just as any other type definition, except that when the compiler translates a declaration of a variable with a parameter list following the type name, the compiler first fills in the parameter value in the type definition to get a complete type definition without parameters. Parameters in type definitions affect the run-time organization of the language implementation in only a few cases (e.g., where a subprogram must accept any data object of the parameterized type as an argument and must be prepared for an argument of possibly different size on each call). In the case of ML, where we can parameterize the operators as well as the type of its arguments, we have actually defined an encapsulated type. We will discuss the implementation of these issues more fully in discussing object-oriented classes in Chapter 7.

6.5 C++ OVERVIEW

History. Just as one person is associated with the development of Pascal (Niklaus Wirth), a single individual is generally credited with development of C++. Starting with C, Bjarne Stroustrup developed an effective language that kept the efficiency of C, yet added the power of object inheritance. To understand C++, it is assumed that C (Appendix A.2) is already known.

During the late 1970s, Stroustrup was working on his Ph.D. at the Computing Laboratory in Cambridge, England. At the time, he programmed in Simula, a derivative of ALGOL, that introduced classes as data objects, and he felt the power of the Simula class to be an effective typing mechanism. When he came to AT&T Bell Telephone Laboratories in the United States, he immediately began to develop extensions to C that incorporated some of these same class features.

One fundamental guideline he followed was that any extensions he developed had to be efficient and not cause C programs to execute more slowly. The extensions he developed, called *C with Classes*, contained the basic class structure that is in C++ today. By 1982, his C with Classes had moderate success within Bell Labs, and he was the guru who had the obligation to maintain the system. To get out of this maintenance role, Stroustrup believed that he had only two options [STROUSTRUP 1993]:

> "(1) Stop supporting C with Classes so that the users would have to go elsewhere (freeing me to do something else),
> "(2) Develop a new and better language based upon my experience with C with Classes that would serve a large enough set of users to pay for a support and development organization (thus freeing me to do something else)."

He chose the latter approach by adding new feature as well as cleaning up inconsistencies in the C with Classes design. In 1984, the name of this effort was changed. C with Classes led some to call the new language *new C*, which led others

Language Summary 6.1: C+- (pronounced "C more or less")

Features: Unlike C++, C+− is a subject oriented language. Each C+− class instance known as a subject, holds hidden members, known as prejudices or undeclared preferences, which are impervious preferences, which are impervious to outside messages, as well as public members known as boasts or claims. The following C operators are overridden as shown:

>	better than
<	worse than
>>	much better than
<<	forget it
!	not on your life
==	comparable, other things being equal.

C+− is a strongly typed language based on stereotyping and self-righteous logic. The Boolean variables TRUE and FALSE (known as constants in less realistic languages) are supplemented with CREDIBLE and DUBIOUS, which are fuzzier than Zadeh's traditional fuzzy categories. All Booleans can be declared with the modifiers strong and weak. Weak implication is said to "preserve deniability" and was added at the request of the D.O.D. to ensure compatability with future versions of Ada. Well-formed falsehoods (WFFs) are assignment-compatible with all Booleans. What-if and why-not interactions are aided by the special conditional evenifnot X then Y.

C+− supports information hiding and, among friend classes only, rumor sharing. Borrowing from the Eiffel lexicon, non-friend classes can be killed by arranging contracts. Note that friendships are intransitive, volatile, and non-Abelian.

Single and multiple inheritance mechanisms are implemented with random mutations. Disinheritance rules are covered by a complex probate protocol. In addition to base, derived, virtual, and abstract classes, C+− supports gut classes. In certain locales, polygamous derivations and bastard classes are permitted. Elsewhere, loose coupling between classes is illegal, so the marriage and divorce operators may be needed:

```
marriage (MParent1, FParent1); // child classes can now be derived
sclass MySclass: public MParent1, FParent1 // define MySclass
sclass YourSclass: public MParent1, FParent2 // illegitimate
divorce (MParent1, FParent1);
marriage (MParent1, FParent2);
sclass YourSclass: public MParent1, FParent2 // OK now
```

Operator precedence rules can be suspended with the directive #pragma dwim, known as the "Do what I mean" pragma. ANSIfication will be firmly resisted. C+−'s slogan is "Be Your Own Standard."

Reference: From S. Kelly-Bootle, "The Devil's AI Dictionary," *AI Expert*, (April 1991), 51. Reprinted in S. Kelly-Bootle, "The Computer Contradictionary," MIT Press, (1995). Reprinted by permission of author.

to call standard C by the name *old C* or *plain C.* C84 was used for a while, and then C++ was suggested by Rick Mascitti of Bell Labs. The use of the ++ operator from C to suggest *successor* or *next* was intentional, as were many of the puns possible on the name. (See Language Summary 6.1.)

The basic language was defined by Stroustrup in 1986, and Version 2.0 was released in June 1989. In 1989, ANSI standard committee X3J16 was organized to produce a draft standard by early 1994, with full standardization being approved approximately 2 years later.

Brief overview of the language. C++ is a language derived from C. The major change is the addition of classes and a mechanism for inheriting class objects into other classes. The design of C++ was guided by three principles:

1. The use of classes would not result in programs executing any more slowly than programs not using classes.
2. To ensure that the addition of classes did not cause other needed features to be omitted, C programs should run as a subset of C++ programs.
3. No run-time inefficiency should be added to the language.

For the most part, the three goals were met. Most C programs can be compiled by a C++ compiler, although there are a few inconsistencies between the languages. Strong typing is stronger than the *weak* strong typing of C. Certain new reserved words have been added to C++. A few other changes were made, as given in this section. C++ uses two forms of comments. As in C, /* ... */ is a comment. C++ adds the format //, which indicates that everything until the end of that line is a comment. Among other additions, input and output are enhanced with the stream functions *cin* and *cout*. Exceptions are added, as well as overloading of operators, and a form of generic class called a *template*.

6.6 SUGGESTIONS FOR FURTHER READING

Three classical articles raising the problems of abstraction and information hiding as central concerns in programming are [DIJKSTRA 1972], [HOARE 1972], and [PARNAS 1972]. The definition and implementation of various forms of abstract data types were the subject of many articles during the 1970s. The languages CLU, ALPHARD, and EUCLID were all described at an ACM conference in 1977 [WORKMAN 1977]. Ada was the first major language to have abstract datatype capabilities [ISO 1994], although Smalltalk predates all of these by almost 10 years. However, it is only recently that Smalltalk has started to achieve mainstream language status, as we describe in Section 7.2.4. Most texts on compiler construction treat stack and static storage-allocation strategies. (See the references for chapter 3.)

6.7 PROBLEMS

1. Write an algorithm for finding the location of the component $V[N]$ of a vector V if V is stored in linked representation, as in Figure 6.1. Assume the address of the descriptor is α, its link field is at offset j, and each component is stored in a separate block with the link stored at offset k in that block.

2. Suppose the declaration of a vector V is given using an enumeration type as the subscript range—for example,

ClassType = (Fresh, Soph, Junior, Senior, Graduate);
V: **array** [ClassType] **of** real;

(a) Show the storage representation (including descriptor) that would be appropriate for V and give the accessing formula for computing the location of a component $V[i]$.

(b) How would the storage representation and accessing formula change if V were declared as

V: **array** [Junior..Graduate] **of** real;

3. Give the accessing formula for computing the location of component $A[I, J]$ of a matrix A declared as:

A: **array** $[LB_1..UB_1,\ LB_2..UB_2]$

where A is stored in *column-major order.*

4. Many computations using matrices involve sequential processing of all the elements of a single row or column. The loop in which the processing is done likely involves references to $A[I, J]$, with the subscript I or J increased by one each time through the loop. In such cases, it is inefficient to compute $lvalue(A[I, J])$ independently on each loop. Instead (assuming subscript I is the one that is varying), $lvalue(A[I, J])$ may be computed more simply from $lvalue(A[I-1, J])$. Give the formula for computing $lvalue(A[I, J])$ in terms of $lvalue(A[I-1, J])$. Extend this formula to arrays of arbitrary dimension where an arbitrary subscript is the one being incremented.

5. In the language SIMSCRIPT, a multidimensional, homogeneous array is represented as a vector of pointers that point to other vectors of pointers to as many levels as the array has dimensions. A 3×4 matrix of numbers is represented by a vector of three pointers, each of which points to another vector of four numbers. Give an algorithm for accessing $A[I, J]$ when such a representation is used. Compare the relative efficiency of accessing and storage use between this representation and the usual sequential representation. Consider both the case of matrices and arrays of higher dimension.

6. For multidimensional arrays, develop the following descriptors:

(a) Show how to develop the descriptor for vector slices of that array given its descriptor.

(b) Design a run-time descriptor for two-dimensional slices (e.g., planes of three-dimensional arrays) that allows the same accessing formula used for ordinary matrices.

(c) For any two-dimensional square array (i.e., declared $A[n, n]$), develop a descriptor for a vector that represents the main diagonal of the array (i.e., $A[i, i]$).

7. Because most hardware provides no direct support, subscript range checking on each access to an array component during a computation can be costly in both execution time and storage for the extra code involved. For a language with which you are familiar, determine the relative cost—in both execution time and storage—of access to a component of a matrix, $A[I, J]$. Preferably, obtain a listing of the object code produced by the compiler for a simple program that includes some array accessing, and determine the instructions generated and their timings for the checked and unchecked cases.

8. Given the representation of Pascal sets using bit strings and assuming that the maximum number of elements in a set must be less than the word length of the underlying hardware computer, give algorithms for implementing the operations of set union, intersection, difference, and the membership test (**in**) using the hardware primitives of *logical and, logical or,* and *logical complement* on entire words.

9. In hash-coding methods for set storage, both the rehashing and sequential-scan techniques for handling collisions encounter difficulties if deletions from the set are allowed. Explain the difficulties encountered.

10. Pick a language and a data structure type in that language. List the *attributes* of data objects of that type. List the *operations* provided for data objects of that type. Determine the storage representation for data objects of that type in your local implementation of the language. Is there a run-time descriptor? What attributes are stored in the descriptor? Do any operations require the allocation or freeing of storage when this storage representation is used?

11. Pick a language and a data structure type in that language. Determine the selection operations provided for selecting individual components or substructures of data objects of that type. For each selection operation (or class of operations), determine (a) whether the existence of the selected component can be determined statically (at compile time), and (b) whether the data type of the selected component can be determined statically. If either existence or data type cannot be determined statically, determine whether you, the programmer, or the language implementation is responsible for checking at run

time whether a selected component exists and is of the correct type before it is used in a computation.

12. Suppose you modified Pascal records (without variants) to allow field names to be integers, and modified the selection of fields to allow integer field names to be computed, so that $R.(I+2)$ could be used to select a component.

(a) Explain why the storage representation of Section 6.1.6 would no longer be adequate.

(b) Modify the storage representation so that it would work, and give the accessing formula (or algorithm) to be used with the new representation to select a component $R.K$, where K is a computed value.

13. Repeat Problem 12, but allow records *with variants.*

14. For a language that allows variant records without tag fields (free-union types) such as Pascal, write a procedure

procedure GIGO(I: integer; **var** R: real;)

that uses a record with two variants whose only purpose is to compromise the type-checking system. *GIGO* takes an argument I of type *integer* and returns the same bit pattern as a result R of type *real* without actually converting the value of I to a real number.

15. For a language with which you are familiar, consider how effective its encapsulation of each primitive data type is by trying to determine how many properties of the storage representations of data objects of that type can be determined by writing test programs. For example:

(a) Arrays. Can you determine whether arrays are stored in row-major or column-major order? Can you determine whether there is a run-time descriptor and its contents and format?

(b) Records. Can you determine the order in which components of the record are stored and whether components are packed or aligned on storage-unit boundaries?

16. In a language of your choice, define an abstract data type *stack of integers* and the operations of *push* and *pop* that insert and delete elements in a stack. Suppose you are part of a programming group that will use stacks of integers in many places in constructing a large program. Explain how your abstract data type may be most effectively set up in the language (using a combination of language-provided protections and coding conventions that the group must follow when working with stacks) so that the storage representation of stacks is hidden and is manipulated only by your *push* and *pop* operations.

17. For a program you have written recently, give a complete specification of the arguments and results of each subprogram. Be sure to include implicit arguments and results in the specifications. Are any of the subprograms history sensitive? Are any of them undefined for some arguments in the domain you specified? List at least one piece of information that is *hidden* by each subprogram.

18. A subprogram that is compiled into a separate code segment and activation record is sometimes said to be *reentrant* because it can be entered (called) during execution a second time before the first activation has terminated. Thus, there may be many simultaneous activations, each sharing the same code segment, as shown in Figure 6.14. For a language of your choice, determine whether subprograms are reentrant. What language feature (or features) allows you to begin a second activation before the first has terminated?

19. For a language of your choice, determine whether *name equivalence* or *structural equivalence* of data types is used. Consider each data type individually (because the rules tend to vary among types) and explain precisely when two variables of that type are considered to have the same type and when a variable (actual parameter) and a formal parameter in a subprogram call are considered to have the same type. Are the rules different for primitive types and programmer-defined types?

20. For data objects of type *record,* give three different possible rules for determining when two records have the same type using structural equivalence as the basic approach. Give two possible rules for determining when two *vectors* have the same type using structural equivalence.

21. The *ord* function is defined as taking a single argument, which must be a value from some enumeration. *ord* returns the integer representing the position of that value in the enumeration sequence (0 if the value is first in the sequence, 1 if it is the second, etc.). However, because a value from an enumeration is represented at run time by the integer representing the position of the value in the sequence anyway, *ord* really has nothing to do. For example, given the enumeration type

$$\text{Class} = (\text{Fresh},\text{Soph},\text{Junior},\text{Senior})$$

and a variable X of type $Class$, the assignment $X := Senior$ actually assigns the value 3 to X, and subsequently $ord(X)$ evaluates to 3. Thus, *ord* gets 3 as its argument and returns 3 as its result, so it does nothing useful (and a Pascal implementation may eliminate any call on *ord* from the executable object code altogether). However, *ord* does have a purpose, but its effect appears during compilation.

(a) Explain the purpose of *ord*. Why does Pascal provide this function when it has no run-time effect at all?

(b) For the variable X defined earlier, explain the actions taken during *execution* for the two program fragments

if $X = Senior$ **then** ...

and

if $ord(X) = 3$ **then** ...

(c) For the two program fragments in part *(b)*, explain the actions taken during *compilation* in type checking the two fragments and the third fragment:

if $X = 3$ **then** ...

22. C++ stream input and output objects *cin* and *cout* are implemented as instances of a *stream* class. Actual reading and writing of data are by overloading the operators << and >>. Give a possible implementation of these functions using standard C input and output functions.

23. Develop a class *rational* in C++ that represents the quotient of two integers a and b (i.e., $\frac{a}{b}$). Overload C++ operations so that statements like

a = b+c;

can be written with a, b, and c being either of type *int* or class *rational*.

(a) Develop the *rational* class for the operators $+$, $-$, and $*$. Include a function $print(x)$ for *rational* argument x that prints out the value of x as $\frac{y}{z}$. If the first argument is *rational*, the function is straightforward. What if the first argument is of type *int*? How would you develop these operators if both arguments are of type *int*? (Note: You need to use **friend** functions.)

(b) Try to extend your solution to include the operator $/$. What problems do you have and how can you solve them? Remember that a/b must give a *rational* result.

24. Assume that language BL includes a stack data structure and three operations:

$NewTop(S, E)$, which adds the element E to the top of stack S,

$PopTop(S)$, which deletes the top element of stack S,

$GetTop(S)$, which returns a pointer to the location in stack S of the current top element.

What is wrong with the design of these three operations? How could they be redefined to correct the problem?

25. A property list might be represented as a set rather than a list because elements are accessed randomly by subscript (attribute name) rather than sequentially. Design a storage representation for property lists using the technique of Section 6.1.7.

26. In SNOBOL4, a property list or *table* (in SNOBOL4 terminology) is created by a statement such as

X = TABLE(50,20)

Tables are stored using a mixed sequential and linked representation. An initial block big enough for 50 subscript-value pairs is created and a pointer to the block is assigned as the value of X. Subscript-value pairs are entered into the table by an assignment such as

X[Age] = 52

which enters the pair $(Age, 52)$ into the table if the subscript Age is not already present. If Age is found, then its value is changed to 52. When 50 pairs have been entered into the initially allocated block, a new block big enough for 20 pairs (the second parameter in the call to the $TABLE$ function) is allocated and linked to the first block. New pairs are now put in the new block until it is full, at which time another block for 20 pairs is allocated. Deletion of a pair is not allowed. Design a detailed storage structure appropriate for such tables, including run-time descriptor, and then give an algorithm for execution of the prior assignment on an arbitrary table.

27. In the syntactic representation of a list in the usual *list notation* (as a sequence of elements in parentheses), the terminating *cdr* pointer to *nil* is implicit (e.g., is written $(A\ B\ C)$ rather than $(A\ B\ C\ nil)$). Occasionally, it is desirable to allow the last element of a list to have a *cdr* pointer to an atom other than *nil*. In this case, an alternative notation—the *dot notation*—may be used. In dot notation, each list element is written as a pair of subelements representing the *car* and *cdr* of the element. The subelements are enclosed in parentheses and separated by a dot. For example, (A) is written $(A.nil)$, $(A\ B)$ is written $(A.(B.nil))$, and, $((A\ B)\ C)$ is written $((A.(B.nil)).(C.nil))$. Now the pair of A and B that cannot be written in list notation can be written $(A.B)$ in dot notation. Write in dot notation:

(a) (A (B C))
(b) (((A)) B (C D))

28. Property lists of atoms that contain properties other than the print name of the atom can never be garbage-collected even if they are entirely inaccessible from any active list structure at the time of garbage collection. Explain why.

29. *The self-reproducing function.* The equivalence of program and data representations in LISP makes it possible to write many subtle programs easily that would be much more difficult in other languages. Some of these have the status of *classical* LISP *problems*, of which the *self-reproducing function problem* is typical. *Write* a LISP *function* SRF *whose value is its own definition.* SRF has no inputs. If SRF is defined as

(defun SRF ()body)

then the result of the call (SRF) is the list structure (*defun SRF ()body*). SRF must construct its result list piecemeal. It cannot access the property list of atom SRF to obtain its definition list.

30. Consider the following ML program:

```
datatype digit = zero | one | two | three | four | five
    | six | seven | eight | nine;
datatype number = sdigit of digit | node of number * number;

fun digitv(one) = 1 | digitv(two) = 2 | digitv(three) = 3
    | digitv(four) = 4 | digitv(five) = 5 | digitv(six) = 6
    | digitv(seven) = 7 | digitv(eight) = 8 | digitv(nine) = 9
    | digitv(zero) = 0;
fun value(node(x,y)) = 10 * value(x) + value(y)
    | value(sdigit(x)) = digitv(x);
```

(a) Trace the execution of each of the following. What value is printed for each?

(1) *value(sdigit(seven))*
(2) *value(node(sdigit(nine), sdigit(three)))*
(3) *value(node(sdigit(three), node(sdigit(one), sdigit(four))))*

(b) Draw the data structure for each expression given in *(a)*.

Chapter 7

Inheritance

In Section 6.2, the concept of encapsulated data types is discussed as a means to designing programs that create new data types with operations that only operate on objects of these new types. For example, to schedule classes, the types *section* and *student* could be defined and operations like *AddToSection* with the signature *student* × *section* → *section* could be implemented to handle adding a new student to a given course section.

Given the program

typedef { *definition* } section;
typedef { *definition* } student;
section NewClass;
student NewStudent;
AddToSection(NewStudent,NewClass);

the details of how *student* and *section* objects are implemented is hidden by the *AddToSection* subprogram. The programmer may consider *student* and *section* as primitive types and *AddToSection* as a primitive function. Only the implementor of the *AddToSection* subprogram need be aware of the actual structure of the various data types. Although such techniques may be employed in any language, we want their use easier and less error-prone. Rather than relying on programmers doing the right thing, we want the language to help us encapsulate data.

We first describe mechanisms for automatically encapsulating data, such as the Ada **package**. We then extend this concept so that operations on these data objects may be automatically derived using a concept called *inheritance*. Such operations are called *methods*. Finally, we extend the concept to full polymorphism on operations.

7.1 ABSTRACT DATA TYPES REVISITED

Recall from Section 6.2 that we define an *abstract data type* as a new data type defined by the programmer that includes

1. A programmer-defined data type,
2. A set of abstract operations on objects of that type, and
3. Encapsulation of objects of that type in such a way that the user of the new type cannot manipulate those objects except by use of the defined operations.

Data abstraction—that is, the design of abstract data objects and operations on those objects—is a fundamental part of programming, as discussed earlier. In a programming language that provides little direct support for data abstraction beyond the ordinary subprogram mechanism, the programmer may still design and use abstract data types, but the concept is not present in the language. Instead, the programmer must use coding conventions to organize the program so that the effect of an abstract data type is achieved. Without language support for the definition of abstract data types, however, encapsulation of a new type is not possible. Thus, if the coding conventions are violated, whether intentionally or not, the language implementation cannot detect the violation. Such programmer-created abstract data types often appear as special subprogram libraries in languages such as C, FORTRAN, and Pascal. Ada, Java, and C++ are among the few widely used languages with data abstraction features.

Type definitions such as those provided by C make it simpler to declare new variables of the type because only the type name is needed in the declaration. However, the internal structure of data objects of the type is not encapsulated. Any subprogram that can declare a variable to be of the new type is also allowed to access any component of the representation of the type. Thus, any such subprogram may bypass the defined operations on the data objects and instead directly access and manipulate the components of the data objects. The intent of encapsulation of an abstract data type definition is to make such access impossible so that the only subprograms that know how data objects of the type are represented are the operations defined as part of the type.

Of the languages described in this book, only Ada, C++, Java, and Smalltalk provide language support for encapsulation of such abstract type definitions. In Ada, such an abstract type definition is one form of a *package*. A package defining an abstract data type *SectionType* might take the form shown in Figure 7.1. The declaration **is private** for type *Section* indicates that the internal structure of section data objects is not to be accessible from subprograms using the package. The actual details of this type are given at the end of the package in the **private** component of the package. Only subprograms within the package definition have access to these private data. Thus, for example, procedures *AssignStudent* and *CreateSection* may access the array *ClassRoll*, which is one component of a *Section*, but any other procedure (outside the package) cannot access this component, although the other procedure may declare a variable to be of type *Section* (and specify a maximum class size as a parameter).

Implementation. Abstract data types defined as Ada packages involve few new implementation ideas. A package provides encapsulation for a set of type definitions

```
package SectionType is
    type StudentID is integer;
    type Section(MaxSize: integer) is private;
    procedure AssignStudent(Sect: in out Section;
        Stud in StudentID);
    procedure CreateSection(Sect: in out Section;
        Instr in integer;
        Room in integer);
    private
        type Section(MaxSize: integer) is
            record
                Room: integer;
                Instructor: integer;
                ClassSize: integer range 0..MaxSize :=0;
                ClassRoll: array (1..MaxSize) of StudentID;
            end record;
    end;

package body SectionType is
    procedure AssignStudent(...) is
            – Statements to insert student on ClassRoll
        end;
    procedure CreateSection(...) is
            – Statements to initialize components of Section record
        end;
    procedure ScheduleRoom(...) is
            – Statements to schedule Section in a room
        end;
    end;
```

Figure 7.1. Abstract data type Section defined in Ada.

and subprograms. Thus, its primary new effect is to restrict the visibility of the names declared in the package so that users of the abstract type cannot gain access to the internal elements of the definition. Once the compiler determines that a given procedure has access to the type definition, the algorithms for data object allocation and accessing from earlier chapters apply.

Having just said that Ada packages do not use new implementation ideas, it is interesting to look at the **package** concept more closely. Each Ada package contains two parts: a specification part and an implementation part. As given in Figure 7.1, the specification for package *SectionType* defines all data, types, and subprograms that are known and made visible to procedures declared in other packages. The implementation of the procedures declared in the specification part of the package are given in the **package body** component. The package body may also include additional data objects and types that are not to be made visible to other packages. In this case, procedure *ScheduleRoom* may only be called from

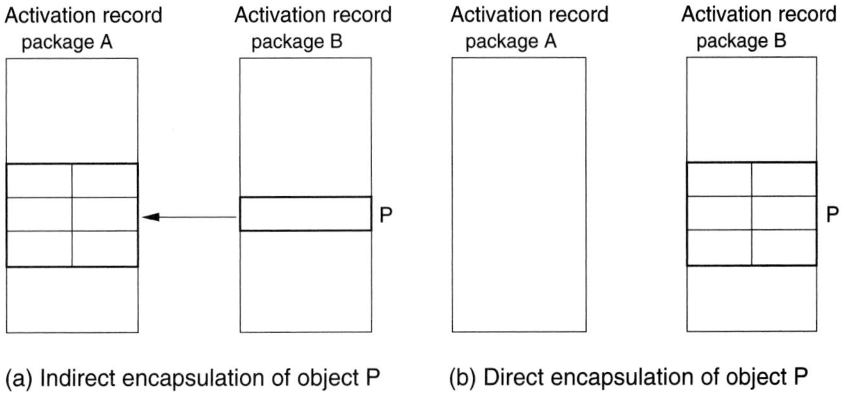

Figure 7.2. Two implementation models for abstract data.

within *AssignStudent* and *CreateSection*; the name is simply not known outside of the package.

The need for the procedure name in the package specification is simple enough; the compiler needs to know the signature of the procedure if it is called from another package, and only the package specification defines the types for each of the formal parameters. Thus, a call to *AssignStudent* from a procedure in another package needs the information that the call requires two actual parameters: one an **in out** argument of type *Section* and the other an **in** parameter of type *StudentID*.

However, why are the private data definitions placed in the package specification? This is information that is known and used only within the body of the package. It would seem simpler to allow such declarations to be placed only within the package body component. To see why Ada has defined packages in this manner, we have to look at the two typical implementations for abstract data types.

Figure 7.2 presents two models for implementing encapsulated data objects. Figure 7.2(a) is an example of *indirect encapsulation*. In this case, the structure of the abstract data type is defined by the package specification A. The actual storage for Object P is maintained in an activation record for Package A. In Package B, which declares and uses object P, the run-time activation record must contain a pointer to the actual data storage.

An alternative implementation is given in Figure 7.2(b), called the *direct encapsulation*. As in the indirect case, the structure of the abstract data object is defined by the specification for Package A. However, in this case the actual storage for Object P is maintained within the activation record for Package B.

Why the difference? In the indirect case, the implementation of the abstract data type is truly independent of its use. If the structure of P changes, only Package A needs to change. Package B only needs to know that Object P is a pointer and does not need knowledge of the format of the data pointed to by P. For large

```
package A is
    type MyStack is private;
    procedure NewStack(S: out MyStack);
    ...
    private
    type MyStackRep;
        – Hidden details of MyStack
    type MyStack is access MyStackRep;
        – B only has pointer to stack
end;
```

(a) Indirect encapsulation

```
package A is
    type MyStack is private;
    procedure NewStack(S: out MyStack);
    ...
    private
    type MyStack is record
        Top: integer;
        A: array (1..100) of integer;
        end record;
        – B has structure of stack
end;
```

(b) Direct encapsulation

Figure 7.3. Two encapsulation examples for Ada data.

systems with thousands of modules, the time saved in not recompiling each module whenever the definition of P changes is significant.

Nevertheless, accessing P has a run-time penalty. Each access of P requires an indirect pointer access to get to the actual storage. Although a single use is not significant, repeated access to P can be costly.

The direct encapsulation case has the opposite characteristics. In this case, data object P is stored within package B's activation record. Accessing of P's components may be faster because the standard-base-plus-offset accessing of data in a local activation record may be used; no indirection through a pointer is necessary. However, if the representation of the abstract object changes, then all instances of its use (e.g., Package B) must also be recompiled. This makes system changes expensive in compilation time, but more efficient in execution.

Ada uses the direct encapsulation model to provide for maximum run-time execution efficiency. Translating the use of an abstract data object (e.g., Package B of Figure 7.2) requires details of the object representation, hence the need for the **private** section in the package specification.

Note, however, that both direct or indirect encapsulation can be used in any program that supports encapsulation, regardless of the model implemented as part of the software architecture of the programming language. Although direct encapsulation is the favored and implied model within Ada, indirect encapsulation is possible if so implemented by the programmer. Figure 7.3 presents Ada segments that demonstrate both implementation strategies. Figure 7.3(a) corresponds to the implementation of Figure 7.2(a) (**access** is a pointer variable in Ada), and Figure 7.3(b) corresponds to the implementation of Figure 7.2(b).

A slight variation to the direct encapsulation of Figure 7.3(b) is given by the type definition:

```
package A is
    type MyStack is record
        Top: integer;
        A: array (1..100) of integer;
        end record;
```

In this case, the activation record organization is the same as direct encapsulation; however, all names are visible within Package B. This is the usual mechanism in languages like Pascal, which provide data types without encapsulation.

Generic Abstract Data Types

The primitive data types built into a language often allow the programmer to declare the basic type of a new class of data objects and then specify several attributes of the data objects as well. This is a simple form of polymorphism, which is discussed in greater detail in Section 7.3. For example, Java provides the basic data type *array* on which several primitive operations such as subscripting are defined. However, in defining the class $Vect$, Java provides a definition of the array $Vect.X$, which is now applied to objects of type *integer*:

```
class Vect { int [ ] X = new int [10] }
```

X is an array of 10 components of type integer, accessible through the subscripts 0, 1, 2, ... , 9. Subprograms may be written to manipulate $Vect$ class objects, but

```
package IntStackType is
    type Stack(Size: Positive) is private;
    procedure Push(I: in integer; S: in out Stack);
    procedure Pop(I: out integer; S: in out Stack);
private
    type Stack(Size: Positive) is record
        StkStorage: array (1 .. Size) of integer;
        Top: integer range 0 .. Size := 0;
        end record;
end IntStackType;
package body IntStackType is
    procedure Push(I: in integer; S: in out Stack) is
        begin
            – Body of Push procedure
        end;
    procedure Pop(I: out integer; S: in out Stack) is
        begin
            – Body of Pop procedure
        end;
end IntStackType;
```

Figure 7.4. Stack of integers abstraction in Ada.

```
generic
    type Elem is private;
package AnyStackType is
    type Stack(Size: Positive) is private;
    procedure Push(I: in Elem; S: in out Stack);
    procedure Pop(I: out Elem; S: in out Stack);
private
    type Stack(Size: Positive) is record
        StkStorage: array (1 .. Size) of Elem;
        Top: integer range 0 .. Size := 0;
        end record;
end AnyStackType;
package body AnyStackType is
    procedure Push(I: in Elem; S: in out Stack) is
        begin
            – Body of Push procedure
        end;
    procedure Pop(I: out Elem; S: in out Stack) is
        begin
            – Body of Pop procedure
        end;
end AnyStackType;
```

Figure 7.5. Generic stack abstraction in Ada.

the operations provided by the base type *array* are still available as well.

A similar structure is desirable for the definition of abstract data types. For example, to define a new abstract type *stack* with operations of *push* and *pop* to insert and delete elements in the stack, the stack might be defined as an Ada package as in Figure 7.4. Note the problem that arises: The type of element in a stack data object is part of the type definition for *stack*, so this definition is for a *stack of integers* data type. A *stack of reals* or a *stack of sections* type requires a separate package definition, although the representation of the stack and of the *push* and *pop* operations may be defined identically.

A *generic abstract type definition* allows such an attribute of the type to be specified separately so that one base type definition may be given, with the attributes as parameters, and then several specialized types derived from the same base type may be created. The structure is similar to that of a type definition with parameters except that here the parameters may affect the definition of the operations in the abstract type definition as well as the type definitions, and the parameters may be type names as well as values. The Ada package of Figure 7.5 shows such a generic type definition for a *generic stack* type in which both the type of element stored in the stack and the maximum size of the stack are defined as parameters.

Instantiation of a generic abstract type definition. A generic package definition represents a *template* that can be used to create particular abstract data types. The process of creating the particular type definition from the generic definition for a given set of parameters is called *instantiation.* For example, given the Ada generic stack type definition in Figure 7.5, it may be instantiated to produce a definition of the *intstack* type equivalent to that in Figure 7.4 by the declaration

package IntStackType **is**
    new AnyStackType(elem => integer);

A stack data type containing sections may be defined by the instantiation

package SetStackType **is**
    new AnyStackType(elem => Section);

Subsequently, integer stacks of different sizes may be declared:

Stk1: IntStackType.Stack(100);
NewStk:IntStackType.Stack(20);

Similarly, section stacks may be declared:

SecStack: SetStackType.Stack(10);

Note that the generic type *AnyStackType* may be instantiated many times for many different values of the parameters, and each instantiation produces another definition for the type name *Stack* within the package. Thus, when stack is referenced in a declaration, it may be ambiguous. Ada requires that the package name precede the type name in the declaration to resolve the ambiguity (e.g., *IntStackType.stack* or *SetStackType.Stack*).

In C++ , a similar concept is called a *template* and may be used to define generic classes—for example:

template <**class** *type_name*> **class** *classname class_definition*

which defines an infinite set of class definitions for all *type_name* arguments.

Implementation. A generic abstract data type, in principle, usually has a straightforward implementation. The parameters to the generic package must be given in the program when the package definition is instantiated. The compiler uses the generic package definition as a template, inserts the specified values for the parameters, and then compiles the definition as if it were an ordinary package definition without parameters. This is comparable to the *#define* macro capability of C. During program execution, only data objects and subprograms appear; the package definition serves primarily as a device to restrict the visibility of these data objects and subprograms. The package does not appear as part of the run-time structure.

If a generic type definition is instantiated many times (as might happen if the generic package were provided in a library), then this straightforward implementation may be too inefficient because the instantiation produces a copy of the entire package, including all the subprograms defined in the package, which must then be completely recompiled. A better implementation would avoid the generation of a new copy of each subprogram and would also avoid the complete recompilation of the entire package. This is discussed further in Section 7.3 when we discuss polymorphism in greater detail.

7.2 INHERITANCE

Information known in one part of a program is often needed and used in another part. For example, the actual parameters of a calling subprogram when referenced as the formal parameters of a called subprogram is a mechanism that passes the data values of the actual parameters into the called subprogram. In this case, this linkage is explicit. There is a concrete subprogram invocation that makes this association.

Often, however, information is passed among program components implicitly. We call the passing of such information *inheritance.* Inheritance is the receiving in one program component of properties or characteristics of another component according to a special relationship that exists between the two components. We have often used inheritance in programming language design.

An early form of inheritance is found in the scope rules for block-structured data. Names used in an inner block may be inherited from the outer block. For example, consider

```
{int i, j;
    {float j, k;
    k = i + j; }
}
```

In $k = i + j$, both j and k are local float variables declared in the current block. However, i is inherited from the outer block, and the declaration of *int j* is blocked from being inherited into the inner block due to the redefinition of j as a *float* variable.

Although scope rules in languages likes Ada, C, and Pascal are a form of inheritance, the term is more often used to refer to the passing of data and functions between independent modules of a program. The C++ **class** is one such example. If a relationship between Class A and Class B is established, written $A \Rightarrow B$, then certain objects within Class A will be implicitly inherited and may be used within Class B. If a certain object X is declared within Class A and is not redefined in Class B, then any reference to Object X within Class B actually refers to Object X of Class A via inheritance, much like the reference to the variable i in the prior C example.

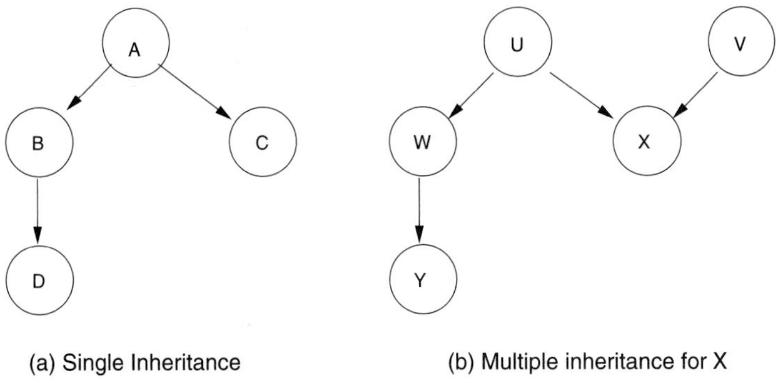

Figure 7.6. Single and multiple inheritance.

If we have $A \Rightarrow B$, we say that A is the *parent* class or *superclass* and B is the *dependent*, *child*, or *subclass* class. A is B's immediate *ancestor*. In Figure 7.6(a), A is the ancestor of both B and C, B and C are siblings, B and C are the immediate descendants of A, and D is a descendant of A. If a class can only have a single parent (Figure 7.6(a)), we say that it has *single inheritance*. If a class can have multiple parents (Figure 7.6(b)), we say that it has *multiple inheritance*.

C++, but not Java, allows for multiple inheritance. Ada 95 has added *tagged* types as a form of inheritance, where the object declared as *tagged private* may be used in a new package with additional components. Examples are:

```
type Calendar is tagged private;
   ...
private
type Calendar is tagged record
    Day: integer;
    Month: integer;
    end record
```

and

```
type AnnualCalendar is new Calendar with record
    Year: integer;
    end record
```

7.2.1 Derived Classes

Classes in languages like C++, Java, and Smalltalk are closely tied to the concept of encapsulation. Classes typically have a part that gets inherited by another class and a part that is used internally and hidden from outside exposure. For example, the Ada integer stacks of Figure 7.4 can be represented in C++ as

```
class intstack
    {private:
    int size;
    int storage(100); }
```

or in Java as

```
class intstack
    {private int size;
    int [ ] storage = new int[100]; }
```

The name *intstack* is a class name known outside of the class, whereas the declarations *size* and *storage* following **private**, as in Ada, represent components of class *intstack* that are known only within the class.

An abstraction includes both data descriptors and functions that may operate on objects of that type. Such functions are often called *methods.* A more complete description of the class *intstack*, including its methods, would be

```
class intstack
    {public:
    intstack() { size=0;}
    void push(int i) { storage[size++]=i;}
    int pop ...
private:
    int size;
    int storage(100);
    }
```

public refers to names that are visible outside of the class definition and may be inherited by other classes. The function *intstack*(), the same name as the class, in the class definition is a special function called a *constructor*, which is called whenever objects of that class are created. Here this function initializes the stack to empty, but in general it can execute any relevant initialization code needed to establish objects of that class. In this example, *push* and *pop* may be used outside of the class definition and are invoked as methods applied to objects of class *intstack* as in *b.push*(7) or j = *b.pop*() for *intstack b*. Names *size* and *storage* are known only within the class definition.

If the function ~*intstack* were defined, then it would be a *destructor* and would be called whenever objects of that class were to be deallocated. In the prior example, the destructor function is not needed. However, if the constructor allocated some additional storage, the destructor would be required to undo that allocation and delete the extra storage.

The notation *b.push*(7) is not as strange as it first appears. Class definitions are similar to C type definitions, only we have extended types with function components. Hence, *b.push* is the *push* function component of Object *b*. This similarity between C++ and Java classes and the C **struct** is not just coincidental. The C declaration

```
class elem {
public:
    elem() { v=0;}
    void ToElem(int b) { v = b;}
    int FromElem() { return v; }
private:
    int v; }

class ElemStack: elem {
public:
    ElemStack() { size=0;}
    void push(elem i)
        { size=size+1; storage[size]=i;}
    elem pop()
        { size=size-1; return storage[size+1]}
private:
    int size;
    elem storage[100]; }

{ elem x;
    ElemStack y;
    int i;
    read(i);          – Get integer value for i
    x.ToElem(i);      – Coercion into type elem
    y.push(x);        – Put x on stack y
    . . .
}
```

Figure 7.7. Derived classes in C++.

struct A {int B}

is just shorthand for the C++ declaration

class A {**public**: int B}

Class definitions, however, may also include function definitions as well as data declarations.

Inheritance in C++ and Java occurs via the use of *derived* classes. For example, if a class creates objects of type *elem* and another class creates stacks of objects of that type, this can be specified by Figure 7.7. The name *ElemStack* following the **class** designation is the derived class, and the name following the colon is the base class (*elem*). (Java uses the keyword **extends** instead of the colon.) If one considers the operations of a class to simply be components of the object definition, then the syntax becomes quite easy to understand. The notation $x.ToElem(\ldots)$ becomes a reference to the *ToElem* method defined in class *elem*, which results in a call on the *ToElem* procedure using object x as an implicit argument.

This example includes several important aspect of using classes to encapsulate data:

1. All public names within class *elem* are inherited by *ElemStack*. These names are also public in *ElemStack* and known to any user of such a stack.

2. The contents of an object of type *elem* are private data and not known outside of the class definition. In this case, *ToElem* and *FromElem* function as coercion operators that convert from type integer to type *elem*. These will always be needed if the internal structure of the class is private.

The keywords *private* and *public* control the visibility of inherited objects. In Java, these are attributes on the data objects. C++ and Java also include the keyword *protected*, meaning that the name is visible to any derived type of the base type, but is not known outside of the class definition hierarchy.

Implementation. Implementing classes does not impose much additional work for the translator. In a derived class, only the inherited names from the base class are added to the local name space for the derived class, and only the public ones are made visible to users of that class. The actual storage representation for the defined objects can be determined statically by the data declarations within the class definition.

If a constructor is present in the definition, then the translator must include a call on that function whenever a new declaration is encountered (i.e., on block entry). Finally, for invocation of methods, such as $x.push(i)$, the translation need only consider this as a call on $push(x, i)$ viewing x as an implicit first argument. Storage management is the same as in Standard C, and the same stack-based organization in C may be used for C++.

Storage management for Java poses more of a problem because arrays are dynamic. The array is declared and storage allocated by the *new* operator. For example,

$$\text{int[ ] NewArray} = \text{new int[10]};$$

creates an array object named *NewArray*, and then the *new* operator dynamically allocates space for 10 integers to assign to *NewArray*. *NewArray* is simply a pointer to this allocated storage. The Java virtual machine needs a dynamic heap storage for allocating arrays.

Each instance of a class has its own data storage consisting of the data objects making up objects of the class as well as pointers to all the methods defined for objects of that class. If the object is derived from some other base class, then that inheritance is handled by the translator and the actual storage for the object contains all of the details of its implementation. We call this a *copy-based approach* toward inheritance, and it is the simplest and most straightforward model to implement.

An alternative implementation model is called the *delegation-based approach.* In this model, any object of a derived class will use the data storage of the base class. Inherited properties are not duplicated in the derived object. This model requires a form of data sharing so that changes to the base object may cause changes to the derived object.

C++ only uses the copy-based approach, but delegation-based sharing does lead to more efficient use of memory (e.g., sharing of inherited properties) and the ability of changes to one object automatically (and instantly) propagating through a hierarchy of derived classes.

Multiple Inheritance

In the previous discussion, C++ classes form a tree structure with multiple derived classes inheriting data and functions from parent classes. This is the model built into Smalltalk, the original object-oriented language. (See Section 7.2.5.) However, C++ also allows new classes to be derived from more than one parent class. In the declaration

class A:B,C { ... }

Class A is derived from *both* Class B and Class C. As long as the set of objects defined by Classes B and C do not overlap, there is no problem in merging those objects in forming Class A. Also neither of these classes poses any problems with the iplementation issues discussed in the previous section.

7.2.2 Methods

The term *object-oriented programming* has been the subject of so much hype in recent years that the term is rapidly losing its meaning. For many, the term has become synonymous with the concept of *encapsulation* described earlier. However, *object orientation* means more than just the combining of data and subprograms into a single module. The inheritance of methods to create new objects provides an additional power that goes beyond simple encapsulation.

For example, consider an extension to the *ElemStack* example given earlier. In our extended example (Figure 7.8), we added the public procedure *MyType* in class *ElemStack*, which prints out the name of the type: "I am type ElemStack." We also made the internal structure of *ElemStack* **protected** so that it may be inherited to any class derived from this class.

In our stack class, we only considered the operations of *push* and *pop*, which append and delete, respectively, an element in the stack. Assume we want a new class *NewStack*, which behaves like an *ElemStack*, but includes the new method *peek*, which returns the value of the top of the stack without changing the stack. By the class definition of Figure 7.8, we seemingly do this. *NewStack* inherits all of the properties of *ElemStack* (all public data and methods) and adds the new method

```
class elem {
public:
    elem() { v=0;}
    void ToElem(int b) { v = b;}
    int FromElem() { return v; }
private:
    int v; }

class ElemStack: elem {
public:
    ElemStack() { size=0;}
    void push(elem i)
        { size=size+1; storage[size]=i;}
    elem pop()
        { size=size-1; return storage[size+1]}
    void MyType() {printf("I am type ElemStack \ n")}
protected:
    int size;
    elem storage[100]; }

class NewStack: ElemStack {
public:
    int peek() {return storage[size].FromElem()}  }
```

Figure 7.8. Method inheritance.

peek. Without even knowing about the operations *push* and *pop* of class *ElemStack* or *ToElem* and *FromElem* of class *elem*, these functions are made available to any object declared as *NewStack*. If these classes are maintained as separate modules maintained by different programmers, changes to the specifications of either *elem* or *ElemStack*, and correspondingly to the implementation of these classes, will be transparent to the definition of *NewStack* and will operate on *NewStack* objects are well as with *ElemStack* objects.

We have a problem, however. For objects of class *NewStack*, the method *MyType* still prints out "I am type ElemStack" because that is the definition of the inherited method from class *elemtype*. We can fix this in two ways:

1. We could simply redefine the method *Mytype* in the *NewStack* class definition:

    void MyType() {printf("I am type NewStack\n")}

Although this would work, it has the complexity of requiring a complete description of each method needing changes in a derived class.

2. We could use a **virtual** function. In a method definition, each subprogram name that is called in the definition is bound to the subprogram that it refers to *at the time of definition of the method.* This is the standard syntactic binding present in languages like C, Pascal, Ada, and FORTRAN and most compiled languages. However, **virtual** subprograms are dynamically bound *at the time of the call of the*

subprogram.

To see the difference, within the class definition of *ElemStack*, we could define *MyType* as follows:

virtual void TypeName() {printf("ElemStack\n")};
void MyType() {printf("I am type", TypeName())}

In class *NewStack* we could define *TypeName* as follows:

virtual void TypeName() {printf("NewStack \n")}

Although the differences between the two approaches are not great in this example, the delayed binding of the virtual method call allows for dynamic changes to the execution behavior of classes. This would be more important in classes where methods such as *MyType* were extremely long and complex. Rather than duplicating this method, with modifications, in each derived class, only a small virtual function of changes to the method need be redefined in each derived class.

Implementation. Virtual methods can be implemented in a manner similar to the central environment table of activation records (Section 9.4.1). Each virtual method in a derived class reserves a slot in the record defining the class. The constructor procedure simply fills in the location of the new virtual procedure, if there is one. If not, it fills in the location of the virtual procedure from the base class.

7.2.3 Abstract Classes

There are times when we would like our class definition to be simply a template for a class and not allow objects to be declared with that definition. Two alternatives to this model are presented: abstract superclasses and *mixin* inheritance.

Abstract superclass. Let us consider the class *ElemStack* with virtual function *TypeName* given earlier. As declared, there would be no prohibition for a user to include

ElemStack X;

in a program and create an instance of class *ElemStack*. However, we could want *ElemStack* to simply be a superclass template and require that all objects using this class be from a derived subclass. In C++, we state this by declaring *TypeName* to be a null virtual function:

virtual void TypeName()=0;

No objects may be created from classes having null virtual functions. Any derived class must redefine this function to create instances of the class.

Mixin inheritance. The model of inheritance presented so far has been $A \Rightarrow B$, where Class B is derived from and is a modification of Class A. There is another form of inheritance called *mixin*, inheritance where we only define the difference between our base class and the new derived class. Consider the class $ElemStack$ considered earlier and the derived class $NewStack$. Rather than defining a new class for $NewStack$, simply define a *delta* class giving the changes. Although this option does not exist in C++, we could represent it using a C++-like notation:

```
deltaclass StackMod
    {int peek() { return storage[size].FromElem();}
    }
```

We would then create our new class as

class NewStack = **class** ElemStack + **deltaclass** StackMod

which would have the semantics of creating a new class $NewStack$, which inherited all of the properties of class $ElemStack$ as modified by the delta class $StackMod$.

The advantage to mixin inheritance is that the delta classes can be applied to any class. Thus, if we had a comparable $ElemQueue$ class, we could create a new class that peeked at the end of the queue by using the same delta class as with stacks:

class newqueue = **class** ElemQueue + **deltaclass** StackMod

This delta class could be applied in numerous situations without the need for complex redefinitions of all class objects.

7.2.4 Smalltalk Overview

History. Smalltalk differs from the other languages in this book in two important respects: (1) It was designed as a total system and not just as a notation for developing programs; and (2) object orientation was a primitive built-in concept, as opposed to an addition of inheritance to the existing type mechanisms in languages like C++ and Ada.

Use of Smalltalk was originally limited by the lack of available implementations. However, that is no longer the case. Smalltalk seems to have a relatively small, but dedicated, following of users.

Smalltalk was developed by Alan Kay at the Xerox Palo Alto Research Center (PARC) in the early 1970s. His project, *Dynabook*, was aimed at a total personal computing environment. This was during the golden age of computing at Xerox PARC, with the development of the Alto and Star PCs, the mouse, a windowed environment (used so effectively by Steven Jobs when at Apple to develop the Macintosh), icons, the ethernet, and Smalltalk. In 1972, Dan Ingalls developed the first implementation of Smalltalk-72, the first practical release of the language.

It has evolved since then, and Smalltalk-80 is the generally accepted standard for describing the language. Because there is no official standard for the language, the name *Smalltalk* refers to a set of highly related and mostly compatible languages.

Initially, Smalltalk needed the total computing environment of a special-purpose computer to execute. Because of this, the spread of Smalltalk has been rather limited. However, several general-purpose implementations of the system now exist, and it is easy to install on large classes of machines such as UNIX workstations and PCs. The language described in this book (as well as the implementation used to test the various programs presented here) is GNU Smalltalk 1.1.1, which is widely available, developed by the Free Software Foundation.

Brief overview of the language. Smalltalk has several features that make it unique among the languages in this book:

Environment design. Smalltalk was designed as a total system: language, computer and programming environment. However, in this book, we consider Smalltalk as a programming language and do not consider the enclosing environment in any detail.

Minimal language design. A small core language defines Smalltalk. Essentially, all you can do in Smalltalk is develop a class as a subclass of other classes and attach methods to each of these classes. The basic statements of Smalltalk define assignment and sequential execution. The real power of the language is the parameter invocation mechanism, called *messages*. Using messages, control structures similar to our usual **if** and **while** structures can be defined.

Smalltalk comes with a predefined set of class definitions written in the Smalltalk source language. When Smalltalk is installed in a computer system, an empty environment image is constructed by including all of these definitions. When you invoke the Smalltalk interpreter, you obtain your own copy of this environment image. Within this image, you build new classes and modify existing classes by adding or changing methods. It would be easy for a system administrator to build a Smalltalk system with an alternative set of predefined class definitions, so it is unclear what is meant by the Smalltalk language. In this book, we consider the set of predefined classes as *the* Smalltalk language.

Smalltalk execution. The execution model for Smalltalk is based on a communication model. Data in Smalltalk consist of objects, and methods are considered to be messages sent to objects. Thus, $1+2$ means that the + message with Parameter 2 is sent to the integer object 1. The + method in this case returns the value 3. It seems a bit bizarre at first, but becomes quite natural after a little practice.

Smalltalk uses a dynamic execution sequencing model. Each method executes with an activation record called a *context*. Because blocks, which contain local variables, may be assigned to a variable, a stack-based last-in first-out storage mechanism is not correct. Smalltalk has to use heap storage for both data object storage and activation record storage. A dynamic garbage collector is typically used, although the semantics of the needed garbage collection are not specified by the language.

7.2.5 Objects and Messages

Smalltalk represents an alternative approach to the development of objects and methods that differs significantly in design from the inheritance models presented earlier in this chapter for Ada and C++. Smalltalk was conceived by Alan Kay at Xerox Palo Alto Research Center during the early 1970s, although many contributed to the eventual design of the language. Smalltalk was designed as a total personal computing environment. As such, it included a language for representing algorithms as well as a computing environment consisting of a windowed screen and a mouse executing on the Xerox Alto workstation. These are all quite common today, but were considered revolutionary when first developed.

A Smalltalk program is composed of a set of class definitions consisting of data objects and methods. All data are encapsulated because only methods of a given class have access to the data within that class definition. Information hiding and encapsulation are inherently built-in features and were not grafted onto the type structure of the language, as was the case with C++.

A Smalltalk program consists of three primary language features:

1. *Class definitions.* These are executable statements that define the internal structure and methods that can be used to create and manipulate objects of a class. Data may be defined that is common across all objects of a given class.

2. *Instantiation of objects.* Specific objects are created for each class definition by invoking creation methods within the class definition. Methods may be defined for instances of a class.

3. *Message passing.* Methods are passed as messages to an object to perform an action. Rather than associating a set of parameters to a function, as is the case with most other languages, in Smalltalk a function (i.e., a method) is associated with a data object. This association of a method with an object is called a *message.*

There are three types of messages in Smalltalk:

1. A *unary* message is simply a method that has no parameter. For example, the predefined method *new* can be invoked to create an object of most classes:

```
x _ Set new
```

creates a new object of class *Set* and assigns it to Variable x. x is now an instance of an object of class *Set*.

2. A *binary* message is principally used for arithmetic operators. $3+6$ refers to the binary method + being sent to the object 3 with the argument 6. The method + returns the object 9 (not surprisingly) for this message.

3. *Keyword* messages have a behavior similar to overloaded functions in languages like Ada and C++. To assign a value to the third element of Array x, the

sequence would be to create the array and then perform the assignment:

x _ Array new:10
x at:3 put:42

The method *new*: is first sent to the *Array* class with Parameter 10 to create a 10-element array that is assigned to Variable x. The keyword method *at*: and *put*: is invoked to assign the third component of x with the value 42. The method name for this assignment is given as the concatenation of the keywords, or method *at:put:*. Another method, *at:*, if sent to an instance of an array, retrieves a value from the array.

The use of the _ as an assignment operator requires a bit of computer history to understand. Originally, the Smalltalk assignment operator was the symbol ←, which, during the 1960s and 1970s, was the same keyboard position as _, hence they had the same internal definition. The use of ← on the keyboard has generally disappeared, but its character position for use in Smalltalk has not changed. Similarly, the operator to indicate a returned value from a method was originally ↑, which shares the keyboard position with ∧. The use of ↑ on keyboards has also generally disappeared.

Sequences of statements may be executed in Smalltalk as a block—for example,

$$[\ :local\_variable \mid statement_1 \ldots statement_n]$$

where *local_variable* is an optional local variable declared in the block. (The leading : prevents syntactic ambiguity in block definitions.) Execution of a block occurs by passing the method *value* to the block, and the result of the execution is the last expression in the block. Thus,

```
| x |
x _ ['This is a string']. "x is assigned the block."
x value print ! "The block assigned to x is evaluated."
```

causes:

1. Local variable x to be declared;
2. x is assigned the block;
3. *x value* causes *This is a string* to be returned, which *print* prints.

Comments are indicated by double quotes in Smalltalk. The symbol ! (often referenced as *bang* in publishing and similarly adopted as computer jargon) is a command for Smalltalk to execute the previous sequence of statements.

Use of keyword parameter passing allows for the creation of many common control structures. The predefined environment for Smalltalk includes for Boolean instances the method *ifTrue:ifFalse:*. Each of these keywords takes a block as argument. For instance, *true ifTrue:ifFalse:* will evaluate the *ifTrue:* block, whereas *false ifTrue:ifFalse:* will evaluate the *ifFalse:* block. Writing these down in a familiar Pascal-like indentation we get the following syntax:

```
x > 2
    ifTrue: ['x is greater than 2' printNl]
    ifFalse: ['x is less than or equal to 2' printNl]
```

In this case, the method > with Parameter 2 is passed to Object x. Method > returns the object *true* or *false* as appropriate. This Boolean object is then passed the keyword method *ifTrue:ifFalse:* with the two blocks as arguments. Depending on which Boolean instance is evaluated, the *ifTrue* : or *ifFalse* : block is executed. (*PrintNl* is similar to method *print* with the addition of a new-line character printed after the object is printed.) Execution behaves much like an if–then–else statement, but the actual execution is radically different. Using this approach, iteration constructs can similarly be developed.

Smalltalk is the only language in this book that is totally based on encapsulation and abstraction. Inheritance is a basic feature of the method-invocation process.

The haphazard way methods may be defined leads to another problem in method definition—ambiguity. For example, consider the following methods:

```
!Datastore class methodsFor: 'Misc'!
asgn: aValue to: bValue
    aValue printNl !
to: aValue asgn: bValue
    aValue printNl !!
```

At first glance, this looks like an ambiguous definition of the method *asgn:to:*. However, *to:asgn:* is a different method:

```
st> Datastore asgn: 8 to: 9 !
Execution begins...
8
st> Datastore to: 9 asgn: 8 !
Execution begins...
9
```

It is important that each keyword method use a unique set of names.

Smalltalk has a small vocal set of adherents. It is an interesting language, but few large commercial systems have been implemented in the language. The lack of easily available translators has hindered its use. Perhaps the easy availability of translators today will change that situation.

Class Inheritance

Smalltalk data are based on a class hierarchy. If any method, which is passed to an object, is not defined within that class, it is passed to the parent class, and so on. The class *Object* is the parent superclass of all classes. Inheritance of methods is thereby a primitive feature of the language. Smalltalk only handles single inheritance with a single-ancestor class, although methods can be passed through multiple levels of parent classes.

In keyword methods, the parameter to the method is explicitly named in the method declaration, as in

```
ifTrue: trueBlock ifFalse: falseBlock
    "Variables trueBlock and falseBlock are parameters
    in body of method."
```

However, how can one access the object that the method is passed to? For example, in $x > 2$, how does the method $>$ access the object x to obtain its value? That is the purpose of the object $self$. It behaves like the *this* parameter in C++.

The need and use of the $self$ object with object hierarchies are demonstrated by the following simple example. Assume you want two classes: *ClassA* and *ClassB* with *ClassB*, being a subclass of *ClassA*. We can define these classes as follows:

```
Object subclass: #ClassA
    instanceVariableNames: ' '
    classVariableNames: ' '
    poolDictionaries: ' '
    category: nil !
ClassA subclass: #ClassB
    instanceVariableNames: ' '
    classVariableNames: ' '
    poolDictionaries: ' '
    category: nil !
```

ClassA is defined as a subclass of class *Object* (just to put it somewhere in the Smalltalk hierarchy), and *ClassB* is a subclass of *ClassA*. *instanceVariableNames* will define the set of local names used in each instantiation of an object of the class, whereas *classVariableNames* will be global data across all instances of class objects. *poolDictionaries* and *category* are not needed here, but are explained in Appendix A.12. However, the syntax of Smalltalk requires that all arguments for keyword methods be given, even with null arguments.

Consider the methods *printIt* and *testIt*, which we add as methods to the class *ClassA* via the *methodsFor* command:

```
!ClassA methodsFor: 'basic'!
    "Add methods to class ClassA"
printIt
    'This is class A' printNl !
testIt
    self printIt !!
```

Each method is defined by giving its name (and parameters, if any), followed by its definition, followed by ! to terminate the definition. !! ends *methodsFor* declarations for *ClassA*.

Application of these methods can be shown by

```
| x | x _ ClassA new. x testIt !
```

which prints,

```
This is class A
```

as expected. Execution proceeds as follows:

1. *new* is passed to class *ClassA*, which passes it to the parent class *Object*.
2. *Object* instantiates the object and assigns it to variable x.
3. The method *testIt* is passed to the instantiated *ClassA* object named x.
4. Method *testIt* is defined as *self printIt*, where *self* refers to object x.
5. The method *printIt* is passed to the object x, which prints the appropriate response.

However, consider what happens when we define a similar method for *ClassB*, which has a *printIt* method but no *testIt* method:

```
!ClassB methodsFor: 'basic'!
printIt
    'This is class B' printNl !!
```

If we write:

```
| x | x _ ClassB new. x testIt !
```

we now get:

```
This is class B
```

Method *testIt* is passed to instance x of class *ClassB*. Because method *testIt* is not defined for Class *ClassB*, *testIt* is passed to the parent class *ClassA*. Here, *testIt* is defined. *self* still refers to object x, but now is of class *ClassB*, so the *printIt* of *ClassB* is invoked rather than the parent method of Class *ClassA* containing the *testIt* method.

7.2.6 Abstraction Concepts

After discussing the role of methods and virtual functions, it is perhaps useful to go back over the role of abstraction in programming languages. Encapsulation is often viewed as a mechanism for divide and conquer to provide intellectual control over the developing program. A programmer is only given access to those data objects that are part of the specification of the segment of the program to be developed.

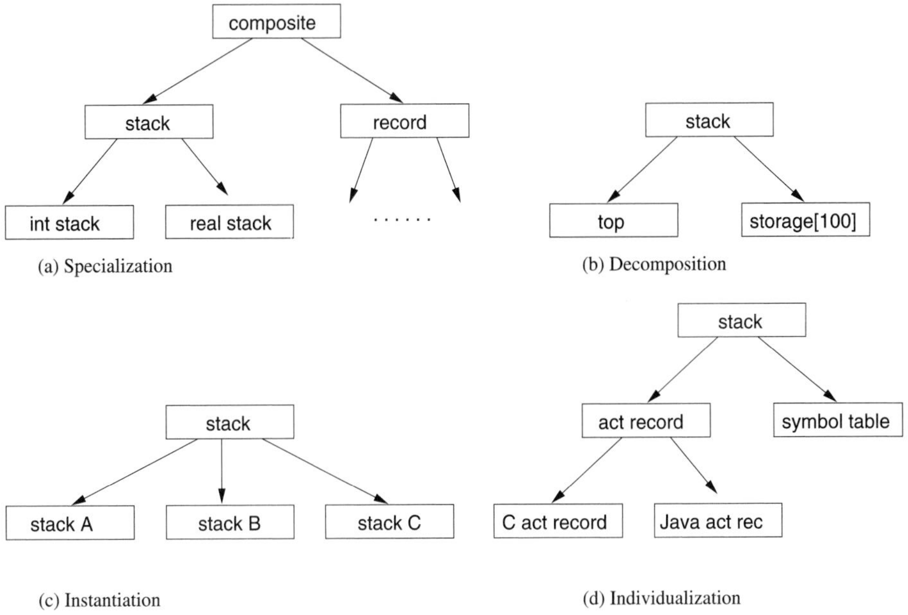

Figure 7.9. Abstraction concepts.

The specification of any other part of the program (and the internal implementation of data that meet those specifications) is outside the domain of knowledge of the programmer. However, we can view abstraction, and the related concept of *inheritance*, as more than just an information wall preventing the programmer from viewing the contents of improper data objects.

Inheritance provides the mechanism for passing information among objects in related classes. If $A \Rightarrow B$ means B is a related class to A, what is the relationship between objects of A and objects of B? Four such relationships exist, as exhibited in Figure 7.9. These summarize the various uses for inheritance in languages.

Specialization. This is the most common form of inheritance, which allows the derived Object B to obtain more precise properties than are present in Object A (Figure 7.9[a]). Thus, a *stack* is more precise than *composite* data, and an *int stack* is more precise than a *stack*, although it retains the essential properties of a stack by inheriting the methods *push* and *pop*. Previously we described $NewStack$ as derived from *ElemStack* by the addition of the *peek* function. We would say that class $NewStack$ is a specialization of class *ElemStack*.

The opposite concept of specialization is *generalization* (e.g., a *stack* is more general than an *int stack* or a *real stack*). Generalization represents the superclass of a set of derived subclasses.

Decomposition. This is the principle of separating an abstraction into its components (Figure 7.9[b]). This is the typical encapsulation mechanism of languages like Ada without the inheritance of methods. For example, a *stack* (externally) consists of a variable *top* and an array *storage*[100] internally. The internal names are not known outside of the defining class. The inverse concept is *aggregation.*

Instantiation. This is the process of creating instances of a class. It is essentially a *copy* operation (Figure 7.9[c]). Declaring instances of a class object in a C++ program is a typical example of instantiation, and it is the process of declaring Object x of Type y in a program:

stack A, B, C;

This causes the execution environment to make three copies of the object of type *stack* and name them A, B, and C.

The inverse concept to instantiation is *classification.* In our example, we would classify A, B, and C as instances of class *stack*.

Individualization. This is the fourth abstraction principle (Figure 7.9[d]), and it is a bit more complex to understand. In this case, similar objects are grouped together for common purposes. The inverse concept is *grouping.* For example, among stacks in a translator, there may be activation records and symbol tables. C and Pascal both implement activation records as stacks, but they are stacks with different characteristics. All of these are instances of specialization. All have the same essential characteristics exemplified by the *push* and *pop* characteristics of a stack. However, the role that a C or Pascal activation record plays in program execution is different, although the underlying structures are similar.

7.3 POLYMORPHISM

The use of parameters to subprograms is one of the oldest characteristics of programming languages. However, in most languages, parameters have one important characteristic: They have an l-value. That is, they are a data object that requires storage in the run-time activation record of the program. It is very familiar to write $P(A, 7)$ or $Q(B, false, \text{`}i\text{'})$. However, statements like $R(integer, real)$ rarely appear, where the parameters refer to types in the language.

Polymorphism means the ability of a single operator or subprogram name to refer to any of a number of function definitions depending on the data types of the arguments and results. We already discussed a limited form of polymorphism in chapter 5, when we discussed overloading of certain operators. In the expressions $1+2$ and $1.5+2.7$, two different + operators are referenced: an integer operator in the first and a real operator in the second. The use of **generic** in Ada allows for limited overloading of functions, where multiple instances of a function are compiled, one for each of the indicated types for the function arguments. Unification in Prolog can also be seen as a form of polymorphism as Prolog attempts to unify a query with the set of rules and facts in the Prolog database.

Polymorphism is generally applied to functions where a type is one of the arguments. Of the languages we discuss, ML and Smalltalk provide for the most general applicability of polymorphism. The identity function, for example, can accept arguments of any type. If we define *ident* as

```
fun ident(x) = x;
```

we get the response

```
- fun ident(x) = x;
val ident = fn : 'a -> 'a
```

from ML, signifying that *ident* is a function that takes an argument of type $'a$ (i.e., any type) and returns an argument of type $'a$ (i.e., the same type) for type parameter $'a$. Thus, passing integer, string, and integer list arguments to ident are all valid:

```
- ident(3);
val it = 3 : int
- ident("abc");
val it = "abc" : string
- ident([1,2,3]);
val it = [1,2,3] : int list
```

In ML, certain operators in a function definition allow for polymorphism, such as equality and operators that make lists out of objects. However, certain operators restrict the domain. For example, arithmetic operators such as + and − limit the results to arithmetic types. However, as explained earlier, + is already overloaded as one of the numeric data types. Because of that, ML definitions such as the previously given

```
fun area(length,width) = length*width;
```

are ambiguous, although $area(1, 2)$ or $area(1.3, 2.3)$ would be unambiguous calls on the function. ML uses a static test on the types of function arguments, although a dynamic test of the types could permit polymorphism for the *area* function.

The difference between ML polymorphism and the Ada generic function is that Ada would compile separate *ident* functions, one to handle each different type of argument. In ML a single instance of the function suffices. In general, functions that use equality (or inequality) and creation of tuples and lists in ML may be polymorphic because these operations do not need to operate on the actual data.

Arguments to ML functions can be of any type (which is statically determined). Therefore, we can write polymorphic functions that take function arguments and apply them to data objects. Consider the following two ML functions: *length* computes the length of a list of integers, and *printit* prints the items of the integer list in order:

```
fun length(nil) =             0
    | length(a::y) =          1+length(y);
fun printit(nil) =            print("\n")
    | prx(a::y: int list) =   (print(a);printit(y));
```

The function *process* can now be invoked with arguments of any type, as long as they are compatible—for example,

```
fun process(f,l) = f l;
```

where $f\ l$ is equivalent to $f(l)$. We thus may have

```
process(printit,[1,2,3]);
123
process(length,[1,2,3]);
3
```

Implementation. For statically typed languages like ML and C++ , polymorphism adds no new complexity. However, languages that allow for dynamic polymorphism (e.g., variants of LISP such as Scheme) pose a problem because the arguments to a polymorphic function must be determined during program execution.

Let us use LISP as an example. A LISP list item contains three fields, which we previously called a type field, a *car* field and a *cdr* field (Section 6.1.7). Because the *car* and *cdr* fields are fixed sizes and the arguments to a polymorphic function can be one of several types, it is necessary for the executing program to determine what the actual type of the argument is.

Two forms of arguments can be passed to a polymorphic function:

1. *An immediate descriptor* occurs when the value to a function is smaller than the size of the fixed field. For example, passing a Boolean, character, or small integer to a function uses less space than the fixed-size object permits. In this case, the actual value is placed in the *car* or *cdr* field, and the extra bits in the field are used to tell the function what the type actually is.

2. *A boxed descriptor* occurs in all other cases. The *car* or *cdr* field will contain a type indicator stating the argument is boxed, and the rest of the field will be the address of the actual object (which will be elsewhere, such as in heap storage)/indexHeap storage. At this address, the complete type information will be given, such as giving the entire structure of the composite data object.

As an example, assume a *car* or *cdr* descriptor field is 5 bytes. Byte 1 is a data type indicator and Bytes 2 to 5 are the data. The following arguments can be passed to a polymorphic function:

1. *32-bit Integer data.* Byte 1=0 signifying integer, bytes 2 to 5 are the 32-bit

integer value.

2. *8-bit character data.* Byte 1=1 signifying character, byte 2= actual character argument, bytes 3 to 5 unused.

3. *1-bit Boolean data.* Byte 1=2 and byte 2= 0 or 1.

4. *Complex record structure.* Byte 1=3 and bytes 2 to 5 are pointer to structure. The r-value at this pointer address contains more information about the actual argument.

Execution of such a polymorphic function will be slower than for a statically typed language like C++ because the executing program must interrogate the arguments before obtaining the argument values. However, in many applications, the power of creating polymorphic functions outweighs the execution inefficiency.

7.4 SUGGESTIONS FOR FURTHER READING

David Parnas was an influential contributor to the development of encapsulated data types in the early 1970s [PARNAS 1972]. Object-oriented development is explored in [HORSTMANN 1997]. The 1977 ACM Conference *Language Design for Reliable Software* was probably the major meeting where proposals for encapsulation mechanisms in languages like Alphard, CLU, Gypsy, Mesa, Euclid, and others were discussed [WORKMAN 1977].

Object-oriented approaches had their start with the development of Smalltalk-72 and its successors [INGALLS 1978], although acceptance of the language was limited due to the limited availability of implementations for it. The general issues of inheritance are discussed more fully in [TAIVALSAAR 1993]. Polymorphism and types are an integral part of ML and are discussed in [ULLMAN 1994].

7.5 PROBLEMS

1. Define a polymorphic function *reverse* in ML that takes a list of objects of some type and reverses the order.

2. Develop a set of functions (e.g., *push*, *pop*, *NewStack*, *top*) in ML that are polymorphic and allow stacks of any type to be created.

3. Assume that the method *print* is defined for instances of class *object*. Explain the execution behavior for the Smalltalk statement 3 *print*.

4. Describe the execution of each of the following Smalltalk expressions:

(a) 2 + 3

(b) 3 + 2

(c) '2' + 3

(d) (2 + 3) print

(e) (2 < 3) ifTrue:['true' print] ifFalse:['false' print]

5. Why doesn't the use of standard ".h" include files in C provide an adequate data abstraction capability for C programs?

6. Why do we need null virtual classes in C++? We could just refrain from allocating objects of this class and simply use subclasses of the superclass.

7. Review the two implementation models for abstract data of Figure 7.2. Which model describes C++ and Smalltalk? How are they implemented?

8. Why is it necessary for Smalltalk to have separate methods for classes and class instances? Could we eliminate one of these mechanisms and still develop Smalltalk programs effectively?

9. Consider the following objects. Develop a class hierarchy for them and define the appropriate set of functions, with inheritance for computing the volume, surface area, and perimeter (as appropriate): box, circle, rectangle, triangle, polygon, line, point, object, quadrilateral, sphere, square, trapezoid, parallelogram, hexagon, pentagon, pyramid, cone.

Chapter 8

Sequence Control

Control structures in a programming language provide the basic framework within which operations and data are combined into programs and sets of programs. To this point, we have been concerned with data and operations in isolation. Now we must consider their organization into complete executable programs. This involves two aspects: control of the order of execution of the operations, both primitive and user defined, which we term *sequence control* and discuss in this chapter, and control of the transmission of data among the subprograms of a program, which we term *data control* and discuss in the next two chapters. This division is convenient because both subjects are rather complex, but it also serves to differentiate sharply two aspects of programming languages that are often confused.

8.1 IMPLICIT AND EXPLICIT SEQUENCE CONTROL

Sequence-control structures may be conveniently categorized into four groups:

1. *Expressions* form the basic building blocks for statements and express how data are manipulated and changed by a program. Properties such as precedence rules and parentheses determine how expressions become evaluated.

2. *Statements* or groups of statements, such as conditional and iteration statements, determine how control flows from one segment of a program to another.

3. *Declarative programming* is an execution model that does not depend on statements, but nevertheless causes execution to proceed through a program. The logic programming model of Prolog is an example of this.

4. *Subprograms*, such as subprogram calls and coroutines, form a way to transfer control from one segment of a program to another. These are developed in chapter 9.

This division is necessarily somewhat imprecise. For example, some languages such as LISP and APL have no statements, only expressions, yet versions of the usual statement sequence-control mechanisms are used.

Sequence-control structures may be either implicit or explicit. *Implicit* (or default) sequence-control structures are those defined by the language to be in effect unless modified by the programmer through some explicit structure. For example, most languages define the physical sequence of statements in a program as controlling the sequence in which statements are executed, unless modified by an explicit sequence-control statement. Within expressions, there is also commonly a language-defined hierarchy of operations that controls the order of execution of the operations in the expression when parentheses are absent. *Explicit* sequence-control structures are those that the programmer may optionally use to modify the implicit sequence of operations defined by the language (e.g., by using parentheses within expressions or **goto** statements and statement labels).

8.2 SEQUENCING WITH ARITHMETIC EXPRESSIONS

Consider the following formula for computing roots of the quadratic equation:

$$root = \frac{-B \pm \sqrt{B^2 - 4 \times A \times C}}{2 \times A}$$

This apparently simple formula actually involves at least 15 separate operations (assuming a square-root primitive and counting the various data references). Coded in a typical assembly or machine language, it would require at least 15 instructions and probably far more. Moreover, the programmer would have to provide storage for and keep track of each of the several intermediate results generated and would also have to worry about optimization: Can the two references to the value of B and A be combined? In what order should the operations be performed to minimize temporary storage and make best use of the hardware? In a high-level language such as FORTRAN, however, the formula for one of the roots can be coded as a single expression almost directly:

ROOT = (-B+SQRT(B**2-4*A*C)) / (2*A)

The notation is compact and natural, and the language processor rather than the programmer concerns itself with temporary storage and optimization. It seems fair to say that the availability of expressions in high-level languages is one of their major advantages over machine and assembly languages.

Expressions are a powerful and natural device for representing sequences of operations, yet they raise new problems. Although it may be tedious to write out long sequences of instructions in machine language, at least the programmer has a clear understanding of exactly the order in which the instructions are executed. But what of the expression? Take the FORTRAN expression for the quadratic formula. Is the expression correct? How do we know, for example, that the expression indicates the subtraction should take place *after* the computation of $4 * A * C$ rather than before? The sequence-control mechanisms that operate to determine the order of operations within this expression are in fact rather complex and subtle.

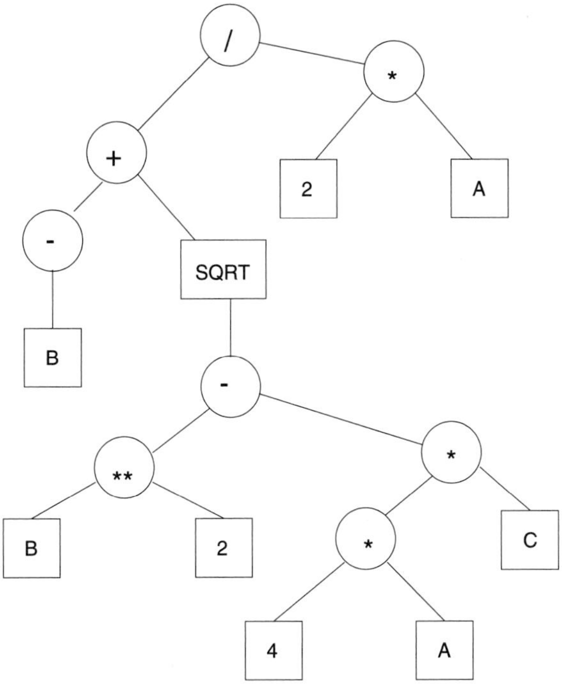

Figure 8.1. Tree representation of quadratic formula.

8.2.1 Tree-Structure Representation

So far, we have considered expressions to be single entities and have ignored the actual syntax and semantics necessary for the evaluation of a given expression. In considering operations within expressions, we call the arguments of an operation its *operands.*

The basic sequence-control mechanism in expressions is *functional composition:* An operation and its operands are specified; the operands may be either constants, data objects, or other operations, whose operands in turn may be constants, data objects, or still other operations to any depth. Functional composition gives an expression the characteristic structure of a tree, where the root node of the tree represents the main operation, nodes between the root and the leaves represent intermediate-level operations, and the leaves represent data references (or constants). For example, the expression for the quadratic formula may be represented (using _ to represent the unary minus operation) by the tree of Figure 8.1.

The tree representation clarifies the control structure of the expression. Clearly the results of data references or operations at lower levels in the tree serve as operands for operations at higher levels in the tree, and thus these data references

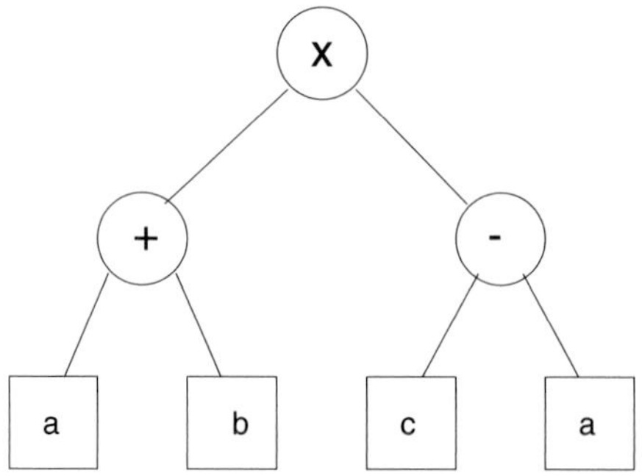

Figure 8.2. Tree form for simple expression: $(a + b) \times (c - a)$.

and operations must be evaluated (executed) first. Yet the tree representation leaves part of the order of evaluation undefined. For example, in the tree in Figure 8.1, it is not clear whether $-B$ should be evaluated before or after $B**2$, nor is it clear whether the two data references to the identifier B may be combined into a single reference. Unfortunately, in the presence of operations with side effects, it may make a difference, as we see later. It is common in a language definition to define the order of evaluation of expressions only at the level of the tree representation and to allow the language implementor to decide on the detailed order of evaluation (such as whether $-B$ or $B**2$ comes first). Before looking at the problems that arise in determining the exact order of evaluation, however, it is appropriate to look at the various syntactic representations for expressions that are in use.

Syntax for Expressions

If we take expressions as characteristically represented by trees, then in order to use expressions within programs some linearization of trees is required (i.e., one must have a notation for writing trees as linear sequences of symbols). Let us look at the most common notations.

Prefix (Polish prefix) notation. In writing function calls, one usually writes the function name preceding its arguments, as in $f(x, y, z)$. We can extend this to all operations in an expression. In prefix notation, one writes the operation symbol first, followed by the operands in order from left to right. If an operand is an operation with operands, then the same rules apply. The tree of Figure 8.2 then becomes $\times + a\ b - c\ a$. Because $+$ is a *dyadic operator* (requires two arguments), it is clear that the arguments for $+$ are a and b. Similarly, the arguments for $-$ must be c and a. Finally, the arguments for $\times$ must then be the $+$-term and the $-$-term. There is no ambiguity, and no parentheses were needed in specifying exactly how to evaluate the expression. Because the Polish mathematician Lukasiewicz invented the parenthesis-free notation, the term *Polish* has been applied to this notation and its derivatives.

A variant of this notation used in LISP is sometimes termed *Cambridge Polish.* In Cambridge Polish notation, parentheses surround an operator and its arguments. An expression then looks like a nested set of lists, where each list begins with an operator symbol followed by the lists representing the operands. In Cambridge Polish, the tree of Figure 8.2 becomes $(\times(+ab)(-ca))$.

Consider the quadratic formula (Figure 8.1) represented in prefix notation (using $\uparrow$ for exponentiation, $\surd$ for $SQRT$, and $\_$ for unary minus):

$$/ + \_\, b \surd - \uparrow b\ 2 \times \times 4\ a\ c \times 2\ a \qquad (Polish)$$
$$(/\ (+\ (\_\, b)(\surd(-(\uparrow b\ 2)(\times(\times 4\ a)c))))(\times\ 2\ a)) \qquad (Cambridge\ Polish)$$

Postfix (suffix or reverse Polish) notation. Postfix notation is similar to prefix notation except that the operation symbol *follows* the list of operands. For example, the expression in Figure 8.2 is represented as $a\ b + c\ a - \times$.

Infix notation. Infix notation is most suitable for binary (dyadic) operations. In infix notation, the operator symbol is written between the two operands. Because infix notation for the basic arithmetic, relational, and logical operations is so commonly used in ordinary mathematics, the notation for these operations has been widely adopted in programming languages and in some cases extended to other operations as well. In infix form, the tree of Figure 8.2 is represented as $(a + b) \times (c - a)$. For operators with more than two arguments (e.g., the C conditional expression), infix is used in a somewhat clumsy manner using multiple infix operators: $(expr?s_1 : s_2)$.

Semantics for Expressions

Each of these three notations—prefix, postfix, and infix—has certain attributes useful in the design of programming languages. They principally differ in how we compute the value for each expression. In what follows, we give algorithms for evaluating (i.e., computing the semantics) for each expression format. We then show that translators have an option of using this process or making minor modifications on it to make expression evaluation more efficient.

Prefix evaluation. With prefix notation, we can evaluate each expression in a single scan of the expression. We need to know, however, the number of arguments for each operation. It is for this reason that we need unique symbols for the dyadic subtraction ($-$) and the unary minus ($\_$) operation to distinguish which is the intended operation (or we must use Cambridge Polish with parentheses).

Aside from saving on parentheses, prefix notation has some value in programming language design:

1. As already stated, the usual function call is already written in prefix notation.

2. Prefix notation may be used to represent operations with any number of

operands, and thus it is completely general. Only one syntactic rule need be learned to write any expression. For example, in LISP, one need master only the Cambridge Polish notation for writing any expression and one has learned most of the syntactic rules of the language.

3. Prefix notation is also relatively easy to decode mechanically, and for this reason translation of prefix expressions into simple code sequences is easily accomplished.

This last point — easy to translate into code sequences — can be demonstrated by the following algorithm. Given prefix expression P consisting of operators and operands, we can evaluate the expression with an execution stack:

1. If the next item in P is an operator, push it on top of the stack. Set the argument count to be the number of operands needed by the operator. (If the number is n, we say that the operator is an n-ary operator.)

2. If the next item in P is an operand, push it on top of the stack.

3. If the top n entries in the stack are operand entries needed for the top n-ary operator (e.g., if $+$ was the last operator on the stack and two operands were added to the stack), we can apply the top operator to these operands. Replace the operator and its n operands by the result of applying that operation on the n operands.

Although this is fairly simple, we have the problem that after pushing an operand on the stack, we still have to check if we have enough operands to satisfy the current top operator. Use of postfix notation avoids that.

Postfix evaluation. Because the operator in postfix notation follows its operands, when an operator is scanned, its operands have already been evaluated. Therefore, evaluation of a postfix expression P, again using a stack, now proceeds as follows:

1. If the next item of P is an operand, place it on the stack.

2. If the next item of P is an n-ary operator, then its n arguments *must be* the top n items on the stack. Replace these n items by the result of applying this operation using the n items as arguments.

As can be seen, the evaluation strategy is straightforward and easy to implement. In fact, it is the basis for generating code for expressions in many translators. During translation (see chapter 3), the syntax for expressions is often converted to postfix. The code generator will then use the prior algorithm to determine the order of generating code to compute the value of the expression.

Infix evaluation. Although infix notation is common, its use in a programming language leads to a number of unique problems:

1. Because infix notation is suitable only for binary operators, a language cannot use only infix notation, but must necessarily combine infix and prefix (or postfix) notations. The mixture makes translation correspondingly more complex. Unary operators and multiargument function calls must be exceptions to the general infix property.

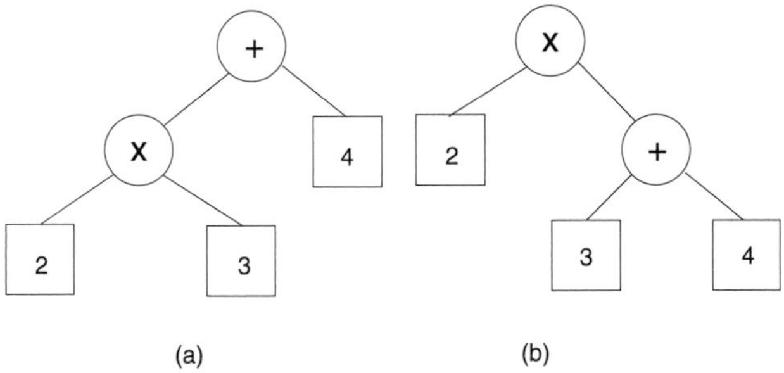

Figure 8.3. Order of evaluation of operators.

Precedence level	**Operators**	**Operations**
Highest precedence	$\star\star$ *abs not*	Exp, abs. value, negation
	$\star$ / *mod rem*	Multiplication, division
	$+$ $-$	Unary addition, subtraction
	$+$ $-$ &	Binary addition, subtraction
	$=$ $\leq$ $<$ $>$ $\geq$	Relational
Lowest precedence	*and or xor*	Boolean operations

Table 8.1. Ada hierarchy of operations.

2. When more than one infix operator appears in an expression, the notation is inherently ambiguous unless parentheses are used.

This last point can be demonstrated by considering the value for the infix expression $2 \times 3 + 4$. You undoubtedly understood this expression to mean the value 10, but it could just as easily have represented the value 14. Figure 8.3 shows why. When you first learned addition and multiplication, you learned this rule: "Do multiplication before addition" (Figure 8.3[a]). However, that is simply a convention, and mathematics could have just as well developed with an alternative assumption of performing addition before multiplication (Figure 8.3[b]). Parentheses may always be used to disambiguate any expression to explicitly indicate the grouping of operators and operands, as in $(a \times b) + c$ or $a \times (b + c)$, but in complex expressions the resulting deep nests of parentheses become confusing.

For this reason, languages commonly introduce implicit control rules that make most uses of parentheses unnecessary. We describe two such examples of implicit rules.

Precedence	Operators	Operator names
17	tokens, a[k], f()	Literals, subscripting, function call
	., ->	Selection
16	++, --	Postfix increment/decrement
15*	++, --	Prefix inc/dec
	~, -, sizeof	Unary operators, storage
	!, & , *	Logical negation, indirection
14	*(typename)*	Casts
13	*, /, %	Multiplicative operators
12	+, -	Additive operators
11	<<, >>	Shift
10	<, >, <=, >=	Relational
9	==, !=	Equality
8	&	Bitwise and
7	∧	Bitwise xor
6	$\vert$	Bitwise or
5	&&	Logical and
4	$\vert\vert$	Logical or
3*	? :	Conditional
2*	=, +=, -=, *=, /=, %=, <<=, >>=, &=, ∧=, $\vert$=	Assignment
1	,	Sequential evaluation

* - Right-associative operations

Table 8.2. C precedence levels for operators.

Hierarchy of operations (precedence rules). The operators that may occur in expressions are placed in a hierarchy or precedence order. The Ada hierarchy is typical (see Table 8.1). In an expression involving operators from more than one level in the hierarchy, the implicit rule is that operators with higher precedence are to be executed first. Thus, in $a \times b + c$, $\times$ is above $+$ in the hierarchy and is evaluated first.

Associativity. In an expression involving operations at the same level in the hierarchy, an additional implicit rule for associativity is needed to completely define the order of operations. For example, in $a - b - c$, is the first or second subtraction to be performed first? Left-to-right associativity is the most common implicit rule, so that $a-b-c$ is treated as $(a-b)-c$. [However, common mathematical conventions say that exponentiation works from right to left: $a \uparrow b \uparrow c = a \uparrow (b \uparrow c)$.]

Precedence works reasonably well for the usual arithmetic expressions because the underlying mathematical model of expression semantics is well known to most programmers. However, as languages evolve with new operators that are not from classical mathematics, precedences break down. C, APL, Smalltalk, and Forth all represent examples of languages that handle extended sets of operators in different ways:

- *C.* C uses an extended set of precedence tables, as given in Table 8.2. Most entries use left-to-right associativity, except for those that are starred. For the most part, the C precedence levels are reasonable. In contrast, Pascal has a strange anomaly in its precedence table. The Boolean expression $a = b \mid c = d$ is invalid because Pascal precedence assumes the unnatural grouping of $a = (b|c) = d$, which is not what the programmer usually means. In Pascal, it is safer to always use parentheses when writing logical expressions.

Language Summary 8.1: APL

Features: Array processsing is APL's strong point. All arithmetic operations are applicable to vectors and arrays, and additional operations exist to create special vectors, e.g., all elements set to given values. Because many of these vector operations are not intuitive, no precedence exists in APL and statements are executed from right to left – a strange quirk until one is used to it.

History: APL was developed by Ken Iverson in the early 1960s as a notation to describe computation. It was later used as a machine architectural language where the behavior of individual instructions could easily be described as vector operations in APL. A third phase in APL's development was an implementation for the IBM 360 in the late 1960s. Because of the conciseness of APL expressions, APL developed a small but devoted following who take pride in developing complex "one-liner" programs.

Example: Sum elements of an array

1	k ← □	Read size of array into k
2	A ← □	Read first element of array
3	A ← A, □	Read next array element, Expand array
4	→ 3 × ι k > ρ A	Size of A (ρ A) compared to k yielding 0 or 1. Generate vector of 0 or 1 (ι operator) and goto (→) statement 3 if result is 1 (i.e., not done yet)
5	□ ← +/A	Add elements of array (+/) and output sum

Reference: A. D. Falkoff, and K. E. Iverson, "The evolution of APL," *ACM History of Programming Languages Conference*, Los Angeles, CA (June 1978) *(SIGPLAN Notices (13)8 [August 1978])*, 47–57.

- *APL.* APL is a language whose primitive operators are designed to operate on arrays and vectors. Almost every APL operator is new in the sense that non-APL programmers find them strange when first studied. Any precedence assignment to APL operators would be artificial, thus, the language is designed with no precedence—all expressions are evaluated in a right-to-left manner. This is reasonable in most APL programs, except that some typical expressions become unintuitive. For example, $a - b - c$, where a, b, and c are integers, is evaluated as $a - (b - c)$, which is the same as $a - b + c$ in languages like ML, FORTRAN, or C. APL is summarized in Language Summary 8.1.

- *Smalltalk.* Smalltalk uses a model like APL. Because the goal with Smalltalk is to develop functions (methods) providing needed functionality, it is never clear what precedence a new function should have. Therefore, precedence is generally omitted and expression evaluation proceeds from left to right. (More about Smalltalk in Section 7.2.5.)

- *Forth.* Forth was a language designed for operating in real-time process control computers. These were developed in the 1960s as small expensive minicomputers. Memory was expensive. Any programming language had to be small, easy to translate, and efficient in execution. As given previously, evaluation of postfix expressions can be performed easily. Forth was a language whose run-time structure was a stack, and its syntax was pure postfix. This allowed translators to be easily installed inexpensively in many applications. With pure postfix, precedence was no longer an issue. Forth is summarized in Language Summary 8.2. It survives today as the basis for Postscript (Section 12.1).

Each of the notations for expressions mentioned here has its own particular difficulties. Infix notation with the implicit precedence and associativity rules and explicit use of parentheses (when required), gives a rather natural representation for most arithmetic, relational, and logical expressions. However, the need for the complex implicit rules and the necessary use of prefix (or other) notation for nonbinary operations makes the translation of such expressions complex. Infix notation without the implicit rules (i.e., with full parenthesization) is cumbersome because of the large number of parentheses required. However, both Cambridge Polish and ordinary mathematical prefix notation share this problem with parentheses. The Polish notation avoids use of parentheses altogether, but one must know in advance the number of operands required for each operator—a condition that is often difficult to satisfy when programmer-defined operations are involved. In addition, the lack of any structuring cues makes reading complex Polish expressions difficult. All the prefix and postfix notations share the advantage of applying to operations with differing numbers of operands.

8.2.2 Execution-Time Representation

We previously gave algorithms for understanding the semantics of expressions written in each of the three common forms. However, if we first transform each expression into its tree representation, we permit the translator to make alternative choices for efficient evaluation of the expression. The first stage of this translation establishes the basic tree control structure of the expression, utilizing the implicit

Language Summary 8.2: Forth

Features: Postfix source language leads to an efficient execution model, even though generally interpreted. System runs on two stacks — a subroutine return stack and an expression evaluation stack. Run-time model very small making it useful on small embedded computers.

History: Forth was developed by Charles Moore around 1970. The name was a contraction of "Fourth Generation Programming Language" with the program name limited to five characters. The language was a replacement for FORTRAN on small minicomputers in the 1970s where space was at a premium and the only input/output device was often a very slow and cumbersome paper tape. Having a resident translator/interpreter made for easy program development on the target system. Forth had limited success, but survives today as the main "engine" that drives Postscript (Chapter 12).

Example: Program to compute: $1^2 + 2^2 + \ldots + 9^2 + 10^2$

(Notation: a, b, c is expression stack. c is stack(top))
: SQR DUP * ; (Defines *square* by: $n \Rightarrow n,\ n \Rightarrow (n * n)$)
: DOSUM SWAP 1 + SWAP OVER SQR + ; ($N,\ S \Rightarrow N + 1,\ S + (N + 1)^2$)
($N, S \Rightarrow S, N \Rightarrow S, (N + 1) \Rightarrow (N + 1), S \Rightarrow$
$(N + 1), S, (N + 1) \Rightarrow (N + 1), S, (N + 1)^2 \Rightarrow$
$(N + 1),\ S + (N + 1)^2$)
3 6 DOSUM . . 22 4 *ok* (Period (.) prints stack(top). Output is $22 = 4^2 + 6$)
0 0 10 0 DO DOSUM LOOP . 385 *ok* (Apply DOSUM from 0 to 9 (Stop at 10))

Reference: E. Rather, D. Colburn, and C. Moore, "The evolution of Forth," *ACM History of Programming Languages Conference II*, Cambridge, MA (April 1993) *(SIGPLAN Notices (28)3 [March 1993])*, 177–199.

rules of precedence and associativity when the expression involves infix notation. In an optional second stage, the detailed decisions concerning order of evaluation are made, including optimization of the evaluation process.

Because of the difficulty of decoding expressions in their original infix form in the program text, it is commonplace to translate into an executable form that may be easily decoded during execution. The following are the most important alternatives in use:

1. *Machine code sequences.* The expression is translated into actual machine code, performing the prior two stages of translation in one step. The ordering of the instructions reflects the sequence-control structure of the original expression. On conventional computers, such machine code sequences must make use of explicit temporary storage locations to hold intermediate results. Machine code representation, of course, allows use of the hardware interpreter,

providing very fast execution.

2. *Tree structures.* Expressions may be executed directly in their natural tree-structure representation (Stage 1) using a software interpreter. Execution (Stage 2) may then be accomplished by a simple tree traversal. This is the basic technique used in (software-interpreted) LISP, where entire programs are represented as tree structures during execution.

3. *Prefix or postfix form.* Expressions in prefix or postfix form (both stages in a single step) may be executed by the simple interpretation algorithm given earlier. In some actual computers based on a stack organization, the actual machine code is essentially represented in postfix form. Prefix representation is the executable form of programs in SNOBOL4 in many implementations. Execution is by a left-to-right scan, with each operation calling the interpreter recursively to evaluate its operands.

Evaluation of Tree Representations of Expressions

Although translation from expressions in programs into tree representations occasionally causes difficulty, the basic translation procedure is straightforward. The second stage, in which the tree is translated into an executable sequence of primitive operations, involves most of the subtle questions of order of evaluation. It is not our concern here to study algorithms for the generation of executable code from the tree representation, but rather to consider the problems of order of evaluation that arise in determining exactly the code to generate.

Problem 1. Uniform evaluation rules. In evaluating an expression or generating code for its evaluation, one would expect the following uniform evaluation rule to apply. For each operation node in the expression tree, first evaluate (or generate code to evaluate) each of its operands and then apply the operation (or generate code to apply the operation) to the evaluated operands. We term this the *eager* evaluation rule because we always evaluate operands first. The exact order in which these evaluations occur should not matter, so that the order of evaluation of operands or independent operations may be chosen to optimize use of temporary storage or other machine features. Under this evaluation rule, for the expression $(a+b)\times(c-a)$ of Figure 8.2, either of the following orders of evaluation would be acceptable.

Order 1. Compute $a+b$ first:

1. Fetch the r-value of a.
2. Fetch the r-value of b.
3. Add a and b, obtaining d.
4. Fetch the r-value of c.
5. Subtract a from c, obtaining e.
6. Multiply d and e, obtaining f, the r-value of the expression.

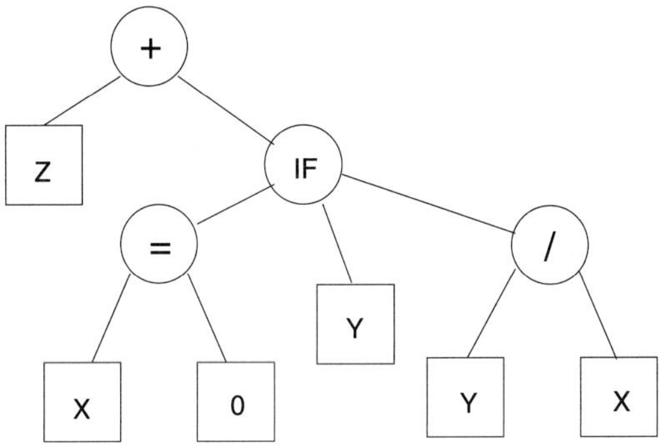

Figure 8.4. An expression containing a conditional.

Order 2. Evaluate operands before any operators:

1. Fetch the r-value of c.
2. Fetch the r-value of b.
3. Fetch the r-value of a.
4. Subtract a from c, obtaining e.
5. Add a and b, obtaining d.
6. Multiply d and e, obtaining f.

This is all quite natural, and one would like to always assume this uniform evaluation rule. Unfortunately, it does not always apply. The best example is the case of expressions containing conditionals (e.g., the C expression $Z + (Y = 0 \; ? \; X \; : \; X/Y)$ has an embedded **if** that computes $\frac{X}{Y}$ if Y is not 0). One would like to treat such a conditional simply as an operation with a funny syntax and three operands, as in Figure 8.4. In fact, in LISP, this is exactly what is done, utilizing the Cambridge Polish notation for conditionals as well as for all other operations. But now we have a problem with the uniform evaluation rule. If we assume that rule and evaluate the operands of the conditional operator in Figure 8.4, we do exactly what the conditional is set up to avoid—namely, dividing X by Y even if Y is zero. Clearly, in this case we do not wish all the operands evaluated before the operation is applied. Instead, we need to pass the operands (or at least the last two operands) to the conditional operation *unevaluated* and let the operation determine the order of evaluation.

The problem with conditionals suggests that perhaps an alternative uniform evaluation rule, often called a *lazy* evaluation rule, would be better: *Never* evaluate operands before applying the operation. Instead, always pass the operands unevaluated and let the operation decide whether evaluation is needed. This evaluation rule works in all cases and thus theoretically would serve. However, implementation turns out to be impractical in many cases, for how is one to simulate the passing of unevaluated operands to operations? This requires substantial software simulation to accomplish. Interpretive languages like LISP and Prolog often use this approach toward expression evaluation, but arithmetic-like languages such as C and FORTRAN would find the overhead of supporting such lazy evaluation prohibitive.

The two uniform evaluation rules suggested earlier—*eager* and *lazy*—correspond to two common techniques for passing parameters to subprograms: transmission *by value* and *by name*, respectively. The details of these concepts and their simulation are discussed in greater depth when parameter transmission is taken up in the next chapter. For our purposes here, it suffices to point out that no simple uniform evaluation rule for expressions (or for generating code for expressions) is satisfactory. In language implementations, one commonly finds a mixture of the two techniques. In LISP, for example, functions (operations) are split into two categories depending on whether the function receives evaluated or unevaluated operands. In SNOBOL4, programmer-defined operations (subprograms) always receive evaluated operands, whereas language-defined primitive operations receive unevaluated operands. ALGOL primitive operations receive evaluated operands, with conditionals being simulated by inline code sequences, but programmer-defined subprograms may receive both evaluated and unevaluated operands.

Problem 2. Side effects. The use of operations that have side effects in expressions is the basis of a long-standing controversy in programming language design. Consider the expression

$$a \times fun(x) + a$$

Before the multiplication can be performed, the r-value of a must be fetched and $fun(x)$ must be evaluated. The addition requires the value of a and the result of the multiplication. It is clearly desirable to fetch the value of a only once and simply use it in two places in the computation. Moreover, it should make no difference whether $fun(x)$ is evaluated before or after the value of a is fetched. However, if fun has the side effect of changing the value of a, then the exact order of evaluation is critical. For example, if a has the initial value 1 and $fun(x)$ returns 3 and also changes the value of a to 2, then the following can be the possible values for this expression:

1. *Evaluate each term in sequence:* $1 \times 3 + 2 = 5$
2. *Evaluate a only once:* $1 \times 3 + 1 = 4$
3. *Call $fun(x)$ before evaluating a:* $3 \times 2 + 2 = 8$

All such values are correct according to the syntax of the language and are determined by the execution order of the expression's components.

Two positions on the use of side effects in expressions have emerged. One position is that side effects should be outlawed in expressions—either by disallowing functions with side effects altogether or simply by making undefined the value of any expression in which side effects might affect the value (e.g., the value of the prior expression). Another view is that side effects should be allowed and that the language definition should make it clear exactly what the order of evaluation of an expression is to be so that the programmer can make proper use of side effects in the code. The difficulty with this latter position is that it makes many kinds of optimization impossible. In many language definitions, the question is simply ignored altogether, with the unfortunate result that different implementations provide conflicting interpretations.

Ordinarily, statements are allowed to have side effects. For example, the assignment operation necessarily produces a side effect—a change in the value of a variable or data structure element. Clearly we expect the side effects produced by one statement to affect the inputs of the next statement in sequence. The problem is whether this sort of interdependence through side effects should be allowed below the statement level in expressions. If disallowed, we need to specify the order of evaluation in expressions only to the tree representation level; expression evaluation, for the programmer, is without tricks, and optimization of expression evaluation sequences by the translator is possible. However, if optimization is not a prime concern, it is often valuable to allow side effects and specify the order of evaluation completely. In this case, we lose much of the reason for distinguishing between statements and expressions in a language. In a number of languages, notably LISP and APL, the distinction between expressions and statements has in fact almost or entirely disappeared. For the programmer, this represents a valuable simplification. Thus, there is no dominant position on side effects in expressions; either approach has its adherents.

Problem 3. Error conditions. A special kind of side effect is involved in the case of operations that may fail and generate an error condition. Unlike ordinary side effects, which usually are restricted to programmer-defined functions, error conditions may arise in many primitive operations (overflow, divide by zero). It is undesirable to outlaw side effects of this sort, yet the meaning and even the occurrence of such error conditions may be affected by differences in the order of evaluation of expression components. In such situations, the programmer may need precise control of the order of evaluation, yet the demand for optimization may preclude this. The solution to these difficulties tends to be essentially ad hoc and varies from language to language and implementation to implementation.

Problem 4. Short-circuit Boolean expressions. In programming, it is often natural to use the Boolean operations *and* (&& in C) and *or* (|| in C) to combine relational expressions such as the C statements

```
if ((A == 0) || (B/A > C)) { ... }
```

and

```
while (( I <= UB) && (V[I] > C)) { ... }
```

In both these expressions, evaluation of the second operand of the Boolean operation may lead to an error condition (division by zero, subscript range error); the first operand is included to ensure that the error does not occur. In C, if the left expression evaluates to *true* in the first example and *false* in the second, then the second expression is never evaluated at all. Logically, this intent makes sense because clearly the value of expression $\alpha \mid\mid \beta$ is *true* if α is *true*, and likewise $\alpha \&\& \beta$ is *false* if α alone is *false*. Unfortunately, the uniform evaluation problem mentioned earlier is also present here. In many languages, both operands are evaluated before the Boolean operation is evaluated. Many programming errors arise from the expectation that the value of the left operand of a Boolean operation may short-circuit the rest of the evaluation if the value of the overall expression may be decided from the value of the left operand alone. A solution to this problem in Ada is to include two special Boolean operations, *and then* and *or else*, which explicitly provide short-circuit evaluation, in addition to the ordinary Boolean operations *and* and *or*, which do not. For example, in Ada,

$$\textbf{if } (A = 0) \text{ or else } (B/A > C) \textbf{ then} \ldots$$

cannot fail because of division by zero, since if $A = 0$, evaluation of the entire expression is terminated and the value is taken to be *true*.

8.3 SEQUENCE CONTROL BETWEEN STATEMENTS

In this section, we take up the basic mechanisms in use for controlling the sequence in which the individual statements are executed within a program, leaving to the next chapter the larger sequence-control structures concerned with programs and subprograms.

8.3.1 Basic Statements

The results from any program are determined by its *basic statements* that apply operations to data objects. Examples of such basic statements include assignment statements, subprogram calls, and input and output statements. Within a basic statement, sequences of operations may be invoked by using expressions, as discussed in the preceding section. For our present purposes, however, each basic statement may be considered as a unit that represents a single step in the computation.

Assignments to Data Objects

Changes to the state of the computation by assigning values to data objects is the major mechanism that affects the state of a computation by a program. Several forms of such statement exist.

Assignment statement. We briefly discussed the assignment statement in Section 5.1.5. The primary purpose of an assignment is to assign to the l-value of a data object (i.e., to its memory location) the r-value (i.e., the data object value) of some expression. Assignment is a central operation defined for every elementary data type. The syntax for an explicit assignment varies widely:

A := B	Pascal, Ada
A = B	C, FORTRAN, PL/I, Prolog, ML, SNOBOL4
MOVE B TO A	COBOL
A ← B	APL
(SETQ A B)	LISP

In C, the assignment is simply an operator, thus we can write: $c = b = 1$, meaning (according to the precedence values of Table 8.2) $(c = (b = 1))$, which undergoes the following evaluation process:

1. b is assigned the value 1.
2. The expression $(b = 1)$ returns the value 1.
3. c is given the value 1.

More often, however, assignment is viewed as a separate statement. Because the Pascal assignment operation returns no explicit result, we use it only at the statement level in an explicit assignment statement:

```
X := B + 2*C;
Y := A + X;
```

Most languages have a single assignment operator. C, however, has several:

$A = B$	Assign r-value of B to l-value of A, return r-value
$A += B\ (-=)$	Increment (or decrement) A by B ($A = A + B$ or $A = A - B$), return new value
$++A\ (--A)$	Increment (or decrement) A then return new value (e. g., $A = A + 1$, return r-value of A)
$A++\ (A--)$	Return value of A then increment (decrement) A (return r-value, then $A = A + 1$)

Although these are all similar, they each have slightly different semantics and may have a different effect in different situations. Because the basic operation of assignment is to assign the r-value of an expression to the l-value of another expression, greater flexibility can be achieved by including operators that affect the l-value and r-value of variables. In C, for example, the unary $*$ operator is an indirection operator that makes the r-value of a variable behave as if it were an l-value. The unary & operator is an address operator that converts an l-value into an r-value. For example, in

```
int i, *p;
p = &i;
*p = 7;
```

we have 1. i is declared as an integer;

2. p is declared as a pointer to an integer;

3. p is set to point to i, i.e., i's l-value is converted to an r-value (&i) and this r-value stored as the r-value of p; and

4. p's r-value is converted to be an l-value ($*p$); it is the l-value of i, so i's r-value is set to 7.

The following C program is a more complete example:

```
main()
    { int *p, *q, i, j;                  /* p and q point to ints */
    int **qq;                            /* qq is pointer to pointer to int */
    i=1; j=2; printf("I=%d; J=%d;\n",i,j);        /* Print i and j */
    p = & i;                             /* p= l-value of i */
    q = & j;                             /* q= l-value of j */
    *p =*q; printf("I=%d; J=%d;\n",i,j);         /* same as i = j */
    qq = & p;                            /* qq points to p */
    **qq = 7; printf("I=%d; J=%d;\n",i,j);}      /* same as i = 7 */
```

The output from the program is:

```
I=1; J=2;
I=2; J=2;
I=7; J=2;
```

Input statement. Most programming languages include a statement form for reading data from the user at a terminal, from files, or from a communications line. Such statements also change the values of variables through assignments. Typically, the syntax is of the form: $read(file, data)$. In C, a call of the $printf$ function causes assignment to the buffer variable of a file. In Perl, simply mentioning the input file causes a read operation (e.g., $X=<STDIN> causes the assignment of the next line of input to variable $\$X$).

Other assigning operations. Parameter transmission (Section 9.3) is often defined as assignment of the argument value to the formal parameter. Various forms of implicit assignment are found as well (e.g., in SNOBOL4, each reference to the variable INPUT causes a new value to be assigned to it), and Prolog goal matching (e.g., resolution) causes implicit assignment to variables. We often can assign an initial value to a variable as part of its declaration.

Forms of Statement-Level Sequence Control

Three main forms of statement-level sequence control are usually distinguished:

- *Composition.* Statements may be placed in a textual sequence so that they are executed in order whenever the larger program structure containing the sequence is executed.

- *Alternation.* Two sequences of statements may form alternatives so that one or the other sequence is executed, but not both, whenever the larger program structure containing both sequences is executed.

- *Iteration.* A sequence of statements may be executed repeatedly, zero or more times (zero meaning execution may be omitted altogether), whenever the larger program structure containing the sequence is executed.

In constructing programs, we are engaged in putting together the basic statements that perform the computation into the appropriate sequences by repeatedly using composition, alternation, and iteration to get the effect desired. Within each of these general control-form categories, we often use variations appropriate for particular purposes. For example, instead of an alternation consisting of only two alternatives, we often need one consisting of several alternatives. The programming language usually provides various sequence-control structures intended to allow these control forms to be easily expressed.

Explicit Sequence Control

Early programming languages were modeled after the underlying actual machine that would execute the program. Because machines consisted of memory locations, early languages (e.g., FORTRAN, ALGOL) modeled these with simple data types directly translatable into machine objects (e.g., C *float* and FORTRAN *real* into hardware *floating point*, C *int* into hardware *integer*) and with simple statements consisting of labels and branches. The transfer of control is most often indicated by use of a **goto** statement to an explicit statement with a given label name.

Two forms of **goto** statement are often present in many languages:

Unconditional **goto**. Within a sequence of statements, an unconditional **goto** such as

goto NEXT

transfers control to the statement labeled *NEXT*. The statement following the **goto** is not executed as part of the sequence.

Conditional **goto**. Within a sequence of statements, a conditional **goto** such as

if A = 0 **then goto** NEXT

transfers control to the statement labeled *NEXT* only if the specified condition holds.

Although a simple statement form, the **goto** has had a rough time for the past 30 years. Its use in programming has been the target of much criticism. Use of **goto** statements leads to an unstructured design of a program, as described next. For example, much of the formal modeling leading to an axiomatic correctness model

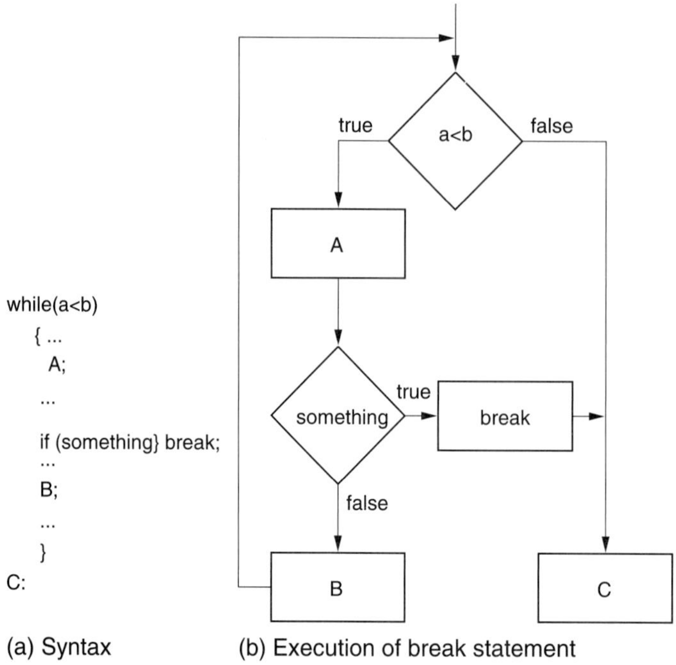
while(a<b)
{ ...
A;
...
if (something} break;
...
B;
...
}
C:
a<b
true
false
A
something
true
break
false
B
C
(a) Syntax
(b) Execution of break statement

Figure 8.5. Structured break statement.

of program design (Section 4.2.4) depends on a reasonable control structure for a program. In fact, the axiomatic model given in that section does not easily permit the inclusion of a **goto** statement.

More important, it has been shown that the **goto** statement is superfluous. (See the Structure Theorem later in this chapter in Section 8.3.3.) Programs can just as easily be written without **goto**s, and most students learn programming in C or Pascal without ever being taught that both languages contain **goto** statements.

Break statement. Some languages such as C, include a **break** statement as a form of structured explicit control. Usually the **break** causes control to move forward in the program to an explicit point at the end of a given control structure. Thus, **break** in C causes control to exit the immediately enclosing **while**, **for**, or **switch** statement. This still gives a one-in, one-out control structure that permits formal properties of a program to be developed (Figure 8.5).

C also includes a related **continue** statement. This causes control to move forward to the end of the current loop body in a **while** or **for** statement. Thus, a **break** will exit a loop, whereas the **continue** will iterate the loop again.

However, the C **break** statement (and the related **switch** statement) does permit sloppy programming in C. One **switch** option will flow right into the next if there is no **break**. Also, it may be confusing about which construct a **break** will exit from. In fact, a misplaced **break** statement was the cause of a major telephone network breakdown in the United States in the early 1990s.

Structured Programming Design

Although most languages define labels and **goto** statements, the 1970s saw considerable controversy over their use. In some new languages (e.g., ML), **goto**s are completely eliminated. The disadvantages of using **goto**s far outweigh any of its advantages.

Lack of hierarchical program structure. It is more important that the program run correctly than be most efficient. Programming language design must reflect these requirements.

The concept of the *one-in, one-out control structure* makes for a more understandable design. A program of more than a few statements is difficult to understand unless statements are organized into groups hierarchically, with each group representing one conceptual unit of the underlying computation. Each of these groups is organized as a few subgroups using one of the control forms, and so on. In the design of a program, this sort of hierarchical organization is essential to allow the programmer to comprehend how all the parts of the program fit together.

Order of statements in the program text need not correspond to the order of execution. Using **goto**s, it is easy to write programs in which control jumps between different sequences of statements in irregular patterns. Then the order in which statements appear in the program has little connection with the order in which the statements are executed and are therefore difficult to understand. Programs with an irregular execution sequence are often called *spaghetti code* (Figure 1.2).

Groups of statements may serve multiple purposes. A program is more easily understood if each group of statements serves a single purpose within the overall program structure (i.e., computes a clearly defined separate part of the entire computation). Often two separate groups of statements may contain several statements that are identical in both. Using **goto**s, we can combine two such groups of statements so that the identical statements are written only once, and control is transferred to this common set during execution of each group. This makes the understanding of this code difficult.

Structured programming. This term is used for program design that emphasizes (1) hierarchical design of program structures using only the simple control forms of composition, alternation, and iteration described earlier; (2) representation of the hierarchical design directly in the program text, using the "structured" control statements described later; (3) program text in which the textual sequence of statements corresponds to the execution sequence; and (4) use of single-purpose groups of statements even if statements must be copied. When a program is written by following these tenets of structured programming, it is usually much easier to understand, debug, verify to be correct, and later modify and reverify. In Section 8.3.3, we give a model for control structures, called the *prime program*, which helps formally define what we mean by a structured program.

8.3.2 Structured Sequence Control

Most languages provide a set of control statements for expressing the basic control forms of composition, alternation, and iteration. One important aspect of the statements discussed next is that each is a *one-in, one-out* control statement, meaning that in each statement there is only one entry point to the statement and one exit point from it. If one of these statements is placed in sequence with some other statements, then the sequence of execution will necessarily proceed from the preceding statement into the one-in, one-out statement through the statement and out to the following statement (provided the statement cannot include an internal **goto** statement that sends control elsewhere). In reading a program constructed only from one-in, one-out control statements, the flow of program execution must match the sequence of statements in the program text. Each one-in, one-out control statement may include internal branching and looping, but control may leave the statement only through its single exit point.

Older languages such as COBOL and FORTRAN contain some one-in one-out control statements, but still rely heavily on **goto** statements and statement labels. Both languages have been difficult to adapt to modern language concepts. COBOL is summarized in Figure 8.6 and Language Summary 8.3.

Compound Statements

A *compound statement* is a sequence of statements that may be treated as a single statement in the construction of larger statements. Often a compound statement is written:

begin
. . .   – Sequence of statements (one or more)
end

In C, C++, Perl, or Java, it is written simply as {...}.

Within the compound statement, statements are written in the order in which they are to be executed. Thus, the compound statement is the basic structure for representing the *composition* of statements. Because a compound statement is a statement, groups of statements representing single conceptual units of computation may be kept together as a unit by the **begin** ... **end** bracketing, and hierarchies of such groups may be constructed.

A compound statement is implemented in a conventional computer by placing the blocks of executable code representing each constituent statement in sequence

Language Summary 8.3: COBOL

Features: COBOL (COmmon Business Oriented Language) has been widely used since the early 1960s for business applications of computers.

History: COBOL has evolved through a sequence of design revisions, beginning with the first version in 1960 and later revisions in 1974 and 1984. COBOL development was organized by the U.S. Defense Department under the direction of Grace Hopper. Some of the ideas within COBOL developed from Univac's FLOWMATIC, including the use of nouns and verbs to describe actions and the separation of data descriptions with commands — two essential attributes of COBOL. A unique goal of COBOL was to develop a language programmed in "natural English." While the resulting language is somewhat readable, it does have a formal syntax, and without adequate training, cannot be programmed easily.

Translation of COBOL into efficient executable code is complex because of the number of different data representations and the large number of options for most statements. Most of the early COBOL compilers were extremely slow, but more recently improvements in compilation techniques have led to relatively fast COBOL compilers, producing fairly efficient executable code.

Example: COBOL programs are organized into four *divisions.* This organization is a result of two design goals: separating *machine-dependent* from *machine-independent* program elements and that of separating data descriptions from algorithm descriptions. The result is a tripartite program organization: The PROCEDURE division contains the algorithms, the DATA division contains data descriptions, and the ENVIRONMENT division contains machine-dependent program specifications such as the connections between the program and external data files. A fourth *IDENTIFICATION* division serves to name the program and its author and to provide other commentary as program documentation.

The COBOL design is based on a static run-time structure. No run-time storage management is required, and many aspects of the language are designed to allow relatively efficient run-time structures to be used (although this goal is less important than that of hardware independence and program transportability).

The language uses an English-like syntax, which makes most programs relatively easy to read. The language provides numerous optional *noise words* that may be used to improve readability. The syntax makes COBOL programs easy but relatively tedious to write because even the simplest program becomes fairly lengthy. Figure 10.1 gives a brief overview of COBOL syntax.

Reference: J. E. Sammet, "The early history of COBOL," *ACM History of Programming Languages Conference*, Los Angeles, CA (June 1978) *(SIGPLAN Notices (13)8 [August 1978])*, 121–161.

```
IDENTIFICATION DIVISION.
PROGRAM-ID. SUM-OF-PRICES.
AUTHOR. T-PRATT.
ENVIRONMENT DIVISION.
CONFIGURATION SECTION.
SOURCE-COMPUTER. SUN.
OBJECT-COMPUTER. SUN.
INPUT-OUTPUT SECTION.
FILE-CONTROL.
     SELECT INP-DATA ASSIGN TO INPUT.
     SELECT RESULT-FILE ASSIGN TO OUTPUT.
DATA DIVISION.
FILE SECTION.
FD INP-DATA LABEL RECORD IS OMITTED.
01 ITEM-PRICE.
     02 ITEM PICTURE X(30).
     02 PRICE PICTURE 9999V99.
WORKING-STORAGE SECTION.
77 TOT PICTURE 9999V99, VALUE 0, USAGE IS COMPUTATIONAL.
01 SUM-LINE.
     02 FILLER VALUE ' SUM ='PICTURE X(12).
     02 SUM-OUT PICTURE $$,$$$,$$9.99.
     02 COUNT-OUT PICTURE ZZZ9.
     ... More data
PROCEDURE DIVISION.
START.
     OPEN INPUT INP-DATA AND OUTPUT RESULT-FILE.
READ-DATA.
     READ INP-DATA AT END GO TO PRINT-LINE.
     ADD PRICE TO TOT.
     ADD 1 TO COUNT.
     MOVE PRICE TO PRICE-OUT.
     MOVE ITEM TO ITEM-OUT.
     WRITE RESULT-LINE FROM ITEM-LINE.
     GO TO READ-DATA.
PRINT-LINE.
     MOVE TOT TO SUM-OUT.
     ... More statements
     CLOSE INP-DATA AND RESULT-FILE.
     STOP RUN.
```

Figure 8.6. Sample COBOL text.

in memory. The order in which they appear in memory determines the order in which they are executed.

Conditional Statements

A *conditional statement* is one that expresses alternation of two or more statements, or optional execution of a single statement—where *statement* means either a single basic statement, a compound statement, or another control statement. The choice of alternative is controlled by a test on some condition, usually written as an expression involving relational and Boolean operations. The most common forms of conditional statement are the **if** and **case** statements.

If statements. The optional execution of a statement is expressed as a *single-branch* **if**, viz.,

if *condition* **then** *statement* **endif**

whereas a choice between two alternatives uses a *two-branch* **if**, namely,

if *condition* **then** $statement_1$ **else** $statement_2$ **endif**

In the first case, a condition evaluating to true causes the *statement* to be executed, whereas a false condition causes the statement to be skipped. In the two-branch **if**, $statement_1$ or $statement_2$ is executed depending on whether *condition* is true or false.

A choice among many alternatives may be expressed by nesting additional **if** statements within the alternative statements of a single **if** or by a *multibranch* **if**:

if $condition_1$ **then** $statement_1$
    elsif $condition_2$ **then** $statement_2$
    ...
    elsif $condition_n$ **then** $statement_n$
    else $statement_{n+1}$ **endif**

Case statements. The conditions in a multibranch **if** often take the form of repeated testing of the value of a variable, as in the following code:

if Tag = 0 **then** $statement_0$
    elsif Tag = 1 **then** $statement_1$
    elsif Tag = 2 **then** $statement_2$
    else $statement_3$
    endif

This common structure is expressed more concisely as a **case** statement, such as in Ada:

```
case Tag is
    when 0 => begin
        statement_0
        end;
    when 1 => begin
        statement_1
        end;
    when 2 => begin
        statement_2
        end;
when others => begin
        statement_3
        end;
end case
```

In general, the variable *Tag* may be replaced by any expression that evaluates to a single value, and then the actions for each of the possible values are represented by a compound statement preceded by the value for the expression that would cause that compound statement to be executed. Enumeration types and integer subranges are particularly useful in setting up the possible values that the expression in a **case** statement may return. For example, if variable *Tag* is defined as having the subrange 0..5 as its type, then during execution of the **case** statement, values for *Tag* of 0, 1, or 2 will cause $statement_0$, $statement_1$, or $statement_2$, respectively, to be executed, and any other value will cause $statement_3$ to be executed.

Implementation. **If** statements are readily implemented using the usual hardware-supported branch and jump instructions (the hardware form of conditional and unconditional **goto**). **Case** statements are commonly implemented using a jump table to avoid repeated testing of the value of the same variable. A *jump table* is a vector stored sequentially in memory, each of whose components is an unconditional jump instruction. The expression forming the condition of the **case** statement is evaluated, and the result is transformed into a small integer representing the offset into the jump table from its base address. The jump instruction at that offset, when executed, leads to the start of the code block representing the code to be executed if that alternative is chosen. The resulting implementation structure for the **case** statement is shown in Figure 8.7.

Iteration Statements

Iteration provides the basic mechanism for repeated calculations in most programs. (Recursive subprograms of the next chapter form the other.) The basic structure of an iteration statement consists of a *head* and a *body*. The head controls the number of times that the body will be executed, whereas the body is usually a (compound) statement that provides the action of the statement. Although the

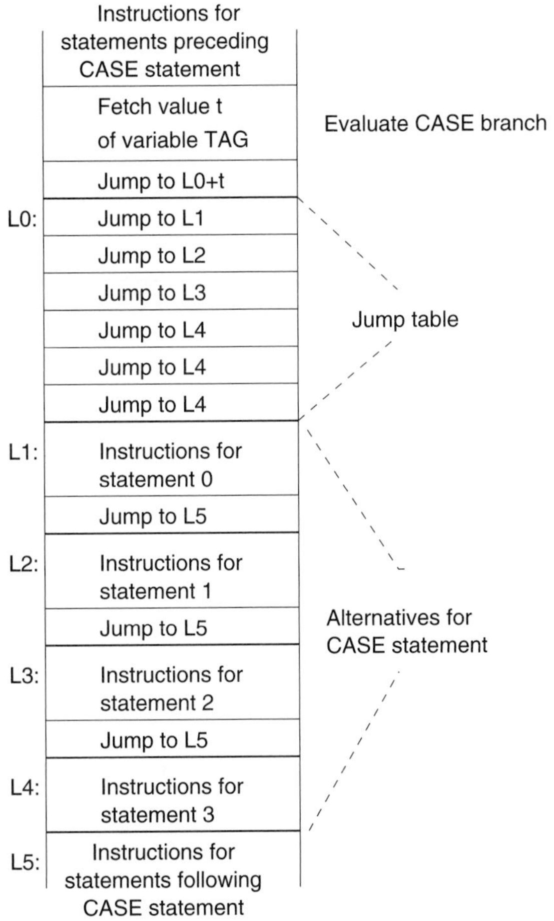

Figure 8.7. Jump table implementation of **case** statement.

bodies of iteration statements are fairly unrestricted, only a few variants of head structure are usually used. Let us look at some typical ones.

Simple repetition. The simplest type of iteration statement head specifies that the body is to be executed some fixed number of times. The COBOL PERFORM is typical of this construct:

perform *body* K **times**

The statement causes K to be evaluated and then the body of the statement to be executed that many times.

However, even this simple statement has some subtle issues. Can K be reevaluated in *body* and change the number of iterations of the loop? What if K is 0 or negative? How does this affect execution?

Although these questions may seem like hairsplitting for this simple iteration statement, the same questions arise in each form of the statement, and thus it is important to look at them in their simplest form here. In each case, it is important to ask: (1) When is the termination test made? and (2) When are the variables used in the statement head evaluated?

Repetition while condition holds. A somewhat more complex iteration may be constructed using a *repeat while* head. A typical form is

while *test* **do** *body*

In this form of iteration statement, the test expression is reevaluated each time after the body has been executed. Note that execution of the body will change some of the values of variables appearing in the test expression; otherwise the iteration, once begun, would never terminate.

Repetition while incrementing a counter. The third alternative form of iteration statement is the statement whose head specifies a variable that serves as a counter or index during the iteration. An initial value, final value, and increment are specified in the head, and the body is executed repeatedly using first the initial value as the value of the index variable, then the initial value plus the increment, then the initial value plus twice the increment, and so on, until the final value is reached. In FORTRAN-77, this is the only form of iteration statement available. The ALGOL **for** statement illustrates the typical structure

for I := 1 **step** 2 **until** 30 **do** *body*

In its general form, the initial value, final value, and increment may be given by arbitrary expressions as in

for K := N-1 **step** 2× (W-1) **until** M× N **do** *body*

Again the question arises as to when the termination test is made and when and how often the various expressions are evaluated. Here the question is of central importance additionally for the language implementor because such iteration statements are prime candidates for optimization, and the answers may greatly affect the sorts of optimizations that can be performed.

Data-based repetition. Sometimes the format of the data determines the repetition counter. Perl, for example, has a **foreach** construct:

foreach $X (@arrayitem) { ... }

For each pass through the loop, scalar variable *$X* will have a value equal to the next element of array *@arrayitem*. The size of the array determines how many times the program loops.

Indefinite repetition. Where the conditions for loop exit are complex and not easily expressible in the usual loop head, a loop with no explicit termination test in the head is often used—for example, in the Ada construct

loop
  ...
  exit when *condition*;
  ...
end loop;

or in Pascal, using a **while** loop with a condition that is always true:

while true **do begin** ... **end**

The C **for** statement permits all of these concepts in one construct:

$$\textbf{for}(expression_1;\ expression_2;\ expression_3)\{body\}$$

Here, $expression_1$ is the initial value, $expression_2$ is the repeat condition, and $expression_3$ is the increment. All of these expressions are optional, allowing for much flexibility in C iterations. Some C sample iteration loops can be specified as follows:

Simple counter from 1 to 10:	**for**(i=1; i<=10; i++){*body*}
Infinite loop:	**for**(;;){*body*}
Counter with exit condition:	**for**(i=1;i<=100 && NotEndfile; i++){*body*}

Implementation of loop statements. Implementation of loop-control statements using the hardware branch/jump instruction is straightforward. To implement a **for** loop, the expressions in the loop head defining the final value and increment must be evaluated on initial entry to the loop and saved in special temporary storage areas, where they may be retrieved at the beginning of each iteration for use in testing and incrementing the controlled variable.

Problems in Structured Sequence Control

A **goto** statement is often viewed as a last resort when the structured control statements described earlier prove inadequate for the expression of a difficult sequence-control structure. Although in theory it is always possible to express any sequence-control structure using only the structured statement forms, in practice a difficult form may not have any natural expression directly using only those statements. Several such problem areas are known, and often special control constructs are provided for these cases that make use of a **goto** statement unnecessary. The most common are the following.

Multiple exit loops. Often several conditions may require termination of a loop. The search loop is a common example: A vector of K elements is to be searched for the first element that meets some condition. The loop terminates if either the end of the vector is reached or an appropriate element is found. Iteration through the elements of a vector is naturally expressed using a **for** loop:

```
for I := 1 to K do
    if VECT[I] = 0 then goto α {α outside the loop}
```

In a language such as Pascal, however, either a **goto** statement must be used to escape from the middle of the loop or the **for** loop must be replaced by a **while** loop, which obscures the information contained in the **for** loop head about the existence and range of the index variable I.

The **exit** statement in Ada and the **break** statement of C provide an alternative construct for expressing such loop exits without use of a **goto** statement:

```
for I in 1 .. K loop
    exit when VECT(I) = 0;
end loop;
```

do-while-do. Often the most natural place to test whether to exit a loop comes not at the beginning or end of the loop, but in the middle, after some processing has been done, as in

```
loop
    read(X)
    if end_of_file then goto α {outside the loop}
    process(X)
end loop;
```

This form is sometimes called the do-while-do because a midpoint **while** can handle this sequence:

```
dowhiledo
    read(X)
    while (not end_of_file)
    process(X)
end dowhiledo
```

Unfortunately, no common language implements this structure, although in C, **if** (*condition*) **break** comes close and Ada's **exit when** is similar.

Exceptional conditions. Exceptions may represent various error conditions, such as unexpected end-of-file conditions, subscript range errors, or bad data to be processed. The statements that handle the processing of these exceptional conditions are often grouped at a special place in the program, such as at the end of the subprogram in which the exception might be detected, or possibly in another subprogram used only to handle exceptions. Transfer from the point where the exceptional condition is detected to the exception handler (group of statements) often is best represented using a **goto** statement in languages that do not implement special exception handling statements. However, Ada and ML provide special language mechanisms for defining exception handlers and for specifying the control transfer needed when an exception is detected. The Ada **raise** statement is typical of this exception handling:

raise BAD_CHAR_VALUE

This statement transfers control to the exception-handling statements that are associated with the exception name BAD_CHAR_VALUE. Exceptions and exception handlers are discussed further in Section 11.1.1.

8.3.3 Prime Programs

Although the collection of control structures presented in this chapter, at first glance, seems like a random assortment of statements, the theory of *prime programs* can be used to describe a consistent theory of control structures. The prime program was developed by Maddux [MADDUX 1975] as a generalization of structured programming to define the unique hierarchical decomposition of a flowchart.

We assume program graphs contain three classes of nodes:

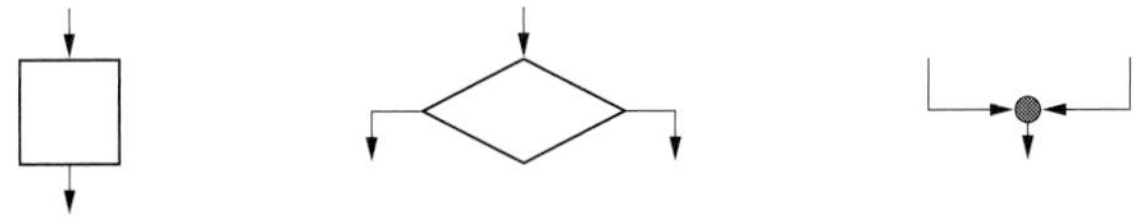

Function nodes represent computations by a program and are pictured as boxes with a single arc entering such a node and a single arc leaving such a node. Intuitively, a function node represents an assignment statement, which causes a change in the state of the virtual machine after its execution.

Decision nodes are represented as diamond-shaped boxes with one input and two output arcs labeled *true* and *false*. These represent predicates, and control flows out of a decision box on either the true or false branch.

A join node is represented as a point where two arcs flow together to form a single output arc.

Every flowchart consists of these three components. We define a *proper program*, which is our formal model of a control structure, as a flowchart that:

1. has a single entry arc,
2. has a single exit arc, and

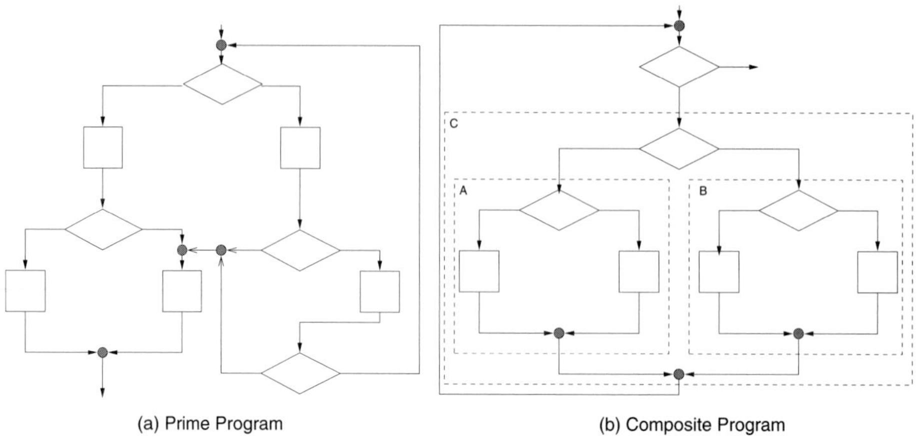

Figure 8.8. Flowcharts.

3. has a path from the entry arc to each node and from each node to the exit arc.

Our goal is to differentiate structured proper programs from unstructured ones. For example, referring to Figure 8.8, there is an obvious qualitative difference between Figure 8.8(a) and Figure 8.8(b). The leftmost flowchart contains a large assortment of arcs that seemingly wander randomly around the graph, whereas the rightmost graph has a nested ordered structure. The prime program defines this concept.

A *prime program* is a proper program that cannot be subdivided into smaller proper programs. If we cannot cut two arcs of the proper program to separate the proper program into separate graphs, then the proper program is prime. (The one exception to this rule is that long sequences of function nodes are considered to be a single prime.) Figure 8.8(a) represents a prime, whereas Figure 8.8(b) is not prime. Dotted boxes A, B, and C all represent nested proper programs within the overall flowchart.

We define a *composite program* to be a proper program that is not a prime. Figure 8.8(b) is composite. By replacing each prime component of a proper program by a function node (e.g., replacing prime components A and B of Figure 8.8[b] by function nodes), we can repeat this process (e.g., by now revealing Box C as a prime) until we achieve a unique prime decomposition of any proper program.

All primes can be enumerated. Figure 8.9 describes all prime programs of up to four nodes. Note that most of these are either ineffective or are the common control structures described earlier in this chapter. Primes (a), (b), (e), and (i) all represent sequences of functions nodes and correspond to the basic block of most languages. Prime (f) is the if–then, (g) is the do–while, (h) is the repeat–until, (j) is the if–then–else, and (k) is the do–while–do of the last section.

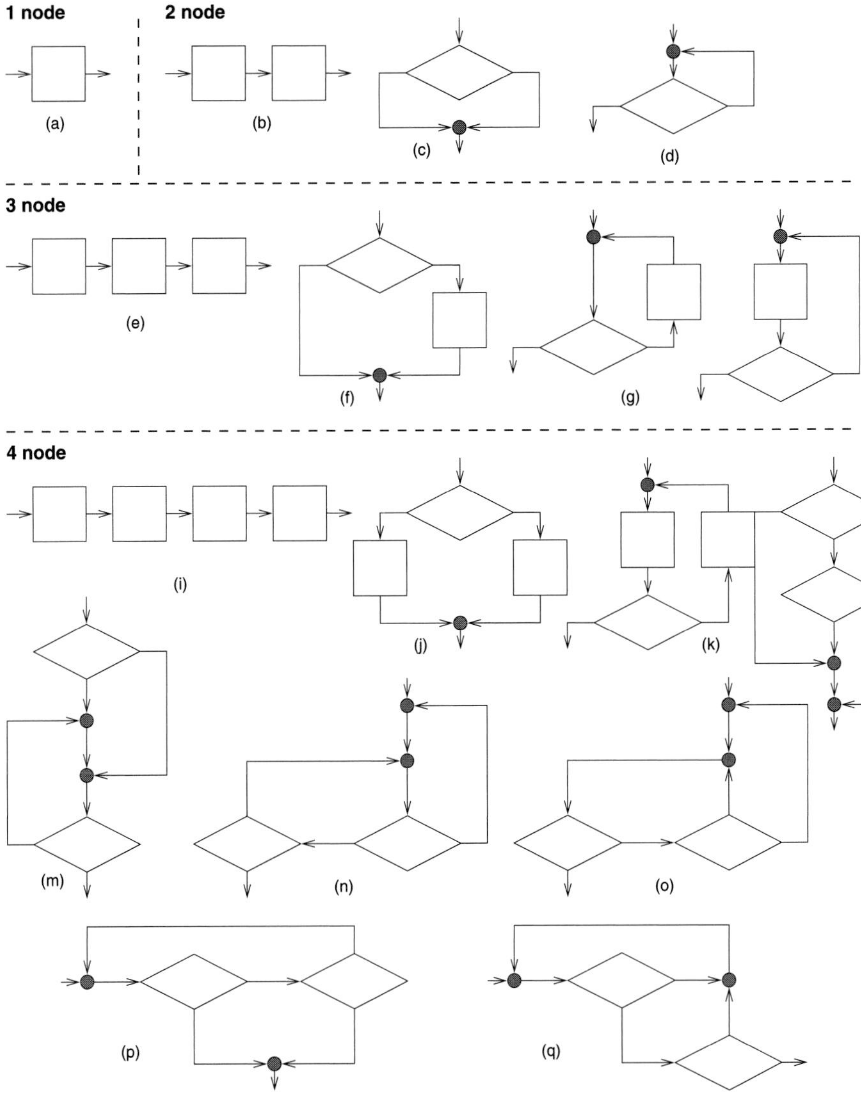

Figure 8.9. Enumeration of prime programs.

Consider Primes (c), (d), and (l) through (q). These all consist of only decision and join nodes. There is no function node, so they do not change the virtual machine state space. Because these primes do not change any data values, they all compute the identity function. However, (c) and (l) always exit (i.e., terminate execution), so they are identity functions on all input data, whereas the others may loop. Once

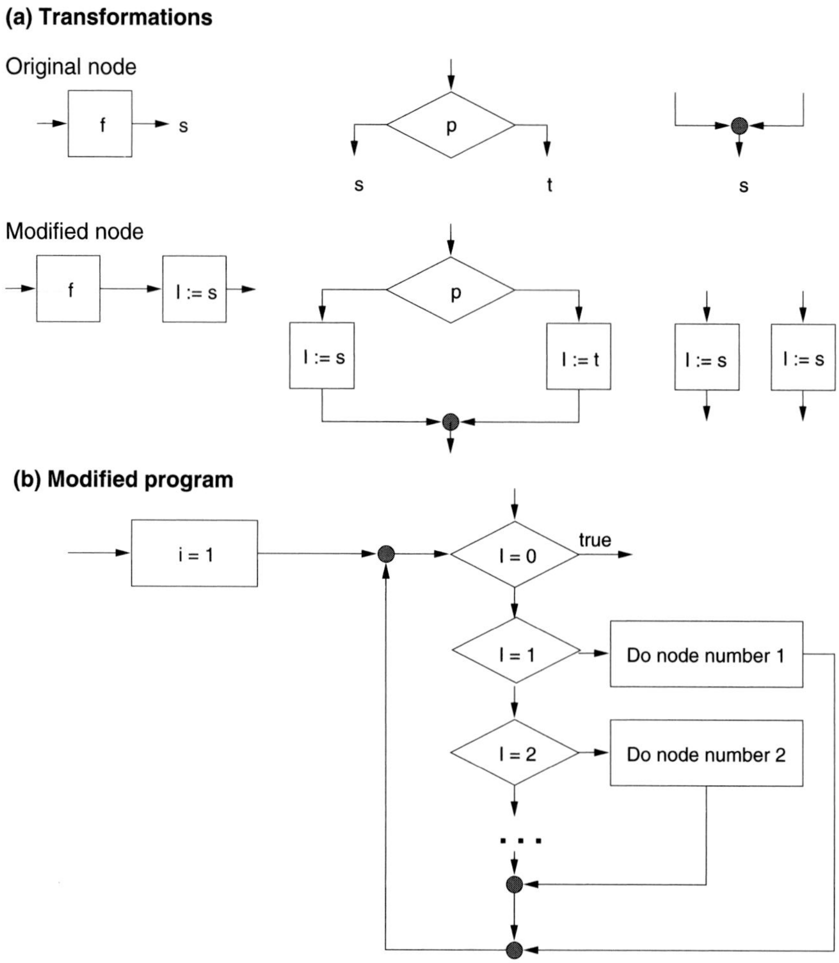

Figure 8.10. The structure theorem.

they loop, they will continue to do so and never exit. These represent partial functions, which exit for only certain input data values. None of these represent effective control structures in a program.

It is not surprising that programming languages have been defined with the set of control structures described in this chapter. They all represent primes with small numbers of nodes. Such primes are easy to understand, and the changes to the state space by executing these primes becomes manageable. By enumerating these primes, it becomes obvious that the do-while-do is a natural control structure that has unfortunately been ignored by language designers.

The structure theorem. When the concept of structured programming developed in the 1970s, there was concern whether using only these control structures would limit the power of such programs. That is, could the program of Figure 8.8(a) be programmed using only the control structures of Figure 8.9? A theorem by Böhm and Jacobini [BOHM and JACOBINI 1966] answered that question. They showed that any prime program could be converted into one using only **while** and **if** statements. Figure 8.10 is an outline of a process similar to the Böhm–Jacobini construction; however, this proof is by Harlan Mills [LINGER et al. 1979]:

1. Given any flowchart, label each node. Label the exit arc with the number 0.
2. Define I to be a new program variable.
3. For each node in the flowchart, apply the transformation described in Figure 8.10(a).
4. Rebuild the program as given in Figure 8.10(b).

It should be clear that I operates like a virtual machine instruction-counter indicating the next statement to execute, and the entire program is simply a series of nested **if** statements within a single **while** loop. This program will operate the same as the original flowchart with the addition of changes to variable I as it executes.

The Böhm and Jacobini result has been cited as a reason why it is *unnecessary* to avoid **go to** statements. One can program any algorithm with or without the **go to** statement and then use the structure theorem to convert the program into a "well-structured" program. Many such structuring machines have been sold to the gullible. Structured programming is not synonymous with good programming. It only means using control structures that are primes with small numbers of nodes. If one starts with bad spaghetti code, then the transformation will simply be to bad structured code.

What the Böhm–Jacobini theorem does provide is an existence proof that all programs *can* be programmed using only the standard control structures. The algorithm does not provide the best solution. That is still up to the programmer to develop. All we know is that there will be some solution *no worse than* the Böhm–Jacobini result and perhaps much better.

8.4 SEQUENCING WITH NONARITHMETIC EXPRESSIONS

In a previous section, we discussed the execution sequence in the evaluation of arithmetic expressions. However, other expression formats are present in languages. Languages like Prolog and ML, designed for processing character data, include other forms of expression evaluation.

8.4.1 Prolog Overview

Unlike other languages in this book, Prolog is not a general-purpose programming language, but instead is oriented toward solving problems using the predicate calculus.

The goal for Prolog was to give the specifications of a solution and allow the computer to derive the execution sequence for that solution, rather than specifying an algorithm for the solution of a problem, such as is the normal case with most languages we have studied. For example, if you have airline flight information of the form

flight(flight_number, from_city, to_city, departure_time, arrival_time)

then all flights from Los Angeles to Baltimore can be specified either as direct flights via the statement

flight(flight_number, Los Angeles, Baltimore, departure_time, arrival_time)

or as flights with an intermediate stop, specified as

flight(flight1, Los Angeles, X, depart1, arrive1),
flight(flight2, X, Baltimore, depart2, arrive2),
depart2 >= arrive1+30

This indicates that you are specifying a city X, which has a flight arriving from Los Angeles, has a flight leaving for Baltimore, and the Baltimore-bound flight leaves at least 30 minutes after the Los Angeles flight arrives to allow time to change planes. No algorithm is specified; we have only indicated the conditions for having a correct solution. If we can state such a set of conditions, the language will provide the execution sequence needed to find the appropriate flight.

History. Development of Prolog began in 1970 by Alain Coulmerauer and Philippe Roussel, who were interested in developing a language for making deductions from text. The name Prolog stands for "PROgramming in LOGic." Prolog was developed in Marseilles, France, in 1972. The principle of resolution by Kowalski from the University of Edinburgh (Section 8.4.5) seemed like an appropriate model on which to develop an inference mechanism. With the limitation of resolution to Horn clauses, unification (Section 8.4.3) led to an effective system where the inherent nondeterminism of resolution was handled by a backtracking process, which could easily be implemented. The algorithm for resolution provided the execution sequence needed to implement the example specifications like the $flight$ relationship given previously.

The first Prolog implementation was completed in 1972 using Wirth's ALGOL W compiler, and the basics of the current language were completed by 1973. Prolog use gradually spread among those involved in logic programming mostly by personal contact and not via commercialization of the product. Several different, but fairly similar, versions exist. Although there is no standard for Prolog, the version developed at the University of Edinburgh has become a widely used variant. Prolog use did not spread until the 1980s. The lack of development of effective Prolog applications inhibited its spread.

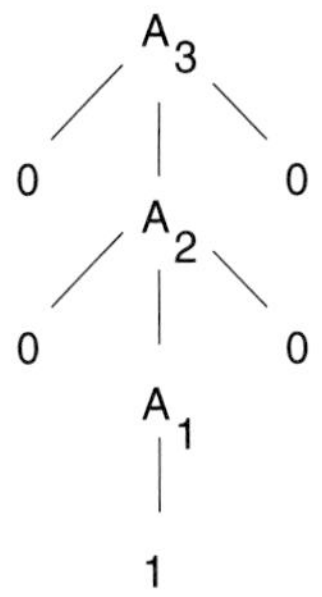

Figure 8.11. SNOBOL4 pattern matching.

Brief overview of the language. A Prolog program consists of a series of facts, concrete relationships among data objects (facts) and a set of rules (a pattern of relationships among the database objects). These facts and rules are entered into the database via a *consult* operation. A program executes by the user entering a query, a set of terms that must all be true. The facts and rules of the database are used to determine which substitutions for variables in the query (called *unification*) are consistent with the information in the database.

Prolog, as an interpreter, prompts the user for input. The user types in a query or function name. The truth ("yes") or falsity ("no") of that query is output, as well as an assignment to the variables of the query that make the query true (i.e., that *unify* the query). If a ";" is entered, then the next set of values that unify the query is printed until no more substitutions are possible, on which Prolog prints *no* and waits for a new query. A carriage return is interpreted as termination of the search for additional solutions.

Execution of Prolog, although based upon the specification of predicates, operates much like an applicative language such as LISP or ML. Developing Prolog rules requires the same recursive thinking that is needed for developing programs in these other applicative languages.

Prolog has a simple syntax and semantics. Because it is looking for relationships among a series of objects, the variable and the list are the basic data structures that are used. A rule behaves much like a procedure, except that the concept of unification is more complex than the relatively simple process of expression substitution for parameters. (See Section 8.4.3.)

8.4.2 Pattern Matching

A crucial operation in languages like Perl, Prolog, and ML is pattern matching. In this case, an operation succeeds by matching and assigning a set of variables to a predefined template. The recognition of parse trees in BNF grammars in Section 3.3.1 is representative of this operation.

For example, the following grammar recognizes odd-length palindromes over the alphabet 0 and 1:

$$A \rightarrow 0A0 \mid 1A1 \mid 0 \mid 1$$

Recognition of the valid string 00100 proceeds as follows:

$$A_1 \text{ matches the center } 1$$
$$A_2 \text{ matches } 0A_10$$
$$A_3 \text{ matches } 0A_20$$

From these three assignments of A_1 to 1, A_2 to $0A_10$, and A_3 to $0A_20$, we can construct the entire parse tree of this string (Figure 8.11). We have already discussed Perl regular expression pattern matching in Section 3.3.3.

SNOBOL4 is a language designed to simulate this feature directly as shown by Language Summary 8.4. Note that the example program is only nine statements long; it would be hard to duplicate that in any other existing language in as short and powerful a set of statements.

SNOBOL4 also has another interesting attribute. Its implementation is designed independently from any actual machine architecture. It is designed for a string processing virtual machine (as described by Figure 2.4 in Section 2.2.2). All that is necessary is to implement the string-processing machine operations as macros on an existing computer to execute SNOBOL4. Because of this, SNOBOL4 was one of the first languages to (1) be available on almost every computer, and (2) have exactly the same semantics in every implementation.

Although SNOBOL4 uses string replacement for its pattern-matching operation, Prolog uses the concept of a relation as a set of n-tuples as its matching mechanism. By specifying known instances of these relations (called *facts*), other instances can be derived. For example, we can consider the relation $ParentOf$ with the following facts:

$ParentOf(John, Mary).$	– John is parent of Mary
$ParentOf(Susan, Mary).$	– Susan is parent of Mary
$ParentOf(Bill, John).$	– Bill is parent of John
$ParentOf(Ann, John).$	– Ann is parent of John

To find the parent of Mary, we simply write the relation $ParentOf(X, Mary)$ and Prolog will try to assign a value for X from the known set of facts in its database and infer that X may be either John or Susan. If we want to find both parents of Mary, then we need a stronger statement. We can develop predicates involving several facts in the database. We want two parents of Mary who are different—that is, we write

$$ParentOf(X, Mary),\ ParentOf(Y, Mary),\ not(X = Y).$$

where the comma separating predicates is an *and* operator (i.e., all of the predicates must be true for the entire relation to be true).

Language Summary 8.4: SNOBOL4

Features: Pattern matching based upon BNF grammars; totally dynamic — including declarations, types, storage allocation, even procedure entry and exit points; implementation uses virtual string-processing macros — rewrite macros for any existing actual computer.

History: Development began in 1962 at AT&T Bell Labs by Ralph Griswold, Ivan Polonsky, and David Farber. The goal was to develop a string processing language for formula manipulation and graph analysis. In the 1950s, Yngve at MIT developed COMIT as a way to handle natural language processing using BNF rules, but the Bell Labs team felt it to be too restrictive for their needs.
Originally called Symbolic Computation Language 7 (SCL7), its name changed to SEXI (String Expression Interpreter), which was doomed for obvious reasons in the 1960s, and then to SNOBOL (StriNg Oriented symBOlic Language) as an intentionally designed unintuitive acronym. Several versions of SNOBOL were developed — SNOBOL, SNOBOL2, SNOBOL3, and SNOBOL4, the last being successful in the 1970s.

Example: Find longest odd length palindrome over 0 and 1in input strings

```
START   GRAMMAR = 0 | 1 | 0 *GRAMMAR 0 | 1 *GRAMMAR 1
*           Set pattern to be BNF grammar
LOOP    NEWLINE = TRIM(INPUT)                 : F(END)
*           Get next line without trailing blanks. If fail, go to END
        NEWLINE (POS(0) SPAN("01") RPOS(0))   : F(BAD)
*           Match line to 0s and 1s.
*           SPAN is string of 0s and 1s
*           POS(0) is first pos. RPOS(0) is last.
        SN = SIZE(NEWLINE)
NEXT    NEWLINE POS(0) GRAMMAR . PALINDROME POS(SN)
-               :S(OK) F(NOTOK)
*           Line matches grammer through POS(SN).
*           If fail, move last pos. If success, print answer.
*           PALINDROME assigned matched part
OK      OUTPUT = "MATCH: " PALINDROME                 :(LOOP)
NOTOK   SN = SN - 1                                   :(NEXT)
BAD     OUTPUT = "IMPROPER INPUT: " NEWLINE           :(LOOP)
END
```

Sample Execution:	Input:	Output:
	11011	MATCH: 11011
	11011101	MATCH: 11011
	11211	IMPROPER INPUT: 11211

Reference: R. E. Griswold, "A history of the SNOBOL programming language," *ACM History of Programming Languages Conference*, Los Angeles, CA (June 1978) *(SIGPLAN Notices (13)8 [August 1978])*, 275–308.

The power of Prolog is in building relations that can be inferred logically from the known set of facts. These relations may be constructed out of other relations, as in $GrandparentOf$:

$$GrandparentOf(X,Y) :- ParentOf(X,Z),\ ParentOf(Z,Y).$$

This means that the relation $GrandparentOf$ is defined to be (written as :–) two $ParentOf$ relations, such that there is some object Z for which Z is the parent of Y and X is the parent of Z. Hence, $GrandparentOf(X, Mary)$ will result in X being either Bill or Ann, but $GrandparentOf(Y, John)$ fails because there is no such fact within our database.

Term Rewriting

Term rewriting is a restricted form of pattern matching that has numerous applications within the programming language domain. Given string $a_1a_2\ldots a_n$ and rewrite rule $\alpha \Rightarrow \beta$, if $\alpha = a_i$, we say $a_1 \ldots a_{i-1}\beta \ldots a_n$ is a *term rewrite* of $a_1a_2 \ldots a_n$. Matching a Prolog query with a rule in the database is a form of rewrite (with substitution; see Section 8.4.3).

We have already discussed term rewriting in Section 3.3.1 in the context of BNF grammars and parsing. Generating a derivation of a string in a language, given some BNF grammar, is just a form of rewriting process. For example, given the grammar

$$\begin{array}{lcl} A & \rightarrow & 0B \mid 1 \\ B & \rightarrow & 0A \end{array}$$

we can generate the string 001 with the following derivation:

$$\begin{array}{lcll} A & \Rightarrow & 0B & \text{using rule } A \rightarrow 0B \\ 0B & \Rightarrow & 00A & \text{using rule } B \rightarrow 0A \\ 00A & \Rightarrow & 001 & \text{using rule } A \rightarrow 1 \end{array}$$

ML uses term rewriting as a form of function definition. For example, the factorial function can be specified rather simply in ML as:

```
fun factorial(n:int)= if n=1 then 1 else n*factorial(n-1);
```

Here the domain for $factorial$ consists of two sets: For $n = 1$, the value returned is 1; for all other positive integers, the returned value is the expression $n*factorial(n-1)$. The **if** statement divides the two cases. This function can be viewed as two separate functions—a constant 1 over the set $\{1\}$ and the value $n * factorial(n - 1)$ over the remaining integers (i. e., $\{n \mid n > 1\}$).

Rather than using the **if** construct to separate the subdomains, we can use term rewriting to indicate each separate case in the function definition:

```
fun fact(1) =          1
   | fact(N:int) =     N * fact(N-1);
```

Here, each subdomain is separated by |. ML will replace the function call by the appropriate definition.

As another example, consider the ML function *length*, which combines term rewriting with a more general pattern-matching operation:

```
fun length(nil) =      0
   | length(a::y) =    1+length(y);
```

nil indicates the empty list and :: is the list concatenation operator. That is, $a :: [b, c, d] = [a, b, c, d]$. In this case, if the domain of the *length* function is the empty list, then the value is 0. Otherwise, if the domain is a list with at least one entry (a), then the value of the function is 1 plus the length of the remainder of the list. ML automatically matches the argument to *length* and assigns the head of the list to a and the tail of the list to y. This feature becomes quite important when we discuss polymorphism in ML (Section 7.3).

8.4.3 Unification

A Prolog database consists of *facts*, as in $ParentOf(Ann, John)$ and *rules*, such as

$$GrandparentOf(X,Y) \text{:-} ParentOf(X,Z),\ ParentOf(Z,Y)$$

An expression containing one or more variables, as in $GrandparentOf(X, John)$, is called a *query*, and it represents an unknown relation. (We give a more precise description of this in the discussion on the resolution principle, which guides Prolog execution, in Section 8.4.5.) The major feature of Prolog is to use pattern matching to discover whether the query is solved by a fact in the database or whether the fact can be deduced by using rules in the database applied to other facts or rules. Prolog uses *unification*—the substitution of variables in relations—to pattern match to determine whether the query has a valid substitution consistent with the rules and facts in the database.

Consider the $ParentOf$ relation given earlier. Assume we want to solve the query

$$ParentOf(X, Mary) = ParentOf(John, Y).$$

In this case, we have the fact that $ParentOf(John, Mary)$ is a solution to both parts of our query. We say that the *instance* $ParentOf(John, Mary)$ *unifies* $ParentOf(X, Mary)$ and $ParentOf(John, Y)$ with the substitution of John for X and Mary for Y because both of these relations yield that fact upon the proper substitution. Unification can be thought of as an extension to the common property of substitution.

Substitution. Substitution is one of the first principles learned in programming. Substitution is the general principle behind parameter passing and macro expansion. For example, consider the C macro[1]

```
#define mymacro(A,B,C) printf("Binary %d%d%d is %d\n",
        A,B,C, 4*(A)+2*(B)+(C))
```

This states that whenever *mymacro*(, ,) is used in a C program, the first argument of *mymacro* replaces A in the definition of the macro, the second argument replaces B, and the third argument replaces C. Thus, writing $mymacro(1, 0, 1)$ is equivalent to writing

```
printf("Binary %d%d%d is %d\n", 1, 0, 1, 4*(1)+2*(0)+(1))
```

Because the *printf* argument string is also a substitution, the earlier statement is actually the same as

```
printf("Binary 101 is 5\n")
```

The arguments being substituted need not be simple integers. *Any* string may be substituted for A, B, and C in the macro expansion. Thus, $mymacro(X + Y, Z/2, Myvar + 3)$ is equivalent to

$$\text{printf(“Binary \%d\%d\%d is \%d\textbackslash n”},X+Y,Z/2,Myvar+3,$$
$$4*(X+Y)+2*(Z/2)+(Myvar+3))$$

The important point to remember is that we are substituting an arbitrary expression for a single variable in the macro definition.

Let us extend this problem to the following *two* macro substitutions:

$$mymacro(X + Y, Z/2, ?);$$
$$mymacro(?, ?, Myvar + 3);$$

The ? symbols represent unknown substitutions. Is it possible for both macro statements to represent the same computation? This is the basic principle behind unification. In this example, the answer is clear. If we let C represent $Myvar + 3$ in the first macro expansion and A and B represent $X + Y$ and $Z/2$, respectively, in the second, then both macro statements will represent the same computation. However, for

$$mymacro(X + Y, Z/2, ?);$$
$$mymacro(?, Z + 7, ?);$$

[1] *printf* prints an output string. The function prints its first string argument using embedded codes to indicate where to put successive arguments into the output string. The sequence "%d" means to print the next argument in the list as an integer. \n is an end-of-line character.

Pattern	F(A,B) = G(A,B)	**Pattern**	F(A,B) = G(A,B) M(C,D) = N(C,D)
Example	F(g(i),h(j))	**Example**	F(John,M(h(v),7))
Substitution	g(i) for A h(j) for B F(A,B) = G(g(i),h(j))	**Substitution**	John for A M(h(v),7) for B F(A,B) = G(John, M(h(v),7)) h(v) for C 7 for D M(C,D) = N(h(v),7)
		Unification	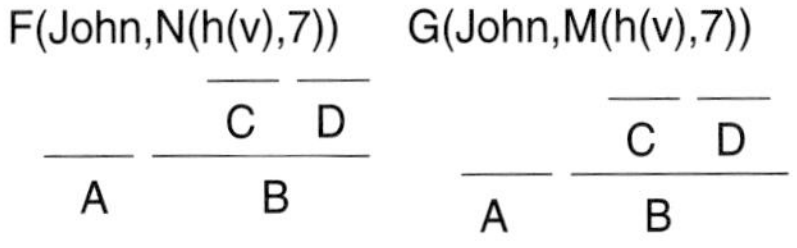

Figure 8.12. Difference between substitution and unification.

no set of assignments to A, B, or C will result in these representing the same computation. The determination of a valid set of substitutions for the question marks is the essence of unification. Whereas substitution is the result of applying new values to macro template arguments, unification is the result of simultaneous substitutions to multiple macro templates to show that all are equivalent under some set of simultaneous substitutions.

General unification. As given earlier, to unify two expression U and V, find substitutions for the variables occurring in U and V that make the two expressions identical. For example, to unify $f(X, John)$ with $f(g(John), Z)$, bind X to $g(John)$ and Z to $John$ to get $f(g(John), John)$ as the unified instance of both expressions. If we unify expressions U and V, we often call the substitutions that are made σ (sigma) and write $U\sigma = V\sigma$.

The difference between substitution and unification is demonstrated in Figure 8.12. When we apply substitution, we have some pattern definition [e.g., $F(A, B)$], which may represent a subprogram signature or a macro definition, and an instance of the pattern [e.g., $F(g(i), h(j))$], which may represent the invocation of the subprogram or a macro expansion. Substitution requires a renaming of the parameters of the pattern definition with the actual values of the instance. However, in unification, we usually have two separate pattern definitions [e.g., $F(A, B)$ and $M(C, D)$] and an instance of a pattern [e.g., $F(John, M(h(v), 7))$]. We would like to know whether there is some assignment to A, B, C, and D that makes the instance of the pattern a substitution of both pattern definitions.

To apply the definition of the patterns, we may have to substitute in *both* directions. In this example, if we substitute $John$ for A in the definition of F and 7 for D in the definition of M, and if we also substitute the patterns $M(h(v),7)$ for B in the definition of F and $h(v)$ for C in the definition of M, our pattern instance represents a valid substitution of both initial pattern definitions to F and M. From our original expression $F(John, M(h(v),7))$, we can get two different results depending on whether we apply the definition for Pattern F or the definition for Pattern M first:

$$\begin{array}{ll} \text{Apply } F \text{ first:} & F(John, M(h(v),7)) = G(John, M(h(v),7)) \\ \text{Apply } M \text{ first:} & F(John, M(h(v),7)) = F(John, N(h(v),7)) \end{array}$$

After applying the second substitution, we get the same result: $G(John, N(h(v),7))$. We say that this set of substitutions *unifies* the pattern instance with both F and M.

Application of unification to Prolog. Assume we have query q with $q = q_1, q_2$, where q_1 and q_2 are subqueries. We first try to unify q_1 with some rule p in the database. If our query q_1 unifies with p in rule

$$p{:}-\ p_1, p_2, \ldots p_n$$

then we may substitute $p\sigma$ for $q_1\sigma$, yielding the new query,

$$p\sigma, q_2\sigma \;=\; p_1\sigma, p_2\sigma, \ldots p_n\sigma, q_2\sigma \;=\; p'_1, p'_2, \ldots p'_n, q'_2$$

where the prime represents the original query modified by the σ transformations. We want to solve this new query.

However, if query q_1 unifies with fact r, then we may replace q_1 with *true* and our query now becomes $true, q_2\sigma \;=\; q_2\sigma \;=\; q'_2$.

This then is the execution process for Prolog. Queries are unified with rules or facts in the database until *true* results. Of course, $false$ may also result, meaning that the wrong rule p or wrong fact r was unified with q_1. An alternative, if any, must then be tried until a valid solution is found. The set of σ transformations needed to resolve this query becomes the answers to our query. The general principle involved here is called *resolution* and is explained in more detail in Section 8.4.5.

A more complete Prolog example is the following set of statements (called *clauses* in Prolog) for defining addition:

1. succ(Y,X) :−Y is X+1.
2. add(Y,0,X) :−Y=X.
3. add(Z,X,Y) :−W is X-1, add(U,W,Y), succ(Z,U).

The *succ* (successor) rule computes $Y = X + 1$ by unifying the variable Y with the sum of X and 1. That is, the value substituted for Y that unifies Y and $X+1$ is the value of $X+1$. (Remember that *is* computes the value of the expression, whereas = means the unevaluated string.) The *add* rules compute the sum by using two facts

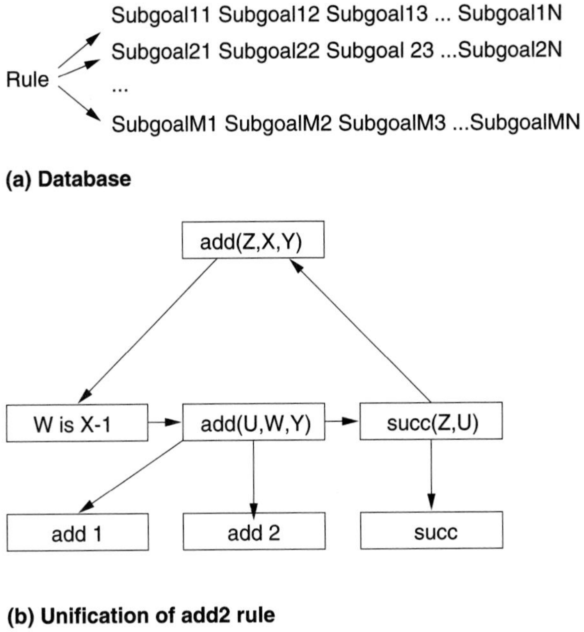

Figure 8.13. Prolog execution.

about addition:

$0 + x = x$ (Rule 2)

$(x + 1) + y = x + (y + 1) = x + succ(y)$ (Rule 3)

Rule 3 reduces addition to an equal number of "subtract 1 from first term" and "add 1 to second term" steps until the first term is 0 (Rule 2).

For example, to compute the sum of 2 and 3, Y must be unified in the query $add(Y, 2, 3)$. Prolog produces as an output

add(Y,2,3).
Y = 5

with $Y = 5$ being the σ transformation that unifies the query with the rules in the database defining addition.

Implementation. Prolog execution is summarized by Figure 8.13 and represents a standard tree-walking algorithm. The set of facts in the Prolog database (Figure 8.13[a]) represents a set of M goals, one for each rule with that relation in the database. For the addition example, *add* would have two possible goals: *add*1 with subgoal $Y = X$, and *add*2 with subgoals $W\ is\ X - 1$, $add(U, W, Y)$, and $succ(Z, U)$ (Figure 8.13[b]).

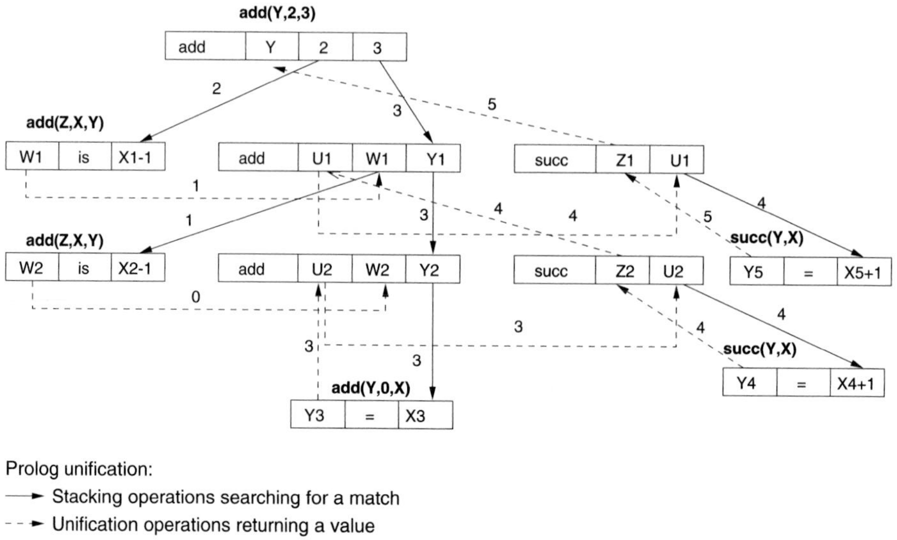

Figure 8.14. Prolog unification.

For each goal (e.g., *add*2 rule), Prolog tries to match each subgoal in succession. First W is unified with $X-1$. This assigns W the value of $X-1$. Prolog then tries to match subgoal $add(U, W, Y)$ by invoking the *add* rules recursively (first *add*1 and then *add*2 looking for a match). If successful, U is the sum of W and Y (i. e., $(X-1)+Y$). If that subgoal is matched, then $succ(Z, U)$ unifies Z with $U+1$ or Z is set to $((X-1)+Y+1) = (X+Y)$. The last subgoal is matched, and the *add*2 rule succeeds with Z being unified with the sum of X and Y.

If any subgoal fails, then a standard backtracking algorithm applies. The previous subgoal is checked for an alternative match. If none is found, then the previous subgoal is checked, and so on. If all subgoals fail, then the rule fails and another *add* rule, if any, is executed.

Using this general tree-walking algorithm, $add(Y, 2, 3)$ is evaluated as follows (Figure 8.14):

1. $add(Y, 2, 3)$ tries to match Rule 3. W_1 is assigned the value $2-1=1$.
2. Prolog tries to unify $add(U_1, 1, 3), succ(Z_1, U_1)$.
3. $add(U_1, 1, 3)$ sets W_2 to 0 and tries to unify $add(U_2, 0, 3), succ(Z_2, U_2)$.
4. $add(U_2, 0, 3)$ succeeds by unifying U_2 with 3 using the first *add* rule.
5. $succ(Z_2, U_2) = succ(Z_2, 3)$ succeeds by unifying Z_2 with 4.
6. Z_2 (i.e., 4) is then unified with U_1 from the relation $add(U_1, 1, 3)$.
7. $succ(Z_1, U_1)$ unifies Z_1 with $U_1 + 1 = 4 + 1 = 5$.
8. Finally, Y is unified with $Z_1 = 5$, which is the value printed.

It should seem clear from this example that stacks play an important role in the implementation of Prolog. Each Prolog clause is stacked, and each subgoal is stacked until a goal match is found.

8.4.4 Backtracking

In describing the Prolog execution behavior for *add* in the previous example, all subgoals matched in the process of computing $add(Y, 2, 3)$. However, what if that is not true? What if some subgoal cannot be unified with a rule in the database? In that case, we say the rule fails.

As given by Figure 8.13, the goals were listed in some order $1..M$. But this is arbitrary, and Prolog simply uses the order in which the facts are entered into the database. At any time, we are trying to match a subgoal. If the match is to succeed, then one of the possible goals will succeed, only we do not necessarily know which one. If we first try an incorrect goal, that goal will fail. In this case, we simply try another possible goal.

If we reach the last possible goal and it too fails, we say that the current subgoal fails. Because we have stacked the set of subgoals we are searching for, we back up to the previous subgoal that matched and try another possible goal for it to match. We call this a general *backtracking* algorithm, which we can describe using Figure 8.13(b):

1. For $Subgoal_{i,j}$ set $k = 1$ as a new goal.
2. Successively try to match $goal_k$ for $k = 1..M$ and return either success or fail, depending upon whether any $goal_k$ succeeds or all fail.
3. If $goal_k$ succeeds, then $Subgoal_{i,j}$ succeeds. Save k and match $Subgoal_{i,j+1}$.
4. If $goal_k$ fails for all k, then $Subgoal_{i,j}$ fails. Back up to $Subgoal_{i,j-1}$ and try the next possible goal $k + 1$ for that subgoal.
5. If $Subgoal_{i,N}$ succeeds, then return success as the result of the parent $goal_k$ that was being searched for.
6. If $Subgoal_{i,j}$ fails for all j, then this goal fails and return fail as the parent's search for $goal_k$.

This algorithm tries all possible matches, searching for success, by successively stacking and unstacking partial results. It is a frequently used (but slow) algorithm that underlies many search strategies.

Prolog uses the function ! (cut) as a fence that always fails on backup. For example, the rule

A :–B,!,C,!,D.

will succeed only if the first goal for B matches and the first goal for C matches and the first goal for D matches. Any attempt to match $Subgoal_{i,j-1}$ in the prior algorithm, where $Subgoal_{i,j-1} =!$, results in failure. Thus, if the first goal for D fails, A fails because no alternative for C is tried as a new goal. Using cuts appropriately prevents unnecessary backtracking on many algorithms.

Backtracking is a general programming technique available in any language that creates tree structures. We can build backtracking algorithms in all of the languages in this book. However, in languages like LISP, where trees are natural consequences of the built-in list data type, backtracking is relatively easy to implement. In Prolog, as we just observed, it is a built-in feature.

8.4.5 Resolution

The predicate calculus has also played an important role in the development of languages—most noticeably, Prolog. During the 1960s, FORTRAN was the dominant language for scientific calculations, whereas LISP was the preferred language for inference- and derivation-based programs. Because LISP used list structures as its basic data type, trees were a natural composite data type handled by LISP programs. If we represent the rule $A\ B\ C \Rightarrow D$ in LISP, the natural data structure is a tree with D as the root and A, B, and C as leaves. Proving D true requires proving the subtrees A, B, and C first. As discussed in Section 8.4.4 on backtracking, LISP is a natural language in which to build such algorithms.

In 1965, Robinson developed the resolution principle, the implementation of which in 1972 became Prolog. Although it is not necessary to fully understand resolution to program in Prolog, it helps to understand the underlying theory behind Prolog execution.

If you have a set of predicates $\{P_1, P_2, \ldots\}$, the general problem is to determine what theorem you can generate from these predicates. In general, if P and Q are predicates, then is $P \Rightarrow Q$ (P implies Q) a theorem?

We start this development with the observation that every predicate can be written in *clausal form*

$$P_1 \wedge P_2 \wedge \ldots P_n \Rightarrow Q_1 \vee \ldots Q_m$$

where each P_i and Q_i are terms. Examples of clausal forms are as follows:

Predicate	Clausal form
$A \Rightarrow B$	$A \Rightarrow B$
$A \wedge B$	$A \wedge B \Rightarrow true$
$A \vee B$	$true \Rightarrow A \vee B$
$\neg A$	$A \Rightarrow false$
$A \wedge \neg B \Rightarrow C$	$A \Rightarrow B \vee C$

We can show this by reducing every predicate to *disjunctive normal form* (i.e., as a sequence of $\vee$ terms). All the negated terms become antecedents and non-negated terms become consequents of the clausal form. The following table is illustrative:

Disjunctive normal form	Clausal form
$A \vee B \vee \neg C \vee D$	$C \Rightarrow A \vee B \vee D$
$\neg A \vee \neg B \vee \neg C \vee D$	$A \wedge B \wedge C \Rightarrow D$

This is a direct consequence of the following transformations:

1. $P \Rightarrow Q$ is equivalent to $\neg P \vee Q$, and
2. (*DeMorgan's law*) $\neg P \vee \neg Q$ is equivalent to $\neg(P \wedge Q)$.

By grouping all the negated terms in the disjunctive normal form for a predicate together, by DeMorgan's law they are equivalent to the negation of the *and* of all the predicates. By Transformation 1, they become the antecedent to the clausal form.

Consider any clausal form:

$$P_1 \wedge P_2 \wedge \ldots P_m \Rightarrow Q_1 \vee Q_2 \vee \ldots Q_n$$

Resolution on this general predicate becomes too complex. But consider the cases where $n = 1$ or $n = 0$. We call such predicates *Horn clauses*. These have the format

$$P_1 \wedge P_2 \wedge \ldots P_m \Rightarrow Q_1$$
$$P_1 \wedge P_2 \wedge \ldots P_m$$

If we reverse the order of antecedent and consequent and replace $\Rightarrow$ by :–, we get the equivalent statements:

$$(1) \quad Q_1{:}-\ P_1 \wedge P_2 \wedge \ldots P_m.$$
$$(2) \quad {:}-\ P_1 \wedge P_2 \wedge \ldots P_m.$$

which are our familiar Prolog clauses. The first represents a rule and the second represents a query. If we consider the case $m = 0$, then we have a Prolog fact: $Q_1{:}-$ *true*, or simply

$$(3) \quad Q_1.$$

The resolution principle on Horn clauses now states that

> Given query $Q_1 \ldots Q_n$ and rule $P_0{:}-P_1 \ldots P_m$, then if we unify Q_1 and P_0, or, as written in Section 8.4.3, $Q_1\sigma = P_0\sigma$, we get equivalent queries.

If we unify Q_1 with P_0 our original query is then equivalent to either
1. $(P_1 \ldots P_m Q_2 \ldots Q_n)\sigma = R_1 \ldots R_{m+n-1}$, if P_0 was a rule, or
2. $(Q_2 \ldots Q_n)\sigma = R_1 \ldots R_{n-1}$, if P_0 was a fact ($m = 0$),

where $R_i = P_j\sigma$ or $R_i = Q_j\sigma$. Eventually, we hope, all of the R_i will unify with facts in our database and result in *true* with a history of transformations giving the results to our query.

This is the essential execution behavior of Prolog. The goal of the Prolog search space is to unify $Q_1 \ldots Q_n$, and Prolog is free to choose any rule P from the database as a hypothesis to try resolution on it. If this succeeds, σ describes the answers to our query; if this fails, we need to try alternative rules P' to search for a valid substitution.

8.5 SUGGESTIONS FOR FURTHER READING

Many of the language texts discussed in chapter 1 describe sequence control issues. The September 1989 *ACM Computing Surveys* [ACM 1989] presents several papers on programming language paradigms, including the necessary control structures. The formal relationship between control structures and formal proof of correctness issues is discussed in [GANNON et al. 1994]. Decision tables are another form of control structure [METZNER and BARNES 1977], and [PRENNER et al. 1972] provided additional information on backtracking algorithms.

8.6 PROBLEMS

1. In C, explain the behavior of the following program fragment:

```
{int i=1
   j=2;
   if (i = j) {printf("true: %d %d\n",i,j);}
      else printf("false: %d %d\n",i,j); }
```

2. A fourth form of expression syntax is called *reverse-Polish prefix*, which is the usual prefix notation written backward. For example, $a + (b \times c)$ is $+\ a \times b\ c$ in prefix, $a\ b\ c \times +$ in postfix, and $c\ b \times a\ +$ in reverse-Polish prefix. Reverse-Polish prefix has properties similar to the usual postfix notation, but occasionally has some advantages over postfix in generating efficient machine language code. Explain why.

3. Give the tree representation for the following, assuming C precedence:

(a) – A – B / C * D / E / F + G
(b) A * B > C + D / E – F
(c) ! A & B > C + D

Repeat this for the precedence defined in Pascal and then Smalltalk.

4. Give all prime programs consisting of five nodes.

5. Show that, for any $n > 1$, there is a prime program of n nodes.

6. One of the major theoretical results supporting the replacement of **go to** statements by structured statements is due to a result by Böhm and Jacobini [BOHM and JACOBINI 1966]. They proved that any proper program may also be programmed using only sequences of statements with **if** and **while** statements. Draw a proper program with several loops and branches. Program this using **go to**s and then using only **if** and **while** constructs. Evaluate both with respect to ease of reading, understanding, and writing of these programs.

7. The Böhm–Jacobini theorem states that any flowchart can be replaced by one with the same functionality that only uses the sequence, **if**, and **while** statements. Show that you do not need the **if**—that is, **while** is sufficient.

8. The Pascal **if** statement has the syntax

if *Boolean_expression* **then** *statement* **else** *statement*

whereas the Ada **if** is

if *Boolean_expression* **then** *statement* **else** *statement* **end if**

Comment on the relative merits of having an explicit terminator to the statement, such as the **end if** of Ada.

9. One of the Pascal iteration statements is given by

for *simple_variable* := *initial_value* **to** *final_value* **do** *statement*

Discuss the merits and implementation details if

(a) *initial_value* and *final_value* are evaluated once when the **for** statement is first executed.

(b) *initial_value* and *final_value* are evaluated each time the program loops back to iterate.

10. Prolog rules can be viewed as logical predicates. The rule a:– b, c will cause a to succeed if b and c both succeed. So we can say a is *true* if the condition $b \wedge c$ is true.

(a) Under what conditions for p, q, r, and s are the following Prolog rules satisfied?

(1)	*(2)*	*(3)*
x :– p,q.	x :– p,!,q.	x :– p,q.
x :– r,s.	x :– r,s.	x :– r,!,s.

(b) Repeat Question *(a)* if we add the rule x:–$fail$ after the two given rules. What if we add this rule first in the database?

11. In the annotated Prolog example of Figure A.16 on page 607, explain what happens if the *for* rule of Line 17 is placed before the *for* rule in lines 11 to 15.

12. *append* can be defined as

```
append(X, Y, Z) :–X= [ ], Y = Z.
append(X, Y, Z) :–X = [A | B ], Z = [A | W], append(B, Y, W).
```

(a) Show that this definition is equivalent to the following definition of *append*:

append([ ], X, X).
append([H|X], Y, [H|Z]) :–append(X, Y, Z).

(b) Trace the execution of the query *append*$([1, 2, 3], [4, 5], Z)$ to show that t Z=[1,2,3,4,5] unifies the *append* query.

Chapter 9

Subprogram Control

In the past few chapters, we have described the process by which languages create data types and data objects of those types. We saw how programs sequence through statements to manipulate such data in memory, and we discussed simple activation record mechanisms by which languages manage storage for the various data objects that are declared. In this chapter, we look at the interaction among subprograms in greater detail and, more important, how they manage to pass data among themselves in a structured and efficient manner.

For most programs, a simple stack structure is sufficient for managing the storage for the executing program. Each new procedure requires a new block of storage, containing the local variables for the procedure, to be added to a stack, and exiting from the procedure is accomplished by popping that block off the stack. In this chapter we will confine ourselves to this model. However, a more dynamic storage mechanism is also needed. In C (using the function *malloc*), C++ , Java, and Pascal (using the function *new*), and implicitly in languages like ML and LISP, a program can arbitrarily create storage for new data objects. In such instances, the program needs a heap storage, which dynamically allocates and frees blocks of storage on demand. We discuss heap storage allocation more fully in chapter 10.

9.1 SUBPROGRAM SEQUENCE CONTROL

How does one subprogram invoke another and then permit the called subprogram to return to the first? The simple subprogram **call** and **return** statement structure is common to almost all programming languages and is the usual mechanism to achieve this result.

Simple subprogram call return. We are accustomed in programming to view programs as hierarchies. A program is composed of a single main program, which during execution may call various subprograms, which in turn may each call other sub-subprograms, and so forth, to any depth. Each subprogram at some point is expected to terminate its execution and return control to the program that called it. During execution of a subprogram, execution of the calling program is temporarily halted. When execution of the subprogram is completed, execution of the calling program resumes at the point immediately following the call of the subprogram. This control structure is often explained by the *copy rule:* The effect of the subprogram **call** statement is the same as would be obtained if the **call** statement were replaced by a copy of the body of the subprogram (with suitable substitutions for parameters and conflicting identifiers) before execution. Viewed in this way, subprogram calls may be considered as control structures that simply make it unnecessary to copy large numbers of identical or nearly identical statements that occur in more than one place in a program.

Before looking at the implementation of the simple call-return structure used for the copy-rule view of subprograms, let us look briefly at some of the implicit assumptions present in this view that may be relaxed to get more general subprogram control structures:

1. *Subprograms cannot be recursive.* A subprogram is *directly recursive* if it contains a call on itself (e.g., if subprogram B contains the statement **call** B); it is *indirectly recursive* if it calls another subprogram that calls the original subprogram or that initiates a further chain of subprogram calls that eventually leads back to a call of the original subprogram.

In the case of simple nonrecursive subprogram calls, we may apply the copy rule during translation to replace subprogram calls by copies of the subprogram body and completely eliminate the need for the separate subprogram (in principle, not in practice). However, if the subprogram is directly recursive, then this is not possible even in principle because the substitution of subprogram call for subprogram body is obviously unending. Each substitution that deletes a **call** statement introduces a new call on the same subprogram, for which another substitution is necessary, and so on. Indirect recursion may allow some subprograms to be deleted but must lead eventually to making others directly recursive. Nevertheless, many algorithms are recursive and lead naturally to recursive subprogram structures.

2. *Explicit* **call** *statements are required.* For the copy rule to apply, each point of call of a subprogram must be explicitly indicated in the program to be translated. For a subprogram used as an *exception handler,* no explicit call may be present.

3. *Subprograms must execute completely at each call.* Implicit in the copy rule is the assumption that each subprogram is executed from its beginning to its logical end each time it is called. If called a second time, the subprogram begins execution anew and again executes to its logical end before returning control. A subprogram used as a *coroutine* continues execution from the point of its last termination each time it is called.

4. *Immediate transfer of control at point of call.* An explicit **call** statement in a program indicates that control is to transfer directly to the subprogram at that point, and thus copying the body into the calling program has the same effect. For a *scheduled subprogram* call, execution of the subprogram may be deferred until some later time.

5. *Single execution sequence.* At any point during execution of a subprogram hierarchy, exactly one program has control. Execution proceeds in a single sequence from calling program to called subprogram and back to calling program. If we halt execution at some point, we may always identify one program that is in execution (i.e., that has control), a set of others whose execution has been temporarily suspended (the calling program, its calling program, etc.), and the remainder, which either have never been called or have completely executed. Subprograms used as *tasks* may execute concurrently so that several are in execution at once.

Of the major languages discussed, only FORTRAN is based directly on the copy-rule view of subprograms. Each of the others allows more flexible structures.

9.1.1 Simple Call-Return Subprograms

Note that the emphasis here is on sequence-control structure (i.e., on the mechanisms for transfer of control between programs and subprograms). Closely tied to each of these sequence-control structures is the question of data control: parameter transmission, global and local variables, and so on. These topics are taken up separately in the next section so that we can keep our focus here on the sequence-control mechanisms. For example, even simple subprogram calls ordinarily arise in two forms: the *function call,* for subprograms that return values directly, and the *procedure* or *subroutine call,* for subprograms that operate only through side effects on shared data.

Implementation. To understand the implementation of the simple call-return control structure, it is important to build a more complete model of what it means to say that a program is *being executed.* For expressions and statement sequences, we think of each as represented by a block of executable code at run time. Execution of the expression or statement sequence means simply execution of the code, using a hardware or software interpreter, as discussed in chapter 2. For subprograms, we need more:

1. There is a distinction between a subprogram *definition* and a subprogram *activation.* The definition is what we see in the written program, which is translated into a template. An activation is created each time a subprogram is called using the template created from the definition.

2. An activation is implemented as two parts: a *code segment* containing the executable code and constants, and an *activation record* containing local data, parameters, and various other data items.

3. The code segment is *invariant* during execution. It is created by the translator and stored statically in memory. During execution, it is used but never modified. Every activation of the subprogram uses the same code segment.

4. The activation record is *created* anew each time the subprogram is called, and it is *destroyed* when the subprogram returns. While the subprogram is executing, the contents of the activation record are constantly changing as assignments are made to local variables and other data objects.

To avoid confusion, we cannot simply talk of "execution of a particular statement S in the subprogram," but rather we must talk of "execution of S during activation R of the subprogram." Thus, to keep track of the point at which a program is being executed, we need two pieces of data, which we consider as stored in two system-defined pointer variables.

Current-instruction pointer. Statements and expressions in a subprogram are represented by instructions of some sort in the executable code produced by the translator and stored in the code segment. We consider that, at any point during execution, there is some instruction in some code segment that is currently being (or just about to be) executed by the hardware or software interpreter. This instruction is termed the *current instruction,* and a pointer to it is maintained in the variable called the *current-instruction pointer* (CIP). The interpreter acts by fetching the instruction designated by the CIP, updating the CIP to point to the next instruction in sequence, and then executing the instruction (which may change the CIP again to effect a jump to some other instruction).

Current-environment pointer. Because all activations of the same subprogram use the same code segment, it is not enough simply to know the current instruction being executed; a pointer to the activation record being used is also needed. For example, when the instruction in the code references a variable X, that variable ordinarily is represented in the activation record. Each activation record for that subprogram has a different data object named X. The activation record represents the referencing environment of the subprogram, so a pointer to an activation record is commonly known as an *environment pointer.* The pointer to the current activation record (current referencing environment) is maintained during execution in the variable we term the *current-environment pointer* (CEP). The activation record designated by the CEP is used to resolve the reference to X.

With the CIP and CEP pointers, it now becomes easy to understand how a program is executed. An activation record for the main program is created (because there is only one such activation, this activation record is often created during translation along with the code segment). The CEP is assigned a pointer to it. The CIP is assigned a pointer to the first instruction in the code segment for the main program. The interpreter goes to work fetching and executing instructions as designated by the CIP.

When a subprogram **call** instruction is reached, an activation record for the subprogram is created and a pointer to it is assigned to the CEP. The CIP is assigned a pointer to the first instruction of the code segment for the subprogram. The interpreter continues from that point, executing instructions in the subprogram. If the subprogram calls another subprogram, new assignments are made to set the CIP and CEP for the activation of that subprogram.

To return correctly from a subprogram call, the values of the CIP and CEP must be saved somewhere by the subprogram **call** instruction before the new values are assigned. When a **return** instruction is reached that terminates an activation of a subprogram, the old values of the CIP and CEP that were saved when the

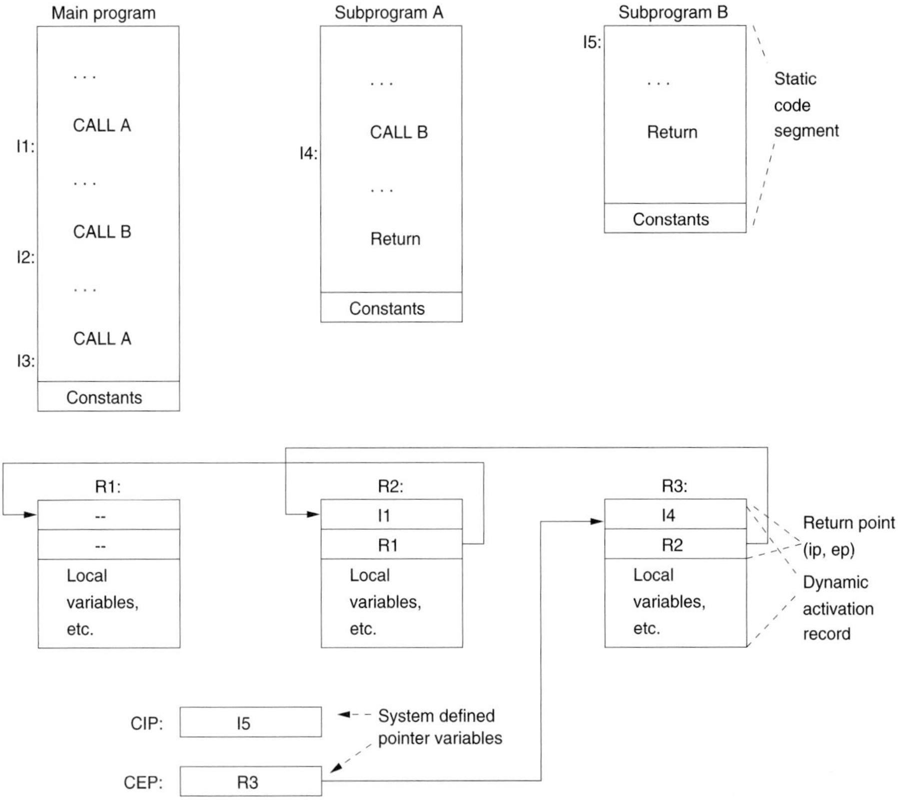

Figure 9.1. Execution state at start of execution of subprogram B.

subprogram was called must be retrieved and reinstated. This reinstatement of the old values is all that is necessary to return control to the correct activation of the calling subprogram at the correct place so that execution of that subprogram may continue.

Where should the **call** instruction save the values of the CIP and CEP before assigning the new values? A convenient place is to store them in the activation record of the subprogram being called. An additional system-defined data object, the *return point,* is included in the activation record. The return point contains space for two pointer values, the pair (instruction pointer, environment pointer [*ip, ep*]). After the **call** instruction creates the activation record, it stores the old values (*ip, ep*) of the CIP and CEP in the return point and assigns the new (*ip, ep*) to the CIP and CEP, thus effecting the transfer of control to the called subprogram. The **return** instruction fetches the old (*ip, ep*) from the return point and reinstates them as the values of the CIP and CEP, thus effecting the return of control to the

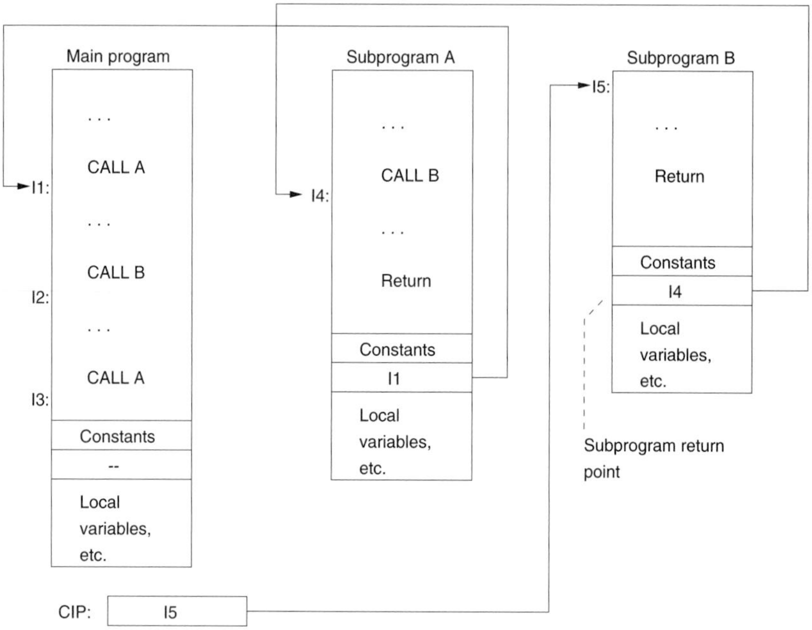

Figure 9.2. Subprogram **call–return** structure.

calling subprogram.

Now if we were to watch the overall pattern of execution of a program, we would see the interpreter plodding along executing the instruction designated by the CIP on each cycle and using the CEP to resolve data references (a subject taken up in detail in the next section). The **call** and **return** instructions swap *(ip, ep)* values in and out of the CIP and CEP to effect transfers of control back and forth to subprograms. If execution were halted at some point, it would be simple to determine which subprogram was currently being executed (look at the CIP and CEP), which subprogram had called it (look at the return point of the subprogram being executed), which subprogram had called that subprogram (look at its return point), and so on. Figure 9.1 shows this organization for a main program and two subprograms, each called at two places.

This model for the implementation of subprogram call and return is general enough to serve as a basis for several of the varieties of subprogram control structure considered later. We note one important property of the copy-rule view of subprograms: At most one activation of any subprogram is in use (i.e., is being enacted) at any point during program execution. A subprogram P may be called many different times during execution, but each activation is complete and terminated before the next activation begins.

From this property, a simpler model of subprogram implementation may be derived, provided we are willing to pay a penalty in storage to increase execution speed. The simpler implementation is to allocate storage for a single activation record of each subprogram statically as an extension of the code segment, rather than creating the activation record at the time of call of the subprogram. In this simpler model (which is used in many implementations of FORTRAN and COBOL), execution of the overall program begins with a code segment and activation record for each subprogram and the main program already present in memory. Execution proceeds without any dynamic allocation of storage when a subprogram is called. Instead, the same activation record is used repeatedly, simply being reinitialized each time the subprogram is called again. Because only one activation is in use at any point, this reuse of the same activation record on each call cannot destroy any information needed from an earlier call because all earlier calls have already terminated.

By allocating a code segment and an activation record as a single block of storage, some other simplifications are also gained. The CEP pointer is no longer needed because the current activation record is always just an extension of the code segment that the CIP designates. A reference in the instructions to a variable X always may be resolved by going to the attached activation record rather than to the CEP. With the CEP omitted, only a single *ip* pointer, the CIP, need be saved and restored on subprogram call and return.

With the more general implementation of call and return, the underlying hardware often provides little support. However, with this simplified implementation, the hardware often provides a *return-jump instruction* that allows a subprogram call to be implemented in a single hardware instruction. The CIP of our model is represented directly by the *program address register* of the hardware (chapter 2). The return-jump instruction stores the contents of this program address register in a memory location or register (often the memory location immediately before the location to which control is transferred) and assigns a designated location as the new value of the program address register (thus effecting a jump to the instruction at that location). The effect is exactly what is desired: The old value of the CIP is saved, and the location of the first instruction of the subprogram code is assigned as the new value. The return from a subprogram is also usually implementable as a single instruction: The saved value is reassigned to the program address register (a jump instruction does this). The result is a simple implementation of subprogram call and return, at a cost in storage due to the static allocation of activation records for all subprograms. An example of this structure is shown in Figure 9.2.

Stack-Based Implementation

The simplest run-time storage-management technique to handle this activation record structure is the stack. Free storage at the start of execution is set up as a sequential block in memory. As storage is allocated, it is taken from sequential

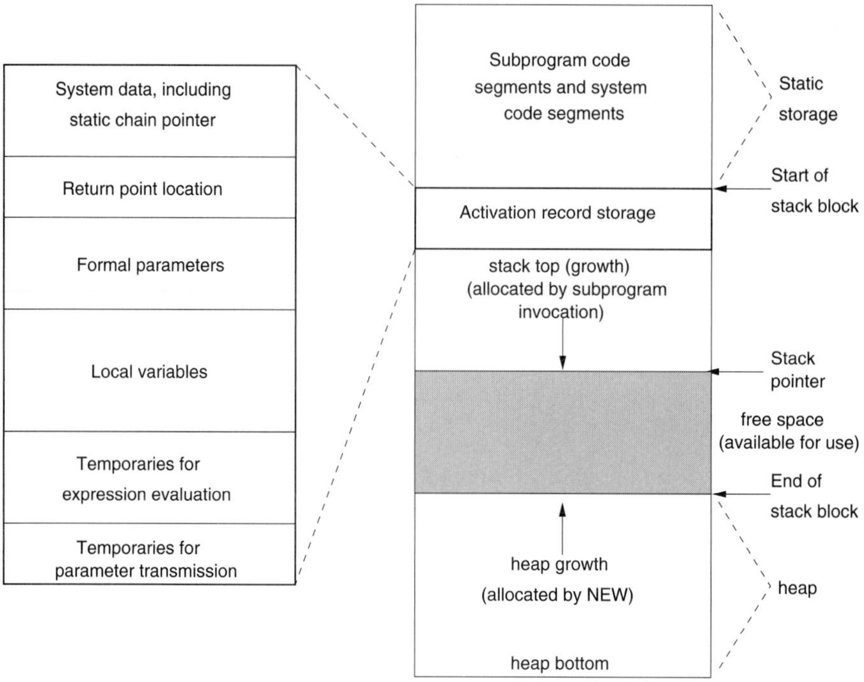

(a) Activation record for one procedure (b) Memory organization during execution

Figure 9.3. C memory organization.

locations in this stack block beginning at one end. Storage must be freed in the reverse order of allocation so that a block of storage being freed is always at the top of the stack.

A single *stack pointer* is all that is needed to control storage management. The stack pointer always points to the top of the stack, the next available word of free storage in the stack block. All storage in use lies in the stack below the location pointed to by the stack pointer. All free storage lies above the pointer. When a block of k locations is to be allocated, the pointer is simply moved to point k locations farther up the stack area. When a block of k locations is freed, the pointer is moved back k locations. *Compaction* occurs automatically as part of freeing storage. Freeing a block of storage automatically recovers the freed storage and makes it available for reuse.

Most C implementations are built around a single central stack of activation records for subprograms together with a statically allocated area containing system programs and subprogram code segments. The structure of a typical activation record for a C subprogram is shown in Figure 9.3(a). The activation record

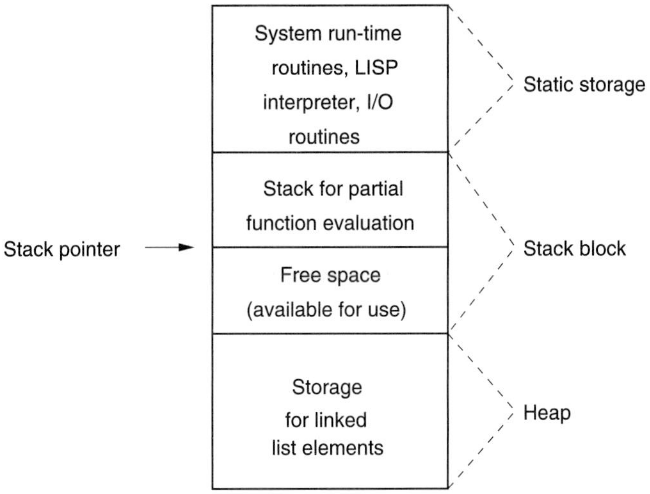

Figure 9.4. LISP memory organization during execution.

contains all the variable items of information associated with a given subprogram activation. Figure 9.3(b) shows a typical memory organization during C execution (the heap storage area is used for storage allocated by *new* and freed by *dispose* and is discussed further in chapter 10).

The use of a stack in a LISP implementation is somewhat different. Subprogram (function) calls are also strictly nested, and a stack may be used for activation records. Each activation record contains a return point and temporaries for expression evaluation and parameter transmission. Local referencing environments might also be allocated in the same stack, except that the programmer is allowed to directly manipulate these associations. Therefore, they are ordinarily stored in a separate stack, represented as a linked list, called the *A-list.* The stack containing return points and temporaries may then be hidden from the programmer and allocated sequentially. LISP implementation also requires a *heap* storage area, which is managed through a free-space list and garbage collection, with a special area and storage manager for full-word data items such as numbers. A typical LISP memory organization is illustrated in Figure 9.4.

9.1.2 Recursive Subprograms

Let us look at one of our subprogram assumptions—no recursion—and investigate language design that permits this feature. Recursion, in the form of recursive subprogram calls, is one of the most important sequence-control structures in programming. Many algorithms are most naturally represented using recursion. In LISP, where list structures are the primary data structure available, recursion is the primary control mechanism for repeating sequences of statements, replacing the iteration of most other languages.

Specification. If we allow recursive subprogram calls, a subprogram A may call any other subprogram, including A, a subprogram B that calls A, and so on. Syntactically, in writing the program, probably nothing changes because a recursive subprogram call looks the same as any other subprogram call. In concept, there is no difficulty provided that the distinction between a subprogram definition and activation is clear. The only difference between a recursive call and an ordinary call is that the recursive call creates a second activation of the subprogram *during the lifetime of the first activation.* If the second activation leads to another recursive call, then three activations may exist simultaneously, and so on. In general, if the execution of the program results in a chain of a first call of Subprogram A followed by k recursive calls that occur before any return is made, then $k+1$ activations of A will exist at the point just before return from the kth recursive call. The only new element introduced by recursion is the multiple activations of the same subprogram that all exist simultaneously at some point during execution.

Implementation. Because of the possibility of multiple activations, we need both the CIP and CEP pointers. At the time of each subprogram call, a new activation record is created, which is subsequently destroyed upon return.

Note that nothing described earlier in Figure 9.1 required that the new activation records be created for *unique* subprograms A and B. Within A, we could have just as easily created a new activation record for A as one for B. In the case where A calls B, the *lifetimes cannot overlap*; for any two activations of A and B, the lifetime of A *completely includes* that of B. This simply says that if instead of A calling B, A called itself recursively, this same property would be true, and the new activation record for A could just be added to the stack containing the older activation record of A.

Each activation record contains a return point to store the values of the (ip, ep) pair used by **call** and **return**. If you observe only the *ep* values stored in the return points in Figure 9.1, you note that they form a linked list that links together the activation records on the central stack in the order of their creation. From the CEP pointer, the top activation record in the central stack is reached. From the *ep* value in its return point, the second activation record in the stack may be reached; from the *ep* value in that activation record, the third activation record in the stack may be reached. At the end of this chain, the last link leads to the activation record for the main program. This chain of links is called the *dynamic chain* because it chains together subprogram activations in the order of their dynamic creation during program execution. (In Section 9.4.2, a related *static chain* is discussed that links activation records together for referencing purposes.)

Conventional computer hardware sometimes provides some hardware support for this central-stack organization, but it is generally somewhat more costly to implement than the simple call-return structure without recursion. There is no difficulty in mixing subprograms implemented in the simple way with those using a central stack, provided the compiler knows which is which when compiling **call** and **return** instructions. Only subprograms that are actually called recursively need the central-stack implementation. Thus, in some languages such as PL/I, subprograms called recursively must be tagged RECURSIVE as part of the subprogram definition; in others, like C and Pascal, the recursive structure is always assumed.

9.1.3 The Pascal Forward Declaration

Recursion in procedure invocation poses a problem with the one-pass strategy, as in the design of many Pascal compiler. For example, if A and B are subprograms and A calls B and B calls A, then if the definition of A appears before the definition of B, then the call to B in A necessarily appears before the definition of B. Reversing the order of the definitions of A and B only reverses the problem. This problem is solved in Pascal by requiring that a **forward** *declaration* be given for whichever of the subprograms is defined last. The **forward** declaration has the form of the signature for the subprogram, including the full parameter list, followed by the word **forward** in place of the subprogram body. An example is

procedure A (*formal_parameter_list*); **forward;**

Following this forward declaration for A, Subprogram B could be defined, and then later the full definition for the body of A is given (but the formal-parameter list is not repeated). The **forward** declaration gives the compiler enough information to correctly compile the call on A found in B, although the complete definition of A has not yet appeared. This is the same principle used in Ada **package** specifications where the signature of a subprogram is given without the details of the subprogram's implementation.

Because the parameter list must not be repeated when the subprogram is later defined, this is a major source of programming errors. The documentation of the subprogram's signature is nowhere to be found near the listing of the body of the subprogram. Misstating parameters as well as misstating call-by-value and reference parameters is a problem. One way to avoid this is to always include a comment giving the parameter list. Therefore, after specifying the **forward** specification, the actual body of the subprogram could be given as

```
procedure A {(formal_parameter_list)};
    begin
    ...
    end
```

The reason for the Pascal emphasis on definition before use of an identifier lies in the mistaken intent that a one-pass compiler is necessary for efficient compilation. A one-pass compiler makes a single sweep through the source program, reading and processing one subprogram definition at a time and generating the executable

```
program anomaly(input,output);
procedure S; {1}
    begin
    writeln('wrong one')
    end;
procedure T;
    {Missing: procedure S; forward; here }
    procedure U;
        begin
        S {2}
        end;
    procedure S; {3}
        begin
        writeln('right one')
        end;
    begin
    U
    end;
begin
T
end.
```

Figure 9.5. A Pascal **forward** anomaly.

object program as it reads in the subprogram. To process the program in one pass, the compiler must have enough information at each point about the meaning of each identifier so that the correct object code can be generated. As discussed in chapter 2, one-pass compilers are not necessary to achieve rapid compilation times, and today, with inexpensive and fast microprocessors, compilation time is not a significant problem.

The rule concerning the **forward** construct brings up a strange anomaly in Pascal, as given in program *anomaly* of Figure 9.5. This program has three possible interpretations:

1. Compilation fails because *anomaly* is an invalid program. The procedure call S at Location 2 is calling the procedure at Location 3, and that is a forward reference without a **forward** declaration.

2. The procedure call at Location 2 is calling the procedure S at Location 1, which is what a simple one-pass compiler would do, even though it is the wrong S within the scope of the call.

3. The program executes with the procedure call at Location 2 calling the procedure S at Location 3. This is the correct procedure to call, even though the superfluous, but required, **forward** is missing.

A careful reading of the Pascal standard [LEDGARD 1984] gives the correct interpretation:

1. Section 6.2.2.1 of the standard states that the *defining point* for $S\{3\}$ is the

second **procedure** S statement.

2. Section 6.2.2.2 and 6.2.2.3 define the region for the defining point $S\{3\}$ as all of procedure T. Hence, the call $S\{2\}$ is an invocation of $S\{3\}$ and not of $S\{1\}$.

3. Section 6.2.2.9 requires that the defining point (e.g., statement $S\{3\}$) for any actual identifier (e.g., $S\{2\}$) occur before its use, which implies the need for the **forward** declaration.

With this explanation, Option 1 is clearly correct, although Option 3, while wrong, is a reasonable interpretation. Option 2 is clearly wrong and the worst choice to use.

By running this program on 13 different Pascal translators covering PCs, Macintoshes, workstations, and various UNIX machines from several vendors, the following results were obtained:

Option 1 (Correct interpretation):	3 compilers
Option 2 (Worst interpretation):	7 compilers
Option 3 (Incorrect, but reasonable):	3 compilers

Clearly only a small minority followed the standard and over half chose the most unreasonable option. (The names of each vendor are not revealed to protect the guilty.) (See Problem 22 at the end of the chapter.)

To further complicate this bizarre example, if you review the issues of language standardization in Section 1.3.3, it is possible for all 13 compilers to still be standards conforming. Because a standards-conforming Pascal compiler only has to compile standards-conforming programs, and this example is not a standards-conforming program, it is unspecified what the compiler should do in this situation. Therefore, all three options are correct with respect to the standard.

9.2 ATTRIBUTES OF DATA CONTROL

The data-control features of a programming language are those parts concerned with the accessibility of data at different points during program execution. The sequence-control mechanisms of the preceding chapter provide the means to coordinate the sequence in which operations are invoked during program execution. Once an operation is reached during execution, it must be provided with the data on which it is to operate. The data-control features of a language determine how data may be provided to each operation, and how a result of one operation may be saved and retrieved for later use as an operand by a subsequent operation.

When writing a program, one ordinarily is well aware of the operations that the program must execute and their sequence, but seldom is the same true of the operands for those operations. For example, a C program contains

$$X := Y + 2 * Z$$

Simple inspection indicates three operations in sequence: a multiplication, an addition, and an assignment. But what of the operands for these operations? One operand of the multiplication is clearly the number 2, but the other operands are marked only by the identifiers X, Y, and Z, and these obviously are not the operands but only designate the operands in some manner. Y might designate a real number, an integer, or the name of a parameterless subprogram to be executed to compute the operand. Perhaps the programmer has erred and Y designates a Boolean value or a string or serves as a statement label. Y may designate a value computed nearby, perhaps in the preceding statement, but equally as likely it may designate a value computed at some point much earlier in the computation, separated by many levels of subprogram call from the assignment where it is used. To make matters worse, Y may be used as a name in different ways in different sections of the program. Which use of Y is current here?

In a nutshell, the central problem of data control is the problem of what Y means in each execution of such an assignment statement. Because Y may be a local or nonlocal variable, the problem involves what are known as scope roles for declarations. Because Y may be a formal parameter, the problem involves techniques for parameter transmission; because Y may name a parameterless subprogram, the problem involves mechanisms for returning results from subprograms. In the following subsection, we first discuss what these problems are. In Section 9.3 we describe in greater details methods for implementing these features.

9.2.1 Names and Referencing Environments

There are two ways that a data object can be made available as an operand for an operation:

Direct transmission. A data object computed at one point as the result of an operation may be directly transmitted to another operation as an operand (e.g. the result of the multiplication $2 \times Z$ is transmitted directly to the addition operation as an operand in the statement $X := Y + 2 \times Z$). In this case, the data object is allocated storage temporarily during its lifetime and may never be given a name.

Referencing through a named data object. A data object may be given a name when it is created, and the name may then be used to designate it as an operand of an operation. Alternatively, the data object may be made a component of another data object that has a name so that the name of the larger data object may be used together with a selection operation to designate the data object as an operand.

Direct transmission is used for data control within expressions, but most data control outside of expressions involves the use of names and the referencing of names. The problem of the meaning of names forms the central concern in data control.

Program Elements That May Be Named

What kinds of names are seen in programs? Each language differs, but some general categories seen in many languages are as follows:

1. Variable names.
2. Formal parameter names.
3. Subprogram names.
4. Names for defined types.
5. Names for defined constants.
6. Statement labels (names for statements).
7. Exception names.
8. Names for primitive operations (e.g., + , *, SQRT).
9. Names for literal constants (e.g., 17, 3.25).

Categories 1 to 3, names for variables, formal parameters, and subprograms form the center of our concern here. Of the remaining categories, most references to names in these groups are resolved during translation rather than during program execution, as discussed earlier. Once the basic ideas underlying data control for variables, formal parameters, and subprogram names are understood, the extension to these new cases is relatively straightforward.

A name in any of the previous categories may be termed a *simple name.* A *composite name* is a name for a component of a data structure. It is written as a simple name designating the entire data structure, followed by a sequence of one or more selection operations that select the particular component of the named structure. For example, if A is the name of an array, then A is a simple name, and $A[3]$ is a composite name. Composite names may be quite complex (e.g., $A[3].Class[2].Room$). In most languages, simple names are represented by identifiers such as X, $Z2$, and $Sub1$, and thus the terms *identifier* and *simple name* are used interchangeably here.

Associations and Referencing Environments

Data control is concerned in large part with the binding of identifiers (simple names) to particular data objects and subprograms. Such a binding is termed an *association* and may be represented as a pair consisting of the identifier and its associated data object or subprogram.

During the course of execution of a program, we observe the following:

1. At the beginning of execution of the main program, identifier associations bind each variable name declared in the main program to a particular data object and bind each subprogram name invoked in the main program to a particular subprogram definition.

2. As the main program executes, it invokes *referencing operations* to determine the particular data object or subprogram associated with an identifier. For example, to execute the assignment

$$A := B + FN(C)$$

four referencing operations are required to retrieve the data objects associated with the names A, B, and C and the subprogram associated with the name FN.

3. When each new subprogram is called, a new set of associations is created for that subprogram. Each of the variable names and formal parameter names declared in the subprogram is associated with a particular data object. New associations for subprogram names may also be created.

4. As the subprogram executes, it invokes referencing operations to determine the particular data object or subprogram associated with each identifier. Some of the references may be to associations created on entry to the subprogram, whereas others may be to associations created back in the main program.

5. When the subprogram returns control to the main program, its associations are destroyed (or become inactive).

6. When control returns to the main program, execution continues as before using the associations originally set up at the start of execution.

In this pattern of creation, use, and destruction of associations, we see the main concepts of data control.

Referencing environments. Each program or subprogram has a set of identifier associations available for use in referencing during its execution. This set of identifier associations is termed the *referencing environment* of the subprogram (or program). The referencing environment of a subprogram is ordinarily invariant during its execution. It is set up when the subprogram activation is created, and it remains unchanged during the lifetime of the activation. The values contained in the various data objects may change, but the associations of names with data objects and subprograms do not. The referencing environment of a subprogram may have several components:

1. *Local referencing environment* (or simply *local environment*). The set of associations created on entry to a subprogram that represent formal parameters, local variables, and subprograms defined only within that subprogram forms the *local referencing environment* of that activation of the subprogram. The meaning of a reference to a name in the local environment may be determined without going outside the subprogram activation.

2. *Nonlocal referencing environment.* The set of associations for identifiers that may be used within a subprogram but that are not created on entry to it is termed the *nonlocal referencing environment* of the subprogram.

3. *Global referencing environment.* If the associations created at the start of execution of the main program are available to be used in a subprogram, then these associations form the *global referencing environment* of that subprogram. The global environment is part of the nonlocal environment.

4. *Predefined referencing environment.* Some identifiers have a predefined association that is defined directly in the language definition. Any program or subprogram may use these associations without explicitly creating them.

Visibility. An association for an identifier is said to be *visible* within a subprogram if it is part of the referencing environment for that subprogram. An association that exists but is not part of the referencing environment of the subprogram currently in execution is said to be *hidden* from that subprogram. Often an association is hidden when a subprogram is entered that redefines an identifier already in use elsewhere in the program.

Dynamic scope. Each association has a *dynamic scope*, which is that part of program execution during which it exists as part of a referencing environment. Thus, the dynamic scope of an association consists of the set of subprogram activations within which it is visible.

Referencing operations. A *referencing operation* is an operation with the signature

$$ref\_op : id \times referencing\_environment \rightarrow data\_object \text{ } or \text{ } subprogram$$

where ref_op, given an identifier and a referencing environment, finds the appropriate association for that identifier in the environment and returns the associated data object or subprogram definition.

Local, nonlocal, and global references. A reference to an identifier is a *local reference* if the referencing operation finds the association in the local environment; it is a *nonlocal* or *global reference* if the association is found in the *nonlocal* or *global* environment, respectively. (The terms *nonlocal* and *global* are often used interchangeably to indicate any reference that is not local.)

Aliases for Data Objects

During its lifetime, a data object may have more than one name (i.e., there may be several associations in different referencing environments, each providing a different name for the data object). For example, when a data object is transmitted by reference (Section 9.3) to a subprogram as a parameter, it may be referenced through a formal parameter name in the subprogram, and it also retains its original name in the calling program. Alternatively, a data object may become a component of several data objects through pointer linkages and thus have several composite names through which it may be accessed. Multiple names for the same data object are possible in various ways in almost every programming language.

When a data object is visible through more than one name (simple or composite) *in a single referencing environment*, each of the names is termed an *alias* for the data object. Where a data object has multiple names, but a unique one

EXAMPLE 9.1. Referencing Pascal Variables.

Figure 7.3 shows a simple Pascal subprogram with the referencing environment for each subprogram marked. Note that identifiers A, D, and C are each declared in two places. Identifier A is a formal parameter name in SUB1 and is also declared as a variable in the main program. Identifier C is a formal parameter in SUB2 and also a variable name in the main program, and D is a local variable name in both SUB1 and SUB2. However, in each referencing environment, only one association for each of these names is visible. Thus, in SUB2, the local association for C is visible, and the global association for C in the main program is hidden. In the statement $C := C + B$ in SUB2 both a local reference to C and a global reference to B in the main program appear.

The predefined referencing environment is not shown. In Pascal it consists of constants such as MAXINT (the maximum integer value) and subprograms such as *read*, *write*, and *sqrt*. Any of these predefined identifiers may be given a new association through an explicit program declaration, and thus the predefined association may become hidden for part of the program.

---

in each referencing environment in which it appears, no problems arise. However, the ability to refer to the same data object using different names within the same referencing environment raises serious problems for both the user and implementor of a language. Figure 9.7 shows two Pascal programs in which an integer variable has two names, I and J, at different points during program execution. In the first program, no aliasing occurs because at no point during execution can both names I and J be used in the same subprogram. In the second program, within subprogram $Sub1$, I and J are aliases for the same data object because I is passed by reference to $Sub1$, where it becomes associated with the name J; at the same time, I is also visible in $Sub1$ as a nonlocal name.

Aliasing is troublesome for the programmer because it makes understanding a program difficult. For example, if, within a program, you see the statement sequence

$$\begin{aligned} &\mathrm{X} := \mathrm{A} + \mathrm{B}; \\ &\mathrm{Y} := \mathrm{C} + \mathrm{D}; \end{aligned}$$

the assignments to X and Y apparently are independent and could take place in either order; if the variable X were not referenced later, the first assignment might be deleted altogether. However, suppose X and C are aliases for the same data object. Then the statements are in fact interdependent, and no reordering or deletion is possible without introducing a difficult error to detect. The possibility of aliasing makes it difficult to verify that a program is correct because no two variable names may be assumed to refer necessarily to different data objects.

```
program main;
var A, B, C: real;
procedure Sub1(A: real);
    var D: real;
    procedure Sub2 (C:real);
        var D: real;
        begin
        – Statements
        C := C+B;
        – Statements
        end;
    begin
    – Statements
    Sub2(B);
    – Statements
    end;
begin
– Statements
Sub1(A);
– Statements
end.
```

Referencing environment for Sub2
Local C, D
Nonlocal A, Sub2 in Sub1
B, Sub1 in main

Referencing environment for Sub1
Local A, D, Sub2
Nonlocal B, C, Sub1 in main

Referencing environment for main
Local: A, B, C, Sub1

Figure 9.6. Referencing environments in a Pascal program.

The problems caused by aliasing for the implementor are similar. As a part of the optimization of program code during translation, it is often desirable to reorder the steps in a computation or delete unnecessary steps. Where aliasing is possible, this cannot be done without additional analysis to ensure that two apparently independent computational steps are not dependent due to aliasing. Because of the problems caused by aliasing, new language designs sometimes attempt to restrict or eliminate altogether features that allow aliases to be constructed.

9.2.2 Static and Dynamic Scope

The *dynamic scope* of an association for an identifier, as defined in the preceding section, is that set of subprogram activations in which the association is visible during execution. The dynamic scope of an association always includes the subprogram activation in which that association is created as part of the local environment. It may also be visible as a nonlocal association in other subprogram activations.

A *dynamic scope rule* defines the dynamic scope of each association in terms of the dynamic course of program execution. For example, a typical dynamic scope rule states that the scope of an association created during an activation of subprogram P includes not only that activation but also any activation of a subprogram called by P, or called by a subprogram called by P, and so on, unless that later subprogram activation defines a new local association for the identifier that hides the original

```
program main(output);
procedure Sub1(var J: integer);
    begin
    ... { J is visible, I is not }
    end;
procedure Sub2;
    var I: integer;
    begin
    ...
    Sub1(I); { I is visible, J is not }
    ...
    end;
begin
...
Sub2 { Neither is visible }
...
end.
```

(a) No aliasing

```
program main(output);
var I: integer;
procedure Sub1(var J: integer);
    begin
    ... { I and J refer to same}
    end; { data object here }
procedure Sub2;
    begin
    ...
    Sub1(I); { I is visible, J is not }
    ...
    end;
begin
...
Sub2 { I is visible, J is not }
...
end.
```

(b) I and J are aliased in Sub1

Figure 9.7. Aliasing in a Pascal program.

association. With this rule, the dynamic scope of an association is tied to the *dynamic chain* of subprogram activations described in Section 9.1.2.

When we look at the written form of a program, the *program text*, we notice that the association between references to identifiers and particular declarations or definitions of the meaning of those identifiers is also a problem. For example, in Figure 9.6, the references to B and C in the statement $C := C + B$ in $SUB2$ need to be tied to particular declarations of C and B as variables or formal parameters. But which declarations? Each declaration or other definition of an identifier within the program text has a certain scope, called its *static scope*.

For simplicity, the term *declaration* is used here to refer to a declaration, subprogram definition, type definition, constant definition, or other means of defining a meaning for a particular identifier within a program text. A declaration creates an association in the program text between an identifier and some information about the data object or subprogram that will be named by that identifier during program execution. The *static scope* of a declaration is that part of the program text where a use of the identifier is a reference to that particular declaration of the identifier. A *static scope rule* is a rule for determining the static scope of a declaration. In Pascal, for example, a static scope rule is used to specify that a reference to a variable X in a subprogram P refers to the declaration of X at the beginning of P, or if not declared there, then to the declaration of X at the beginning of the subprogram Q whose declaration contains the declaration of P, and so on.

Static scope rules relate references with declarations of names in the program text; dynamic scope rules relate references with associations for names during program execution. What should the relation be between the two? Clearly the scope rules must be *consistent*. For example, if the static scope rules for Pascal relate the reference to Variable B in the statement $C := C + B$ in Figure 9.6 to the declaration of B in the main program, then the dynamic scope rules must also relate the reference to B at run time to the data object named B in the main program. There may be several declarations for B in the program text and several data objects named B in various subprogram activations during execution. Thus, maintaining the consistency between static and dynamic scope rules is not entirely straightforward. Several different approaches are considered next.

The importance of static scope. Suppose a language makes no use of static scope rules. Consider a statement such as $X := X + Max$ that occurs in a subprogram. Without static scope rules, nothing about the names X and Max can be determined during translation of the program. During execution of the program, when the statement is reached, a referencing operation must first find the relevant associations for X and Max, and then the type and other attributes of X and Max must be determined. Does there exist an association for each identifier? Is Max a subprogram name, variable name, statement label, type name, or formal parameter name? If X is a variable name, is it of a type that can be added to Max? None of these questions can be answered until the attempt to reference names X and Max is made during execution. Moreover, each time the statement is executed, the entire process must be repeated because the associations for X and Max may change between two executions of the statement. LISP, SNOBOL4, and APL make almost no use of static scope rules. Thus, each reference to a name in these languages requires a rather complex and costly interpretation process to be invoked during execution that first finds the relevant association for the name (if any) and then determines the type and attributes of the associated data object or subprogram.

Static scope rules allow much of this process to be performed once during program translation rather than repeatedly during execution for most references to names in a program. For example, if the assignment statement $X := X + Max$ appears in Pascal, and Max is defined by a constant declaration **const** $Max = 30$ somewhere in the program, then the static scope rules of Pascal allow the reference to Max to be related to this (or some other) declaration of Max during translation. The Pascal compiler can then determine that Max always has the value 30 when this statement is executed and may translate the statement into executable code that simply adds 30 to X, with no referencing operation for the name Max. Similarly, if the Pascal static scope rules allow the reference to X to be related to the declaration $X : real$ somewhere in the program text, then the Pascal compiler may perform static type checking—that is, it may determine that when the statement is executed, (1) an association relating X to a data object will exist, (2) that data object will be of type real, and (3) its value will be of the right type to serve as an argument for the addition operation. The compiler cannot tell from the declaration the *location* of the data object that X references (because the location is determined dynamically during execution and may be different on different executions of the statement), nor can the compiler determine the *value* of X (because it is also determined dynamically during execution). However, the static type checking makes program execution much faster and more reliable (because type errors are detected for all program paths during translation).

Static scope rules allow many different sorts of connections to be established between references to names and their declarations during translation. Two were mentioned earlier: relating a variable name to a declaration for the variable and relating a constant name to a declaration for a constant. Other connections include relating type names to type declarations, relating formal parameters to formal parameter specifications, relating subprogram calls to subprogram declarations, and relating statement labels referenced in **goto** statements to labels on particular statements. In each of these cases, a different set of simplifications may be made during translation that make execution of the program more efficient.

Static scope rules are also important for the programmer in reading a program because they make it possible to relate a name referenced in the program to a declaration for the name without tracing the course of program execution. For example, the static scope rules of Pascal allow a reference to X in a statement to be related to a declaration for X elsewhere in the program without any consideration for the sequence of subprogram calls that lead from the main program to the actual execution of the statement. Thus, the static scope rules make the program easier to understand.

9.2.3 Block Structure

The concept of *block structure*—as found in *block-structured languages* such as Pascal, PL/I, and Ada—deserves special mention. Block-structured languages have a characteristic program structure and associated set of static scope rules. The concepts originated in the language ALGOL 60, one of the most important early languages. Because of their elegance and effect on implementation efficiency, they have been adopted in other languages.

In a block-structured language, each program or subprogram is organized as a set of nested blocks. The chief characteristic of a *block* is that it introduces a new local referencing environment. A block begins with a set of declarations for names (variable declarations, type definitions, constant definitions, etc.) followed by a set of statements in which those names may be referenced. For simplicity, we shall consider a block as equivalent to a subprogram declaration, although the exact definition of a block varies from language to language. The declarations in a block define its local referencing environment. This local environment is invariant during the execution of the statements that form its body. In C, there is a block structure, but it only exists within a single subprogram. This provides the ability of providing nonlocal names without any of the overhead for subprogram activation. We discuss this later.

```
program Main;
    - Local declarations for Main;                                  Start Main
    procedure Sub1;                                                     |
        - Local declarations for Sub1;                      Start Sub1  |
        procedure Sub3;                                         |       |
            - Local declarations for Sub3;  Start Sub3          |       |
            begin                               |               |       |
            - Statements for Sub3;              |               |       |
            end {Sub3};                     End Sub3            |       |
        procedure Sub4;                                         |       |
            - Local declarations for Sub4;  Start Sub4          |       |
            begin                               |               |       |
            - Statements for Sub4;              |               |       |
            end {Sub4};                     End Sub4            |       |
        begin                                                   |       |
        - Statements for Sub1                                   |       |
        end {Sub1};                                         End Sub1    |
    procedure Sub2;                                                     |
        - Local declarations for Sub2                       Start Sub2  |
        begin                                                   |       |
        - Statements for Sub2                                   |       |
        end {Sub2};                                         End Sub2    |
    begin                                                               |
    - Statements for Main;                                              |
    end {Main}.                                                     End Main
```

Figure 9.8. Static block structure of a program.

The nesting of blocks is accomplished by allowing the definition of one block to entirely contain the definitions of other blocks. At the outermost level, a program consists of a single block defining the main program. Within this block are other blocks defining subprograms callable from the main program; within these blocks may be other blocks defining subprograms callable from within the first-level subprograms, and so on. Figure 9.8 illustrates the typical layout of a block-structured program. In languages such as C and Ada, the outermost level may consist of several independent nests of blocks (each of which may be compiled separately), but it is sufficient here to consider only a single nest.

The *static scope rules* associated with a block-structured program are as follows:

1. The declarations at the head of each block define the local referencing environment for the block. Any reference to an identifier within the body of the block (not including any nested subblocks) is considered a reference to the local declaration for the identifier if one exists.

2. If an identifier is referenced within the body of the block and no local declaration exists, then the reference is considered a reference to a declaration within the block that immediately encloses the first block. If no declaration exists

there, then it refers to a declaration in the block that immediately encloses that block, and so on. If the outermost block is reached before a declaration is found, then the reference is to the declaration within that outermost block. Finally, if no declaration is found there, the declaration in the predefined language environment is used, if any, or the reference is taken to be an error. The predefined environment thus acts like a block enclosing the outermost block (or blocks) of the program.

3. If a block contains another block definition, then any local declarations within the inner block or any blocks it contains are completely hidden from the outer block and cannot be referenced from it. Thus, inner blocks encapsulate declarations so that they are invisible from outer blocks.

4. A block may be named (usually when it represents a named subprogram). The block name becomes part of the local referencing environment of the *containing block*. For example, if a Pascal main program contains a subprogram definition that begins

   procedure P(A: real);

   then the procedure name P is a local name in the main program, whereas the formal parameter name A is part of P's local environment. Within the main program, P may be referenced, but A may not.

Note that, using these static scope rules, a declaration for the same identifier may occur in many different blocks, but a declaration in an outer block is always hidden within an inner block if the inner block gives a new declaration for the same identifier.

These static scope rules for block-structured programs allow every reference to a name within any block to be associated with a unique declaration for the name during program translation (if the reference is not an error), with little explicit action by the programmer other than to provide the proper *local* declarations in each block and the proper nesting of blocks. The compiler for the language may provide static type checking and other simplifications of the run-time structure based on use of the static scope rules. For these reasons, block structure has been adopted as a program structure in many major languages.

9.2.4 Local Data and Local Referencing Environments

We now begin to look at the various data-control structures used in programming languages. Local referencing environments, which form the simplest structure, are treated in this section. The sections that follow consider nonlocal environments, parameters, and parameter transmission.

The *local environment* of a subprogram Q consists of the various identifiers declared in the head of Subprogram Q (but not Q). Variable names, formal parameter names, and subprogram names are the concern here. The subprogram names

```
procedure R;
    ...
end;
procedure Q;
var X: integer := 30;     – initial value of X is 30
begin
    write (X);            – print value of X
    R;                    – call subprogram R
    X := X + 1;           – increment value of X
    write (X)             – print value of X again
end;
procedure P;
    ...
    Q;                    – call subprogram Q
    ...
end;
```

Figure 9.9. Local referencing environment: retention or deletion?

of interest are the names of subprograms that are defined locally within Q (i.e., subprograms whose definitions are nested within Q).

For local environments, static and dynamic scope rules are easily made consistent. The static scope rule specifies that a reference to an identifier X in the body of Subprogram Q is related to the local declaration for X in the head of Subprogram Q (assuming one exists). The dynamic scope rule specifies that a reference to X during execution of Q refers to the association for X in the current activation of Q (note that, in general, there may be several activations of Q, but only one will be currently in execution). To implement the static scope rule, the compiler simply maintains a table of the local declarations for identifiers that appear in the head of Q, and, while compiling the body of Q, it refers to this table first whenever the declaration of an identifier is required.

Implementation of the dynamic scope rule may be done in two ways, and each gives a different semantics to local references. Consider Subprograms, P, Q, and R with a local variable X declared in Q in Figure 9.9. Subprogram P calls Q, which in turn calls R, which later returns control to Q, which completes its execution and returns control to P. Let us follow variable X during this execution sequence:

1. When P is in execution, X is not visible in P because X is local to Q.

2. When P calls Q, X becomes visible as the name of an integer data object with initial value 30. As Q executes, the first statement references X and prints its current value, 30.

3. When Q calls R, the association for X becomes hidden, but it is retained while R executes.

4. When R returns control to Q, the association for X becomes visible again. X still names the same data object, and that data object still has the value 30.

5. Q resumes its execution, X is referenced and incremented, and then its new value, 31, is printed.

6. When Q returns control to P, the association for X again becomes hidden, but two different meanings might be provided for this association:

   Retention. The association for X might be *retained* until Q is called again, just as it was while Q called R. If the association is retained, then when Q is called the second time, Q is still associated with the same data object, which still has its old value, 31. Thus, the first statement executed will reference X and print the value 31. If the entire cycle repeats and Q is called a third time, X will have the value 32, and so on.

   Deletion. Alternatively, the association for X might be *deleted* (i.e., the association binding X to the data object might be broken, and the data object destroyed and its storage reallocated for some other use). When Q is called a second time, a new data object is created and assigned the initial value 30, and the association with X is re-created as well. The first statement in Q then prints the value 30 every time Q is executed.

Retention and deletion are two different approaches to the semantics of local environments and are concerned with the *lifetime* of the environment. C, Java, Pascal, Ada, LISP, APL, and SNOBOL4 use the deletion approach: Local variables do not retain their old values between successive calls of a subprogram. COBOL and many versions of FORTRAN use the retention approach: Variables do retain their old values between calls. PL/I and ALGOL provide both options; each individual variable may be treated differently.

Implementation

In discussing the implementation of referencing environments, it is convenient to represent the local environment of a subprogram as a *local environment table* consisting of pairs, each containing an identifier and the associated data object, as shown in Figure 9.10. As discussed previously, the storage for each object is represented as a type (as discussed in chapter 6) and its location in memory as an l-value (as discussed in chapter 5). Drawing a local environment table this way does not imply that the actual identifiers (e.g., "X") are stored during program execution. Usually they are not. The name is only used so that later references to that variable will be able to determine where that variable will reside in memory during execution. Using local environment tables, implementation of the retention and deletion approaches to local environments is straightforward.

```
procedure SUB(X:integer);
   var Y: real;
       Z: array [1..3] of real;
   procedure SUB2;
      begin
      ...
      end {Sub2};
   begin
   ...
   end {Sub};
```

Subprogram definition

Name	Type	Lvalue contents
X	integer	Value parameter
Y	real	Local value
Z	real	Local array Descriptor: [1..3]
SUB2	procedure	Pointer to code segment

(Compile time) Local environment table for procedure SUB

Figure 9.10. Pascal local environment table for subprogram Sub.

Retention. If the local environment of subprogram *Sub* of Figure 9.10 is to be retained between calls, then a single local environment table containing the retained variables is allocated as part of the *code segment* of *Sub*, as shown in Figure 9.11.

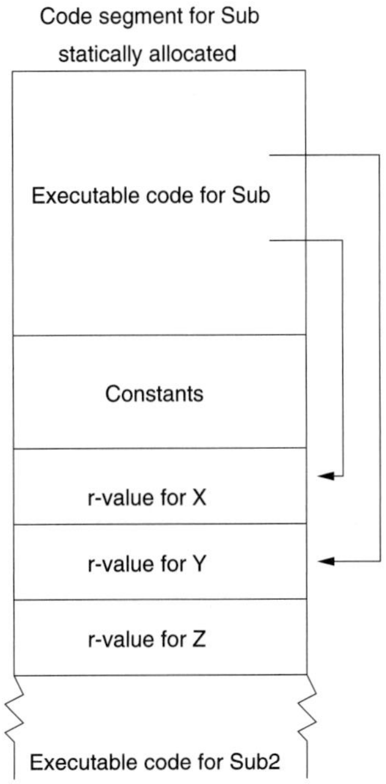

Figure 9.11. Allocation and referencing of retained local variables.

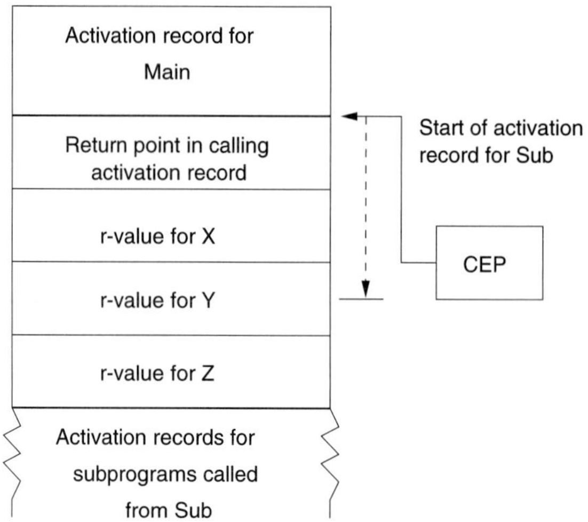

Figure 9.12. Allocation and referencing of deleted local variables.

Because the code segment is allocated storage statically and remains in existence throughout execution, any variables in the local environment part of the code segment are also retained. If a variable has an initial value, such as the value 30 for Y, then the initial value may be stored in the data object when the storage is allocated (just as the value for a constant in the code segment would be stored). Assuming each retained local variable is declared at the start of the definition of *Sub*, the compiler can determine the size of each variable in the local environment table and compute the offset of the start of the data object from the start (the base address) of the code segment. When a statement within the code references a variable Y during execution, the offset of Y is added to the base address of the code segment to find the location of the data object associated with Y. The identifier "Y" is not needed during execution and is not stored at all.

With this implementation of retention for the local environment, no special action is needed to retain the values of the data objects; the values stored at the end of one call of *Sub* will still be there when the next call begins. Also no special action is needed to change from one local environment to another as one subprogram calls another. Because the code and local data for each subprogram are part of the same code segment, a transfer of control to the code for another subprogram automatically results in a transfer to the local environment for that subprogram as well.

Deletion. If the local environment of *Sub* is to be deleted between calls and recreated anew on each entry, then the local environment table containing the deleted variables is allocated storage as part of the activation record for *Sub*. Assuming the activation record is created on a central stack on entry to *Sub* and deleted from the stack on exit, as discussed in Section 9.1, deletion of the local environment follows automatically. Assuming each deleted local variable is declared at the start of the definition of *Sub*, the compiler again can determine the number of variables and the size of each in the local environment table and may compute the offset of the start of each data object from the start of the activation record (the base address). Recall that the CEP pointer (current-environment pointer) is maintained during execution so that it points to the base address of the activation record in the stack for the subprogram that is currently executing at any point. If *Sub* is executing and references Variable Y, then the location of the data object associated with Y is found by adding the offset for Y to the contents of the CEP. Again the identifier "Y" need not be stored in the activation record at all; only the data objects are needed. Figure 9.12 shows this implementation. The dotted arrow shows the offset computed for a reference to Y.

Both the retention and deletion approaches are easy to implement in our general model of subprogram implementation as given in Section 8.3.2. Several additional points deserve notice:

1. In the implementation of the *simple* call-return structure described earlier, retention and deletion in the absence of recursion lead to essentially the same implementation because there is never more than one activation record that may be allocated statically. However, if initial values are provided for variables, two different meanings for initialization result. (See Problem 2.)

2. *Individual variables* may readily be given either treatment, with those whose values are to be retained allocated storage in the code segment and those whose values are to be deleted allocated storage in the activation record. This is the approach used in PL/I, where a variable declared STATIC is retained and a variable declared AUTOMATIC is deleted.

3. A *subprogram name,* which is associated with a declaration for the subprogram in the local environment, may always be treated as retained. The association of name and definition may be represented as a pointer data object in the code segment, where the pointer points to the code segment representing the subprogram.

4. A *formal-parameter* name represents a data object that is reinitialized with a new value on each call of the subprogram, as described in Section 9.3. This reinitialization precludes retaining an old value for a formal parameter between calls. Thus, formal parameters are appropriately treated as deleted associations.

5. If *recursive* subprogram calls are allowed, then multiple activations of a subprogram *Sub* may exist as separate activation records in the central stack at the same time. If a variable Y is treated as deleted, then each activation

record will contain a separate data object named Y, and, as each activation executes, it will reference its own local copy of Y. Ordinarily separate copies of Y in each activation are what is desired, and thus for languages with recursion (or other subprogram control structures that generate multiple simultaneous activations of a subprogram) the deletion of local environments is ordinarily used. However, retention of some local variables is often of value. In ALGOL 60, for example, a local variable declared as **own** is treated as a retained variable, although the subprogram containing the declaration may be recursive. If multiple activations of a subprogram *Sub* reference the retained Variable Y, then there is only one data object Y that is used by every activation of *Sub* and its value persists from one activation to another.

Advantages and disadvantages. Both retention and deletion are used in a substantial number of important languages. The retention approach allows the programmer to write subprograms that are *history sensitive* in that their results on each call are partially determined by their inputs and partially by the local data values computed during previous activations. The deletion approach does not allow any local data to be carried over from one call to the next, so a variable that must be retained between calls must be declared as nonlocal to the subprogram. For recursive subprograms, however, deletion is the more natural strategy. Deletion also provides a savings in storage space in that local environment tables exist only for those subprograms that are in execution or suspended execution. Local environment tables for all subprograms exist throughout execution using retention.

9.3 PARAMETER TRANSMISSION

A data object that is strictly local is used by operations only within a single local referencing environment (e.g., within a single subprogram). Data objects, however, are often *shared* among several subprograms so that operations in each of the subprograms may use the data. A data object may be transmitted as an explicit parameter between subprograms, but there are numerous occasions in which use of explicit parameters is cumbersome. For example, consider a set of subprograms that all make use of a common table of data. Each subprogram needs access to the table, yet transmitting the table as an explicit parameter each time it is needed is tedious. Such data sharing is usually based on sharing of identifier associations. If Subprograms P, Q, and R all need access to the same variable X, then it is appropriate to simply allow the identifier X to have the same association in each subprogram. The association for X becomes part of the local environment for one of the subprograms, and it becomes a common part of the *nonlocal* environment of the others. Sharing of data objects through nonlocal environments is an important alternative to the use of direct sharing through parameter transmission.

Explicitly transmitted parameters and results are the major alternative method for sharing data objects among subprograms. In contrast to the use of nonlocal referencing environments, where sharing is achieved by making certain nonlocal names visible to a subprogram, data objects transmitted as parameters and results are transmitted without a name attached. In the receiving subprogram, each data object is given a new *local name* through which it may be referenced. The sharing of data through parameters is most useful when a subprogram is to be given different data to process each time it is called. Sharing through a nonlocal environment is more appropriate where the same data objects are used on each call. For example, if Subprogram P is used on each call to enter a new data item into a table shared with other subprograms, then typically the table would be shared through references to a nonlocal environment and the data item would be transmitted as an explicit parameter on each call of P.

Four basic approaches to nonlocal environments are in use in programming languages: (1) explicit common environments and implicit nonlocal environments based on (2) dynamic scope, (3) static scope, and (4) inheritance. In the following subsections, we discuss parameter transmission and three of these nonlocal environment methods. In the next chapter we separately cover the concept of inheritance.

9.3.1 Actual and Formal Parameters

We first consider the sharing of *data* through parameters, and then later the use of parameters to transmit *subprograms* and *statement labels.* In the preceding chapters, the term *argument* is used for a data object (or a value) that is sent to a subprogram or primitive operation as one of its operands (i.e., as a piece of data to use in processing). The term *result* refers to a piece of data (data object or value) that is returned from an operation at the end of its execution. The arguments of a subprogram may be obtained both through parameters and through nonlocal references (and, less commonly, through external files). Similarly, the results of a subprogram may be returned through parameters, through assignments to nonlocal variables (or files), or through explicit function values. Thus, the terms *argument* and *result* apply to data sent to and returned from the subprogram through a variety of language mechanisms. In narrowing our focus to parameters and parameter transmission, the terms *actual parameter* and *formal parameter* become central.

A *formal parameter* is a particular kind of local data object within a subprogram. The subprogram definition ordinarily lists the names and declarations for formal parameters as part of the specification part (heading). A formal parameter name is a simple identifier, and the declaration ordinarily gives the type and other attributes, as for an ordinary local variable declaration. For example, the C procedure heading

SUB(int X; char Y);

defines two formal parameters named X and Y and declares the type of each. The declaration of a formal parameter, however, does not mean the same thing as a declaration for a variable. The formal parameter, depending on the parameter transmission mechanism to be discussed shortly, may be an alias to the actual parameter data object or may simply contain a copy of the value of that data object.

An *actual parameter* is a data object that is shared with the caller subprogram. An actual parameter may be a local data object belonging to the caller, it may be a formal parameter of the caller, it may be a nonlocal data object visible to the caller, or it may be a result returned by a function invoked by the caller and immediately transmitted to the called subprogram. An actual parameter is represented at the point of call of the subprogram by an expression, termed an *actual-parameter expression,* that ordinarily has the same form as any other expression in the language (e.g., such as an expression that might appear in an assignment statement). For example, the subprogram SUB specified earlier might be called with any of the following types of actual parameter expressions:

Procedure Call in P	Actual Parameter in P
SUB(I,B)	I, B: local variables of P
SUB(27,true)	27, true: constants
SUB(P1,P2)	P1, P2: formal parameters of P
SUB(G1,G2)	G1, G2: global or nonlocal variables in P
SUB(A[I],D.B1)	Components of arrays and records
SUB(I + 3,FN(Q))	Results of primitive or defined functions

The syntax for procedure calls in C is typical of many languages. The subprogram call is written in prefix form, as discussed in Section 8.2, with the subprogram name first, followed by a list of actual parameter expressions in parentheses (other notations are used, however, such as infix notation in APL, Cambridge Polish in LISP). For simplicity, we adopt the conventional C prefix representation and speak of *actual-parameter lists* and *formal-parameter lists* to indicate the sequence of actual and formal parameters designated in a subprogram call and subprogram definition, respectively.

When a subprogram is called with an actual-parameter expression of any of the prior forms, the expression is *evaluated* at the time of the call before the subprogram is entered. The data objects that result from the evaluation of the actual-parameter expressions then become the actual parameters transmitted to the subprogram. The special case in which the actual-parameter expressions are *not* evaluated at the time of call, but are passed *unevaluated* to the subprogram, is treated separately later.

Establishing the Correspondence

When a subprogram is called with a list of actual parameters, a correspondence must be established between the actual parameters and the formal parameters listed in the subprogram definition. Two methods are described in turn.

Positional correspondence. The correspondence is established by pairing actual and formal parameters based on their respective positions in the actual- and formal-parameter lists; the first actual and first formal parameters are paired, then the second in each list, and so on.

Correspondence by explicit name. In Ada and some other languages, the formal parameter to be paired with each actual parameter may be named explicitly in the calling statement. For example, in Ada, one could call *Sub* with the statement

Sub(Y => B, X => 27);

which pairs actual parameter *B* with formal parameter *Y* and actual parameter 27 with formal parameter *X* during the call of *Sub*.

Most languages use positional correspondence exclusively, so examples here use this method. Ordinarily, the number of actual and formal parameters must correspond so that the pairing is unique. However, some languages relax this restriction and provide special conventions for interpreting missing or extra actual parameters. For simplicity here, all parameters are assumed to be paired.

9.3.2 Methods for Transmitting Parameters

When a subprogram transfers control to another subprogram, there must be an association of the actual parameter of the calling subprogram with the formal parameter of the called program. Two approaches are often used: The actual parameter may be evaluated and that value passed to the formal parameter, or the actual data object may be passed to the formal parameter. We describe this by a two-step process:

1. Describe the implementation details of the parameter transmission mechanism.
2. Describe the semantics of how the parameters will be used.

Several methods have generally been devised for passing actual parameters as formal parameters. The first four that are described next are the most common: call by name, call by reference, call by value, and call by value-result.

Call by name. This model of parameter transmission views a subprogram call as a substitution for the entire body of the subprogram. With this interpretation, each formal parameter stands for the actual evaluation of the particular actual parameter. Just as if the actual substitutions were made, each reference to a formal parameter requires a reevaluation of the corresponding actual parameter.

This requires that, at the point of call of the subprogram, no evaluation of the actual parameters are made until they are actually referenced in the subprogram. The parameters are transmitted unevaluated, and the called subprogram determines when, if ever, they are actually evaluated. Recall from our earlier discussion of uniform evaluation rules that this possibility was useful in treating operations such as the *if–then–else* conditional as ordinary operations. In primitive operations, the technique is occasionally useful; in programmer-defined subprograms, its utility is more problematic because of the cost of implementation. Parameter transmission by name plays a major role in ALGOL and is of considerable theoretical importance. However, it has considerable execution overhead so is not deemed a popular method to use.

The basic call-by-name rule may be stated in terms of substitution: The actual parameter is to be substituted everywhere for the formal parameter in the body of the called program before execution of the subprogram begins. Although this seems straightforward, consider the problem of even the simple **call** $Sub(X)$. If the formal parameter in Sub is Y, then X is to be substituted for Y throughout Sub before Sub is executed. This is not enough, however, because when we come to a reference to X during execution of Sub, the association for X referenced is that *back in the calling program* not the association in Sub (if any). When X is substituted for Y, we must also indicate a different referencing environment for use in referencing X. We may also introduce ambiguity if X is already a variable known to Sub.

Not surprisingly, the basic technique for implementing call by name is to treat actual parameters as simple parameterless subprograms (traditionally called *thunks*). Whenever a formal parameter corresponding to a by-name actual parameter is referenced in a subprogram, the thunk compiled for that parameter is executed, resulting in the evaluation of the actual parameter in the proper referencing environment and the return of the resulting value as the value of the thunk.

Call by reference. Call by reference is perhaps the most common parameter transmission mechanism. To transmit a data object as a call-by-reference parameter means that a *pointer* to the location of the data object (i.e., its l-value) is made available to the subprogram. *The data object does not change position in memory.* At the beginning of execution of the subprogram, the l-values of actual parameters are used to initialize local storage locations for the formal parameters.

Passing call-by-reference parameters occurs in two stages:

1. In the calling subprogram, each actual-parameter expression is evaluated to give a pointer to the actual-parameter data object (i.e., its l-value). A list of these pointers is stored in a common storage area that is also accessible to the subprogram being called (often in a set of registers or the program stack). Control is then transferred to the subprogram, as described in the preceding chapter (i.e., the activation record for the subprogram is created [if necessary], the return point is established, etc.).

2. In the called subprogram, the list of pointers to actual parameters is accessed to retrieve the appropriate r-values for the actual parameters.

During execution of the subprogram, references to formal parameter names are treated as ordinary local variable references (except that there may be a hidden pointer selection). On termination of the subprogram, results are returned to the calling program through the actual-parameter data objects as well.

Call by value. If a parameter is *transmitted by value* (called *by copy* in Ada 95), the value (i.e., r-value) of the actual parameter is passed to the called formal parameter. The implementation mechanism is similar to the call-by-reference model, except that

1. On invoking a subprogram, a call-by-reference parameter passes its l-value, whereas a call-by-value parameter passes its r-value.
2. On reference in the subprogram, a call-by-reference parameter uses the l-value stored in the formal parameter to access the actual data object, whereas in call by value, the formal parameter contains the value that is used.

From this discussion, it should be clear that, with call by reference, we have an alias to the actual parameter, whereas in call by value we have no such reference. Once an actual parameter is passed by value, the formal parameter has no access to change the value of the actual parameter. Any changes made in the formal-parameter values during execution of the subprogram are lost when the subprogram terminates.

Call by value-result. If a parameter is *transmitted by value-result,* the formal parameter is a local variable (data object) of the same data type as the actual parameter. The value (i.e., r-value) of the actual parameter is copied into the formal-parameter data object at the time of call so that the effect is the same as if an explicit assignment of actual parameter to formal parameter were executed. During execution of the subprogram, each reference to the formal-parameter name is treated as an ordinary reference to a local variable, as with call by value. When the subprogram terminates, the final contents of the formal-parameter data object are copied into the actual-parameter data object, just as if an explicit assignment of formal parameter to actual parameter were executed. Thus, the actual parameter retains its original value until termination of the subprogram, when its new value is assigned as a result of the subprogram.

Value-result parameter transmission developed from Algol-W, a language developed by Nicklaus Wirth as a successor to ALGOL during the 1960s prior to his development of Pascal. Implemented on an IBM 360 computer, call by reference was relatively inefficient because there was no way to access the r-value of an actual parameter in one instruction. There was no indirect memory load operation. To speed up execution, value-result transmission made all parameters local variables directly addressable by the current activation record pointer.

Both call by reference and call by value-result are widely used and, in most normal situations, give the same result. However, all four techniques—call by name, call by reference, call by value, and call by value-result—have differences that can lead to similar programs having different semantics, as is shown later.

Call by constant value. If a parameter is *transmitted by constant value,* then no change in the value of the formal parameter is allowed during program execution (i.e., no assignment of a new value or other modification of the value of the parameter is allowed, and the formal parameter may not be transmitted to another subprogram except as a constant-value parameter). The formal parameter thus acts as a *local constant* during execution of the subprogram. Because no change in its value is allowed, two implementations are possible. The formal parameter may be treated exactly as a parameter transmitted by value so that it is a local data object whose initial value is a copy of the actual-parameter value. Alternatively, it may be treated as a parameter transmitted by reference so that the formal parameter contains a pointer to the actual-parameter data object.

Both call by value and call by constant value protect the calling program from changes in the actual parameter. Thus, from the viewpoint of the calling program, the actual parameter is only an input argument for the subprogram. Its value cannot be modified by the subprogram either inadvertently or to transmit results back.

Call by result. A parameter *transmitted by result* is used only to transmit a result back from a subprogram. The initial value of the actual-parameter data object makes no difference and cannot be used by the subprogram. The formal parameter is a local variable (data object) with no initial value (or with the usual initialization provided for local variables). When the subprogram terminates, the final value of the formal parameter is assigned as the new value of the actual parameter, just as in call by value-result.

Most languages implement one or two of the transmission mechanisms. FORTRAN implements call by reference, whereas Pascal implements both call by value and call by reference. A parameter X : *integer* is a call-by-value parameter, whereas **var** X : *integer* is a call-by-reference parameter. (Note, however, that this is a source of many Pascal errors. By forgetting to include the **var** keyword, the parameter is a value parameter and any changes made to its value will not be reflected back into the calling subprogram. This error is subtle and extremely hard to find at times.) In contrast, C only implements call by value. The use of pointers, however, allows the programmer to build call-by-reference arguments. Passing an argument i by reference to procedure *mysubroutine* is via the expression $\&i$, which passes the l-value of i. The call will be written as $mysubroutine(\&i)$ to a procedure declared as $myprocedure(int\ *x)$, which declares x as a pointer to an integer. Forgetting to include the appropriate dereferencing operators (& and $*$) can lead to many C programming errors.

9.3.3 Transmission Semantics

The previous discussion forces the programmer to be aware of how parameters are actually implemented before deciding what mode of parameter transmission to use. However, this goes against many language design criteria where the programmer should not be unduly concerned about the underlying implementation details. In Ada, for example, a different approach is used. Rather than describing the mode of transmission, the *role* of the parameter is specified. The parameter may be an **in** parameter whose value will be passed in from the actual parameter to the formal parameter and then used in the subprogram, the parameter may be an **out** parameter whose value is generated by the subprogram and then passed back to the actual parameter on subprogram exit, or it may be an **in out** parameter whose value is both passed in and then the resulting value passed back to the actual parameter. Ada is defined so that the implementor may choose alternative transmission methods for some of these. For the programmer, the particular method used makes no difference in the final result, provided the called subprogram terminates normally and provided the called subprogram cannot also access the actual parameter through an alias.

In the original definition of Ada (Ada 83), the language implementor had the option of choosing between call by reference and call by value for **in** and **out** parameters. This caused conformance problems because *correct* programs could give different results when compiled by different *correct* compilers. Because of this, in the Ada 95 revision to the language, parameter transmission was revised:

Elementary data types (e.g., scalars like integer, real, or Boolean) are passed by constant value if an **in** parameter or value-result if an **out** or **in out** parameter.

Composite data types (e.g., arrays and records) are passed by reference.

This has simplified Ada parameter transmission, but still leaves the opportunity for confusing execution as Problem 23 at the end of the chapter demonstrates.

Explicit Function Values

In most languages, a single result may be returned as an explicit *function value* rather than as a parameter. The subprogram must be declared to be a function subprogram, and the type of the result returned must be declared as part of the subprogram specification, as in the C declaration: $float\ fn(int\ a)$, which specifies fn to be a function subprogram returning a result of type *real*. Within the function subprogram, the result to be returned as the function value may be specified in one of two ways. One method, used in C, is to designate the function value to be returned by an explicit result expression given as part of the **return** statement that terminates execution of the subprogram (e.g., **return** $2 * x$ to designate that the value $2 * x$ is to be returned as the function value). An alternative method, used in Pascal, is to designate the value to be returned by an assignment of the value to the *function name* within the subprogram (e.g., $fn := 2 * x$). In this latter method, the subprogram may contain several assignments to the function name. The function value returned is the last value assigned to the function name before the subprogram terminates. With either method, the function value may best be considered as an extra implicit out parameter from the subprogram.

9.3.4 Implementation of Parameter Transmission

Because each activation of a subprogram receives a different set of parameters, storage for the formal parameters of a subprogram is ordinarily allocated as part of the activation record of the subprogram, rather than in the code segment. Each formal parameter is a local data object in the subprogram. If a formal parameter P is specified in the subprogram heading as being of a particular type T (i.e., the actual parameter transmitted is of type T), then the formal parameter is implemented in one of two ways depending on the method of parameter transmission being used (as discussed earlier). Either P is treated as a local data object of Type T (whose initial value may be a copy of the actual parameter's value) or P is treated as a local data object of type *pointer to* T (whose initial value is a pointer to the actual-parameter data object). The former method is used for parameters transmitted by value-result, by value, and by result; the latter is used for parameters transmitted by reference. Either method may be used to implement parameters transmitted by constant-value. An explicit function value may be treated with the former method. If the language does not provide a type specification for formal parameters (as in LISP, APL, and SNOBOL4), then the formal parameter may be implemented as a local pointer variable, but the pointer may point to a data object of arbitrary type.

The various actions associated with parameter transmission are split into two groups: those associated with the *point of call* of the subprogram in each calling subprogram and those associated with the *entry and exit* in the subprogram. At the point of call, in each calling subprogram, each actual-parameter expression is evaluated, and the list of pointers to actual-parameter data objects (or sometimes just copies of their values) is set up. Note that it is important that this evaluation take place at the point of call in the referencing environment of the calling subprogram. When the actual parameters have been determined, control is transferred to the called subprogram. Ordinarily this involves a change in the CIP and CEP pointers, as discussed in chapter 8, to transfer control to the start of the executable code for the subprogram and also to change the referencing environment to that appropriate for the called subprogram.

After the transfer of control to the subprogram, the *prologue* for the subprogram completes the actions associated with parameter transmission by either copying the entire contents of the actual parameter into the formal parameter or copying the pointer to the actual parameter into the formal parameter. Before the subprogram terminates, the *epilogue* for the subprogram must copy result values into the actual parameters transmitted by result or value-result. Function values must also be copied into registers or temporary storage provided by the calling program. The subprogram then terminates and its activation record is lost, so all results ordinarily must be copied out of the activation record before termination.

The compiler has two main tasks in the implementation of parameter transmission. First it must generate the correct executable code for transmission of parameters, return of results, and each reference to a formal-parameter name. Be-

```
Q(int i, int *j)
    { i=i+10;
    *j=*j+10;
    printf("i=%d; j=%d;\n",i,*j);
    }

(a) Called subprogram
```

```
P()
    {int a, b;
    a = 2;
    b = 3;
    Q(a,&b);
    printf("%d %d\n",a,b);
    }

(b) Calling subprogram
```

Figure 9.13. C value and reference parameters.

cause most languages provide more than one parameter transmission method, the executable code required in each case is often slightly different. This code generation is also difficult because it often involves coordinated actions taken at each point of call, in the subprogram prologue, and in its epilogue. The second major task of the compiler is to perform the necessary static type checking to ensure that the type of each actual-parameter data object matches that declared for the corresponding formal parameter. For this checking, the compiler must know the specification of the subprogram being called (number, order, and type of parameters) but need not know the internal structure of the subprogram body. This specification must be available at each point of call of the subprogram. In many languages, particularly where subprograms may be compiled separately from each other, if a subprogram Q is called from a subprogram P, then a separate specification for Q must be provided when compiling P, although Q is defined elsewhere, to allow the compiler to perform the necessary static type checking and to generate the appropriate code for parameter transmission at each point of call.

Parameter Transmission Examples

The combination of parameter transmission method with the different types of actual parameters leads to a variety of effects. Some examples are of use in explaining the subtleties. For these examples, call *by reference* and call *by value* are the two methods used. The differences that result from using other methods are taken up in some of the problems. C is used as the base for these examples. In our version of C, a formal-parameter name that is preceded by $*$ in the subprogram heading is transmitted by reference, whereas one without the $*$ is transmitted by value.

Simple variables and constants. Figure 9.13(a) shows a C subprogram Q with two formal parameters: i, transmitted by value, and j, transmitted by reference. Suppose we write a subprogram P that calls Q with two integer variables, a and b, as actual parameters, as in Figure 9.13(b). If P is executed, the results printed by the two *write* statements are: 12 13 2 13. Let us follow each parameter in turn.

When P calls Q, the actual-parameter expressions a and $\&b$ are evaluated (i.e., a referencing operation is invoked to determine the current association of the names a and b). Each name represents an integer variable data object so the actual parameters transmitted are the r-value of a and the l-value of b. Because a is being transmitted by value, formal parameter i is represented as a local integer variable within Q. When Subprogram Q begins execution, the value of a at the time of the call is assigned as the initial value of i. Subsequently, a and i have no further connection. Thus, when i is assigned the new value 12, a is not changed. After the call to Q is complete, a still has the value 2.

In contrast, Parameter b is transmitted by reference. This means that j is a local variable in Q of type *pointer to integer*. When Q begins execution, the pointer to data object b is stored as the r-value of j. When 10 is added to the value of j, j does not change. Instead, each reference to j (the r-value of j, which is the l-value of b) is followed by a pointer value selection operation so that the reference to j actually gives access to the location of the data object b. As a result, the assignment to j, although it looks similar to the assignment to i, actually means something quite different. The value of actual parameter b is changed to 13. When the values of the formal parameters i and j are printed in Q, the results are 12 and 13. After return to P, when the values of the corresponding actual parameters a and b are printed, only b has changed value. The value 12 assigned to i in Q is lost when Q terminates because local variables in Q are deleted at termination. The value of j, of course, is also lost, but this is the pointer, not the value 13.

Data structures. Suppose we write a different version of Q in which the formal parameters are vectors. There is a problem in writing this example in C because C does not normally pass array values by value. Instead, the procedure declaration *sub*1(*int a*[20]) is interpreted the same as if *sub*1(*int* $*$ *a*) were written. In other words, C interprets array parameters the same as in Ada 95 by passing a pointer to the array (its l-value) rather than passing the r-value (a copy of the array). Because of this, this part of the example will be given in Pascal, which will copy the r-value of a call-by-value array parameter into the subprogram:

```
type vect = array [1 . . 3] of integer;
procedure Q(k: vect; var l: vect);
    var n: integer;
    begin
        k[2] := k[2] + 10;
        l[2] := l[2] + 10;
        for n := 1 to 3 do write(k[n]);
        for n := 1 to 3 do write(l[n])
    end;
```

We might write procedure P as given in Figure 9.14.

When P is executed, the values printed are: 6 17 8 6 17 8 6 7 8 6 17 8.

```
procedure P;
    var c,d: vect;
        m: integer;
    begin
        c[1] := 6; c[2] := 7; c[3] := 8;
        d[1] := 6; d[2] := 7; d[3] := 8;
        Q(c,d);
        for m := 1 to 3 do write(c[m]);
        for m := 1 to 3 do write(d[m])
    end;
```

Figure 9.14. Data structure parameters.

To follow the transmission of c and d as parameters, we first note that the evaluation of the actual-parameter expressions c and d in P leads to pointers to the blocks of storage for the vectors c and d within P's activation record (just as for a and b earlier). These pointers are transmitted to Q. Because vector c is transmitted by value, the corresponding formal parameter k is a local array in Q having the same shape as c (three components plus a descriptor). The three values in Vector c are copied into the corresponding positions of k, and thereafter c and k have no further contact. Thus, on return to P, Vector c is unmodified by the assignment to k in Q. However, Vector d transmitted by reference is modified by the assignment to formal-parameter vector l because l is not a vector, but only a pointer to a vector. When Q begins execution, l is initialized to point to Vector d, and each subsequent reference to l in Q leads via this pointer to d. Thus, the assignment to $l[2]$ modifies $d[2]$. The printed values reflect these distinctions. Figure 9.15 shows the run-time stack at the end of execution of Q.

In general, a data structure such as an array or record that is transmitted by value is copied into a local data structure (the formal parameter) in the called subprogram. The subprogram works on this local copy and has no access to the original. A data structure transmitted by reference is not copied, and the called subprogram works directly on the actual-parameter data structure (using the formal-parameter pointer for access).

Components of data structures. Suppose we go back to the procedure Q in Figure 9.13(a), but instead of simple variables or constants, we pass components of data structures as parameters to Q—for example, by writing P as

```
P()
    {int c[4];
    int m;
    c[1] = 6; c[2] = 7; c[3] = 8;
    Q(c[1],&c[2]);
    for (m = 1;m<=3; m++) printf("%d\n",c[m]);
    }
```

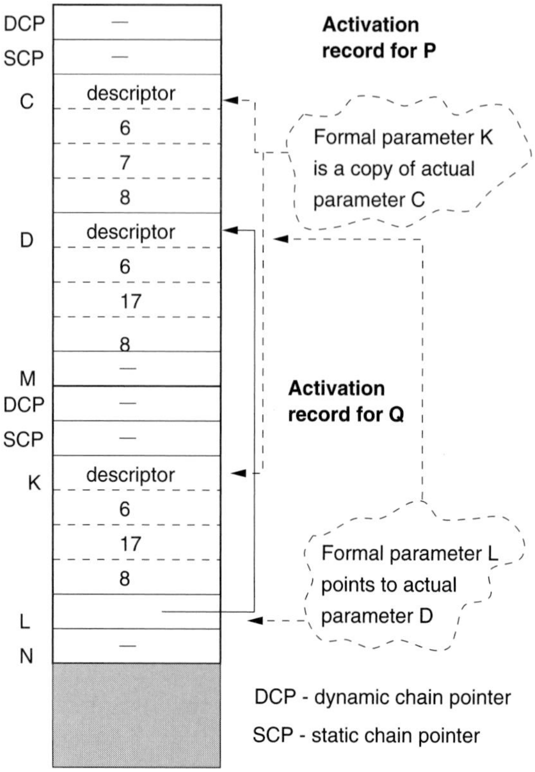

Figure 9.15. Run-time stack before Q terminates.

When P is executed, the values printed are: 16 17 6 17 8.

Transmission of $c[1]$ by value follows the same pattern as before. The expression $c[1]$ is evaluated by referencing c and then selecting its first component. The result is the r-value of that component. Formal parameter i is initialized to this r-value as before, so the rest of the actions are the same. Similarly, $\&c[2]$ is evaluated and a pointer to the component transmitted. Assignments within Q then directly change the component of c via the pointer stored in formal parameter j.

The components of c are represented in storage *exactly like simple variable data objects of the same type.* Within Q, the code that is executed to manipulate i and j is the same regardless of whether the call of Q is $Q(a, b)$ or $Q(c[1], c[2])$. If the components of c were represented in storage differently from simple variables a and b (e.g., if they were packed in some way), then a special conversion would have to be made before Q was called to convert the actual parameters to the proper representation (whatever is expected by Q), store the converted parameters in temporary storage, and pass pointers to the temporary storage to Q. For call by value, this conversion might be acceptable. However, for call by reference, the resulting pointer is no longer a pointer to the original data object, so assignments to the formal parameter no longer modify the actual parameter directly. For this reason, transmission of components of packed arrays and records is often prohibited (e.g., in Pascal).

Array components with computed subscripts. Suppose Subprogram R has two integer parameters transmitted by reference:

```
R(int *i, int *j)
    {*i = *i + 1;
    *j = *j + 1;
    printf("%d %d\n",*i,*j);
    }
```

The previous definition of P with R substituted for the call to Q yields

```
P()
    {int c[4];
    int m;
    c[1] = 6; c[2] = 7; c[3] = 8;
    m = 2;
    R(&m,&c[m]);
    for (m = 1; m<=3; m++)printf("%d\n",c[m]);
    }
```

What values are printed when P is executed now? Note that m has the value 2 initially; however, because it is a reference parameter, its value is changed to 3 in R before $c[m]$ is incremented via the pointer in j. Does the statement $*j = *j + 1$ then add 1 to $c[2]$ or $c[3]$? Clearly it must be $c[2]$ that is incremented, not $c[3]$, because the actual-parameter expression $c[m]$ is evaluated *at the time of call of R* to get a pointer to a component of c. At the time of call of R, m has the value 2, so it is a pointer to $c[2]$ that is transmitted to R. R knows nothing of the existence of $c[3]$ because within R, the pointer to $c[2]$ appears the same as a pointer to any other integer data object. Thus, the values printed are: 3 8 6 8 8. (A different effect appears if parameters are transmitted *by name*.)

Pointers. Suppose an actual parameter is a simple variable of type *pointer* or a data structure such as an array or record that contains l-values (pointers to data objects) as components. For example, suppose X in P is declared as $vect * x$ and the corresponding formal parameter in Q is declared likewise: $vect * h$. Regardless of whether h is declared as transmitted by value or by reference, the effect of transmitting x as the actual parameter is to allow Q to directly access the vector to which x points. If transmission is by value, then Q has its own copy of the l-value that x contains, so both x and h point to the same vector. If transmission is by reference, then h contains a pointer to x that contains a pointer to the vector. As a general rule, whenever the actual-parameter data object contains a pointer or pointer components, the data objects designated by these pointers are directly accessible from the subprogram, regardless of the method of parameter transmission. Note that if a linked list (or other linked data structure) is transmitted *by value* as a parameter to a subprogram, this usually means that only the pointer to the first element is copied during transmission; the entire linked structure is not copied into the subprogram. It is because of this property of pointer variables and the addition of various l-value and r-value operators in C that C does not need an explicit call-by-reference mechanism and call by value is sufficient.

Results of expressions. If we wish to pass an expression by reference, such as expression $a + b$ in $Q(\&(a + b), \&b)$, the translator must evaluate the expression at the point of call, store the resulting value in a *temporary storage location* in P, and transmit a pointer to that location to the procedure Q as the parameter. Execution of Q continues as before. Transmission by reference leads to the formal parameter containing a pointer to the temporary storage location in P. Because this location has no name by which it can be referenced in P, any assignment made to it by Q does not change a value that P can later reference. Thus, Q cannot transmit a result back to P through the reference parameter. Both C and Pascal prohibit this case where the transmission is by reference because assignments to the formal parameter have no observable effect in the calling program (and thus a parameter transmitted by value should be used).

Aliases and Parameters

The possibility of aliases (multiple names for the same data object in a single referencing environment) arises in connection with parameter transmission in most languages. As explained in Section 9.2.1, aliases are a problem in understanding and verifying the correctness of programs and in program optimization. An alias may be created during parameter transmission in one of two ways:

1. *Formal parameter and nonlocal variable.* A data object transmitted as an actual parameter by reference may be directly accessible in the subprogram through a nonlocal name. The formal-parameter name and the nonlocal name then become aliases because each refers to the same data object. Figure 9.7 shows an example of this type of aliasing.

2. *Two formal parameters.* The same data object may be transmitted as an actual parameter by reference in two positions in the same actual-parameter list. The two formal-parameter names then become aliases because the data object may be referenced through either name. For example, Procedure R defined with the Pascal specification

procedure R(**var** i,j: integer);

could be called by P using $R(m, m)$. During execution of R, both i and j contain pointers to the same data object m in P; thus i and j are aliases. FORTRAN prohibits this form of aliasing.

Subprograms as Parameters

In many languages, a subprogram may be transmitted as an actual parameter to another subprogram. The actual-parameter expression in this case consists of the *name* of the subprogram. The corresponding formal parameter is then specified as of *subprogram* type. In Pascal, for example, a subprogram Q may be defined with a formal parameter R of type procedure or function, as in

procedure Q(x:integer; **function** R(y,z: integer): integer);

and Q may then be called with a function subprogram as its second parameter [e.g., the call $Q(27, fn)$, which invokes Q and passes function subprogram fn as a parameter]. Within Q, the subprogram passed as the parameter may be invoked by using the formal-parameter name, R, for example, $z := R(i, x)$ invokes the actual-parameter subprogram (fn in the prior call) with the actual parameters i and x. Thus, $R(i, x)$ is equivalent to $fn(i, x)$ in this case. On a different call, if the actual parameter is function subprogram $fn2$, then $R(i, x)$ invokes $fn2(i, x)$.

Two major problems are associated with subprogram parameters:

Static type checking. When a subprogram parameter is called using the formal-parameter name [e.g., $R(i, x)$], it is important that static type checking be possible to ensure that the call includes the proper number and type of actual parameters for the subprogram being called. Because the actual name of the subprogram being called is not known at the point of call (in the example, it is fn on one call and $fn2$ on another), the compiler cannot ordinarily determine whether the actual parameters i and x in the call $R(i, x)$ match those expected by fn or $fn2$ without additional information. What the compiler needs is a full specification for formal parameter R that includes not only the type *procedure* or *function,* but also the number, order, and type of each parameter (and result) of that procedure or function (e.g., as given in the specification for Q). Then within the subprogram Q, each call of R may be checked statically for the correctness of its parameter list. In addition, at each call of Q, the actual parameter that corresponds to R may be checked as to whether its specification matches that given for R. Thus, fn and $fn2$ must both have the same number, order, and type of parameters as specified for R.

Nonlocal references (free variables). Suppose that a subprogram such as fn or $fn2$ contains a reference to a nonlocal variable. For example, suppose fn references z and $fn2$ references $z2$ and neither subprogram contains a local definition for the variable referenced. Such a nonlocal reference is often termed, in mathematics, a *free variable* because it has no local binding within the subprogram definition. Ordinarily when a subprogram is called, a nonlocal referencing environment is set up, and this nonlocal environment is used during execution of the subprogram to provide a

```
program Main;
    var X: integer;
    procedure Q(var I:integer; function R(J:integer):integer);
        var X:integer;
        begin
        X := 4;
        write("In Q, before call of R, I=", I, "X=", X);
        I := R(I);
        write("In Q, after call of R, I=", I, "X=", X)
        end;
    procedure P;
        var I: integer;
        function FN(K:integer):integer;              | In FN,
            begin;                                   | I and X
            X := X+K;                                | are free
            FN := I+K;                               | variables
            write("In P, I=", I, "K=", K, "X=", X)   | here
            end;                                     |
        begin
        I := 2;
        Q(X,FN);
        write("In P, I=", I, "X=", X)
        end;
    begin
    X := 7;
    P;
    write("In Main, X=", X)
    end.
```

Figure 9.16. Free variables as subprogram parameters in Pascal.

meaning for each reference to a nonlocal variable (as described in the next sections). However, suppose that a subprogram fn that contains a nonlocal reference is passed as a parameter from a calling subprogram P to a called subprogram Q. What should be the nonlocal environment used when fn is invoked within Q [by using the corresponding formal parameter R, e.g., $R(i, x)$ to invoke $fn(i, x)$]? The simplest answer is to say that the nonlocal environment should be the same as that used if the call $R(i, x)$ were simply replaced by the call $fn(i, x)$ in subprogram Q, but that turns out to be the wrong answer in most cases. Figure 9.16 illustrates the difficulty. Function fn contains nonlocal references to both x and i. According to the Pascal static scope rules, x references the x declared in the main program and i references the i declared in Procedure P. However, P passes fn as a parameter to Q, and it is Q that actually calls fn via the formal-parameter name R. Q has local definitions for both i and x, and fn cannot be allowed to incorrectly retrieve these local variables when it is called.

This problem of free variables in functions passed as parameters is not unique to languages like Pascal, which use static scope rules and block structure. It also occurs in LISP and other languages that use the most recent association rule for nonlocal referencing. The general solution is to invoke the following rule about the meaning of free variables in functional parameters: A nonlocal reference (reference to a free variable) should mean the same thing during the execution of the subprogram passed as a parameter as it would *if the subprogram were invoked at the point where it appears as an actual parameter in the parameter list.* For example, in Figure 9.16, the subprogram fn appears as an actual parameter in the parameter list of the call to Q within P. Thus, the nonlocal references to x and i in fn, regardless of where fn is actually called later (in this case, within Q), are to mean just what they would mean if fn were called where Q is called within P.

To correctly implement this rule for the meaning of nonlocal references within subprograms passed as parameters, it must be possible to re-create the correct nonlocal environment at the point of call of the subprogram parameter so that it executes using the correct nonlocal environment. In the static chain implementation of nonlocal referencing, as discussed in Section 9.4.2, this is fairly straightforward. All that is necessary is to determine the correct static chain pointer for the subprogram parameter and pass that along as part of the information transmitted with a subprogram parameter. The subprogram parameter then becomes a pair of pointers (CP, SCP), where CP is a pointer to the code segment for the subprogram and SCP is the static chain pointer to be used when the subprogram is invoked. This pair may be passed through many levels of subprogram until it becomes time to invoke the subprogram. At that point the activation record is created, the transmitted SCP is installed, and execution of the subprogram code segment proceeds as for any other call.

Figure 9.17 illustrates the main steps in execution of the Pascal program of Figure 9.16. To illustrate the interplay between static (SCP) and dynamic chains (DCP), as well as subprogram parameters and nonlocal referencing, the example shows the values of variables, return points, and static chain pointers during the main steps in execution of the program. The behavior of the program is as follows:

IN Q:	BEFORE CALL OF R, I=7, X=4
IN FN:	I=2, K=7, X=14
IN Q:	AFTER CALL OF R, I=9, X=4
IN P:	I=2, X=9
IN Main:	X=9

Statement Labels as Parameters

Many languages allow a statement label to be passed as a parameter to a subprogram and then used as the object of a **goto** statement within the subprogram. Besides the usual difficulties associated with the use of **goto** statements, as described in chapter 8, this mechanism introduces two new difficulties.

Which activation should be used? A statement label refers to a particular instruction in the code segment of a subprogram during execution. However, a **goto** cannot simply transfer control to that instruction by changing the CIP in the usual

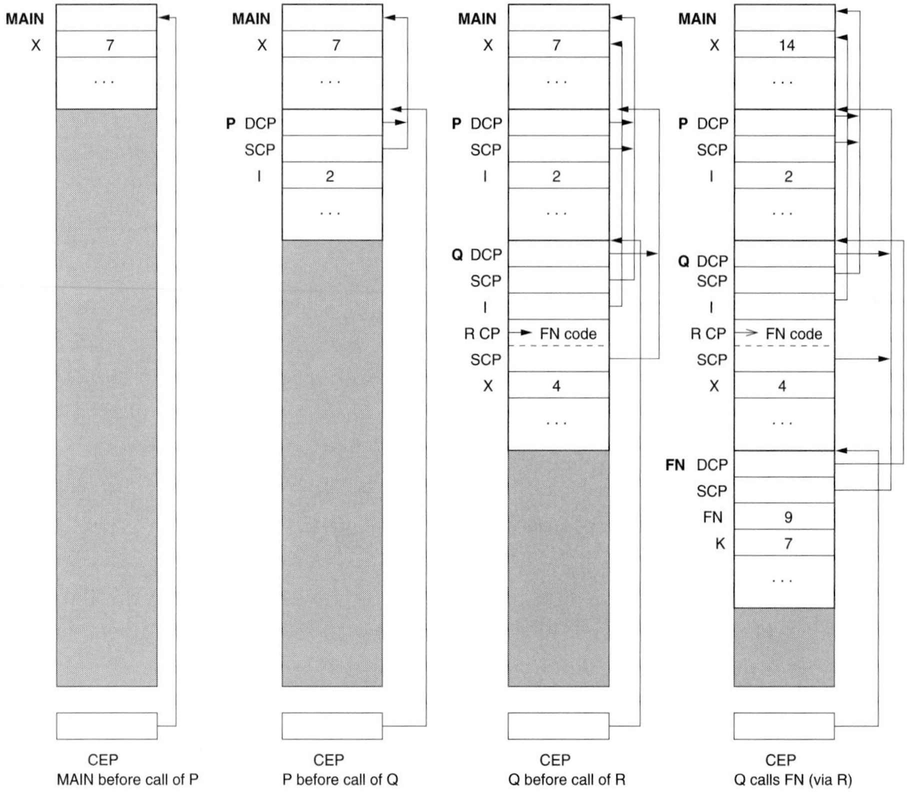

Figure 9.17. Snapshots of the central stack during Pascal execution.

way because the code segment may be shared by several activations of the subprogram. The statement label, when passed as a parameter, must designate an instruction *in a particular activation* of the subprogram. Thus, the label becomes a pair (instruction pointer, activation record pointer) that is transmitted as the parameter.

How is the **goto** *to a label parameter implemented?* When a **goto** is executed that designates a formal parameter of type label as its object, it does not suffice to simply transfer control to the designated instruction in the designated activation in most cases. Instead, the dynamic chain of subprogram calls must ordinarily be unwound until the designated subprogram activation is reached. That is, the current subprogram executing the **goto** statement must be terminated, then the subprogram that called it, then that subprogram's caller, and so on until the subprogram activation designated in the **goto** is reached. That activation then begins executing at the instruction designated by the **goto** rather than at the instruction designated by the original return point. Depending on the details of the language definition and implementation, especially regarding the final values of value-result and result parameters in such aborted calling chains, this process may be fairly complex to implement correctly.

9.4 EXPLICIT COMMON ENVIRONMENT

A *common environment* set up explicitly for the sharing of data objects is the most straightforward method for data sharing. A set of data objects that are to be shared among a set of subprograms is allocated storage in a separate named block. Each subprogram contains a declaration that explicitly names the shared block. The data objects within the block are then visible within the subprogram and may be referenced by name in the usual way. Such a shared block is known by various names: *COMMON block* in FORTRAN; in Ada it is a form of a *package;* in C single variables tagged *extern* are shared in this way. *Classes* in C++ and Smalltalk provide this feature, but that is not the normal purpose for classes. (See chapter 7.) The term *common environment* is appropriate in our setting here.

Specification. A common environment is identical to a local environment for a subprogram except that it is not a part of any single subprogram. It may contain definitions of variables, constants, and types, but no subprograms or formal parameters. The **package** specification in Ada is an example:

```
package Shared_Tables is
    Tab_Size: constant integer := 100;
    type Table is array (1 . . Tab_Size) of real;
    Table1, Table2: Table;
    Curr_Entry:integer range 1 . . Tab_Size;
end
```

The package specification defines a type, constant, two tables, and an integer variable that together represent a group of data objects (and type definitions) that are needed by several subprograms. The package definition is given outside of any subprograms that use the variables.

If a subprogram *P* requires access to the common environment defined by this package, then an explicit **with** statement is included among the declarations of *P*:

```
with Shared_Tables;
```

Within the body of *P*, any name in the package may now be used as if it were part of the local environment for *P*. We use the qualified name *package name.variable name* to reference these names. Thus, we can write in *P*

```
Shared_Tables.Table1(Shared_Tables.Curr_Entry) :=
    Shared_Tables.Table2(Shared_Tables.Curr_Entry) + 1;
```

without any further declaration of any of these names. The package name must be used as a prefix on each name because a subprogram may use many packages, some of which may declare the same name. (If there are no such conflicts, the package name prefix may be avoided by a **use** statement in Ada—for example, **with** Shared_Tables; **use** Shared_Tables.) In general, any number of other subprograms may use the same common environment by including the statement **with** Shared_Tables, and any number of common environments may be used by a single subprogram.

Implementation. In FORTRAN and C, each subprogram using the common environment must also include declarations for each shared variable so that the compiler knows the relevant declarations although the common environment is also declared elsewhere. In Ada, the compiler is expected to retrieve the declaration for the common environment from a library or another part of the program text when a **with** statement is encountered during compilation of a subprogram.

The declarations for the common environment are added to the compiler symbol table as an additional set of local names that may be referenced in the subprogram. Each reference to a name in the subprogram body is then looked up in the table in the usual way for purposes of static type checking and generation of executable code.

At run time, a common environment is represented as a block of storage containing the data objects declared in the definition. Because the data objects are potentially of mixed type and their declarations are known during compilation, the block may be treated as if it were a *record*. The name of the block represents the name of the record, and the individual variables in the block represent the components of the record. References to individual variables within the block are then translated into the usual base-address-plus-offset calculation for record component references.

The block of storage representing a common environment must continue to exist in memory for as long as any of the subprograms that use it are still potentially callable because each activation of any of these subprograms may access the block. Thus, the block is ordinarily allocated storage statically so that it is set up at the beginning of program execution and is retained throughout execution. There may be many such common blocks in memory, interspersed with the blocks representing code segments for subprograms and other statically allocated blocks of run-time storage.

A subprogram that references a data object in a common block must know the base address of the block. A simple implementation is to allocate a location in the code segment for the subprogram to contain a pointer to the block (i.e., to contain the base address of the block). These pointer linkages between a subprogram and the common blocks that it uses are similar to the linkages between a subprogram and the code segments for the subprograms that it calls. One of the primary tasks of the link editor, which assembles a collection of subprograms and common blocks in

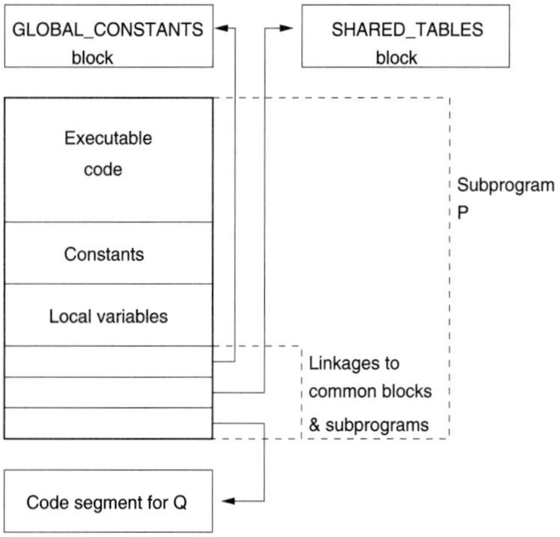

Figure 9.18. Linkage to common blocks in subprograms.

memory prior to the start of execution, is the storing of the actual linkage pointers in each code segment as required for execution. Figure 9.18 illustrates this structure. During execution, a reference to a data object in a common environment is handled by taking the base address of the appropriate common block from the code segment for the subprogram making the reference and adding the precomputed offset to get the actual memory location of the shared data object.

Sharing Explicit Variables

A related form of explicit sharing of data objects is that of providing a means for a data object in the *local* environment of a subprogram to be made visible to other subprograms. Thus, instead of a group of variables in a common environment separate from any subprogram, each variable has an owner—the subprogram that declares it. To make a local variable visible outside the subprogram, an explicit *export definition* must be given, such as the **defines** declaration in the following code:

```
procedure P(. . .);
    defines X, Y, Z;   - X, Y, and Z become available for export
    X, Y, Z: real;     - Usual declarations for X, Y, and Z
    U, V: integer;     - Other local variables
begin . . . end;       - Statements
```

Another subprogram that needs access to an exported variable uses an explicit *import definition* to import the variable (e.g., by including a **uses** declaration naming both the subprogram and the exported variable):

```
procedure Q(. . .);
    uses P.X, P.Z;      - Imports X and Z from P
    Y: integer;         - Other declarations
begin . . . end;        - Statements may include references to X and Z.
```

This is the model present in C with the *extern* declaration.

Implementation. The effect is similar to use of a variable in a common environment. Storage for an exported local variable must be retained between activations of the subprogram defining it so it ordinarily would be allocated storage in the code segment for the subprogram, as for ordinary retained local variables. Referencing of such a variable from another subprogram that imports it then uses the base address of the code segment for the exporting subprogram and adds the appropriate offset.

9.4.1 Dynamic Scope

An alternative to the use of explicit common environments for shared data is the association of a *nonlocal environment* with each executing subprogram. The nonlocal environment for a subprogram P consists of a set of local environments of other subprogram activations that are made accessible to P during its execution. When a variable X is referenced in P and X has no local association, then the nonlocal environment is used to determine the association for X. What should be the nonlocal environment for P? In block-structured languages, the static scope rules determine the implicit nonlocal environment for each subprogram. This fairly complex approach is considered in the next section. A simpler, but less widely used, alternative is considered here—use of the local environments for subprograms in the current dynamic chain.

Consider a language in which local environments are deleted on subprogram exit and in which subprogram definitions are not nested within one another. Each is defined separately from the others. This case, present in APL, LISP, and SNOBOL4, has no static program structure on which to base scope rules for references to *nonlocal* identifiers. For example, if a subprogram P contains a reference to X and X is not defined locally within P, then which definition for X in some other subprogram is to be used? The natural answer is found by considering the *dynamic chain* of subprogram activations that leads to the activation of P. Consider the course of program execution: Assume the main program calls a subprogram A, which calls B, which calls P. If P references X and no association for X exists in P, then it is natural to turn to the subprogram B that called P and ask if B has an association for X. If B does, then that association for X is used. Otherwise, we go to the subprogram A that called B and check whether A has an association for X. We have used the *most recently created association* for X in the dynamic chain of subprogram calls leading to P. This meaning for a nonlocal reference is termed the *most recent association rule*; it is a referencing rule based on dynamic scope.

If the nonlocal environment is determined by the most-recent-association rule, no static scope rules are used (i.e., no attempt is made during program translation to determine the definition associated with a reference to an identifier that is not defined locally in the subprogram). During program execution, when a data object X is created as part of the activation of subprogram P, the *dynamic scope* of the association for X becomes all the activations of subprograms called by P or by those subprograms, and so on. X is visible within this dynamic scope (except where it is hidden by a later subprogram that has its own local association for X). Viewed from the other direction, the *nonlocal environment* of a subprogram activation P consists of the entire dynamic chain of subprogram activations leading to it.

The most troublesome aspect of this nonlocal environment is that it may *change* between activations of P. Thus, on one activation of P, when a nonlocal reference to X is made, the most recent association in the calling chain may have X as the name of an array. On a second activation of P, invoked through a different sequence of prior subprogram calls, the dynamic chain may change so that the most recent association for X is as the name of a character string. On a third activation of P, there may be no association for X in the calling chain at all so that the reference to X is an error. This variability in the association for X means that *dynamic type checking* is required. Thus, the method is only used in languages such as LISP, APL, and SNOBOL4 where dynamic type checking is used for other reasons.

Implementation. Implementation of the most recent association rule for nonlocal references is straightforward given the central-stack implementation for storing subprogram activation records. The local environment for each subprogram is made part of its activation record. On entry to the subprogram, the activation record is created; on return, the activation record is deleted.

Suppose that a subprogram P calls Subprogram Q, which calls R. When R is executing, the central stack might look like Figure 9.19. To resolve a nonlocal reference to X, the stack is searched beginning with the local environment for R and working back through the associations in the stack until the most recent association for X is found. As the figure shows, some of the associations in the stack will be hidden by later associations for the same identifier.

This implementation of the most-recent-association rule is costly. The search required at each nonlocal reference takes time and reintroduces the necessity of storing some representation of the *identifiers* in the local association tables because the position of the association for X may differ in each local table. Thus, no base-address-plus-offset computation is possible in nonlocal referencing.

How may searching for nonlocal references be avoided? A tradeoff is possible between the cost of nonlocal referencing and the cost of subprogram entry and exit, which may be advantageous if nonlocal referencing is assumed to be much more frequent than subprogram entry and exit (i.e., if the nonlocal environment is likely to be used more frequently than it is modified).

The alternative implementation uses a central table common to all subprograms—the *central referencing environment table*. The central table is set up to contain at

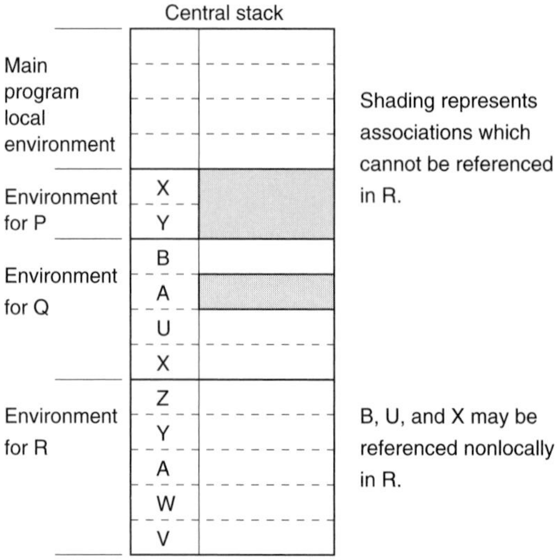

Figure 9.19. Active referencing environment during execution.

all times during program execution *all the currently active identifier associations* regardless of whether they are local or nonlocal. If we assume, also for simplicity, that the set of identifiers referenced in any of the subprograms may be determined during translation, then the central table is initialized to contain one entry for each identifier regardless of the number of different subprograms in which that identifier appears. Each entry in the table also contains an *activation flag* that indicates whether that particular identifier has an active association as well as space for a pointer to the object of the association.

All referencing in subprograms is direct to this central table using the base-address-plus-offset scheme described previously. Because the current association for Identifier X is always located at the same place in the central table, regardless of the subprogram in which the reference occurs and regardless of whether the reference is local or nonlocal, this simple referencing computation is adequate. Each reference requires only that the activation flag in the entry be checked to ensure that the association in the table is currently active. By use of the central table, we have obtained our objective of relatively efficient nonlocal referencing without search.

Subprogram entry and exit are more costly because each change in referencing environment requires modification of the central table. When Subprogram P calls Q, the central table must be modified to reflect the new local environment for Q. Thus, each entry corresponding to a local identifier for Q must be modified to incorporate the new local association for Q. At the same time, if the old table entry for an identifier was active, the entry must be saved so that it may be reactivated when Q exits to P. Because the entries that require modification are likely to be

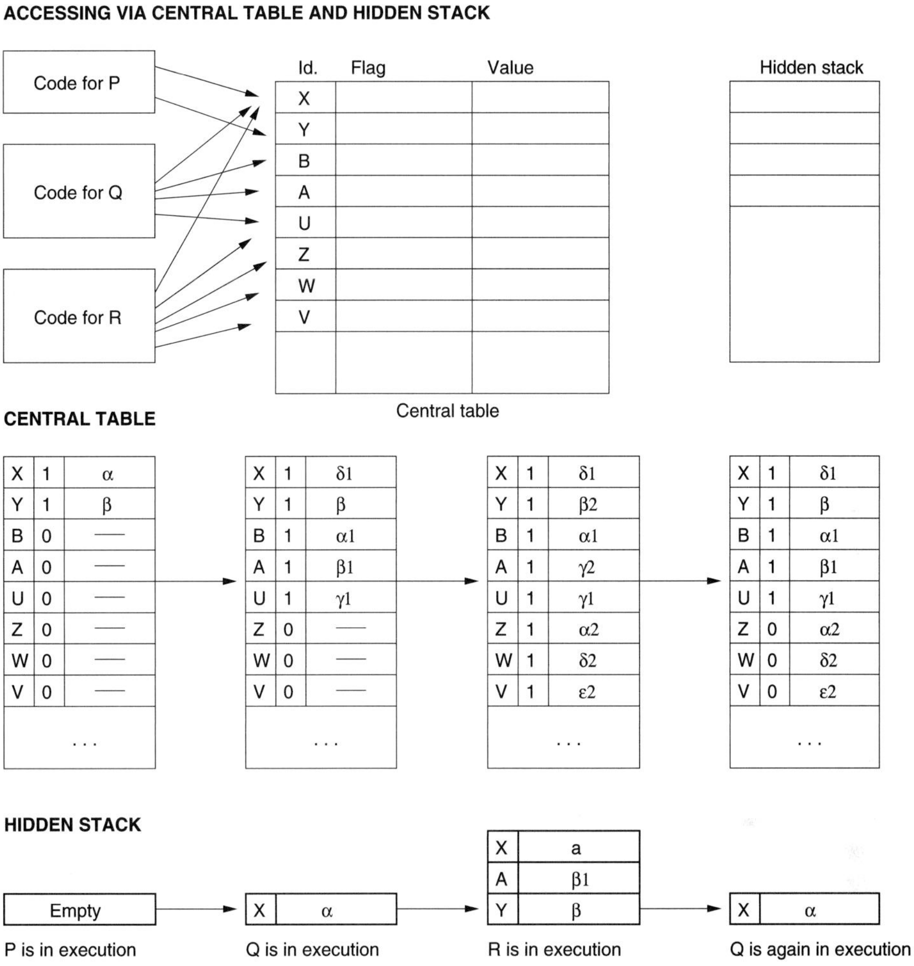

Figure 9.20. Central environment table for nonlocal referencing.

scattered throughout the central table, this modification must be done piecemeal, entry by entry. On exit from Q, the associations deactivated and saved on entry to Q must be restored and reactivated. Again an execution-time stack is required, as in the earlier simulations, but it is used here as a *hidden stack* to store the deactivated associations. As each local identifier association is updated on entry to Q, the old association is stacked in a block on the hidden stack. On return from Q, the top block of associations on the stack is restored into the appropriate positions in the central table. This central table simulation is shown in Figure 9.20. An additional advantage accrues when using the central table if the language does not allow new references to be generated during execution. In this case, as was the case earlier in regard to local tables, the identifiers may be dropped from the table because they will never be used, having been replaced by the base-address-plus-offset computation. (In a sense, the identifier is simply represented by its table offset during execution.)

9.4.2 Static Scope and Block Structure

In languages such as Pascal and Ada that utilize a block-structured form for programs, the handling of nonlocal references to shared data is more complex. If you look again at the static scope rules for block-structured programs given in Section 9.2.3, you note that each reference to an identifier within a subprogram is associated with a definition for that identifier in the program text, even if the identifier is not local to the subprogram. Thus, the nonlocal referencing environment of each subprogram during execution is already determined by the static scope rules used during translation. The implementation problem is to retain consistency between the static and dynamic scope rules so that a nonlocal reference during program execution is correctly related to the data object corresponding to the definition for that identifier in the program text.

Figure 9.21 shows an example of the static scope rules for a block-structured Pascal program. Subprogram R is called from Subprogram Q, which is called from P. Subprograms P and Q and the main program define a variable X. Within R, X is referenced nonlocally. The static scope rules define the reference to X as a reference to the X declared in the main program, not as a reference to either of the definitions for X within P or Q. The meaning of the nonlocal reference to X is independent of the particular dynamic chain of calls that leads to the activation of R, in contrast to the most recent association rule of the preceding section, which relates X to the X either in P or in Q depending on which subprogram called R.

The static scope rules are straightforward to implement in the compiler. As each subprogram definition is processed during compilation, a local table of declarations is created and attached to a chain of such local tables that represent the local environments of the main program and other subprograms within which this subprogram is nested. Thus, in compiling R, the compiler adds the local table of declarations for R to the chain containing only the main program definition. During compilation, this chain is searched to find a declaration for a reference to X, starting with the local declarations for R and proceeding back down the chain to the declarations in the main program. When compilation of R is complete, the compiler deletes the local table for R from the chain. Note the similarity with the searching for a meaning for X done with the most-recent-association rule described in Section 9.4.1. However, this search for a declaration for X is done during *compilation*, not during execution. The chains of local tables of declarations represent the static nesting of subprogram definitions in the program text rather than the dynamic subprogram calling chain during execution.

During program execution in a block-structured language, a central stack is used

```
program Main;
    var X, Y: integer;
    procedure R;
        var Y: real;
        begin
        ...
        X := X+1; { Nonlocal reference to X }
        ...
        end {R};
    procedure Q;
        var X: real;
        begin
        ...
        R; { Call procedure R }
        ...
        end {Q};
    procedure P;
        var X: Boolean;
        begin
        ...
        Q; { Call procedure Q }
        ...
        end {P};
begin { begin Main }
...
P; { Call procedure P }
    ...
end.
```

Figure 9.21. Pascal procedure with nonlocal references.

for subprogram activation records. The local environment for each subprogram is stored in its activation record. The difficulty in maintaining static scope using dynamic scope rules becomes apparent in Figure 9.22, which shows the contents of the central stack during execution of Subprogram R of Figure 9.21. When R is executing and the nonlocal reference to X is encountered, the referencing operation must find the association for X in the main program, rather than that in Subprogram Q, which called R. Unfortunately, a simple search down the stack leads to the association for X in Q. The problem is that the sequence of local tables in the stack represents the *dynamic nesting* of subprogram *activations*—the nesting based on the execution-time calling chain. However, it is the *static nesting* of subprogram *definitions* that now determines the nonlocal environment, and the stack as currently structured contains no information about static nesting.

To complete the implementation, it is necessary to represent the static block structure during execution in such a way that it may be used to control nonlocal referencing. Observe that in many respects the rule for nonlocal referencing in this case is similar to that for nonlocal referencing using the most recent association

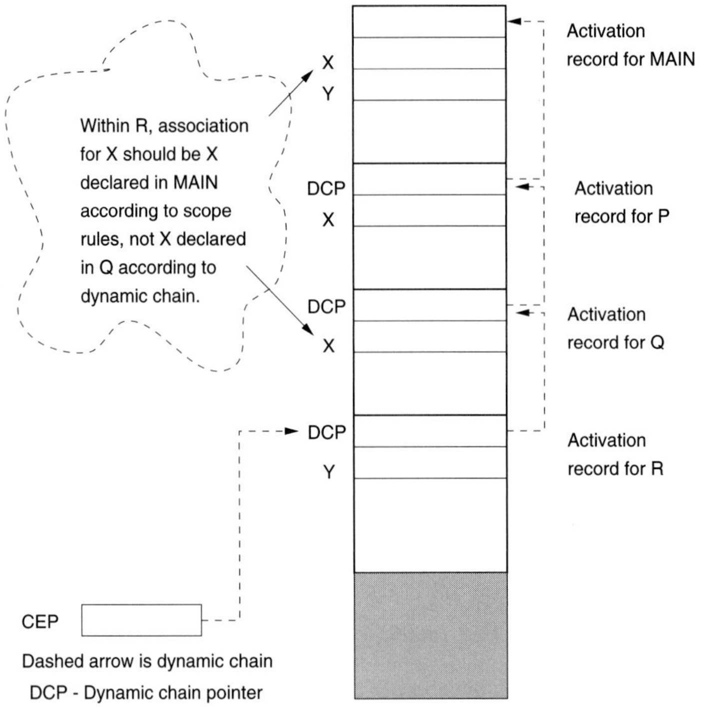

Figure 9.22. Incomplete central stack during execution using static scope.

rule: To find the association to satisfy a reference to X, we search a chain of local environment tables until an association for X is found. However, the chain of local environment tables to search is not composed of *all* the local tables currently in the stack, but only those *that represent blocks or subprograms whose definition statically encloses the current subprogram definition in the original program text.* The search then is still down some of the tables in the stack, but only those tables that are actually part of the referencing environment.

Static chain implementation. These observations lead to the most direct implementation of the correct referencing environment: the *static chain* technique. Suppose that we modify the local environment tables in the stack slightly so that each table begins with a special entry—the *static chain pointer.* This static chain pointer always contains the base address of another local table further down the stack. The table pointed to is the table representing the local environment of the statically enclosing block or subprogram in the original program. (Of course, because each local environment table is just a part of an activation record, we may use the base address of the activation record, rather than just the base address of the local environment part.)

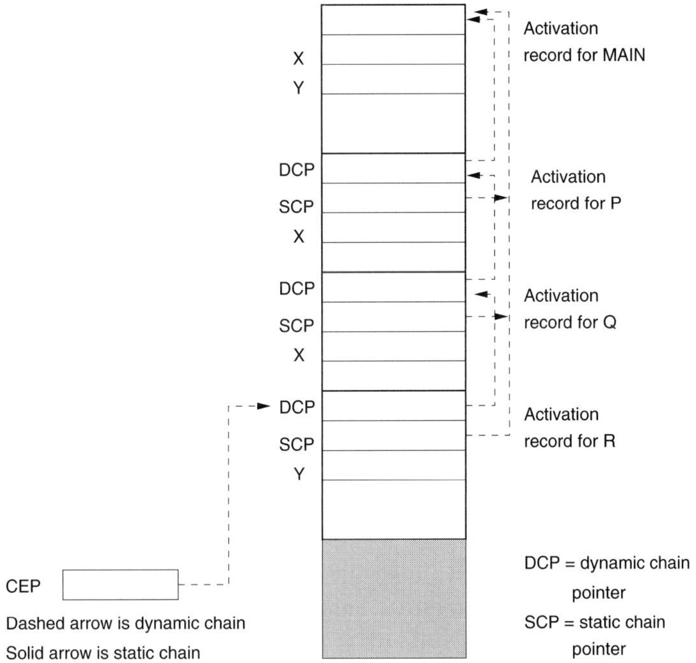

Figure 9.23. Central stack during execution.

The static chain pointers form the basis for a simple referencing scheme. To satisfy a reference to X, we follow the CEP pointer to the current local environment on top of the stack. If no association for X is found in the local environment, then we follow the static chain pointer in that local table down the stack to a second table. If X is not in that table, the search continues down the static chain pointers until a local table is found with an association for X. The first one found is the correct association. Figure 9.23 illustrates the static chain for the Pascal program of Figure 9.21.

Although this seemingly requires a *search* of each statically linked environment until X is found, this is not necessarily so. As the compiler creates the local environment table for each local declaration (e.g., Figure 9.10), it keeps track of which subprograms are statically nested within that environment. For each reference to X, the compiler *counts* the number of enclosing environments it must search (at compile time) to find the correct association to X. Then it generates code to follow the static chain pointer that many times to arrive at the appropriate activation record containing the association for Variable X. This avoids having to keep the name of the identifier within the execution stack, as previously stated.

This is a fairly efficient implementation, generally requiring n accesses of the static chain pointer to access a variable declared at Level k when used at Level $k+n$. With subprograms rarely nested more than 4 or 5 deep (with 2 or 3 being typical), n is rarely greater than 1 or 2, but in languages like Pascal can be arbitrarily large. However, we can do even better. We can access any correct environment with only one reference to a static chain pointer, as we describe shortly.

The static chain technique allows straightforward entry and exit of subprograms. When a subprogram is called, its activation record is created on top of the stack. At this time the appropriate static chain pointer must be installed in it, pointing to an activation record further down the stack. On exit, it is only necessary to delete the activation record from the stack in the usual way; no special action is needed for the static chain pointer.

How can we determine the appropriate static chain pointer to install on entry to a subprogram? Suppose that Subprogram R is called from Subprogram Q and that R is defined in the original program text nested directly within $Main$, as in Figure 9.22. When R is entered during execution, the appropriate static chain pointer is back to the activation record for $Main$. At the point of call, the activation record for Q is on top of the stack and that for R is to be stacked on top of Qs. How is it determined that the proper static chain pointer is the one to $Main$? Observe that the identifier "R," the subprogram name, is referenced nonlocally in Q in the call statement invoking R. If "R" is determined (at compile time) to be defined at one level of nesting out from the call statement in Q, then at run time the static chain pointer for R should point to the activation record one step back down Q's static chain. Thus, at the point of call in Q, the static chain pointer for R can be determined to point to the activation record for $Main$ because $Main$'s activation record is one step back down Q's static chain. The situation is exactly as if R were defined as a local variable in $Main$ that was referenced nonlocally in Q, except that after following the static chain from Q to the appropriate activation record, no offset is added. Instead, the activation record found is made the object of R's static chain pointer after R's activation record is created.

Display implementation. To see how to improve on the static chain implementation for nonlocal variable accessing, we need a few preliminary observations:

1. For any subprogram R, when R is in execution (and its local environment table is therefore on top of the stack), the length of the static chain leading from R's local table down the stack (and ultimately to the table for the main program) is *constant* and simply equal to the depth of static nesting of subprogram R's definition back in the original program at compile time, which is fixed throughout execution. For example, if R is defined within a block that is directly contained within the outermost block of the program, then the static chain for R during execution always has length 3—R's local table, the local table for the directly containing block, and the local table for the outermost block (the main program). In Figures 9.21 and 9.23, for example, the static chain for R always has length 2.

2. In this chain of constant length, a nonlocal reference will always be satisfied at exactly the same point in the chain. For example, in Figure 9.23, the nonlocal reference to X in R will always be satisfied by the second table in the chain. Again, this fact is a simple reflection of the static program structure. The number of levels of static nesting that one must go out from the definition of R to find the declaration for X is fixed at compile time.

3. The position in the chain at which a nonlocal reference will be satisfied may be determined at compile time. We used this fact in counting the number of static chain pointers to follow in our static chain implementation earlier. For example, we may determine at compile time that a reference to X in R will be found in the second table down the static chain during execution. In addition, we know at compile time the relative position of X in that local table. Thus, for example, at *compile time*, we can conclude that the association for X will be the second entry in the second table down the static chain during execution.

The basis for an efficient referencing operation is now apparent. Instead of explicitly searching down the static chain for an identifier, we need only skip down the chain a fixed number of tables, and then use the base-address-plus-offset computation to pick out the appropriate entry in the table. We represent an identifier in the form of a pair (chain position, offset) during execution. For example, if X referenced in R is to be found as the third entry in the first table down the chain, then in the compiled code for R, X may be represented by the pair (1, 3). This representation provides a rather simple referencing algorithm.

In this implementation, the current static chain is copied into a separate vector, termed the *display*, on entry to each subprogram. The display is separate from the central stack and is often represented in a set of high-speed registers. At any given point during execution, the display contains the same sequence of pointers that occur in the static chain of the subprogram currently being executed. Figure 9.24 illustrates the display for the example of Figure 9.21.

Referencing using a display is particularly simple. Let us adopt a slightly modified representation for identifiers during execution. Again, pairs of integers are to be used, but let the 3 in a pair like (3,2) represent the number of steps back from the *end* of the chain to the appropriate activation record (rather than down from the start of the chain as before). The second integer in the pair still represents the offset in the activation record. Now, given a nonlocal reference such as (3,10), the appropriate association is found in two steps:

1. Consider the first entry (3) as a subscript into the display. $base\_address = display[3]$ assigns $base\_address$ to be a pointer to the base address of the appropriate activation record.

2. Compute the location of the desired entry as base address plus offset, as in $base\_address + 10$.

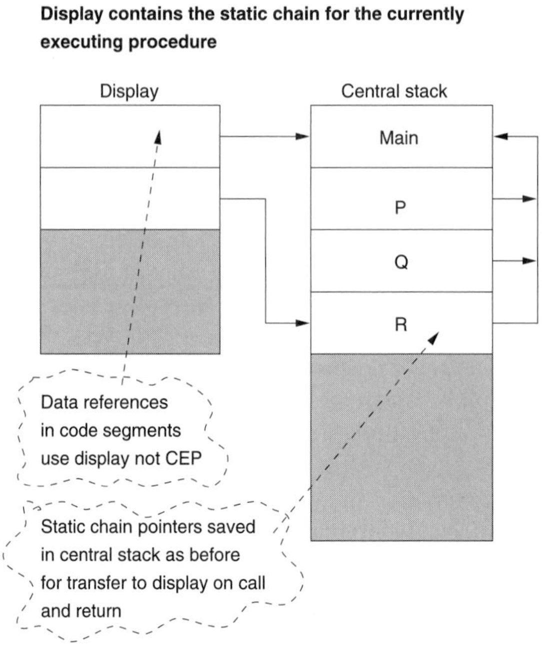

Figure 9.24. Central stack and display during execution.

Ordinarily these two steps combine into one using indirect addressing through the display entry. If the display is represented in high-speed registers during execution, then only one memory access per identifier reference is required.

Although referencing is simplified using a display, subprogram entry and exit are more difficult because the display must be modified on each entry and exit to reflect the *currently active* static chain. The simplest procedure is to maintain the static chain pointers in the central stack, as described earlier, and reload the display with the appropriate static chain pointers on each entry and exit using instructions inserted by the compiler into the prologue and epilogue of each subprogram code segment.

Declarations in Local Blocks

Languages like C allow the declaration of variables local to a block of statements, nested within a procedure (Figure 9.25). At first glance, it appears that each of the blocks requires a separate activation record for storage of these variables. However, there is one important difference between these blocks and the previous discussion of procedure activation records. Due to the dynamic nature of procedure calls, we can never be sure (in general) which procedures are currently in execution.

```
real proc1( parameters )
    {int i, j;
    ... /* statements */
        {int k, l; ... /* statements */ }
        {int m, n;
        ... /* statements */
            {int x; ... /* statements */ }
            {int y; ... /* statements */ }
            } }
```

Figure 9.25. Local declarations in C.

Thus, if the prior blocks each represent procedures, it might be that the block containing k and the block containing m are both in execution simultaneously (e.g., the block containing k calls the block containing m), hence they would need separate activation records.

However, in the prior C example, this is impossible. Within the block containing Variable k, we cannot be within the scope of variable m. Similarly, if we are in the scope of x, we cannot be within the scope of y. This permits a simple storage strategy, which is analogous to the storage structure for variant records of Figure 6.9. Variables k and l can use the same storage locations as m and n because they cannot be active at the same time, and all of this storage is allocated with the enclosing procedure. All that the local declarations do is define the visibility—the set of statements—where each variable may be used. The storage exists for the entire procedure activation. This is summarized in Figure 9.26.

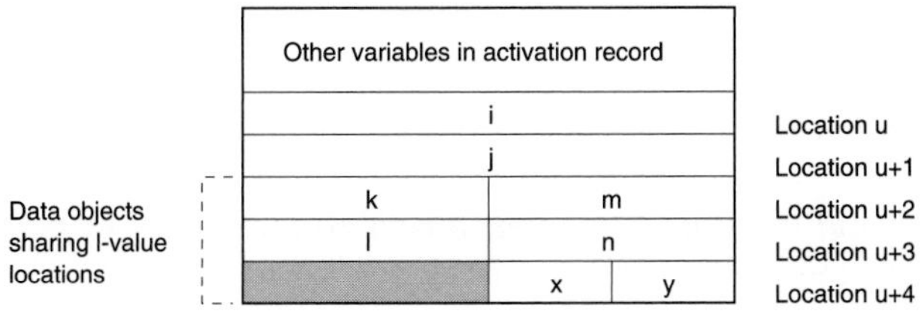

Figure 9.26. Overlapping variable storage in activation record.

9.5 SUGGESTIONS FOR FURTHER READING

Most of the books and papers referenced in chapter 1 that deal with subprogram-level control structures also deal with the associated problems of referencing environments, shared data, and parameters. The translator writing texts given in chapter 3 describe how to compile such structures.

9.6 PROBLEMS

1. When local referencing environments are deleted between subprogram activations, using a central stack as in C, it sometimes appears as if values are *retained.* For example, in most C implementations, if procedure *Sub* has a local variable X and *Sub* assigns the value 5 to X on the first call, then on a second call, if X is (inadvertently) referenced before it is assigned a new value, sometimes X still has its old value 5. However, in the same program, a third call on *Sub* may find X *not* retaining its old value from the second call.

   (a) Explain this apparent anomaly: In what circumstances could an activation of *Sub* that references an uninitialized variable X find that X still had the value assigned on a previous call? In what circumstances would X not have its previously assigned value?

   (b) Write a simple C program and determine the effects of trying this process on your local implementation.

2. Suppose a language allows initial values to be specified for local variables, as in the Ada declaration

   X: integer := 50

   which initializes X to 50. Explain the two meanings that such an initialization might have in the cases (a) local variables are *retained* between calls and (b) local variables are *deleted* between calls.

3. Pascal (and many other languages) allow *pointer* type variables to be used together with a *new* operation to construct data objects. Pascal also uses the deletion approach to local referencing environments. The combination has a high potential to generate *garbage* (inaccessible storage) during program execution. Explain the difficulty.

4. For a program you have written recently in a language that uses *static scope rules,* take each subprogram and list the names in (a) its local referencing environment, (b) its nonlocal referencing environment, (c) its global referencing environment, and (d) its predefined referencing environment. Then invert the problem: For a name declared in each of these referencing environments, list (a) the subprogram definitions in its static scope, and (b) the subprogram activations in its dynamic scope.

5. The goal of *information hiding* in a subprogram design is often made difficult if the language does not allow any local data to be retained between calls (as in Pascal). Give an example of a situation in Pascal in which deletion of local environments makes it necessary for a data object to be made visible outside a subprogram, although the subprogram is the only routine that should have access to the data object.

6. In the *display* implementation of nonlocal referencing in block-structured languages, can the *maximum* size of the display be predicted during compilation of a program? How?

7. In languages such as Pascal that use static scope rules and allow recursive subprogram calls, it is sometimes difficult to relate a nonlocal reference in one subprogram to a particular variable in another subprogram if there are several recursive activations of that second subprogram in existence. For example, suppose A, B, C, and D are the subprograms of program $Main$, and A is called by $Main$. Suppose A calls B, B calls A recursively, A calls C, and then C calls D.

(a) If D makes a nonlocal reference to Variable X in A, then which "X" is visible in D—that in the first activation of A or the second?

(b) With the calling and nonlocal referencing patterns assumed here, only *four* different static nestings of the definitions of A, B, C, and D are possible. Draw the four possible static nestings (e.g., as in Figure 9.8).

(c) For each of the four static nestings, draw the run-time stack at the time that "X" is referenced in D, showing the activation records for A, B, C, and D and the static and dynamic chains. For each case, give the run-time representation of "X" as a pair (n,m) and explain which data object X the nonlocal reference to "X" in D must retrieve given this run-time structure. Assume the static chain pointer implementation of nonlocal referencing.

8. Suppose that you wish to modify Pascal so that nonlocal referencing is based on dynamic scope (most recent association) rather than static scope.

(a) How would the organization of the central run-time stack have to be modified? What information could be deleted from each subprogram activation record? What information would need to be added to each activation record?

(b) Explain how a nonlocal reference would be resolved in this modified implementation.

(c) Give two examples of error checks that would have to be done at run time (that can be done at compile time if static scope is used).

9. Suppose that you wished to design a language that used *(1)* retained local environments, *(2)* no recursive subprogram calls, and *(3)* nonlocal references based on dynamic scope. Design an implementation for such a language. Explain how the referencing environment is represented. Explain the actions taken on subprogram call and return. Explain how nonlocal referencing is implemented.

10. Explain why it is *impossible* in a language with only parameters transmitted by value or name, such as ALGOL, to write a subprogram *Swap* of two parameters that simply swaps the values of its two parameters (which must be simple or subscripted variables). For example, *Swap* called by $Swap(X, Y)$ should return with X having the original value of Y and Y the original value of X. Assume that *Swap* works only for arguments of type integer.

11. Consider the following program. Give the three numbers printed in the case that Y is transmitted to P (a) by value, (b) by reference, (c) by value-result, and (d) by name.

```
program Main(...);
    var Y: integer;
    procedure P(X: integer);
        begin X := X + 1; write (X,Y) end;
    begin
    Y := 1; P(Y); write(Y)
    end.
```

12. Consider the following program in a language with static scope:

```
program main(input,output);
    var i,j,k,m: integer;
    procedure Q(var i: integer; m: integer);
        begin
        i:=i+k;
        m:=j+1;
        writeln(i,j,k,m)
        end;
    procedure P(var i: integer; j:integer);
        var k: integer;
        begin
        k:=4;
        i:=i+k;
        j:=j+k;
        Q(i,j)
        end;
begin
i:=1;
j:=2;
k:=3;
P(i,k);
writeln(i,j,k)
end.
```

Fill in the following table for each *writeln* statement assuming the given parameter-passing mechanisms:

Parameter mode	i	j	k	m
Pascal, as written				
All parameters are call by reference				
All parameters are call by value				
All parameters are call by value-result				

13. References to arrays using computed subscripts [e.g., $A(I)$] are sometimes considered a form of *aliasing*. For example, the two composite names $A[I]$ and $A[J]$ may be considered to be aliases. Explain why these array references create some of the same problems for the programmer and implementor as other types of aliases.

14. FORTRAN requires that the declaration for each data object shared through a common environment be given again in each subprogram that uses the data object. This allows each subprogram definition to be compiled independently because each contains full declarations for shared data objects. Suppose the programmer inadvertently gives a slightly different declaration in each of two subprograms $Sub1$ and $Sub2$, which share a variable X. What happens if $Sub1$ and $Sub2$ are compiled independently and then linked and executed? Assume that the actual data object X is represented at run time according to the declaration given in $Sub1$ rather than that in $Sub2$.

15. Suppose that Subprogram Q in Figure 9.13 on page 383 were called from within P using constants as actual parameters [e.g., $Q(2,3)$ instead of $Q(a,\&b)$]. Although transmission of a constant by reference is not legal in C, it is allowed in many languages, so assume it is valid here. Remember that (1) a constant data object is ordinarily allocated storage in the code segment of the calling subprogram, and (2) an actual-parameter expression consisting of a single constant is a special case of the more general case of an arbitrary expression appearing as an actual parameter. Give two methods by which transmission of a constant by value and by reference might be implemented. Method 1 uses no temporary storage in the caller; Method 2 does. (Method 1 used for transmission by reference may lead to constants that change value; e.g., in some FORTRAN implementations, you can write a program that adds 1 and 2 and gets 4.) Write such a program and try it on your local implementation. [*Hint:* Try the equivalent of

Sub(1); X := 2; X := X + 1; **print**(X)

and write *Sub* so it changes the literal 1 to have value 2.]

16. *Jensen's device.* Parameters transmitted by name allow use of a programming trick known as *Jensen's device.* The basic idea is to transmit by name as separate parameters to a subprogram both an expression involving one or more variables and the variables. By adroit changes in the values of the variables, coupled with references to the formal parameter corresponding to the expression, the expression may be evaluated for many different values of the variables. A simple example of the technique is in the general-purpose summation routine *Sum*, defined in ALGOL as follows:

```
real procedure Sum (Expr, Index, LB, UB);value LB, UB;
    real Expr; integer Index, LB, UB;
    begin real Temp; Temp := 0
    for Index := LB step 1 until UB do Temp:=Temp+Expr;
    Sum := Temp
    end Sum;
```

In this program *Expr* and *Index* are transmitted by name and *LB* and *UB* by value. The call of

Sum(A[I],I,1,25)

will return the sum of the first 25 elements of Vector *A*. The call

Sum(A[I] ⋆ B[I],I,1,25)

will return the sum of the products of the first 25 corresponding elements of Vectors *A* and *B* (assuming that *A* and *B* have been appropriately declared). The call

Sum(C[K,2],K,-100,100)

will return the sum of the second column of Matrix C from $C[-100, 2]$ to $C[100, 2]$.

(a) What call to *Sum* would give the sum of the elements on the main diagonal of a matrix *D* declared as **real array** D[1:50, 1:50]?

(b) What call to *Sum* would give the sum of the squares of the first 100 odd numbers?

(c) Use Jensen's device to write a general-purpose *Max* routine that will return the maximum value from a set of values obtained by evaluating an arbitrary expression *Expr* containing an index *Index*, which varies over a range from *LB* to *UB* in steps of *Step* size (an integer).

(d) Show how the effect of Jensen's device may be obtained by using subprograms as parameters in a language without parameter transmission by name.

17. In FORTRAN and Ada, the same syntax is used for referencing array components and calls to function subprograms. For example, in $A + B(C, D)$, B may be a two-dimensional array or a subprogram with two parameters. If all array and subprogram names are declared, the syntax is unambiguous. However, if a declaration is missing, the compiler or loader may have problems. Under what conditions could the compiler infer the correct interpretation for a missing declaration?

18. FORTRAN 90 is a major change to FORTRAN in that it permits dynamic storage in some instances. List the features that require the translator to allocate storage dynamically.

19. Because FORTRAN 77 has only static storage, how would you implement a recursive function such as $factorial(n)$?

20. *(a)* What changes to the run-time organization of C would be required to add the statement

int A[n]

which would allocate an array of size n and name it A, assuming n is a variable declared in another block?

(b) Can this be done in Java? Why?

21. The storage allocation operation *malloc* in C is often implemented as a call on the storage allocator provided by the operating system. The operating system provides a central heap, used by all programs, *malloc* (and $free$) allocate (and return) storage when called from your C program from this central heap. Because *malloc* requires a call to the operating system for this service, it can be a time-consuming operation. An alternative implementation of *malloc* provides a local heap storage area within each C program. Here *malloc* use is inexpensive. (Pascal *new* is implemented this way.)

Suppose your program design requires frequent use of *malloc* to allocate small blocks of storage from a heap.

(a) Investigate your local C implementation to determine the cost of using *malloc* as provided in C for this purpose.

(b) Compare that cost to an implementation of a heap and *malloc* that you could do yourself as part of your program. Consider two cases: (i) Your program allocates blocks only of one size, and (ii) your program allocates blocks of many different sizes.

22. Referring back to program *anomaly* in Figure 9.5, determine which option your local Pascal translator uses to resolve **forward** declarations.

23. Because Ada allows actual parameters to be paired with formal parameters by using the *names* of the formal parameters in the call statement, the formal parameter names become *visible* in the caller. Ordinarily formal parameter names are local to the called subprogram and are not visible in the caller. Explain the effect on ease of modification of a subprogram caused by the visibility of its formal parameter names.

Chapter 10

Storage Management

In chapter 9 we discussed a stack structure for subprogram control. However, most languages also have the ability to dynamically allocate and free the storage for data objects in a somewhat arbitrary manner. Storage for such objects is said to come from a *heap.* In many implementations the stack begins at one end of memory in a computer and the heap is at the other end. If the two structures—the stack and the heap—ever meet, then the program is out of memory and halts. In this chapter, we discuss various methods for managing the heap storage requirements for a programming language. Storage management for data is one of the central concerns of the programmer, language implementor, and language designer. In this section, the various problems and techniques in storage management are considered.

Typically languages contain many features or restrictions that may be explained only by a desire on the part of the designers to allow one or another storage-management technique to be used. Take, for example, the restriction in FORTRAN to nonrecursive subprogram calls. Recursive calls could be allowed in FORTRAN without change in the syntax, but their implementation would require a run-time stack of return points—a structure necessitating dynamic storage management during execution. Without recursive calls, FORTRAN may be implemented with only static storage management. It is a dramatic break with the past that, in the latest FORTRAN 90 standard, limited dynamic storage is permitted. Pascal is carefully designed to allow stack-based storage management, LISP to allow garbage collection, and so on.

Although each language design ordinarily permits the use of certain storage-management techniques, the details of the mechanisms and their representation in hardware and software are the task of the implementor. For example, although the LISP design may imply a free-space list and garbage collection as the appropriate basis for storage management, there are several different garbage-collection techniques from which the implementor must choose based on available hardware and software.

Although the programmer is also deeply concerned with storage management and must design programs that use storage efficiently, the programmer is likely to have little direct control over storage. A program affects storage only indirectly through the use or lack of use of different language features. This is made more difficult by the tendency of both language designers and implementors to treat storage management as a *machine-dependent* topic that should not be directly discussed in language manuals. Thus, it is often difficult for a programmer to discover what techniques are actually used.

10.1 ELEMENTS REQUIRING STORAGE

The programmer tends to view storage management largely in terms of storage of data and translated programs. However, run-time storage management encompasses many other areas. Some, such as return points for subprograms, have been touched on previously. Let us look at the major program and data elements requiring storage during program execution.

Code segments for translated user programs. A major block of storage in any system must be allocated to store the code segments representing the translated form of user programs, regardless of whether programs are hardware- or software-interpreted. In the former case, programs are blocks of executable machine code; in the latter case, blocks are in some intermediate form.

System run-time programs. Another substantial block of storage during execution must be allocated to system programs that support the execution of the user programs. These may range from simple *library routines*, such as sine, cosine, or print-string functions, to software interpreters or translators present during execution. Also included here are the routines that control run-time storage management.

User-defined data structures and constants. Space for user data must be allocated for all data structures declared in or created by user programs including constants.

Subprogram return points. Subprograms may be invoked from different points in a program. Therefore, internally generated sequence-control information, such as subprogram return points, coroutine resume points, or event notices for scheduled subprograms, must be allocated storage.

Referencing environments. Storage of referencing environments (identifier associations) during execution may require substantial space, as, for example, the LISP A-list (Appendix A.6).

Temporaries in expression evaluation. Expression evaluation requires the use of system-defined temporary storage for the intermediate results of evaluation. For example, in evaluation of the expression $(x+y) \times (u+v)$, the result of the first addition may have to be stored in a temporary while the second addition is performed. When expressions involve recursive function calls, a potentially unlimited number of temporaries may be required to store partial results at each level of recursion.

Temporaries in parameter transmission. When a subprogram is called, a list of actual parameters must be evaluated and the resulting values stored in temporary storage until evaluation of the entire list is complete. Where evaluation of one parameter may require evaluation of recursive function calls, a potentially unlimited amount of storage may be required, as in expression evaluation.

Input–output buffers. Ordinarily input and output operations work through buffers, which serve as temporary storage areas where data are stored between the time of the actual physical transfer of the data to or from external storage and the program-initiated input and output operations.

Miscellaneous system data. In almost every language implementation, storage is required for various system data: tables, status information for input–output, and various miscellaneous pieces of state information (e.g., reference counts or garbage-collection bits).

Besides the data and program elements requiring storage, various operations may require storage to be allocated or freed. The following are the major operations:

Subprogram call and return operations. The allocation of storage for a subprogram activation record, the local referencing environment, and other data on call of a subprogram is often the major operation requiring storage allocation. The execution of a subprogram return operation usually requires freeing of the storage allocated during the call.

Data structure creation and destruction operations. If the language provides operations that allow new data structures to be created at arbitrary points during program execution (rather than only on subprogram entry—e.g., *new* in Java), then these operations ordinarily require storage allocation that is separate from that allocated on subprogram entry. The language may also provide an explicit destruction operation, such as the Pascal *dispose* and the C *free* function, which may require that storage be freed. Java has no explicit destruction operation; garbage collection is employed.

Component insertion and deletion operations. If the language provides operations that insert and delete components of data structures, storage allocation and freeing may be required to implement these operations (e.g., the Perl *push* function adds an element to an array).

Although these operations require explicit storage management, many other operations require some hidden storage management to take place. Much of this storage management activity involves the allocation and freeing of temporary storage for housekeeping purposes (e.g., during expression evaluation and parameter transmission).

10.2 PROGRAMMER- AND SYSTEM-CONTROLLED STORAGE

To what extent should the programmer be allowed to directly control storage management? On the one hand, C has become very popular because it allows extensive programmer control over storage via *malloc* and *free*, which allocate and free storage for programmer-defined data structures. On the other hand, many high-level languages allow the programmer no direct control; storage management is affected only implicitly through the use of various language features.

The difficulty with programmer-controlled storage management is twofold: It may place a large and often undesirable burden on the programmer, and it may also interfere with the necessary system-controlled storage management. No high-level language can allow the programmer to shoulder the entire storage-management burden. For example, the programmer can hardly be expected to be concerned with storage for temporaries, subprogram return points, or other system data. At best a programmer might control storage management for local data (and perhaps programs). Yet even simple allocation and freeing of storage for data structures, as in C, are likely to permit generation of garbage and dangling references. Thus, programmer-controlled storage management is dangerous to the programmer because it may lead to subtle errors or loss of access to available storage. Programmer-controlled storage management also may interfere with system-controlled storage management, in that special storage areas and storage-management routines may be required for programmer-controlled storage, allowing less efficient use of storage overall.

The advantage of allowing programmer control of storage management is that it is often extremely difficult for the system to determine when storage may be most effectively allocated and freed. The programmer often knows quite precisely when a particular data structure is needed or when it is no longer needed and may be freed.

This dilemma is by no means trivial and is often at the heart of what language to use on a given project. Does one provide protection for the programmer by using a language with strong typing and effective storage-management features with a corresponding decrease in performance? Or does one need the performance characteristics (e.g., storage management and execution speed) with an increase in risk that the program may contain errors and fail during execution? This is one of the fundamental debates in the software engineering community. This book does not solve this debate, but a major goal is to provide the reader with the appropriate details to make an intelligent choice in these matters.

Storage-Management Phases

It is convenient to identify three basic aspects of storage management:

Initial allocation. At the start of execution, each piece of storage may either be allocated for some use or free. If free initially, it is available for allocation dynamically as execution proceeds. Any storage-management system requires some technique for keeping track of free storage as well as mechanisms for allocation of free storage as the need arises during execution.

Recovery. Storage that has been allocated and used, and that subsequently becomes available, must be recovered by the storage manager for reuse. Recovery may be very simple, as in the repositioning of a stack pointer, or very complex, as in garbage collection.

Compaction and reuse. Storage recovered may be immediately ready for reuse or compaction may be necessary to construct large blocks of free storage from small pieces. Reuse of storage ordinarily involves the same mechanisms as initial allocation.

Many different storage-management techniques are known and in use in language implementations. It is impossible to survey them all, but a relative handful suffice to represent the basic approaches. Most techniques are variants of one of these basic methods.

10.3 STATIC STORAGE MANAGEMENT

The simplest form of allocation is *static allocation*—allocation during translation that remains fixed throughout execution. Ordinarily storage for the code segments of user and system programs is allocated statically, as is storage for I/O buffers and various miscellaneous system data. Static allocation requires no run-time storage-management software, and, of course, there is no concern for recovery and reuse.

In the usual FORTRAN implementation, all storage is allocated statically. Each subprogram is compiled separately, with the compiler setting up the code segment (including an activation record) containing the compiled program, its data areas, temporaries, return-point location, and miscellaneous items of system data. The loader allocates space in memory for these compiled blocks at load time, as well as space for system run-time routines. During program execution, no storage management need take place.

Static storage allocation is efficient because no time or space is expended for storage management during execution. The translator can generate the direct l-value addresses for all data items. However, it is incompatible with recursive subprogram calls, with data structures whose size is dependent on computed or input data, and with many other desirable language features. In the next few subsections of this chapter, we discuss various techniques for *dynamic* (run-time) *storage management.* However, the reader should not lose sight of the importance of static allocation. For many programs, static allocation is quite satisfactory. Two of the most widely used programming languages, FORTRAN and COBOL, are designed for static storage allocation (although as stated previously, FORTRAN 90 now permits dynamic arrays and recursive procedures). Languages like C, which have dynamic storage, also permit static data to be created for efficient execution.

10.4 HEAP STORAGE MANAGEMENT

The third basic type of storage management after stack and static allocation is termed *heap storage management.* A *heap* is a block of storage within which pieces are allocated and freed in some relatively unstructured manner. Here the problems of storage allocation, recovery, compaction, and reuse may be severe. There is no single heap storage management technique, but rather a collection of techniques for handling various aspects of managing this memory.

The need for heap storage arises when a language permits storage to be allocated and freed at arbitrary points during program execution, as when a language allows creation, destruction, or extension of programmer data structures at arbitrary program points. For example, in ML, two lists may be concatenated to create a new list at any arbitrary point during execution, or the programmer may dynamically define a new type. In LISP, a new element may be added to an existing list structure at any point, again requiring storage to be allocated. In both ML and LISP, storage may also be freed at unpredictable points during execution.

It is convenient to divide heap storage management techniques into two categories depending on whether the elements allocated are always of the same fixed size or of variable size. Where fixed-size elements are used, management techniques may be considerably simplified. Compaction, in particular, is not a problem because all available elements are the same size. We consider the fixed-size case in this section, leaving the variable-size case until the following section.

10.4.1 LISP Overview

History. LISP was first designed and implemented by John McCarthy and a group at the Massachusetts Institute of Technology around 1960 [MCCARTHY 1961]. The language has become widely used for computer science research, most prominently in the area of artificial intelligence (e.g., robotics, natural language processing, theorem proving, intelligent systems). Many versions of LISP have developed over the past 30 years. Of all the languages described in this book, LISP is the one language that is neither standardized nor dominated by one particular implementation.

LISP is different from most other languages in a number of aspects. Most striking is the equivalence of form between programs and data in the language, which allows data structures to be executed as programs and programs to be modified as data. Another striking feature is the heavy reliance on recursion as a control structure, rather than the iteration (looping) that is common in most programming languages.

As stated earlier, LISP had its beginnings at MIT around 1960. During the 1960s and 1970s, various versions of the language were developed. These versions included MacLisp at MIT, Interlisp by Warren Teitelman for the DEC PDP-10, Spice LISP, and Franz LISP. Interlisp was the dominant dialect during most of this era. During the latter part of the 1970s, Gerald Sussman and Guy Steele developed a variant as part of research in models of computation that was known as *Schemer.* Because of six character name limitations, it was shortened to just Scheme. This is the version that has had the most impact on university use of the language.

In April 1981, a meeting was held among the various LISP factions to try and coalesce the various dialects into a single LISP language, which became known as Common LISP for lack of a better common name. The name Standard LISP was already taken by one of these dialects. The basic structure of Common LISP developed over the next 3 years.

The era from 1985 to the early 1990s was probably the height of popularity for LISP. AI research was prospering; at many universities, perhaps 75% or more of entering graduate students were declaring AI as their area of specialization. In 1986, technical working group X3J13 met to standardize Common LISP, and an effort was started to merge the Scheme and Common LISP dialects. This failed, and in 1989 the IEEE developed an IEEE standard for Scheme. About this time, the effects of object orientation in languages like C++ and Smalltalk were being felt, and the Common LISP Object System (CLOS) was written. Finally in 1992, X3J13 developed a draft for Common LISP at over 1,000 pages—larger than the standard for COBOL. It seems strange that a language with such a simple, clean, basic design can grow out of control.

From the beginning, LISP was criticized for slow execution, especially on the standard von Neumann computer described in chapter 2. Just as the original *car* and *cdr* functions were modeled on the IBM 704 hardware, alternative machine architectures were devised for speeding up LISP execution. Several companies developed machines designed for rapid LISP execution. However, around 1989, a garbage-collection strategy for standard von Neumann architectures was developed that was competitive with special-purpose LISP hardware. Because of this, none of the LISP companies survived to be long-term commercial successes.

Brief overview of the language. LISP programs run in an interactive environment (ordinarily). As a result, a main program does not exist in the usual form. Instead, the user at a terminal enters the main program as a sequence of expressions to be evaluated. The LISP system evaluates each expression as it is entered, printing the result automatically at the terminal. Ordinarily some of the expressions entered are function definitions. Other expressions contain calls on these defined functions with particular arguments. There is no block structure or other complex syntactic organization. The only interactions between different functions occur through calls during execution.

LISP functions are defined entirely as expressions. Each operator is a function that returns a value, and subprograms are written as single (often complex) expressions. Various special constructs have been added to the language to make this pure expression syntax appear somewhat like the ordinary *sequence of statements* syntax, but the expression form remains basic.

Data in LISP are rather restricted. *Literal atoms* (symbols) and *numeric atoms* (numbers) are the basic elementary types. Linked lists and property lists (represented as a special case of linked lists) form the basic data structures. All descriptor processing is done during execution, and no declarations of any sort are necessary.

LISP provides a wide variety of primitives for the creation, destruction, and modification of lists (including property lists). Basic primitives for arithmetic are provided. Run-time program translation and execution are also provided as primitives, and programs may be created and executed dynamically.

LISP control structures are relatively simple. The expressions used to construct programs are written in strict Cambridge Polish form and may include conditional branching. The *prog* feature provides a simple structure for writing expressions in a sequence. Recursive function calls are heavily emphasized in most LISP programming.

Comments in LISP usually begin with a semicolon, which indicates that the remainder of the line is a comment.

LISP referencing is primarily based on the *most recent association* rule for nonlocal referencing, often implemented using a simple linked list of current associations, the *A-list*, which is searched for the current association each time an identifier is referenced.

Function parameters are transmitted either all by value or all by name depending on the classification of the function, with transmission by value being the usual case.

LISP is most easily implemented with a software interpreter and software simulation for all primitives. Most implementations also provide a compiler that can be used to compile selected function definitions into machine code. These compiled functions are then executable by the hardware interpreter (but still require software simulation for many operations). LISP is rather poorly suited for compilation because most bindings are not made until execution. A complex storage-management structure based on a garbage-collected heap is used as the primary storage for data and programs.

10.4.2 Fixed-Size Elements

Assume that each fixed-size element allocated from the heap and later recovered occupies N words of memory. Typically N might be 1 or 2. Assuming the heap occupies a contiguous block of memory, we conceptually divide the heap block into a sequence of K elements, each N words long, such that $K \times N$ is the size of the heap. Whenever an element is needed, one of these is allocated from the heap. Whenever an element is freed, it must be one of these original heap elements.

Initially the K elements are linked together to form a *free-space list* (i.e., the first word of each item on the free list points to the first word of the next item on the free list). To allocate an element, the first element on the free-space list is removed from the list and a pointer to it is returned to the operation requesting the storage. When an element is freed, it is simply linked back in at the head of the free-space list. Figure 10.1 illustrates such an initial free-space list, as well as the list after allocation and freeing of a number of elements.

Recovery: Reference Counts and Garbage Collection

Return of newly freed storage to the free-space list is simple, provided such storage may be identified and recovered. However, identification and recovery may be quite

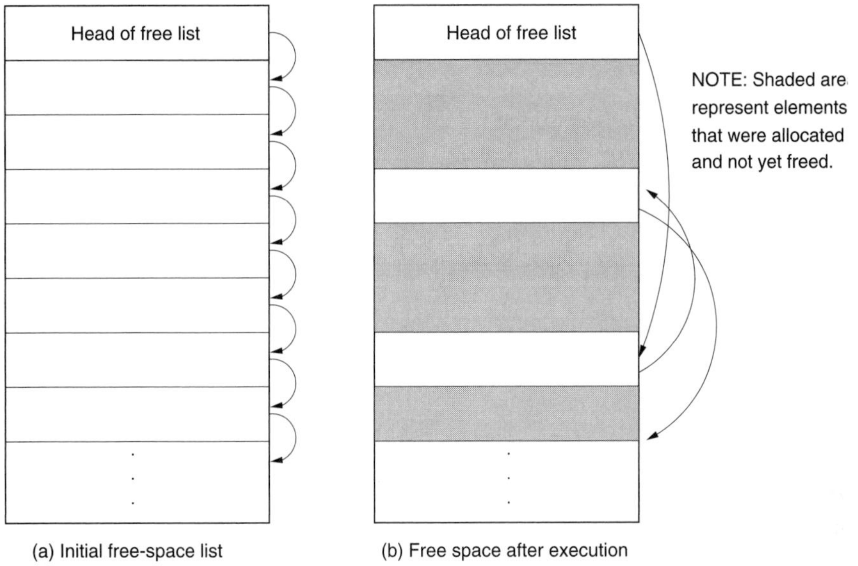

Figure 10.1. Free-space list structure.

difficult. The problem lies in determining which elements in the heap are available for reuse and therefore may be returned to the free-space list. Three solutions are in fairly wide use.

Explicit return by programmer or system. The simplest recovery technique is that of *explicit return*. When an element that has been in use becomes available for reuse, it must be explicitly identified as free and returned to the free-space list (e.g., a call to *dispose* in Pascal). Where elements are used for system purposes, such as storage of referencing environments, return points, or temporaries, or where all storage management is system controlled, each system routine is responsible for returning space as it becomes available for reuse through explicit call of a *free* routine with the appropriate element as a parameter.

Explicit return is a natural recovery technique for heap storage, but unfortunately it is not always feasible. The reasons lie with two old problems: garbage and dangling references. We first discussed these problems in chapter 5 in connection with destruction of data structures. If a structure is destroyed (and the storage freed) before all access paths to the structure have been destroyed, any remaining access paths become dangling references. However, if the last access path to a structure is destroyed without the structure being destroyed and the storage recovered, then the structure becomes garbage. In the context of heap storage management, a dangling reference is a pointer to an element that has been returned to the free-space list (which may have also been reallocated for another purpose). A garbage element is one that is available for reuse but not on the free-space list, and thus it has become inaccessible.

If garbage accumulates, available storage is gradually reduced until the program may be unable to continue for lack of known free space. If a program attempts to modify through a dangling reference a structure that has already been freed, the contents of an element on the free-space list may be modified inadvertently. If this modification overwrites the pointer linking the element to the next free-space list element, the entire remainder of the free-space list may become defective. Even worse, a later attempt by the storage allocator to use the pointer in the overwritten element leads to completely unpredictable results (e.g., a piece of an executable program may be allocated as free space and later modified). Similar sorts of problems arise if the element pointed to by the dangling reference has already been reallocated to another use before a reference is made.

The explicit return of heap storage facilitates creating garbage and dangling references. It is easy in such cases for the programmer to inadvertently create garbage or dangling references. For example, consider the C statements

```
int *p, *q;                /* p and q are pointers to integers */
...
p = malloc(sizeof(int));   /* allocate an int and set l-value in p */
p = q;                     /* oops – l-value previously in p now lost */
```

or

```
int *p, *q;                /* p and q are pointers to integers */
...
p = malloc(sizeof(int));   /* allocate an int and set l-value in p */
q = p;                     /* save l-value of allocated space in q */
free(p);                   /* oops – dangling reference still in q */
```

It may be equally difficult for the run-time system to avoid creating garbage or dangling references. In LISP, for example, linked lists are a basic data structure. One of the primitive LISP operations is *cdr*, which, given a pointer to one element on a linked list, returns a pointer to the next element in the list (Figure 10.2[a]). The element originally pointed to *may* have been freed by the *cdr* operation provided the original pointer given *cdr* was the only pointer to the element. If *cdr* does not return the element to the free-space list at this point, it becomes garbage. However, if *cdr* does return the element to free space and other pointers to it exist, then they become dangling references. If there is no direct way to determine whether such pointers exist, then the *cdr* primitive must potentially generate garbage or dangling references.

Owing to these problems with explicit return, alternative approaches are desirable. One alternative, called *reference counts*, requires explicit return but provides a way to check the number of pointers to a given element so that no dangling references are created. A second alternative, called *garbage collection*, is to allow garbage to be created but no dangling references. Later if the free-space list becomes exhausted, a *garbage-collector* mechanism is invoked to identify and recover the garbage.

Reference counts. The use of reference counts is the simpler of the two techniques. Within each element in the heap some extra space is provided for a *reference counter.* The reference counter contains the *reference count* indicating the number of pointers to that element that exist. When an element is initially allocated from the free-space list, its reference count is set to 1. Each time a new pointer to the element is created, its reference count is increased by 1. Each time a pointer is destroyed, the reference count is decreased by 1. When the reference count of an element reaches zero, the element is free and may be returned to the free-space list.

Reference counts allow both garbage and dangling references to be avoided in most situations. Consider the LISP *cdr* operation again. If each list element contains a reference count, then it is simple for the *cdr* operation to avoid the previous difficulties. *cdr* must subtract 1 from the reference count of the element originally pointed to by its input. If the result leaves a reference count of zero, then the

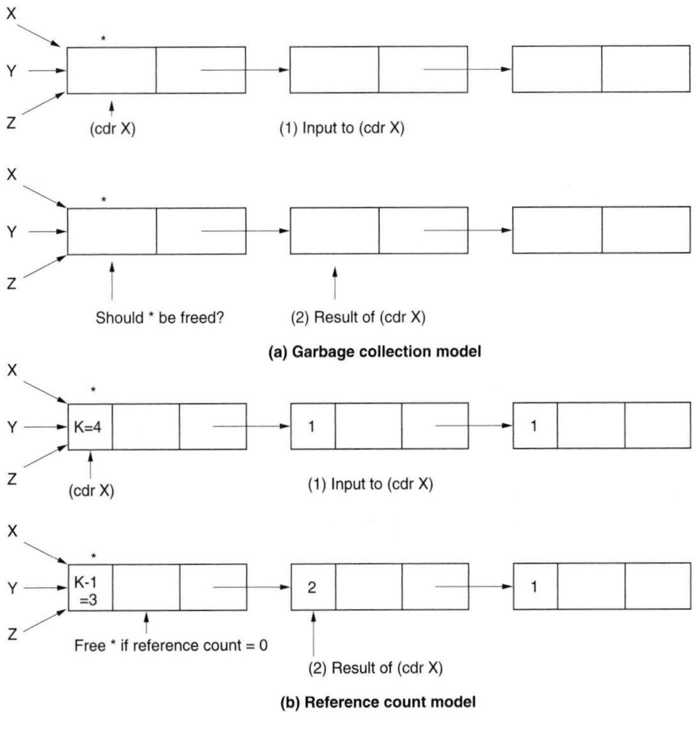

Figure 10.2. LISP *cdr* operation.

element may be returned to the free-space list, and if nonzero, then the element is still pointed to by other pointers and cannot be considered free (Figure 10.2[b]).

Where the programmer is allowed an explicit *free* or *erase* statement, reference counts also provide protection. A *free* statement decrements the reference count of the structure by 1. Only if the count then is zero is the structure actually returned to the free-space list. A nonzero reference count indicates that the structure is still accessible and the *free* command should be ignored.

The most important difficulty associated with reference counts is the cost of maintaining them. Reference-count testing, incrementing, and decrementing occur continuously throughout execution often causing a substantial decrease in execution efficiency. Consider, for example, the simple assignment $P := Q$, where P and Q are both pointer variables. Without reference counts, it suffices to simply copy the pointer in Q into P. With reference counts, we must do the following:

1. Access the element pointed to by P and decrement its reference count by 1.
2. Test the resulting count; if zero, return the element to the free-space list.
3. Copy the l-value stored in Q into P.
4. Access the element pointed to by Q and increment its reference count by 1.

The total cost of the assignment operation has been increased substantially. Any similar operation that may create or destroy pointers must also modify reference counts. In addition, there is the cost of the extra storage for the reference counts. Where elements are only one or two locations in length to begin with, storage of reference counts may substantially reduce the storage available for data. However, this technique is popular with parallel processing systems because the cost of maintaining the reference counts is spread among the users of the data, whereas in the following garbage-collection model, retrieving data becomes quite expensive.

Garbage collection. Returning to the basic problems of garbage and dangling references, we may readily agree that dangling references are potentially far more damaging than garbage. Garbage accumulation causes a drain on the amount of usable storage, but dangling references may lead to complete chaos because of random modification of storage in use. Of course, the two problems are related: Dangling references result when storage is freed too soon, and garbage when storage is not freed until too late. Where it is not feasible or too costly to avoid both problems simultaneously through a mechanism such as reference counts, garbage generation is clearly preferred to avoid dangling references. It is better not to recover storage at all than to recover it too soon.

The basic philosophy behind garbage collection is simply to allow garbage to be generated to avoid dangling references. When the free-space list is entirely exhausted and more storage is needed, the computation is suspended temporarily and an extraordinary procedure instituted—a *garbage collection*—which identifies garbage elements in the heap and returns them to the free-space list. The original computation is then resumed, and garbage again accumulates until the free-space list is exhausted, at which time another garbage collection is initiated, and so on.

Because garbage collection is done only rarely (when the free-space list is exhausted), it is allowable for the procedure to be fairly costly. Two stages are involved:

Mark. In the first stage, each element in the heap that is active (i.e., that is part of an accessible data structure) must be marked. Each element must contain a *garbage-collection bit* set initially to on. The marking algorithm sets the garbage-collection bit of each active element off.

Sweep. Once the marking algorithm has marked active elements, all those remaining whose garbage-collection bit is on are garbage and may be returned to the free-space list. A simple sequential scan of the heap is sufficient. The garbage-collection bit of each element is checked as it is encountered in the scan. If off, the element is passed over; if on, the element is linked into the free-space list. All garbage-collection bits are reset to on during the scan (to prepare for a later garbage collection).

The marking part of garbage collection is the most difficult. Because the free-space list is exhausted when garbage collection is initiated, each element in the heap is either active (i.e., still in use) or garbage. Unfortunately, inspection of an element cannot indicate its status because there is nothing intrinsic to a garbage element to indicate that it is no longer accessible from another active element. Moreover, the presence of a pointer to an element from another heap element does not necessarily indicate that the element pointed to is active; it may be that both elements are garbage. Thus, a simple scan of the heap that looks for pointers and marks the elements pointed to as active does not suffice.

When is a heap element active? Clearly, an element is active if there is a pointer to it from *outside the heap* or from another *active* heap element. If it is possible to identify all such outside pointers and mark the appropriate heap elements, then an iterative marking process may be initiated that searches these active elements for pointers to other unmarked elements. These new elements are then marked and searched for other pointers, and so on. A fairly disciplined use of pointers is necessary because three critical assumptions underlie this marking process:

1. Any active element must be reachable by a chain of pointers beginning outside the heap.
2. It must be possible to identify every pointer outside the heap that points to an element inside the heap.
3. It must be possible to identify within any active heap element the fields that contain pointers to other heap elements.

LISP satisfies these three assumptions, which permits garbage collection on LISP data. However, if any of these assumptions are unsatisfied, then the marking process will fail to mark some active elements. For example, in C, Assumptions 2 and 3 may not necessarily be true. If garbage collection were used in C, the result might be recovery of active elements and thus the generation of dangling references.

EXAMPLE 10.1. LISP Storage allocation.

The relationship between the LISP heap and the LISP stack is demonstrated by Figure 5.9. In this figure it is assumed that:

- The heap storage contains 15 items of which 9 are currently on the $free$ list [Figure 5.9(a)].
- The following two definitions have been entered by the user:

```
(defun f1(x y z) (cons x (f2 y z)))
(defun f2(v w) (cons v w))
```

The execution of the expression (f1 'a '(b c) '(d e)) proceeds as follows:

1. $f1$ is invoked and arguments x, y, and z are added to the stack using the 9 available heap entries from the $free$ list [Figure 5.9(b)].
2. $f2$ is invoked with pointers to its arguments v and w [Figure 5.9(c)].
3. The $free$ list is empty. The garbage collector first marks the items pointed to from the stack and then in a second pass puts all remaining items onto the $free$ list [Figure 5.9(d)].
4. The value for $f2$ is computed and put on stack [Figure 5.9(e)].
5. The value for $f1$ is computed and put on stack [Figure 5.9(f)]. The LISP system would automatically display this result to the user.
6. All items in the computation are now garbage. When the $free$ list is next empty, they will be reclaimed by the next garbage collection.

The manner in which these assumptions are satisfied in a typical LISP implementation is instructive. First, each heap element is formatted identically, usually with two pointer fields and a set of extra bits for system data (including a garbage-collection bit). Because each heap element contains exactly two pointers, and these pointers are always in the same positions within the element, Assumption 3 is satisfied. Second, there is only a small set of *system data structures* that may contain pointers into the heap. Marking starting from these system data structures is guaranteed to allow identification of all external pointers into the heap, as required by Assumption 2. Finally, it is impossible to reach a heap element other than through a chain of pointers beginning outside the heap. For example, a pointer to a heap element cannot be computed by addition of a constant to another pointer. Thus, Assumption 1 is satisfied. Example 10.1 shows how the LISP stack, heap, and garbage collection all interact during program execution.

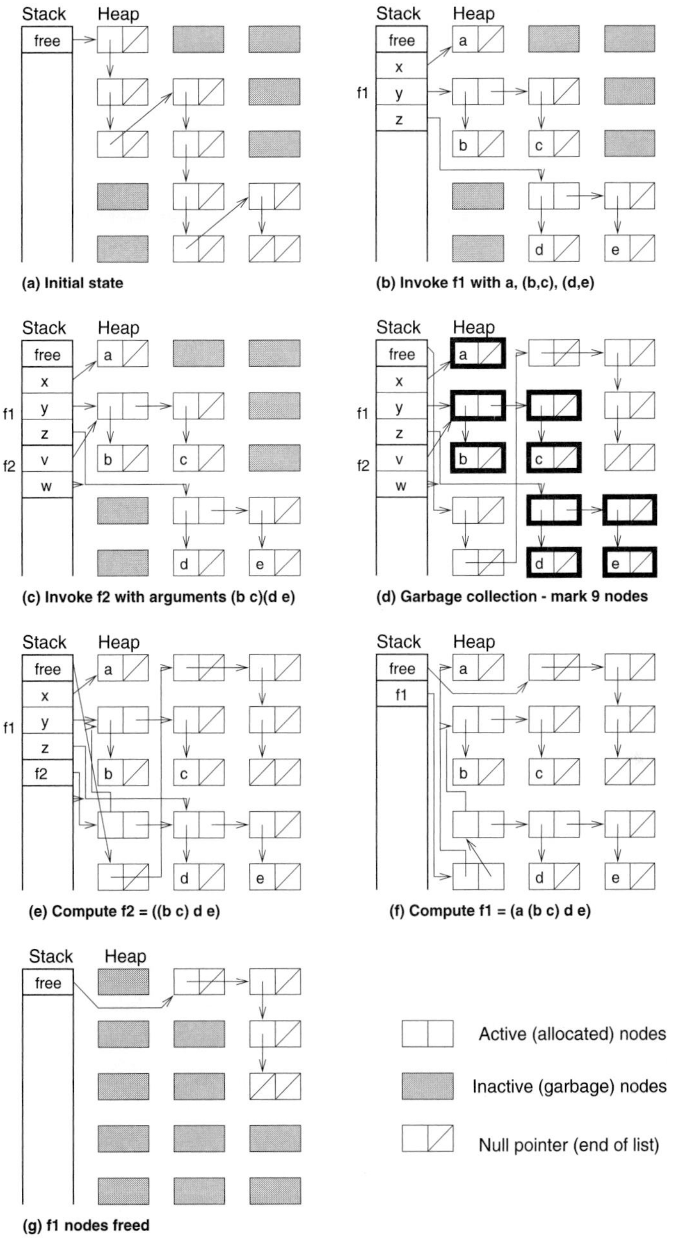

Figure 10.3. LISP heap and stack storage allocation.

10.4.3 Variable-Size Elements

Heap storage management—where the programmer controls the allocation and recovery of variable-size elements—is more difficult than with fixed-size elements, although many of the same concepts apply. Variable-size elements arise in many situations. For example, if space is being used for programmer-defined data structures stored sequentially, such as arrays, then variable-size blocks of space are required or activation records for tasks might be allocated in a heap in sequential blocks of varying sizes.

The major difficulties with variable-size elements concern reuse of recovered space. Even if we recover 2 five-word blocks of space in the heap, it may be impossible to satisfy a later request for a six-word block. This problem did not arise in the simpler case of fixed-size blocks; recovered space could always be immediately reused.

Initial Allocation and Reuse

With fixed-size elements, it was appropriate to split the heap immediately into a set of elements and then base initial allocation on a free-space list containing these elements. Such a technique is not acceptable with variable-size elements. Instead we wish to maintain free space in blocks of as large a size as possible. Initially then we consider the heap as simply one large block of free storage. A *heap pointer* is appropriate for initial allocation. When a block of N words is requested, the heap pointer is advanced by N and the original heap pointer value returned as a pointer to the newly allocated element. As storage is freed behind the advancing heap pointer, it may be collected into a free-space list.

Eventually the heap pointer reaches the end of the heap block. Some of the free space back in the heap must now be reused. Two possibilities for reuse present themselves because of the variable size of the elements:

1. Use the free-space list for allocation, searching the list for an appropriate-size block and returning any leftover space to the free list after the allocation.

2. Compact the free space by moving all the active elements to one end of the heap, leaving the free space as a single block at the end and resetting the heap pointer to the beginning of this block.

Let us look at these two possibilities in turn.

Reuse Directly from a Free-Space List

The simplest approach, when a request for an N-word element is received, is to scan the free-space list for a block of N or more words. A block of N words can be allocated directly. A block of more than N words must be split into two blocks: an N-word block, which is immediately allocated, and the remainder block, which is returned to the free-space list. A number of particular techniques for managing allocation directly from such a free-space list are used:

1. *First-fit method.* When an N-word block is needed, the free-space list is scanned for the *first* block of N or more words, which is then split into an N-word block, and the remainder, which is returned to the free-space list.

2. *Best-fit method.* When an N-word block is needed, the free-space list is scanned for the block with the *minimum* number of words greater than or equal to N. This block is allocated as a unit if it has exactly N words or is split and the remainder returned to the free-space list.

By keeping elements in the free-space list in size order, it makes allocation fairly efficient. You only have to scan the list until you find the appropriate size needed. However, there is a corresponding cost of adding entries into the free-space list by having to search the list looking for the appropriate place to add the new entry.

Recovery with Variable-Size Blocks

Before considering the memory compaction problem, let us look at techniques for recovery where variable-size blocks are involved. Relatively little is different here from the case of fixed-size blocks. Explicit return of freed space to a free-space list is the simplest technique, but the problems of garbage and dangling references are again present. Reference counts may be used in the ordinary manner.

Garbage collection is also a feasible technique. Some additional problems arise with variable-size blocks, however. Garbage collection proceeds as before, with a marking phase followed by a collecting phase. Marking must be based on the same pointer-chain-following techniques. The difficulty now is in collecting. Before, we collected by a simple sequential scan of memory, testing each element's garbage-collection bit. If the bit was on, the element was returned to the free-space list; if off, it was still active and was passed over. We should like to use the same scheme with variable-size elements, but now there is a problem in determining the boundaries between elements. Where does one element end and the next begin? Without this information, the garbage cannot be collected.

The simplest solution is to maintain along with the garbage-collection bit in the first word of each block, active or not, an integer *length indicator* specifying the length of the block. With the explicit length indicators present, a sequential scan of memory is again possible, looking only at the first word of each block. During this scan, adjacent free blocks may also be compacted into single blocks before being returned to the free-space list, thus eliminating the partial-compaction problem discussed later.

Garbage collection may also be effectively combined with full compaction to eliminate the need for a free-space list altogether. Only a simple heap pointer is needed in this case.

Compaction and the Memory Fragmentation Problem

The problem that any heap storage management system using variable-size elements faces is that of memory *fragmentation.* One begins with a single large block of free space. As computation proceeds, this block is progressively fragmented into smaller pieces through allocation, recovery, and reuse. If only the simple first-fit or best-fit allocation technique is used, it is apparent that free-space blocks continue to split into ever smaller pieces. Ultimately one reaches a point where a storage allocator cannot honor a request for a block of N words because no sufficiently large block exists, although the free-space list contains in total far more than N words. Without some compaction of free blocks into larger blocks, execution will be halted by a lack of free storage faster than necessary.

Depending on whether active blocks within the heap may be shifted in position, one of two approaches to compaction is possible:

1. *Partial compaction.* If active blocks *cannot* be shifted (or if it is too expensive to do so), then only adjacent free blocks on the free-space list may be compacted.

2. *Full compaction.* If active blocks *can* be shifted, then all active blocks may be shifted to one end of the heap, leaving all free space at the other in a contiguous block. Full compaction requires that when an active block is shifted, all pointers to that block be modified to point to the new location.

10.5 SUGGESTIONS FOR FURTHER READING

Most texts on compiler construction treat stack and static storage allocation strategies (see the references for chapter 3). Techniques for heap storage management have been widely studied. For example, see [SHAFFER 1996]. [COHEN 1981] gave a compact survey of garbage-collection methods. [MULKERS et al. 1994] described a method to perform compile-time analysis of a program to avoid dynamic garbage collection at run time.

Operating systems also provide storage-management facilities that often overlap the facilities provided by programming languages. *Virtual memory systems* are now commonly provided by many operating systems to provide storage allocation in fixed-size *pages* or variable-size *segments.* These facilities may support but usually do not supplant heap storage management provided by the language implementation. Discussion of storage management by the operating system is a topic in most texts on operating systems.

10.6 PROBLEMS

1. Analyze the storage-management techniques used in a language implementation available to you. Consider the various elements requiring storage mentioned

in Section 10.1. Are there other major run-time structures requiring storage besides those mentioned in Section 10.1?

2. An alternative garbage-collection strategy is to have two storage areas. During the first-pass *marking phase*, copy each referenced object to the head of the other storage area. In that way, once all active nodes are marked, garbage collection is complete. Now allocate from the second storage area. When this fills, compact the storage back into the first area. Compare this algorithm to the two-pass mark-sweep algorithm given on page 426.

3. Analyze the primitive operations used in a language with which you are familiar. Which operations require storage to be allocated or freed? Is the size of the storage block always the same or are blocks of variable size required? Is storage allocated and freed only on subprogram entry and exit or at unpredictable points during execution? What does the overall pattern of storage allocation and freeing suggest about the storage management structures used in the language implementation? Can you prove that a heap of fixed- or variable-size blocks is required? Can you prove that only a central stack is sufficient?

4. As Figure 9.3(b) illustrates, most Pascal implementations use a single large block of storage for both the central stack and the heap. The stack and heap grow toward each other from opposite ends of the storage block during execution, allocating storage from the block of free space between. Suppose the stack and heap meet because the free space is entirely used up. Explain the options available to the implementor if *(a)* the next request is for a new block from the stack, or *(b)* the next request is for a new block from the heap.

5. One of the striking features of a garbage collection as a method of storage recovery is that its cost is *inversely proportional* to the amount of storage recovered (i.e., the less storage recovered, the more it costs to perform a garbage collection).

(a) Explain why this is so.

(b) When a program is just about to run out of storage altogether, it often performs a series of lengthy and costly garbage collections (that recover very little storage) before it terminates altogether. Give a method for avoiding repeated useless garbage collections of this sort.

6. In an early list-processing extension to FORTRAN, each list has a special header (containing a reference count). When a list is freed, instead of returning all the list elements to the head of the free-space list, only the list header is returned, and it is placed at the *end* of the free-space list (using a special pointer to the end of the free-space list). Thus, the cost of returning a list to free space is minimal. The list elements are returned to the free-space list only when the header of the list reaches the top of the free-space list. What is the advantage of this technique for shifting the cost of freeing the list elements from the time of *recovery* of the list to the time of *reuse* of the storage?

7. *Full-word* data items such as numbers present problems in garbage collection. Ordinarily the data take up the entire heap element, with no extra bit available for garbage-collection marking. Usually in such cases, all such full-word elements are placed in a special section of the heap and all the garbage-collection bits for these full-word elements are placed in a special packed array (a *bit vector*) outside the heap. Assuming that the full-word data items are numbers (and thus contain no pointers to other heap elements), design a garbage-collection algorithm that allows the possibility of pointers to full-word items in the heap. The algorithm should include marking and collecting. Maintain a separate free-space list for the full-word portion of the heap.

8. The text states that, in parallel processing applications, reference counts are the preferred method for garbage collection of dynamic storage. Why would a mark-sweep algorithm be ineffective in that environment?

9. Give an algorithm for the *collection* of marked blocks during garbage collection in a heap with variable-size elements. Assume that the first word of each block contains a garbage-collection bit and a length indicator. Compact all adjacent blocks during the collection.

10. Design a storage-management system for a heap B of variable-size blocks under the following assumptions:

(1) B is used only to store arrays of real numbers (one word per number). Arrays always have at least two elements.

(2) Each array block is accessible only through a single external pointer stored in the array descriptor. All array descriptors are stored in a Block A separate from Heap B.

(3) Requests for blocks to be allocated from the heap occur at random (and frequently) during execution.

(4) Blocks are explicitly returned to free status when arrays are destroyed. This also occurs randomly and frequently during execution.

(5) Permanent loss of storage through memory fragmentation cannot be tolerated. (Note that a one-word free block can never be reused.)

These assumptions are basically the ones behind APL data storage. Your design should specify: *(1)* The *initial organization* of the heap block B, together with any special external structures needed for storage management (e.g., free-space list heads), *(2)* The *storage-allocation* mechanism, given a request for a block of N words from B, *(3)* The *storage-recovery* mechanism, given a call on the storage manager with the address of a block of M words to be freed, and *(4)* The *compaction* mechanism, if any, including a specification of how it works and when it is invoked.

11. Implementations of Pascal have handled the *dispose* operation in various ways.

The following have been some of the strategies employed:

(a) Have *dispose*(*P*), when executed, do nothing except assign *nil* as the value of pointer variable *P*. Implement heap storage management using a single pointer to the current top (first free location) in the heap. Advance the pointer to allocate storage when *new* is called. Never retreat the pointer.

(b) Implement heap storage management as in part *(a)*, using a single pointer that is advanced by *new*, but have *dispose* both assign *nil* to its pointer parameter *P* and also move the heap top pointer back to the position below the data object to which *P* points so that storage for *P* is recovered and returned to the heap. [*Hint*: Consider the sequence *new*(*P*); *new*(*Q*); *dispose*(*P*);.]

(c) Implement the heap using a free-space list for variable size blocks of storage, as described in Section 10.4. Use a first-fit or best-fit allocation strategy for storage requested by *new*. Implement *dispose* so that it sets its pointer parameter *P* to *nil* and returns the block of storage to which *P* points to the free-space list.

Discuss the problems of garbage, dangling references, and fragmentation that result with each of these possible implementations of *new* and *dispose*.

12. The **this** pointer is useful for creating linked lists. Consider the following **class** definition:

```
class LinkedList
    {public: AddToList(LinkedList *X) // Add X to list here
    private: LinkedList *PreviousListItem, *NextListItem;};
```

Develop the code for *AddToList* that inserts the argument after the current location (**this** pointer) in the list, as in

```
LinkedList A[10];
int i, j;
...
// Insert A[j] after A[i]
A[i].AddToList(&A[j])
```

Chapter 11

Distributed Processing

Computing has evolved from a solitary activity on a single machine in the 1950s and 1960s into a federation of cooperating activities that often span the globe. Client–server systems, local area networks, and the World Wide Web (WWW) are all examples where a set of machines in different locations need to communicate to process relevant information. The basic problem these are all trying to solve is that a single machine is not large or fast enough to solve our computing problems, which leads to the need for several machines to work cooperatively to solve a problem. In this chapter we discuss the evolution of programming language design that has allowed such developments to proceed.

11.1 VARIATIONS ON SUBPROGRAM CONTROL

In this section, we discuss variations on subprogram design. The **call-return** procedure activation (from Section 9.1) with static and dynamic linkage to data objects was based on scope rules, which allow us to implement many current programming languages. However, to provide for additional features in our subprogram structure, such as coroutines, exceptions, and tasks, we consider variations to this basic mechanism.

First, recall that the subroutine linkage described in Section 9.1 was based on five assumptions:

1. Subprograms cannot be recursive.
2. Explicit **call** statements are required.
3. Subprograms must execute completely at each call.
4. Control must be transferred immediately at the point of call.
5. There must be a single execution sequence.

We already looked at the first assumption—recursion. Let us change the other assumptions and investigate the form of subroutine mechanism that results.

11.1.1 Exceptions and Exception Handlers

During execution of a program, events or conditions often occur that might be considered exceptional. Rather than continue with normal program execution, a subprogram needs to be called to perform some special processing, including being able to handle the following situations:

Error conditions to process an error such as an arithmetic operation overflow or reference to an array element with a subscript out of bounds.

Unpredictable conditions that arise during normal program execution such as the production of special output headings at the end of a printer page or an end-of-file indicator on an input file.

Tracing and monitoring during program testing such as printing trace output during program testing when the value of a variable changes.

Although it is usually possible to insert an explicit test in the program to test for these exceptional conditions, such extra statements can obscure the program's basic structure. It is simpler to relax the requirement that subprograms must be invoked by explicit calls and provide a way that a subprogram may be invoked when a particular condition or event occurs. Such a condition or event is usually termed an *exception* or a *signal,* and the subprogram that performs the special processing is termed an *exception handler.* The action of noticing the exception, interrupting program execution, and transferring control to the exception handler is called *raising the exception.* In Ada, there is a class of exceptions called *checks* or conditions that require code to be executed at run time. For example, $Index\_Check$ is a $Constraint\_Error$ exception that is raised when an array bound is invalid.

Exception Handlers

Because an exception handler is invoked without an explicit call, it ordinarily does not require a name or parameters. The definition of an exception handler typically contains only

1. A set of declarations of local variables (if any), and
2. A sequence of executable statements.

To provide the connection between exceptions and their handlers, each class of exceptions is given a name. Some exceptions may be predefined in the language (e.g., $Constraint\_Error$, $Program\_Error$, $Storage\_Error$ or $Numeric\_Error$ in Ada). Others may be programmer-defined (e.g., the program may include a declaration "Underflow: **exception**" or "Overflow: **exception**"). Each exception handler is then paired with the name (or names) of the exception(s) that it is to handle. Usually all the exception handlers are grouped at the beginning or end of the larger program or subprogram where the exception might occur. The Ada structure is typical:

```
procedure Sub is
    Bad_Data_Value: exception;
            -other declarations for Sub
begin
            -statements for normal processing in Sub
exception
    when Bad_Data_Value =>
        -handler for bad data values
    when Constraint_Error =>
        -handler for predefined exception Constraint_Error
    when others =>
        -handler for all other exceptions
end;
```

Raising an exception. An exception may be raised by a language-defined primitive operation (e.g., an addition or multiplication operation might raise the exception Constraint_Error). Alternatively, an exception may be raised explicitly by the programmer using a statement provided for that purpose, such as the Ada statement

```
raise Bad_Data_Value;
```

which might be executed in a subprogram after determining that a particular variable or input file contained an improper value.

In a subprogram, if an explicit **raise** statement is used and the subprogram contains a handler for the exception raised, as, for example, when the statement

```
if X = 0 then raise Bad_Data_Value end if;
```

appears within the body of the procedure *Sub*, then the **raise** statement transfers control to the associated handler, which then exits the procedure. One of the major uses for **goto** statements in languages without explicit exception-handling features is to provide transfers to exception-handling code, as discussed in Section 8.3.2.

Data may be passed to the exception handler, as demonstrated by the following ML example. Normal action in ML is to terminate the procedure. However, if a handler is provided, the handler is executed and control returns to the point of the error, as in

```
exception BadDenominator of int;
fun InnerDivide(a:int,b:int):real=
    if b=0 then raise BadDenominator(b)
        else real(a)/real(b);
fun Divide(a,b)= InnerDivide(a,b) handle
    BadDenominator(b) => (print(b); "is bad denominator, 0 used"; 0.0);
```

In this case, the program invokes the function *Divide*, which calls the function *InnerDivide*. *InnerDivide* invokes the execution of the actual divide operation to be handled by the BadDenominator exception. In this case, the handler prints a message and returns the real value 0.0 for the *Divide* function and execution continues. (Note that no types need be specified for the arguments and returned value from function *Divide*. ML tries to infer the correct type and, in this case, can do so from the explicit types given for *InnerDivide*.)

Exceptions are processed in C++ and Java (although not every C++ translator has implemented exceptions) via the **try** clause. C++ raises an exception by throwing the exception, and the exception is handled by catching the exception. The syntax is similar to ML, although, unlike ML, execution halts after handling an exception:

```
try {
    statement1;
    statement2;
    ...
    if BadCondition { throw ExceptionName};
        }
catch ExceptionName { // Do something for exception
        } // End of Exception
    }
```

Propagating an exception. Often in constructing a program, the place at which an exception occurs is not the best place to handle it. For example, one subprogram may have the function of reading data values from a file and passing them to a nest of subprograms to be processed. Suppose that several different types of bad data values may be found on the file and each subprogram tests for a different class of such errors, but the response in all cases is the same: Print an error message and advance the file past the bad data. In this case, the handler might properly be a part of the subprogram that reads the file, and each subprogram might properly raise the exception *Bad_Data_Value*. When an exception is handled in a subprogram other than the subprogram in which it is raised, the exception is said to be *propagated* from the point at which it is raised to the point at which it is handled.

The rule for determining which handler handles a particular exception is usually defined in terms of the *dynamic chain* of subprogram activations leading to the subprogram that raises the exception. When an exception P is raised in Subprogram C; then P is handled by a handler defined in C if there is one. If there is none, then C terminates. If Subprogram B called C, then the exception is propagated to B and raised again at the point in B where B called C. If B provides no handler for P, then B is terminated, the exception propagates to B's caller, and so on. If no subprogram or the main program provides a handler, then the entire program is terminated and a standard language-defined handler is invoked. For example, in the previous ML example, the function *InnerDivide* raised the *Bad_Denominator* exception, which was propagated to the handler in the *Divide* function, which then returned a programmer-defined value as a result of handling that exception.

One important effect of this rule for propagating exceptions is that it allows a subprogram to remain as a programmer-defined abstract operation even in processing exceptions. A primitive operation or a subprogram may suddenly interrupt its normal processing and raise an exception. To the caller, the effect of a subprogram's raising an exception is the same as a primitive operation's raising an exception if the subprogram does not handle the exception. If the exception is handled within the subprogram, then the subprogram returns in the normal way, and the caller is never aware that an exception has been raised.

After an exception is handled. After a handler completes the processing of an exception, there is a sticky question as to where control is to be transferred because there was no explicit call of the handler. Should control return to the point where the exception was raised (which may be several levels of subprogram distant)? Should control return to the statement in the subprogram containing the handler where the exception was raised after being propagated? Should the subprogram containing the handler be terminated, but terminated normally, so it appears to its caller as if nothing had happened? The latter solution is that adopted in Ada; ML provides several options, and other languages have chosen other alternatives.

Implementation

Exceptions come from two sources: (1) conditions detected by the virtual machine, and (2) conditions generated by the semantics of the programming language. In the former case, operating system exceptions may be raised directly by hardware interrupts or traps, such as arithmetic overflow, or they may be raised in support software, such as end-of-file condition. In C, the programmer has direct access to these signals processed by the operating system. The programmer may *enable* an interrupt (e.g., the *sigaction* function in Unix, which specifies a procedure that gets invoked when the given signal is raised).

The programming language may provide for additional exceptions by having the language translator insert additional instructions into the executable code. For example, to detect the exception Index_Check caused by an array subscript that was too large or too small, the translator inserts an explicit sequence of instructions at each reference to an array, such as $A[I, J]$, to determine whether the values of I and J are within the declared bounds. Thus, unless the hardware or operating system provides the exception checking, checking for an exception requires some software simulation. Often the cost of this software checking, in both code storage and execution time, is large. For example, it may take longer to perform the subscript bounds check on $A[I, J]$ than it does to access the element of the array. Because of this extra cost, most languages provide a means to turn off checking for exceptions in parts of the program where the programmer determines it is safe to do so [e.g., **pragma** *Supress*(*Index_Check*) in Ada].

Once the exception is raised, transfer of control to a handler in the same program is usually implemented by a direct jump to the start of the handler code. Propagation of exceptions back up the dynamic chain of subprogram calls can make use of the dynamic chain formed by the return points of the subprogram activation records in the central stack as discussed previously. In proceeding up the dynamic chain, each subprogram activation must be terminated using a special form of **return** instruction to both return control to the caller and raise the exception in the caller again. The sequence of returns continues up the dynamic chain until a subprogram is reached that has a handler for the exception raised.

Once the appropriate handler is found, it is invoked as in an ordinary subprogram call. When the handler terminates, however, it may also terminate the subprogram that contains it, thus leading to two normal subprogram returns, one immediately after the other. Once the dynamic chain has been unwound in this way to a final normal return to a subprogram, that subprogram continues its execution in the usual manner.

Assertions

Related to exceptions is the concept of an assertion. An assertion is simply a statement implying a relation among data objects in a program, as in the C++ statement:

```
#include < assert.h >
...
assert (x>y+1);
```

The predefined macro in C++ generates:

```
if (x>y+1) { /* Print error message */ }
```

It is an effective way to test for errors without complex coding cluttering up the design of the source program. After the program is developed, the **assert** can remain as documentation within the program (see Section 4.2.4), and the macro can be altered to generate no program statements and remain simply as a comment.

11.1.2 Coroutines

Suppose that we drop Restriction 3 in Section 11.1 to allow subprograms to return to their calling program before completion of execution. Such subprograms are termed *coroutines*. When a coroutine receives control from another subprogram, it executes partially and then is suspended when it returns control. At a later point, the calling program may *resume* execution of the coroutine from the point at which execution was previously suspended.

Note the symmetry that has now been introduced into the calling and called program structure. If A calls Subprogram B as a coroutine, B executes awhile

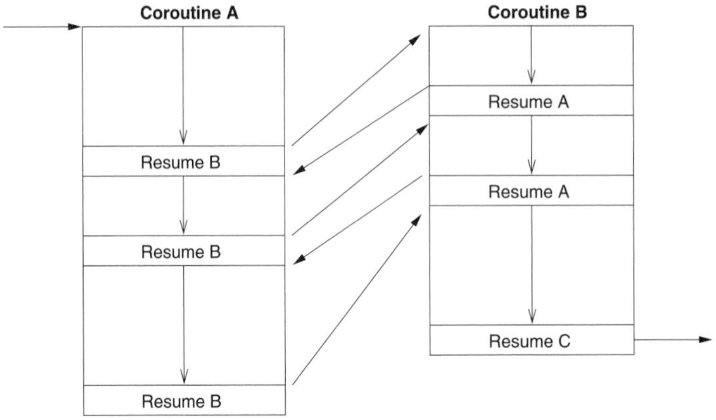

Figure 11.1. Control transfer between coroutines.

and returns control to A, just as any ordinary subprogram would do. When A again passes control to B via a **resume** B, B again executes awhile and returns control to A, just as an ordinary subprogram. Thus, to A, B appears as an ordinary subprogram. However, the situation is similar when viewed from Subprogram B. B, in the middle of execution, *resumes* execution of A. A executes awhile and returns control to B. B continues execution awhile and returns control to A. A executes awhile and returns control to B. From Subprogram B, A appears much like an ordinary subprogram. The name *coroutine* derives from this symmetry. Rather than having a parent–child or caller–callee relationship between the two subprograms, the two programs appear more as equals—two subprograms swapping control back and forth as each executes, with neither clearly controlling the other (Figure 11.1).

Coroutines are not currently a common control structure in programming languages outside of discrete simulation languages. (See Section 11.1.3.) However, they provide a control structure in many algorithms that is more natural than the ordinary subprogram hierarchy. Moreover, the simple coroutine structure may be readily simulated in many languages using the **goto** statement and a *resume point* variable specifying the label of the statement at which execution is to resume.

Implementation. The **resume** instruction that transfers control between coroutines specifies the resumption of some particular activation of the coroutine. If there are multiple recursive activations of a coroutine B, then the statement **resume** B has no clear meaning. For this reason, it is simplest to think of coroutines in a context where at most one activation of a given coroutine exists at a time. This restriction allows us to use an implementation for coroutines similar to that used for the simple call-return structure in Section 8.3.2. A single activation record is allocated storage statically at the beginning of execution as an extension of the code segment for the coroutine. A single location, now called the *resume point,* is reserved in the activation record to save the old *ip* value of the CIP when a **resume** instruction transfers control to another coroutine. However, unlike the return point in a simple subprogram, this resume point location in a coroutine B is used to store the *ip* value *for B itself.* Execution of a **resume** B instruction in coroutine A then involves two steps:

1. The current value of the CIP is saved in the resume point location of the activation record for A.

2. The *ip* value in the resume point location of B is fetched from B's activation record and assigned to the CIP to effect the transfer of control to the proper instruction in B.

Because there is no explicit return instruction, B does not need to know that A gave it control.

Control structures in which subprograms may be invoked either as coroutines or ordinary subprograms and in which coroutines may be recursive (i.e., may have multiple simultaneous activations) require more complex implementations.

11.1.3 Scheduled Subprograms

The concept of *subprogram scheduling* results from relaxation of the assumption that execution of a subprogram should always be initiated immediately on its call. One may think of an ordinary subprogram call statement as specifying that the called subprogram is to be scheduled for execution immediately, without completing execution of the calling program. Completion of execution of the calling program is rescheduled to occur immediately on termination of the subprogram. The exception-handling control structure may also be viewed as a means of subprogram scheduling. The exception handler executes whenever a particular exception is raised.

Generalizing further, other subprogram scheduling techniques are possible:

1. Schedule subprograms to be executed before or after other subprograms, as, for example: **call** B **after** A, which would schedule execution of Subprogram B after execution of Subprogram A is completed.

2. Schedule subprograms to be executed when an arbitrary Boolean expression becomes true, as, for example,

   $$\textbf{call } \mathrm{B} \textbf{ when } X = 5 \textbf{ and } Z > 0$$

   Such scheduling provides a sort of generalized exception-handling feature; B is called whenever the values of Z and X are changed to satisfy the given conditions.

3. Schedule subprograms on the basis of a simulated *time scale,* as, for example,

   $$\textbf{call } \mathrm{B} \textbf{ at } \mathrm{time} = 25 \textbf{ or call } \mathrm{B} \textbf{ at } \mathrm{time} = \mathrm{CurrentTime} + 10$$

Such scheduling allows a general interleaving of subprogram calls scheduled from different sources.

4. Schedule subprograms according to a priority designation, as, for example,

   call B **with priority** 7

   which would activate B when no other subprogram with higher priority has been scheduled.

Generalized subprogram scheduling is a feature of programming languages designed for discrete system simulation, such as GPSS, SIMSCRIPT, and SIMULA, although the concepts have wide applicability. Each of the prior scheduling techniques appears in at least one of the simulation languages mentioned. The most important technique in system simulation is the third in the list: scheduling based on a simulated time scale. We emphasize this technique in our discussion.

When we speak of subprogram scheduling, we mean scheduling of subprogram *activations* because this scheduling is a run-time activity in which the same subprogram may be scheduled to be activated at many different points during execution. In generalized subprogram scheduling, the programmer no longer writes a main program. Instead, the main program is a system-defined *scheduler program* that typically maintains a list of currently scheduled subprogram activations ordered in the sequence in which they are to be executed. Statements are provided in the language through which subprogram activations may be inserted into this list during execution. The scheduler operates by calling each subprogram on the list in the indicated sequence. When execution of one subprogram terminates, execution of the next subprogram on the list is initiated. Usually provision is also made for ordinary subprogram calls, sometimes simply by allowing a subprogram to suspend its own execution and schedule immediate execution of another subprogram.

In simulation languages, the most common approach to subprogram scheduling is based on a type of generalized coroutine. Execution of a single subprogram activation proceeds in a series of *active* and *passive* phases. During an active phase, the subprogram has control and is being executed; in a passive phase, the subprogram has transferred control elsewhere and is awaiting a resume call. However, rather than each coroutine directly transferring control to another coroutine when it switches from active to passive, control is returned to the scheduler, which then transfers control to the next subprogram on its list of scheduled activations. This transfer of control may take the form of a resume call if the subprogram is already partially executed or an entirely new activation of the subprogram may be initiated.

The coroutine scheduling concept is particularly direct using a simulated time scale. Assume that each active phase of execution of a subprogram may be scheduled to occur at any point on an integer time scale beginning at time $T = 0$. T is a simple integer variable that always contains the value of the current time on the simulated scale. Execution of an active phase of a subprogram always occurs instantaneously on this simulated time scale (i.e., the value of T does not change during execution of an active phase of a subprogram). When a subprogram completes an active phase and returns control to the scheduler, the scheduler updates the value of T to that at which the next subprogram on the list of scheduled subprograms is to be activated and transfers control to that subprogram. The newly activated routine partially executes and returns control to the scheduler, which again updates T and activates the next routine on the list.

11.2 Parallel Programming

The final restriction from Section 9.1 to consider is the restriction to a single execution sequence in executing a program. More generally, several subprograms might be executing *simultaneously*. Where there is a single execution sequence, the program is termed a *sequential program* because execution of its subprograms proceeds in a predefined sequence. In the more general case, the program is termed a *concurrent* or *parallel* program. Each subprogram that can execute concurrently with other subprograms is called a *task* (or sometimes a *process*).

In the control sequences discussed so far, we have assumed that there is always a predetermined thread of control describing the execution of a program. This is very much in line with the von Neumann architecture we have been assuming for the actual computer hardware. However, parallel designs play an important role in programming.

Computer systems capable of executing several programs concurrently are now quite common. A *multiprocessor* system has several central processing units (CPU) sharing a common memory. A *distributed* or *parallel* computer system has several computers (possibly hundreds), each with its own memory and CPU, connected with communication links into a network in which each can communicate with the others. In such systems, many tasks may execute concurrently.

Even on a single computer, it is often useful to design a program so that it is composed of many separate tasks that run concurrently on the *virtual* computer, although on the actual computer only one can be executing at any one instance. The illusion of concurrent execution on a single processor is obtained by interleaving execution of the separate tasks so that each executes a portion of its code, is swapped out to be replaced by another task that executes a portion of its code, and so on. Operating systems that support *multiprogramming* and *time sharing* provide this sort of concurrent execution for separate user programs. Our concern here, however, is with concurrent execution of tasks *within a single program.*

The major stumbling block is the lack of programming language constructs for building such systems. For the most part, standard languages like C are used with additional function calls to the operating system for enabling parallel tasks. However, programming language design can help.

Principles of Parallel Programming Languages

Parallel programming constructs add complexity to the language design because several processors may be accessing the same data simultaneously. To consider parallelism in programming languages, the following five concepts must be addressed:

1. *Variable definitions.* Variables may be either *mutable* or *definitional.* Mutable variables are the common variables declared in most sequential languages. Values may be assigned to the variables and changed during program execution. A definitional variable may be assigned a value only once. The virtue of such a variable is that there is no synchronization problem. Once assigned a value, any task may access the variable and obtain the correct value.

2. *Parallel composition.* Execution proceeds from one statement to the next. In addition to the sequential and conditional statements of sequential programming languages, we need to add the *parallel* statement, which causes additional *threads of control* to begin executing. The **and** statement of Section 11.2.1 and the operating system $fork$ function called from C are examples of such structures.

3. *Program structure.* Parallel programs generally follow one of the following two execution models: (a) They may be *transformational,* where the goal is to transform the input data into an appropriate output value. Parallelism is applied to speed up the process, such as multiplying a matrix rapidly by multiplying several sections of it in parallel. (b) They may be *reactive*, where the program reacts to external stimuli called *events.* Real-time and command-and-control systems are examples of reactive systems. An operating system and a transaction processing system, such as a reservation system, are typical examples of such reactive systems. They are characterized by generally having nondeterministic behavior because it is never explicit exactly when an event will occur.

4. *Communication.* Parallel programs must communicate with one another. Such communication will typically be via *shared memory* with common data objects accessed by each parallel program or via *messages* where each parallel program has its own copy of the data object and passes data values among the other parallel programs.

5. *Synchronization.* Parallel programs must be able to order the execution of its various threads of control. Although nondeterministic behavior is appropriate for many applications, in some an ordering must be imposed. For example, it is possible to design a compiler where the scanner and parser execute in parallel, but you have to make sure that the scanner has read in the next token before the parser operates on it to parse the program. The communication mechanism, described earlier will generally implement this.

In the subsections that follow, we discuss some of these issues in greater detail.

11.2.1 Concurrent Execution

The principal mechanism for installing parallel execution in a programming language is to create a construct that allows for parallel execution. The **and** statement,

$$statement_1 \ \textbf{and} \ statement_2 \ \textbf{and} \ \ldots \ \textbf{and} \ statement_n$$

performs this task and has the semantics that each of the various $statement_i$ execute in parallel; the statement following the **and** statement does not begin until all the parallel statements terminate.

Although conceptually simple, it provides the full parallel power we need for parallel execution. For example, if an operating system consists of a task to read from a terminal, a task to write to a screen, and a process to execute a user program, we could specify this operating system as

```
call ReadProcess and
call WriteProcess and
call ExecuteUserProgram;
```

Sequences for parallel execution are only part of the problem. Correct handling of data is another concern. Consider the following:

```
x:=1;
x:=2 and y := x+x; (*)
print(y);
```

Because the two statements labeled (*) may execute in parallel, we cannot predict which will terminate first. Therefore, y may be assigned the value 2 (if the assignment to y is executed first), 4 (if the assignment to x is performed first), or even 3 (if the assignment to x is made between the two accesses of x in the assignment to y). We need to coordinate data access across concurrent programs. We discuss this further in the discussion of *semaphores* in Section 11.2.5.

Implementation. There are two basic ways to implement an **and** construct. Notice that if all the parallel tasks may execute in parallel, there is no assumption made as to their order of execution. We could simply execute them in sequence. If the original **and** construct is correct, then replacing the **and** by the sequential ";" and a **while** statement would allow for correct execution. For example, the prior example could be rewritten by the compiler as

```
while MoreToDo do
    MoreToDo := false;
    call ReadProcess;
    call WriteProcess;
    call ExecuteUserProgram
end
```

If, for example, the *ReadProcess* tried to read data that were not yet ready to be processed, it could simply set *MoreToDo* to *true* and return. This loop will repeat as long as each subprogram still has not terminated.

A more direct way to implement this construct is to use the parallel execution primitives of the underlying operating system. For example, in C, the compiler could execute a *fork* function that creates two processes executing in parallel. Each process would continue to execute until it terminates. The code generated by the C compiler would look something like the following:[1]

```
fork ReadProcess;
fork WriteProcess;
fork ExecuteUserProgram;
wait /* for all 3 to terminate */
```

Facilities to support concurrent tasks are still rather rare in high-level programming languages. No widely used language provides for the **and** construct mentioned here. Only Ada provides tasks and concurrent execution, although the close association of C to the operating system allows programs in C to invoke the *fork* operating system function to create concurrent tasks.

11.2.2 Guarded Commands

A second class of constructs concerns nondeterministic execution where it cannot be determined which statement to execute next. The **and** construct is generally deterministic because only one of the parallel statements will actually execute next on a given computer. However, the concept of the **and** is parallel execution, and its implementation is often a sequential pass through each of the statements.

True nondeterminacy was proposed in the 1970s by Dijkstra with the concept of the *guarded command* as a means to simplify both program development and program verification [DIJKSTRA 1975]. So far, all of the control structures in this chapter are deterministic. That means that each part of the statement has a specific order of execution. However, there are times when nondeterminacy makes a software design easier, much like the discussion with nondeterministic finite-state automata as given in Section 3.3.2.

A nondeterministic execution is one where alternative execution paths are possible. This condition arises frequently in the execution of concurrent programs. If there are n processes ready to execute in a system, it is not always clear which one will be the next to execute. Although this is a common problem in operating system design, it is often not encountered in single program development, mostly because we have not had the tools (e.g., programming language statements) at our disposal to think in nondeterministic ways.

[1]This example is only partially correct to keep it simple. C would actually have to first invoke the *fork* function to create two processes and then *exec* to call this process.

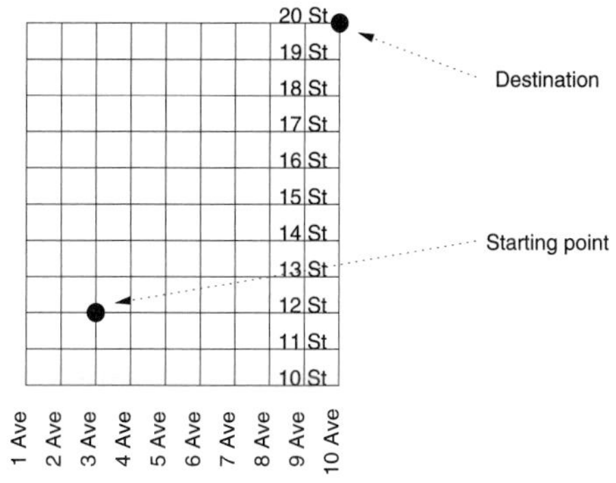

Figure 11.2. Nondeterministic travel in a city.

Consider as a simple example a city consisting of north–south running avenues and east–west running streets (Figure 11.2). If you are at Third Avenue and Twelfth Street, what is the path to get to Tenth Avenue and Twentieth Street? If told to program this in a conventional language, typically two different programs designs are possible:

Design 1	**Design 2**
Move east from 3 *to* 10 *Ave.*	*Move north from* 12 *to* 20 *St.*
Move north from 12 *to* 20 *St.*	*Move east from* 3 *to* 10 *Ave.*

However, numerous other paths are possible. If the city has interesting highlights, then you will never see the sights at Eighth Avenue and Sixteenth Street, for example. In fact, you can specify all paths for this program as

while not at destination **do arbitrarily**
  if not at 10th Ave., go east 1 **or**
  if not at 20th St., go north 1
  end

Any solution that follows this arbitrary (i.e., nondeterministic) route is a valid solution to the original problem. We soon see that Dijkstra's guarded commands are a general solution to this problem.

Guards. The basic concept is the *guard,* which is written as: $\rightarrow$. If B is a *guard* (i. e., condition) and S is a *command* (i.e., statement), then a guarded command, $B \rightarrow S$ means that statement S is enabled or ready for execution if guard B is *true*. We use guards in **guarded if** and **repetitive** statements.

Guarded if statement. If B_i is a set of conditions and S_i is a set of statements, the **guarded if** is written as

$$\textbf{if } B_1 \rightarrow S_1 \,\|\, B_2 \rightarrow S_2 \,\|\, \ldots \,\|\, B_n \rightarrow S_n \textbf{ fi}$$

which has the meaning that at least one of the guards *must* be true and the execution is that of a corresponding command.

Note that this differs from previous constructs we have studied: It differs from the standard **if-then** because the usual case does not require a guard to be true. Further, it is not the same as the LISP *cond*, where the statement to execute was the first one in the sequence with a true condition. The guarded **if** is defined with true nondeterminacy. We arbitrarily choose any S_i to execute as long as B_i is true.

Guarded repetition statement. This is the generalization to the sequential **while** statement and is similar to the **guarded if**: If B_i is a set of guards and S_i is a set of commands, the guarded **do** is written as:

$$\textbf{do } B_1 \rightarrow S_1 \parallel B_2 \rightarrow S_2 \parallel \ldots \parallel B_n \rightarrow S_n \textbf{ od}$$

Execution proceeds as follows: If some guards B_i are true, one of the corresponding S_i is executed. This process repeats as long as some guard is true. If no guard is true initially, the **do** is skipped, which is similar to the behavior of the usual **while** statement. As in the guarded **if**, nondeterminacy is introduced into the execution if more than one guard is true at the same time.

Guarded commands often make many algorithms easier to develop or understand. Consider our city-walking problem given earlier. We can specify the general solution nondeterministically as follows:

$$\begin{array}{l} \text{Ave} = 3; \quad \{\text{At } 3^{rd} \text{ Avenue}\} \\ \text{St} = 12; \quad \{\text{At } 12^{th} \text{ Street}\} \\ \textbf{do} \quad \text{Ave} < 10 \rightarrow \text{Ave} = \text{Ave} + 1 \\ \quad\quad \parallel \text{St} < 20 \rightarrow \text{St} = \text{St} + 1 \textbf{ od} \end{array}$$

All executions that start at 3×12 and end at 10×20 are valid executions of this program.

No common language has truly implemented guarded commands as defined by Dijkstra. However, the concept of nondeterministic execution does arise in the design of operating system software. The role of such guarded commands in the use of tasks and subprograms is addressed more fully in Section 11.2.4.

11.2.3 Ada Overview

History. Although originally designed for military applications, Ada is a general-purpose language applicable to solve most programming problems. It has a block structure and data type mechanism similar to Pascal, although it has extensions for real-time and distributed applications. It provides a more secure form of data encapsulation than Pascal, and the latest revision of the Ada standard increases the ability to develop objects and provide for method inheritance.

The Ada language is unique in this book because it became an international standard before there were any working translators for the language. The goal, led by the U.S. Department of Defense, was to design a language and freeze the design with a standard before there were incompatible variations. This was achieved to a limited degree in 1983, although imperfections in the language led to a 1995 revision of the standard.

In the late 1970s, there was interest by the U.S. Department of Defense (DOD) to develop a single language for use in embedded real-time systems. The Higher Order Language Working Group (HOLWG) was created to design such a language to avoid the previous chaos. One survey conducted by HOLWG listed some 500 languages used to support diverse military applications. Through a series of successively more precise specifications from 1975 to 1978 ("Strawman," "Woodenman," "Tinman," "Ironman," and finally "Steelman"), the requirements for such a language were defined. Although the initial goal was to either use or enhance an existing language (most likely Pascal, ALGOL 68, or PL/I), it was soon realized that no current language would fulfill the needs for this application domain and a new language was needed.

To short circuit the 20 years or so that would be required to fully develop a new language, a novel approach was tried. Contracts were given to several developers to design such a language, and the results of this design competition were subject to an intense industry and academic study to compress experiences about the language into a few short months. Of the 17 submitted proposals, 4 finalists were chosen. Of the 4 finalists, code-named "red," "green," "yellow," and "blue," the green language of Jean Ichbiah of France was chosen in 1979 as the winning design. Although initially called DOD-1, the name was soon changed to Ada in honor of Ada Lovelace, an early pioneer in computing and supporter of Charles Babbage, designer of an early mechanical computing engine in the 1850s.

Pascal was the starting point for the design of Ada, but the resulting language is different in many major aspects from Pascal. Most prominently, Ada is a much larger and more complex language than Pascal, and it includes several major features that have no analogue in Pascal—in particular, tasks and concurrent execution, real-time control of tasks, exception handling, and abstract data types. The language was standardized in 1983 as both a U.S. commercial standard, a U.S. military standard, and an international standard [ISO 1995].

To ensure that translators adhered to the standard, the DOD created the Ada Joint Program Office (AJPO) to oversee military uses of Ada and develop the Ada Compiler Validation Suite (ACVS)—a series of tests that an Ada translator had to pass to be considered an implementation of the language. For U.S. military applications, an ACVS validation was required for any compiler used on such a project, although for academic or commercial use of the language no such validation was required.

The use of the ACVS was another departure from the usual standardization process. Subsets or extensions to the standard were not permitted in any certified translator. Conformance was strictly defined as the contents of the language reference manual, nothing more and nothing less, although this rule was relaxed somewhat. For example, a simple processor managing the emission control system for an automobile had little use for a complex file management system. Such functions were not required in Ada compilers needed for this application domain if the target system did not have those capabilities.

The first effective Ada translators did not appear until 1986 or 1987. These new translators as well as academic experimentation with the language (faculty do not feel bound by such protocols as the ACVS) led to suggestions about revisions or extensions to the language. In 1988, the AJPO created the Ada 9X committee, in conjunction with ISO, to revise the standard. The "9X" was because the effective date could not be estimated as such work always takes longer than anticipated. 9X turned out to be 95. Aside from cleaning up problems with the 1983 standard, major changes in the new edition included better object oriented data, hierarchical libraries, and a better tasking model for processes. This chapter describes the 1983 language and indicates how the newer standard modifies these features.

Brief overview of the language. Ada is intended to support the construction of large programs by teams of programmers. An Ada program is ordinarily designed as a collection of larger software components called *packages*, each representing an abstract data type or a set of data objects shared among subprograms.

An Ada program consists of a single procedure that serves as a main program. This main program declares variables and executes statements, including calls on other subprograms. However, these data types and subprograms are often part of separately defined packages, which are simply imported from a program library as needed. The Ada program may involve a set of separate tasks that are to execute concurrently. If so, then these tasks are often directly initiated by the main program and form the top level of the program structure.

Ada provides a broad range of built-in data types, including integers, reals, enumerations, Booleans, arrays, records, character strings, and pointers. Abstraction and encapsulation of programmer-defined data types and operations are provided through the package features. The encapsulation mechanism allows the internal structure of data objects and subprograms to be made invisible so that true abstraction of both data and operations is enforced.

Sequence control within a subprogram utilizes expressions and statement-level control structures similar to those in Pascal. An extensive set of features are available for exception handling. Subprogram-level sequence control includes the ordinary subprogram call and return with recursion. In addition, exceptions may cause subprograms to be terminated. The most notable aspect of the sequence-control features of Ada, however, is the provision of tasks that may be executed concurrently and controlled using a time clock and other scheduling mechanisms.

The data-control structures of Ada utilize the static block-structure organization as in Pascal. However, the language also provides means for nonlocal references to type names, subprogram names, and other identifiers in an explicit common environment defined by a package, where often the same identifier may be used in many different packages. Each formal parameter in a subprogram is tagged as **in**, **out**, or **in out**.

The Ada virtual computer utilizes a central stack for each separate task. Each stack is used to create and delete subprogram activation records during execution of that task. Because tasks may run concurrently, they may execute subprograms independently of each other. A heap storage area is also required for programmer-constructed data objects. Because the separate tasks in an Ada program may potentially be executed by separate computers, the storage areas utilized by each task may be distributed among the memories of the various computers. The distributed nature of data storage and task execution produces special problems in Ada implementation that are not present in the other languages discussed here.

11.2.4 Tasks

The basic idea behind tasks is quite simple. Consider a subprogram A being executed in the normal fashion. If A calls Subprogram B, then ordinarily execution of A is suspended while B executes. However, if B is initiated as a *task*, then execution of A continues while B executes. The original execution sequence has now split into two parallel execution sequences. Either A or B or both may now initiate further tasks, allowing any number of parallel execution sequences to coexist.

In general, each task is considered a *dependent* of the task that initiated it. When a task is ready to terminate, it must wait until all its dependents have terminated before it may terminate. Thus, the splitting into multiple execution sequences is reversed as tasks terminate, coalescing into fewer and fewer sequences until finally only a single sequence remains. In normal circumstances, each of these top-level tasks controls a major part of the system (often now a distributed computer system); once initiated, they are expected to run forever.

Task Management

The definition of a task in a program differs little from the definition of an ordinary subprogram, except for defining how the task synchronizes and communicates with other tasks. Most of the body of a task definition contains ordinary declarations and statements concerned with the processing performed by the task while working independently of other tasks. In Ada, which is our primary example here, a task definition takes the form

```
task Name is
        - Declarations for synchronization and communication
    end;
task body Name is
        - Usual local declarations as found in any subprogram
    begin -Sequence of statements
    end;
```

Initiating execution of a task may take the form of an ordinary subprogram call. For example, in many implementations of PL/I, a task B is initiated by executing the statement

call B (*parameters*) **task**;

In Ada, the method is somewhat different. The definition of task, as given earlier, is included among the declarations of some larger program structure such as the main program. When that larger program structure is entered, all the tasks declared within it are automatically initiated. Thus, no explicit **call** statement is needed; the tasks begin execution concurrently as soon as the larger program structure is entered.

Multiple simultaneous activations of the *same* task are often required in applications. For example, consider a computer system that controls a set of user terminals. The primary task might be the program that monitors the status of all the terminals. When a user logs on at a terminal, this task, *Monitor*, initiates a new task, *Terminal*, to control the interactions with the user at that particular terminal. When the user logs off, the *Terminal* task terminates. The *Monitor* task, of course, runs continuously except in the case of a catastrophic system failure. When several users are logged on simultaneously at different terminals, several activations of the task *Terminal* are required, one for each user.

If a task is initiated using an ordinary subprogram call, as in PL/I, then repeatedly executing a **call** suffices to create multiple activations. In Ada, the task definition described earlier may be used to create only a single task activation owing to the implicit initiation of tasks. Thus, the task *Monitor* would probably be defined as before. For the task *Terminal*, multiple activations are required, and they must be created and initiated by *Monitor* as needed. In Ada, *Terminal* is defined as a *task type*:

task type Terminal **is**
    -Rest of definition in the same form as above
end;

Definition of *Terminal* as a task type allows an activation of the task to be treated as a type of data object, in the same way that an ordinary type definition is used to define a class of data objects, as described in Section 6.3. Enaction (e.g., creation and initiation) of a new task activation is then the same as a new data object using a type definition as a template. To create several activations and give them the names A, B, and C, the Ada programmer writes the declarations as ordinary variable declarations:

A: Terminal;
B, C: Terminal;

These declarations appear at the beginning of a larger program structure; on entry to this larger program the three activations of *Terminal* are created and initiated. Alternatively, a pointer variable may be defined whose value is a pointer to a *task activation*, as in

type TaskPtr **is access** Terminal;	-Defines pointer type
NewTerm: TaskPtr := **new** Terminal;	-Declares pointer variable

Variable *NewTerm* points to an activation of a task of type *Terminal* that is created at the time *NewTerm* is created.

Once a task is initiated, the statements in its body are executed in sequence, just as for an ordinary subprogram. When a task terminates, it does not return control; its separate parallel execution sequence simply ends. However, a task cannot terminate until its dependents have terminated; when it does terminate, any task of which it is a dependent must be notified so that that task may also terminate. A task terminates when it completes execution of the statements in its body; a task that never terminates is written to contain an infinite loop that cycles continuously (until an error occurs).

11.2.5 Synchronization of Tasks

During the concurrent execution of several tasks, each task proceeds *asynchronously* with the others; that is, each task executes at its own speed independently of the others. Thus, when Task A has executed 10 statements, Task B, which was initiated at the same time, may have executed only 6 statements or no statements or it may have already run to completion and terminated.

For two tasks running asynchronously to coordinate their activities, the language must provide a means of *synchronization* so that one task can tell the other when it completes execution of a particular section of its code. For example, one task may be controlling an input device and the second task processing each batch of data as it is input from the device. The first task reads in a batch of data, signals the second that a batch has arrived, and then begins preparation for input of the next batch of data. The second task waits for the signal from the first task, processes the data, signals the first that it has completed the processing, and then waits again for the signal that another batch has arrived. The signals sent between the tasks allow the tasks to synchronize their activities so that the second does not start processing data before the first has finished reading these in, and so that the first does not overwrite data that the second is still processing.

Tasks that are synchronizing their activities in this way are somewhat like coroutines. The signals serve to tell each task when to wait and when to proceed—somewhat like the use of resume calls between coroutines to signal a coroutine to proceed. However, with coroutines, there is only a single execution sequence, whereas here there may be several.

Interrupts. Synchronization of concurrent tasks through the use of interrupts is a common mechanism found in computer hardware. If Task A wishes to signal to Task B that a particular event has occurred (e.g., completion of a particular segment of code), then Task A executes an instruction that causes execution of Task B to be interrupted immediately. Control is transferred to a subprogram or code segment whose sole purpose is to handle the interrupt by performing whatever special actions are required. When this interrupt handler completes its execution, Task B continues its execution from the point where the interrupt occurred. This method of signaling is similar to the exception-handling mechanisms described in Section 11.1.1 and is often used for that purpose. For example, in a hardware computer, a task that handles an input–output device may synchronize with the central processor through the use of interrupts. In high-level languages, however, interrupts have several disadvantages as a synchronization mechanism: (1) The code for interrupt handling is separate from the main body of the task, leading to a confusing program structure; (2) a task that wishes to wait for an interrupt must usually enter a *busy waiting loop*—a loop that does nothing but cycle endlessly until the interrupt happens; and (3) the task must be written so that an interrupt at any time can be correctly handled, which usually requires that data shared between the task body and the interrupt routine be protected in special ways. Because of these (and several other) problems with interrupts, high-level languages usually provide other mechanisms for synchronization.

Semaphores. A *semaphore* is a data object used for synchronization between tasks. A semaphore consists of two parts: (1) an integer counter, whose value is always positive or zero, that is used to count the number of signals sent but not yet received; and (2) a queue of tasks that are waiting for signals to be sent. In a *binary semaphore*, the counter may only have the values zero and one. In a *general semaphore*, the counter may take on any positive integer value.

Two primitive operations are defined for a semaphore data object P:

signal(P). When executed by a task A, this operation tests the value of the counter in P; if zero, then the first task in the task queue is removed from the queue and its execution is resumed; if not zero or if the queue is empty, then the counter is incremented by one (indicating a signal has been sent but not yet received). In either case, execution of Task A continues after the *signal* operation is complete.

wait(P). When executed by a task B, this operation tests the value of the counter in P; if nonzero, then the counter value is decremented by one (indicating that B has received a signal) and Task B continues execution; if zero, then Task B is inserted at the end of the task queue for P and execution of B is suspended (indicating that B is waiting for a signal to be sent).

signal and *wait* both have simple semantics that require the principle of *atomicity*. Each operation completes execution before any other concurrent operation can access its data. Atomicity prevents certain classes of undesirable nondeterministic events to occur. For example, if we let $atom(S)$ stand for the atomic execution (i.e., cannot be interrupted) of Statement S, the nondeterministic example of Section 11.2.1 can be rewritten as

```
x:=1;
x:=2 and atom(y := x+x);
print(y);
```

In this case, the result may be either 2 or 4, depending on which statement executes first, but we avoid the undesirable result of 3 as an answer.

As an example of the use of semaphores and the *wait* and *signal* operations, consider again the two tasks that cooperate to (1) input a batch of data (Task A), and (2) process a batch of data (Task B). To synchronize their activities, two binary semaphores might be used. Semaphore *StartB* is used by Task A to signal that input of a batch of data is complete. Semaphore *StartA* is used by Task B to signal that processing of a batch of data is complete. Figure 11.3 shows the structure of Tasks A and B using these semaphores.

Semaphores have some disadvantages for use in high-level language programming of tasks: (1) A task can wait for only one semaphore at a time, but often it is desirable to allow a task to wait for any of several signals; (2) if a task fails to *signal* at the appropriate point (e.g., because of a coding error), the entire system of tasks may *deadlock* (i.e., the tasks may each be waiting in a semaphore queue for some other task to signal so that no task remains executing); and (3) programs involving several tasks and semaphores become increasingly difficult to understand, debug, and verify. In essence, the semaphore is a relatively low-level synchronization construct that is adequate primarily in simple situations.

The semaphore has an additional drawback in current environments. The semantics of *signal* and *wait* imply that all tasks accessing the semaphore share memory. With the growth of multiprocessing systems and computer networks, this is not necessarily so. The use of *messages* is related to the semaphore, but is not restricted to a shared memory space.

Messages. A message is a transfer of information from one task to another. It provides a way for each task to synchronize its actions with another task, yet the task remains free to continue executing when not needing to be synchronized. The

```
task A;
begin
    – Input first data set
    loop
        signal(StartB) – Invoke task B
        – Input next data set
        wait(StartA) – Wait until Task B
                finishes with data
    endloop;
end A;
```

```
task B;
begin
    loop
        wait(StartB) – Wait for
            task A to read data
        – Process data
        signal(StartA) – Tell Task
            A to continue
    endloop;
end B;
```

Figure 11.3. Synchronization of tasks using *signal* and *wait*.

basic concept is similar to a pipe. A message is placed into the pipe (or *message queue*) by a *send* command, whereas a task waiting for a message will issue a *receive* command and accept a message from the other end of the pipe. The sending task is free to continue to execute, sending more messages and filling the message queue, whereas the receiving task will continue to execute as long as there are pending messages waiting to be processed.

For example, a typical application is the *producer–consumer* problem. The producer task obtains new data (such as reading input from the keyboard), whereas the consumer task uses that data (such as compiling the program just typed in). If we let $send(to, message)$ mean that the task is sending $message$ to task to and $receive(from, message)$ mean that the task is waiting for a message to be placed in $message$ from task $from$, we can program the producer task as

```
task Producer;
begin
    loop – while more to read
        – Read new data;
        send(Consumer,data)
    endloop;
end Producer
```

and the consumer task as

```
task Consumer;
begin
    loop – while more to process
        receive(Producer,data);
        – Process new data
    endloop;
end Consumer
```

Messages are quite versatile. Problem 1 at the end of the chapter investigates how we can use messages to simulate semaphores.

Implementation of message passing is more complex than it might seem. Several tasks may simultaneously attempt to send messages to a single receiving task. If some of these messages are not to be lost, the implementation must include a mechanism to store the messages in a queue (usually called a *buffer*) until the receiver can process them. Alternatively, the sending task (rather than just its message) can be made to wait in a queue until the receiver is ready to receive the message. The latter method is used in Ada, where a sending task must rendezvous with the receiving task (and thus synchronize with it) before the message may be transmitted.

Guarded commands. As described in Section 11.2.2, we defined the guarded command as a way to add nondeterminacy into programming. Synchronization is a form of nondeterminacy because it is not always clear which task is the next one to execute. The guard forms a good model for task synchronization.

The guarded **if** command in Ada is termed a **select** statement and has the general form (Ada makes some further restrictions not mentioned here)

> **select**
>   **when** $condition_1$ => $statement_1$
>   **or when** $condition_2$ => $statement_2$
>   ...
>   **or when** $condition_n$ => $statement_n$
>   **else** $statement_{n+1}$ -optional else clause
>   **end select;**

Like the guarded **if**, each of the conditions is termed a *guard*, and each statement is a *command*. One of the guards that evaluates to true determines which statement to execute next. Although guarded commands may be used as part of a variety of task-synchronization mechanisms, their use in the Ada rendezvous mechanism illustrates the concept well.

Rendezvous. Ada uses a synchronization method very similar to the message, but requires a synchronization action with each message. When two tasks synchronize their actions for a brief period, that synchronization is termed a *rendezvous* in Ada. Suppose that one task A is used to input data, as in the previous example, and the second task B processes the data. However, assume B *copies* the data into a local data area before processing it so that A may input a new batch without waiting. Now a rendezvous is necessary to allow A to signal to B that a new batch of data is ready. Task A must then wait while B copies the new data into its local area, and then both tasks may continue concurrently until A has input a new batch of data and B has processed the last batch, at which point another rendezvous takes place.

A rendezvous point in B is called an *entry*, which in this example might be named *DataReady*. When Task B is ready to begin processing a new batch of data, it must execute an **accept** statement:

> **accept** DataReady **do**
>   -statements to copy new data from **A** into
>   local data area of B
> **end;**

When Task A has completed the input of a new batch of data, it must execute the *entry call*: *DataReady*. When Task B reaches the **accept** statement, it waits until Task A (or some other task) executes an entry call for the entry *DataReady* named in the **accept** statement. Similarly, when Task A reaches the entry call *DataReady*, it waits until B reaches the **accept** statement. When both are at that point, the rendezvous takes place: A continues to wait while B executes all the statements contained within the **do ... end** of the **accept** statement. Then the rendezvous is complete, and both A and B continue their separate executions.

To see how guarded commands might be used to allow B to wait for any of several rendezvous, suppose B is extended so that it can process data from any of three input devices, each controlled by separate tasks—$A1$, $A2$, and $A3$. Each of the three input tasks runs concurrently with B and each other. When an input task has a batch of data ready to be processed, it executes the corresponding entry call, *Ready*1 (in task $A1$), *Ready*2 (in task $A2$), or *Ready*3 (in task $A3$). When one of these entry calls is issued, Task B may be waiting already or B may still be processing a previous batch of data. If B were waiting already, then without a guarded-command structure, B could not wait for any of *Ready*1, *Ready*2, and *Ready*3, but instead would have to wait for only one of these. To wait for any one of the three, B executes the guarded command

```
select accept Ready1 do
    -Copy data from A1 into local area of B
    end;
or accept Ready2 do
    -Copy data from A2 into local area of B
    end;
or accept Ready3 do
    -Copy data from A3 into local area of B
    end;
end select;
```

When B reaches this statement, it waits until $A1$, $A2$, or $A3$ signals the appropriate entry call. The entry call is accepted (if more than one is signaled at the same time, only one is accepted) and the rendezvous takes place as before. Note that the explicit guards **when** *condition* => and the **else** clause have been omitted here because all three **accept** statements are to be available for execution when the **select** statement is reached. In some cases, however, an explicit guard might be included. For example, each input device might have an associated status indicating whether it was operating properly. The rendezvous might be made conditional on the status of each device:

```
select
    when Device1Status = ON => accept Ready1 do ... end;
or when Device2Status = ON => accept Ready2 do ... end;
or when Device3Status = connected => accept Ready3
        do ... end;
else ...            - No device is ready; do something else
end  select;
```

Tasks and Real-Time Processing

A program that must interact with input–output devices or other tasks within some fixed time period is said to be operating in *real time*. Programs monitoring automobile performance, controlling your microwave oven, and even managing your digital watch may need to react in times under 100 milliseconds for correct performance. Thus, for example, Task A that wishes to rendezvous with Task B may not be able to delay more than a fixed length of time before proceeding even without starting the rendezvous. In real-time computer systems, failure of part of the hardware of an external input-output device often leads to a task's being abruptly terminated. If other tasks wait on such a failed task, the entire system of tasks may deadlock and cause the crash of the system.

The special demands of real-time processing requires that the language include some explicit notion of *time*. In Ada, there is a language- defined package called *Calendar* that includes a type *Time* and a function *clock*. A task waiting for a rendezvous may watch the clock, as in

```
select DataReady;
or delay 0.5;        - Wait at most .5 seconds
end select;
```

This is a guarded command with no explicit guards, so either alternative is available for execution, thus avoiding a system crash if .5 seconds elapses and *DataReady* is still not enabled.

Tasks and Shared Data

Each different treatment of subprogram control structures (e.g., coroutines, exception handlers, tasks, and scheduled subprograms), as discussed in Section 11.1, leads to somewhat different structures for shared data. In most cases, these structures are straightforward variations on the concepts presented in the preceding sections, but tasks present special problems due to the concurrent execution involved. There are two issues: (1) storage management, and (2) mutual exclusion.

Storage management in tasks. Tasks are defined as several execution sequences executing simultaneously within a given program. Typically this is represented as several sets of procedures executing independently and communicating with one another using some of the mutual exclusion mechanisms described later. Each of the tasks needs its own storage management, usually a stack. Because each task executes independently, this gives the implementor a difficult problem: How does one implement multiple stacks on a single computer?

Several solutions to this problem are described in Figure 11.4. Figure 11.4(a) represents the usual approach for single tasks as represented in languages like Pascal or C, where the stack and heap are created at opposite ends of main storage; if they ever meet, there is no more space available and the program must terminate. All

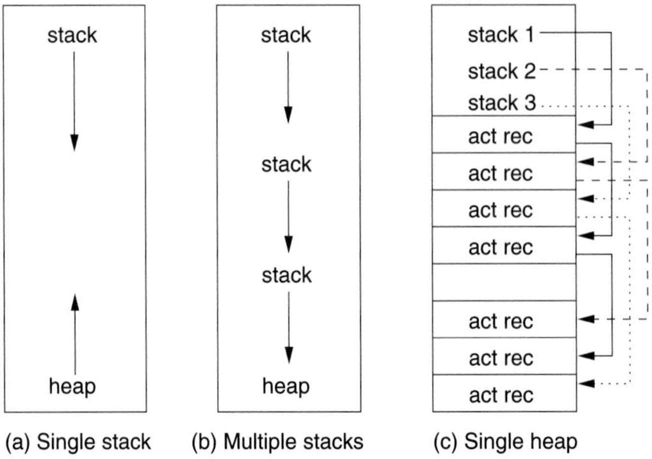

Figure 11.4. Activation records in a task environment.

space is used efficiently, although, as described in Section 10.4.3, some space may be unusable due to memory fragmentation in the heap.

If there is enough memory, Figure 11.4(b) may be used. Each task has its own stack in a separate place in memory. Again, if any stack overlaps the next segment of memory, the program must terminate. With modern virtual memory systems, this is an effective solution. For example, a program may have an address space of a billion locations, but only the few thousand actually used are in real memory. If each task has its stack starting sufficiently far apart (e.g., $stack_1$ at location 100 million, $stack_2$ at 200 million, $stack_3$ at 300 million, *heap* at 400 million), then they are unlikely to overlap. Thus, the storage management of the underlying operating system can be used to manage these multiple stacks with little additional help needed by the language translator other than setting up the initial stack address.

For systems with only limited memory (e.g., there is no virtual memory system or the virtual memory address space is relatively small), the previous option may not be realistic. Figure 11.4(c) may be used. In this case, all memory is a heap, and each stack consists of activation records allocated from the heap and linked together. This will always work and, for example, was the storage mechanism used for the early PL/I compilers. This, however, is a high overhead option. All procedure activations and returns require time-consuming calls to the system memory allocator rather than using the efficient stack-based model. If each activation record is of a unique size, memory fragmentation, which does not occur in the stack model, becomes a critical problem. Timing comparisons using this model often show that essentially all of the execution time is spent in the system memory-allocation routines, and there is little the programmer can do to speed up such programs. This third option is not desirable, but often there is little choice if one needs to implement independently

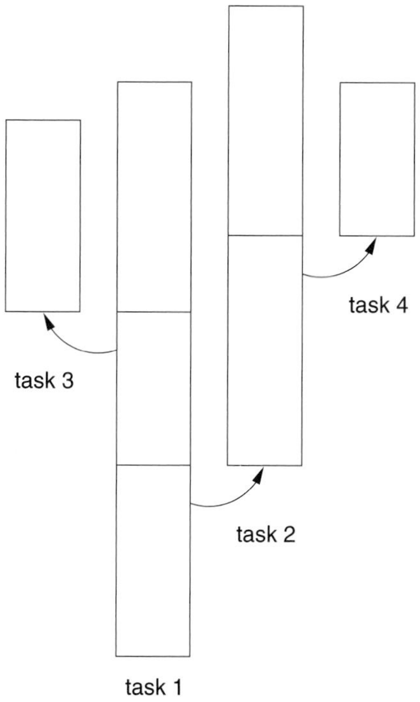

Figure 11.5. Cactus stack model of multiple tasks.

executing tasks using a small memory address space.

Because a task requires its own central stack area to store the activation records of subprograms that it calls, execution begins with a single stack for the main procedure. As tasks are initiated, each requires a new stack area. The original stack thus has split into several new stacks, which may split again if more tasks are initiated. This storage management structure is usually known as a *cactus stack* because it resembles the splitting of the arms of a saguaro cactus (Figure 11.5). The connection of the stack of the newly initiated task to the stack of the program unit within which it is statically nested must be maintained at run time because of the possibility that the task may make nonlocal references to shared data back in the stack of the original program unit. Thus, a link such as a static chain pointer must be maintained to allow such nonlocal references to be satisfied correctly at run time.

Mutual exclusion. If Task A and Task B each have access to a single data object X, then A and B must synchronize their access to X so that Task A is not in the process of assigning a new value to X while Task B is simultaneously referencing that value or assigning a different value. For example, if Variable X has the value

1 and Task A executes the statement

if X > 0 **then** X := X + 1;

and B executes the statement

if X > 0 **then** X := X − 2;

then X may end up with the value 0 (if A goes first), the value −1 (if B goes first), or possibly the value 2 (if A and B happen to interleave their actions by attempting to execute both statements concurrently). To ensure that two tasks do not simultaneously attempt to access and update a shared data object, one task must be able to gain *exclusive access* to the data object while it manipulates it. There are several different approaches to solve the problem of mutual exclusion when tasks work on shared data. We previously described semaphores and atomicity in Section 11.2, which can be used for data synchronization. Other mechanisms are described in turn.

Critical Regions

A *critical region* is a sequence of program statements within a task where the task is operating on some data object shared with other tasks. If a critical region in Task A is manipulating data object X, then mutual exclusion requires that no other task be simultaneously executing a critical region that also manipulates X. During execution of Task A, when it is about to begin execution of the critical region, A must wait until any other task has completed a critical region that manipulates X. As Task A begins its critical region, all other tasks must be locked out so that they cannot enter their critical regions (for Variable X) until A has completed its critical region. Critical regions may be implemented in tasks by associating a semaphore with each shared data object (or group of objects). The shared data objects ordinarily are made part of an explicit common environment (or several common environments) that is accessible to each task.

Monitors

Another approach to mutual exclusion is through the use of a monitor. A *monitor* is a shared data object together with the set of operations that may manipulate it. Thus, a monitor is similar to a data object defined by an abstract data type as described in Section 6.2. A task may manipulate the shared data object only by using the defined operations so that the data object is encapsulated, as is usual for data objects defined by abstract data types. To enforce mutual exclusion, it is only necessary to require that at most one of the operations defined for the data object may be executing at any given time.

The requirement for mutual exclusion and encapsulation in a monitor makes it natural to represent the monitor as a task. The shared data object is made a local data object within the task, and the operations are defined as local subprograms within the task. For example, suppose the shared data object is a table, *BigTable*, and two operations, *EnterNewItem* and *FindItem*, are defined. Mutual exclusion is necessary so that one task will not be entering a new item at the same time that another task is attempting to find an item at the same position in the table. In Ada, the monitor might be represented as a task *TableManager*, with two entries, *EnterNewItem* and *FindItem*, defined as shown in Figure 11.6. Within *TableManager*, *BigTable* is a local variable. A **select** statement with two **accept** alternatives is used to allow the monitor to respond to requests from other tasks to perform one or the other of the operations *EnterNewItem* or *FindItem* in such a way that only one such operation is ever in execution at once. Two tasks may simultaneously request items to be entered or looked up in the table. For example, Task *A* may execute the entry call statement

EnterNewItem(...);

and Task *B* may execute concurrently the entry call

FindItem(...);

The first entry call received by *TableManager* is processed (i.e., the rendezvous takes place as described in Section 11.2). If the second entry statement is executed before the first is processed by *TableManager*, the second task must wait. Thus, *BigTable* is protected from simultaneous access by two tasks.

Message Passing

Another solution to the problem of shared data between tasks is to prohibit shared data *objects* and provide only the sharing of data *values* through passing the values as messages. This is just the message concept discussed previously for task synchronization. Using message passing as the basis for data sharing ensures mutual exclusion without any special mechanism because each data object is owned by exactly one task, and no other task may access the data object directly. The owner Task *A* may send a copy of the values stored in the data object to Task *B* for processing. *B* then has its own local copy of the data object. When *B* has finished processing its local copy, *B* sends a copy of the new values to *A*, and *A* then changes the actual data object. Task *A*, of course, may continue to change the actual data object while *B* changes its local copy.

11.3 HARDWARE DEVELOPMENTS

One way to allow a machine to solve more complex problems is to make it run faster. Although machines have been getting faster yearly, about a factor of two every 3 years, the basic problem has remained. The control memory and CPU are

```
task TableManager is
    entry EnterNewItem(...);
    entry FindItem(...);
end;
task body TableManager is
    BigTable: array (...) of
    procedure Enter(...) is
        – Statements to enter item in BigTable
    end Enter;
    function Find(...) returns ... is
        – Statements to find item in BigTable
    end Find;
begin
        – Statements to initialize BigTable
    loop – Loop forever to process entry requests
        select
            accept EnterNewItem(...) do
                – Call Enter to enter received item in BigTable
            end;
        or accept FindItem(...) do
                – Call Find to look up received item in BigTable
            end;
        end select;
    end loop;
end TableManager;
```

Figure 11.6. A monitor represented as an Ada task.

always about an order of magnitude faster than the larger main memory. Therefore, a computer often spends much of the time simply waiting for the hardware to bring in data from the larger main memory into the faster control memory.

Two approaches have been tried to solve this problem. In one case, software has been designed to allow for more efficient use of the hardware. Statements like the **and** statement discussed in Section 11.2.1 allow for programmers to code concurrent programs. This permits the hardware to execute more efficiently by executing another program when one program is blocked waiting for data.

The alternative is to develop more effective hardware. Building CPUs with larger control memories limits the number of times main memory must be accessed to retrieve data. The use of a cache memory between main memory and the control memory gives an effective speedup of the control memory. However, no matter how fast we make computers, applications are constantly being designed that require even more computer resources.

In addition, the nature of computing is changing. No longer are computers housed in their separate temples. Powerful workstations exist on millions of desktops. This book is being composed on a personal computer connected to the international Internet computer network. The concept of client–server computing where computational tasks are distributed among a set of computers is changing the nature of software. Although Section 4.2 emphasized that we want to verify the correctness and termination of a program, for many applications (e.g., the telephone network, an airline, or hotel reservation system), the program should *never* terminate. Termination could cost the user of the program a significant amount in lost revenue.

To address these concerns, we briefly describe some of the emerging trends in computing today and what we believe will be the effects of these on language design. We separate these trends into hardware and software developments.

As described in Sec, 2.1.1, a computer consists of a CPU that executes instructions, a small fast control memory, and a larger slower main memory. Because of the speed differential between the CPU and main memory, the CPU is often waiting for data to be retrieved—the so-called *von Neumann bottleneck*. As described in chapter 2, the cache memory is one hardware solution to this problem that is totally transparent to the programmer. The hardware automatically manages the cache, and the addition of a cache to a computer system has little effect on programming language design.

This statement is not totally accurate. Managing the cache could aid performance. If a program loop were 32 bytes long and if each cache segment were also 32 bytes long, greater efficiency could be achieved in starting the loop at a cache segment boundary, allowing the entire loop to fit within one cache segment rather than requiring two segments to contain the loop. This would free up an additional cache segment for another data item. Although this would allow the cache to have an additional item and be marginally faster, the speedup would be insignificant compared with the major impact of simply having the cache.

To improve overall performance of the computer's hardware, there are two general approaches: (1) Improve the performance of a single CPU, and (2) develop alternative architectures that allow for increased performance. We discuss each approach in the next two subsections.

11.3.1 Processor Design

One obvious method for improving performance is to increase the speed of the CPU. In this section, we discuss the standard CPU design, often called the complex instruction set computer (CISC). We then discuss the reduced instruction set computer (RISC) as a method for improving system performance.

CISC computers. An early approach to increasing the performance of computers was to minimize the movement of data between main memory and the CPU. By making instructions more powerful, fewer instructions would be needed even if it took longer to execute each instruction. This gave rise to the CISC architecture. Although early machines typically had only a few instructions (e.g., move data to or from main memory, apply simple arithmetic operations on data in control memory, branch to a new instruction address), more recent machines may have hundreds of available operations. These are often broken down into instruction subfields:

[operation] [source data] [destination data]

The source of an instruction could be a main memory location, a control memory location, an indexed address in main memory, or a constant value. The same could be true for the destination (except for constant value). The operation could be a byte operation on that data, a word operation, arithmetic (e.g., $+$, $\times$), logical (e.g., $\wedge$, $\vee$), conditional (e.g., $>$, $\leq$), or transfer (e.g., **goto**). Complex operations, such as **do** loop indexing, array element accessing, and conversion between integer and real formats, are often single built-in operations due to their prevalence in most programming languages.

The CISC approach puts a burden on the compiler writer to use the new instructions effectively. For example, in the personal computer world, the Intel 80286 processor used 16-bit data and the Microsoft MS-DOS operating system was built to execute on that machine. This software also executed on the faster i486 and Pentium processors, which contained 32-bit instructions. However, the programs designed for the older 80286 did not use the newer hardware effectively, and compiler vendors had to upgrade their compilers to generate instructions that effectively used the more powerful instructions in the faster CPUs.

RISC computers. The addition of more and more complex instructions means that a greater and greater number of CPU cycles are needed to execute each instruction. Although machine speeds have been increasing to 100MHz, 200MHz, 600MHz, and greater, the number of cycles to execute each instruction also increases from 1 to 2, 3, 4, and so on. Thus, although machines are getting much faster, the underlying complexity of the CPU is also growing, with current microprocessors containing over 3 million components on a single chip. Such complexity often leads to hardware errors in the design of the chip.

To avoid the spiraling speedup and increased chip complexity, an alternative architecture (RISC) was proposed in the 1970s. The concept was to restrict CPU complexity as much as possible to make full use of the machine's fast cycle time. Thus, a machine with a cycle time of 400MHz should execute 400 million instructions per second. Although such a machine might require more instructions than the corresponding program on a CISC computer, the belief was that the increased speed of the machine would more than offset the additional instructions that would be necessary to execute.

A RISC CPU incorporates several design principles, all contributing to rapid execution:

Single-cycle execution. Every instruction should execute in one cycle (but subject to pipelining).

Pipelined architecture. Execution of an instruction requires several stages for execution—for example, the following:

1. Retrieve instruction from main memory.
2. Decode operation field, source data, and destination data.
3. Get source data for operation.
4. Perform operation.

A pipelined architecture performs this sequence in several stages, with successive instructions at each stage. Thus, while Instruction 1 is executing, Instruction 2 is retrieving source data, Instruction 3 is being decoded, and Instruction 4 is being retrieved from memory. Each individual instruction takes four machine cycles to execute, but each cycle completes the execution of another instruction, thus executing instructions at the full cycle rate of the CPU if we can keep four instructions always in the pipeline. This is a major *if* and puts a burden on the language designer, as we discuss next.

Large control memory. To avoid main memory accessing, a large set of registers (often 100 or more) is provided. This increases the number of data items in control memory at any one time, avoiding the need to retrieve data from main memory.

Fast procedure invocation. Activation record allocations (chapter 9) are often time-consuming. By using the large number of control registers in a RISC processor, the run-time activation record stack is often handled within the control memory. Subprogram call and return are often implemented as single RISC instructions.

This design often has a major impact on translator writers. For example, with a standard CISC design, the statement $E = A + B + C + D$ will have the postfix $EAB + C + D+ =$ and will execute as follows

1. Add A to B, giving sum.
2. Add C to sum.
3. Add D to sum.
4. Store sum in E.

However, in pipelined architectures, Instruction 2 cannot retrieve source data *sum* (the result of adding A to B [Stage 3 in the pipeline example]) until the previous instruction stores that result (Stage 4 in the pipeline). This causes the processor to wait a cycle on Instruction 2 until Instruction 1 completes its execution. A more intelligent translator would develop the postfix $EAB + CD + + =$, which would allow $A + B$ to be computed in parallel with $C + D$ and avoid the delay. An even more intelligent translator would intermix two independent statements, such as

$$E=A+B+C+D$$
$$J=F+G+H+I$$

with the postfix $AB + FG + CD + HI + (1)(3) + (2)(4) + E(5) = F(6) =$, where the operand numbers indicate the *operation number* within that expression. In this case, each statement executes with no interference from the other, and the processor executes at the full speed of the pipeline. However, this is a major headache for the language translator to sort out all the interferences between statements. For example, if the second assignment were $J := E + G + H + I$, the operation $EG+$ could not execute until the result of the assignment to E was completed. To make matters worse, to simplify processor design as much as possible, the responsibility of making that determination is often left to the language translator; the hardware will simply pick up the incorrect value and continue.

Transfer instructions pose additional constraints. For example, for rapid execution of the **if** statement

if expr **then** $stmt_1$ **else** $stmt_2$

the execution sequence on most RISC machines will be as follows:

Evaluate *expr*
Fill pipeline with $stmt_1$
If *expr* false then empty pipeline and fill with $stmt_2$.

By assuming the expression will be true, the RISC processor can start executing the **then** branch without causing the processor to halt for a few cycles for the pipeline to catch up. However, if the result is false, it is important that no spurious calculations from the **then** branch be stored incorrectly. Developing programs where most branches are true could speed up execution on such machines.

11.3.2 System Design

Hardware speedup is generally accomplished in two ways. In one, the pipelined architecture described for RISC machines has multiple instructions executing on the same data at the same time. An alternate approach is to have multiple instructions operating on several data objects at the same time—the Multiple Instruction Multiple Data (MIMD) computer.

Multiprocessors are not new developments. Two or more CPUs executing under control of a single operating system have been around for over 20 years. In the simple case, the operating system simply assigns a different user program to each processor, and there is little interference between the two programs. Overall system performance is enhanced by the two processors, but there is little impact on the execution of a single program.

Figure 11.7 presents three approaches toward multiple CPU architectures. Figure 11.7(a) represents the usual approach toward multiple CPUs. Several processors communicate with several memory modules using a single data path called a *bus*. The design is the simplest of all those considered, but has the relatively severe drawback that there may be *interference* between the data access of one CPU with the data accesses of others. Because of this, total system performance of p processors of k MHz each will be much less than $p \times k$.

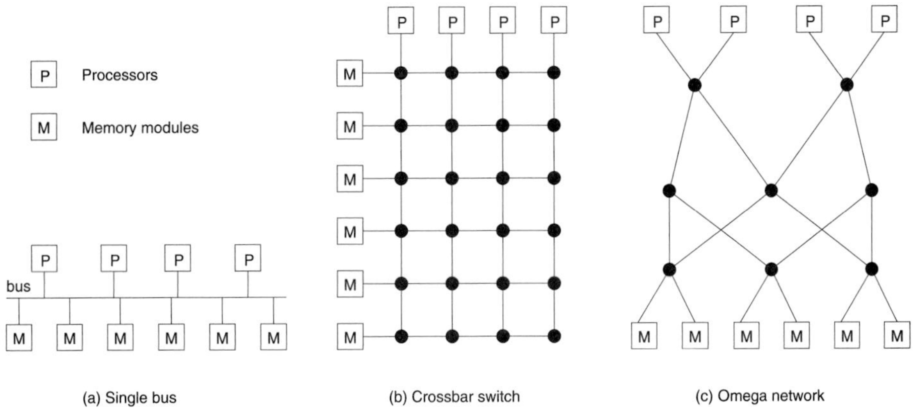

Figure 11.7. System architectures for multiprocessors.

A second model is the crossbar switch of Figure 11.7(b). In this model, each processor may be separately connected to a separate memory module. Although we could achieve performance of $p \times k$ MHz with this arrangement, if there are m memory modules, we would need $m \times p$ switches. This greatly increases the costs of such systems.

A compromise between these two models is the *omega network* approach (Figure 11.7[c]). Here we have a set of switches that allows each processor to be routed to each memory module. There is some speed delay over Alternative 2 because of the need to set up the network routing for the data, yet it is faster than Alternative 1 because there will be few cases of data interference. Costs are less than Alternative 2, but higher than Alternative 1 because fewer switches are needed.

With each of these designs, the operating system may simply assign a different program to execute on each processor. In such cases, the hardware is transparent to programming language design, and each processor is simply executing a sequential program. However, if the operating system assigns several of the processors to a single program, then language design is crucial in these cases, and the task synchronization issues of Section 11.2.5 must be addressed.

Massively parallel computers. With the multiprocessor architecture, we may have hundreds or even thousands of interconnected processors. We call such machines *massively parallel computers*. The problem, then, is how to divide a given program into enough small pieces so that each processor may execute independently without the data needs of one constantly interfering with the data needs of another.

We can separate the parallelism issue into *high-level* and *low-level* approaches. High-level approaches depend on language constructs provided by the programmer to signify parallel execution. The **and** statement of Section 11.2.1 is one method that the programmer can use to tell the translator to schedule each separate statement on a separate processor. Unfortunately, programmers are rarely able to manually parallelize a program effectively, so such approaches do not work well in practice.

In low-level parallelism, primitive language constructs that may be parallelized are found by the translator. The most important examples are in array processing. In many applications (e.g., fluid flow, weather forecasting, airflow over an aircraft wing), the solution depends on a matrix of points of finer and finer granularity. Matrices of millions of points are not uncommon, and multiplying two of these together takes millions or billions of calculations. Because matrix multiplication requires the multiplication of Row i of Matrix A to Column j of Matrix B, for all i and j, a cache memory has little effect on performance because data are retrieved from all over memory. Instead, for low-level parallelism, the matrix is automatically divided into small segments, and each segment is processed by a different processor. Often such matrices are *sparse,* meaning that most of the elements are zero. If so, many of these submatrix segments are zero and can be ignored. Language constructs like slices are important in writing algorithms to take advantage of these architectures.

11.4 SOFTWARE ARCHITECTURE

Most programming languages are based on a discrete model of execution, That is, the program begins execution, and then, in some order,

1. Reads relevant data from the local file system,
2. Produces some answers,
3. Writes data to the local file system.

This description clearly shows the presence of two classes of data: temporary or *transient data*, which have a lifetime being the execution of the program, and *persistent data*, which has a lifetime transcending the execution of the program. Traditionally, transient data are the objects defined by the given programming language and encompass most of the objects described earlier. Persistent data have generally been in the realm of database system or file systems. Programs execute by reading persistent data into transient data within the program and then rewriting the transient data back into the persistent storage when execution terminates.

11.4.1 Persistent Data and Transaction Systems

For most applications, the separation of data into transient and persistent objects is a satisfactory situation and has served us well for many years. However, there are applications where this model can be very inefficient. Consider a reservation system (e.g., airline or hotel). Here we would like the reservation program to be executing continually because reservation calls may occur at any time. However, in this case, it is inefficient to read in the persistent data describing the state of reservations, update this state with the new information, and then rewrite the reservation back to the persistent store.

We could redo the reservation system by having the entire database be an array in the reservation program and simply have the program loop waiting for new requests. This would avoid the necessity of rereading the data each time we needed to update the reservation database. The problem is that if the system failed (e.g., by programming error or power loss to the computer), all transient data are lost. We would lose the contents of our reservation system.

We can solve this by use of a *persistent programming* language. In this case, there is no distinction between transient and persistent data. All changes to transient program variables are immediately reflected in changes to the persistent database, and there is no need to first read data into transient storage. The two concepts are the same, resulting in reliability in the storage system if the system should fail during execution. We refer to a persistent programming language as one that does not explicitly mention data movement (e.g., between persistent and transient storage).

Smalltalk (Section 7.2.5) has aspects of persistence. The user's environment of classes and methods remains the same from one execution to the next. However, data local to a given method are lost when execution of the method terminates. There are some persistent languages (e.g., χ [SAJEEV and HURST 1992]), however, that do preserve data integrity in face of failure.

Design of a persistent programming language requires many of the same concepts used to develop traditional languages like C or Pascal. However, persistence requires a few additional design constraints [SAJEEV and HURST 1992]:

1. *Need a mechanism to indicate an object is persistent.* The usual approach is to assume all data are transient and indicate which objects are persistent.

2. *Need a mechanism to address a persistent object.* The underlying operating system file structure is often used, but that is not necessary. The language can develop its own model of persistent storage. However, one needs a mechanism for two different programs in this language to access the same persistent object.

3. *Need to synchronize simultaneous access to an individual persistent object.* There are well-developed methods for doing this, such as the use of semaphores described previously in Section 11.2.5.

4. *Need to check type compatibility of persistent objects.* Because of the multiple programs that need to access a given persistent object, name equivalence of objects is often difficult to use. For this reason, structural equivalence is the preferred method in persistent languages.

11.4.2 Networks and Client–Server Computing

As the prior discussion suggests, programs typically are written to access local data stores, produce answers, and terminate. The computer is considered a machine to be used to solve a given problem. As machines became faster and more expensive, multiprogramming systems were developed and terminals were added as a way to allow more individuals to access a computer at the same time.

The situation began to change in the early 1980s as minicomputers and later microprocessors (i.e., personal computers) evolved. With machines becoming smaller and dispersed geographically, there was interest in developing techniques for these dispersed machines to communicate. Beginning in the 1970s with the Arpanet and continuing into the 1990s with the Internet, the technology of communicating across high-speed communication lines developed. Today virtually all computers have the ability to communicate with other computers using high-speed communication lines. Protocols such as X.25 and TCP/IP allow for the reliable transfer of information between two such machines. We call processors linked by communication lines a computer *network*.

In Section 11.3, *tightly coupled* systems are described. In such systems, the execution of several programs is handled in parallel using multiprocessor architectures and hardware techniques such as pipelining. The use of communication lines allows for the development of *loosely coupled* systems. In such systems, each processor has its own memory and disk storage, but communicates with other processors to transfer information. Systems developed on such architectures are called *distributed systems*.

Distributed systems can be *centralized*, where a single processor does the scheduling and informs the other machines as to the tasks to execute, or *distributed* or *peer-to-peer*, where each machine is an equal and the process of scheduling is spread among all of the machines. In a centralized system, a single processor will inform another processor of the task to execute. When completed, the assigned processor will indicate that it is ready to do another task. In the peer-to-peer model, one processor may broadcast a message to all the processors, and a given processor that is currently inactive could respond with the message "I'll do it." Alternatively, each machine in the network will individually invoke a task on a specified machine elsewhere in the network. In this way, work gradually gets propagated around the network.

The growth of PCs has changed this model. In the early 1980s, terminals were the typical method to communicate with a large mainframe computer. As PCs started to populate the desktop, programs running in the PC simulated the terminal. In this way, the PC could operate locally as a separate computer and also act as a terminal to a larger mainframe.

As PCs became faster, it was soon apparent that the PC could solve many of the computational tasks currently being performed on the large mainframe. In this way, data were retrieved from the large mainframe and processed locally. For example, a large company financial database could exist on the mainframe while a spreadsheet program could run on the PC to compute local statistics. The large mainframe program became known as the *server* while the program running on the PC became known as the *client.* Client–server computing required that problems be divided into segments, parts requiring centralized control such as database lookup, and parts requiring local computation such as spreadsheet calculations.

As microprocessors grew even more powerful, many mainframe applications could just as easily be processed on workstations. The mainframe shrunk, but the client–server model was still viable. Today we have many applications written using this approach. For example, a centralized data repository retrieves data as the server while the client executes on a local workstation doing calculations, performing word processing, or evaluating the data in some other manner.

The major impact this has had on programming language design is the lack of a global data store for the program. Both the client and server only have limited access to the total information content of the program. Programs need to be divided into separate pieces to effectively compute an answer. We have already discussed some of the techniques needed to address these problems. Tasks in Ada are one form of separating programs into independent pieces. The *Remote Procedure Call* (RPC) is another. An RPC syntactically looks like any other subprogram call except that the operating system will enact a program possibly on another processor. RPCs are related to message communication and often are implemented as a *send–receive* message strategy of a client sending an RPC message to a server, the server waiting on a *receive* for the message, and then responding back to the client in a similar manner.

The WWW has spawned interest in a form of client–server computing called a *mediator* architecture (Figure 11.8). A mediator is a software module that uses encoded knowledge about sets of data to create information for a higher class of application. In this organization, a user interacts with a client software product (e.g., a Web browser), which then communicates with a server. The server has access to multiple data resources and extracts information from several of them to create new information for the user. We discuss this further in Section 12.2.

In general, client–server programming does not require major changes to the underlying language as long as some message mechanism is added, such as the RPC call or some other. However, program design becomes more complex. The program must be divided to minimize communication traffic across the network. For example, one could multiply a matrix in the client by asking for each row and column from the server as needed, but the resulting message traffic would swamp the network and make the system generally unusable.

11.5 SUGGESTIONS FOR FURTHER READING

[CHANDY and KESSELMAN 1991] and [WYATT et al. 1992] discussed parallel systems. Articles by [BURGESS et al. 1994], [JOHNSON and JOHNSON 1991],

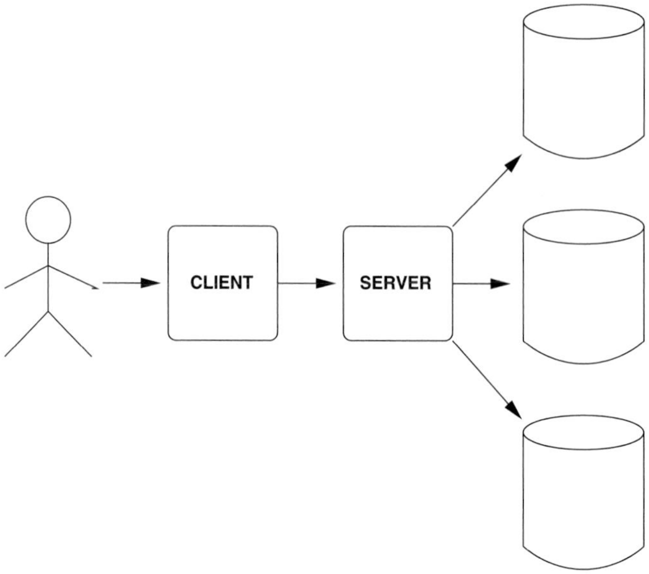

Figure 11.8. Client-server mediator architecture.

and [SMITH and WEISS 1994] summarized the design of RISC machines, and the article by [TANENBAUM 1990] described designs of several RISC architectures. Development of parallel algorithms for MIMD machines is described in the article by [LOPEZ et al. 1992]. The survey in [DUNCAN 1990] gives an overview of parallel architecture designs. Massively parallel architectures are discussed in [FURHT 1994] and [TANENBAUM et al. 1992]. Persistent languages are described in [ATKINSON and BUNEMAN 1987].

11.6 PROBLEMS

1. Is it possible to implement semaphores *signal* and *wait* by using messages *send* and *receive*? Write two procedures *signal*(P) and *wait*(P) that communicate via messages, but have the semantics of the *signal* and *wait* semaphores. What problems with atomicity do you have with your solution? *signal* and *wait* can be used by sets of tasks using the same semaphore. How can *send* and *receive* be generalized to more than a single sender and receiver?

2. One of the more difficult problems in concurrent applications is the answer to the question, "What time is it?" Synchronizing clocks across a network of machines can be difficult because you want the time to be exactly the same across a network, yet it takes a finite amount of time to propagate a given time to all machines.

(a) Think of a method to pass the time to the various processors of a multiprocessing system so that each machine has exactly the same time.

(b) What is the problem with a system having separate *time* and *date* functions to access the current time and date? (Consider the problem of function atomicity when accessing the time and date close to midnight. For this reason, most systems today have a single *TimeAndDate* function.)

3. Parameter transmission by reference and value-result ordinarily give the same effect (for the programmer). However, if a subprogram terminates because of an exception and the exception propagates to a handler outside the subprogram (or alternatively a **goto** to a nonlocal statement label is used), the two methods of parameter transmission may lead to different effects. Suppose Y has the value 5 in subprogram $Sub1$, Y is transmitted to $Sub2$, and $Sub2$ assigns 7 to Y and then raises an exception that propagates to a handler in $Sub1$. Explain what value Y might have in $Sub1$ after the exception is handled in the cases *(a)* transmission by reference and *(b)* transmission by value-result.

4. Consider a system with multiple processors, each having a cache memory. The cache coherence problem is when one processor updates its cache and another processor needs to access those data before the first processor has time to rewrite the cache contents into main memory. Because the cache memory is associated with the CPU and not the main memory, discuss ways the hardware can be designed to solve this problem.

5. With some RISC processors, the execution of the assignment statement

```
while some condition do
    – Some statement here
    C=A+B
    end
```

will be as follows:

```
Load control memory with A
Load control memory with B
Add two values (i.e., compute A + B)
Goto while statement
Store control memory into C
```

Explain how the store to C can occur *after* the jump to the top of the **while** loop and still be correct.

6. The *remote procedure call* has the syntax of a function call such as

$$\textbf{call } NewFunction(p_1, p_2, p_3)$$

except that the called procedure may be executing elsewhere on a computer network. The values of the arguments are transferred to the called procedure, and the returned value is transmitted back to the caller. *(a)* Explain how to implement a remote procedure call using messages as the underlying synchronization mechanism. How would you implement this if the various parameters could be call by value? *(b)* Call by reference? *(c)* Call by result?

Chapter 12

Network Programming

Computers are often thought of as electronic *calculators* or *number* crunchers due to their initial applications of computing ballistics tables, processing payrolls, or solving differential equations to predict the weather. However, the nature of computing is changing as we use computers today to fly airplanes, drive cars, play games, process documents, and speak to us. In keeping with these trends to non-numeric applications, language design is following suit. Some of this has been discussed in the existing text. LISP, Prolog, and Java all represent languages useful for inferring facts about data. In this chapter, we look at the evolution of textual information. Although chapter 11 presented some initial concepts on distributed processing and client–server computing, desktop publishing, the explosion of the Internet and the growth of the World Wide Web (WWW) has greatly increased interest in languages for processing text. In this chapter, we look at Postscript as a language for describing documents. We then look at the WWW and the various languages it utilizes for managing its information flow.

Translator models. When we discuss text processing, we have to extend our concept of a compiler. In chapter 2 we discussed interpreters, virtual machines and binding times to discuss how translators interact with the data of a program. To understand text-processing applications, we have to look at translators from a different point of view. We can discuss translators classified by the form of the output they produce in three ways:

1. **Interpretation.** The output is the solution to the problem posed to the translator. For example, given the question, "What is the meaning of life, time, and everything?"[1], the translator will simply write the number 42.[2] For the code

```
sum=0; I=0;
while I<10 do
    { I=I+1; sum=sum+I; }
```

[1] From Douglas Adams' brilliant book *Hitchhiker's Guide to the Galaxy* [ADAMS 1979].

[2] Don't ask us why 42; ask Mr. Adams.

the translator would simply output the code: $sum = 55$. In this instance, the translator acts as an interpreter and executes the query to output the desired answer.

2. **Compilation.** In this case, the translator produces an algorithm (i.e., a program) that will compute the answer. This corresponds to the typical compiler. A C compiler will produce a program for a hardware-implemented machine that can execute the program to produce the desired answer, such as for the previous C program. We have several common machine architectures (e.g., Intel Pentium, Apple PowerPC, various RISC processors). A compiler will develop the set of instructions unique to that specific machine architecture that will be used for the computation.

3. **Semantic description.** The translator produces a description of the output. For example, instead of simply writing "42," the output from the question "What is the meaning of life, time, and everything?" could be given as ⟨integer⟩ ⟨binary value⟩ 101010 ⟨end⟩. Note that this is more general than simply writing 42. The output of 42 assumes that the reader knows the context of this answer—that numbers are given in base 10. For example, on the planet Frammis, where inhabitants count in octal (base 8), the digits 42 represent the binary number 100010, which is our decimal number 34. That is a very different value. However, the semantic description includes the semantic information necessary to interpret the answer within any frame of reference, using any base, and printed using any character set, not necessarily the usual Arabic numerals we are used to.

For numeric calculations, most of the world has adapted to Arabic numerals. However, the same is not true for word-processing applications. Readers of Japanese, Hebrew, Arabic, Korean, and other character sets need to have text presented in their own alphabet. For languages that process text, it is more important that we keep track of the frame of reference in addition to the answer. For text applications, then, the three forms of translators given earlier have the following meaning:

1. **Interpretation.** This would represent the specific output format. For text it could be a set of bits representing the page to be displayed. For a page that is 1,000 bits wide by 1,200 bits long, 1,200,000 bits would be required for a black-and-white description of this page—or about 150K bytes of data. Although data-compression techniques can reduce this amount significantly, it still represents an inflexible method of creating and storing such information. In general, this approach is not used for these applications.

2. **Compilation.** In this model, the translator converts the document into an executable program that executes to create its own image; that is, a program written for a virtual machine that executes a set of commands to create an

image. This is the process used by Postscript. The Postscript virtual machine accepts Postscript commands that have the effect of painting a blank sheet of paper with the appropriate image. When the paper is finished, a print command causes the page to be displayed or printed. Translators that produce Postscript produce a program that creates the final document in its formatted description by executing on the Postscript virtual machine. In Section 12.1, we describe Postscript further.

3. **Semantic description.** In this case, we describe what attributes the final document has, but not the details of how it actually looks. For example, Microsoft uses Rich Text Format (RTF) for saving documents using its Word word-processing applications. Other processors can be written to read and write RTF format. This provides a series of commands describing each attribute of the document, much like the description of the number 42 as an integer and binary number given earlier. For WWW use, HyperText Markup Language (HTML) has become the standard description of text. In Section 12.2, we describe HTML, and we look at Java as an extension to the document-processing capabilities of Web applications.

12.1 DESKTOP PUBLISHING

The programming languages in this book are based on traditional programming language concepts where source programs are compiled for execution by a virtual machine. Under control of this virtual machine, data are read in and processed, and then results are printed. It is part of this programming model that programs are *implemented* and then documentation *written* describing the program.

However, documentation is just another form of data, and the writing of a document involves concepts similar to writing a program. For example, this book has a top-level design in terms of chapter topics and section topics within chapters. As the text was written, references to locations in the text were defined and referenced elsewhere. This book has a certain style in terms of the size of each page, location of page numbers and headings on each page, font used for text, placement of tables and figures, and so on. Although such texts were previously developed manually using simple machines like typewriters, the growth of the personal computing market has given rise to desktop publishing.

12.1.1 LaTeX Document Preparation

With desktop publishing, the user is responsible for the generation of all aspects of document preparation. To simplify this process, languages for processing documents have been created. This book was processed by TeX (TeX), developed by Donald Knuth, using the LaTeX (LaTeX) macros, developed by Leslie Lamport. For lack of a better term, we often refer to the compiling of the book as various chapters are processed by the TeX program.

TEX executes much like a traditional compiler. As described in Section 3.2, a first pass of TEX creates a symbol table to keep track of section numbers, page numbers, and figure numbers. In the second pass, an output format is generated with the correct values inserted in the document.

For example, the source input to LATEX for the previous paragraph would look like

```
\TeX executes very much like a traditional compiler. As described
in Section \ref{translation.sec}, a first pass of \TeX creates a
symbol table to keep track of section numbers, page numbers, and
figure numbers. In the second pass, an output format is generated
with the correct values inserted in the document.
```

The macro \TeX in this LATEX source prints out the name of TeX in its fancy font, \ref refers to an address of a previous section of the book, which in this case is the label given the name *translation.sec* and is stored by Pass 1 of TEX in the symbol table as the value 3.2. This is then used by Pass 2 of the process to insert the actual value in the printed document.

However, unlike traditional compilation concepts like data storage, subprogram invocation, and types, a publishing program is concerned about page layout and space. For example, this book requires a three-pass execution of TEX. During Pass 1, the text is placed on lines and pages according to a predefined style (either built into TEX or defined by the user's own style guide) and the various references and bibliographic citations are stored in a symbol table. During Pass 2, these citations are placed where referenced elsewhere in the text, and the table of contents is produced. During Pass 3, the table of contents, figures, and citations are all placed in their proper locations. For reports with no table of contents, only two passes are needed, and it is possible for a complex TEX document to take a larger number of passes, but two or three are typical.

LATEX creates *environments* that make TEX easier to use. These behave much like C or Pascal scope rules of variable definitions. For example, one can begin and end a list of items. The list may be numbered or just bulleted. Starting new sections or subsections automatically adjusts the appropriate section numbers. LATEX has a syntax similar to the block-structured style of a programming languages.

Figure 12.1 describes the structure of a typical document processed by LATEX. By invoking LATEX, the *latex.tex* document is read into TEX to create commands for chapters, sections, subsections, figures, tables, lists, and the numerous other structures needed to write simple documents. The *documentstyle* command (in LATEX) allows the user to add other style features. The required *article* parameter causes *article.sty* to be read in to tailor *latex.tex* with commands needed for an article. For example, there are no chapters in *articles*, but for style *book* (i.e., *book.sty*), chapters are defined. 11*pt* defines the size of the text font (11-point type), and *art*11*.sty* is read giving additional information on line and character spacing for 11-point type. The TEX program along with *article.sty* and *art*11*.sty*

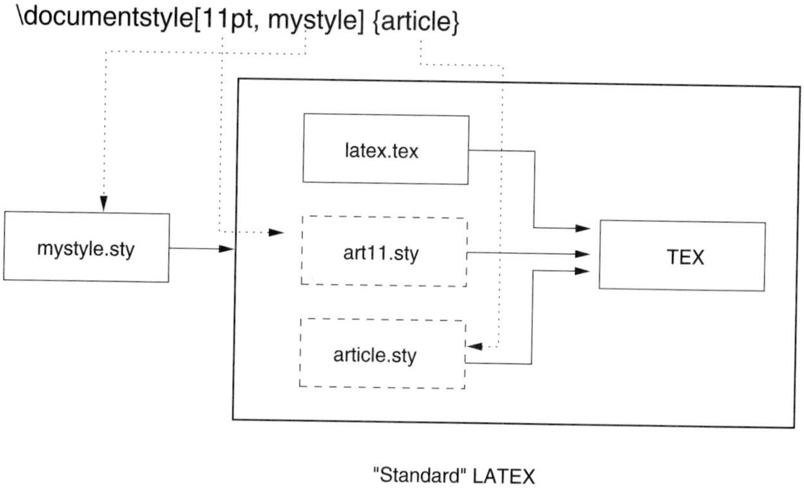

Figure 12.1. Structure of LaTeX.

form the standard way to process a LaTeX article. LaTeX similarly defines styles for reports, books, slides, and letters as well.

A user may want to tailor this style further. Prentice Hall, for example, has a style for its books. This book has chapter and section headings at the top of each page, the page size is not the LaTeX default, spacing between paragraphs and between sections are different, and so on. The parameter *mystyle* informs TeX to read in *mystyle.sty* with additional style commands that further refine what TeX will do for book formatting instructions.

Implementation. Systems like TeX compile the document for execution on a word-processing virtual machine. A common format is Postscript (described later). After compiling the document, the output file is executed on the Postscript virtual machine for viewing or printing. An advantage to this approach is that the original source document is the basic ASCII text, which is viewable by any text editor.

LaTeX uses a style guide to direct compilation of a document. In this way, the style of the document and the text can be kept separate. Writing a paper for a conference only requires the parameter *twocolumn* to be added to the *documentstyle* macro to change the formatting from one to two columns per page, with no change to the document. This allows a single document file to be used for multiple purposes as long as the style information is kept separate. However, it is sometimes hard to understand what the finished document will look like.

12.1.2 WYSIWYG Editors

An alternative strategy is the What You See Is What You Get (*WYSIWYG*) editor. In this case, the file is preformatted to its final output representation. All fonts, spacing, figures, tables, and section numbers are included in their proper places. All editing updates are immediately reflected in the screen display. This provides for easier editing, but makes changing styles somewhat harder to accomplish. This form of desktop publishing is most common on PC-based editing systems, such as Microsoft's Word or Corel's WordPerfect.

Implementation. In this case, the document is embedded with appropriate editing and formatting commands, and the word-processing program is a virtual machine designed to display those commands. The problem with this approach is that each WYSIWYG word-processing program has defined its own virtual machine architecture. Thus, a file prepared for execution by one word-processing program is often not viewable by another word-processing program.

Notations such as *rich text format* (RTF) have solved this problem somewhat. RTF is a notation for describing the execution of a word-processing virtual machine using a standard notation. Thus, any word-processing system that has built a translator from RTF to its own internal virtual machine has the ability to process documents generated by another WYSIWYG program. The use of RTF has greatly expanded the ability to move documents from one word-processing system to another.

Page Description Languages

Systems like TEX are designed for document writing. Another class of textual language is the page description language, such as Postscript by Adobe Systems or HTML, which is used to describe pages on the WWW of the Internet. In this case, Postscript is generally the output language from a system like TEX and is used to draw the text onto the page. Most Postscript printers have Postscript interpreters built into them, and a Postscript document is actually executed by the printer as it places text and figures onto the page. Again, as with TEX, Postscript has a defined syntax and can be described by many of the techniques discussed in this book. We discuss HTML in further detail later in this chapter.

12.1.3 Postscript

Postscript was developed by John Warnock and Chuck Geschke of Adobe Systems [ADOBE 1990] in the early 1980s. It was initially used as the printing engine of Apple computers, but soon became a widely used standard for most computer systems. Postscript interpreters (either as software or hardware components) exist for printing documents on almost every current computer system in use today.

Postscript uses the model of painting text (or pictures) onto a blank page. When

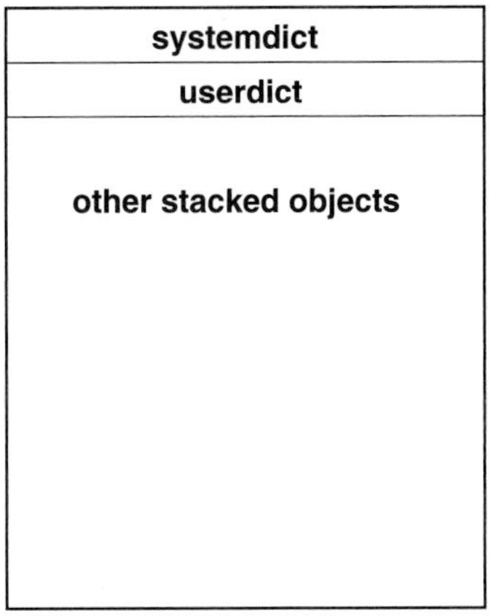

Figure 12.2. Postscript execution model.

the page is finished, it is printed and a new page is started. This is the compilation method of translation given earlier. Each Postscript document consists of a program that prints successive pages onto a printer (or display screen).

A Postscript program consists of four components:

1. *An interpreter for performing calculations.* A simple postfix execution stack is the basic model.

2. *A language syntax.* This is based on Forth, which was described earlier (Figure 8.2.1).

3. *Painting extensions.* An extension to Forth with painting commands for managing the process of painting text and pictures on a sheet of paper.

4. *Conventions.* A series of conventions, not part of the formal Postscript language, that various printers use for consistency in presentation. Use of these conventions makes it easier for transporting Postscript documents from one system to another.

Each component is described in the sections that follow.

12.1.4 Postscript Virtual Machine

A Postscript program consists of a sequence of commands that represent the postfix of the algorithm necessary to paint the document. This sequence manipulates a stack, as shown in Figure 12.2. Postscript execution begins with two entries initially on the stack, which the program may not remove:

- *Systemdict* is the system dictionary, which represents the initial binding of Postscript objects to their internal representation.

- *Userdict* is the user dictionary, which represents the new definitions included within this execution of a Postscript program. This may include redefinition of primitive objects already defined in *systemdict*.

Execution stacks. Postscript actually manages four stacks:

1. The *operand* stack contains the operands as they are stacked, executed, and unstacked.
2. The *dictionary* stack contains only dictionary objects. This stack defines the scope and context of each definition.
3. The *execution* stack contains executable objects. For the most part, these are functions in intermediate stages of execution.
4. The *graphics state* stack manages the context for painting objects on the page and are discussed shortly.

A Postscript program is written as a sequence of ASCII characters. The program is broken down into a sequence of tokens. As each token is read, its definition is accessed in the stack (by first looking in *userdict* and then *systemdict*) and then executed by an appropriate action.

Names are executable objects and generally consist of any characters except whitespace (e.g., AName, abc, A.Name). In general, names cause their values to be looked up in the dictionary stack and their values executed. Thus, the name *add* causes the definition in *systemdict* to be accessed. This definition causes the top two operand stack entries to be added together. Of course, the user can write a new definition for *add* and place it in *userdict* to redefine the *add* primitive. Figure A.15 on page 602 is an example of a simple Postscript program.

Literals are names preceded with a slash (/). This causes the name to be placed on the operand stack rather than having its value looked up. This allows the l-value of *add* (i.e., its name) to be placed in the stack rather than its r-value (i.e., the add procedure) invoked. For example, when defining a new function, before the definition is entered in the dictionary, it is first necessary to place the name and its definition in the operand stack and then execute the name *def*. The name *def*, when looked up in *systemdict*, will cause the top two entries in the operand stack (which should be the new function name and its executable definition) to be added as a new entry in *userdict*.

Painting Commands

So far we have described a language much like Forth, which uses a simple postfix evaluation virtual machine. Operands are stacked and operators use stack contents for their arguments. What gives Postscript its power is the ability to paint information on the page.

The name *show* is used to place text onto the page, *moveto* moves the cursor around the page, and *showpage* is used to display a completed page. The page is assumed to be white. Objects drawn on the page are opaque, meaning any object will erase an object it overwrites. Erasing part of a page is simply to write a white object onto that space.

The origin is the lower left bottom of the page and locations are given as (x, y) coordinates, with x being the horizontal distance and y being the vertical distance from the origin. Distance is measured in points, 72 to the inch, although the *scale* command can change that.

Example picture. To demonstrate some of these graphics capabilities, we will extend Figure A.15, which is the Postscript translation of the Forth program given in Figure 8.2.1, with a picture of a simple truck. Figure 12.3 is our modified program, with Lines 14 to 30 inserted between Lines 12 and 13 of the previous postscript program.

box is a new function that creates a 1 by 3 rectangle. Note that this is 1 point by 3 points, $\frac{1}{72} \times \frac{3}{72}$ of an inch, which is much too small to be seen. We use the scale command on Line 19 to enlarge this. *Newpath* starts a path. The cursor is moved to the origin by the *moveto* command, and then *lineto* is used to create a series of line segments. *Closepath* is used to close the path into a closed figure.

Line widths are set to .1 and the color is set to degrees of gray by the *setgray* command. Black is 0; white would be 1. In Line 18, the current graphics environment is saved to later restore it. All scaling changes that follow are reset to the original value when we restore the current graphics state. We then scale the x and y coordinates so that each point now represents an inch (72 points). A 1 by 3 rectangle now represents a one-inch by three-inch box.

To place the truck on the page (Line 20), we translate the origin by 2 (which is 2 inches now due to scaling) in the x direction and 5 inches in the y direction. The origin (0,0) is now near the numbers printed by Lines 1 to 12 of this program. *box stroke* draws the 1 by 3 box in the translated location, and stroke fills in the line segments. (We also could have filled in the box with the *fill* command, as we show on the next line.) We then translate the origin to place the various parts of the truck and its tires. Line 24 defines a tire as a unit circle.

The complete program is given in Figure 12.3 and the completed picture is given in Figure 12.4. Note that we added the comment line %! at the beginning. This is a Postscript convention (see page 490) that is often needed to inform programs, such as printing programs, that the file really represents a Postscript program.

Space filling commands. One of the more interesting properties of Postscript is the ability to fill shapes with a pattern. We already used the *box fill* command on line 21 of our truck picture. However, a difficult problem is this: When are you inside or outside of an arbitrary shape? Two algorithms are implemented:

1. *Nonzero winding rule.* This is the method used by the *fill* operator. Draw a line from a point to infinity. For each segment of the shape boundary that crosses the line segment from left to right, add one; for each segment that

```
%! This is a Postscript file
%Same as earlier Forth program
/Helvetica findfont
20 scalefont
setfont
200 400 moveto
/formatit {10 10 string cvrs show} def
/sqr {dup mul} def
/dosum {exch 1 add exch 1 index sqr add} def
3 6 dosum 2 copy formatit ( ) show formatit
clear
200 375 moveto
0 0 0 1 9 {pop dosum} for formatit
% Lets draw a truck
/box {newpath 0 0 moveto 0 1 lineto 3 1 lineto 3 0 lineto
   closepath} def
.1 setlinewidth 0 setgray
gsave
72 72 scale
2 5 translate box stroke
3.2 0 translate .5 .5 scale box fill
0 1 translate .6 .6 scale box fill
grestore
/tire {newpath 1 0 moveto 0 0 1 0 360 arc closepath} def
.5 setlinewidth 10 10 scale
16 34 translate tire stroke
3 0 translate tire stroke
17 0 translate tire stroke
3 0 translate tire stroke
8 0 translate tire stroke
showpage
```

Figure 12.3. "18 wheeler" Truck program.

crosses from right to left, subtract one. If the final count is zero, then the point is outside the shape; otherwise it is inside.

2. *Even–odd rule.* This is the algorithm used by the *eofill* operator. Draw a line segment from the point to infinity. If it crosses an odd number of shape boundary segments, the point is inside the shape; if an even number of segments, then it is outside the segment.

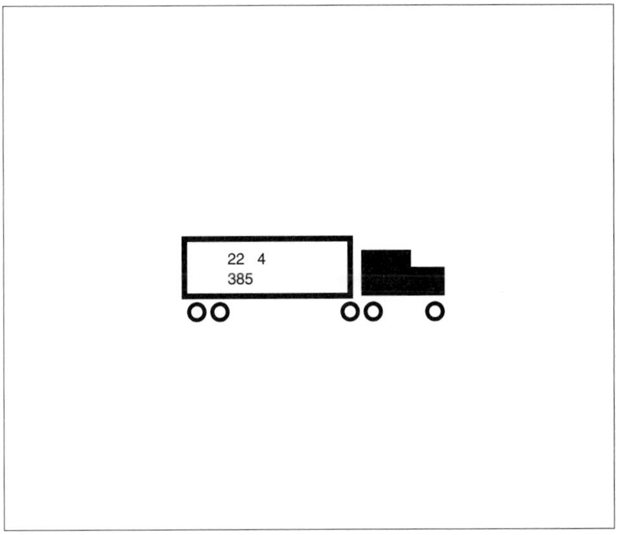

Figure 12.4. Excellent art work by the authors.

The differences among filling operators are given in Figure 12.5. The star is defined by the procedure

/star {newpath 1 0 moveto 6 4 lineto 0 4 lineto 5 0 lineto
3 6 lineto closepath} def

The leftmost start is drawn by the commands *star stroke*, the center star by *star fill*, and the right star by *star eofill*.

Figure 12.5. Stroke, fill, and eofill commands.

Document Conventions

What has been described so far is enough Postscript in which to write programs that create interesting documents. However, there are some conventions that are often used and sometimes required by various Postscript virtual machines. These are generally comments (which can be ignored), but often convey information to the Postscript interpreter. This prologue is often at the beginning of the file.

The most important is that the leading comment should be

%!

This informs the interpreter that the file is a Postscript program. Most programs that generate Postscript place their name on this line. A minimally conforming program contains %!PS in its initial line. Each page of a document is usually bracketed by a *save* and a *restore* command to isolate that page from the effects of other pages. Structuring conventions begin with %% until the first line that doesn't contain this comment. Some of these conventions are as follows

DocumentFonts: a list of fonts used in the document.

Title: an arbitrary string giving the title of the document.

Creator: the name of the person or program that created the file.

CreationDate: the date and time of creation.

Pages: the number of pages in the document.

BoundingBox: the four values that represent the lower left and upper right corners of the page that are actually painted by the program. This allows the pages to be inserted into other documents.

Postscript summary. Postscript was developed to be a virtual machine architecture that can be used to create printable documents. In most applications, the Postscript of a document is not meant to be read by a programmer. However, the syntax is quite simple and easily understood. There are educational programs that teach Postscript as a programming language. It has a simple syntax and semantics, and the availability of programs to display Postscript documents on the screen means that everyone has access to the virtual machine interpreter on which to test their Postscript programs.

Postscript has been developed further by Adobe with the creation of their Portable Document Format (PDF). PDF is a form of compressed Postscript. PDF readers are freely available over the Internet, and most Web browsers can display PDF files. PDF has become ubiquitous for the transmission and display of formatted documents. Giving away PDF display programs was a shrewd move for Adobe because they sell the Acrobat program needed to create PDF documents.

12.2 THE WORLD WIDE WEB

The growth of the Internet and the activity of *surfing the net* has led to a growth in the interest in the semantic description languages mentioned at the beginning of this chapter. In this section, we discuss the Internet, how it was developed, and where it came from. We provide a brief overview of Java's role as an Internet process. Finally, we discuss HTML and the role it plays in displaying information and in navigating around the WWW.

12.2.1 The Internet

During the 1960s, computers moved away from the batch-oriented model of computing toward an interactive model using terminals. (See Section 1.2.2.) As machines became more powerful, there was a desire to share information among users on different systems.

In the late 1960s, the U.S. Department of Defense Advanced Research Projects Agency (ARPA) began a project to see whether several computers, widely separated geographically, could be linked together to enable users at a terminal on one system to access the resources (e.g., the programs and data) on another computer. This was the beginning of the ARPANET. It is beyond the scope of this book to cover this in great detail. Suffice it to say that data communications—sending messages reliably from one computer to another—was the major obstacle.

The initial ARPANET began in 1970 as a three-node network linking BBN in Cambridge, Massachusetts, with UCLA and SRI in California using 56 kilobit lines. Gradually over time, more military installations and universities were added to the ARPANET until several hundred sites were available by the mid-1970s.

Communication between two computers was handled via *messages*. A message was broken down into fixed-length strings called *packets*, and the packets were sent from computer to computer until the original message was reassembled at the receiving node. To ensure that messages destined for another computer arrived reliably, a formal communication model—called a *protocol*—was developed. For the ARPANET, this developed as the Transmission Control Program/ Internet Protocol (TCP/IP).

TCP/IP was a low-level communication mechanism that simply determined that a sequence of bytes destined for a specific computer arrived there uncorrupted. It was generally too complex for users to use directly for accessing a computer. Therefore, several other protocols were developed that users could invoke, and these new protocols would be implemented in programs that actually transmitted the data using TCP/IP. For the ARPANET, three protocols were widely used:

- *Telnet.* Telnet is a protocol that makes the sending computer—the computer the user is actually working on—behave like a terminal connected to the distant computer. Using the terminology of distributed computing, the user is connected to a client computer, which acts like a terminal, and the terminal program is communicating using the telnet protocol to a distant *host* computer, which is providing the server program. This allows a user at one location to log into a computer at another location and appear to the distant computer as a local user. With telnet, a user at a computer at one university could log into the computer at another university and use the facilities of that second computer as if the user were directly connected at that second university.

- *SMTP.* SMTP is Simple Mail Transport Protocol. This provides the basic e-mail (electronic mail) that has become so ubiquitous today. Mail programs (e.g., Berkeley mail, Microsoft Outlook, Eudora, Lotus Notes) each have their own mechanisms for creating mail messages, saving messages in the user's file system, and processing additional commands. However, all compile messages into the same syntax that adheres to the SMTP protocol. The mail program then sends the message through the Internet, and the previously described TCP/IP protocol ensures that the message arrives at its destination. Adherence to this protocol is what allows e-mail to be so successful. E-mail can be sent by anyone and can be read by almost anyone else regardless of what mail program they are using. Contrast this to the almost chaos that reigns when word processing documents are written by one word-processing program and tried to be read by another.

- *FTP.* FTP is File Transfer Protocol. For many years, this was the standard way to retrieve data from a distant machine. FTP provided a mechanism to move a file from one machine to another. One would invoke the FTP client on a local machine, log onto the distant server machine using the FTP protocol, and then retrieve the desired documents from the distant machine or send documents from the user's machine to the distant machine. To permit general availability of documents, FTP permitted the *anonymous* login. Users could use FTP to get to a distant host computer, use the special login name *anonymous* that required no password, and have the ability to retrieve documents from a specified file directory. This was an early mechanism to permit the dissemination of information to any interested user.

Weaknesses in the FTP mechanism are apparent. First of all, one had to know explicitly which machine to access to retrieve the desired data. One also had to have access to the files of that machine to retrieve the information. The anonymous login partially solved that. One had to know exactly where on the file system the desired information was. Despite these weaknesses, FTP was the standard file transmission mechanism for many years until HTML changed all that. More about HTML later.

In the mid-1980s, ARPA decided to stop supporting the ARPANET. As a research activity, the concept had been proved, and ARPA was not in the business of providing what was becoming a commercial service. By this time, it had grown to several thousand computers worldwide. The academic world, the military, and high-technology companies were heavy users of this system. The U.S. National Science Foundation (NSF) took over the backbone network in the United States—the set of high-speed telephone lines that provided the basic TCP/IP communications traffic between host computers. The name of the network gradually evolved into the

Internet. Attached to this backbone, local networks (a state, a university, a large company) were added until the Internet became this amorphous collection of computers all continually chattering to one another. Commercial providers, now called Internet Service Providers (ISPs; e.g., Microsoft Network, Compuserve, AOL), established links to the Internet so that individuals on their home computers could use a modem to dial into their local ISP to be on the Internet. Today no one can accurately determine how many millions of users actually have access to this network. Once on the Internet, users could use their existing protocols (SMTP, FTP, Telnet) to send e-mail, retrieve files, and log into distant host computers.

By the early 1990s, the NSF also wanted to get out of the networking business, and various commercial communications companies took over management of the network. Growth has continued and today there are millions of users. The actual numbers are impossible to determine due to the lack of any centralized control of Internet resources. Transmission speeds have increased from the initial 56-kilobit lines, to 1-megabit lines to 100 million bits per second on fiberoptics cables, although individual users working at home typically are connected via 33.6-kilobit or 56-kilobit-per-second modems. One of the newer advances is high-speed home access with users using their cable TV lines to get megabit access to the Internet.

Creation of the Web

By the late 1980s, there was widespread interest in being able to easily transfer files. As already explained, FTP was a cumbersome process. The WWW (or the Web) was developed as additional protocols to the three widely used protocols (Telnet, SMTP, and FTP) mentioned earlier. Physicists—principally Tim Berners-Lee at CERN, the high-energy particle research laboratory near Geneva, Switzerland—desired a mechanism to access and transfer documents by computer that was simpler than the standard FTP server. They developed the concept of the semantic description given earlier in this chapter. One server program would display a document, and a client program, called a *browser*, would read and understand the displayed document. The power of their system was that the displayed document contained pointers to other documents—something the computer science community calls *hypertext*. An earlier version of hypertext was Apple Computer's HyperCard product for the Macintosh, but the real power of the CERN development was to allow hypertext links to documents that existed on other computers connected to the Internet.

The protocol developed was the HyperText Transport Protocol (HTTP). Each pointer became known as a *Uniform Resource Locator* (URL). Document location was reduced to invoking a Web browser on your local machine, typing in a URL for the document you wanted to access, connecting to a Web server on the distant machine that contained the location of the typed in URL, and displaying the document obeying the HTTP protocol. By clicking with your mouse on URLs embedded within the displayed document as hypertext links to locate other documents, the user could navigate from Web server to Web server.

This process was vastly superior to the FTP mechanism that was used earlier. Web browsers totally changed the nature of the Internet. The National Center for Supercomputer Applications (NCSA) Mosaic browser was released in 1993. It made it easy for anyone to access documents by using a point-and-click interface to navigating with URLs and hyperlinks. Now the Internet was no longer the tool of the research community and could be used by anyone to access and retrieve information. As long as a browser and the displayed document obeyed the HTTP protocol, any browser can communicate with any Web server. This moved the Internet out of the realm of the *techie* user and into mainstream computer (and non-computer) applications.

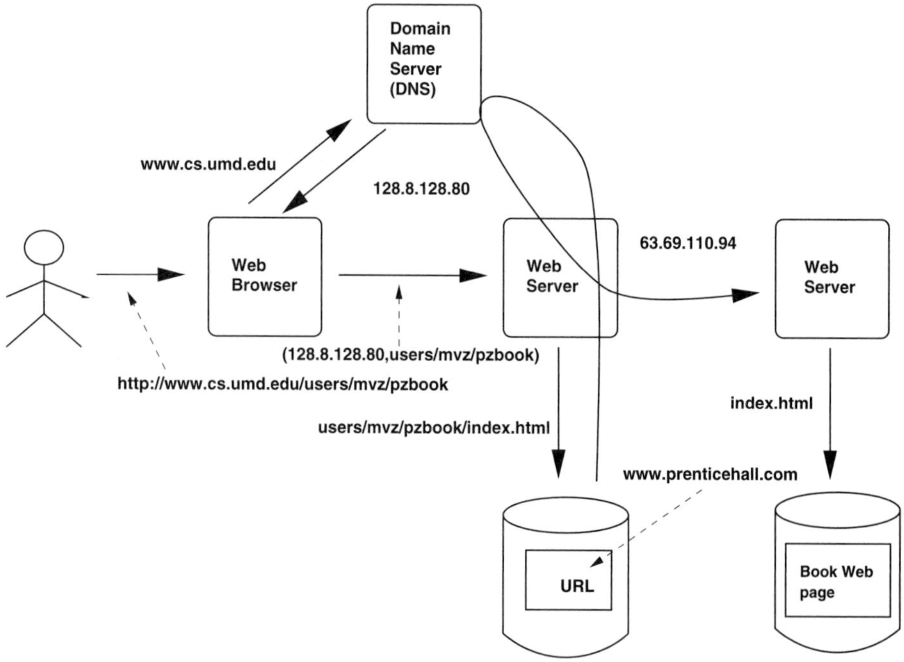

Figure 12.6. Accessing Web Pages.

Figure 12.6 is an example that shows the mediator architecture of the WWW. Assume that you want to find the Prentice-Hall Web site for information about this book. The steps in the process are as follows:

1. The user types in the URL for the *home page*—a page of information about an individual or a topic. This would be *http://www.cs.umd.edu/users/mvz/pzbook*. This URL consists of two parts: a *Domain name* (*www.cs.umd.edu*), which is the name of the machine containing the desired web page, and a file on that machine, which is the desired Web page with information about this book (*users/mvz/pzbook*).

2. The Web browser sends the domain name to one of several special Internet

machines called *Domain Name Servers* (DNS). The DNS returns the Internet Protocol (IP) address for that domain name. Every machine on the Internet has a unique domain name and unique IP address. The IP address is a sequence of four 8-bit bytes usually written as four numbers separated by periods. (In this example, the DNS entry would be 128.8.128.80.)

3. The web browser sends the file name (*users/mvz/pzbook*) to the Web server at IP address 128.8.128.80. A HTTP Daemon (HTTPD) program on this machine is the main interface between a web server and the Internet. This program is constantly monitoring the computer's connection to the Internet, looking for appropriate HTTP messages. A *Daemon* is a program in an operating system that is always executing. Print programs, memory management programs, and scheduling programs are typical daemons in most operating systems. To implement the Web, an HTTP Daemon has to be installed on a server computer.

4. In this example, the Web server appends the name *index.html* because the given file (*users/mvz/pzbook*) was a directory and not a file. (On PCs, it will append *index.htm* or *default.htm* typically.)

5. The contents of the file *users/mvz/pzbook/index.html* are sent back to the Web browser and displayed to the user.

6. If the user now clicks on the URL for Prentice-Hall that appears on the Web page (*www.prenticehall.com*), the process is repeated and the Prentice-Hall server at IP address 63.69.110.94 is accessed and the appropriate Web page is displayed.

In a similar manner, a user can point and click and then navigate around the world looking at Web pages until the desired information is found.

Portals. To make navigation easier, certain Web sites are now known as *portals*—entrance sites to the WWW. These sites have programs known as *search engines.* A search engine is a query processor in which you enter a question. The result of that query is a list of WWW locations that answer the question. By clicking on the relevant links, the user can visit various locations to obtain information.

Search engines often operate as *Web crawlers.* Beginning at one location, the Web crawler follows all links on that Web page to find other Web pages. Because of this interconnection, the entire WWW can be reached. A Web crawler will construct a database abstracting all pages, and a query to the search engine will retrieve information from that database.

For example, professors at a university may have home pages. On those pages may be links to a department home page and a university home page. The universities where they obtained their degrees may also be listed as well as companies or organizations in which they are associated. Because of this expanding network, the entire Internet can generally be reached. Different search engines differ in how they classify information in response to a query. Most of this is proprietary information, which often results in very different answers to the same query when different search engines are used.

HTML

An important part of Web navigation is the ability to display Web pages from a Web server and find and activate URLs to move from one Web site to another. HTML is the semantic description language developed by the original CERN group. It creates a virtual machine that Web browsers are programmed to execute to perform Web functions. As for the actual details of the notation for creating this new protocol, CERN decided to use a version of Standard Generalized Markup Language (SGML) that they called HyperText Markup Language (HTML).

SGML. We will first look at the general SGML notation and then look at the HTML instance of SGML.

History of SGML. Development of SGML began in the late 1960s as a means to format a particular document using descriptive tags. Rather than using proprietary keywords, a document could be classified according to a predefined set of terms, such as *section heading*, *title*, *figure*, and so on. In this manner, semantic information about a document could be carried along with the actual contents. In the late 1960s, the Graphic Communications Association Composition Committee, with ideas from William Tunnicliffe, Stanley Rice, and Norman Scharpf, developed the GenCode(R) concept to identify the different generic codes needed for different documents. In 1969, Charles Goldfarb of IBM, with Edward Mosher and Raymond Lorie developed the Generalized Markup Language (GML) to identify components of a document with a specific nested syntax. In 1978, the American National Standards Institute (ANSI) set up a standards group to merge the concepts of GenCode(R) and GML. This developed into SGML, which was standardized in 1986 as ISO standard 8879.

SGML syntax. A document consists of text, which is an unstructured sequence of characters. However, within the text can be SGML *elements*. The semantics of elements are unspecified, but their syntax is given. Elements are bracketed by a start-tag and an end-tag notation. For example, the *zork* element begins with the tag ⟨zork⟩ and terminates with the end tag ⟨/zork⟩. All text between these tags belongs to this element. For example,

⟨zork⟩ I am a zork ⟨/zork⟩

identifies "I am a zork" as the contents of the *zork* element.

In cases where the ending of an element is unambiguous, the end-tag can be omitted. For example, if we define a report as an SGML document consisting of a title, author, abstract, and body of text, we could give its description as

⟨report⟩
⟨title⟩ text ⟨/title⟩
⟨author⟩ text ⟨/author⟩
⟨abstract⟩ text ⟨/abstract⟩
⟨body⟩ text ⟨/body⟩
⟨/report⟩

or as

⟨report⟩
⟨title⟩ text
⟨author⟩ text
⟨abstract⟩ text
⟨body⟩ text
⟨/report⟩

because each section flows unambiguously into the next.

If we define the body of a report to be a sequence of sections, each consisting of nested sections, to an unlimited depth, then each section is defined by the syntax

⟨section⟩ text ⟨/section⟩

However, in this case, the end-tag would be required because it would not be unambiguously known where the end occurred.

An important part of SGML is that it separates the attributes of a document from its presentation. We could print the ⟨report⟩ using any type font and not destroy the essential meaning of the document. We could print the ⟨title⟩ element in 20-point font and the ⟨author⟩ element in 16-point font, or we could print everything in 10-point font. All this is outside of the scope of the document. As we later see, this poses a problem in HTML, where the HTML file is both a description of what a Web page contains and a description of how it will be displayed.

SGML could be used to handle more significant presentation issues. For example, as described in Section 1.3.4, the date is often displayed in different formats in different countries. To receive a message that "There will be a meeting on 11/10/01" has a very different interpretation in the United States than in Europe. If this is an internal memo of an international company, it would not be clear if the meeting is on the 10th day of November or the 11th day of October. However, if this memo were in SGML, we could have an appropriate ⟨date⟩ element and write the statement as

⟨memo⟩ There will be a meeting on
    ⟨! This is a SGML comment – – Give date⟩
    ⟨date⟩ ⟨month⟩ 11 ⟨day⟩ 10 ⟨year⟩ 2001 ⟨/date⟩.
⟨/memo⟩

Different client mail systems—one for the European employees and one for the U.S. employees—would display the ⟨date⟩ element correctly for each user.

The set of elements are described in an SGML component called the Document Type Declaration (DTD), which provides for a grammatical definition of the available tags for a given document. Although there are other components of SGML, this is a sufficient introduction for our tour of HTML.

HTML Syntax and Semantics. When CERN developed the initial concept of a hypertext browser, SGML became the basis for their notation. The language was called HyperText Markup Language and most files are given as *name.html* by convention. (On PCs, which have three-character filename extensions, this is often given as *name.htm*.) The default file to read when a Web browser tries to access a new computer is usually the name *index.html*. For example, if you want to access updated information about this book, the authors have set up a Web home page at the University of Maryland. By entering the address

http://www.cs.umd.edu/users/mvz/pzbook/

your Web browser will look for the file *index.html* in this directory, and then display it.

HTML files obey the SGML syntax given previously. The minimal HTML document has the syntax

⟨html⟩
⟨title⟩ Document title ⟨/title⟩
⟨body⟩ Text of document ⟨/body⟩
⟨/html⟩

Case is ignored for tags. Thus, ⟨html⟩ and ⟨HTML⟩ are the same. In addition, tags can sometimes have optional arguments.

The text of the body of the document can have additional structure. Some of the more important elements of HTML are as follows:

1. *Sections.* These separate parts of a document. ⟨h1⟩ is a major heading. These are usually printed in large letters. Note that this ⟨h1⟩ tag mixes semantic content (the major heading of a Web page) with a presentation issue (use a large font). Because Web browsers have freedom in displaying HTML tags, a given Web page may look very different when displayed by different browsers.

   ⟨h2⟩ and ⟨h3⟩ provide for subheadings of a document and are displayed in smaller fonts. ⟨hr⟩ draws a horizontal line on the document, and the tag width (e.g., ⟨hr width = 50%⟩) specifies how long the line should be. ⟨p⟩ starts a new paragraph, and ⟨br⟩ (break) starts a new line with no indentation.

2. *Presentation.* These affect how a document may look. Exactly how they are displayed is not specified, and individual browsers have wide latitude in presentation format. ⟨b⟩ displays text in bold fonts, and ⟨i⟩ is italics. ⟨blink⟩ displays blinking text (which is very annoying and should not be used). ⟨pre⟩ is preformatted text that is displayed as it exists in the HTML file with all embedded spaces and newline characters. It was an attempt to provide standardized formatting independent of browser. In general, HTML ignores whitespace characters as it formats the text for presentation.

   ⟨center⟩ centers the text, and ⟨blockquote⟩ formats a long quotation.

3. *Lists.* Lists of items can be displayed in various ways: ⟨li⟩ starts the next item in a list. This is terminated by either the end of the list or the next list item. (There is no ⟨/li⟩.) Lists may be numbered (ordered list) with the tag ⟨ol⟩ or unordered (unordered list) with the tag ⟨ul⟩. Definition lists lists (⟨dl⟩) have the embedded tags ⟨dt⟩ for the term being defined and ⟨dd⟩ for the definition of the term.

4. *URLs.* The power of HTML is in its links to other HTML resources. The concept of the Uniform Resource Locator (URL) is the mechanism that provides this linkage. In specific tags of an HTML document, the URL of another HTML document can be accessed. The general syntax of a URL is

   http://location/pathname/file

   where

   http : signifies that the location is an HTML document using the HTTP protocol,

   // states that it is on another machine, and

   location is the domain name of that machine on the Internet. The Domain Name Server is a machine that translates a domain name into an IP address, the actual location of the machine on the Internet.

   pathname/file is the location of the file on the machine at address *locaiton*. If the URL points to a local file, then the leading // can be omitted.

   Accessing another document is given by the tag ⟨a⟩. ⟨a HREF = url location⟩ text ⟨/a⟩ causes *text* to be highlighted in some way by the Web browser. Clicking the mouse on this text causes the browser to link to this new HTML file at address *url location* and display it. This is the basic mechanism used to surf the net.

5. *Image URLs.* ⟨IMG SRC = file location ALT = text⟩ causes pictures at file location *file location* to be displayed on the screen. ALT indicates *text* that should be displayed if the browser cannot display the picture. The parameter *align* (with values *top*, *middle*, or *bottom*) causes succeeding text to be aligned with the top, middle, or bottom line of the figure. This is extremely limiting in that only one line of text can appear next to a picture. Pictures can typically be GIF-formatted or JPEG-formatted.

   In defining a URL, we have the strange syntax in the HREF option of specifying "http:". This is because a hyperlink to another HTML Web page using the HTTP protocol is only one possible option of a hypertext link. Others are possible. The general syntax of these URLs is

   method://location/pathname/file

which indicates that the URL that is given should be accessed via the chosen *method.* HTML files via the HTTP protocol is only one way to create hyperlinks in a document. Others include the following:

- *FTP* - Access the URL using the FTP protocol. This is used to transmit files to the browser, especially non-HTML files. HTML files can be easily transmitted directly by the browser.
- *GOPHER* - Access the URL using the gopher protocol. Gopher is an earlier protocol for accessing information on the Internet. It was just gaining popularity when HTML arrived on the scene and replaced it.
- *MAILTO* - The URL in this case is an e-mail address, and clicking on this URL causes the Web server to create a mail message that is sent to that address.
- *FILE* - The URL specified here is a local file. Based upon the extension to the file name, an appropriate viewer will be invoked. That is, *report.ps* will open a Postscript viewer for the file, *picture.tif* will open a graphics view in TIFF format, *sound.au* represents an audio file, and so on. This permits the Web browser to have full access to the local file system of the user's computer. There is no distinction between local files and foreign URLs.
- *NEWS* - The URL of *news.group* will invoke the local news server to access that news group.

One of the weaknesses of the WWW is that each browser has to know about each of these protocols. If a new protocol is developed, then each browser needs to be updated to handle this new feature. Given the amorphous and sometimes chaotic growth of the Internet, this is a recipe for potential disaster. Java was developed to handle this problem, as we discuss later.

6. *Tables.* Tables can be created with a ⟨table⟩ element. Tables can have borders and consist of so many lines by so many columns.

   The tag *border* = *number* creates a box *number*-thick around the table as a border. Before each new row, the tag ⟨tr⟩ starts this new table row, and the tag ⟨td⟩ refers to the next item in that row. ⟨th⟩ heading ⟨/th⟩ gives a cell heading, and ⟨caption⟩ text ⟨/caption⟩ places a caption after the table.

Applets

As given so far, HTML is a passive language. The browser simply displays Web pages in HTML and uses embedded URLs on that page to navigate from one HTML file to another displaying information or pictures. That by itself is a valuable service that allows users to search for information from a variety of sources and has greatly changed the behavior of millions of individuals in looking for products, performing research, or looking for information.

However, Web servers have additional features that permit a more active role for the server. It can acquire information from the client browser (i.e., from the user) and provide for alternative behavior. We are in effect using the Web server to execute programs, and programming web pages has become the latest change to our programming paradigms. These executable web pages have become known as *applets* or mini-applications. Some of these are available on all Web servers. Sun Microsystems has developed Java, which is a language designed for applet execution. We discuss applets in Section 12.2.3.

Forms. Forms are a method for passing information between a user at a Web browser and a Web server. Information is entered by the user, based upon embedded commands in the HTML file. This information is passed to a program on the server system. This is the Common Gateway Interface (CGI) file. Web servers typically have a specific *cgi-bin* directory containing these CGI programs. The syntax of the ⟨form⟩ element is given as

⟨form method = "type" action = "cgi script to execute"⟩ text ⟨/form⟩

where *type* can be either *get* or *post*. Using *Get*, the data are passed to the CGI script program as the variable QUERY_STRING , whereas with *post*, the information is passed to the CGI program through the normal read process. The CGI script can be a C or Java program, but is most often a shell program or a TCL or Perl script. We already discussed Perl as a process scripting language with strong features for processing regular expressions back in chapter 3. Perl has turned out to be well suited for the processing of HTML forms as well. We briefly discuss Perl scripts in Section 12.2.2.

Several elements provide for the information that can be passed to this CGI program:

⟨input type = textname = "name" size = number⟩ causes (in most browsers) a window of size *number* of characters to open on the screen. The pair (*name*, *user input*) will be passed to the CGI program when the data are *submitted.* This can be handled as an associative array data item in Perl to associate the given name with the text that a user enters.

The tag ⟨input type = submit value = "send"⟩ creates a button with the label *send*, which, when clicked, causes the data entered in the form to be sent to the CGI program. The tag ⟨input type = "reset" value = "Reset form"⟩ creates a button labeled *Reset form* and clears all data from the form to allow for reentering new data before submission.

Other types are implemented for the ⟨input⟩ tag. ⟨input type = password⟩ is similar to *text* except that the input does not appear on the browser screen. As its name implies, it is useful for typing in passwords. ⟨input type = checkbox⟩ creates a box that can be checked (i.e., a toggle button or a push pin icon);

⟨input type = radio⟩ creates a radio button for other toggles with the same name. ⟨textarea name = "name" rows = "num1" cols = "num2"⟩ is like ⟨input⟩ except that a box $num1 \times num2$ is opened on the browser window. Using forms, CGI scripts, and building HTML files dynamically allow the Web to behave like any other computing environment. One can build query systems, games, and other features that have made surfing the net so popular.

12.2.2 CGI Scripts

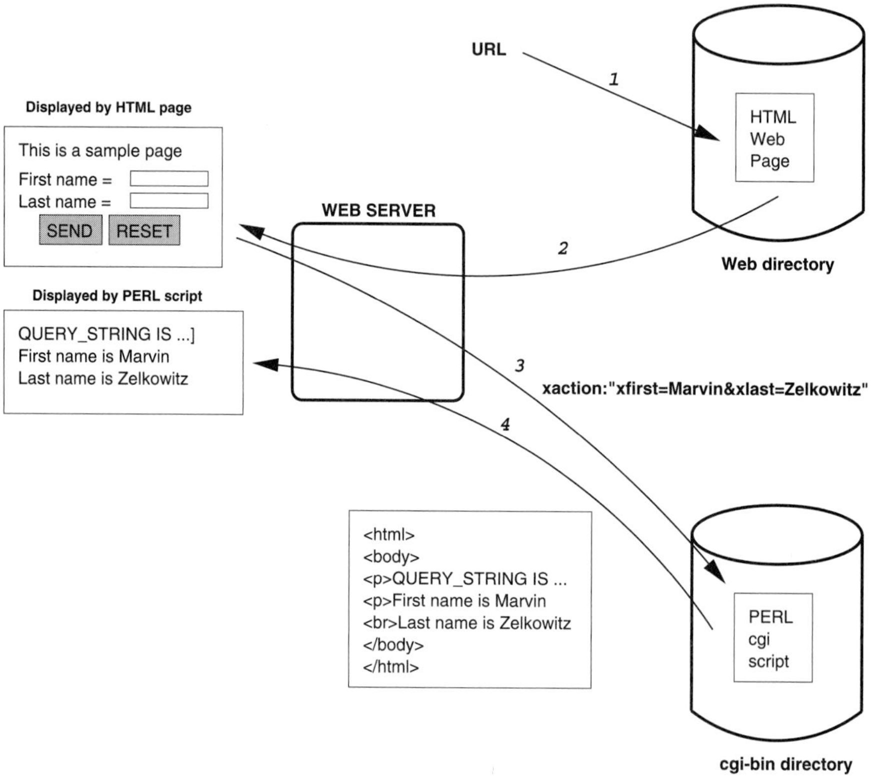

Figure 12.7. CGI scripts.

Figure 12.7 shows the interaction between a Web page and a cgi script written in Perl. It is a simple example of a client–server interaction. By typing in the URL into a Web browser (Link 1 in Figure 12.7), the appropriate HTML file is passed to the Web browser and the Web page is displayed (Link 2 of Figure 12.7). After the appropriate information is added to the Web page, the *SEND* button causes the data to be sent to the Perl script *xaction* (Link 3). The Perl program processes the

```
<HTML>
<HEAD>
<TITLE>cgi-test</TITLE>
</HEAD>
<BODY>
<p> This is a sample page to read
two data items from the web page:
<form action="cgi-bin/xaction" method=get>
<p>First name=<input type=text name=xfirst size=10>
<br>Last name=<input type=text name=xlast size=20>
<br> <input type=submit value=SEND>
<input type=reset value=RESET>
</form>
</BODY>
</HTML>
```

(a) Web page

```
#!/usr/bin/perl
print "Content-Type: text/html\n\n";
print "<html><head>\n";
print "<title>Sample PERL script</title>\n";
print "</head><body>\n";
print "<p>Query_string is $ENV{'QUERY_STRING'}\n";
foreach ( split( /&/, $ENV{'QUERY_STRING'}) )
    { ( $key, $val ) = split( /=/, $_, 2 );
    $tmp{$key} = $val; }
print "<p>First name is <b>$tmp'xfirst'</b>\n";
print "<p>Last name is <b>$tmp'xlast'</b>\n";
print "</body></html>\n"
```

(b) xaction PERL cgi script

Figure 12.8. HTML and Perl scripts.

data and creates an HTML page that is displayed on the user's Web browser. This page contains the information passed to it earlier (Link 4).

The actual code to cause this interaction is given in Figure 12.8. The interaction between the Web page written in HTML and the cgi script is given as the ⟨form⟩ element in Figure 12.8(a). The sequence of actions described by this figure is as follows:

1. The ⟨action⟩ tag in the ⟨form⟩ element states that the cgi program *xaction* will be activated when the *submit* tag is entered.

2. The text entered in the first rectangle will be associated with the name *xfirst* by the first ⟨input⟩ element, and the text entered in the second rectangle will be associated with the name *xlast* by the second ⟨input⟩ element. *xfirst* and *xlast* are arbitrary names created by the Web page designer.

3. When the user clicks on the *SEND* button (assuming *Marvin* is typed into the first rectangle and *Zelkowitz* into the second), the *xaction* program is invoked and is passed to the environment variable *QUERY_STRING* with the value "xfirst=Marvin&xlast=Zelkowitz."

At the server end of the process, the Perl program *xaction* operates as follows:

1. The script first informs the operating system that it is a Perl program (Line 1 of Figure 12.8[b]).

2. The output from this program will be sent back to the Web browser. We want it to be an HTML page to be displayed. The *Content-Type : text/html* tells the Web browser of the data to be presented—a text Web page written in HTML.

3. Each Perl print statement generates the next part of the HTML to display. The program dynamically creates a Web page in HTML to display.

4. The essential part of the algorithm in *xaction* is the **foreach** loop. The first *split* function divides the *QUERY_STRING* parameter in the operating system environment (variable $ENV of the Perl program) created by the HTML ⟨form⟩ into a sequence of strings using & as the delimiter. This creates the array ($xfirst = Marvin$, $xlast = Zelkowitz$). The **foreach** statement and *split* function can each handle an arbitrary number of names.

5. The second *split* creates the association of *$key* and *$val* for each sequence member created by the *split* function. Thus, the pairs ($xfirst, Marvin$) and ($xlast, Zelkowitz$) are created. The associative array *$tmp* is created so that *$tmp{'xfirst'}* and *$tmp{'xlast'}* can be accessed to extract the two arguments.

This example only shows the basic interaction between Web pages and cgi scripts. There are other considerations:

1. Once the parameters are decoded by the **foreach** statement, the Perl program may access files within the server to retrieve relevant information, order a product for the Web user, or perform any other computational task.

2. The *split* operation as given previously is not quite complete. The *submit* operation on the Web form actually changes all blanks to + symbols. Thus, + must be changed back to a blank via the Perl substitution pattern

   ```
   $key=~s/+/ /g;
   ```

   which causes a global substitution (the final *g*) of each + back into a blank.

3. Special symbols, transmitted as binary data %xx, must be converted into their ASCII character code given by *xx*:

   ```
   $key=~s/%([0-9a-f]{2})/pack("c",hex($1))/gie;
   ```

   This last command is a substitution that matches % followed by two characters from the Set 0 to 9 and a to f (i.e., the 16 symbols used to represent hexadecimal [base 16] numbers), which then packs them into a single character. That is, the two hexadecimal digits each represent 4 bits and collectively are the 8-bit representation of the special symbol. This symbol then replaces the %xx in the original string.

12.2.3 Java Applets

The existing Web structure with HTML documents being read by Web servers and displayed by Web browsers has four limitations, although it is clear that the Web has greatly exceeded the initial design goals developed by the physicists at CERN:

1. For each change or addition to a protocol, all browsers need to be updated. It does no good to just update the server to display the new format because the display process resides in the browser client.

2. The amount of information an HTML process can access is limited to the few simple keystrokes generated by the ⟨form⟩ elements of a document. It would be useful for HTML programs (e.g., the CGI scripts) to access large data files on the browser system.

3. Control of the interaction is now handled by the server with the embedded HTML commands in Web pages. This ties up the server, especially at sites that are popular with many user *hits* per day. It would be more efficient if control could be managed by the client browser with the server being in more of a supporting role.

4. Displaying Web pages is limited by the transmission speed of the communications line. Typically the user client machine is idle, waiting for information while the data are being downloaded to a user's machine at a low speed of 33.6K bits per second or even at the slightly faster 56K bits per second. With an increase in large video, picture, and audio components to Web pages, this time delay is growing.

One way to handle this would be for some server interaction to execute on the browser platform. Instead of transferring HTML data to the server, the server could transmit a small program to the browser and execute the application on the browser machine. This would eliminate some of the load off the server and might decrease the amount of information that has to be transmitted from server to browser.

Java is a programming language with a syntax similar to C++ with some of the semantics of C++ and Smalltalk. Java programs are initially compiled into a machine-independent interpreter code using a notation called *bytecodes* for a Java Virtual Machine. Java was designed as a vehicle for executing programs on the client browser.

Security of these browsers is crucial for their acceptance. It must not be possible for a browser to download a malicious applet from another source, which then destroys the client's file system. The Java Virtual Machine is designed to have run-time checks to ensure that this doesn't happen. However, this is really a systems validation issue and outside of the realm of the Java language.

Sun initially developed a Web browser called HotJava that included a Java interpreter. However, since 1995, Java is processed by virtually all Web browsers.

Java adds a new feature to Web browsing. Whereas previous browsers needed to know about all protocols and file formats (e.g., http, ftp, gif, au), a Java browser did not need to know about any of them. When a hyperlink URL is activated, the method is checked: if it is not available, the browser will look for it on the browser system and then on the server system. If found, it will transfer it (if necessary) to the browser client, and then execute it as a local applet.

For example, with HotJava, if HotJava finds an *http* hyperlink, it will first transport the *http* applet, which has been written in Java, and then execute it. Only those servers implementing a method need have a Java applet for it. The browser, in turn, need know nothing about it—only the ability to acquire it if necessary.

This allows for a somewhat orderly growth of Web functionality. If a company develops a new protocol, it can implement its server with it and supply a Java applet to handle this new method. The browser, when it finds this new method, can download the applet and then execute it. One feature (or danger depending on your point of view) of this approach is that the company can first charge for accessing this new applet and provides for a source of revenue that is currently missing from most Web access. Of course, there are those who say Web access should not have a charge. Free access probably cannot survive forever, but a reasonable charging scheme needs to be developed. One pitfall to this is that a company may simply use an existing protocol, but change its name to stimulate revenue. One hopes that such charades will fail because if not, the entire Internet may fail. Internet growth and usage has survived principally on the universality of access to Internet resources.

A side effect of this approach is that, once the applet is executing on the client system, it could access the file system of the user. The Java Virtual Machine is supposed to ensure that this cannot happen. Of course, an important consideration is security of the user system. One must be extremely careful that the browser that accesses an applet does not permit it to contain a computer virus (the ability to change executable programs on the user's machine to destroy files) or a Trojan horse (the ability to take over control of the user's computer).

Active applets. The use of CGI scripts permit a Web page designer to pass information back and forth between a Web server and a user using a Web browser. However, the use of CGI scripts is limited because the information available via the HTML ⟨form⟩ element is limited. Java applets allow for additional information to be processed because Java is a full programming language and not limited to a simple fill in the blanks of the HTML ⟨form⟩.

For processing Java source programs in HTML, the ⟨applet⟩ element

$$\langle \text{applet code} = \textit{Java bytecode}\ \text{width}=num_1\ \text{height}=num_2 \rangle$$

was added. This element will cause *Java bytecode*—an executable Java program in the same directory as the HTML web page—to execute. The results will be in a box that is num_1 pixels wide by num_2 pixels high.

For example, to execute the traditional "Hello World" program, the following Java program in file *hello.java* can be written:

```
import java.awt.*; /* applet library */
public class   hello extends   java.applet.Applet {
    public void paint(Graphics x) {
        x.drawString("Hello World", 100, 100);
    }
}
```

Compiling this program by the Java compiler creates the file *hello.class*. This file can now be executed by a Web page, so it is placed in an appropriate directory that can be read by the Web browser.

HTML to invoke this applet is the following:

```
⟨html⟩
⟨body⟩
⟨applet code = "hello.class" width = 200 height = 200⟩
⟨/applet⟩
⟨/html⟩
```

If the URL for this HTML page is passed to the Web browser, the ⟨applet⟩ element causes the *hello.class* Java program to execute. In this case, the *paint* command is used by Java to write its output to the HTML page (much like the Postscript *showpage* command earlier). In this small applet, the *paint* command that is given overrides the default *paint* command, and "Hello World" is displayed.

12.2.4 XML

HTML, as an instance of SGML, has a fixed set of semantic rules for each of its elements. As explained previously, there are conflicts between the semantics of what a document contains (e.g., header elements, paragraph elements, list elements) and presentation issues (e.g., fonts, colors, height and width of objects). To address these, toward the end of the 1990s, the WWW Consortium (W3C) developed Extensible Markup Language (XML) as a possible replacement for HTML for displaying Web pages.

XML is another instance of SGML. An XML document consists of a set of elements using the SGML syntax ⟨element name⟩. As with SGML documents, a document type declaration (DTD) document describes the semantics of each element type. However, as with HTML, some of these are becoming standard, and many XML documents can be processed with no external DTD.

An XML document begins with ⟨?xml XMLVersionNumber ?⟩ and consists of nested ⟨name⟩ *text* ⟨/name⟩ element sections. Elements with no ending tag are given as ⟨name/⟩.

Many of the concepts from HTML carry over to XML. URLs from HTML are Uniform Resource Indicators (URI) in XML and can be specified as *simple links* in XML:

<a xml:link="simple" href="usual http URL" >

Elements consist of markups and content. There are six types of markup

1. *Elements.* These are the types of items familiar from HTML and are given as ⟨name⟩ text ⟨/name⟩.
2. *Attributes.* These are tags associated with the start of an element. The prior URL example includes href="usual http URL" as an attribute.
3. *Entity references.* Symbols such as < have special meaning. To insert this into a document, an entity reference, &lt, is used instead. <start> is the same as <start>. Several other symbols are also entity references.
4. *Comments.* Comments are denoted ⟨! − −text − −⟩.
5. *Processing instructions.* These are given as ⟨?name PIName ?⟩. Applications should process *PIName* applications they recognize and ignore others. This is a mechanism to pass specific protocol information to an application that processes an XML page.
6. CDATA. These are characters ignored by the markup process and passed directly to the application. In ⟨![CDATA[text]]⟩, *text* is passed directly to the application.

The major difference between XML and HTML is that DTDs can be specified for documents using the element ⟨!DOCTYPE...⟩. This provides a syntax and a semantics for the elements of an XML document that is not simply the default values for the associated tags in HTML. For example, HTML Web pages can be specified in XML using the DTD

<!DOCTYPE HTML PUBLIC "HTML specification document URI" >

Each industry (e.g., banks, e-commerce, library repositories) can define a DTD that specifies the semantics of the information that it needs to process. This will permit specific XML Web pages to be processed more effectively than using the simpler HTML format.

12.3 SUGGESTIONS FOR FURTHER READING

Details of Postscript can be found in the *Postscript Language Reference Manual* [ADOBE 1990]. The use of TeX is explored by its author [KNUTH 1984], and Lamport's LaTeX extensions are described in [LAMPORT 1986]. More on networking is found in [DAVIE et al. 1999], and additional information on Web developing is in [BERNERS-LEE 1996].

12.4 PROBLEMS

1. (a) How many passes would it take LaTeX to create this book? Note that this book has a table of contents, various chapters with section headings, and an index. What data are created on each pass? What is the maximum number of passes needed?

2. Write a Postscript program that prints a post advertising the course this book is being used in. Make sure your poster includes several lines of text and at least five picture items.

3. Give some ways in which you could develop a compressed form of Postscript to transmit a Postscript document using fewer bytes.

4. Describe some of the ways in which HTML mixes up the semantic content of a Web page with the presentation of that page on the display screen.

5. What would be the advantages and disadvantages of using Postscript rather than HTML as the Web display language?

6. Why is Perl suited for CGI scripts? Why is C a poor choice to use instead of Perl?

Appendix A

Language Summaries

In this book we have emphasized the syntax and semantics from 13 different notations: Ada, C, C++, FORTRAN, HTML, Java, LISP, ML, Pascal, Perl, Postscript, Prolog, and Smalltalk. HTML was covered fairly thoroughly in chapter 12. In this appendix, we present sample programs for the other 12 languages that are discussed in some detail in this book, and we give the basic syntactic and semantic rules necessary to write simple programs in each of these languages.

A.1 ADA

Annotated Example

Figure A.1 presents an example of an array summation program. Here we use the encapsulation provided by Ada packages to implement information hiding. For the data input

```
4 1 2 3 4 5 1 2 3 4 5 0
```

the program produces the output

```
  1  2  3  4
SUM =  10
  1  2  3  4  5
SUM =  15
```

Line 1. `ArrayCalc` is the package specification that collects the array data for this program. All details about `ArrayCalc` that are to be known outside of this package must be given in this specification.

Line 2. `Mydata` is a data type that is known outside of the package. However, the type is `private`, meaning that it is only possible to declare objects of type `Mydata` and pass them to functions declared within package `ArrayCalc`.

Lines 3–4. Subprograms `sum` and `setval` are defined in this specification. Only the signature of the two subprograms are given to permit calls on these subprograms to be compiled from other packages.

```
package ArrayCalc is
     type Mydata is private;
     function sum return integer;
     procedure setval(arg:in integer);
     private
         size: constant:= 99;
         type myarray is array(1..size) of integer;
         type Mydata is record
             val: myarray;
             sz: integer := 0;
             end record;
         v: Mydata;
end;
package body ArrayCalc is
    function sum return integer is
        temp: integer;
    -- Body of function sum
        begin
        temp := 0;
        for i in 1..v.sz loop
            temp := temp + v.val(i);
            end loop;
        v.sz:=0;
        return temp;
        end sum;
    procedure setval(arg:in integer) is
        begin
        v.sz:= v.sz+1;
        v.val(v.sz):=arg;
        end setval; end;
with Text_IO; use Text_IO;
with ArrayCalc; use ArrayCalc;
procedure main is
     k, m: integer;
begin -- of main
     get(k);
     while k>0 loop
         for j in 1..k loop
            get(m); put(m,3);
            setval(m);
            end loop;
         new_line; put("SUM =");
         put(ArrayCalc.sum,4);
         new_line; get(k);
         end loop;
end;
```

Figure A.1. Ada example to sum an array.

Line 5. The keyword `private` indicates that all remaining information in this package specification may not be used by subprograms defined outside of package `ArrayCalc`.

Line 6. `size` is defined to be the constant 99. The scope of this constant is the package `ArrayCalc`.

Lines 8–12. `Mydata` and `v` are local data to the package.

Line 14. This begins the implementation part of package `ArrayCalc`, which gives implementation details for each subprogram declared in the package specification.

Line 17. Comments in Ada begin with `--` and continue for the rest of the line.

Lines 18–25. This `begin` block is the body of function `sum`.

Lines 20–22. Iteration is handled by the `loop` statement. There are several variations. In this subprogram, the `for` variation iterates with `i` taking on successive values from `1` to `v.sz`. Note that `i` is not declared, but is implicitly declared as a local variable within the loop statement.

Lines 26–30. These lines define the subprogram `setval`. `arg` is defined as an input-only argument, like call by value in Pascal.

Line 31. `with` indicates that the predefined package `Text_IO` is to be used within the following Ada component. All objects defined by `Text_IO` are prefixed by the name of the package. Because `Text_IO` is the standard input and output package, functions `Text_IO.get` and `Text_IO.put`, among others, are defined.

The `use` command allows Ada to search the `Text_IO` package first to define scopes of objects. Instead of using `Text_IO.put`, the program need only contain the name `put`.

Line 32. The package `ArrayCalc` will also be used in the following Ada component.

Line 33. An Ada program consists of a main procedure that may call other subprograms in various packages. `main` is our name for the main program in this example.

Line 36. The `get` function is defined in `Text_IO` to read data. It is an overloaded function, so the argument can be an integer variable (as in `k` here), a string variable, or the pair (file, object), allowing reads from data files. Because each set of arguments are unique, the Ada compiler knows which `get` function to call.

Line 39. `get` will read in integer `m`. `put`, defined in `Text_IO`, prints it argument. The optional second argument gives the field width of the object as printed. Thus, `m` is printed as three characters (with leading blanks for numbers less than 100).

Line 40. The procedure `setval` in package `ArrayCalc` is called and passed the argument `m`. Because of the `use` command on line 32, it is not necessary to fully qualify the name as `ArrayCalc.setval`.

Line 42. `new_line` is a function defined in `Text_IO`, which prints an end-of-line symbol. The `put` function prints `SUM =`. Note how this is a *different* function call from the `put` on Line 40 because this one prints a string, whereas the `put` on line

39 prints an integer. Overload resolution determines which function to invoke.

Line 43. Here the fully qualified name is given. Because of the `use` command on Line 32, `sum` could have been used instead. The fully qualified name is needed if the same function name is used in several packages within the scope of the current statement, and overload resolution could not distinguish between them. In this case, the number returned from `sum` is printed as four characters of output.

A.1.1 Data Objects

The basic types described in this section extend only slightly the data types available in Pascal. However, the Ada facilities for programmer definition of new types are considerably more powerful than those provided by Pascal, and the package facility allows encapsulation of type definitions and subprograms to obtain true data abstractions.

Primitive Data Types

Types such as *integer*, *real* (called *float* in Ada), *character*, *Boolean*, and *string* are *predefined* types, defined in package *Standard*, which is automatically known within each Ada program. These types are actually defined using a more primitive set of type constructors. Examples of these constructors are *enumerations*, *arrays*, and *records*. For example, both *Boolean* and *character* are defined as *enumerations*, and *string* is defined as a vector of *characters*. Because the type-definition mechanism is used for both primitive and programmer-defined types, many of the examples in this section may include type definitions.

Variables and constants. Any data object may be defined as either a constant or a variable. Any declaration beginning with the keyword **constant** is a constant. An initial value must be given, and this value cannot be changed during execution. If the keyword **constant** is omitted, the same declaration defines a variable data object. An initial value may be given, and the value may be modified through assignment. For example, a constant *MaxSize* and a variable *CurrentSize* may be declared by

MaxSize: **constant** integer := 500;
CurrentSize: integer := 0;

Ada constants may be arrays and records as well as elementary data objects, as in

WeekDays: **constant array**(1..5) **of** string(1..3) :=
("MON", "TUE", "WED", "THU", "FRI")

Ada includes many predefined *attributes* that designate important bindings or properties of a data object, data type, subprogram, or the underlying hardware computer. The attribute name (prefixed by ') is used with the name of the object to retrieve the value of the attribute. For example, one of the attributes of any vector data type, *Vect*, is the lower bound on its subscript range, denoted *Vect'First*. The upper bound is *Vect'Last*. By using these attributes, a program may be written so that it is independent of the particular type definition of *Vect*. Thus, if the definition of *Vect* is modified, the program statements using *Vect'First* and *Vect'Last* may remain the same. Predefined attributes exist for most of the basic data types discussed next; other attributes are taken up in subsequent sections as appropriate.

Numerical data types. Integers, floating-point reals, and fixed-point reals are the basic numeric data types. Declarations are similar to Pascal using the attributes **range** (for integers) and **digits** (for float), which specify the range in values the object may take:

```
type DayOfYear is range 1..366;    -- An integer value from 1 to 366
MyBirthday: DayOfYear := 219;      -- MyBirthday initialized to August 7
type Result is digits 7;           -- float type of 7 digits
Answer: Result;                    -- 7-digit float variable
```

Programs may access a hardware-provided fixed-point real-number representation if one exists. To define a fixed-point type, the program declares the required maximum difference between two consecutive values of the type, called the *delta value*. For example, to specify a range of decimal fixed-point numbers with two digits after the decimal point, a delta value of .01 would be declared:

```
type SmallAmount is delta 0.01 range -100.0..100.0;
```

The usual arithmetic operations are provided for fixed-point numbers. If the hardware does not directly provide an appropriate fixed-point number representation, the floating-point representation may be used by an implementation, provided the specified accuracy constraints are satisfied (i.e., numbers must provide at least the accuracy specified by the delta value).

Enumerations. Enumerations may be defined using a Pascal-like style of definition and implementation. For example, the definition

```
type class is (Fresh, Soph, Junior, Senior);
```

defines an enumeration type that may then be used in variable declarations. Unlike Pascal, an enumeration cannot be defined directly in a variable declaration, but must be defined in a separate type definition. The run-time representation of enumeration values uses the position number for each literal value, starting with 0 for the first value listed, 1 for the second value, and so on. The basic relational comparisons (equal, less than, etc.) are provided for enumeration values, as well as the successor and predecessor functions and assignment.

The same literal name may be used in several enumerations (unlike Pascal, where all enumeration literals must be distinct). Such a literal name is said to be *overloaded.* For example, given the prior definition of *class*, the definition

type BreadStatus **is** (Stale, Fresh);

overloads the literal name *Fresh*. In some contexts, the compiler may be able to resolve the overloading directly (e.g., in the assignment $B := Fresh$ where B is of type *class*). To specify explicitly which meaning of *Fresh* is intended at a point in the program where both the types *class* and *BreadStatus* are visible, the programmer may qualify the literal name with the name of the base type (e.g., *class*(*Fresh*) or *BreadStatus*(*Fresh*)).

Character and Boolean types. These are defined in the package *Standard* to be specific enumerations.

Pointer data types. A pointer type, called an **access** type, together with a primitive function **new**, creates a new data object (allocating storage in a heap area) and returns a pointer to it, which may then be assigned to a variable of an access type. A variable cannot be directly declared to be of an access type; instead, a type definition such as

type *access_typename* **is access** *typename*;

must be used, and then variables may be declared to be of the defined access type. A variable of access type is thus constrained to point to data objects of only a single type. All variables of access types have the null pointer value, *NULL*, as their initial value by default, unless an explicit pointer value is assigned in the declaration.

A block of storage may be set aside for allocation of storage for all data objects of a particular access type using the statement

for *access_typename* **use** *expression*

where the expression gives the size of the block of storage to be reserved. Any subsequent use of **new** for that access type allocates storage within the reserved block.

Structured Data Types

Vectors and arrays. An array data object may be declared with any number of dimensions with arbitrary subscript ranges and any type of component. For example, the declaration

Table: **array** (1..10,1..20) **of** float;

creates a 10×20 matrix of real numbers. Subscripting is used to select components (e.g., $Table(2,3)$).

Type definitions may be used to declare classes of array data objects. Ada fixes a defect in Pascal by not including the bounds of an array as part of the type designation. Ada allows an array type definition to be given without a particular subscript range for one or more dimensions. When a variable is declared as being of that type, the particular dimensions to be used for that data object are then given. For example, the array type definition might be

```
type Matrix is
    array (integer range <>, integer range <>) of float;
```

where <>, called a box, indicates a subscript range to be filled in when a variable of type *Matrix* is declared. A later variable declaration would then provide the particular subscript range for the *Matrix* data object—for example,

```
Table: Matrix(1..10,1..20);
```

The subscript range need not be an integer range; it may be a range from any enumeration type. Also the subscript bounds may be defined by expressions that involve computed results—for example,

```
NewList: array (1..N) of ListItem;
```

where N is a variable with a computed value. Each time the subprogram containing this declaration is entered, a new length of vector *NewList* is created depending on the value of N at the time of entry.

Subscripting may be used to select a *slice* out of a vector instead of a single component, where a *slice* is defined as a contiguous subvector of the original vector. For example, the reference *NewList*(2..4) results in selection of the three-component slice composed of the second through fourth components of *NewList*.

Initialization. Array components may be assigned initial values in the declaration that created the array, as in:

```
PowerOfTwo: array (1..6) of integer := (2,4,8,16,32,64);
```

Character strings. Character strings are treated as a predefined vector type using two other predefined types—*positive* (the positive integers) and *character* (enumerating the characters defined in package *Standard*):

```
type string is array (positive range <>) of character;
```

A particular string data object may then be declared by giving the maximum length (as subscript range) for the string:

```
MyString: string(1..30);
```

File data types. Files and input–output operations in Ada are defined as abstract data types using several predefined packages. Besides these packages, an implementation would ordinarily supply additional input–output packages built using the basic data types and operations defined in the predefined packages (e.g., a package for graphic output to a terminal).

User-Defined Types

Record data objects in Ada are similar to Pascal records. A record may have any number of components of arbitrary type. If the record has several variants, the variant components must come at the end. Unlike Pascal, however, a record with variants must always have a tag field, called the *discriminant* (fixing another defect in the Pascal definition), that explicitly indicates at run time which variant currently exists. Selection of a component that does not currently exist in the variant part of a record may be detected at run time and an exception raised.

In Ada, unlike Pascal, a record data object must be defined by first using a *type definition* to define the structure of the record and then giving a variable declaration using the type name. Similarly, if a component of a record is itself a record, then that record structure must be defined as a separate type definition; the second record definition cannot be nested inside the definition of the larger record.

A *default initial value* may be given for any component of a record, as in:

```
type Birthday is
    record
        Month: string(1..3) := "Jan";
        Day: integer range 1..31 :=17;
        Year: integer range 1950..2050 := 1969;
    end record;
```

Every data object of type *Birthday* has the initial value ("Jan", 17, 1969) unless an initial value assignment is given in the declaration in which case the stated initial values are used. If variable *MyDay* is declared, as in:

```
MyDay : Birthday;
```

then *MyDay* has the default initial values for its components. However, if *YourDay* is declared:

```
YourDay : Birthday := ("MAR", 13, 1968);
```

or, alternatively,

```
YourDay : Birthday := (Month => "MAR", Day => 13,
        Year => 1968);
```

then the given initial values are used in place of the default values.

Type declarations may include parameters, called *discriminants*, to define similar data objects. For example, to define a record type that contains information about each month, including a vector of reals having one entry for each day of the month, the following definition might be used:

```
type Month (Length : integer range 1..31) is
    record
        Name : string(1..3);
        Days : array (1..Length) of float;
    end record;
```

Then individual records of type *Month* may be declared, as in

```
Jan : Month(31);
Feb : Month(28);
```

in order to get a *Days* vector of the correct length in each record. Attributes *Days'First* and *Days'Last* may be used to access each component without having to know the explicit bounds information for each month.

A second method for using a single record type definition to define similar but not identical record data objects is to use a variant record structure similar to that in Pascal. The tag field, used to indicate which variant is present, is always listed as a discriminant in the record type definition (in the same form as given above). For example, an employee record might appear as

```
type WageType is (hourly, salaried);
type EmployeeRec (PayType : WageType) is
    record
        Name: string(1..30);
        Age: integer range 15..100;
        case PayType is
            when Hourly =>
                Hours: float;
                HourlyRate: float;
            when Salaried =>
                MonthlyRate: float;
    end record;
```

and then particular data objects might be declared, such as

```
President: EmployeeRec(Salaried);
Chauffeur: EmployeeRec(Hourly);
```

where the variant chosen never changes during execution (e.g., the wage type of *President* never changes to *Hourly*).

- all types
  - elementary
    - scalar
      - discrete
        - enumeration
          - character
          - Boolean
          - other enumeration
        - integer
          - signed integer
          - modular integer
      - real
        - floating point
        - fixed point
          - ordinary fixed point
          - decimal fixed point

- *all types continued*
  - *elementary continued*
    - access
      - access to object
      - access to subprogram
  - composite
    - array
      - string
      - other array
    - untagged record
    - tagged
    - task
    - protected

Numeric and nonlimited do not fit into this hierarchy

Figure A.2. Ada subtype hierarchy.

If the variant of a record data object is to change at run time, an assignment to the entire record variable must be made; the discriminant value cannot be changed in any other way. Such an assignment overwrites the block of storage representing the record with a complete set of new values, including a new discriminant value.

Subtypes. Any defined type gives a name to a class of data objects having certain attributes. A *subtype* of that *base type* consists of a subset of those data objects that meet a particular *constraint*. A constraint for the base type *integer* would be a restriction to a subrange of the integers; a constraint for an array base type defined with unspecified *integer* subscript range (<>) would be a particular subscript range. A constraint for a base type defined as a record with a discriminant would be a particular value for the discriminant (which might determine a particular variant of the record).

A subtype is defined using the syntax

subtype *subtypename* **is** *basetypename constraint*;

as in

subtype GraphScale **is** integer **range** -20..20;
subtype Executive **is** EmployeeRec(Salaried);

A subtype does not define a new type; it simply defines a subset of the data objects defined by the base type. In particular, the same operations that can be used on data objects of the base type can be used on objects of the subtype, and data objects of different subtypes of the same base type may be mixed as operands in an expression.

Derived types. A derived type is similar to a subtype, but a derived type is a *new type*—different from the base type. The syntax for a derived type definition is

type *DerivedTypeName* **is new** *basetypename*;

where the base type might be defined with a constraint (and thus actually be a subtype). For example, we might have

type Meters **is new** integer;
type Liters **is new** integer;

A derived type is allowed to use all the operations defined on the base type (or subtype). However, because the derived type is a distinct type from the base type, operations cannot be applied to mixtures of operands of the base type and the derived type. For example, given the earlier definitions, "+" is defined for base type *integer*, and thus it is also defined for derived types *Meters* and *Liters*. However, if X, Y, and Z are variables of types *integer*, *Meters*, and *Liters*, respectively, then no pair of these variables may be added together (e.g., $X+Z$ is invalid). Thus, by use of a derived type, the programmer is protected against the inadvertent addition of two variables that represent distinct kinds of data, although the base representation of the data may be identical (all represented as integers in this example).

A.1.2 Sequence Control

Ada execution is statement oriented, much like FORTRAN and Pascal.

Expressions

Infix notation is used for the usual binary arithmetic, relational, and Boolean operations. Prefix notation is used for unary operations (+, -, and NOT), and function calls use the ordinary mathematical prefix representation "*functionname*(*argument list*)." In the absence of parentheses, the following precedence order is followed (highest precedence operations listed first):

** (exponentiation)							
*	/	**mod**	**rem**				
+	−	**abs**	**not**	(unary + and −)			
+	−	&	(binary + and −)				
=	/=	<	<=	>	>=	**in**	**not in**
and	**or**	**xor**	**and then**	**or else**			

Operations with the same precedence are associated from left to right. Note that Ada contains the *short-circuit* Boolean operations **and then** and **or else**, which evaluate only their first operand whether that value is enough to determine the value of the expression. The operations **in** and **not in** are used to test if a value is within a particular range or satisfies a particular constraint.

Statements

The statement sequence-control structures are the usual conditional statements (**if** and **case**) and iteration statements (**loop**). Three forms of loop statement are provided, and an **exit** statement allows direct exit from a loop. A limited form of **goto** statement is also provided. All the major control statements terminate with the keyword **end** followed by the initial keyword of the statement (e.g., **end if, end loop**), so that separate **begin–end** pairs are seldom needed to bracket component statements in Ada.

Assignment. The Ada assignment statement is similar to the Pascal assignment. Assignment of a complete set of values to a record variable is also possible using either of these forms:

```
MyDay := ("DEC",30,1964);
MyDay := (Year => 1964, Month => "DEC", Day => 30);
```

If statements. The **if** statement has the general form

```
if Boolean expression then
    – statement sequence
elsif Boolean expression then
    – statement sequence
elsif Boolean expression then
...
else
    – statement sequence
end if;
```

where any of the **elsif** (else if) or **else** parts may be omitted.

CASE statements. The general form of the **case** statement is

```
case expression is
    when choice | ... | choice => statement sequence;
    when choice | ... | choice => statement sequence;
...
when others => statement sequence
end case;
```

Each choice indicates either one or a range of possible values for the expression at the head of the statement; that is, it is a literal value or a subrange of integer values (or values from some other enumeration)—for example,

```
case GradeLevel is
    when Fresh => statements;
    when Soph | Junior => statements;
    when Senior => statements;
end case;
```

One important requirement is that the set of choices include all the possible values for the expression, or that the final case be **when others** to explicitly indicate an action for all the remaining values. Thus, no run-time error is possible because of computation of a value for the **case** expression for which no action is specified. If no action is required for some choice, the statement part may be the keyword **null**.

Loop statement. The basic iteration statement has the form

loop
  – sequence of statements
end loop

Because no loop header is given to indicate a termination condition, this form of loop iterates endlessly until terminated by an explicit **exit**, **goto**, or **return** statement or an exception.

Controlled iteration may be created via **while** or **for** forms of the loop statement. The **while** has the syntax

while *Boolean expression*

and the **for** clause has the two forms

for *variable name* **in** *discrete_range*
for *variable name* **in reverse** *discrete_range*

where *discrete_range* may be a subrange of an enumeration or integer type (e.g., 1..10 or *Fresh..Junior*). The keyword **reverse** indicates that the iteration begins with the final value of the range assigned to the given variable and works down to the initial value. Examples of **for** loops are given in Figure A.1.

An important feature of the **for** loop is that the *variable name* given in the **for** clause is *not* declared as an ordinary local variable, as in Pascal. Instead, it is declared *implicitly* by its occurrence in the **for** clause, and it may be referenced only within the loop. Once the loop is exited, this variable disappears and can no longer be referenced. This structure allows a number of important loop optimizations to be performed by the Ada compiler.

Exit statement. The **exit** statement has the form

exit when *Boolean_expression*;

or simply **exit**. When an **exit** statement is executed, it transfers control to the end of the innermost enclosing loop (if the condition indicated by the Boolean expression is satisfied). Alternatively, loops may be labeled and the **exit** statement may give the label of the enclosing loop to be exited—for example,

exit OuterLoop **when** A(I,J) = 0;

Goto statement. **Goto** statements are provided in Ada, but their use is tightly restricted. In general, a **goto** may transfer control only to another statement within the same subprogram and at the same or an outer level of statement nesting.

Input and output. Ada has no built-in input and output features. These are handled by overloaded functions in predefined packages. For example, the package *Text_IO* contains the definitions of the simple form of textual input and output functions needed to write simple Ada programs.

The function *get*(*arg*) will read in a numeric or string argument from the standard input (keyboard). *put*(*arg*) will write to the standard output. *put*(*arg*, *fw*) will write *arg* as a field of *fw* characters. *new_line* will write an end of line symbol.

Conversion between string and numeric data can also be handled by *get* and *put*. The function *get*(**in** *string*, **out** *number*, **out** *last*) assigns to *number* the numeric value of the first 1..*last* characters of *string*. Similarly, *put*(**out** *string*, **in** *number*) assigns to *string* the value of *number*.

get and *put* may also be used for data files. Files are defined as **limited private** with the **private** component of the package declared *implementation defined*. The functions *open*(**in out** *File_Type*, **in** *File_Mode*, **in** *File_Name*) may be used to open string *File_Name* with *mode* defined as (*In_File*, *Out_File*, *Append_File*) and *close*(**in out** *File_Type*).

Pragmas. A **pragma** is a statement used to convey information to the compiler. It is not considered to be part of the language. That is, if all pragmas are deleted from a correct program, the program should compile and have the same semantics as before. However, the pragma provides valuable information to the translator to tailor the compilation for a specific application.

The general form of a pragma is

pragma *PragmaName* (*parameters*)

where *PragmaName* is either predefined in the language or defined by an implementation. Some pragmas control compiler functions, such as the generation of a program listing (**pragma** LIST). However, the majority are intended to allow some control over the run-time structure of a particular subprogram. For example, **pragma** INLINE(*subprograms*) specifies that calls on the listed subprograms are to be replaced by inline code sequences whenever possible; **pragma** OPTIMIZE(TIME **or** SPACE) specifies that the subprogram within which it occurs should be compiled so as to minimize its execution TIME or storage SPACE requirements.

Exceptions. At the end of each program unit (subprogram, block, task, or package), a set of exception handlers may be specified. These handlers may be used to process exceptions raised within the program unit or propagated to the unit from some called subprogram that does not handle the exception. Each exception has a name. There are a few predefined exceptions, such as CONSTRAINT_ERROR (raised when a subscript is out of its declared range, when a subrange constraint is violated in an assignment, etc). All other exceptions are declared using the form

exceptionname: **exception**

An exception handler begins with the names of the exceptions that it handles, followed by a sequence of statements that take the action appropriate for handling the exception. The general syntax for the exception handlers is

```
exception
    when exception_name | ... | exception_name
        => statement_sequence;
    ...
    when others     => statement_sequence;
```

where each sequence of statements may handle one or more named exceptions. The **others** handler need not be specified. However, if it is, it handles all exceptions not named in previous handlers.

An exception is raised either implicitly, by a primitive operation, or explicitly, by the execution of a statement

raise *exception name*

When an exception is raised, control is transferred to the handler in the currently executing program unit if that unit has a handler for it. If no handler is present, then the exception is propagated up the dynamic chain of subprogram calls to the most recently called subprogram that does have a handler for it, or ultimately to a system-defined handler if no program-defined handler is present. Exceptions are not propagated from a task.

Once an exception has been processed by a handler, the subprogram (or other program unit) terminates execution normally and transfers control back to its caller. Thus, the exception handler in Ada is viewed as *completing* the execution of the subprogram body that was interrupted when the exception was raised. There is no provision for resumption of execution of the program unit in which the exception occurred. An exception handler may partially process the exception and then propagate the same exception to a handler back up the dynamic chain by executing the statement **raise** with no exception name.

Tasks. A task is a subprogram that may be executed concurrently with other tasks. This was described in greater detail in Section 11.2.

Embedded applications. Because Ada is designed to run embedded applications, it often needs special access to the underlying hardware on which it is executing. Some of these features are the following.

Address specifications. The particular location in memory at which a data object, subprogram, or task is to be located at run time may be specified, using the statement

```
task taskname is
    – entry declarations
end;
task body taskname is
        – sequence of declarations
    begin
        – sequence of statements
    exception
        – exception handlers
end;
```

Figure A.3. Ada task structure.

for *object_name* **use at** *memory_address*

where the memory address is given as the value of an expression.

Interrupts. It is often important in embedded systems for a program to be able to process interrupts generated by the hardware or external devices. Such an interrupt may be associated with an entry name for a task using

for *entry_name* **use at** *interrupt_address*

When an interrupt occurs, it acts as a highest priority entry call on the task with the given entry. Thus, the task responsible for processing the interrupt may respond immediately if it is waiting at an appropriate **accept** statement for the entry.

Standard Functions

Ada includes many predefined packages that define the usual functions. Some common ones include the following:

Ada.Strings.Fixed	Fixed-length string functions
Ada.Strings.Bounded	Variable-length string functions
Ada.Strings.Unbounded	Unbounded-length functions
Ada.Numerics.Generic_Elementary_Functions	Trigonometric functions

Packages

The Ada package provides for encapsulation. Ada 95, however, adds additional features for object-oriented inheritance.

A package definition has two parts: a *specification* (containing a *visible part* and a *private part*) and a *body*. The specification provides the information necessary for the correct use of the package; the body provides the encapsulated local variables and subprogram definitions, as well as the bodies of subprograms callable from

```
package packagename is
    – declarations of visible data objects
private
    – complete definitions of private data objects
end;
package body packagename is
    – definitions of data objects and subprograms declared
    – in the specification part above
begin
    – statements to initialize the package when first instantiated
exception
    – exception handlers
end;
```

Figure A.4. Ada package specification.

outside the package. In some cases, a package does not need to have a body. The general form of a package definition is given in Figure A.4.

The visible part of the package specification (everything preceding the keyword **private**) defines what the outside user of the package can make use of in a program. If type definitions are given in the visible part, the user can declare variables of those types; if variables and constants are defined, they may be referenced, and so on.

If the package defines an abstract data type, we want the user to declare variables of the abstract type, but we do not want the detailed type definition to be visible. In this case, the type definition in the visible part is

type *typename* **is private**;

and the complete type definition is given in the private part of the specification (e.g., Lines 6–12 from Figure A.1).

It would seem logical to place the private components of a package in the body of the package rather than in the specification part to keep the names hidden from the other packages. However, because of implementation considerations, this is not so. This issue is described more fully in Section 7.1.

Limited private types. Usually it is desirable to have the primitive operations of assignment and the tests for equality and inequality available automatically even for a private type, so that A := B is defined for A and B of private types. In Ada, these are the only operations provided directly for a private type without explicit programmer definition. However, in many cases, even these operations should not be predefined for a private type. If the programmer declares the type as **limited private**, then no operations at all are predefined for the type.

Generic packages. A generic package specification has parameters giving the types of particular package elements, the sizes of particular arrays in the package, and so forth. For example, a generic package that defines the abstract type *stack* might have a parameter giving the type of component stored in the stack. The general form is

> **package** *actual_package_name* **is**
> **new** *generic_package_name* (*parameters*);

Instantiation of a package is an operation done by the compiler. At compile time, each reference to a formal parameter name within the package is replaced by the actual parameter in the statement that instantiates the package. The resulting package can then be compiled in the same way as an ordinary package. The generic package and its instantiation have no effect on the run-time structure; only the resulting package (after the instantiation) actually is compiled into run-time data objects and executable code. However, because instantiation of generic packages is a rather frequent operation in Ada, especially where library packages are involved, most Ada compilers optimize this operation in various ways, often by a partial precompilation of the generic package, leaving only those aspects directly dependent on the parameters to be compiled anew at each instantiation.

Inheritance

Ada 95 has extended the package concept to include inheritance. Previously explicit packages had to be included using the **with** construct or derived types had to be used. Ada 95 adds the concept of a *type extension* with the new type called a *tagged* type. For example, if the type *Mydata* of Figure A.1 were declared as

> **type** Mydata **is tagged record**
> val: myarray;
> sz: integer := 0;
> **end record**;

then we could have defined another object, such as *Doublestack*, as

> **type** Doublestack **is new** Mydata **with**
> **record**
> Newdata: myarray;
> **end record**;

Doublestack would have the components *val* and *sz* as inherited components from *Mydata*. By use of tagged types, Ada 95 allows for new packages to be developed without the need to recompile existing package definitions.

Each tagged type contains a *class* attribute (e.g., *class* as in *Mydata'class* and *Doublestack'class*, which can be used for dynamic binding). *Doublestack* is a member of the same class as *Mydata* because it is derived from it.

Tagged objects may also be declared as **abstract**, as in

```
#include <stdio.h>
const int maxsize=9;
main()
   {int a[maxsize];
   int j,k;
   while( (k=convert(getchar())) != 0) {
      for(j=0; j<k; j++) a[j] = convert(getchar());
      for(j=0; j<k; j++) printf("%d ", a[j]);
      printf("; SUM= %d\n", addition(a,k));
      while(getchar() != '\n');
      } }
/* Function convert subprogram */
int convert(char ch)
   {return ch-'0';}
/* Function addition subprogram */
int addition(v, n)
   int v[ ], n;
   {int sum,j;
   sum=0;
   for(j=0; j<n; j++) sum=sum+v[j];
   return sum;
   }
```

Figure A.5. C example to sum an array.

type Mydata **is abstract tagged with null record**

giving the name of the object, its class designator, but no storage definition. The definition of *Mydata* can be filled in by a type extension. This provides a template for the type, and tagged types must be defined to use this object.

Calling a primitive operation with an actual parameter of a tagged type results in a run-time binding of the actual subprogram to call. This differs from Ada 83 and provides the essential features of a dynamic object-oriented execution model for Ada 95.

A.2 C

Annotated Example

Figure A.5 is a C program to sum the elements of an array. In this example, an input of

41234
0

will produce an output of

```
1 2 3 4 ; SUM= 10
```

Line 1. The standard input–output library stdio.h is to be used in this program. This is a preprocessor statement that gets expanded before translation begins. The contents of file `stdio.h` are included as part of the program at this point.

Line 2. `maxsize` is defined to be an integer constant with value 9. A preprocessor statement could have also been used with similar results:

#define maxsize 9

Line 3. Execution begins here. Some function must have the name `main`.

Line 4. Integer array `a` is declared with subscripts ranging from 0 to 8.

Line 6. `getchar()` is a function defined in `stdio.h`, which reads in the next character of input. Because char variables are subtypes of integers, the integer value of the character is read in. For example, on systems that use ASCII characters, the digit 2 is the character with the bit value 0110010, which is 62 in octal or 50 in decimal. However, the program wants the numeric value 2, which is what the function `convert` (lines 13–14) does.

The value that is read in is assigned to `k`. Note that assignment here is just an operator and the expression `k=convert(getchar())` assigns the next input number to `k` and returns that as the value of the expression. If the value is not 0, then the following statements (lines 7–11) are executed. Therefore, a value of 0 will terminate the loop and the program by falling off the end of procedure `main`.

Line 7. The `for` statement reads in successive values for the array (using the `convert` function and stdio function `getchar`). The first argument of the `for` is executed on entry to the statement, and is usually the initial value for the loop (`j=0`). The second argument is the continuation condition (loop as long as `j<k`), whereas the third argument is the operation at the end of the loop (`j++` or add one to `j`).

Line 8. This `for` statement is similar to the prior one to print out the array. The `printf` function prints out its character string argument. The `%d` indicates that C is to take the next argument and print it in integer format at that point in the string.

Line 10. The program reads characters until the end-of-line marker is read. This `while` statement has a null statement body.

Line 11. These braces end the block beginning on Line 6 and the body of the mainprogram from Line 4.

Line 12. A comment. These may be placed anywhere a blank character may be placed.

Line 14. It is not necessary to know the ASCII value for digits. All that you have to know is that '0' is 0, '1' is one more than '0' with a value of 1, '2' is 2 more than '0' with a value of 2, and so forth. The expression `ch-'0'` will return the single digit value that is needed.

Lines 16–17. This is the old C style for parameters. The names are placed in the argument list, and their types follow. Note that the array bounds are not specified.

A.2.1 Data Objects

C is strongly typed, but there are very few types, so strong typing is only marginally helpful. Data may be integer, enumerated types, or float (for floating point). Structured data may be arrays, strings (a form of array), or records like struct or union.

Primitive Data Types

Variables and constants. C identifiers are any sequence of letters, digits, and the underscore (_) character and must not start with a digit. C ".h" header files often use internal variables names beginning with underscore, so it is best to avoid that convention in your own programs. Case is important in C; abc and ABC are distinct names.

Integers may be specified in the usual integer format (e.g., 12, -17), or as octal constants containing a leading 0 (e.g., 03 = decimal 3, 011 = decimal 9, 0100 = decimal 64). A character literal is written between quotes (e.g., '*A*', '*B*', '1'). The character \n stands for the end of line character, and \0 is the *null* symbol, which is needed in string processing. The actual ASCII character codes may be specified using numeric codes. Thus, \062 is ASCII character 62 (octal), which is the same as '2'.

Discrete values may be created by *enumeration types*, another form of integer data:

enum *typename* { *list of values* } *name*

An example is

```
enum colors {red, yellow, blue} x, y, z;
x= red;
y = blue;
```

The values for the enumerated type need be listed only once. A second declaration for *colors* may be written as

```
enum colors a, b, c;
```

Floating-point constants have an embedded decimal point (e.g., 1.0, 3.456) or have an exponent (e.g., 1.2e3 = 1200., .12e-1 = .012).

String constants are specified as characters enclosed by ″ (e.g., "abc", "1234"). However, strings are really character arrays with null terminators. Therefore, the string "123456" is really the sequence 123456\0 and can be processed as if it were declared as either of the following:

```
char arrayvar[ ] = "123456"; /* arrayvar of length 7 */
char *arrayptr = "123456"; /* arrayptr points to the characters */
```

Numeric data types. Integers come in several variations. Type *short* is an integer that uses the least number of bits effectively for the given implementation. For many personal computer implementations, this usually means a 16-bit signed integer that has a maximum value of 32,767. It may also be larger — such as a 32-bit integer. Type *long* is the longest hardware implementation for integers on that particular hardware. It is usually 32 bits, but can be larger. Type *int* is the most efficient implementation for that particular hardware. *int* may be the same as *short*, may be the same as *long*, or may have some value intermediate to those lengths.

As the annotated example demonstrated, type *char* is also a subtype of integer— in this case, a 1-byte value. Thus, any characters read in may be manipulated like any other integer value.

There are no Boolean or logical data; integers serve this purpose. $TRUE$ is defined as any nonzero integer value and $FALSE$ is the value zero. Bit operators may be used to set and reset various bits in integers. Although several bits in a single word may be used to store different Boolean values (e.g., the binary number 101 = decimal 5 could mean "A is true, B is false, C is true"), it is often better to use separate *int* variables for this purpose.

Constants may be defined either using the #define preprocessor statement, as given earlier, or by the *const* declaration:

const *type name* = *value*

Pointer data. Pointers may point to any data. $*p$ indicates that p is a pointer to an object. For example, the statements

```
int *p;
p = (int *) malloc(sizeof(int));
p = 1
```

do the following:

1. Allocate a pointer p that will point to an integer.
2. Allocate enough memory to hold an integer and saves the l-value of that memory as the r-value of p.
3. Using the r-value of p, store the integer 1 into the memory space allocated and pointed to by p.

Structured Data Types

Arrays. Arrays are one dimensional with indices beginning with 0 (e.g., *int* $a[3]$). Multidimensional arrays of any number of dimensions may be defined:

int a[10][5]

These arrays are stored in *row-major* order. The effect is that the array is stored as if it were declared as

thing a[10]

where type *thing* is an integer array of length 5.

Strings are arrays of characters, as described previously. String functions generally use null-terminated strings (i.e., arrays of characters terminated with the null character: $''abcdef'' = abcdef\backslash 0$).

User-Defined Types

C can create records of structured data, called **struct**s. The syntax is similar to the enumerated constants given previously. Thus,

struct MarylandClass {int size; char instructor[20];} CMSC330, CMSC630;

defines a structure *MarylandClass* containing a *size* component and a 20-character array *instructor* component, with two variables named $CMSC330$ and $CMSC630$ of type *MarylandClass*. And

struct MarylandClass CMSC430;

defines a new variable $CMSC430$ as another *MarylandClass*, referring to the same *struct* definition.

Members of the structure are accessed via a qualified name (dot) notation. $CMSC330.size$ will be the integer size component of that structure, and the qualified name $CMSC330.instructor$ will be the instructor component of that structure.

The **struct** declaration creates a new type. Paradoxically, the **typedef** declaration is really a name substitution and not a new type definition. Accordingly,

typedef int newint;

defines *newint* to be the same as *int*. It is generally used in **struct** definitions. Thus,

```
typedef struct NewClass { ... } MarylandClass;
MarylandClass A;
MarylandClass B;
```

defines *MarylandClass* to be the **struct** definition *NewClass*, and the type definition defines Variables A and B to also be of type *struct NewClass*.

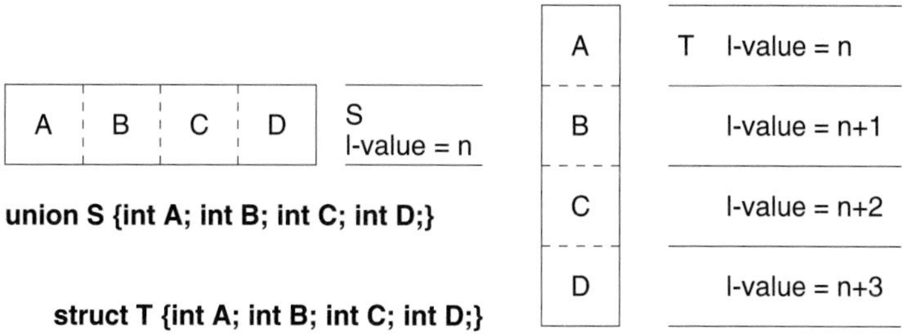

Figure A.6. Storage for union S and struct T.

Union. A **union** is a type definition that is syntactically like the **struct** type definition, but semantically like the Pascal variant record on Page 224. The difference between a **union** and a **struct** type is given in Figure A.6. With *union S*, each component of S has an l-value, which is the same as the l-value of S. Each component occupies the same storage location. In *struct T*, the l-value for A is the same as the l-value for T, but the others are all different. Each component has its own storage location.

Storage representation. Integers, float, and characters are stored in their natural format, and arrays do not need descriptors. Pointers are simply the l-value of the object to which they point. There is little overhead in accessing these objects.

Pointers and arrays are closely related. The array

```
int A[10]
```

may also be accessed as a pointer variable:

```
int *arrayptr;
arrayptr = &A[0]; /* arrayptr points to A[0] */
```

The expression $*((arrayptr) + (i))$ is the same as $a[i]$.

If q is a **struct**, such as

```
struct q {int a; int b; }
```

then the sequence

```
struct q *p;
p = (struct q *) malloc(sizeof(struct q));
```

as in the previous example, allocates memory for **struct** q and saves its address in p. The operator $\rightarrow$ (written ->) is then used to access components of this **struct**. Component a is referenced as $p \rightarrow a$ and Component b is referenced as $p \rightarrow b$. Note that $p \rightarrow a$ is *exactly* the same as $(*p).a$.

Initialization. Any statically allocated variable may be initialized, as in

int i= 12;

If an array is to be initialized, a list of items is specified:

int a[4]= (1,2,3,4); char string[4] = "abc";

This latter example initializes the array *string* to *abc*\0. Space in the array must be reserved for the final null character.

A.2.2 Sequence Control

Expressions

One of C's strengths is the number of operators that may manipulate numeric data. (It is also a weakness because there are now many ways to accomplish similar operations.) The set of C operations and their precedence levels were given earlier in Table 8.2.

It is important to remember the distinction between bitwise and logical operators. The bitwise *and* in 5 & 4 will result in an expression value of 4 because it ands the bits individually:

$$5 \ \& \ 4 = 0101 \ \& \ 0100 = 0100 = 4$$

but the logical *and* in the expression 5 && 4 results in a value of 1 because it operates as follows:

$$a \ \&\& \ b = \quad if \ a = 0 \ then \ 0 \ else \ if \ b = 0 \ then \ 0 \ else \ 1$$

The other logical operators are handled in a similar manner. They always return a value of 0 or 1.

The expression "if ($a = b$)" assigns b to a and returns the value of a. Be careful if you really mean the equality test "if (a==b)."

Coercions. Coercions generally occur if there is no loss of information, as from a *char* to *int* type. Coercions may be forced by writing a unary *cast* before a value. Thus, $a + (int)b$ coerces b to type *int* before adding it to a.

Statements

Blocks. The sequence {*statement list*} may be used wherever a statement is needed. Also, any block may declare local variables:

{int i, j; ...}

However, as explained in Section 9.4.2, the storage for i and j will be allocated when the storage for the entire procedure containing this block is allocated.

Expression statements. Any expression may be used as a statement. In particular, the assignment statement $a = b$ is really the assignment expression.

Conditional statement. C has the usual **if then** and **if then else** constructs:

if then:	if(*expression*) *statement*
if then else:	if(*expression*) *statement* else *statement*

With nested **if** statements, the **else** statement is associated with the nearest **if**.

Iterative statements. There are three iterative statements in C—**while**, **do**, and **for**:

while: while(*expression*) *statement*; means to execute *statement* as long as *expression* remains true.

do: do *statement* while(*expression*); means to execute *statement* and then test the *expression*. If true, then the **do** is repeated. This is often called the **repeat until** in Pascal and other languages, except the test expression continues the loop if true.

for: for($expr_1$; $expr_2$; $expr_3$) *statement*; is a form of iteration, and executes as follows:

1. If present, $expr_1$ is evaluated. Often it is an initialization statement like $J = 0$, but need not be.
2. If present, $expr_2$ is evaluated. If the result is 0, then the **for** terminates. It usually defines the stopping condition of the loop, like $J < 10$.
3. *statement* is executed.
4. If present, $expr_3$ is executed. It is usually the increment, such as J++ or add one to J.
5. Repeat process with Step 2.

Switch statement. The **switch** is like a multiway branch, often called a **case** statement. It has the syntax

switch(*expression*)
  {case $constant_1$: $StatementList_1$;break;
  case $constant_2$: $StatementList_2$;break;
  case $constant_3$: ...;
  default: $StatementList_n$;}

The *expression* is evaluated and control passes to the case label with the correct constant value or to the default statement if no label matches.

The **break** is important here and is a real weakness of C because one case statement will flow into the next if there is no transfer of control.

Statements to transfer control. The four statements that transfer control are **break**, **continue**, **goto**, and **return**.

break causes the smallest (syntactically) enclosing **while**, **do**, **for**, or **switch** statement to terminate. It is essentially a goto statement to the first statement that follows this enclosing compound statement. As given earlier, it is important for the **switch** statement to avoid one case from flowing into the next.

continue transfers control to the bottom of the smallest enclosing **for**, **do**, or **while** statement. It causes the program to go to the next iteration of that loop.

goto *branchlabel* transfers control to statement with label *branchlabel*. As in FORTRAN, it is a poor statement, and its use is unnecessary and should be avoided. The **break** and **continue** statements nested within the iteration statements are all the transferring mechanism that is needed.

return will return from a procedure. If the procedure was called as a function, the syntax is: return *expression*.

Preprocessor statements. **define**, **ifdef**, **ifndef**, **include**, **if**, **undef**, and **else** are preprocessor statements that begin with the symbol #, which has no other function in C. With older C translators, the # symbol must be the first symbol on the line; however, in many current translators, blanks are allowed to precede the #.

#define names a sequence of tokens, as in

$$\#\text{define } name\ SequenceOfTokens$$

Constants may be defined, as in

$$\#\text{define TRUE 1}$$

Note that

$$\#\text{define TRUE} = 1$$

is incorrect because the value of TRUE would be "= 1", not just "1".

#define can also be used for macro definitions, such as

$$\#\text{define } name(Var_1, Var_2, \ldots, Var_n) \qquad SequenceOfTokens$$

where the *vars* are replaced by their actual arguments when used, as in

$$\#\text{define abs(A,B) A<B ? A: B}$$

abs may then be used in any expression. $abs(newvar, oldvar)$ results in the expression $newvar < oldvar?newvar : oldvar$ being compiled by the translator.

#include adds text from a file into the program:

$$\#\text{include} < filename >$$
$$\#\text{include " } filename \text{ "}$$

The first adds *filename* from the system library, which for UNIX systems is usually */usr/include*. The second adds *filename* from the same directory as the source program being compiled. The convention is that interface definitions are stored in ".h" #include files and are copied in as needed.

#ifdef is used to check if a name has been defined previously. If defined, then the sequence of statements is added to the source program:

#ifdef *VariableName*
statements
#endif

Similarly, **ifndef** adds the statements if the *VariableName* is not defined.

#if conditionally adds text based upon the value of a constant expression.

#undef makes a name no longer defined: #undef *VariableName*.

#else can be used to start an else clause for #if, #ifdef, or #ifndef failure.

Input and Output

C has no specific input or output statements. Input and output are handled by a prespecified set of functions that are defined in the header file *stdio.h*. Input and output are described under "Standard Functions" in the following section on subprogram and storage management.

Standard Functions

Much of the power of C results from the rich library of functions that aid program generation. Many of these are direct interfaces to the operating system. There is no attempt in this book to cover all of these. However, the following are some of the more important ones you need in simple programs.

Standard input and output. These functions are defined in stdio.h. For simple input and output routines, *getchar* for character input and *printf* for simple formatted output are the most important.

The files *stdin* and *stdout* are predefined as the standard input file (generally keyboard) and standard output file (generally display screen), respectively. These names may generally be omitted in parameter lists. For example, reading characters from a file requires the function *getc(filename)*, whereas reading from the keyboard requires just *getchar* with no file name. *getchar* is just defined to be *getc(stdin)*.

EOF is defined as a constant and used to indicate end-of-file conditions. (It is usually the value -1 to distinguish it from any valid character that can be read.)

int getchar() returns the next character of the input stream (*stdin*).

*int getc(FILE * filename)* returns the next character from *filename*.

FILE $*$ *fopen*(*char* $*$ *filestring*, *char* $*$ *filetype*) opens the file *filestring* for input (if *filetype* = "*r*"), for new output (if *filetype* = "*w*"), or to append to existing file (if *filetype* = "*a*"). Files *stdin* (normal input), *stdout* (normal output) and *stderr* (error output) are opened automatically.

putchar(*char* x) prints character x on *stdout*.

putc(*char* x, *FILE* $*$ *filename*) outputs x into file *filename*.

fgets(*char* $*$ s, *int* n, *FILE* $*$ *filename*) reads in an array of characters from *filename*. s is a pointer to an array of characters. The function reads in characters until either

1. A new line is seen
2. An end of file is reached, or
3. $n - 1$ characters have been read in.

A null termination \0 is appended to string in s.

feof(*FILE* $*$ *filename*) returns TRUE if an end of file was reached on a previous read.

int printf(*string*, *arguments*) prints *string* on *stdout*. If the line is to appear on the terminal, *string* should terminate with an end-of-line character \n. If the *string* contains %d or %i, the next argument from the parameter list is printed in integer format. If it is %s, then the next argument is assumed to be a null-terminated string and printed. %c means a character for the next argument, %f is floating-point data without an explicit exponent, whereas %e means print the E exponent. %o is octal output.

int sprintf(*char* $*$ s, *string*, *arguments*) is the same as *printf* except that the string is written into s.

Memory allocation functions. These are defined in malloc.h.

void $*$ *malloc*(*int value*) allocates storage block of size *value* and returns a pointer to it.

int sizeof(*typename*) returns size of object of type *typename*. This is often used with *malloc*, as in

$$ptrvar = (newtype*)malloc(sizeof(newtype));$$

int free(*char* $*$ *mallocptr*) returns storage pointed to by *mallocptr*, which was originally allocated by *malloc*.

String functions. These are defined in string.h.

char $*$ *strcat*(*char* $*$ $s1$, *char* $*$ $s2$) appends $s2$ onto the end of $s1$ and returns pointer to $s1$.

char $*$ *strncat*(*char* $*$ $s1$, *char* $*$ $s2$, *int* n) appends up to n characters of $s2$ onto the end of $s1$ and returns pointer to $s1$ (or all of $s2$ if less than size n).

int strcmp(*char* $*$ $s1$, *char* $*$ $s2$) returns a value less than 0 if $s1$ is lexicographically less than $s2$, 0 if they are equal, and a value greater than 0 if $s1$ is greater than $s2$.

int strncmp$(s1, s2, n)$ is like *strcmp* except that it compares only up to n characters of $s2$.

char $*$ *strcpy*(*char* $*$ $s1$, *char* $*$ $s2$) overwrites $s1$ with $s2$. A pointer to $s1$ is returned.

char $*$ *strncpy*(*char* $*$ $s1$, *char* $*$ $s2$, *int* n) copies the first n characters of $s2$ into $s1$.

int strlen(*char* $*$ *string*) returns the length of the *string*.

Conversion functions. These are defined in stdlib.h.

double strtod(*char* $*$ *string*, *char* $**$*ptr*) converts a string to *float* and sets *ptr* to point to the character following the last converted character of *string*. If *ptr* is null, nothing is set.

long strtol(*char* $*$ *string*, *char* $**$*ptr*, *int base*) converts a string to a long integer. *base* is the number base of the input data. Values of 2, 8, and 10 are most useful.

The functions *atoi*(*char* $*$*string*) (ASCII to integer), *atol* (ASCII to long), and *atof* (ASCII to float) exist from older versions of C.

A.3 C++

Annotated Example

Figure A.7 presents a modification of the C example of Section A.2 to read in an array of integers and print out their sum. The example is perhaps a bit more complex than it needs to be to demonstrate the use of classes, inheritance, and stream I/O.

Line 1. stream.h is the standard C++ library for input and output functions *cin* and *cout*. The standard C library stdio.h may also be used.

Line 2. C++ uses an Ada-like comment starting from // to the end of line as well as the C comment /* ... */.

Lines 3–5. A class `DataConvert` is defined.

Line 4. All objects declared in class `DataConvert` will have a `protected` access class. This means that the function `convert` on Line 5 will only be visible in any derived class from class `DataConvert`.

Line 5. Function `convert` converts a character representing a digit into its numeric equivalent (e.g., *convert*('1') = 1, *convert*('3') = 3, ...), as given in the C program of Figure A.5.

Line 6. `DataStore` is a derived class from class `DataConvert`. The function `convert` declared in class `DataConvert` (written as `DataConvert::convert`) is visible in this class definition.

Line 7. `public` means that the declarations from Lines 8 to Line 19 are visible outside of the class definition.

```
1   #include <stream.h>
2        // This is C++ IO streams. stdio.h also works
3   class DataConvert {
4   protected:
5   int convert(char ch) {return ch-'0';}};

6   class DataStore: DataConvert{
7   public:
8   int initial(char a)
9        {ci=0;
10        return size = convert(a);};
11  void save(char a)
12       {store[ci++]=convert(a);};
13  int setprint() { ci=0; return size;};
14  int printval() { return store[ci++];};
15  int sum()
16      {int arrsum;
17       arrsum=0;
18       for(ci=0;ci<size;ci++)arrsum=arrsum+store[ci];
19       return arrsum;}
20  private:
21  const int maxsize=9;
22  int size;  // Size of array
23  int ci;    // Current index into array
24  int store[maxsize];};

25  main()
26     {int j,k;
27     DataStore x;
28     while((k=x.initial(cin.get()))!=0)
29          {for(j=0;j<k;j++)x.save(cin.get());
30          for(j=x.setprint(); j>0; j--)cout << x.printval();
31          cout << "; SUM=" << x.sum() << endl;
32          while(cin.get()!='\n');}}
```

Figure A.7. C++ example to sum an array.

Lines 11–12. The class DataStore creates a data abstraction of the stored data by encapsulating the actual values in an array that is not visible outside of the class definition.

Line 13. `setprint` returns the count of how many elements to print, and then `printval` is called repeatedly to return successive values.

Line 14. The next value from the array is returned. This function must be called because the array is encapsulated from outside the class and may not be accessed without using a function defined in the class. If the array `store` were public, this function would not be needed.

Line 20. All declarations following this attribute are **private** and may only be used within this class definition.

Line 25. Start of main program.

Lines 26–27. `j` and `k` are local variables. Object `x` of class `DataStore` is our array storage object.

Line 28. This is similar to Line 6 of Figure A.5. The sequence of actions is: (1) The function `get` of class `cin` defined in `stream.h` is called to return a single character; (2) the function `DataStore::initial` (Line 8) is called to convert the size of the array and save it in variable `x.size`; and (3) the size of the array is set to `k`; if it is not 0, then the array is processed.

Line 29. The **for** statement calls the `get` function for each number in the array and saves it in `x.store` by invoking `DataStore::save`.

Line 30. `DataStore::setprint` initializes the **for** statement, which counts down to 0 and prints each element of the array by invoking `DataStore::printval`. The stream function `cout` works by piping data to the function. Thus, to print a, b, and c, either of the following could be written:

$$cout \ << \ a \ << \ b \ << \ c$$

or

$$\begin{array}{lll} cout & << & a \\ cout & << & b \\ cout & << & c \end{array}$$

Line 31. The sum is printed by calling `DataStore::sum`. The object `endl` piped to `cout` prints an end-of-line character and causes the line to be printed.

Line 32. The function `get` in class `cin` is called to flush the rest of the current input line until the end-of-line character "$\backslash n$" is reached.

A.3.1 Data Objects

Primitive data in C++ are the same as in C.

Primitive Data Types

C++ uses the same *int* and *float* primitive data as C.

User-Defined Types

In addition to *int* and *float*, programs may use C **struct** and **typedef** to create structured data objects.

C++ includes the ability to define a **class**. A class is an extension to a **struct** with the addition of subprograms (*methods*) as additional components to the structure.

The syntax of a class is given by

class *classname*
{$class\_component_1$;
$class\_component_2$;
...
$class\_component_n$; }

where each *class_component* is either a data object declaration or a method declaration.

Data object declarations may be **const** declarations, **struct** declarations, or declarations of data objects of any type or class. In C++ the reserved word **struct** need not appear in the declaration of a variable of that type. For **struct** *Myclass*, data objects may be declared as

Myclass A, B, C;

Method declarations are the specifications of functions or procedures that may be invoked as operators of the class. The complete specification may be given or else just the signature header to the function giving its parameters need be specified. This latter form is similar to the **package** specification of Ada where the details of the function are specified elsewhere in the package body. This header information is needed to generate code to call the function from outside of the class definition.

Each member of a class has an *access control* attribute that describes the visibility of that member. Each *class_component* may have access control **public**, meaning its name is known outside of the class; **protected**, meaning that the name may only be used in a derived class; or **private**, meaning that it may only be used within the class definition containing the declaration.

The access control attribute precedes the *class_component* designation, as in

protected: void setvalue(int *a, int b) { *a = b; }

which returns, using call by reference, the r-value of *b* to the object passed as the l-value in *a*.

Once an access control attribute is set, it remains the default until changed. If no access control attribute is specified, **private** is assumed.

Friend classes. The **protected** and **private** access control is sometimes more restrictive than desired. Sometimes a class may allow another class to have access to its private data. This can be specified by one class declaring the other class as a **friend** and allowing it access to its inner structure. For example, in the example of Figure A.7, class *DataStore* was made a derived class of *DataConvert* to have access to protected method *convert*. Instead, *DataStore* could be a base class and be made a **friend** in *DataConvert*:

```
class DataConvert
    {protected:
    int convert(char  ch) {return ch-'0';}
    friend class DataStore; };
```

In this case, *DataConvert* :: *convert* would be visible within *DataStore*.

The scope of a *class_component* is the name of the class where it is declared. For example, in

```
class newclass
    {protected: void setvalue(int *a, int b) { *a = b; };
    public: int x; }
```

each component may be specified as *newclass* :: *setvalue* and *newclass* :: *x*.

For method declarations, the body of the method may be specified outside of the class definition, as in

```
class newclass
    {protected: void setvalue(int *a, int b);
    public: int x; }
newclass::setvalue(int *a, int b) { *a = b; };
```

Allocation of classes. Data objects of a defined class are declared the same as any data object, such as objects of the *newclass* class given earlier:

```
newclass W
```

The components of this object are referenced the same as a **struct** would be referenced: data object *W.x* and method *W.setvalue*.

This pointers. In instances of the **class** *newclass* given earlier, such as

```
newclass i, j
```

a call of *setvalue* on object *i* would be specified as *i.setvalue*(&*m*, *n*) and would be translated as if *newclass* :: *setvalue*(&*i*, &*m*, *n*) were written. That is, to distinguish among the various instantiations of objects of class *newclass*, the single copy of the method *setvalue* is invoked with a pointer to the actual data object *i*. Similarly, a call on *j.setvalue* will invoke the call $newclass :: setvalue(\&j, \&m, n)$. The value of this first pointer to the actual data argument is called the **this** pointer and may be used within method declarations.

For example, given a class definition

```
class myclass
    {methods;
private:
    myclass *Object; }
```

the component *Object* will be a pointer to an object of *myclass*. A method that sets the *Object* pointer of one *myclass* object to point to another *myclass* object may be given as:

```
myclass i, j; // Declare two objects
i.setpointer(j.getpointer()); // Pass pointer of j to i
```

where *getpointer* and *setpointer* are defined as

```
myclass::getpointer() { return this;}
myclass::setpointer(myclass *X) {Object = X;}
```

Initialization. If a method is declared with the same name as the class, it is called a *constructor* and is called whenever an object of that class is allocated storage. Constructors must not return a value or have a return type in their declarations. Similarly, a method with the name ∼ *classname* is called a *destructor* and is called whenever storage for a class is deallocated. For example, the code

```
class rational
    { public:
    rational(int a; int b) { numerator = a; denominator = b; }
    ~ rational() { numerator = 0; denominator = 0; }// Destroy value
    private:
    int numerator;
    int denominator;
    ... }
main()
    {rational NewValue(1,2);
```

allocates *NewValue* as an object of type *rational* with components of 1 and 2. Adding the declaration

```
rational() {numerator = 1; denominator = 1;}
```

to the **class** definition adds default declarations of *rational* objects so that initial values are not needed.

```
rational x, y, z;
```

Derived classes. Information from one class may be passed to another class using a derived class designation:

$$\begin{array}{l}\textbf{class}\ \mathit{derivedclass}\text{: } \mathit{baseclass} \\ \quad \{\mathit{class\_component}_1; \\ \quad \mathit{class\_component}_2; \\ \quad \ldots \\ \quad \mathit{class\_component}_n;\ \}\end{array}$$

where *derivedclass* is the name of the new class being defined, and *baseclass* is the base class used to derive the new class. All **public** and **protected** components in the base class become public and protected components in the derived class unless the name is redefined in the derived class.

All components of the base class may be given a default access class as in

$$\textbf{class}\ \mathit{derivedclass}\text{:}\mathit{access\_class}\ \mathit{baseclass}\ \{\ \ldots\ \}$$

where *access_class* is **public**, **protected**, or **private**.

Virtual functions. In most cases, the association of a method and the source program that must be executed is determined statically at translation time. However, we can delay that binding to run time by the use of *virtual* functions. A function is given an attribute of **virtual** in its class definition, as in

virtual void setvalue(int *a, int b);

Any use of the name *setvalue* will use the latest copy of the function *setvalue* if it has been redefined in a derived class.

If a class definition is to be used only as a base class, with all data objects being declared in a derived class, we call such classes *abstract*. We can define an abstract class as a class containing a null virtual function:

$$\textbf{virtual}\ \mathit{void\ setvalue}(\mathit{int}\ *a,\ \mathit{int}\ b)\ =\ 0;$$

No object may be declared if it has a null virtual function. A derived class containing a null virtual function must redefine this function if it is to be used to create objects of that derived class.

Templates. C++ includes a form of generic function called a *template*. A template has the syntax

template <**class** *type_parameter*> **class** *classname definition*

where *definition* is either a class definition or a function definition.

The template *classname* < *actualtype* > is used to describe a class declaration. For example, in

```
1  #include <stream.h>
2  template<class stacktype, int size> class allstack
3      {public: stacktype stg[size];};
4  allstack<int,10> x;
5  allstack<float,20> y;
6  main()
7      {x.stg[4] = 7.5; // int array
8      y.stg[4] = 7.5; // float array
9      cout << x.stg[4] << ' ' << y.stg[4] << endl; }
```

Lines 2–3 create a template class named *allstack*, which has a *type* parameter *stacktype* and an integer parameter *size* that creates data storage of an array named *stg* of size *size* and of type *stacktype*. Lines 4–5 create an object x, which is an *allstack* whose internal storage is a integer array of size 10, and an object y, which is an *allstack* whose internal storage is a real array of size 20.

The translation and execution of this program produces the output

Compiler error messages:
sample.cc: In function ‘int main ()’:
sample.cc:7: warning: float or double assigned to integer data type
% execute
7 7.5

with the warning message indicating that 7.5 was really cast as an integer in the assignment to $x.stg[4]$, but remained a float in the assignment to $y.stg[4]$.

Storage Representation

class objects may be stored the same as **struct** objects. Invoking a method *classobject.methodname(parameter)* is really a compile time translation into

$$classname :: methodname(\&classobject, parameter)$$

The only complexity is when virtual functions are invoked because the actual function to be called may have been redefined in a derived class. All that is required is to have a jump table stored in the class object for each inherited virtual function. If this is updated with any new virtual functions in derived classes, this data object will always point to the current virtual function to call.

A.3.2 Sequence Control

C++ includes the same statements as C. C++ has added exception handling, although not every C++ translator includes this feature.

Expressions

C++ expressions are the same as C expressions.

Statements

All C statements may be used in C++.

Default function parameters. Parameters to functions may have default values by initializing them in their definition:

myfunction (int a; int b = 7); ...

can be invoked as $myfunction(5, 12)$ setting $a = 5$ and $b = 12$, or as $myfunction(6)$ setting $a = 6$ and $b = 7$. Parameters are filled in order so any default parameters must be on the right. (Note: This is an error-prone construct especially if the program has overloaded function names with differing parameter lists. To avoid confusion, avoid this form of function call.)

Try statement. The **try** statement is used to handle program-defined exceptions:

```
try
    {statement1;
    statement2;
    ...
    if BadCondition { throw ExceptionName};
    }
catch ExceptionName { // Do something for exception
    } // End of Exception
    }
```

Within any procedure enacted from this **try** block, a **throw** of a condition causes the associated **catch** statement to be executed. After such execution, the procedure terminates.

The **catch** statements, overloaded function definitions, are tested in order until one is found that matches the appropriate **throw** statement. For example,

throw "This is bad data."

may be caught by a handler:

catch (char *ErrorString) { /* Do something */ }

Input and Output

Input and output streams have been defined as a standard set of functions. Functions *cout* and *cin*, and related functions, are defined in the next section.

Overloading. In C++, two functions can be overloaded (i. e., given the same name) if they have distinct signatures. For example:

```
int Myfunction(int a, int b) { ... }; // Function A
int Myfunction(int a) { ... }; // Function B
```

represent two distinct functions A and B.

When a function name is defined twice in a program, C++ will do the following:

1. If signatures match exactly, the second function will be considered a redeclaration of the first.
2. If the arguments match, but the return values do not, the second function is considered an error.
3. If the arguments do not match, the functions are considered overloaded.

Operator symbols may also be overloaded in **class** definitions by specifying a function beginning with the term **operator** followed by the symbol being overloaded. For example, a function + to return the first character of a string can be defined as

```
#include <stream.h>
class thing
    {public: char operator+(){return stg[0];};
    char stg[4]; };
main() {thing x; x.stg="abc"; cout << "print x[0]: " << +x << endl;}
```

where the first argument is an object of the implied class name *thing*. This program produces the output

```
print x[0]: a
```

A binary *char* operator for + would have the signature

```
char operator+(thing string) ...
```

and the components of the second argument would be referenced as *string.stg*. The first argument could be referenced as *this−> stg*.

The signature of overloaded operators must be compatible with the signatures of their predefined functionality. That is, + may be unary or binary, but ! may be unary only, for example.

An overloaded operator, such as *thing_data* + *int_data*, would be defined as a function within the *thing_data* class with argument *int_data*. Therefore, the left argument to the binary operator defines the class that contains the function definition. In this case, class *thing* contains the function

operator+ (int x){...}

To write the function *int_data + thing_data*, you need a function that takes an argument of class *thing* applied to an *int* class. However, *int* is a built-in type. We get around this problem by defining the function as a **friend** class in the *thing* class definition:

friend operator+ (int x, thing y){...}

In all cases, however, at least one of the arguments to + must be from a user-defined class.

Implicit conversions. The **operator** construct can be used to define implicit conversions (casting). Given a class object *thing*:

operator *type*() { **return** ... }

will be invoked whenever an object of type *thing* is used and an object of type *type* is needed. If

operator char() { **return** stg[0] }

is added to the *thing* **class** definition, then the following has the same effect as the prior overloaded + operator:

main() {thing x; x.stg="abc"; cout << "print x[0]: " << (char) x << endl;}

Standard Functions

All C functions may be used in C++. C++ also includes a set of standard stream input and output functions defined in header file *stream.h*.

cout << *item* adds *item* to the output stream. Several items may be appended in one statement, as in: *cout* << $item_1$ << $item_2$.... The specific item *endl* adds an end-of-line character and prints the line. The function *cout.put* will place a single character argument into the output stream.

cin reads data in a free format. *cin* >> *a* >> *b* reads the first item into *a* and the second into *b*. If a single character is desired, the function *cin.get* will perform this action. (*get* is similar to the *stdio.h* function *getchar*.)

*getline(char * b, int bsize, char delim =' \n')* will read a block of at most *bsize* − 1 characters and store it in array *b* with a null \0 appended to the end. *Delim* determines the final character to read, which is normally the end-of-line character.

Memory allocation. C++ does not need to use the operating system function *malloc* for memory allocation. The functions *new* and *delete* were added to the language.

```
      PROGRAM MAIN
        PARAMETER (MAXSIZ=99)
        REAL A(MAXSIZ)
 10     READ (5,100,END=999) K
100     FORMAT(I5)
          IF (K.LE.0.OR. K.GT.MAXSIZ) STOP
          READ *,(A(I),I=1,K)
          PRINT *,(A(I),I=1,K)
          PRINT *,'SUM=',SUM(A,K)
          GO TO 10
999     PRINT *,"All Done"
        STOP
        END
C SUMMATION SUBPROGRAM
      FUNCTION SUM(V,N)
        REAL :: V(N) ! New style declaration
        SUM = 0.0
        DO 20 I = 1,N
          SUM = SUM + V(I)
 20       CONTINUE
        RETURN
        END
```

Figure A.8. FORTRAN example to sum an array.

new typename allocates an instance of *typename* and returns a pointer to it. If the call is *new classname*, an object of that class is allocated and a pointer to it is returned.

delete object will delete the storage previously allocated to *object* via a *new* function call.

A.4 FORTRAN

Annotated Example

The example given in Figure A.8 presents the summation of a vector. As a holdover from its batch-processing roots, numeric statement labels are given in columns 2 to 5, and a C in Column 1 indicates a comment. All statements require one line unless column 6 has a nonblank character, indicating a continuation of the previous statement.

Blanks are ignored so spaces may be freely inserted into the source program to increase readability, such as indicating the nesting of blocks of statements in Figure A.8. Unfortunately, most FORTRAN programmers still adhere to the rule that statements begin on Column 7. This is only a guideline, and good programs include plenty of white space for improved legibility. The sequential line numbers at the left of Figure A.8 are not part of the program; they are just for the discussion.

Line 1. Program name is `MAIN`.

Line 2. `MAXSIZ` is a programmer-defined constant. The value of 99 is actually what the translator uses, not the name `MAXSIZ`, in translating this program.

Line 3. A real array of size 99, with bounds ranging from 1 to 99, is declared. Lower bounds are assumed to be 1.

Line 4. This reads in the size of the array into `K`, which because undeclared, is an integer variable. The 5 after the `READ` refers to an input file. This refers to the usual input (e.g., keyboard). A 6 refers to the usual output file (e.g., display).

Line 5. This `FORMAT` statement says that the data will be integer format (I format) and take five places on the input line. F format is "fixed" real. For example, the real number 5.123 would have format F5.3 meaning it takes five characters and three are to right of the decimal point.

Line 7. This `READ` statement reads in value of the array elements from `A(1)` through `A(K)`. Rather than using a FORMAT statement, as in `READ(5,101)`, the asterisk indicates a list-directed READ, which parses real numbers sequentially from the input stream. Variable `I` is only given a value within this statement.

Line 10. FORTRAN 77 has no **while** construct. This statement transfers control back to statement label 10 to read the next array data in. Lines 4 through 10 effectively form the construct

while not_end_of_file **do**
  Process next array
  end

Line 13. End of main program unit.

Line 14. A comment. These may appear anywhere in a program.

Lines 15–22. Function subprogram `SUM`. This function is compiled separately from the main program. Information from the main program is not used to pass information to the compiler. The erroneous line

FUNCTION SUM(V,N,M)

would also compile but may fail when the loader tries to merge this subprogram with the main program.

Line 16. Although array is given as `V(N)`, it refers to the statically allocated parameter, real array `A(99)` of Line 3 when used on Line 9. This line shows the style of declarations for FORTRAN 90 by adding the symbol ::, and FORTRAN 90 also allows embedded comments using the designator !.

Line 18. This `DO` loop sets `I` to 1, and then increments `I` until `I` equals `N`. The statement label indicates the end of the loop. If the increment is not 1, then a third parameter may be given, as in

DO 20 J= 2,20,2

which sequences J through all even integers from 2 to 20.

Line 19. A value is returned in a FORTRAN function by assigning a value to the name of the function.

Line 20. `CONTINUE` is a null statement that is simply a placeholder for a statement label. Here it ends the DO loop.

A.4.1 Data Objects

Variables and constants. Variable names are from 1 to 31 characters long, begin with a letter, and contain letters, digits and _. FORTRAN is case insensitive; PRINT, print, PrInT, and PRint all refer to the same name. FORTRAN traditionally was written with only upper case letters, but the current practice is to mix upper and lower case letters, as in most other languages.

Variables do not have to be explicitly declared. An explicit declaration such as

```
REAL A, B, SUM
DOUBLE PRECISION Q, R
LOGICAL :: T
```

may be given. The definition of T shows the FORTRAN 90 syntax for declarations. If no explicit declaration appears, a *naming convention* based on the first character of the variable name determines the type. The default naming convention specifies that names beginning with I-N are *integer* variables; all others are *real* variables. However, the programmer may change the naming convention used in any subprogram by beginning the subprogram definition with an IMPLICIT statement. For example, the statement

IMPLICIT INTEGER (A-Z)

at the start of a subprogram causes the type *integer* to be assumed for all variables not explicitly declared. The declaration

IMPLICIT NONE

in FORTRAN 90 turns off all implicit declarations of variables and indicates as an error any variable that is used without a declaration. This is a good practice to put in every program.

Programmer-defined constants may be included by the use of a PARAMETER statement at the beginning of a subprogram:

PARAMETER (KMAX=100, MIDPT=50)

The implicit type determined by the naming convention applies to defined constants as well or may be explicitly stated

REAL, PARAMETER :: EPSILON = .0012

Static type checking is used in FORTRAN, but the checking is incomplete. Many language features, including arguments in subprogram calls and the use of COMMON blocks, cannot be statically checked, in part, because subprograms are compiled independently. Constructs that cannot be statically checked are ordinarily left unchecked at run time in FORTRAN implementations.

Numeric data types. The numeric types *integer*,*real*, and *double-precision (real)* are usually represented directly using hardware number representations. Type *complex* is represented as a pair of real numbers, stored in a two-word block.

An extensive set of primitive operations for arithmetic and for conversion between the four numeric types is provided. The basic arithmetic operations (+, −, ∗, /) and exponentiation (∗∗) are supplemented by a large set of predefined intrinsic functions that include trigonometric and logarithmic operations (*sin*, *cos*, *tan*, *log*), square root (*sqrt*), maximum (*max*) and minimum (*min*), as well as explicit type-conversion functions for the various numeric types. The usual relational operations on numeric values are also provided, represented as follows:

Operator	Meaning	Operator	Meaning
.EQ.	equal	.NE.	not equal
.LT.	less than	.GT.	greater than
.LE.	less than or equal	.GE.	greater than or equal

Logical data type. The Boolean type is called LOGICAL, with the constants .TRUE. and .FALSE. The operations .NOT., .AND., and .OR. represent the basic Boolean operations; .EQV. and .NEQV. represent Boolean equivalence and its negation, respectively.

LOGICAL expressions can be constructed in the usual way with numeric data [e.g., $(A.LT.7).OR.(B.GE.15)$].

Pointer variables. Older FORTRANs do not include pointer variables because all data are statically allocated. Therefore, building list structures in FORTRAN often means using large arrays with the index of the array serving as the pointer to the next list element. This works effectively when all allocated structures are of the same type. However, it is difficult to write programs that create arbitrary data structures. FORTRAN 90 does add pointers as a new typed data object.

Pointers are declared as

INTEGER, POINTER :: P

which indicates that P is a pointer to an integer. The r-value of P is set to the l-value of X by P=>X.

X must be a legal *target* of a pointer, specified by

INTEGER, TARGET :: X

Using a pointer in an expression is the same as using the value of its r-value (i. e., the pointer is automatically dereferenced):

```
P1=>X
P2=>Y
P1=P2 ! Same as X = Y
```

Dynamic storage for a pointer $P1$ is allocated via an $ALLOCATE(P1)$ statement, and the storage is freed via $DEALLOCATE(P1)$.

Structured Data Types

Arrays. The subscript ranges for arrays must be explicitly declared, either in a DIMENSION statement (which allows the component type to be determined by the implicit naming convention) or by declaring the array and its component type using one of the declarations mentioned earlier—for example,

```
REAL M(20), N(-5:5)
DIMENSION I(20,20)
```

If the lower subscript bound is omitted, it is assumed to be 1. Array I is assumed INTEGER unless an IMPLICIT statement redefined the naming convention for I. An array may have up to seven dimensions.

Subscripts are used to select array components using the same syntax as for function calls [e.g., $M(3)$ or $N(I+2)$].

Unlike most language definitions, FORTRAN arrays are stored in *column-major order*. That is, a matrix is stored sequentially by columns rather than by rows. No descriptor is stored with an array; if needed, it must be stored separately. For example, in the two-dimensional array access $A(7,9)$ (referring back to Section 6.1.5), because all bounds for the array are known at compile time, the accessing formula

$$lvalue(A(7,9)) = VO + 7 \times S + 9 \times E$$

can be computed by the translator because VO, S, and E are all known and constant.

Arrays are statically allocated, as are all data in FORTRAN, unless the ALLOCATABLE attribute is given.

Character strings. Fixed-length character-string variables may be declared. For example,

```
CHARACTER S*10, T*25
CHARACTER(LEN=7) U
```

defines S and T to contain character strings of length 10 and 25, respectively, and U as a seven-character string in FORTRAN 90. The IMPLICIT declaration may also be used to provide a default length and CHARACTER type for variables not explicitly declared. Arrays of character strings and functions that return character strings as their values may also be defined. The concatenation operation (//) allows two-character strings to be joined. The relational operations (.EQ., .GT., etc.) are also defined for character strings using lexicographic ordering.

The character positions in the value of a character-string variable are numbered from 1 to the declared bound. A substring of a character string may be selected using the syntax

$$CharVariableName(FirstCharPosn : LastCharPosn)$$

Either the first or last character position indicators may be omitted, and the default of $FirstCharPosn = 1$ and $LastCharPosn = DeclaredBound$ is used.

The format conversions provided by the input–output operations may also be invoked to convert a character string stored in a variable or array into internal binary storage representations in another variable or array of numeric or logical type (or vice versa). The same READ, WRITE, and FORMAT statements are used, but the UNIT specification is now a variable name. For example,

```
READ (UNIT=A, FMT=200) M, N
```

specifies that the data are to be read from character string variable A, just as if A were an external file converted to internal integer representation and stored in M and N.

User-Defined Types

FORTRAN 77 has no mechanism for creating user types. All types are predefined in the language. FORTRAN 90 introduces a TYPE statement. For example, to generate variable length strings, a type $VSTRING$ could be defined:

```
TYPE VSTRING
    INTEGER :: SIZE
    CHARACTER(LEN=20):: LEN
END TYPE VSTRING
```

Declarations are similar to other FORTRAN 90 declarations:

TYPE(VSTRING) :: MYSTRING

Note that % is used as a selector: *MYSTRING%SIZE* or *MYSTRING%LEN*.

A.4.2 Sequence Control

Expressions

An expression may be used to compute a single number, logical value, or character string. Associativity of primitive operations is from left to right for all operations except ** (exponentiation), which associates from right to left. Parentheses may be used to control the order of evaluation in the usual way. The primitive operations have the following precedence order (from highest to lowest):

```
**
/
+ -
//
.EQ. .NE. .LT. .GT. .LE. .GE.
.NOT.
.AND.
.OR.
.EQV. .NEQV.
```

Statements

Assignment. The assignment statement has the syntax

variable = *expression*

where the r-value of *expression* is assigned to the l-value of *variable*, as in

```
X = Y + Z
A(1,2) = U + V − A(I,J)
```

The *variable* and *expression* may both be numeric, logical, or character. Assignment to a variable of type CHARACTER causes the assigned string to be adjusted to the declared length of the receiving variable, either by truncation (if too long) or extension with blanks (if too short).

Conditional statement. Four conditional branching statements are provided: the traditional IF constructs of FORTRAN 77 as well as a CASE statement in FORTRAN 90.

An *arithmetic* IF statement provides a three-way branch depending on whether the value of an arithmetic expression is negative, zero, or positive:

$$\text{IF}(expr)\ label_{neg\_value},\ label_{zero\_value},\ label_{pos\_value}$$

The *label*'s are statement labels to which control is to be transferred. This is considered obsolete and may be deleted from a future version of the language.

A *logical* IF statement allows only execution of a single statement if the value of a logical expression is true:

$$\text{IF}(expr)\ statement$$

A *block* IF statement allows an *if ... then ... else ... endif* alternation of statements without the use of statement labels. The form is

```
IF test_expression THEN
        -sequence of statements on separate lines
ELSE IF test_expression THEN
        -sequence of statements on separate lines
        ...
ELSE
        -sequence of statements on separate lines
END IF
```

where the ELSE IF or ELSE parts may be omitted. Note that because of the statement-per-line syntax of FORTRAN, each of the IF, ELSE IF, ELSE, and END IF delimiters must appear as a separate line in the program.

The CASE statement added in FORTRAN 90 has the syntax

```
SELECT CASE expression
CASE (case_selector)
    block_of_statements
... – Other cases
CASE DEFAULT
    block_of_statements
END SELECT
```

where *expression* must evaluate to an integer, character string, or logical value and the *case_selector* must be a constant or a range in values of constants, such as **case** $(1:3, 5:6, 9)$, which indicates selection if the expression has a value of 1, 2, 3, 5, 6, or 9.

The DEFAULT case is optional; if no *case_selector* matches the *expression*, the statement is skipped.

Iteration statement. The FORTRAN 90 iteration statement has the form

```
DO loop_control
    block_of_statements
END DO
```

If *loop_control* is omitted, this represents an infinite loop. Exit from the loop must be via an EXIT statement.

For an iterative loop with a fixed number of iterations, the syntax is

$$\text{DO } label\ init\_var = init\_val,\ final\_val,\ increment$$

where *init_var* is a simple integer variable to be used as a counter during repeated executions of the body of the loop. *init_val* is an expression specifying the initial value of the counter, *final_val* likewise specifies the final value, which when reached by the counter, terminates the loop, and *increment* specifies the amount to be added to the value of *init_var* each time through the loop. If omitted, the increment is 1.

Null statement. The CONTINUE statement is a null statement that is used as a placeholder for a statement label. Its main use is as the end of a DO loop or as the object of a GOTO. This permits the statement label to remain at a fixed spot, while any other statements may be modified if necessary.

Subprogram control. The CALL statement is used to invoke a subprogram, and is given as

$$\text{CALL } subprogram\_name(param\_list)$$

where the parameter list is a sequence of actual parameter names or expressions.

Function subprograms are subprograms that return a value and are simply used in an expression, as in $2 + myfun(1, 23, .TRUE.)$. Values are returned from functions by assigning to the name of the function before executing the RETURN statement:

$$\begin{array}{l}\text{MYFUN} = 27\\ \text{RETURN}\end{array}$$

The function name may be used as a local variable within the subprogram. Previous versions of FORTRAN, with its static storage structure, did not permit recursion; FORTRAN 90 allows for recursion and dynamic storage.

Program execution terminates with a STOP statement.

Subprograms return to the calling program with a RETURN statement.

Input and Output

Both sequential and direct-access files are supported and an extensive set of input–output operations is provided. Nine statements are used for input-output operations: READ, WRITE, and PRINT specify the actual transfer of data; OPEN, CLOSE, and INQUIRE allow the status, access method, and other properties of a file to be set or queried; and BACKSPACE, REWIND, and ENDFILE provide positioning of the file-position pointer.

A textfile (sequence of characters) in FORTRAN is termed a *formatted* file; other files are *unformatted.* READ, WRITE, and PRINT statements convert data values from internal storage representations to character form during transfer to formatted files. Data transfer to an unformatted file leaves the data in their internal representation. A READ, WRITE, and PRINT to a formatted file may be *list-directed*, which means that no explicit format specification is given; an implicit, system-specified format is used instead, as in Figure A.8. Alternatively, an explicit format may be provided by the programmer:

label FORMAT (*sequence_of_FORMAT_specifications*)

The *label* is designated in the READ, WRITE, or PRINT statement. For example, to read a sequence of integers formatted eight per line in five-character fields, the READ and FORMAT statements might be

```
    READ 200, N, (M(K), K=1,7)
200 FORMAT (8I5)
```

This may also be specified by placing the format specification directly in the READ statement:

```
READ "(8I5)" N, (M(K), K=1,7)
```

The READ statement specifies that the first integer is read into Variable N and the next seven into the components 1 — 7 of Vector M. The FORMAT statement specifies "I"(integer) format, five digits per integer, repeated eight times across the line beginning in the first-character position. A large number of possible format specifications are provided for the various kinds of numeric and character data. Some of the more useful are (w = size of field and d = number of decimal digits) as follows:

Field	Data Type	Example Use
Iw	Integer	I5 = 12345
Fw.d	Fixed (real)	F6.2 = 123.56
Ew.d	Exponential (real)	E10.2 = -12.34E+02 = 1234
wX	Skip	Skip w character positions
Aw	Character	A6 = abcdef
"literal"	Constant	"abcdef" prints out as those 6 characters

It is generally safe to place the data right justified in the field. Leading blank characters will be interpreted as 0 in reading numeric data.

Each READ or WRITE statement begins a new line of input or output. For each item in the input or output list, the next FORMAT item is processed until the end of the data list is reached. If there are more data items than FORMAT items, then the FORMAT statement is restarted on a new line of data.

To specify an exception handler for an end-of-file condition or an error during an input-output operation, a statement number is provided in the READ or WRITE statement designating a statement in the subprogram executing the READ or WRITE to which control should transfer if the exception is raised. For example,

READ (UNIT=2, FMT=200, END=50, ERR=90) N, (M(K), K=1,7)

is the extended form of the READ, which specifies a transfer to statement number 50 on an end-file condition and statement number 90 on an error. The $UNIT = 2$ designation specifies that the file is to be found on the input device numbered 2.

The format specifications used to control input and output are treated as character strings. During translation, they are stored in character-string form and interpreted dynamically by the READ, WRITE, and PRINT procedures as needed during execution. A format specification (character string) may be dynamically created or read in during program execution and subsequently used to control input–output conversions. The result is a flexible and powerful input–output system.

A.5 JAVA

Annotated Example

Figure A.9 is a Java program to sum the elements of an array. In this example, an input of

41234

will produce an output of

```
1234; SUM=10
```

This example is quite similar to the C++ example of Figure A.7 and shows the similarity in these languages.

Line 1. The standard input-output library java.io.* is to be used in this example.

Lines 2–3. Java classes are similar to C++ classes. The *public* access type is an attribute on a function or data object.

Line 4. Java uses the *extends* keyword to define derived classes.

Lines 12–15. The basic function design is similar to both C and C++.

Line 19. Arrays are handled differently from C and C++. *store* is defined to be an integer array (*int*[]), and then storage of the correct size is allocated by the *new* operator.

Line 21. The main program must be declared as *public* and *static*.

Line 24. The class *DataStore* is referenced as object x in this class and is initialized by the *new* operator.

```
import java.io.*;
class DataConvert {
public int convert(byte ch) {return ch-'0';}};
class DataStore extends DataConvert {
public void initial(int a)
    {ci=0;
    size=a;};
void save(int a)
    {store[ci++]=a;};
int setprint() { ci=0; return size;};
int printval() { return store[ci++];};
int sum()
     {int arrsum = 0;
     for(ci=0;ci<size;ci++)arrsum=arrsum+store[ci];
     return arrsum;};
private static int maxsize = 9;
int size;  // Size of array
int ci;    // Current index into array
int[] store = new int[maxsize];};
class sample {
public static void main(String argv[])
     {int sz,j;
     byte[] Line = new byte[10];
     DataStore x = new DataStore();
     try{
         while((sz= System.in.read(Line)) != 0)
              {int k = x.convert(Line[0]);
              x.initial(k);
              for(j=1;j<=k;j++)x.save(x.convert(Line[j]));
              for(j=x.setprint(); j>0; j--)
                   System.out.print(x.printval());
              System.out.print("; SUM=");
              System.out.println(x.sum());}}
     catch(Exception e){System.out.println("File error.");}
     } // End main
     } // End class sample
```

Figure A.9. Java example to sum an array.

Line 25. The *try* and *catch* (Line 34) clause are needed to handle input and output errors.

Line 26. *System.in.read* reads in a line of input into the byte array *Line*.

Lines 27–33. This is the same algorithm as the C++ program. *System.out.print* writes its argument to the standard output file. *System.out.println* adds an end-of-line marker to the line.

A.5.1 Data Objects

Primitive data. Numeric data can be 8-bit, 16-bit, 32-bit or 64-bit signed integer data. Most integer is either *int* or *long*. There are also 32-bit (*float*) and 64-bit (*double*) real data that follow IEEE Standard 754. Java also stores data as *byte* and *short*, although these are coerced into *int* to perform any operations on them.

Character data are stored using *unicode*. Unicode is an international standard that creates 16-bit characters. For example,

$$\text{char x} = \text{'a'}$$

creates an object x with the unicode value for the character a.

Boolean data can have the values of *true* or *false*. Unlike C, Boolean is not an integer value.

Structured data objects. Arrays are explicitly defined in the language. For instance,

$$\text{Newvalues Mydata[ ]}$$

declares *Mydata* as an array of *Newvalues*, where *Newvalues* is a class object you define. However, to actually allocate the array, you would invoke the *new* function, as in the following to allocate a 100-element array:

$$\text{Mydata} = \text{new Newvalues[100];}$$

To actually allocate each element of the array, you would also need to do, for each i,

$$\text{Mydata[i]} = \text{new Newvalues()}$$

Both could be accomplished in one step; for example,

$$\text{int[ ] Mydata} = \text{new int[100];}$$

allocates *Mydata* as a 100-element array; so

The *length*() method to array objects returns the length of the array:

$$\text{Mydata.length()}$$

will return 100 in this case as in C++.

Strings are objects with a syntax similar to that of C. Accordingly,

String Publisher = "Prentice Hall";

instantiates a string object initialized to "Prentice Hall". The + operator for strings means concatenation; hence,

System.out.println(Publisher + " is the publisher of this book.");

will print out "Prentice Hall is the publisher of this book." *length*() is also defined as a method for string objects.

There is no need for C *struct* data because the C++ class structure permits composite data by simply defining a class containing the several defined objects.

A.5.2 Sequence Control

Statements. Java has the usual C control structures: **if**, **for**, and **while**. There is no **goto** statement. You exit loops by the C **continue** or **break** statement by placing a label on the loop to exit:

```
OuterLoop: for(i=0, i<j, i++) {
    ...
    if (true exit condition){break OuterLoop;}
    ...
}
```

Class definitions. Java class definitions are similar to C++ class definitions in defining instance variables and methods for a new class, but have aspects of Smalltalk in that the superclass of a new class is explicitly given, as in

```
class Newvalues extends Object {
    public double x; /* instance variable */
    public int y; /* instance variable */
    Newvalues() { ... } /* Constructor for Newvalues */
    }
```

where *Newvalue* is a subclass of the superclass *Object* and consists of the two instance variables x (a double real value) and y (an integer).

Java uses a large predefined class library. *java.io.∗* is the standard input-output library and *java.awt.∗* is the standard applet library when Java executes haspart of an HTML Web page.

As given previously, C-like declarations are used to allocate instances of this class object; thus,

Newvalues Mydata[ ]

creates a (blank) array *Mydata*, each of whose elements are of type *Newvalues*.

As with C and C++, the same selector syntax is used to refer to the components of object *Mydata*: *Mydata*[17].*x* and *Mydata*[17].*y*.

Also the same as C++, the method *Newvalues*() can be defined to give the instance variables *x* and *y* explicit values on instantiation.

We can pass parameters to the constructor as in

```
Newvalues(double a; int b) {
    this.x = a;
    this.y = b; }
```

A method to be invoked when an object is deallocated is the *finalize*() method (similar to C++'s ~ *classname* destructor).

Other methods can be specified in a class definition and invoked the same way as in C++.

Java has no explicit function call or even a need for one. Method access (as in *out.println*(*string*)) is an implicit function invocation.

Subclass definitions. Java has the same sub-classing structure of C++. A subclass *Newclass* is a subclass of *Olderclass* by the class definition

```
class Newclass extends Olderclass { ... }
```

Newclass inherits all the instance variables of *Olderclass*, and method invocation to *Newclass* (as in *Newclass.functionX*) is passed to *Olderclass.functionX* if *functionX* is not a method defined in class *Newclass*.

Access control. Instance variables in Java are public, private, and protected. Public names are available everywhere, private names are accessible only in that class definition, and protected are available in subclasses of that class.

If none of those access control names are used, the access control is assumed to be *friendly*, or available to any class definition in the same package as the given class, but not elsewhere (a form of semipublic).

Variables in a class definition are usually *instance* variables, meaning that they are in every instance of an object of that class. To have a variable that is common across all instances of a given class, use the attribute *static*. For example, if you are creating a linked list structure, each linked list would be of class *LinkedObject*. There would be a declaration

```
static FreeListType FreeList;
```

that would be common across all instances of a *LinkedObject* to manage the allocation of new list elements from a common list. Methods common across all instances of a class and able to access class variables only can also be declared with the attribute *static*.

C++ 's virtual methods are called *abstract* in Java and are defined similarly to C++ 's virtual methods:

abstract void MethodName(); /* Null body */

Threads. Java allows for some level of multiprocessing through threads. For example, the HotJava browser has a garbage collector executing in parallel with the browser that is displaying the user's HTML files. This avoids halting displays while waiting for the garbage collection to finish. Also a method to display a graphic can be a separate thread from one displaying text, allowing for more rapid transfer of useful information.

Threads are defined by the *new Thread(object)* command. The *synchronized* attribute (*synchronized void startSort()*) on multiple-method definitions prevents more than one of them from executing at a time, and thus avoids deadlock situations.

Standard Functions

Java was designed to ease the building of Web pages. As such, it includes the Abstract Window Toolkit (AWT) class library for building user interfaces. This includes the ability to create frames, show them on the screen, and add menus, scroll bars, and text. The following methods only give some of the functionality, which is available; the class library is too complex to provide more than that here.

AWT creates a hierarchy of classes. At the top level are graphics, components (buttons, containers [e.g., frames], text area) and borders. Various subclasses are used to create complex structures for display. A Window object has no borders or menubar. It can generate a *WindowOpened* or a *WindowClosed* event that can be used to instantiate the window. Frames are windows with a title and border, which also allows more events than a window allows.

show() displays a frame (a subclass of a window) on the screen.

Frame("framename") creates a new frame with the name "framename."

setSize(M, N) adjusts the frame to be *M* by *N* pixels.

MenuBar() creates a menubar in a frame.

MenuItem("name") creates a menu item named "name."

Button("name") creates a button named "name."

add(object) adds *object* (e.g., menu or button) to the frame.

drawstring("text", X, Y) places "text" at pixel location (X,Y) in the frame.

A.6 LISP

Annotated Example

Our annotated example in Figure A.10 again sums an array of integers. In this case, we type the functions directly into LISP. Our particular LISP has the function

```
1  %lisp
2  >; Store values as a list of characters
3  >(define (SumNext V)
4             (cond ((null V) (progn (print "Sum=") 0))
5             (T  (+ (SumNext (cdr V)) (car V)) ) ))
6  SUMNEXT
7  >; Create vector of input values
8  (defun GetInput(f c)
9             (cond ((eq c 0) nil)
10            (T (cons (read f) (GetInput f (- c 1))))))
11 GETINPUT
12 >(defun DoIt()
13            (progn
14            (setq infile (open '"lisp.data"))
15            (setq array (GetInput infile (read infile)))
16            (print array)
17            (print (SumNext array))))
18 DOIT
19 >(DoIt)
20
21 (1 2 3 4)
22 "Sum="
23 10
24 10
```

Figure A.10. Sum of a vector of numbers in LISP.

(*load "filename"*), which will read the LISP function definitions from a file. The symbol $>$ is the prompt from LISP.

Line 1. Invoke LISP interpreter.

Line 2. A comment in LISP is from the ; to the end of the line.

Line 3. `SumNext` is a function declared to have one parameter `V`. It returns the sum of the entries in its parameter. The definition for `SumNext` is the expression on Lines 4–5.

Line 4. `cond` looks for the first $< \mathit{predicate}, \mathit{expression} >$ pair that is true. This first pair has the predicate `null V`, which will be true after the last input value has been processed. The function prints out `SUM=` and returns.

The construct `progn` sequentially executes a sequence of expressions, in this case, the `print` function followed by the expression 0 as a default value.

Line 5. If the vector `V` is not null (the usual case), the predicate `t` becomes the default case for the `cond` on Line 4. Vector `V` less the first member is passed to `SumNext` recursively, and upon return, the head of `V` is added to the previously computed sum.

Line 6. LISP prints out the name of the function `SUMNEXT` as the result of Lines 3–5.

Lines 7–11. These lines define `GetInput`, which has two parameters: the input file pointer, `f`, and the count of vector elements remaining to be read, `c`. This function definition shows the `defun` syntax for function definition rather than the Scheme `define`. `GetInput` returns a list of the data values that are read in.

Line 9. The `cond` first checks for the count `c` to be 0, and if so, returns the null list.

Line 10. If the count is not 0, `GetInput` creates a new vector by reading an atom from the file `f` and adds it to the head of the list returned from the recursive call to `GetInput` with parameters `f` and the count decreased by 1.

Lines 12–18. This defines the main control function for the program. `DoIt` has no parameters.

Line 13. `progn` here causes the expressions on Lines 14–17 to be executed sequentially.

Line 14. The `open` function opens the file `lisp.data` and returns a file pointer. `setq` assigns this file pointer to the variable `infile`. The sequence of actions is that the argument `open` is evaluated, and then the assignment to `infile` is made.

Line 15. The function `GetInput` is called (Lines 8–10) with parameters `infile`, which was defined on Line 14 and the result of the `read` function, which will be the count of the number of vector elements to sum. `setq` assigns this input data to the variable `array`.

Line 17. The input data (list `array`) are passed to the function `SumNext` defined on Lines 3–5, which returns the sum of the members of the list.

Line 19. The function `DoIt` is called.

Lines 20–24. If `lisp.data` contains the input

4 1 2 3 4

then Lines 20–23 give the output that is produced. The number 10 is printed twice in this example—once as a result of the `print` function on Line 17, and once as the returned value from the call to `DoIt`.

A.6.1 Data Objects

Primitive Data Types

The primary types of data objects in LISP are lists and atoms. Function definitions and property lists are special types of lists of particular importance. Arrays, numbers, and strings usually are also provided, but these types play a lesser role.

Variables and constants. A LISP **atom** is the basic elementary type of data object. An atom is sometimes called a *literal atom* to distinguish it from a number (or *numeric atom*), which is also classified as an atom by most LISP functions. Syntactically, an atom is just an identifier—a string of letters and digits beginning with a letter. Upper and lower case distinction for identifiers is usually ignored. Within LISP function definitions, atoms serve the usual purposes of identifiers; they are used as variable names, function names, formal parameter names, and so on.

A LISP atom is not simply an identifier, however, at run time. An atom is a complex data object represented by a location in memory, which contains the type descriptor for the atom together with a pointer to a *property list*. The property list contains the various properties associated with the atom, one of which is always its *print name*, which is the character string representing the atom for input and output. Other properties represent various bindings for the atom, which may include the function named by the atom and other properties assigned by the program during execution.

Whenever an atom appears as a component of another data object such as a list, it is represented by a pointer to the memory location serving as the run-time representation of the atom. Thus, every reference to the atom *ABC* during execution of a LISP program appears as a pointer to the same location in memory.

Every atom also ordinarily appears as a component in a central, system-defined table called the *object list* (*ob_list*). The *ob_list* is usually organized as a hash-coded table that allows efficient lookup of a print name (character string) and retrieval of a pointer to the atom with that print name. For example, when a list is input that contains the character string "ABC," representing the atom *ABC*, the *read* function searches the *ob_list* for the entry "ABC," which also contains a pointer to the storage location for the atom *ABC*. This pointer is inserted into the list being constructed at the appropriate point.

Numbers (numeric atoms) in integer or floating-point format may be used. The hardware representation is used, but a run-time descriptor is also required, so each number typically uses two words. However, this representation coordinates well with that used for literal atoms; a number is an atom with a special type designator and a pointer to the bit string representing the number instead of a pointer to a property list.

Strings in LISP are represented as string of symbols. Be aware that the single quote (′) is interpreted as the *quote* function for literal (unevaluated) arguments to functions.

Property lists. Each literal atom has an associated property list accessible via a pointer stored in the memory location representing the atom. A property list is simply an ordinary LISP list, differing only in that its elements are logically paired into an alternating *property name/property value* sequence. If an atom is a function name, its property list contains the property name giving the function type and a pointer to the list representing the function definition. Other properties may be added by the programmer as desired, and certain primitives also add properties.

Structured Data Types

Most LISP implementations provide some type of vector or array data object. However, there is little uniformity in treatment between different implementations, reflecting the relative lack of importance of vectors and arrays in most LISP programming. A typical implementation provides a function *mkvect*(*bound*) that creates a vector data object with subscript range 0 to a given *bound*. Each component of the vector may contain a pointer to any LISP data object; initially all pointers are set to *nil*. A function *getv*(*vector*, *subscript*) returns the pointer stored in the indicated component of the argument vector. Thus, *getv* is the LISP version of subscripting to retrieve the value of a vector component. *putv* is used to assign a new value to a vector component.

Programmer-defined functions are written in the form of lists for input, as seen in Figure A.10. The LISP input routines make no distinction between function definitions and data lists, but simply translate all lists into the internal linked-list representation. Each atom encountered is looked up in the *ob_list* and the pointer to the atom retrieved if it already exists or a new atom created if not.

Initialization and assignment. Direct assignment does not play as central a role in LISP programming as it does in other languages. Many LISP programs are written entirely without assignment operations, using recursion and parameter transmission to get the same effect indirectly. However, assignment is used within *prog* segments, where the LISP program takes on the ordinary sequence-of-statements form. The basic assignment operator is *setq*. The expression (*setq* x *val*) assigns the value of *val* as the new value of variable x; the result of the expression is the value of *val* (thus *setq* is a function, but its value is usually ignored). The primitive *set* is identical to *setq* except that the variable (which is just an atom) to which assignment is made may be computed. For example, (*set* (*car* L) *val*) is equivalent to (*setq* x *val*) if Atom x happens to be the first element of list L. *rplaca* and *rplacd* allow assignment to the *car* and *cdr* fields, respectively, of any list element. For example, (*rplaca* L *val*) assigns the value of *val* as the new first element of list L, replacing the current first element.

A.6.2 Sequence Control

LISP does not distinguish between LISP data and LISP programs, leading to a simple design for the LISP interpreter. LISP execution is interesting compared with other languages in this book, in that the basic interpreter can be described in LISP. The function *apply* is passed a pointer to the function to be executed, and *apply* interprets the definition of that function using a second function *eval* to evaluate each argument.

The LISP translator is simply the *read* function. *read* scans a character string from the input file or terminal looking for a complete identifier or list structure. If a single identifier is found, it is looked up in the ob-list to obtain a pointer to the corresponding atom (or to create a new atom if none is found with that print name). If a list structure is found, beginning with "(", then each item in the list is scanned until a matching ")" is found. Each list item is translated into internal form and a pointer is inserted into the list as a *car* pointer at the appropriate point. Numbers are translated into their binary equivalents with a descriptor in a separate word. If a sublist is found, beginning with another "(", then *read* is called recursively to build the internal representation of the sublist. A pointer to the sublist is then inserted as the *car* pointer of the next component of the main list. Note that this translation process does not depend on whether the list is a function definition or a data list; all lists are treated the same way.

Execution of a LISP program consists of the evaluation of a LISP function. Sequencing normally occurs by function call (which may be recursive) and by the conditional expression.

Expressions

A LISP program consists of a sequence of function definitions, where each function is an expression in Cambridge Polish notation.

Conditionals. The conditional is the major structure for providing alternative execution sequencing in a LISP program. The syntax is

(cond $alternative_1$
    $alternative_2$
    ...
    $alternative_n$
    (T $default\_expression$))

where each $alternative_i$ is ($predicate_i$ $expression_i$).

cond executes by evaluating each $predicate_i$, in turn, and evaluating $expression_i$ of the first one returning true (T). If all predicates are false, $default\_expression$ is evaluated.

Operations on atoms. The operations on atoms typically include the test function *atom*, which distinguishes between a pointer to a list word and a pointer to an atom (by checking the descriptor of the word); *numberp*, which tests whether an atom is a literal atom or a number; *eq*, which tests whether two literal atoms are the same (by simply testing if its two arguments point to the same location); *gensym*, which generates a new atom (and does not put it on the ob_list); *intern*, which puts an atom on the *ob_list*; and *remob*, which removes an atom from the *ob_list*.

LISP contains the basic arithmetic primitives: +, -, *, /, and a few others. The syntax is the same as for other LISP operations; thus, $A + B * C$ is written

(+ *A* (∗ *B* *C*)). All arithmetic operations are generic operations, accepting arguments of either real or integer data type and making type conversions as necessary.

The relational operation *zerop* tests for a zero value; *greaterp* and *lessp* represent the usual greater-than and less-than comparisons. The results of these operations are either the atom *nil*, representing *false*, or *T*, representing *true* (any non-*nil* value ordinarily represents *true* in LISP).

There is no Boolean data type in LISP. The Boolean operations *and*, *or*, and *not* are provided as functions. The *and* operation takes an arbitrary list of unevaluated arguments; it evaluates each in turn and returns a *nil* result if any of its arguments evaluates to *nil*. The *or* operation works in a similar manner.

Operations on lists. The primitives *car* and *cdr* retrieve the *car* pointer and *cdr* pointer of a given list element, respectively. Effectively, given a list *L* as operand, (*car L*) returns a pointer to the first list element, and (*cdr L*) returns a pointer to the list with the first element deleted.

The *cons* primitive takes two pointers as operands, allocates a new list element memory word, stores the two pointers in the *car* and *cdr* fields of the word, and returns a pointer to the new word. Where the second operand is a list, the effect is to add the first element to the head of this list and return a pointer to the extended list.

car, *cdr*, and *cons* are the basic operations for selecting list components and constructing lists. By using *cons* any list may be constructed element by element. For example,

(cons A (cons B (cons C nil)))

constructs a list of the three elements referenced by *A*, *B*, and *C*. Similarly, if *L* = (*A B C*) is a list, then (*car L*) is *A*, (*car* (*cdr L*)) is *B*, and (*car* (*cdr* (*cdr L*))) is *C*. By using *car*, *cdr*, and *cons* appropriately, any list may be broken down into its constituent elements, and new lists may be constructed from these or other elements.

The primitive *list* may be used to replace a long sequence of *cons* operations. *list* takes any number of arguments and constructs a list of its arguments, returning a pointer to the resulting list.

quote allows any list or atom to be written as a literal in a program, as described in Section 6.1.7.

The *replaca* primitive is used to replace the *car* pointer field in a list word with a new pointer; *replacd* is used to change the *cdr* pointer. These two primitives must be used with care in LISP because they actually modify the contents of a list word as well as returning a value, and thus they have *side effects.* Because of the complex way that lists are linked in LISP, these side effects may affect other lists besides the list being modified.

null tests if a list is empty (equals the atom *nil*), *append* may be used to concatenate two lists, and *equal* compares two lists for equality of corresponding elements (applying itself recursively to corresponding pairs of elements).

Operations on property lists. Basic functions are provided for insertion, deletion, and accessing of properties on property lists. *put* is used to add a property name/property value pair to a property list; *get* returns the current value associated with a given property name; and *remprop* deletes a name/value pair from a property list. For example, to add the name/value pair (*age*, 40) to the property list of atom *mary*, one writes

(*put* '*mary* '*age* 40)

Later in the program, the *age* property of *mary* may be retrieved through the function call

(*get* '*mary* '*age*)

Deletion of the *age* property of *mary* is accomplished by the call

(*remprop* '*mary* '*age*)

The primitives that define functions also may modify property lists for special property names such as *expr* and *fexpr*. (See later.)

Input and Output

Input and output are simply function calls. (*read*) will read the next atom from the keyboard. Lines 14 and 15 from Figure A.10 show how a data file can be opened by the function *open* and read via the call (*read file_pointer*).

(*print object*) will print an object in a readable format.

Function Definition

The *defun* function is used to create new functions. The syntax of this function is

(*defun function_name*(*arguments*)*expression*)

where *arguments* are the parameters to the function and the body of the function is a single expression (which may be a sequence of *progn* or other complex execution sequences).

Alternatively, in Scheme, the syntax

(*define* (*function_name arguments*) *expression*)

can be used to define a function.

When LISP was first developed in the early 1960s, the function definition was based on the lambda expression, as we discussed in Section 4.2.2. Lambda expressions can be used to define functions, as in

$$(define\ function\_name\ (lambda(parameters)(body)))$$

where the function name and each parameter name are just atoms, and the body is any expression involving primitive or programmer-defined functions.

The action of function declaration is quite simple. Definitions of interpreted functions are ordinarily stored as an attribute-value pair on the property list of the atom representing the function name. For an ordinary function, such as defined previously, the attribute name *expr* is used, and the associated value is a pointer to the list structure representing the function definition. Thus, the call to *define* earlier is equivalent to the call:

$$(put\ 'function\_name\ 'expr\ '(lambda(parameters)(body)))$$

Many LISP systems reserve a special location in the atom (header block) for the definition of the function named with that atom, to avoid the necessity to search the property list for the function definition each time the function is called. The special location designates the type of function (*expr*, *fexpr*, etc.) and contains a pointer to the list structure representing its function definition. In these implementations, special primitives are usually provided to directly get, insert, and delete a function definition from the special location.

Standard Functions

Many of the following functions are present in most LISP implementations. However, it would be best to check a local reference manual for the language before using them.

List Functions (*car L*) returns the first element of list L. (*caar L*) = (*car*(*car L*)), and so on.

(*cdr L*) returns list L less the first element. (*cddr L*) = (*cdr*(*cdr L*)), and so on. *car* and *cdr* may be intermixed, as in (*caddr L*) = (*car*(*cdr*(*cdr L*))).

(*cons x y*) returns a list L such that (*car L*) $= x$ and (*cdr L*) $= y$.

(*list x y z*) returns the list ($x\ y\ z$).

(*quote x*) (or $'x$) does not evaluate x.

Predicates (*atom x*) returns true if x is an atom.

(*numberp x*) returns true if x is a number.

(*greaterp x y*) returns true of $x > y$ and (*lessp x y*) returns true if $x < y$.

(*null x*) returns true if x is the null atom, *nil*.

(*and x y*) returns $x \wedge y$.

(*or x y*) returns $x \vee y$.

(*not x*) returns $\sim x$.

(*eq x y*) returns true if x and y are the same atoms or the same lists. (*equal x y*) returns true if x and y are lists with the same elements.

Arithmetic Functions $(+\ x\ y)$ returns $x + y$ for atoms x and y. Similarly for *, −, and /.

$(rem\ x\ y)$ returns $remainder\ of\ x/y$.

Input and Output Functions Many of these functions differ across different LISP implementations.

$(load\ filename)$ will read in file $filename$ as a sequence of LISP definitions. It is the major interface with the file system for loading programs.

$(print\ x)$ prints item x. Scheme also calls it *display*.

$(open\ filename)$ will open the file $filename$ and returns a file pointer to it. The common way to use this is to save the file pointer via a *setq* function:

(setq infile (open '*filename*))

and use the variable $infile$ in a *read* statement.

$(read)$ will read from the terminal the next atomic symbol (number, character, or string). $(read\ filename)$ will read from file pointer $filename$ the next atomic symbol if $filename$ was previously opened.

$(help)$ or $(help\ 'command)$ may provide useful information.

$(trace\ function\_name)$ will trace the execution of $function\_name$ as an aid to determining errors in a program.

(bye) exits from LISP.

Abstraction and Encapsulation

Basic LISP does not include data abstraction features. However, Common LISP does include the Common LISP Object System (CLOS). CLOS was the result of merging four object-oriented extensions to LISP in the mid-1980s: New Flavors, CommonLoops, Object LISP, and Common Objects [STEELE and GABRIEL 1993]. CLOS has the following features:

1. Multiple inheritance is supported using *mixin* inheritance (Section 7.2.3).
2. Generic functions.
3. Metaclasses and metaobjects.
4. An object creation and initialization technique that permits user control of the process.

A.7 ML

Annotated Example

Figure A.11 presents our sample program to sum an array of elements. ML runs as an interpreter, and this example uses Standard ML of New Jersey.

```
1  %editor prog.sml
2  fun digit(c:string):int = ord(c)-ord("0");
3  (* Store values as a list of characters *)
4  fun SumNext(V) = if V=[ ] then (print("\n Sum="); 0)
5                    else (print(hd(V));
6                    SumNext(tl(V))+digit(hd(V)));
7  fun SumValues(x:string):int= SumNext(explode(x));
8  fun ProcessData() =
9       (let val infile = open_in("data.sml");
10           val count = digit(input(infile,1))
11      in
12           print(SumValues(input(infile,count)))
13      end;
14      print("\n"));
15 %editor data.sml
16 41234
17 %sml
18 - use "prog.sml";
19 [opening prog.sml]
20 val digit = fn : string -> int
21 val SumNext = fn : string list -> int
22 val SumValues = fn : string -> int
23 val ProcessData = fn : unit -> unit
24 val it = () : unit
25 - ProcessData();
26 1234
27  Sum=10
28 val it = () : unit
```

Figure A.11. Sum of an array in ML.

Lines 1–14. The editor is called to create the program. It could have been typed directly into ML rather than included by the `use` command on Line 18.

Line 2. Functions must be declared before they are used. `digit` takes a one-character string as argument, returns an integer value, and, as given in the earlier C examples of Section 1.5, converts the character to an integer. "1" is one more than "0," "2" is 2 more than "0," and so on. `ord` returns the integer value of the first character of its string argument.

Line 3. This is a comment in ML.

Lines 4–6. This defines the function that recursively takes off the leading digit from the array and adds its value to the sum.

Line 5. If the list is not empty, then another value must be computed. The head of the list is printed. Lines 5 and 6 form a sequence of two expressions to be evaluated as part of the `else` expression.

Line 7. This initializes the sum of list elements. The input string is converted to a list of characters by the built-in function `explode`, and then `SumNext` computes the values for each character in the list.

Line 9. The `let` expressions on Lines 9 and 10 are evaluated before the expression on Line 12 is evaluated. `infile` is initialized to be a pointer to the data file. The side effect of this expression is to open the data file.

Line 12. `count` was initialized to the number of characters to read. That many characters are read, and the resulting string is passed to `SumValues` for processing. The resulting value is printed.

Line 14. A final *newline* is printed.

Lines 15–16. The editor is invoked to create the data file.

Lines 17–18. Standard ML is started, and the file `prog.sml` is read in as a series of function definitions.

Lines 19–24. Output from ML indicating that it was processing the function definitions from the input file. The signatures for functions `digit`, `SumNext`, `SumValues`, and `ProcessData` are printed.

Line 25. The function `ProcessData()` is invoked.

Lines 26–28. Output from ML indicating that the program worked. Exit from ML is by an end-of-file indicator, usually the *controlD* character.

A.7.1 Data Objects

Primitive Data Types

Variables and constants. ML has integer (*int*) constants (e.g., 1, 2, 3, 4), reals (*real*) (e.g., 1.2, 3.4, 10.E3) using the usual notation, Boolean (*bool*) (i.e., true or false), and Strings (*string*) (e.g., "1", "abc"). For both integers and reals, negative numbers use the tilde (~), and ML is case-sensitive, so *True* and *ABC* differ from *true* and *abc*. Only *true* and *false* are Boolean values.

ML uses the C convention to represent control characters. To embed control characters within a string, use \n for *newline*, \" for " or else it will be interpreted as a string-ending symbol, \t for the *tab* character, and \ddd where *ddd* is the three-digit octal code for a character.

Identifiers are strings of symbols starting with a letter or apostrophe (') and containing letters, digits, and underscore (_). Identifiers beginning with apostrophes are considered type identifiers.

Structured Data Types

ML contains tuples, lists, and records as structured objects.

A **tuple** is a sequence of objects separated by commas and enclosed in parentheses. (12, "abc", 3) is a tuple of type $int * string * int$. These may be nested to any depth. The tuple

(2, "a", (3, 4.3), "xyz" , (true, 7))

has type $(int * string * (int * real) * string * (bool * int))$.

The ith member of a tuple can be accessed as $\#i$. For example, the second member of a tuple is given as #2, as in: $\#2(2, 4, 6) = 4$.

A **list** is a tuple consisting of objects of a single type. Four strings in a list would be ["a", "b", "c", "d"], and the resulting type is indicated as *string list*. Similarly, [[1,2], [3,4]] would be of type *int list list* or a list of lists of integers.

The function *nil* stands for the empty list.

A **record** in ML uses the syntax $\{label_1 = value, label_2 = value, \ldots\}$, with components selected by the *#label* operator. Tuples are actually special cases of records. The tuple (10, 23, "a") is an instance of the record {1=10, 2=23, 3="a"}.

Initialization. A pure applicative language does not have the concept of an assignment to storage. However, in ML, a value may be bound to an identifier by the **val** construct. Thus,

val $identifier = expression$

binds the value of the *expression* to the name $identifier$. For example: **val** $X = 7$ prints out

val X = 7 : int

indicating that X has the value 7 and is of type *int*. ML also has a reference type, which corresponds more closely to data storage. This is described later.

Note that = is not an assignment, but a unification operator that causes ML to associate a new copy of the identifier X to the value 7. This can be demonstrated by omitting the **val**. In response to an input of $X = 8$, ML prints

val it = false : bool

indicating that the unification of the current value of X (i.e., 7) with the value of 8 is false, and *false* is returned.

User-Defined Types

User types can be defined with the **datatype** statement:

datatype identifier = type_expression

For example, *direction* can be specified as

```
- datatype direction = north | east | south | west;
    con east : direction
    con north : direction
    con south : direction
    con west : direction
```

which creates four constants of type *direction*. We have created a type similar to enumerated types in C and Pascal. The statement

```
- val NewDirection = north;
```

sets the type of *NewDirection* to be *direction*, with value *north*.

We can extend this to include tree-structured data types. For example,

```
- datatype Mydirection = dir of direction;
    datatype Mydirection
    con dir : direction → Mydirection
```

creates a type *Mydirection* consisting of selector function *dir*.

Objects of type *Mydirection* are given as tuples (e.g., *dir*(*north*)), as in

```
- val Heading = dir(north);
val Heading = dir north : Mydirection
```

Without the tuple, we get a direction value:

```
- val NewHeading = north;
val NewHeading = north : direction
```

Components of a data type look like function calls:

```
- val NewDirection = dir(NewHeading);
val NewDirection = dir north : Mydirection
```

The power of the data type is to create arbitrary tree-structured data structures. For example, Figure A.12 displays a tree consisting of *NumEntry* and *CharEntry* nodes. The specification would be

```
- datatype Tree = Empty |
    NumEntry of int * Tree * Tree |
    CharEntry of string * Tree;
datatype Tree
    con CharEntry : string * Tree → Tree
    con Empty : Tree
    con NumEntry : int * Tree * Tree → Tree
```

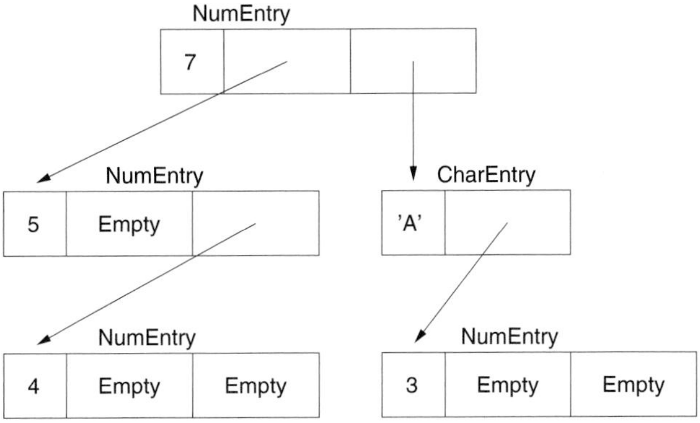

Figure A.12. ML tree-structured datatype.

signifying that datatype *Tree* consists of three alternative parts, a *CharEntry*, a *NumEntry*, and an *Empty* entry.

The structure of Figure A.12 is given by

```
- val NewTree=NumEntry(7,NumEntry(5,Empty,NumEntry(4,Empty,Empty)),
= CharEntry("A" , NumEntry(3, Empty, Empty)));
val NewTree =
    NumEntry
        (7,NumEntry (5,Empty,NumEntry (4,Empty,Empty)),
        CharEntry ("A",NumEntry (3,Empty,Empty))) : Tree
```

Accessing components of datatypes is demonstrated by the following program:

```
datatype object = pair of int * int;
fun CreatePair(a,b) = pair(a,b);
fun CreateTwo(a,b,c,d) = CreatePair(a,b) :: CreatePair(c,d) :: [ ];
fun PrintFirst(pair(x,y)::z) = print(x)
| PrintFirst(x) = print("Error\n");
fun PrintThird(x::y) = PrintFirst(y)
| PrintThird(x) = print("Error\n");
```

Execution of

```
val x = CreateTwo(1,2,3,4);
```

results in

```
val x = [pair (1,2),pair (3,4)] : object list
```

and execution of

```
PrintFirst(x);
PrintThird(x);
```

results in

```
1
3
```

A.7.2 Sequence Control

Expressions

Arithmetic expressions use the following precedence for expressions:

$\sim$	Unary minus
$*$, $/$, *div*, *mod*	Multiplicative operators
$+$, $-$	Additive operators

The full set of arithmetic relationships can be used: =, <>, >=, <=, <, and >.

Boolean expressions. These may be combined with *andalso*, *orelse*, and *not* predicates. *andalso* is similar to *and*, but is designed for lazy evaluation. The right operand is evaluated only if the left operand is true. Similarly, the right operation of *orelse* is evaluated only if the left operand is false.

String expressions. Concatenation is specified by $\wedge$: "abc" $\wedge$ "def" = "abcdef". The empty string is given by "".

If expression. As an applicative language, ML has no concept of the *conditional statement*. Instead, the conditional expression is used, as in C:

if *expression* **then** *true_part* **else** *false_part*

Because every expression must be well defined, the **else** part is not optional as it often is with an **if** statement.

While expression. The **while** expression is given by

while $expression_1$ **do** $expression_2$

and has the obvious interpretation of evaluating $expression_2$ as long as $expression_1$ remains true. However, due to the applicative nature of ML execution, how can $expression_1$ change its value? $expression_2$ must change the association of a variable in the local environment. ML also has the concept of a *reference variable*, whose value may be changed.

List expressions. The functions $hd(L)$ for head of a list L, and $tl(L)$ for tail of a list L, perform operations very similar to *car* and *cdr* in LISP. The LISP *cons* operation is given in ML by ::. $hd(L) :: tl(L) = L$.

ML also has a join operation that merges two lists: $[1,2]@[3,4] = [1,2,3,4]$. Note that for $x :: y$, if x is of type $'a$, then y must be of type $'a\ list$. However, for $x@y$, both x and y must be of type $'a\ list$.

Coercions between lists and strings are given by the built-in functions *explode* and *implode*. *explode* converts a string into a list of single-character strings, whereas *implode* takes a *string list* and returns a single string.

Statements

ML has no real concept of a statement, but instead a program is a function evaluation. Much like LISP, execution proceeds by recursive procedure call. Each expression is terminated by a semicolon (;).

Sequential execution can be simulated by executing the sequence

$$(expression_1; expression_2; \ldots; expression_n)$$

Each expression is evaluated in sequential order.

Function Definition

Functions are defined as

fun *function_name* (*parameters*) = *expression*;

where *function_name* is the name of the function and *expression* is the expression to be evaluated. *parameters* give the parameters for the function in the usual context. However, unlike other languages, the type of the parameter may be omitted if it can be inferred from context.

For example, the sum of two numbers can be specified as

```
- fun sumit(a:int, b:int):int = a+b;
val sumit = fn : int * int → int
```

indicating that *sumit* takes two *int* arguments, returns an *int*, and the name *sumit* has type *function* with signature $int * int \rightarrow int$.

Any one of these specifications of *int* uniquely determines the other two types, so the following are also equivalent:

```
- fun sumit(a, b):int = a+b;
- fun sumit(a, b:int) = a+b;
- fun sumit(a:int, b) = a+b;
```

However, one of the *int* specifications must be given because

- fun sumit(a, b) = a+b;

is ambiguous; it is not clear whether *int* or *real* is meant.

This simple syntax permits powerful polymorphic functions. Consider the following function that shuffles a list by placing the head of the list at the end. It joins the tail of a list with a list consisting of only the first member:

```
- fun shuffle(x) = tl(x) @ [hd(x)];
val shuffle = fn : 'a list → 'a list
- shuffle([1,2,3]);
val it = [2,3,1] : int list
```

Function *shuffle* operates on any list of type *'a* and returns a list of the same type. However, when *shuffle* is applied to the concrete list [1,2,3], a specific *int list* type is returned.

ML also permits a form of pattern matching to define functions as described earlier in Section 8.4.2. We can define our own join operation as follows:

```
fun append(a,b) = if a=nil then b else hd(a) :: append(tl(a),b);
```

We can consider this as two separate domains in which to define *append*. If *a* is nil, we return *b* as the value. If *a* is not nil, we perform another operation. ML allows us to specify the separate domains for the function:

```
fun app(nil,b) = b
   | app(a,b) = hd(a) :: app(tl(a),b);
```

For the domain where the first argument is nil, *b* is the value; otherwise, *hd(a) :: app(tl(a), b)* is the value.

The real power of pattern matching is in accessing components of complex data types. Consider the structure represented by Figure A.12. An object *X* of type *Tree* is defined by the following components:

```
NumEntry * Tree * Tree
CharEntry * Tree
Empty
```

Assume we want a function *last* that accesses the rightmost component of the figure. We can specify this as

```
fun last(NumEntry(I,T1,T2))= if T2=Empty then if T1=Empty
            then NumEntry(I,T1,T2) else last(T1) else last(T2)
    | last(CharEntry(C,T1))= if T1=Empty then CharEntry(C,T1)
            else last(T1)
    | last(Empty) = Empty;
```

where each subdomain of *last* recursively chooses the rightmost subtree. When we apply it to the variable *NewTree*, which we previously set to be the structure in the figure, we get the *NumEntry* with the integer component 3:

```
- last(NewTree);
val it = NumEntry (3,Empty,Empty) : Tree
```

As expressions. In the definition of a pattern, it sometimes is useful to be able to access the entire pattern. **As** performs this action. For example,

```
fun AStart(L as "a"::b) = F1(L)
    AList(a) = F2(a)
```

will call (1) $F1$ with argument L if it is a list with "a" as first element and (2) function $F2$ otherwise.

Recursive functions. ML permits recursive functions but, like most other languages, has a problem with indirect recursion. If A calls B and B calls A, which to declare first? In Pascal, this is solved by the **forward** declaration.

Because ML performs static type checking, the type of a function must be known before it appears in an expression. Indirect recursion is handled by the **and** expression, which causes all functions to effectively be declared simultaneously:

fun *first_rec_fcn* = ...
    and *second_rec_fun* = ...
    and *last_rec_fun* = ...;

Input and Output

The *print* function performs simple output. The character "\n" can be used to end a line of output. The function *open_in(filename)* opens a file for input and returns a pointer to a file descriptor of type *instream*. The function *input(file_ptr, n)* reads in *n* characters from the file and returns a *string*. The function *end_of_stream(file_ptr)* returns *true* if the end of file has been reached.

Exceptions

ML allows users to define exceptions. An exception is defined as

exception *exception_name*

and is invoked by

raise *exception_name*

where *exception_name* is the name of the exception. Exceptions may be handled by the **handle** clause:

$$expression \ \textbf{handle} \ handler$$

If *raise* is invoked within *expression* or any function called from *expression*, then *handler* will be invoked. The *handler* is of the format

$$\begin{aligned} handler(pattern_1) &\ => \ expression_1 \\ handler(pattern_2) &\ => \ expression_2 \\ \ldots & \\ handler(pattern_n) &\ => \ expression_n \end{aligned}$$

For example, an exception *myerror* raised as **raise** myerror(2) can be handled as

$$\begin{aligned} myerror(1) &\ => \ expression_1 \\ myerror(2) &\ => \ expression_2 \end{aligned}$$

Standard Functions

Input–Output Functions *use filename* causes *filename* to be read in as a program.

print(x) prints out primitive object x.

open_in("*filename*") opens *filename* and returns a pointer of type *instream* to the open file.

input(*file_ptr*, *size*) returns a string of length *size* consisting of the next *size* characters from open file *file_ptr*.

end_of_stream(*file_ptr*) is true if the end of file has been reached.

Other Functions #*i* returns the ith component of a tuple.

hd(*list*) returns the first element of *list*.

tl(*list*) returns a list consisting of the second through the last element of *list*.

explode(*string_val*) converts *string_val* into a list of single-character strings.

implode(*list*) takes a *string list* and returns a string. For example, the function call *implode*(["a","bc"]) returns "*abc*".

size(*str*) returns the number of characters in string *str*.

ord(x) returns the integer value of character x.

chr(i) returns the character represented by the integer i.

inc(i) is equivalent to i :=!$i+1$ for *ref int i*, and *dec*(i) is equivalent to i :=!$i-1$ for *ref int i*.

Abstraction and Encapsulation

Structures. ML includes the concept of a module, called a **structure** with the syntax

structure *identifier* = **struct**
element$_1$
element$_2$
...
element$_n$ **end**

where each $element_i$ is a declaration of a type, value, or function. For example, a simple list module that defines functions to create a new list, add an element to a list, delete an element from a list, and compute the size of a list can be declared:

```
- structure ListItem = struct
= val NewList = nil;
= fun add([ ],y)= y :: nil |
=       add(x,y) = x @ [y];
= fun size(x) = if x=[ ] then 0 else 1+size(tl(x));
= fun delete(x) = tl(x)
= end;
```

The resulting signature is:

```
structure ListItem :
    sig
        val NewList : 'a list
        val add : 'a list * 'a → 'a list
        val delete : 'a list → 'a list
        val size : 'a list → int
    end
```

Note that the structure is polymorphic and can be used to create lists of any type (specified as $'a$) in the signature.

The **open** declaration

open *structure_name*

creates a dynamic scope for a structure and adds the signature of the structure to the current environment, eliminating the need to explicitly name the structure, such as in the following *int* list:

```
- open ListItem;
open ListItem
val add = fn : 'a list * 'a → 'a list
val size = fn : 'a list → int
val delete = fn : 'a list → 'a list
val NewList = [ ] : 'a list
- val a = NewList;
val a = [ ] : 'a list
- val b = add(a,3);
val b = [3] : int list
- val c = size(b);
val c = 1 : int
```

The signature of a structure defines the interface, much like an Ada **package** or C++ **class**. We can define a new structure that is a restriction on the general structure. For example, we can define *int* lists that are restricted to integer lists and do not contain the *delete* function by defining this new signature using the **signature** declaration

```
signature IntListSig = sig
    val NewList : int list;
    val add : int list * int → int list;
    val size : int list → int
end;
```

and a new structure created to look like the original *ListItem* only restricted to the *IntListSig* signature, by using an alternative form of **structure**:

```
structure IntList : IntListSig = ListItem;
```

At this point, we can invoke *NewList* and *add* to create integer lists, but *delete* is not part of our restricted environment:

```
- val i = IntList.NewList;
val i = [ ] : int list
- IntList.add(i,7);
val it = [7] : int list
- IntList.delete(i);
Error: unbound variable or constructor: delete in path IntList.delete
```

Abstraction. The use of **signature** to create restrictions on a structure is one method for hiding the names of functions, such as the previous example of hiding the *delete* function in the structure *IntList*. The SML of NJ implementation also includes an **abstraction** construct:

abstraction *abstraction_type* : *abstraction_signature* = *structure_def* which performs a similar function. Similarly, an

abstype *datatype_name* **with** *declarations* **end**

may be used to create new data types, except that the constructors of the data objects are not exported from the type definition, providing true abstractions.

Arrays. ML implements arrays as a structure:

open Array adds the array functions to the current environment,

$array(m, n)$ returns an array with subscripts ranging from 0 to $(m - 1)$ and each element initialized to n,

$sub(a, i)$ returns the value of $a[i]$, and

$update(a, i, val)$ assigns to $a[i]$ the value val.

A.8 PASCAL

Annotated Example

Figure A.13 presents a similar version of the previously given FORTRAN and C programs. An array of real data is read, the values of the individual items are printed, and the sum of all the values is computed and then printed. If the input file *sample.data* contains

```
3
12 14 16
4 1.2 1.4 1.6 1.0
```

then the output from the program will be

```
        12.00      14.00      16.00
  sum = 42.0000
         1.20       1.40       1.60       1.00
  sum = 5.2000
```

Line 1. `main` is defined as the name of the program. The file `input` refers to the standard input file (keyboard), `output` refers to the standard output file (display terminal), and `infile` refers to a data file used within the program. Only files used within the program need be mentioned here.

Line 3. `Vector` is defined as a new type, an array from 1 to 99, where each data object is of type *real*. Both lower and upper bounds must always be specified.

Lines 4–6. **var** defines the global variables used by the program. In this case, `infile` is a *textfile* containing the input data. The files *input* and *output* do not need to be declared.

```
1        program main(input,output,infile);
2        const size = 99;
3        type Vector = array  [1..size] of real;
4        var infile: text;
5            a: Vector;
6            j,k: integer;
7        function sum(v: Vector; n: integer): real;
8           var temp: real;
9           i: integer;
10          {Body of function sum}
11          begin
12          temp := 0;
13          for i := 1 to n do temp := temp + v[i];
14          sum := temp
15          end ;{sum}
16      begin {of main}
17           reset(infile,'sample.data');
18           while not (eof(infile)) do
19              begin
20              read(infile, k);
21              for j := 1 to k do
22                  begin
23                  read(infile, a[j]);
24                  write(a[j]:10:2)
25                  end;
26              writeln;
27              writeln('sum = ',sum(a,k):6:4);
28              readln(infile)
29              end
30     end.
```

Figure A.13. Pascal example to sum an array.

Line 7. The function `sum` is declared. It has call-by-value parameters `v` of type *Vector* and `n` of type *integer*. If call by reference were needed, the parameters would be `var v: Vector`, for example. `sum` returns a value of type *real*.

Line 10. Comments in Pascal use set braces as bracketing symbols.

Line 13. **for** statement where `i` varies from 1 to `n`. If the **for** statement body consists of more than one statement, then a **begin–end** statement will bracket the sequence of statements. (See Lines 22–25.)

Line 14. Functions return a value by assigning a value to the name of the function.

Line 17. **reset** opens a file for input. In this case, it associates the operating system file *sample.data* with the internal data object `infile`. If the data come from the standard keyboard input, no **reset** is needed. The **rewrite** statement opens a file for writing.

Line 20. Read the first value of `k` from file `infile`. If this input were from the keyboard, the file name could be omitted. This is a free-form of input. Pascal will read characters up to a comma or blank and try to translate what was read into integer format. If the type of `k` were character, then only one character from the input file would be read.

Line 24. Write this vector value onto the standard output file (e.g., display screen) because no file name was given as the first data object to write. The optional terms `10:2` state to print out 10 decimal digits for the number, with 2 being fractional digits. If this is omitted, Pascal uses a default formatting. Successive **write** statements are appended on the same line, unless a **writeln** is used (Line 26).

Line 26. Add an end-of-line symbol to previous output. This ends the previous line of output (printing of array values).

Line 27. Write out the string `SUM =`, call the function `sum` to compute the sum, and then print out the sum using 6 digits with 4 being fractional digits. Because it is a **writeln** statement, add an end-of-line symbol to the output. **write** could have also been used if no end-of-line symbol were wanted.

Line 28. Read the file `infile` to the end of the current line.

Line 30. File end of program, ending with the final period.

A.8.1 Data Objects

Pascal is mostly strongly typed, with array bounds being declared as part of the type. The specifications for the various Pascal primitive data types are generally straightforward, with a few simple restrictions intended to allow efficient implementation.

Primitive Data Types

Variables and constants. Every variable name (and most other identifiers) used in a Pascal program must be declared explicitly at the beginning of a program or subprogram. Complete static type checking is performed for both local and nonlocal variable references for each operation used in a program.

The syntax of Pascal requires that constants be declared first, followed by local variables and subprogram declarations. However, many compilers loosen these requirements and permit declarations in any order.

Constant declarations are given by

$$constant\_name = constant\_value$$

but note that an expression is not allowed on the right side of a constant definition, so one constant cannot be defined in terms of the value of another defined constant.

Numerical data types. Data objects of type *integer*, ordinarily represented using the hardware integer number representation, are provided. Arithmetic and relational operations are defined using the usual infix notation for the binary operations: +, -, *, *div* (division), *mod* (remainder), =, <> (inequality), <, >, <= (less than or equal), and >= (greater than or equal). The largest integer value is the value of the predefined constant *maxint* (set by the implementor to reflect the largest conveniently representable integer value).

The predefined type *real* corresponds to a hardware floating-point representation. A simple set of operations is supported, again using the usual infix notation: +, -, *, =, <>, <, >, <=, >=, and / (division). No exponentiation is provided, but some basic arithmetic functions are built in (e.g., *sin* [sine], *cos* [cosine], and *abs* [absolute value]).

An enumeration type may be defined using the syntax

$$type\_name \;=\; (literal_1,\ literal_2, \ldots literal_k)$$

where the literals are programmer-chosen identifiers. The literals represent a sequence of values, ordered as listed, so that $literal_1 < literal_2$, and so on.

A subrange of the sequence of values defined by *integer* or by an enumeration type may be specified using the syntax:

$$first\_value..last\_value$$

(e.g., 2..10 or *Soph..Senior*). An enumeration or a subrange of an enumeration may be used to specify an array subscript range. For example, the declaration

Q: **array** [Class] **of** integer;

gives an array of four components selected by Q[Fresh], Q[Soph], and so on.

Boolean data type. A predefined Boolean data type is specified as the enumeration

boolean = (false,true)

The Boolean operations *and*, *or*, and *not* are primitive, as well as the relational (and other) operations available for any enumeration type. The Boolean values are implemented as the values 0 and 1.

Character data type. A predefined type *char* is defined as an implementation-defined enumeration, listing the available characters in the character set in the order of their collating sequence. Besides the relational operations *succ*, *pred*, and *ord* available for any enumeration type, the operation *chr* takes an integer argument in the range 0 up to the number of characters (minus one) in the character set and returns the corresponding character value.

Pointers. A data object may contain a pointer to another data object. The type of the first data object is then declared to be ↑ *second_type*, where *second_type* is the type of the data object pointed to. A variable may be declared to be of pointer type using the syntax

$$variable\_name: \ \uparrow type$$

and the value of the variable may then be either the null pointer, denoted *nil*, or an actual pointer to a data object of the declared type.

No operations are defined on pointer values except assignment (which copies the pointer value), the relational operations = and <> (notequal), which compare pointer values, and the operation *new*, which allocates an instance of a type and returns a pointer to it.

Structured Data Types

Array data type. The basic array data structure in Pascal has only a single dimension with an arbitrary subscript range, which may be defined as an integer subrange or an enumeration. The subscript range must be fixed at compile time permitting the compiler to perform all address calculations during compilation and thus not need descriptors during program execution. Array components may be of any type, either primitive or programmer-defined. Thus, an array of records, an array of files, and an array of sets are all possible structures. An array is declared as

array [*subscript_range*] **of** *component_type*

A multidimensional array is constructed out of single-dimensional arrays by constructing a one-dimensional array whose components are each a one-dimensional array (i.e., a vector of vectors). For example, to define a 3×6 matrix of real numbers, the declaration might be

array [1..3] **of** **array** [1..6] **of** real

For convenience, the declaration of a multidimensional array may be shortened by listing all the subscript ranges together:

array [1..3,1..6] **of** real

The latter form also allows use of a simpler subscripting syntax for selecting array components (e.g., A[3,4] instead of A[3][4]).

A **character string** is represented in Pascal as a (probably optional **packed**) array, each of whose components is a single character. Because the subscript range of an array is fixed during compilation, this representation of strings corresponds to the fixed declared length representation discussed in chapter 5. The only operations provided for character-string data are the relational operations (=, <, etc.), which apply to strings of the same length. The result is determined by the ordering of characters defined in the enumeration of the *char* type (discussed earlier). Assignment to a character-string variable is allowed, but only of another string of the same length. Character strings may be output to textfiles, but they must be read in a character at a time to an ordinary variable or array with components of type *char*.

Record data type. The basic record data type is described fairly completely in Section 6.1.6.

Sets. Pascal provides a limited form of *set* data type. A set is composed of a set of components, each from some base type, which is restricted to be an enumeration or integer subrange containing less than some maximum number of values. The maximum is determined by the implementor and ordinarily corresponds to the number of bits in one or several words of storage in the underlying hardware computer. The set may then be implemented as a sequence of Boolean values (single bits), where each bit corresponds to one possible element in the base set. If a bit is *true*, then the element is in the set value; if *false*, the element is not in the set value.

The syntax for declaration of a set type is

$$type\_name = \textbf{set of } base\_type$$

where the base type is as described previously. A variable of a set type may then have as its value any subset of the values of the base type, including the empty set (written [ ]). A literal constant representing a set value may be written

$$[value, \ldots, value]$$

where each *value* is either a single value or a subrange of values from the base set.

The operations provided for sets are union (syntax "+"), intersection ("*"), and difference ("-"). The relational operations =, <>, <=, and >= are also defined for set types, where the latter two operations denote a test for the inclusion of one set in another (e.g., $A <= B$ means: "Is A a subset of B?"). To test whether a particular value is in a set, the operation **in** is used. For example, *Soph* **in** *S* means: "Is the value Soph in the set represented by the current value of S?"

Files and input-output. Sequential files are the only type of file structure provided in Pascal. The syntax for declaring a file is

$$\textbf{file of } component\_type$$

where *component_type* may be any type except a file or pointer type. Thus, the components of a file may be arrays, records, or other structured data objects, in addition to data objects of elementary types.

The first line of a program has the syntax:

program *program_name* (*file_list*);

where *file_list* is a list of file names provided from some external environment to the program. These files must be declared in the local declarations for the main program. Other local files may be declared within the main program or subprogram just as for variables of any other type. These local files may be used as scratch files, which are written during one part of the program and later are read by another part of the program. Local files disappear on exit from the program or subprogram in which they are declared, just as any other locally declared data objects in Pascal.

When a file is declared, the file name is also used as the name of a buffer variable, referenced as *file_name*↑. This buffer variable is not declared explicitly but may be referenced and assigned in the program. For example, if F is declared as

F: **file of** integer

then within the program declaring F, the assignment $F\uparrow := 2$ or $X := F\uparrow$ is valid. The buffer variable is the data object representing the local temporary storage for a single component of the file. Two predefined procedures *get* and *put* are used to move data from the file to the buffer variable (*get*) or from the buffer variable to the file (*put*).

User-Defined Types

Pascal creates new types by the declaration

type *type_name* = *type_definition*

Type definitions in Pascal are used only during compilation. The compiler enters the information from type definitions into its symbol table and then uses the information to perform static type checking of variable references and to lay out the structure of subprogram activation records. Type definitions do not exist during program execution.

Two variables are considered to have the same type in some cases if the variables are declared using the same type name. In other cases, they have the same type if the declared types have the same structure. Thus, Pascal uses a mixture of *name* and *structural* equivalence for determining whether two variables have the same type. Name equivalence is used in most cases for determining whether formal and actual parameters in subprogram calls have the same type; structural equivalence is used in most other situations.

A.8.2 Sequence Control

Expressions

Pascal uses only four precedence levels for evaluation of expressions. From highest to lowest, these are as follows:

not
$\star$, /, *div*, *mod*, *and*
+, −, *or*
=, <>, >=, <=, <=, >= , *in*

and terms are evaluated from left to right within each precedence level. Note that this is counterintuitive from normal use. Operator *and* usually has a lower precedence than arithmetic operators. For example, the segment

var A, B: boolean;
...
if A *and* B=false **then** ...

has the interpretation

if (A *and* B)=false **then** ...

rather than what was probably intended:

if A *and* (B=false) **then** ...

The first interpretation is true if either A or B is false, whereas the second implies A is true and B is false. As a precaution, with Boolean data, always use parentheses in expressions.

Within a Pascal expression, no coercions of types are performed except to convert an *integer* operand to type *real* where required by the context.

Statements

Compound statements. The Pascal compound statement is bracketed by **begin** and **end**:

begin
  statement
  ...;
  statement
end

Conditional statements. Both **if** and **case** statements are provided.

If statement. The simple one- and two-branch conditional statements have the following two forms:

> **if** *Boolean_expression* **then** *statement*
> **if** *Boolean_expression* **then** *statement* **else** *statement*

When the two forms are combined, as in

$$\textbf{if } A = 0 \textbf{ then if } B < C \textbf{ then } S_1 \textbf{ else } S_2;$$

the ambiguity discussed in Section 8.3.2 regarding the execution sequence is resolved by always pairing an **else**-part with the nearest preceding unmatched **then**.

Case statement. The **case** statement takes the form

```
case expression of
    constant: statement;
    ...
    constant: statement
end
```

where the constants represent possible values of the expression.

When a **case** statement is executed, the expression in the head of the statement is evaluated and the value is used to determine which of the following statements is executed next. If the value does not match one of the constants labeling any of the following statements, then it is considered a run-time error.

Iteration statements. Three forms of iteration statement are provided in Pascal. The two basic forms, the **while** and **repeat** statements provide for the loop termination test to be made before each iteration (**while**) or after each iteration (**repeat**). The syntax for these statements is

> **while** *Boolean_expression* **do** *statement*
> **repeat** *statement_sequence* **until** *Boolean_expression*

In either case, the body of the loop may be a sequence of statements, but an explicit **begin** ... **end** compound statement must be used to bracket the sequence for the **while** statement.

The third form of iteration statement is a **for** loop, which provides iteration while incrementing or decrementing a counter. The syntax for both forms of **for** is:

> **for** *simple_variable* := *initial_value* **to** *final_value* **do** *statement*
> **for** *simple_variable* := *initial_value* **downto** *final_value* **do** *statement*

where the **to** form indicates an increment of one in the value of the simple variable after each iteration and **downto** indicates a decrement of one. No other increments are allowed in Pascal. The initial and final values are specified by arbitrary expressions that are evaluated at the time of initial entry to the loop. Assignments to the controlled variable within the loop are prohibited.

Error-prone constructs. A Pascal statement may be labeled with an integer label, and control may then be transferred to it using a **goto** statement. As repeated numerous times in this text, use of these features is unnecessary and generally leads to programs that are more difficult to debug.

Input-output statements. For most input and output operations, the low-level functions *get* and *put* and the statements *read* and *write* provide all the functionality that is needed.

Get and put functions. When a new component is to be written to a file, two steps are necessary: (1) The value for the new component must be assigned to the buffer variable for the file, and (2) the procedure *put* must be called to transfer the data from the buffer variable to the file, inserting a new component at the end of the file with the specified value and advancing the file position indicator past the new component. For example, the two statements $F\uparrow := 2; put(F)$ must be executed to write the value 2 on file F. A similar sequence is required to read the value of the current component from the file into a local variable (e.g., $X := F\uparrow; get(F)$ copies the current component [in the buffer variable $F\uparrow$] into Variable X and then advances the file to the next component, bringing its value into the buffer variable $F\uparrow$).

Read and write statements. Because most file processing involves many repetitions of these two-step sequences, predefined statements **read** and **write** are provided that combine the sequences into a single procedure call. For example, **read**(F, X) is equivalent to $X := F\uparrow; get(F)$.

Readln, writeln statements, and textfiles. A textfile is a file of single-character components declared using the predefined type *text*. A textfile is presumed to be organized into lines, which are sequences of characters ending with a special end-of-line character. Textfiles may be processed using the ordinary file operations, *get* and *put*, and **read** and **write** statements. However, **read** and **write** are extended to allow a variable of other than character type to be used as an argument (e.g., **read**(F, N) is allowed, where N is an integer variable rather than being of type *char*). When given an argument of numeric rather than character type, **read** and **write** provide automatic conversion between the character representation on the file and the internal binary representation needed for the value of the variable. **read** scans the input file until a complete number of the required type is found; **write** provides automatic formatting of the output data on the output file. **readln** and **writeln** procedures provide the same actions as **read** and **write**, but they also advance the file to a new line before they terminate.

Standard Functions

Input and Output Functions

rewrite(f) opens file f for output. In many implementations, this is given as *rewrite*$(f, filename)$, which associates external string "$filename$" with the internal Pascal file f. *reset*(f) or *reset*$(f, filename)$ opens File f for input.

put(f) moves the data object in the file buffer $f\uparrow$ into the output file. *get*(f) moves the next data object from the file into $f\uparrow$. *read*, *readln*, *write*, and *writeln* are actually procedures but were described previously under Pascal statements.

$eof(f)$ returns true if f is at the end of file. If f is *input*, it can be written as just eof. *eoln*(f) returns true if f is reading the end-of-line character. Unfortunately, Pascal always converts the end-of-line character to a space, so it cannot be explicitly checked, as is possible in C.

Storage-Management Functions *new*(p) allocates a data object of the same type as the underlying type of pointer variable p and sets the r-value of p to point to this data object. *dispose*(p) frees the storage pointed to by the r-value of pointer p. This storage must have been previously allocated by a call to *new*.

Arithmetic Functions *abs*(x), *sqr*(x), *sin*(x), *cos*(x), *exp*(x), *ln*(x), *sqrt*(x), and *arctan*(x) compute, respectively, absolute value, square, sine, cosine, e^x, natural logarithm, square root, and arc tangent of their argument.

trunc and *round* are two functions for converting from *real* to type *integer*. *trunc*(x) returns an integer such that $0 \leq x - trunc(x) < 1$, if x is positive or 0, and $-1 < x - trunc(x) \leq 0$ if x is less than 0. $round(x) = trunc(x + .5)$ if x is positive or 0 and equal to $trunc(x - .5)$ if x is negative.

pack and *unpack* are used to convert from character arrays to packed arrays. *pack*(a, i, z) means to pack Array z with components of Array a starting at $a[i]$. *unpack*(z, a, i) means to unpack Array z into Array a starting at $a[i]$.

Ordinal Functions

ord(x) returns the index of x within its enumerated type. *chr*(x) returns the character represented by integer x. *succ*(x) returns the value of the next item of an enumerated type. It is an error if the next item doesn't exist. *pred*(x) returns the value of the previous item of an enumerated type. It is an error if the previous item doesn't exist.

```
1   #!/usr/bin/perl
2   @inputdata = split(/ /, <STDIN>);
3   $count = 0;
4   foreach $nextone (@inputdata)
5       {print "$nextone";
6        $count = $count + $nextone;};
7   print "Sum = ";
8   print "$count\n";
```

Figure A.14. Perl example to sum an array.

A.9 PERL

Annotated Example

Figure A.14 is a Perl program to sum the elements of an array. In this example, an input of

1 2 3 4

will produce an output of

1234
SUM = 10

A Perl program consists of a sequence of statements, each ending with a semicolon. The first line of the program is a pseudocomment beginning with the comment symbol #, followed by !. It gives the name of the program that will execute the script. A typical first line is

#!/usr/bin/perl

Line 1. Inform the operating system that this shell script will be interpreted by the *Perl* program.

Line 2. Read the input data and separate at each blank into array *inputdata*.

Lines 4-6. Access each input value in *inputdata* and add to *count*.

Line 4. For each loop iteration, *nextone* is assigned the next element in the array.

Lines 7-8. Print out answers as well as final endline character.

A.9.1 Data Objects

Primitive data. Scalar variables begin with the symbol $ and have the type of integer, character, or string. Strings are enclosed with single quotes (' '). To have the string evaluated when executed, double quotes are used (" "). Therefore,

```
$x = 'mvz';
print 'My initials are $x';
```

will print *My initials are* $\$x$, whereas

```
$x = 'mvz';
print "My initials are $x";
```

will print *My initials are mvz.*

For many functions, $_ is the default argument name if none is given.

Boolean data, like in C, are integer values. Zero means *false*, and nonzero means *true*.

Array data. Array names are prefixed with @. Implicit arrays are created by assignment; for example,

```
@classStanding = ('freshman', 'sophomore', 'junior', 'senior');
```

creates a 4-element array with indices from 0 to 3. Accessing an array element uses the $ symbol (e.g., $\$classStanding[2]$) because it is a scalar value.

Arrays are dynamic. The *push* function added elements to an array, as in $push(@classStanding, 'gradstudent')$, which adds a fifth element to the array.

Associative arrays. Arrays can be viewed as relationships between a *key* and a *value*. Perl uses associative arrays to save these relationships. Such arrays use the % symbol. Thus,

```
%GPA = ( 'Tom', 3.6,
    'George', 2.6,
    'Sam' 3.2 )
```

creates a 3-element associative array. Further,

```
print "GPA of Tom is $GPA{'Tom'}";
```

will print 3.6. Note that the array (usually prefixed with @) is given with the scalar $. This is because the array reference is a scalar and not an array object.

The use of **foreach** $name (key %GPA) allows programs to go through each member of an associative array to process the associated *value* field.

Regular expressions. A regular expression is enclosed in slashes and is matched with the operator =~. $\$x$ =~ *thing* is true if *thing* is contained within $\$x$. Nonmatch is the operator ! ~.

The following operators can be used in regular expressions:

.	Matches any single character (except newline)
∧	Matches the beginning of the string
$	Matches the end of the string
*	Matches zero or more of the previous character
+	Matches one or more of the previous character
?	Matches zero or one of the previous character
[abc]	matches one of a, b, or c
[∧abc]	Matches none of a, b, or c
[a-z]	Matches anything in the range from a to z
a|b	matches a or b where a or b can be patterns

Specific symbols used in these patterns (e.g., |, ∧) can be specified in a regular expression by prefixing the \ symbol.

Placing the pattern in parentheses (as in /([a-z])/) causes the matched symbol to be placed in variable $1 (through $9). Each parenthesis gets the next system variable. This has uses in string substitution.

Substitution. The construct *s/rexpr/value/* causes a pattern match and a substitution of *value* if a match is made. *s/rexpr/value/g* replaces all such occurrences. The Perl variables $1 through $9 can be used in the substitution by writing them as \1 through \9.

A.9.2 Sequence Control

Statements. Perl has the usual language control structures. Perl executes one statement at a time. Each statement ends in a semicolon. The assignment statement is typical, but its handling of arrays is unusual:

```
@x = @y;      # Assign array y to array x
$x = @y;      # Assign the length of the array to x
$x = "@y";    # Evaluate y. Turn list into a string and assign to x
```

The looping construct

foreach $indexvar (@arrayvalue) { statement };

assigns *$indexvar* to successive values of the array and executes *statement*. Perl has a **for** state as in C, as well as a **while-do** and **do-until**. Predicates follow the C conventions. Equality is the operator ==, inequality is the operator ! =, string equality is *eq* and string inequality is *ne*.

The general conditional is the **if** as in

if (*expression*)
  then { *then – statement* }
  elseif (*expression*) { *first – alternative* }
  elseif (*expression*) { *second – alternative* }
  else {*last – alternative* };

Reading from a file requires use of the filename, hence,

$x = <STDIN>;

reads the next input from the standard input file (e.g., keyboard). The statement
open(filename, $stringvalue);
opens the file $*stringvalue* and **close**(filename) closes that file. The UNIX shell conventions on file access are also used:

```
open(myfile, ">$file");     # Open file for output
open(myfile, ">>$file");    # Open file for appending
open(myfile, "<$file");     # Open for input
```

Functions. *push(array, scalar)* adds an element to an array and *pop(array)* returns the last element of the array.

The function *key* returns the first member of an associative array relationship, whereas *value* returns the second member of that relationship.

split(rexpr, stringvar) uses *rexpr* as a regular expression to split a string into an array. @*x* = *split*(/ /, $*y*); will separate string $*y* at each blank and create an array @*x* containing all the pieces. If no string argument is given, *split* uses the argument $_.

chop deletes the end of line symbol from the string.

tr (translate) translates a string from one set of symbols to another. *tr/a−z/A−Z/*; translates the argument $_ from lower case to upper case letters.

Subroutines. Subroutines have the syntax

sub name { statements }

Subroutines are called as in &name, and arguments are passed in the array variable @_. The returned value is the last value computed. As an example,

local ($x, $y);

creates local variables in subroutines.

A.10 POSTSCRIPT

A.10.1 Data Objects

Primitive data. Postscript data consist of the following objects:
Numbers can be integers (e.g., 1, 3, -42) or reals (e.g., -1.234, 1.2E-10).

```
 1: %Same as Forth program on page 248 of text
 2: /Helvetica findfont
 3: 20 scalefont
 4: setfont
 5: 200 400 moveto
 6: /formatit {10 10 string cvrs show} def
 7: /sqr {dup mul} def
 8: /dosum {exch 1 add exch 1 index sqr add} def
 9: 3 6 dosum 2 copy formatit ( ) show formatit
10: clear
11: 200 375 moveto
12: 0 0 0 1 9 {pop dosum} for formatit
13: showpage
```

Figure A.15. Postscript program.

Compound data. Compound data consist of various components grouped together, which in turn consist of the following elements:

Arrays are primitive objects in brackets ([,])—for example,

[123 4 567] % An array of three integers
(Comments begin with %)

[123 abc /xyz] % An array of an integer, a name, and a literal name

Strings are any sequence of characters enclosed in parentheses:

(This is a string)

Procedures are sequences of Postscript tokens enclosed in set braces ({, }):

{dup mul} % Squares a number by duplicating the top of stack and then multiplying by itself.

As an example of a Postscript program, Figure A.15 is the Postscript version of the Forth program in Figure 8.2.1.

Line 1. A comment starts with %.

Line 2. The name (literal) Helvetica is placed on the operand stack and then *findfont* replaces the name with the font definition on the operand stack. Helvetica is a fairly standard sans-serif font. Times-Roman is the usual serif font.

Line 3. *scalefont* scales the Helvetica font to 20 points. Normal text is usually 11 or 12 point. Distances are measured in points, 72 to the inch.

Line 4. The current font on the operand stack (Helvetica scaled to 20 points) is made the current font. All text painted on the page will use this font until changed.

Line 5. The cursor is moved to coordinates (200,400), or roughly 3 inches from the left margin and almost 6 inches from the bottom of the page. The origin (location (0,0)) is assumed to be the lower left corner of the page.

Line 6. *formatit* is defined as a function in *userdict* that places the integer at the top of the operand stack onto the page. It creates a string of 10 zeros (10 *string*), takes the top operand stack entry, converts it to base 10, places it into the string (*cvrs*), and then paints the string at the current cursor position on the page (*show*).

Line 7. *sqr* is defined as a function that duplicates the top stack entry and multiplies the two top entries together (i.e., squares the top stack entry).

Line 8. Function *dosum* takes the operands n and S and produces $n+1$ and $S+(n+1)^2$. (See explanation in Figure 8.2.1. *exch* is used instead of Forth's *swap* and 1 *index* replaces Forth's *over*.)

Line 9. Try *dosum* with arguments 3 and 6 producing 4 and 22. Make a copy of the 4 and 22 and print 22, print a string of 3 spaces, and then print 4 at the current cursor position.

Line 10. Clear the stack of the remaining 4 and 22.

Line 11. Move cursor down about one third of an inch (25 points).

Line 12. 0 1 9 *proc for* will place 0, 1, 2, ..., 9 on the top of the stack and then evaluate *proc*. On each iteration, *pop* (to get rid of the index) and *dosum* are called, letting operand stack become: $(0,0) \Rightarrow (1,1) \Rightarrow (2,5) \Rightarrow (3,14) \Rightarrow (4,30) \ldots$ (10,385). The top of the stack (385) is then painted on the page (*formatit*).

Line 13. The painted page is then printed.

Sample Postscript operators. For each operator, the number of arguments (top stack entries) needed to execute the operator and the number of resulting values pushed on the stack are indicated. The usual binary operator (such as *add*), which takes two arguments and replaces them with a single result, is given as (2,1).

add (2,1) – *Add* takes the top two entries and replaces them by their sum.

aload (1,n+1) – Place the elements of the array argument onto the stack below the array.

array (1,1) – Create an array of length equal to argument.

astore (n+1,1) – Store n elements into top array argument.

Boolean (2,1) – Compare the top two operand entries and set the top of stack to true or false. *Boolean* can be *eq*, *ne*, *ge*, *gt*, *le*, or *lt*. In addition, there are operators for *and*, *or*, *not*, and *xor* with their usual interpretation.

clear (n,0) – Pop all entries off the stack.

cleartomark (n,0) – Pop all elements down to the mark on the stack.

copy (n+1,2n) – The n stack entries after the top value of n are duplicated on the stack.

counttomark (n,n+1) – Count the number of arguments from the mark and place value on stack.

currentfont (0,1) – Place current font on stack. (Can use this to resize current font without knowing what the current font is—e.g., currentfont 2 scalefont setfont will double to size of the current font.)

cvrs (3,1) – a b c cvrs stores number a in base b into string c and returns the substring containing a. Thus, 123 10 10 *string* returns the string (123). 123 2 10 *string* will convert 123 and return it as a string of binary bits.

def (2,0) – /a b def will take literal name a and function definition b and create an entry for a in *userdict*. Usually, b is given as a list of operations $\{x\ y\ z\}$.

div (2,1) – *Div* takes the top two entries and replaces them by their quotient.

dup (1,2) – *Dup* takes the top stack entry and duplicates it on stack.

exch (2,2) – *Exch* exchanges the position of the two two stack elements.

findfont (1,1) – Take name and place in the stack the appropriate font from the system dictionary.

for (4,a) – a b c proc for places a, then $a + b$, then $a + 2b$, ... until c on the stack and then invokes *proc*. The index argument remains on the stack unless *proc* removes it.

forall (2,a) – s proc forall invokes *proc* for each element of string s.

if (2,0) b proc if executes *proc* if b is true.

ifelse (3,0) b proc1 proc2 ifelse executes *proc*1 if b is true and *proc*2 is b is false.

index (n+2,n+3) – The sequence $a\ b\ c\ \ldots d\ n\ index$ will take the nth stack element and duplicate it on the top of the stack. $n = 0$ is the current top element, $n = 1$ is the next, and so on. *Dup* can be replaced by 0 *index*.

length (1,2) – Place the number of elements in array argument onto the top of the stack.

mark (0,1) – Place mark on stack.

moveto (2,0) – The two arguments represent the x and y coordinates from the lower left corner of the page. Size is represented in points, 72 to the inch.

mul (2,1) – *Mul* takes the top two entries and replaces them by their product.

pop (1,0) – This removes the top stack element.

quit (0,0) – This terminates the execution of Postscript.

repeat (2.1) – n proc repeat causes *proc* to be executes n times.

rmoveto (2,0) – This sets the new position relative to the current position.

roll (n+2,n) – a b c ... d m n roll causes the top m objects to be rolled circularly n positions.

scalefont (2,1) – Take the font and a scale factor and replace by an operand font entry that represents the appropriately sized font.

setfont (1,0) – Take the scaled font entry and make it the current font to be used in printing.

show (1,0) – Place top stack entry and place it on page.

showpage (0,0) – Print current page and reset page to blank.

string (1,1) – Creates a string consisting of zeros, the length of which is the argument (e.g., 10 string creates a string of 10 zeros.)

sub (2,1) – *Sub* takes the top two entries and replaces them by their difference.

Environment operators. These save and restore the state of the Postscript interpreter.

save and restore (0,1) and (1,0) – *Save* places a copy of the current environment on the stack, and *restore* restores the saved environment. This is useful, for example, if scaling and translation are later applied to the environment and you desire to go back to the previous state. These commands also save the graphics state.

gsave and grestore (0,1) and (1,0) – *gsave* saves the current graphics state, and *grestore* restores it as the current state.

A.10.2 Painting Commands

These commands are useful for painting pictures on the page.

arc (5,0) – x y r a b arc draws an arc with center coordinates x and y, radius r from angle a (in degrees) to angle b. For example, to draw a circle centered at coordinates x and y, do:

```
x y moveto
z y r 0 360 arc
```

where z is $x + r$.

closepath (0,0) – This closes the path back to the previous *newpath* command.

currentpoint (0,2) – This places the current coordinates on the stack.

eofill (0,0) – This will paint the current path with the fill color (see *setgray*). To erase an area, set the fill color to white. This operator uses the even–odd rule for strange-shaped objects.

erasepage (0,0) – Paint page white (i.e., erase all contents of page).

fill (0,0) – This will paint the current path with the fill color (see *setgray*). To erase an area, set the fill color to white.

lineto (2,0) – This draws a line from the previous point to this new point.

newpath (0,0) – Sets the current location as a new path.

scale (2,0) – Scale the new coordinate system relative to the old coordinate system (i.e., multiply each x and y coordinate by the arguments to *scale*).

setdash (2,0) – a b setdash sets the pattern for producing line segments. a is an array, whose elements are accessed circularly and specify the sequence of solid and blank line segments. b specifies the distance into the array to start, measured in line distances not array indices. The following are some examples:

[ ] 0 setdash	A solid line
[1] 0 setdash	One unit solid, one unit blank, one unit solid, ...
[1] 1 setdash	Same as above, only start with blank segment
[1 2 3] 2 setdash	1 unit blank, 3 solid, 1 blank, 2 solid, 3 blank, ...

setgray (1,0) – Sets current color as shades of gray. 0 is black and 1 is white.

setlinecap (1,0) – Determines how line segments are joined in a path, 0 is butt-ended, 1 is rounded, 2 is square.

setlinewidth (1,0) – Sets current width of line.

stroke (0,0) – Draw a line along current path.

translate (2,0) – Translate the user space by relative distances given by the arguments. This changes to location of the origin from the lower left corner to elsewhere on the page (if arguments are positive).

A.11 PROLOG

Annotated Example

In this example, as with previous languages, we show a Prolog program that sums a vector of numbers. To keep the problem simple, we assume that the input data have the form of a Prolog relation: $datavals(number\_items, [list\_items])$. Figure A.16 shows the execution of this program.

Lines 1–3. These invoke the editor to create the data file. Input will be a fact `datavals`, which contains a count and a list of numbers to sum.

Line 4. This invokes the editor to create the program. The program could have been typed directly into Prolog from the keyboard by a `consult(user)` instead of a `consult('pgm.prolog')` on Line 21.

Line 5. This defines the main goal of the program, the resolving of the predicate `go`. `go` is resolved if Lines 5 to 9 are resolved. `go` first reconsults the database by reading the file `data.prolog` and adds any facts into the database, in this case, the fact `datavals` of Line 3.

Line 6. This has the effect of assigning (actually unifying) `A` to the first item of `datavals`, the count of elements (`A` = 4), and `B` to the vector of elements (`B` = [1,2,3,4]).

Line 7. INSUM is set to 0. `is` is required, = means identity, and simply unifies both objects to be the same if possible.

Line 8. This line creates a for-loop using recursion. The rule will execute for `I` times (`I` being number of items in Vector `B`), passing in Vector `B` and current sum `INSUM` and return `OUTSUM = INSUM + elements of B`. Because the `for` rule will print out each data value, `nl` prints out a newline character.

Line 9. On return from the `for` rule, `OUTSUM` has the desired sum.

Line 10. Comments in Prolog are like comments in C and may be placed anywhere.

Lines 11–17. These define the `for` rule. The semantics of the rule are to execute the rule `I` times. If `I` is not 0, then this rule continues to execute; if it fails, then Prolog backtracking will execute the second `for` rule on Line 17.

```
1  %editor data.prolog
2       /* Read in data as a Prolog Relation */
3       datavals(4,[1,2,3,4]).
4  %editor pgm.prolog
5        go :- reconsult('data.prolog'),
6             datavals(A,B),
7             INSUM is 0,
8             for(A,B,INSUM,OUTSUM),nl,
9             write('SUM ='),write(OUTSUM),nl.
10       /* for loop executes 'I' times */
11       for(I,B,INSUM,OUTSUM) :- not(I=0),
12            B=[HEAD|TAIL],
13            write(HEAD),
14            NEWVAL is INSUM+HEAD,
15            for(I-1,TAIL,NEWVAL,OUTSUM).
16      /* If I is 0, return INSUM computed value */
17      for(_,_,INSUM,OUTSUM) :- OUTSUM = INSUM.
18      not(X) :- X, !, fail.
19      not(_).
20 %prolog
21 | ?- consult('pgm.prolog').
22 {consulting /aaron/mvz/book/pgm.prolog...}
23 {/aaron/mvz/book/pgm.prolog consulted, 30 msec 1456 bytes}
24 yes
25 | ?- go.
26 {consulting /aaron/mvz/book/data.prolog...}
27 {/aaron/mvz/book/data.prolog consulted, 10 msec 384 bytes}
28 1234
29 SUM =10
30 yes
```

Figure A.16. Prolog example to sum an array.

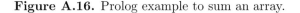

Line 15. The new partial sum and the shorted TAIL vector are passed to the `for` rule again recursively with the count decreased by 1.

Lines 17. Line 17 is the second `for` rule that is executed if the first `for` rule fails. The first one will fail if `not(I=0)` fails (i.e., `I` is 0). In this case, we ignore the first two arguments and simply unify the sum of the array (`OUTSUM`) with the value we have been computing (`INSUM`). Note that if we reversed the order of the two `for` rules on Lines 11–15 and 17, then this second rule will be executed first in all cases and the program will not work as desired.

Lines 18–19. This is the standard definition of `not` as explained in the text.

Line 20. Now that the data and program files have been created, invoke Prolog.

Line 21. Read in the rules from file `'pgm.prolog'`. `consult(user)` could have been entered and the rules typed directly into the program.

Lines 22–24. This is output from Prolog saying that the file was read successfully.

Line 25. The input `go.` signifies a query, defined on Lines 5–9, which defines success for the program.

Lines 26–27. Output from Prolog as a result of reading the data file on Line 6.

Lines 28–29. Desired output from the program.

Line 30. `go` from Line 25 succeeds. Exit from Prolog is often an end of file indicator (e.g., *controlD*).

A.11.1 Data Objects

Primitive Data Types

Variables and constants. Prolog data include integers (1, 2, 3, ...), reals (1.2, 3.4, 5.4, ...), and characters ('a', 'b', ...). Names beginning with a lower case letter represent concrete facts if part of a fact in the database or if upper case represent variables that may be unified with facts during Prolog execution. The scope of a variable is the rule within which it is used.

Structured Data Types

Objects may be atoms (string constants and variables) or lists. A list is represented as $[A, B, C, \ldots]$. The notation $[A|B]$ is used to indicate A as the head of the list and B as the tail of the list:

```
?- X = [A|B], X=[1,2,3,4].  – Query 2 definitions of X
                            – Print out unification of A, B and X
A = 1,
B = [2,3,4],
X = [1,2,3,4]
```

The string *'abcd'* represents the list $['a','b','c','d']$.

The variable _ is an arbitrary unnamed variable. Thus, $[A \mid \_]$ matches A with the head of any list.

User-Defined Types

There are no real user data types; however, rules defining relationships may act as if they were user types.

Storage Representation

Rules and facts are stored as linked lists in memory. The basic execution of Prolog is similar to the tree-walking linked list structure described earlier for LISP.

A.11.2 Sequence Control

Given a query, Prolog uses unification with backtracking, as described in Sections 8.4.3 and 8.4.4, as mechanisms to manage storage. There is no real concept of local or global environments. All rules have local context.

Because of the way unification has been implemented, a query such as

$$q_1, q_2, \ldots, q_n$$

first evaluates q_1, then q_2, and so on. This has the appearance of sequential order for any rule. In addition, rules are stored in the order of their being entered in the database. Thus, *not* may be defined as

```
not(X) :–X, !, fail.
not(_).
```

rather than

```
not(_).
not(X) :–X, !, fail.
```

In this latter case, *not*(_) would be checked first and would always succeed.

Expressions

Arithmetic operations +, -, *, *mod*, and / are defined. Relations such as =, =< (note this is not written <=), <, >, and >= are also defined. However, the equality operator = means "same as," so $X = 1 + 2$ means that X is the same as the expression 1+2. The operator *is* means evaluate; X *is* 4+1 results in an assignment of 5 to X:

```
| ?- X = 1+2.
X = 1+2 ? – X assigned expression '1+2'
yes
| ?- X is 1+2.
X = 3 ? – X assigned value 3
yes
```

Because of this meaning of the = operator, expressions such as $1 + 3 = 2 + 2$ will be false. To evaluate these, you need to define an equality function that uses the *is* construct to force the evaluation of both terms:

```
samevalue(X,Y) :–A is X, B is Y, A=B.
```

Then $samevalue(1 + 4, 2 + 3)$ will return true.

Statements

Facts. Facts are relationships that are stated during a *consult* operation, which adds new facts and rules to the database. They are n-tuples $f(a_1, a_2, \ldots, a_n)$ and state the relationship among the n arguments according to relationship f. In response to the function that adds data to the database, *consult*(*user*), the user could enter

```
employer(zelkowitz,university).
employer(smith,nasa).
employer(pratt,nasa).
publisher(zelkowitz,prenticehall).
publisher(pratt,prenticehall).
controlD
```

These relationships are invariant. They cannot be unified to some other value.

Rules. Rules are implications that are stated during a *consult* operation. They have the syntax

```
employed(X) :-employer(X,_). /* X is employed if X has an employer*/
employedby(X) :-employer(X,Y), write(Y).
```

employed only checks that *employer*(*X*, *something*) is in the database, so the employer is ignored. However, *employedby*(*X*) uses the relationship *employer*(*X*, *Y*) to write out the name of the employer:

```
employed(pratt).
yes
employedby(zelkowitz).
university
yes
```

Queries. Queries consist of a sequence of terms ending with a period:

$$q_1,\ q_2,\ \ldots, q_n.$$

We want an association for the variables in each term to be such that all terms are true. Execution proceeds by unifying q_1, possibly by referring to its definition in the database and, if true, unifying q_2 with its definition. If unification fails at any point, the process backs up to the previous correct choice and tries an alternative, as given earlier in Section 8.4.3.

Rules may be combined to make complex queries. For example, the question "Who works for NASA and has a book published by Prentice Hall?" can be expressed as the query

```
employer(X,nasa),publisher(X,prenticehall).
X = pratt ?
yes
```

Although *zelkowitz* and *pratt* both unify *publisher*(*X*, *prenticehall*), only *pratt* unifies with *employer*(*X*, *nasa*).

Cuts. The process of query evaluation often requires considerable backtracking. To save time, the *cut* was introduced. Cut (!) indicates that if backtracking must be applied, the pattern fails. The effect of a cut is to limit the search space for a solution. Use of cut will never add a solution that could not be found without a cut, but may eliminate some valid solutions.

For example, if the prior query were written as

```
employer(X,nasa),!,publisher(X,prenticehall).
```

then the query would fail. *employer*(*smith*, *nasa*) would unify first, but *smith* would fail to unify with *publisher*(*X*, *prenticehall*). Normally, Prolog would backtrack and search for another relationship *employer*(*X*, *nasa*), but the cut says not to do that backtracking. Cut has no effect in the forward direction.

Problems with negation. Negation is defined as:

```
not(X) :-X, !, fail.
not(_).
```

Note that this is not the same as *return true if X is false*. If *X* is true, then *not*(*X*) will evaluate *X* as true, fail on *fail*, but the cut forces failure of the rule. If *X* is false, then the first rule fails, but *not*(_) succeeds. However, the first rule may fail if *X* is false or if *X* is simply not in the database. The difference can be seen in the following two queries:

```
X is 5, not(X=10).
not(X=10), X is 5
```

In the first case, *X* unifies with 5 and not(X=10) succeeds. In the second case, *X* first unifies with 10 and fails so the unification with 5 is never executed.

Input and Output

For many simple queries, the default output of the unified variables is sufficient for writing out answers. However, a *write* function also exists to write out any string. *write*('*abc*') prints out *abc*. The function *nl* writes out a new-line symbol.

Standard Functions

Most Prolog systems include several built-in functions to aid in program generation:

consult(*filename*) reads the file *filename* and appends new facts and rules into the database. *filename* can also be written as '*filename*' if the file name has nonidentifier embedded characters in it. *consult(filename)* can often be specified as simply [*filename*].

reconsult(filename) overwrites relationships in the database.

fail always fails.

see(filename) reads input from *filename* as a series of rules.

write(term) writes out *term*.

tell(filename) redirects *write* output to *filename*.

told closes the file from a previous *tell* and redirects *write* output to the standard display terminal.

nl goes to the next line (of input and output).

atom(X) is a predicate that returns true if X is an atom (string constants or variable names).

var(X) is a predicate that returns true if X is a variable.

integer(X) is a predicate that returns true if X is an integer.

trace turns on trace debugging by showing each step in program execution. *notrace* turns it off.

A.12 SMALLTALK

Annotated Example

We again present our array summation example. In this version, we store the data in the file *data*. For the input data

412345123450

the program of Figure A.17 produces the output

1 2 3 4 SUM =10
1 2 3 4 5 SUM =15

Line 1. This defines `Datastore` as a subclass of class `Array`.

Line 2. This null list indicates that each instance of objects of class `Datastore` has no local variables. In this example, all data are manipulated in the class definition. In general, each instance of a class object will have its own set of local variables.

Line 3. The variables `DataFile`, `ArrIndex`, `Storage`, and `Size` are all global variables in the class object for `Datastore`.

Lines 4–5. These are needed for correct definition of the keyword method but are beyond the scope of these examples. The bang (!) indicates the end of the subclass definition.

Line 6. This indicates the start of methods that are defined for the class `Datastore`—that is, method invocations of the form

```
Array variableSubclass: #Datastore
      instanceVariableNames: ''
      classVariableNames: 'DataFile ArrIndex Storage Size'
      poolDictionaries: ''
      category: nil !
!Datastore class methodsFor: 'instance creation'!
new
     DataFile _ FileStream open:'data' mode: 'r'.
     Storage _ Array new: 99.
     Size _ 99.
     self reset !!
!Datastore class methodsFor: 'basic'!
asgn: aValue
    ArrIndex _ ArrIndex + 1.
    Storage at: ArrIndex put: aValue !
getval
    ArrIndex _ ArrIndex + 1.
    ^Storage at: ArrIndex !
nextval
    ^((DataFile next) digitValue - $0 digitValue)!
reset
    ArrIndex _ 0 !!
|k j sum|
Datastore new.
"Initialize k"
[(k _ Datastore nextval) > 0]
    whileTrue: [1 to: k do: [(j _ Datastore nextval) print.
                             Character space print.
                             Datastore asgn: j].
                Datastore reset.
                sum _ 0.
                ' SUM =' print.
                1 to: k do: [ sum _ sum + Datastore getval].
                sum printNl.
                Datastore reset] !
```

Figure A.17. Smalltalk example to sum an array.

Datastore methodname

Line 7. Method `new` is being defined. This method will open the input data file and initialize an array to contain the data.

Line 8. The file `data` is set to mode `'r'` for *read*. The `FileStream` class will return a descriptor object for this file, which is assigned to the variable `DataFile`, which is a global variable in the class definition of subclass `Datastore` from Line 3.

Line 9. The method `new:` is sent to the `Array` class with Parameter `99`. A 99 element array is returned and assigned to `Storage`, which is declared on Line 3.

Line 11. The method `reset` is sent to the object represented by `self`, which is the object that `new` was originally sent to. This effectively invokes the method `reset` for class `Datastore` defined on Line 21. The double bang indicates the end of the invocation methods defined for class `Datastore` on Line 6.

Line 12. Basic operational methods are defined for class `Datastore`.

Lines 16–18. Unary method `getval` increments the array index `ArrIndex` and returns (∧) the array element using the `at:` method for instances of arrays, in this case for `Storage`.

Lines 19–20. Method `nextval` for file object `DataFile` will return the next character from the file. The method `digitValue` passed to this character will return the integer value of that ASCII character. Subtracting the value of the character 0 will result in the correct numerical value for an integer digit [e.g., Character 0 ($0) will return integer 0, character 1 ($1) will return integer 1, etc.].

Line 23. `k`, `j`, and `sum` are defined as local variables. All variables are declared without types because types are assigned dynamically.

Line 24. The `new` method of Line 7 is invoked for class `Datastore` to open the input file and allocate the data array.

Line 25. This is a Smalltalk comment.

Line 26. Method `nextval` is passed to class `Datastore` to return the next integer value from the file. This object is assigned to Variable `k` and compared to the value `0`. The result of this block is either the object `true` or the object `false`.

Lines 27–29. The method `whileTrue:` has a block as an argument and is passed to the previous Boolean object on Line 26. If passed to `false`, the block is ignored; if passed to `true`, the block is executed and the conditional block on Line 26 is evaluated again. That is, a standard while loop is executed.

The actual block represents an iterative do construct. The method `to:do:` takes a count `k` and a block of statements and passes them to the integer object `1`. The effect is to iterate the block from `1` through `k`.

`Datastore nextval` returns the next character in the file, assigns it to Variable `j`, and then prints the value of `j`. The period is a statement separator.

Lines 30–32. Method `reset` in class `Datastore` is invoked and `sum` is assigned the value 0. The string `'SUM ='` is printed.

Line 34. The value of `sum` is printed. `printNl` inserts a new-line character after printing.

Line 35. The array is reset for the next summation. The bang indicates execution of the statements between Lines 23 and 34.

A.12.1 Data Objects

Variables are strings of letters starting with a lower case letter. The Smalltalk convention is to give variables multiple word names with successive words beginning with an upper case letter, as in *anInteger*, *aParameter*, *theInput*, *myInputFile*, and so on. Global data start with an upper case letter. Data shared across objects (i.e., declared in the class definition of the object) all begin with uppercase names. Strings are enclosed by single quotes, and character data are represented as the character prefixed by the symbol \$. Thus, the letter "a" is given as \$a. Execution is dynamic. Therefore, types are not specified for a variable, but set, changed, and interrogated during execution.

Primitive Data Types

Classes define types in the language. The set of predefined classes are listed in Figure A.18.

Structured Data Types

Smalltalk has no built-in structured data. Data objects are created by the class-definition methods.

Arrays. Arrays are created by using the *new*: keyword method for class *Array*, where the parameter to *new*: is the size of the array. Values are stored in the array by the keyword method, as described in Section 7.2.5:

arrayVariable at:*index* put:*arrayvalue*

The *at*: method retrieves values:

arrayVariable at:*index*

Sets. Sets are created by the *new* method to the class *Set*. Keyword method *add* : places a new object into a set, method *remove* : deletes the object from a set, and method *includes* : returns *true* or *false* depending on whether the argument is in the set.

Other structures. Smalltalk comes with predefined class definitions for linked lists, bags (i.e., sets allowing duplicate members), and the other classes given in Figure A.18. Check for other predefined class definitions, which should be online on your local system. The method *inspect* applied to an object can be used to determine attributes of each such class.

Class

- Object
  - Autoload
  - Behavior
    - ClassDescription
      - Class
      - Metaclass
  - BlockContext
  - Boolean
    - False
    - True
  - CFunctionDescriptor
  - CObject
  - Collection
    - Bag
    - MappedCollection
    - SequenceableCollection
      - ArrayedCollection
        - Array
        - ByteArray
        - CompiledMethod
        - String
        - Symbol
      - Interval
        - LinkedList
      - Semaphore
      - OrderedCollection
        - SortedCollection
    - Set
      - Dictionary
        - IdentityDictionary
        - SystemDictionary

(Continued)

- Object (superclass – continued)
  - Delay
  - FileSegment
  - Link
    - Process
    - SymLink
  - Magnitude
    - Character
    - Date
    - LookupKey
      - Association
    - Number
      - Float
      - Integer
    - Time
  - Memory
    - ByteMemory
    - WordMemory
  - Message
  - MethodContext
  - MethodInfo
  - ProcessorScheduler
  - SharedQueue
  - Stream
    - PositionableStream
      - ReadStream
      - WriteStream
        - ReadWriteStream
          - FileStream
    - Random
    - TokenStream
  - UndefinedObject

Figure A.18. Smalltalk predefined class hierarchy.

User-Defined Types

Smalltalk handles user functions and polymorphism by the inheritance of methods in class definitions.

Storage Representation

Smalltalk uses dynamic storage and pointers. Each variable has a pointer to an appropriate context for objects of that class.

A.12.2 Sequence Control

Expressions are executed in order. Statements are separated from the next statement by a period. Method definition is terminated by !, and a class definition is terminated by !!.

Expressions

Expressions are extremely simple in Smalltalk. There are only three precedence levels:

Unary method
Binary method
Keyword method

Within any given level, execution is from left to right. For example, $2 + 3 * 4$ has two binary methods with the same precedence, so the correct interpretation is: $((2 + 3) * 4)$ or 20, and not the *expected* 14. This is perhaps the most unusual part of the language, and one must be careful using this.

Be careful also with expressions such as: $1+2$ *print*. Because *print* is unary, the factorization is $1 + (2$ *print*), which is not what was probably desired. Parentheses can always be used to force a given semantic meaning for an expression.

Smalltalk defines the usual set of relational methods (e.g., <, <=, =, >, >=). The *notequal* method is given by ~=.

Several additional computational methods are defined. Some of the more useful are the following:

//	Quotient (Integer division)
\\	Remainder
gcd:	Greatest common divisor (i. e., m gcd:n for integers m and n)

Statements

Declarations. The syntax |*variable*| defines a local variable whose scope continues until the end of the current method definition (indicated by !).

Assignment. The basic assignment statement is

variable _ *expression*

where *expression* is evaluated and assigned to *variable*. The expression may be data or an executable block, which is the way the **if** statement is constructed. In GNU Smalltalk, := may be used in addition to the operator _ for assignment.

Block. The block has the syntax

[:*local_variable* | *statement_list*]

where *local_variable* is optional and represents a list of one or more local variables whose scope is the block. Sending the method *value* to a block causes the block to be executed. Typically blocks will be assigned to a variable x and then executed by passing the message *value* to that block as in: x *value*.

Conditional. A conditional is created by passing the method *ifTrue:ifFalse:* to the objects *true* or *false*. *true* will evaluate the block argument *ifTrue*, whereas *false* will evaluate the block argument *ifFalse*:

Boolean expression
    ifTrue: [*block*]
    ifFalse: [*block*]

Boolean expression will evaluate to either *true* or *false*. This value will be passed the keyword message *ifTrue:ifFalse:* and will perform the appropriate action.

Iteration statements. Similar to the conditional, keyword methods may be used to create loop constructs:

Simple iteration. The *timesRepeat:* method will pass a block to an integer and iterate the block that many times. Thus,

count timesRepeat:*block*

will execute the block *count* times.

Fixed repetition. The Smalltalk code

initial_value to: *final_value* by: *increment* do: [*block*]

is similar to the FORTRAN loop:

DO I = *initial_value*, *final_value*, *increment*
    statement_list
    END DO

As in FORTRAN, the *by:* value is optional. The current index of the loop can be accessed by specifying a local variable in the loop:

initial_value to:*final_value* by:*increment* do: [:*loopVar* | *block*]

While repetition. A construct similar to the **while** statement of other languages can be specified as

[*Boolean_expression*]
    whileTrue: [*block*]

where *block* will be executed as long as *Boolean_expression* returns *true*.

Input and Output

The classes *ReadStream*, *WriteStream*, and their subclasses provide input and output functions.

The method *print* can be sent to any class to print its value. *printNl* is the same as *print*, except it appends a new-line character at the end of the output.

The method *fileIn*: for class *FileStream* reads and executes a file. For example,

FileStream fileIn: *filename*

causes the file *filename* to be read in and processed by Smalltalk. It allows programs to be read in and executed during program execution.

The method *open:mode*: for class *FileStream* opens a file; thus,

FileStream open:*filename* mode:*mode*

returns a file descriptor for the file named *filename*, which is open for input (if mode is 'r') or for output (if mode is 'w').

The method *next* for instances of class *FileStream* returns the next character of the file. If *f* was opened by the above *open:mode*: method, then

f next

returns the next character in *f*.

Class Definitions

Class definitions consist of four components:

1. A class name.
2. The superclass of the class.
3. Declaration of the variables available to instances of the class.
4. Methods used by instances of the class.

Subclasses are defined using the syntax

superclass subclass: #*newClassName*
    instanceVariableNames: *instanceVariables*
    classVariableNames: *classVariables*
    poolDictionaries: ' '
    category: nil !

where *newClassName* is the new subclass name, *instanceVariables* is a list of all variables allocated storage in each instance of a new object, hence forms the structure of the new subclass, and *classVariables* is a list of variables common across all instances of a class. *category* is defined as a documentation aid so that common methods can be grouped together; it has no effects on the semantics of the language. Variables listed in *poolDictionaries* allow shared variables to be used in specified classes of the system outside of the normal inheritance hierarchy.

Method definition. Methods that are defined on instances of a class are added to a class definition by

!*className* methodsFor: '*usage*'!
$method_1$
    $statement\_list_1$!
$method_2$
    $statement\_list_2$!
    ...
$method_n$
    $statement\_list_n$!!

where *usage* defines the category of method being defined.

If the method is to create instances of the class and is part of the class definition, the syntax is

!*className* class methodsFor: '*usage*'!

For example, Figure A.17 shows method declaration for instance creation and basic operations for class *Datastore*.

Storage Management

Local referencing environment. Object inheritance forms the basis for the local referencing environment. If a method is not found in the object it is passed to, then its parent object class is invoked. Similarly, only variables defined in the class definition or declared locally to a method are accessible within the method.

Accessing the instance of the class that a method has been sent to is performed by the object *self*. To force a method to look at a parent class, the object *super* is referenced, as in

```
new
    ∧ super new
```

which causes the method *new* to first invoke the method *new* in the parent class and return that instance. This provides for modifying the semantics of a given method in a subclass yet also allows invocation of the parent method.

Common referencing environment. All class names are globally known, so class objects may be invoked from any method. The object *Smalltalk* provides for a global dictionary. The method *at:put:* can initialize any object, giving it a global name. For example,

```
Smalltalk at:#x put:(Array new:20)
```

creates a global object x that is initialized to be a 20-element array object.

Parameter passing. All parameters are passed by value because the dynamic storage model simply copies any parameter to new storage and will garbage collect the freed storage later.

Return from a method. An object is returned from a method by the syntax $\wedge$*object*. If $\wedge$ is not specified, then the object containing the called method is returned.

Standard Functions

There are many predefined functions in the predefined class definitions in the default environment when Smalltalk is first invoked. Several have already been described. Other useful ones include the following.

Class Character. *Character value:anInteger* returns the character represented by *anInteger*.

x digitValue returns the integer value of character x. As with C, ($2 digitValue) - ($0 digitValue) will give value 2.

Print Functions. *print* causes the value of an object to be printed. *printNl* is similar except it adds a new-line character after printing. Actually, *print* sends message *printOn:filename* to the object *self*. This allows any class to modify what it prints about itself:

```
printOn: stdOutput
    super printOn:stdOutput. "Do default output"
    ... ! "Do special output for this class object"
```

System Functions. The dictionary object *Smalltalk* provides for many system functions. Some of these are:

The *inspect* method will print internal information about the structure of any object.

quitPrimitive exits from Smalltalk (i.e., *Smalltalk quitPrimitive*). The end-of-file character (often *control D*) may also be entered from the terminal to end the program.

system:command causes *command* to be executed by the operating system. For example, *Smalltalk system:'ls'* will print the names of the local files on UNIX systems.

A.13 SUGGESTIONS FOR FURTHER READING

The appropriate ANSI documents describe the standard definitions for FORTRAN 90 [ANSI 1990], C [ANSI 1989], and COBOL [ANSI 1985].

A good summary of FORTRAN 90 features is given in [BRAINERD et al. 1990]. The book [HARBISON and STEELE 1995] is a good overview of C. The early development of both FORTRAN and COBOL is described in the 1978 ACM History of Languages Conference [WEXELBLAT 1981], whereas the development of C is covered in the second ACM History of Languages Conference in 1993 [ACM 1993].

A history of Pascal is summarized by Wirth [WIRTH 1993]. A clear description of the language was published by Jensen and Wirth [JENSEN and WIRTH 1974], and an annotated version of the standard gives some good pointers on how to use the language [LEDGARD 1984]. Further critical comments about the language can be found in [WELSCH et al. 1977]. A comparison between Pascal and C was published in [FEUER and GEHANI 1982].

Using Pascal as a base, Concurrent Pascal [BRINCH HANSEN 1975] and Modula [WIRTH 1988] were developed as systems programming languages. However, neither has made much headway against the onslaught of C as a systems programming language.

The development and history of Ada is described by [WHITAKER 1993]. The book [BOOCH 1983] gives a more complete description of programming in Ada than is possible here, whereas [ISO 1995] describes the standard.

The development of C++ from C is described in [STROUSTRUP 1993]. Details of C++ are presented in several recent books [LIPPMAN 1998], [POHL 1996], and [STROUSTRUP 2000].

The history of Smalltalk is given in [KAY 1993]. A more complete description of the standard Smalltalk-80 language is given in [GOLDBERG 1984]. An alternative development of an object-oriented language is presented in the language Eiffel by Bertrand Meyer [MEYER 1990].

LISP has suffered through the lack of a common language definition. The original language is described in an easily read book by McCarthy [MCCARTHY 1961]. The Scheme dialect can be found in [ABELSON et al. 1985]. Common LISP is defined in the book by Steele [STEELE 1990], and the book by [GRAHAM 1994] is a good introduction to Common LISP. The fractious history of LISP is well summarized in [STEELE and GABRIEL 1993].

The specification of Standard ML is described in [MILNER et al. 1989], while the book by Ullman [ULLMAN 1994] presents a clear description useful to learn the language. The development of the AT&T Standard ML compiler, used to develop the examples in this book, is given in [APPEL and MACQUEEN 1991].

The interest in functional languages greatly increased in the late 1970s after Backus gave his Turing Award lecture criticizing the von Neumann bottleneck in conventional programming languages [BACKUS 1978]. As an alternative to ML,

Miranda, a language developed by David Turner, has properties similar to ML [BIRD and WADLER 1988]. Miranda is purely functional, whereas ML does permit assignment.

The early development of logic programming is presented in [KOWALSKI 1988], and the history of Prolog is summarized in [COLMERAUER and ROUSSEL 1993]. The use of the language is described in [CLOCKSIN and MELLISH 1987] and [STERLING and SHAPIRO 1986].

References

[ABELSON et al. 1985] Abelson, H., G. J. Sussman, and J. Sussman, *Structure and Interpretation of Computer Programs*, MIT Press, Cambridge, MA (1985).

[ABRAMS and ZELKOWITZ 1994] Abrams, M. D., and M. V. Zelkowitz, Belief in Correctness, National Computer Security Conference, Baltimore, MD (October, 1994), 132–141.

[ACM 1989] *ACM Computing Surveys: Special Issue on Programming Language Paradigms* (21)3 (1989).

[ACM 1993] *ACM History of Programming Languages Conference II*, Cambridge, MA (April 1993) *[SIGPLAN Notices (28)3 (March 1993)].*

[ADA 1980] *Formal Definition of the Ada Programming Language,* Honeywell, Inc. (preliminary) (1980).

[ADAMS 1979] Adams D., *Hitchhiker's Guide to the Galaxy*, (1979).

[ADOBE 1990] Adobe Systems Inc., *Postscript Language Reference Manual*, Addison-Wesley, Reading, MA (1990).

[AHO et al. 1988] Aho, A., R. Sethi, and J. D. Ullman, *Compilers: Principles, Techniques and Tools*, Addison-Wesley, Reading, MA (1988).

[ANSI 1985] ANSI, American National Standard Programming Language COBOL, X3.23, ANSI, New York (1985).

[ANSI 1989] ANSI, American National Standard Programming Language C, X3.159, ANSI, New York (1989).

[ANSI 1990] ANSI, American National Standard Programming Language FORTRAN 90, X3.198, ANSI, New York (1990).

[APPEL and MACQUEEN 1991] Appel, A. W., and D. B. MacQueen, Standard ML of New Jersey, in *Third International Symp. on Programming Language Implementation and Logic programming*, M. Wirsing (Ed.), Springer-Verlag, New York (1991).

[ATKINSON and BUNEMAN 1987] Atkinson, M. P., and O. P. Buneman, Types and Persistence in Database Programming Languages, *ACM Computing Surveys* (19)2 (1987), 105–190.

[BACKUS 1960] Backus, J., The Syntax and Semantics of the Proposed International Algebraic Language of the Zurich ACM-GAMM Conference, *Information Processing,* UNESCO, Paris (1960), 125–132.

[BACKUS 1978] Backus, J., Can Programming Be Liberated from the von Neumann Style? A Functional Style and Its Algebra of Programs, *Comm. ACM* (21)8 (1978), 613–641.

[BERNERS-LEE 1996] Berners-Lee T., WWW: Past, present, and future. *IEEE Computer* (29)10 (1996) 69–77.

[BIERMANN 1990] Biermann, A., *Great Ideas in Computer Science: A Gentle Introduction*, MIT Press, Cambridge, MA (1990).

[BIRD and WADLER 1988] Bird, R., and P. Wadler, *Introduction to Functional Programming*, Prentice-Hall, Englewood Cliffs, NJ (1988).

[BOHM and JACOBINI 1966] Böhm, C., and G. Jacobini, Flow Diagrams, Turing Machines, and Languages with only Two Formation Rules, *Comm. ACM* (9)5 (1966), 366–371.

[BOOCH 1983] Booch, G., *Software Engineering with Ada*, Benjamin/Cummings, Menlo Park, CA (1983).

[BRAINERD et al. 1990] Brainerd, W. S., C. H. Goldberg, and J. C. Adams, *Programmer's Guide to FORTRAN 90*, McGraw-Hill, New York (1990).

[BRINCH HANSEN 1975] Brinch Hansen, P., The Programming Language Concurrent Pascal, *IEEE Trans. on Soft. Engr.* (1)2 (1975), 199–207.

[BROWN et al. 1992] Brown, A., A. Earl, and J. McDermid, *Software Engineering Environments*, McGraw-Hill International, London (1992).

[BURGESS et al. 1994] Burgess, B., N. Ullah, P. van Overen, and D. Ogden, The PowerPC 603 Microprocessor, *Comm. ACM* (37)6 (1994), 34–42.

[CARDELLI 1984] Cardelli, L., Compiling a Functional Language, *Symp. on LISP and Functional Programming*, ACM (1984), 208–217.

[CHANDY and KESSELMAN 1991] Chandy, K. M., and C. Kesselman, Parallel Programming in 2001, *IEEE Software* (8)6 (1991), 11–20.

[CHOMSKY 1959] Chomsky, N., On Certain Formal Properties of Grammars, *Information and Control* 2 (1959), 137–167.

[CLOCKSIN and MELLISH 1987] Clocksin, W. F., and C. S. Mellish, *Programming in Prolog*, Springer-Verlag, Berlin (1987).

[COHEN 1981] Cohen, J., Garbage Collection of Linked Data Structures, *ACM Computing Surveys* (13)3 (1981), 341–368.

[COLMERAUER and ROUSSEL 1993] Colmerauer, A., and P. Roussel, The Birth of Prolog, *ACM History of Programming Languages Conference II*, Cambridge, MA (April 1993) *[SIGPLAN Notices (28)3 (March 1993)]* 37–52.

[CONWAY and MAXWELL 1963] Conway, R., and W. L. Maxwell, CORC: The Cornell Computing Language, *Comm. of the ACM* (6)6 (1963), 317–321.

[CONWAY and WILCOX 1973] Conway, R. W., and T. Wilcox, Design and Implementation of a Diagnostic Compiler for PL/I, *Comm. ACM* (16)3 (1973), 169–179.

[DAHL et al. 1972] Dahl O., E. Dijkstra, and C. A. R. Hoare, *Structured Programming*, Academic Press, New York (1972).

[DAVIE et al. 1999] Davie B., L. Peterson, D. Clark, *Computer Networks: A Systems Approach*, Morgan Kaufmann, San Francisco, CA (1999).

[DERSHEM and JIPPING 1995] Dershem, H., and M. Jipping, *Programming Languages: Structures and Models*, PWS Publishing Co., Boston (1995).

[DIJKSTRA 1972] Dijkstra, E., Notes on Structured Programming. In [DAHL et al., 1972], 1–82.

[DIJKSTRA 1975] Dijkstra, E. W., Guarded Commands, Nondeterminacy, and Formal Derivation of Programs, *Comm. ACM* (18)8 (1975), 453–457.

[DUNCAN 1990] Duncan, R., A Survey of Parallel Computer Architectures, *IEEE Computer* (23)2 (1990), 5–16.

[FALKOFF and IVERSON 1978] Falkoff, A. D., and K. E. Iverson, The Evolution of APL, *ACM History of Programming Languages Conference*, Los Angeles, CA (June 1978) *[SIGPLAN Notices (13)8 (August 1978)]*, 47–57.

[FEUER and GEHANI 1982] Feuer, A., and N. Gehani, A Comparison of the Programming Languages C and Pascal, *ACM Computing Surveys* (14)1 (1982), 73–92.

[FISCHER and LEBLANC 1988] Fischer, C. N., and R. LeBlanc, *Crafting a Compiler,* Benjamin Cummings, Menlo Park, CA (1988).

[FURHT 1994] Furht, B., Parallel Computing: Glory and Collapse, *IEEE Computer* (27)11 (1994), 74–75.

[GANNON et al. 1994] Gannon, J. D., J. M. Purtilo, and M. V. Zelkowitz, *Software Specification: A Comparison of Formal Methods*, Ablex, Norwood, NJ (1994).

[GOLDBERG 1984] Goldberg, A., *Smalltalk-80: The Interactive Programming Environment,* Addison-Wesley, Reading, MA (1984).

[GRAHAM 1994] Graham, P., *On Lisp: Advanced Techniques for Common Lisp*, Prentice-Hall, Englewood Cliffs, NJ (1994).

[GRISWOLD 1975] Griswold, R., *String and List Processing in SNOBOL4: Techniques and Applications*, Prentice-Hall, Englewood Cliffs, NJ (1975).

[GRISWOLD 1978] Griswold, R. E., A History of the SNOBOL Programming Language, *ACM History of Programming Languages Conference*, Los Angeles, CA (June, 1978) *[SIGPLAN Notices (13)8 (August 1978)]*, 275–308.

[GUTTAG 1980] Guttag, J. V., Notes on Type Abstraction (Version 2), *IEEE Trans. on Software Engineering* (6)1 (1980), 13–23.

[HARBISON and STEELE 1995] Harbison, S. P., and G. L. Steele, *C: A Reference Manual*, 4th edition, Prentice-Hall, Upper Saddle River, NJ (1995).

[HOARE 1972] Hoare, C. A. R., Notes on Data Structuring. In [DAHL et al., 1972], 83–174.

[HOARE 1973] Hoare, C. A. R., and N. Wirth, An Axiomatic Definition of the Programming Language Pascal, *Acta Informatica* 2 (1973), 335–355.

[HOARE 1974] Hoare, C. A. R., and P. E. Lauer, Consistent and Complementary Formal Theories of the Semantics of Programming Languages, *Acta Informatica* 3 (1974), 135–153.

[HORSTMANN 1997] Horstmann C. S., *Practical Object-Oriented Development in C++ and Java*, John Wiley & Sons, New York (1997).

[IBM 1966] IBM, The Man Behind FORTRAN, *IBM Computing Report* (2)4 (November 1966), 7–10, 19.

[IEEE 1985] IEEE, *Binary Floating Point Arithmetic*, Standard 754, IEEE, New York (1985).

[INGALLS 1978] Ingalls, D. H., The Smalltalk-76 Programming System: Design and Implementation, *ACM Symp. on the Principles of Programming Languages*, (January 1978).

[ISO 1994] Intermetrics, Ada 95 Rationale, (January 1995).

[ISO 1995] ISO, Ada 95 Reference Manual, ISO/IEC 8652:1995, International Organization for Standardization/International Electrotechnical Committee (December, 1994).

[JENSEN and WIRTH 1974] Jensen, K., and N. Wirth, *Pascal User Manual and Report*, Springer-Verlag, New York (1974).

[JOHNSON and JOHNSON 1991] Johnson, M., and W. Johnson, *Superscalar Microprocessor Design*, Prentice-Hall, Upper Saddle River, NJ (1991).

[JONES 1990] Jones, C. B., *Systematic Software Development Using VDM*, Prentice-Hall, Englewood Cliffs, NJ (1990).

[KAY 1993] Kay, A., The Early History of Smalltalk, *ACM History of Programming Languages Conference II*, Cambridge, MA (April 1993) *[SIGPLAN Notices (28)3 (March 1993)]*, 67–95.

[KELLY-BOOTLE 1995] Kelly-Bootle, S., *The Computer Contradictionary*, MIT Press, Cambridge, MA (1995).

[KNUTH 1968] Knuth, D. E., Semantics of Context-Free Languages, *Mathematical Systems Theory* 2 (1968), 127–145.

[KNUTH 1973] Knuth, D., *The Art of Computer Programming*, Vols 1 to 3, Addison-Wesley, Reading, MA (1968, 1969, 1973).

[KNUTH 1984] Knuth, D. E., *The TEXbook*, Addison-Wesley, Reading, MA (1984).

[KOWALSKI 1988] Kowalski, R., The Early History of Logic Programming, *Comm. ACM* (31)1 (1988), 38–43.

[KURTZ 1978] Kurtz, T. E., BASIC, *ACM History of Programming Languages Conference*, Los Angeles, CA (June 1978) *[SIGPLAN Notices (13)8 (August 1978)]*, 103–118.

[LAMPORT 1986] Lamport, L., *LaTeX: A Document Preparation System*, Addison-Wesley, Reading, MA (1986).

[LEDGARD 1984] Ledgard, H., *The American Pascal Standard with Annotations*, Springer-Verlag, New York (1984).

[LINGER et al. 1979] Linger, R. C., H. D. Mills, and B. I. Witt, *Structured Programming: Theory and Practice*, Addison-Wesley, Reading, MA (1979).

[LIPPMAN 1998] Lippman, S. B., *C++ Primer*, Third Edition, Addison-Wesley, Reading, MA (1998).

[LOPEZ et al. 1992] Lopez, L. A., K. A. Valimohamed, and L. G. Schub, An Environment for Painless MIMD System Development, *IEEE Software* (9)6 (1992), 67–76.

[LOUDEN 1993] Louden, K., *Programming Languages: Principles and Practice*, PWS-Kent, Boston, MA (1993).

[LUCAS and WALK 1969] Lucas, P., and K. Walk, On the Formal Description of PL/I, *Ann. Rev. Auto. Prog.* (6)3 (1969), 105–182.

[MADDUX 1975] Maddux, R., A Study of Program Structure, Ph.D. dissertation, University of Waterloo (July 1975).

[MANO and KIME 1999] Mano, M., and C. Kime, *Logic and Computer Design Fundamentals*, Prentice-Hall, Upper Saddle River, NJ (1999).

[MARCOTTY et al. 1976] Marcotty, M., H. Ledgard, and G. Bochman, A Sampler of Formal Definitions, *ACM Computing Surveys* (8)2 (1976), 191–275.

[MARTIN 1992] Martin, A., *Internationalization Explored*, Uniforum, San francisco, CA (1992).

[MCCARTHY 1961] McCarthy, J., *LISP 1.5 Programmer's Manual*, 2nd edition, MIT Press, Cambridge, MA (1961).

[METZNER and BARNES 1977] Metzner, J., and B. Barnes, *Decision Table Languages and Systems*, Academic Press, New York (1977).

[MEYER 1990] Meyer, B., *Eiffel: The Language* Prentice-Hall, Upper Saddle River, NJ (1990).

[MILNER et al. 1989] Milner, R., M. Tofte, and R. Harper, *The Definition of Standard ML*, MIT Press, Cambridge, MA (1989).

[MORGAN 1970] Morgan, H., Spelling Correction in Systems Programs, *Comm. ACM* (13)2 (1970).

[MULKERS et al. 1994] Mulkers, A., W. Winsborough, and B. Bruynooghe, Live-Structure Dataflow Analysis for Prolog, *ACM Trans. on Prog. Lang. and Systems* (16)2 (1994), 205–258.

[PARNAS 1972] Parnas, D. L., On the Criteria to be Used in Decomposing Systems into Modules, *Comm. ACM* (15)12 (1972), 1053–1058.

[PERRY and KAISER 1991] Perry, D., and G. Kaiser, Models of Software Development Environments, *IEEE Trans. on Soft. Eng.* (17)3 (1991), 283–295.

[POHL 1996] Pohl, I., *C++ distilled: A Concise ANSI/ISO Reference and Style Guide*, Addison-Wesley, Reading, MA (1996).

[PRENNER et al. 1972] Prenner, C., et al., An Implementation of Backtracking for Programming Languages, in *Control Structures in Programming Languages* (Special Issue), *SIGPLAN Notices* (7)11 (1972).

[RADA and BERG 1995] Rada, R., and J. Berg, Standards: Free or Sold?, *Comm. ACM* (38)2 (1995), 23–27.

[RATHER et al. 1993] Rather, E., D. Colburn, and C. Moore, The Evolution of Forth, *ACM History of Programming Languages Conference II*, Cambridge, MA (April 1993) *[SIGPLAN Notices (28)3 (March 1993)]*, 177–199.

[RITCHIE 1993] Ritchie, D. M., The Development of the C Language, *ACM History of Programming Languages Conference II*, Cambridge, MA (April 1993) *(SIGPLAN Notices (28)3 (March 1993))*, 201–208

[ROSEN 1967] Rosen, S., *Programming Systems and Languages*, McGraw-Hill, New York (1967).

[SAJEEV and HURST 1992] Sajeev, A. S. M., and A. J. Hurst, Programming Persistence in χ, *IEEE Computer* (25)9 (1992), 57–66.

[SAMMET 1969] Sammet, J., *Programming Languages: History and Fundamentals*, Prentice-Hall, Englewood Cliffs, NJ (1969).

[SAMMET 1972] Sammet, J., Programming Languages: History and Future, *Comm. ACM* (15)7 (1972), 601–610.

[SAMMET 1978] Sammet, J. E., The Early History of COBOL, *ACM History of Programming Languages Conference*, Los Angeles, CA (June 1978) *[SIGPLAN Notices (13)8 (August 1978)]*, 121–161.

[SCOTT 1972] Scott, D., Lattice Theory, Data Types and Formal Semantics, *Formal Semantics of Programming Languages* [R. Rustin (Ed.)], Prentice-Hall, Englewood Cliffs, NJ (1972), 65–106.

[SEBESTA 1998] Sebesta, R., *Concepts of Programming Languages*, 4th edition, Benjamin Cummings, Redwood City, CA (1998).

[SETHI 1996] Sethi, R., *Programming Languages: Concepts and Constructs*, 2nd edition, Addison-Wesley, Reading, MA (1996).

[SHAFFER 1996] Shaffer C., *A practical introduction to data structures and algorithm analysis*, Prentice-Hall, Upper Saddle River, NJ (1996).

[SMITH and WEISS 1994] Smith, J. E., and S. Weiss, PowerPC 601 and Alpha 21064: A tale of Two RISCs, *IEEE Computer* (27)6 (1994), 46–58.

[SPIVEY 1989] Spivey, J. M., An Introduction to Z and Formal Specifications, *Software Engineering Journal* (4)1 (1989), 40–50.

[STANSIFER 1995] Stansifer, R., *The Study of Programming Languages*, Prentice-Hall, Englewood Cliffs, NJ (1995).

[STEELE 1990] Steele, G., *Common LISP: The Language*, 2nd edition, Digital Press, Bedford, MA (1990).

[STEELE and GABRIEL 1993] Steele, G. L., and R. P. Gabriel, The Evolution of LISP, *ACM History of Programming Languages Conference II*, Cambridge, MA (April 1993) *[SIGPLAN Notices (28)3 (March 1993)]*, 231–270.

[STERLING and SHAPIRO 1986] Sterling, L., and E. Shapiro, *The Art of Prolog*, MIT Press, Cambridge, MA (1986).

[STROUSTRUP 1993] Stroustrup, B., A History of C++: 1979–1991, *ACM History of Programming Languages Conference II*, Cambridge, MA (April 1993) *[SIGPLAN Notices (28)3 (March 1993)]*, 271–297.

[STROUSTRUP 2000] Stroustrup, B. *The C++ programming language, Special Edition*, Addison-Wesley, Reading, MA (1990).

[TAIVALSAAR 1993] Taivalsaari, A., On the Notion of Object, *J. of Systems and Software*, (21)1 (1993), 3–16.

[TANENBAUM 1990] Tanenbaum, A., *Structured Computer Organization*, 3rd edition, Prentice-Hall, Englewood Cliffs, NJ (1990).

[TANENBAUM et al. 1992] Tanenbaum, A. S., M. F. Kaashoek, and H. E. Bal, Parallel Programming Using Shared Objects and Broadcasting, *IEEE Computer* (25)8 (1992), 10–19.

[TUCKER et al. 1991] Tucker, A. B. (Ed.), Computing Curricula 1991, *Comm. ACM* (34)6 (1991), 68–84.

[TURING 1936] Turing, A., On Computable Numbers, with an Application to the Entscheidungs-Problem, *Proc. London Math. Soc.* 42 (1936), 230–265.

[ULLMAN 1994] Ullman, J. D., *Elements of ML Programming*, Prentice-Hall, Englewood Cliffs, NJ (1994).

[WELSCH et al. 1977] Welsch, J., W. Sneeringer, and C. A. R. Hoare, Ambiguities and Insecurities in Pascal, *Software–Practice and Experience* (7)6 (1977), 685–696.

[WEXELBLAT 1981] Wexelblat, R. (Ed.), *History of Programming Languages*, Academic Press, New York (1981).

[WIRTH 1988] Wirth, N., *Programming in Modula-2*, Springer-Verlag, Berlin (1988).

[WIRTH 1993] Wirth, N., Recollections About the Development of Pascal, *ACM History of Programming Languages Conference II*, Cambridge, MA (April 1993) *[SIGPLAN Notices (28)3 (March 1993)]*, 333–342.

[WHITAKER 1993] Whitaker, W. A., The Ada Project: The DOD Higher Order Language Working Group, *ACM History of Programming Languages Conference II*, Cambridge, MA (April 1993) *[SIGPLAN Notices (28)3 (March 1993)]*, 299–332.

[WYATT et al. 1992] Wyatt, B, K. Kavi, and S. Hufnagel, Parallelism in Object-Oriented Languages: A Survey, *IEEE Software* (9)6 (1992), 56–65.

[WORKMAN 1977] Workman, D., *ACM Conference on Language Design for Reliable Software*, Raleigh, NC, *SIGPLAN Notices* (12)3 (March 1977).

[ZELKOWITZ 1993] Zelkowitz, M. V., The Role of Verification in the Software Specification Process, *Advances in Computers* 36, Academic Press (1993), 43–109.

Index